Indians of North America

Indians of

North America

Second Edition, Revised

Harold E. Driver

THE UNIVERSITY OF CHICAGO PRESS
Chicago and London

International Standard Book Number: 0-226-16466-7 (*clothbound*)
0-226-16467-5 (*paperbound*)
Library of Congress Catalog Card Number: 79-76207

The University of Chicago Press, Chicago 60637
The University of Chicago Press, Ltd., London

To Wilhelmine

Contents

Illustrations

xi

PLATES
(*Following page 188*)

MAPS
(*Following page 566*)

Preface to the Second Edition

SINCE the first edition was published in 1961 there has been an increased interest on the part of students, laymen, and anthropologists alike in what the Indians of the twentieth century have been doing, especially in the recent years of the 1960's. To meet this demand, the author has deleted the last chapter of the first edition and substituted for it five new chapters on ethnohistory and culture change after A.D. 1492. These terminal chapters divide the continent along national lines, with separate chapters or sections for Mexico, the United States, Alaska, Canada, and Greenland. Because most readers of this book are likely to be residents of the United States and are most concerned with the Indians in this nation, two of these chapters are devoted to the United States.

The five terminal chapters are more concerned with the facts of ethnohistory than with the broad trends or processes of acculturation theory. The author was more impressed with the wide variation in the responses of Indians to Whites than with the overall uniformities which could be pigeonholed under a double handful of theoretical concepts. At the same time, contrasts have been made between the Spanish and the English treatment of Indians in the colonial period, and between the policies and programs of the new governments—Mexico, the United States, Canada, and Denmark—in the later period. The twentieth century is given more space than any other, perhaps as much as the other four historic centuries combined.

The first chapter, on archeology, has been rewritten entirely to include the many discoveries since 1961 and to emphasize the growth of the civilizations in Meso-America. Dancing has been added to the chapter on music by Wilhelmine Driver, and the music of Meso-America has been given fuller treatment.

The order of two chapters has been changed. The chapter on language, originally 25, has been moved forward to become 3. This has been done to familiarize the reader near the beginning with the terms for language families and subfamilies, which are used through-out the book to localize information of all kinds. The genetic language classification of Voegelin and Voegelin (1966) replaces the older scheme of the first edition. The original Chapter 14, "Property and Inheritance," has now become 16 so that it will follow the two chapters on kinship instead of preceding them. Property was owned and inherited by kinship groups, and their structures must be known in order to understand the discussion about property.

The Circum-Caribbean area has been dropped from the text, although it is left on the maps. It is included in the *Handbook of South American Indians*, edited by Julian H. Steward, in *Native Peoples of South America*, by Steward and Louis Faron, and in other general works on South America. Its geographical and historical affiliations are with South America rather than with North America.

The chapter on horticulture has been drastically revised in light of new research by archeologists and botanists. Intentional diffusion by man of domesticated plants across the Pacific before A.D. 1492 has been abandoned as an explanation in favor of independent domesti-cation in the two hemispheres for all genera and species except the sweet potato, which seems to have been first domesticated in the New World and subsequently diffused to Polynesia within the time span A.D. 1-1492. The list of Meso-American domesticated plants has been expanded, but the new entries are of minor importance in the native culture.

About 150 new references have been cited and added to the ter-minal bibliography, most of them with dates in the 1960's. The illustrations remain the same except for the deletion of one line draw-ing; Maps 1, 2, 6, 31, and 37 have been revised. The index retains most of the original entries, to which several hundred new ones have been added.

The criticism made by some reviewers that the first edition of this book lacked functionally integrated descriptions of the cultures of single tribes has not been acted upon because four other books with a wealth of such descriptions have appeared since: *The Americas on the Eve of Discovery*, edited by Harold E. Driver, 1964; *The Native Americans*, by Robert F. Spencer, Jesse D. Jennings, *et al.*, 1965; *This Land Was Theirs*, by Wendell H. Oswalt, 1966; *The North American Indians*, edited by Roger C. Owen, James J. F. Deetz, and Anthony D. Fisher, 1967. These books supplement each other as well as this book.

I wish to thank the reviewers and teachers of courses on Indians for their suggestions for improving the book, especially David Barreis, David Damas, William N. Fenton, Nelson H. H. Graburn, June Helm, Melville Jacobs, Volney Jones and Evon Vogt. My wife Wilhelmine and I are especially grateful to George Herzog for his meticulous and helpful criticism of the revised version of the chapter on music and dance, as well as for suggestions for the language chapter. I wish also to acknowledge the help of Nancy O. Lurie of the University of Wisconsin at Milwaukee and Joseph Jorgensen of the University of Michigan, who read the first draft of the terminal chapters on the areas north of Mexico and made valuable marginal notes, most of which were incorporated in the final draft. I am also grateful to Frank Essene of the University of Kentucky for verbal comments on both the old and the new material which improved its quality, and to Daniel Crowley of the University of California, Davis, for giving the typing of the first draft of the terminal chapters priority over his own work. I wish, further, to thank Patricia Rademaker of Davis, California, and Peggy Wagner and Janice Perry of Bloomington, Indiana, for a careful typing job. My greatest debt, however, is to my wife Wilhelmine, who criticized and edited every word of the manuscript from the first to the final draft, read and summarized a number of Spanish sources, and contributed enormously to the thought of the book as well as to the mechanics of the writing.

Indians of North America

1

Origin and Prehistory

RECENT discoveries by Louis S. B. Leakey and others in east Africa have pushed back the first appearance of fossil men (hominids) in the Old World to about two and a half million years ago (Patterson and Howells, 1967). Still older fossils, intermediate between apes and men, demonstrate beyond all reasonable doubt that man evolved from fossil monkey and ape ancestry in the Old World. In the New World, in contrast, all fossil human bones so far discovered have been classed as *Homo sapiens sapiens* (doubly wise man), the subspecies to which all living forms of man belong. It is obvious that until man had evolved into a full-fledged human being with the ability to make fire, fur clothing, and semisubterranean houses, and to capture arctic game, he could not have lived in the arctic climate of Siberia in the Pleistocene and eventually worked his way east over a land bridge into Alaska and the New World. Although in the preceding Tertiary epoch there were warmer periods, which made it possible for monkeys to get to South America, this was before any form of man existed, and the records show that these monkeys did not serve as the springboard for evolution upward to man in the New World.

There is abundant evidence of the presence of man in the New World as early as about 10,000 B.C., and no trained anthropologist doubts these facts. A growing number, however, believe that the earliest entry of man into the New World from Siberia took place as early as about 40,000 B.C. The evidence consists of large quantities of crude chipped stone implements found mostly on the surface in both North and South America and not yet dated accurately. None of these implements can pass as a spear point or arrowhead; so this early horizon has been labeled pre-projectile-point (Krieger, 1964). Such tools were probably used in the butchering and skinning of game killed with spears or clubs of wood, which is rarely preserved in the soil more than a few years. At a later date, perhaps between 25,000 and 10,000 B.C., hunters from Siberia may have come over a land bridge bringing both unifacial and bifacial chipped stone spear points of a widespread Eurasian Levallois-Mousterian tradition. Although these tools appeared earlier in Europe and western Asia (50,000 to 150,000 B.C.), they survived in the marginal area of Siberia until the period 25,000 to 10,000 B.C. and may have given rise to the later lanceolate and fluted stone blade forms of America.

Although the Eskimos have regularly and frequently negotiated Bering Strait in hide boats filled with trade goods in historic times, and archeological evidence suggests that they and their ancestors have paddled their way back and forth across this strait for several millenia (Giddings, 1960: 128, 133), the earliest immigrants to the New World were not Eskimos and more likely walked across on a land bridge as much as 1,000 miles wide at its maximum. There is overwhelming zoological and geological evidence of land bridges from Siberia to Alaska at several times during the Pleistocene. The native animals in northern Asia and North America are so much alike that zoologists have combined the two areas into a single major life zone. Geologists estimate that during the maximum periods of the major glaciations the ice cap was a mile high over vast areas of land and as much as 9,000 feet high in some localities. The enormous amount of water contained in these ice caps came ultimately from the oceans in the form of fog and clouds and later fell in the form of snow, which still later became compressed into solid ice. The result was a lowering of the ocean level by as much as several hundred feet. Because the ocean bottom at Bering Strait today is only about 120 feet deep, it is clear that a modest lowering of ocean depths could produce a land bridge there.

Recently assembled evidence indicates that there were two land bridges in the late Pleistocene between Siberia and Alaska which might have been used by early immigrants to the New World (Müller-Beck, 1966: 1203–4). The first existed between about 50,000 and 40,000 B.C., and the second between about 26,000 and 8000 B.C. The second was wider than the first and reached its maximum width of 1,000 miles at about 18,000 B.C. However, the climate during the time of the earlier land bridge was a little milder and more favorable to man than it is today, and it was at this time that the woolly mammoth, caribou, and other species later hunted by early man first migrated from Asia to North America. At the time of both of these land bridges the climate was so cold that a people not equipped with tailored fur clothing and pit houses could not have survived in what is now the

Bering Sea area. The landscape of the land bridge was arctic tundra, without trees, and temperatures were about as cold as those of the tundra today. Evidence of pit houses and fur clothing has been found in Mongolia near Lake Baikal at sites dated between 13,000 and 8000 B.C., and may well have been continuously distributed across the land bridge into Alaska. An impediment to migration into North America over this second bridge was an ice barrier just south of Alaska between about 21,000 and 11,000 B.C. That this ice barrier was broken by ice-free corridors, and that human groups were traversing it at this time, is suggested by the apparently sudden appearance of Paleoindians at many localities in the Americas around 10,000 B.C. or soon after. The evidence of early man in Tierra del Fuego by about 8000 B.C. suggests that his ancestors had passed through this so-called ice barrier thousands of years earlier.

Spruce pollen recently collected by Colinvaux (1967) on the Pribilof Islands in the Bering Sea proves that spruce forests extended farther to the west in Alaska at about 8000 B.C. than they do at present. This, in turn, shows that the climate at the land bridge was a little milder for a short period at this time than it is today, although it was never mild enough in the late Pleistocene for the forests of Siberia and Alaska to join one another on the land bridge.

Physically, Indians resemble Asians more closely than they do any other major physical type in the Old World; but resemblance is closer to the marginal Mongoloids of Indonesia, west central Asia, and Tibet than to the central ones of Mongolia, China, or Japan. The marginal Mongoloids represent an earlier and less specialized racial type than do the central Mongoloids. The American Indians sprang from the ancestors of this marginal Mongoloid population, which at one time covered most of Asia north and east of India. These marginal Mongoloids share more physical characteristics with Europeans than do the central Mongoloids; this fact is explained by the hypothesis that the separation of Europeans and Mongoloids had not progressed very far when the latter in northeast Asia began to migrate into Alaska via the land bridge across Bering Strait.

The physical anthropologist Imbelloni (1958) has classified the Indians of both continents into 11 subvarieties; Georg Neumann (1952) has divided the Indians of North America north of Mexico into 8 subvarieties. Neumann postulated that all but one of his subvarieties represented a separate migration of a physical subtype already differentiated from the others when it entered the New World.

At the opposite pole is the theory of Marshall Newman (1962), who postulates that most of the physical variations among subvarieties of American Indians are to be explained by adaptations of a single ancestral type to the various environments of the New World. The truth of the matter probably lies somewhere between these extreme views.

A recent quantitative test by Long (1966) of the reality of Georg Neumann's subvarieties in the eastern United States found strong supporting evidence for some, no evidence at all for others, and postulated a new Iroquoian group not distinguished by Neumann. Although no published criticism of Marshall Newman's environmental explanation has been as explicit, it seems likely that the populations in California, the Southwest, the Southeast, and central Mexico were not as stable and free of migration as he believes. Language classification alone suggests many migrations into these areas during the past 5,000 years and probably earlier (Map 37; Voegelin and Voegelin, 1966). Whole languages do not spread by relay diffusion, but require the migration of considerable numbers of speakers or of a powerful political and military elite, such as that of the Romans in their colonies. The plethora of unrelated language families and phyla found in the areas that Marshall Newman considered the most stable calls for more migration than his theory can tolerate. If we allow for the immigration of several distinct subtypes into the New World and also permit a moderate amount of adaptation to environment, we arrive at a more plausible explanation of the physical subvarieties of the American Indians. It has been a complicated development which cannot be explained by any single overriding process, as Newman and Neumann have agreed in more recent writings.

Until recently linguists have been unable to relate any of the languages and language groups of the Americas with those of Asia. Swadesh (1962) has finally assembled considerable evidence to indicate that the Eskimo-Aleutian languages of the North American Arctic are historically related to the Kamchadal-Chukchi-Koryak group in Siberia. The former group is called Eskaleutian, and the latter Chukotian. These two language families diverged from a common ancestral language about 2500 B.C., as estimated from glottochronology. This is the strongest case of its kind so far. Earlier attempts by Shafer (1952) and Swadesh (1952) to relate Athapaskan to the Sino-Tibetan phylum were less conclusive. As more and more comparative linguistic knowledge accumulates, we may anticipate more evidence on the historical relationship of other language groups in Asia and the Americas, but the time depths are likely to be great.

The earliest major culture type to emerge unchallenged in the archeological record is the Big-Game Hunting tradition. It flourished in the grasslands which covered not only the area now known as the Great Plains but also parts of the Southwest and the Eastern Woodland. It is characterized by lanceolate projectile points retouched on both sides. These fall into several major types: the fluted Clovis, Folsom, and related forms; the single-shouldered Sandia; and the groups called Plano. Although none of these so far discovered can be dated with certainty earlier than 10,000 B.C., they may be several millenia older in light of their possible derivation from older Old World forms and the excellent workmanship that suggests the need of an apprentice period of development. The demise of this Big-Game tradition began as early as 8000–7000 B.C. in some localities, but it survived in the Plains area to as late as 4000 B.C. Because the weapon points were much larger and heavier than the arrowheads of historic hunting peoples, it is universally assumed that they were attached to the ends of spears which could either have been thrust and retained in the hands or hurled like a javelin. Some might have been thrown with the spear-thrower, although there is no direct evidence of this implement in this early period.

From 10,000 to 8000 B.C. the principal animals hunted were the mammoth and mastodon, huge animals larger than any modern elephant. As these animals became scarcer, an extinct bison larger than any form alive today was the most important animal; this species gave way later to the smaller bison hunted by historic Plains Indians. Although these Big-Game Hunters certainly killed and ate smaller game too and even ate a little vegetable food from time to time, their principal occupation and diet centered in the big game. They have left no evidence of houses or of food storage pits, suggesting that they were constantly on the move. They must have had a close-knit social organization with a maximum of teamwork within their hunting parties in order to kill such large animals as the mammoth. The Big-Game Hunting culture gave rise to the Archaic traditions of the Plains and Eastern Woodlands.

From about 9000 to 5000 B.C. a cultural tradition called Old Cordilleran flourished in the northwestern part of North America from the Rocky Mountain divide to the Pacific Ocean and from Alaska south to Oregon. This is distinct from the Big-Game Hunting tradition, and, although the two overlap in time, they occupied mutually exclusive areas. The most diagnostic single trait of the Old Cordilleran Culture is a willow-leaf-shaped stone point chipped on both sides and retouched on all edges. These points are thought to have been used as points on spears or darts and possibly also as knives in a wooden or horn handle. They are associated with other chipped stone tools presumably used for chopping, cutting, scraping, and perforating—all suggesting a predominantly hunting subsistence. No seed-grinding stones occur in this tradition. The Old Cordilleran tradition was the forerunner of the later cultures that appeared in the Arctic, Northwest Coast, Plateau, and parts of California.

A third major early culture is called the Desert tradition, which was found in the Great Basin, the Southwest, and Northeast Mexico. The two most diagnostic traits are baskets and milling stones to grind wild seeds. The baskets were used to collect the seeds, to carry them home, to store them, and to boil them by means of hot stones placed in water in the basket. Projectile points were broader and shorter and generally smaller than those of the Big-Game Hunters or the Old Cordillerans. They were mounted on darts or spears hurled with the aid of the spear-thrower. Animals of various sizes were hunted, but the larger ones were most often wild sheep, antelope, and deer, although some bison bones have also been found in Desert sites. Beginning about 8500 B.C., this Desert tradition persisted with little change in the Great Basin area of Nevada, Utah, eastern Oregon, and southern Idaho until the middle of the nineteenth century. The Paiute and Shoshoni Indians are the descendants of the Desert people. Because there were never any desert areas in Alaska and Canada, the Desert tradition must have arisen after the early Indians had reached the desert area well within the boundaries of what is now the United States. The ancestors of the earliest Desert people were probably the Old Cordillerans.

THE FIRST FARMERS

The earliest archeological sites in the highlands of central and southern Mexico reveal a hunting culture generically akin to those of the Big-Game Hunters and Old Cordillerans. By about 7000 B.C. the peoples of these areas were subsisting principally on wild plants, and the first evidence of farming also appears at this time. Caves in the mountains of southern Tamaulipas have yielded evidence for the domestication of the bottle gourd (*Lagenaria*), the chili pepper (*Capsicum annum* or *frutescens*), and the summer squash or pumpkin (*Cucurbita pepo*) during the Infiernillo phase, from 7000 to 5000 B.C. In the same horizon the remains of a number of wild plants, such as maguey (*Agave*), the cactus pear (*Opuntia*), and the runner bean (*Phaseolus coccineus*), have been found at camp sites in these caves. All of these plants were eaten except the gourd, which was used as a container. These people made twilled and checkered mats, rod-foundation baskets, and net bags. The latter two were used to collect and store the plant products. They also made chipped stone projectile points, scrapers, and choppers used in hunting, butchering, and dressing hides, but remains of plants far outnumber those of animals, suggesting that these people possessed a Desert culture.

In Tamaulipas, stone mortars and manos, used for grinding plant seeds, first appear between 5000 and 3000 B.C. It is estimated that at this time wild plants provided about 80 per cent of the diet, domesticated plants about 7 per cent, and wild animals about 13 per cent. Maize (corn) (*Zea mays*) did not appear in this area until 2500 B.C., and squash (*Cucurbita moschata*) not until 2000 B.C., when domesticated plants furnished about 20 per cent of the diet. The house remains in the open sites of this period suggest a more sedentary way of life. Permanent farming villages with pottery were achieved in the next millenium, 2000–1000 B.C.

Four hundred miles to the south, in what is now the Mexican state of Puebla, a partly independent but parallel development of farming cultures was going on at the same time. Cave sites in the Tehuacán Valley at about 6,000 feet altitude have yielded the first evidence of farming in the El Riego period, 7000 to 5000 B.C. One plant—squash (probably *Cucurbita moschata* or *mixta*)—may have been domesticated. Remains of wild plants, such as grasses, maguey, and cactus pear, were found in abundance, but animal bones were rare, suggesting that subsistence was heavily biased toward plants. Man-made objects found in the caves include bell-shaped pestles and mortars, crude milling stones and manos, string nets, coiled baskets, and twined blankets of plant fibers.

In the next later horizon in Puebla, 5000 to 3400 B.C., more plants appear. The most significant one is corn, which dates from about 5000 B.C.; at that time it was a tiny primitive form with a pod around each kernel. Although no cobs or grains of corn have yet been recovered from any earlier archeological sites, pollen analysis of much earlier soils reveals that wild corn existed as early as 80,000 B.C. This completely demolishes speculation that corn may have originated in the Old World. Other plants were avocados, chili peppers, gourds, amaranth, tepary beans, zapotes, and squash (*C. moschata*). The last-named was a domesticate, as the others may have been at this date and are definitely known to have been in later periods. The fact that plants harvested in both fall and spring seasons were found side by side in the same time levels suggest occupation of the same cave all or most of the year.

The earliest cotton (*Gossypium*) appeared about 5800 B.C. in sites occupied by human beings, but it was probably wild. It became increasingly more common, and by the Abejas phase, 3400–2300 B.C., was widely used and probably domesticated. The pumpkin (*C. pepo*) first appears in Puebla at about 3000 B.C.

Recent excavations in Oaxaca by Flannery *et al.* (1967) yielded evidence of a third center of early domestication. Small black beans (*Phaseolus* sp.) and squash seeds (*Cucurbita* sp.) first appear at about 7000 B.C., and these were soon followed by other species of plants. By 1500 B.C., permanent villages, relying principally on farming with irrigation from shallow wells in the corn fields, were established.

This evidence suggests that agriculture may have had multiple origins in Mexico, because most of the earliest domesticated plants in the three areas were of different species. Once plants were domesticated, however, they were relayed from one area to another by intervening peoples, thus establishing diffusion as an important contributor to culture growth. Much of the growth of farming in Mexico took place during a hot and dry period called the Altithermal, which extended from about 5000 to 2500 B.C. It is possible that the failure of wild plant crops to thrive in this adverse climatic phase encouraged the Indians to plant, cultivate, and eventually irrigate the wild species that needed such care. Then, when the climate became moister and cooler, around 2000 B.C., agriculture experienced a leap forward and soon became the dominant means of subsistence.

In the Southwest, which includes Arizona, New Mexico, Sonora, Chihuahua, and parts of Utah, Colorado, and Texas, the earliest evidence of farming is the corn or maize from Bat Cave, New Mexico, dated between 3500 and 2500 B.C. It was a small pod-popcorn, similar to that from Tamaulipas dated at 2500 B.C. It was most likely the result of relay diffusion from Mexico, probably up the Sierra Madre Occidental to the Mogollon Mountains of southern New

Mexico and Arizona. Although the evidence for squashes or pumpkins and the gourd is more shaky, it is probable that these domesticates diffused along with maize. The red kidney bean (*Phaseolus vulgaris*) arrived in the same area by 1000 B.C. along with improved maize varieties. These domesticated plants would not have been accepted by the earlier Southwesterners, who were principally hunters; but the later Desert peoples of this area had been subsisting mostly on wild plants for thousands of years before knowledge of domesticated plants reached them from Mexico, and were sufficiently plant-conscious to learn from the outside how to cultivate the new species. By about the beginning of the Christian era the cultivation of these plants had spread more widely and had laid the groundwork for the emergence of three separate traditions: the Mogollon, the Anasazi, and the Hohokam. The Mogollon survived in northern Mexico until about A.D. 1700; the Anasazis became the historic Pueblos, and the Hohokam probably the historic Pimans. About A.D. 700 the Patayan culture began to farm on the Colorado River, and has survived in the historic period as the River Yumans.

In the Eastern Woodlands, farming was first introduced about 1000 B.C., either from the Southwest or from Tamaulipas, Mexico. It became associated with burial mounds and pottery, which had made their first appearances about 1500 B.C. and 2500 B.C. respectively (Jennings, 1968: 185). The first plants to be cultivated were squashes, pumpkins, and gourds, introduced from the south or west, along with a number of endemic species, including the sunflower, pigweed, marsh elder, and goosefoot. Maize came along a few centuries later, apparently from the Southwest. As early as 500 B.C., at least squash had been relayed as far north as the Saginaw Valley in Michigan.

Perhaps the most famous and widespread tradition of this period in what is now the eastern half of the United States was that of the Hopewell people, who flourished from 200 B.C. to A.D. 400. Although they cultivated maize and probably other plants, they subsisted principally on game and wild plants. Their mounds and village sites extend from Kansas to Ohio and from Wisconsin and Michigan to the Gulf of Mexico. The culmination of prehistoric Indian cultures in this area is that of the Mississippian peoples, A.D. 700–1500, who, by A.D. 700–900, were raising much larger quantities of maize, beans, squashes, pumpkins, sunflowers, and gourds. The climactic period for the Mississippians was from A.D. 1200 to 1500. De Soto came upon them in his famous explorations, 1539 to 1542, and found huge fields of maize and other plants, large mounds on which temples and palaces were erected, and witnessed the arrival of male and female chiefs on litters carried on the shoulders of commoners.

CIVILIZATIONS

It was noted above that the peoples of southern Mexico stepped up their farming activities at about 2000 B.C. and became more sedentary. The first great civilization to emerge in this area was that of the Olmecs in southern Veracruz and Tabasco from 1500 B.C. to perhaps A.D. 300. They built the first religious centers with man-made mounds of earth, on which temples of perishable materials were probably erected, and carved a number of stone monuments, the most impressive being huge stone heads up to eight feet high and weighing as much as thirty tons. At the other extreme, they made hollow, baby-faced pottery figurines, some of which were small enough to be concealed in one hand. Olmec sculpture was both in the round and in relief. It portrayed human beings and mythical half-animal and half-human gods, of which the anthropomorphized jaguar was the most recurrent. The characteristic mouth has full lips and turned-down corners. At La Venta, the largest Olmec ceremonial center, 800 to 400 B.C., the complex of mounds and monuments extended for two kilometers; the largest structure was a rectangular earth mound seventy by 120 meters at the base and thirty-two meters high at one end. The population that built such a religious and political center must have numbered thousands. They lived principally on cultivated plants, and were led by a chief or overlord with the power to compel them to work at least part time on these large public works. At Tres Zapotes, the latest Olmec center, a stela carved with a bar-and-dot numerical date, equivalent to our 31 B.C., is the oldest archeological · evidence so far of writing and the Long Count calendar in the New World. These apparently were Olmec contributions to Meso-American culture, although these accomplishments reached their greatest development in the hands of the Mayas.

During the middle pre-classic period, 1000 to 300 B.C., Olmec civilization spread west and south into what are now the Mexican states of Puebla, Morelos, Guerrero, Oaxaca, and Chiapas, and even into Guatemala. It served as a base for the greater civilizations of the lowland Maya, those in the Mexican highlands at Monte Albán in

Oaxaca, and at Teotihuacán in the Valley of Mexico, and many other smaller and lesser-known nations.

The first settlers in the Maya lowlands arrived after 1000 B.C. and, by about the time of Christ, had constructed a number of religious centers comparable to the somewhat earlier ones of the Olmecs. During their classic period, A.D. 300 to 900, the Mayas surpassed all other American civilizations. This was followed by an invasion of Toltecs from central Mexico, a subsequent decline, and a sort of leveling off of achievement by the time the Spanish arrived in the sixteenth century.

The material achievements of the Mayas include a stone architecture, using both the post-and-beam principle and the corbeled arch, and the construction of pyramids up to seventy meters in height in the ceremonial centers of their towns. On top of the high pyramids were temples, while lower earthworks were crowned with lower and longer buildings thought to have housed royalty and nobility. All pyramids and buildings were at least faced with solid stone, on which elaborate art was carved. As many as twenty such ceremonial centers were occupied and fully in operation at the same time in the classic period.

The Maya were the most intellectually advanced of all Indian peoples. Their knowledge of mathematics, astronomy, and the resulting calendar exceeded that of the Greeks and Romans. But their writing never advanced beyond the ideographic glyph stage, and has never been completely deciphered and translated. Mayan art is generally ranked first among pre-Columbian art styles, but it is so different from Old World forms of artistic expression that comparison is difficult.

A second great civilization to develop from the Olmec base was that of the Zapotecs at Monte Albán in Oaxaca, 600 B.C. to A.D. 900. In the earliest phase, about 500 B.C., the Zapotecs produced large, flat-topped mounds, carved stone monuments, hieroglyphs, numerals, and a calendar. In phase III, A.D. 600 to 900, Monte Albán was one of the largest religious and political centers in all of Meso-America. It was built on a hilltop which had been leveled, creating a plaza in the center, surrounded on four sides by platforms, pyramids, temples, palaces, and a ball court. There were many tombs of royalty and nobility, one of which produced the finest and most valuable collection of gold, silver, and copper jewelry so far discovered at any single archeological site in the New World. Some of the tombs are painted with interior frescoes of men, gods, and hieroglyphs. A distinctive feature of the site is the large number of burial urns on which the figure of a seated god has been modeled in clay. The site was abandoned after A.D. 900 except as a burial place for Zapotecan and later Mixtecan royalty and nobility.

A third great culture to stem from the Olmec base is that at Teotihuacán in the Valley of Mexico northeast of Mexico City, 200 B.C. to A.D. 600. The first phase, 200 B.C. to A.D. 1, produced platform ceremonial mounds and closely packed residential structures covering three square miles. This civilization reached its climax in the second and third phases, A.D. 1 to 600, when seven square miles were occupied by two large pyramids, several temples and palaces, thousands of wall-to-wall rooms that apparently housed families, and a long concourse connecting the two pyramids and the principal temple, that of Quetzalcoatl, the feathered serpent god. The largest pyramid, called (later by the Aztecs) the Pyramid of the Sun, is 210 meters square at the base with a flat top sixty-four meters above the surrounding plain. The best examples of stone carving are the heads of the feathered serpent god on the temple dedicated to him. The city of Teotihuacán certainly dominated the Valley of Mexico and may have been the capital of a kingdom of wider extent. Its population is estimated at from 10,000 to 100,000 persons. There is a little evidence of hieroglyphic writing and a calendar, both of central Mexican types differing from those of the Maya. The power of this great city ended suddenly about A.D. 600, when it was sacked and burned by an enemy army.

After the fall of Teotihuacán, central Mexico was dominated by the Toltecs at their capital city at Tula in Hidalgo from about A.D. 950 to 1160. The Aztecs first appeared on the scene about the time that Tula was destroyed (A.D. 1160), and may even have had a hand in its destruction. Like the Toltecs before them, they moved in from the north and only gradually became acculturated to the way of life of the more civilized peoples already in the Valley of Mexico. It was not until A.D. 1428 that the Aztecs gained the ascendancy in the Valley of Mexico, but by A.D. 1502 they were operating an economic and military empire that stretched from coast to coast and extended southeast all the way to Guatemala. They, in turn, were defeated by the Spanish in 1521.

The majority of American scholars view the great Indian civilizations as largely historically independent of those in the Old World, although some contacts across the Pacific are not denied. Willey

(1966: 19–24) assembles a representative sample of the arguments that have been offered for trans-Pacific diffusion. Wauchope (1962) debunks a large number of untenable speculations about the origin of the Indians and their cultures. The view of this volume is that we must give almost all the credit to the Indians, even though we concede a few diffusions from the Old World.

A comparison of rates of cultural evolution in the New World with those in the Old World shows that American Indian cultures developed faster from their first appearance until about 7000 B.C. The Levallois-Mousterian base in Siberia, from which the Indian traditions stemmed, was 10,000 to 20,000 years behind the demise of this base in Europe, the Middle East, and North Africa. By the time the Indians began to farm, about 7000 B.C., they were only about two thousand years behind the earliest farming in the Old World, about 9000 B.C. (Wright, 1968). From this time on, however, the Indians fell behind, and remained in a stage of incipient agriculture for about five thousand years. It was not until after 2000 B.C. that their farming provided more food than did their hunting and gathering. In the Old World, in contrast, permanent villages and towns with wall-to-wall adobe brick rooms were achieved by 6000 B.C., suggesting that farming was already the dominant means of subsistence. Cities with populations in the tens of thousands do not appear in the New World until about the beginning of the Christian era, while in the Old World there were a number of such cities by 3000 B.C.

In the field of technology, bronze was known by 3500 B.C. and iron by 1500 B.C. in the Old World, while the Indians did not invent bronze until A.D. 1150 (in Peru) and knew nothing of iron until Europeans introduced it. Similarly, hieroglyphic writing was established by 3000 B.C. and the alphabet by 1000 B.C. in the Old World, while the Indians were not using hieroglyphs until almost at the beginning of the Christian era and never did invent an alphabet.

On the other hand, the mathematics, astronomy, and calendar of the Mayas were more advanced than those of the Greeks, Romans, or any other Old World civilization earlier than, or contemporary with, that of the Mayas. Whatever evaluation one makes of the largely independent growths of civilization in the two hemispheres, the conquest of the Indians by Europeans throttled any further independent development on the part of the Indians and robbed the world of the further original achievements they surely would have contributed if they had not been subjugated.

REFERENCES

COLINVAUX, 1967; FLANNERY *et al.*, 1967; GIDDINGS, 1960; GRIFFIN, 1967; IMBELLONI, 1958; JENNINGS, 1968; JENNINGS AND NORBECK, 1964; KRIEGER, 1964; MÜLLER-BECK, 1966; NEUMANN, 1952; NEWMAN, 1962; PATTERSON AND HOWELLS, 1967; SWADESH, 1962; VOEGELIN AND VOEGELIN, 1966; WAUCHOPE, 1962, 1966; WILLEY, 1966; WRIGHT, 1968.

2

Culture Areas

THE word "culture," as used by anthropologists and other social scientists, refers to the entire way of life of a people, not just the visual arts, music, dancing, drama, and literature. The chapter headings in this volume, with the partial exception of that on the origin of the Indians, all refer to culture, each to a different aspect of it. A culture area is a geographical area occupied by a number of peoples whose cultures show a significant degree of similarity with each other and at the same time a significant degree of dissimilarity with the cultures of the peoples of other such areas. In theory the delimitation of culture areas must be based on a representative sample of all aspects of the cultures of all the peoples being thus classified. The determination of significant degrees of similarity and dissimilarity is ultimately a statistical problem, but working approximations may be arrived at by other means, partly intuitive, by scholars familiar with a region.

The culture area, in its current stage of development, is a convenient way of describing the ways of life of hundreds of peoples covering a whole continent or a larger part of the earth's surface. Few readers are familiar with even a hundred names of Indian tribes, and the many names on Maps 38–44 at the end of this volume are much too numerous to be repeatedly mentioned in a book of this kind. Therefore the entire North American continent, from the Arctic to Panama, has been divided into seventeen culture areas, which are relatively easy to remember (Map 2). With this simple scheme it is possible to give the approximate geographical distribution of some detail of Indian life, such as the custom of scalping, in a few words. As is evident from the many maps to follow, most details of culture do not fit the areas exactly. Nevertheless, the areas provide a convenient framework for introducing some degree of order in the plethora of detail available about North American Indians.

In some respects the culture areas of the anthropologist are like the

17

geographical regions of the geographer, and the dominance of geographical terms in the culture area labels is designed to help the reader remember where the areas are located. The boundaries of such areas on maps unavoidably give a false impression by overemphasizing the sharpness of the break. Most boundaries are actually the approximate lines where the two neighboring types of phenomena are present in equal amounts. In one direction the first features become progressively more dominant, while in the opposite direction the second features become more and more noticeable.

For example, if you drive from New York to San Francisco you encounter a number of geographical zones. You start on a coastal plain, originally covered with broad-leaved trees, and as you proceed west you gain in altitude until you have reached the modest ranges of the Appalachians in Pennsylvania. Here trees of the pine family appear along with the broadleaves. After leaving the mountains around Pittsburgh, you travel through the slightly rolling Ohio country which gradually becomes flatter and flatter in Indiana and Illinois. If the natural vegetation had been undisturbed by the White man, you would notice at about the Indiana-Illinois line a balance between equal amounts of the forest, through which you have traveled so far, and a treeless prairie. As you proceed west in Illinois the forest cover gradually gives way to the tall grass of the prairie which dominates the landscape until you arrive in Nebraska. There at about the 100th meridian the grass becomes shorter and the trees still fewer. The first really abrupt change comes when you strike the magnificent peaks of the Rockies, which rise 9,000 feet above the mile-high plains at Denver. You suddenly find yourself in a wonderland of snow-capped peaks, coniferous trees, and cascading mountain streams. But before you are out of Colorado, the land becomes drier and sagebrush makes its appearance, anticipating the deserts of the Great Basin. The Great Basin is so labeled because the streams there do not reach the ocean but flow inward to lakes, such as Great Salt Lake, or lose themselves in desert sands. After about a day's drive on the desert, you suddenly reach the eastern slopes of the Sierra Nevada which rise abruptly from the desert floor. Again you see the snow-capped peaks and coniferous forest which give way in California to valley grasslands and low coastal mountains.

If you could have traveled the same route in 1600, before Indian cultures had been disturbed by the Whites, you would have noticed similar changes in their way of life. You might travel for hundreds of miles with no appreciable change in Indian housing, clothing, and customs, and then suddenly you would notice abrupt changes within a few miles. In most cases, however, the change would be gradual. The permanent houses of the eastern United States would become salted with portable tipis in the prairie area before they were abandoned entirely in favor of the tipi out on the open plains. Nevertheless, it is convenient to draw a boundary at the line where the frequency of portable tipis matches that of stationary houses. The boundaries of culture areas, therefore, are generally the lines at which the two ways of life are in balance and only occasionally represent an abrupt change. A brief description of the culture areas follows.

Arctic.—The home of the Eskimo in Alaska, Canada, and Greenland, this area is divided into a western portion, which includes the Aleut on the Aleutian Islands as well as the Eskimo of Alaska, and a combination central and eastern division, which embraces all the Eskimo from the Mackenzie River delta east to Greenland. The Alaskan Eskimo and Aleuts have been much influenced by both the cultures of Siberia on the west and of the Northwest Coast on the southeast. The Central and Eastern Eskimo retain more of the early and distinctive features of their way of life because they lived in greater isolation, with less contact with Indians to the south. The Eskimo in every locality but one or two had access to the sea and lived most of the year on the shoreline where they could obtain sea mammals.

Sub-Arctic.—This area lies directly south of the Arctic, as the name implies, in a belt of coniferous forest broken here and there by treeless tundra. It includes interior Alaska and most of interior Canada and was the home of the snowshoe and toboggan Indians who spoke languages of the Athapaskan and Algonquian families. For convenience this huge area has been split into three subdivisions: the Yukon Sub-Arctic in Alaska and Yukon Territory, Canada, drained by the Yukon River system; the Mackenzie Sub-Arctic in Northwest Territories and the northern parts of British Columbia, Alberta, Saskatchewan, and Manitoba, drained by the Mackenzie River; and the Eastern Sub-Arctic in Ontario, Quebec, and adjacent parts of Manitoba, and coast of Labrador. Indians speaking languages of the Athapaskan family occupied the Yukon and Mackenzie regions, while people speaking Algonquian languages lived in the eastern part. The caribou and the moose were the principal sources of food over most of the Sub-Arctic, and the many streams, lakes, and swamps made travel in the birch bark canoe almost universal.

Northwest Coast.—This area includes the coastline from the panhandle in southeastern Alaska through British Columbia, Washington, and Oregon, to the northwestern corner of California. These Indians subsisted principally on fish, lived in plank houses, and enjoyed a considerable surplus of the necessities of life. Those in Alaska and British Columbia are famous for their totem poles, which may be seen in many large museums. The culture of this area competes with that of the Arctic as the most distinctive or the most foreign of aboriginal North America. This is due partly to the geographical environment but also to its history, which shows much evidence of contact with Asia. The great emphasis on the acquisition of material goods, their display on public occasions, and the emergence of social classes and hereditary slavery set it off sharply from other nonfarming culture areas of the continent.

Plateau.—This region is named after the Columbian plateaus drained by the Columbia River system. It includes parts of British Columbia. It is a difficult area to characterize because its culture exhibits influences from both the Northwest Coast and the Plains, and the semidesert environment of the southern portion gives it something in common with the Great Basin as well. In the central part of the Plateau we find democratic peoples entirely free of the emphasis on rank of the Northwest Coast; they are also peaceful peoples largely lacking the war drive of the Plains Indians. Fish was the staple food over most of this region as one might suspect from the large numbers of salmon taken in its streams in modern times.

Plains.—This area stretches from central Alberta all the way south to the Mexican border. It is bounded on the west by the Rocky Mountains and on the east by the Missouri River. It includes parts of Alberta, Saskatchewan, Montana, Wyoming, Colorado, the Dakotas, Nebraska, Kansas, Oklahoma, and Texas. The Plains Indians are the ones best known to most people in the United States today. They ate the meat of the buffalo, rode horses after A.D. 1600, lived in conical tipis, and did not farm. After acquiring the horse, they became the most nomadic of all Indians and fought the White man bravely to defend their lands until as late as the 1870's. This was the home of the Blackfoot, Crow, Sioux (Dakota), Cheyenne, and Comanche Indians, among others.

Prairies.—This region matches pretty closely our modern Middle West. It includes all of Wisconsin, Michigan, Illinois, Iowa, and

Missouri, and parts of the Dakotas, Minnesota, Nebraska, Kansas, Oklahoma, Texas, Arkansas, Tennessee, Kentucky, and Indiana. These Indians were much like those of the Plains except that they farmed and lived in permanent villages near their farms part of the year. Most of them also hunted the buffalo as well as other animals. Such familiar peoples as the Pawnee, Omaha, Iowa, Osage, and Illinois lived in this area.

East.—This area extends from a little beyond the St. Lawrence River in Canada to the Gulf of Mexico and from the eastern boundary of the Prairies area to the Atlantic. It includes all of New York and the Middle Atlantic states, southern New England, and most of the Southern states as far west as Louisiana. The Iroquois of New York state belong in this region, as do the Five Civilized Tribes of the South. These peoples were more sedentary than those of the Prairies, subsisted to a greater extent on farm crops, and were organized into the largest political units north of Mexico. The European colonists settling in the United States contacted these Indians and learned from them to raise corn, beans, and pumpkins, as well as tobacco.

California.—This culture area includes about two-thirds of the modern state of that name. Although the area is small, it is famous for its great diversity of physical type, speech, and culture. In spite of the absence of farming, population was fairly dense but the political unit, called the tribelet, numbered only a few hundred. These Indians suffered a decline after the Spanish arrived in 1770, and the Gold Rush of 1849 put an end to their independence. The names of these peoples, such as Maidu, Miwok, Pomo, and Yokuts, are not generally familiar today.

Great Basin.—This area includes all of Nevada and Utah and parts of California, Oregon, Idaho, Wyoming, and Colorado. It is one of the driest regions in the United States and was inhabited by Shoshonis, Paiutes, and Utes. These peoples obtained a meager living from wild species of plants and animals available in their deserts and mountains. They lived in small family groups or bands until they got horses from the Spanish or from other Indians. Along with the horses came other influences from the Plains area, and those living east of Great Salt Lake adopted the buffalo-hide tipis, Plains dress, and Plains customs after that time.

Baja California.—This small area is left separate because it does not fit very well with any of the neighboring areas. Most of it is desert, but in the south rainfall is heavier. From the number of village names left by the Spanish Padres, population appears to have been greater in the more favorable southern environment. Although none of these Indians farmed, their diet was superior to that of the Great Basin peoples because of sea foods. Few localities are more than fifty miles from the sea, and settlements were more numerous on the shore than inland. They were missionized by the Spanish before the California Indians and died of malnutrition and European diseases in such numbers that few survive today. Little is known about them.

Southwest.—This area includes most of Arizona, New Mexico, all of the Mexican states of Sonora and Sinaloa, and the western parts of Chihuahua and Durango. Because much of the land is desert, settlements tended to be in oasis-like spots near streams. All of these Indians farmed, although some much more than others. Many of them lived in villages or towns, hence the name Pueblo for the village dwellers of northern New Mexico and Arizona, such as Hopi and Zuñi. The Navaho and Apache also belong in this area, as do such lesser-known tribes as the Mohave and Yuma. Of the Mexican tribes, the Yaqui are known to many people in the United States today, and the Tarahumara may be familiar to those who have toured Mexico. On the whole the Indians in New Mexico and Arizona have been less disturbed by our own westward expansion than those in any other part of the United States, and they still retain many of their Indian attitudes and customs which make them interesting to tourists. The Navaho are now the largest tribe in the United States, with a population of about 100,000 in 1969.

Northeast Mexico.—This desert region was formerly inhabited by the wild Chichimecs, who harassed the Spanish during the entire colonial period. They lived exclusively on wild plants and animals and were experts with the bow and arrow. They were extremely warlike and cost the Spanish many times as much in blood, sweat, tears, and money as did the successful campaign of Cortés against Montezuma and the Aztecs. On many occasions the Chichimecs fought to the last man to defend themselves against the Spaniards and, when captured, often escaped or committed suicide rather than acquiesce in a life of farming and peace. Today the few survivors of the Chichimecs live on little farms of their own or work as laborers on the farms and ranches of the Mexicans, but the oldest ones, who still speak no Spanish, remember the wild tales of the good old days when they raided the Spanish wagon trains to and from the silver mines at Zacatecas.

Meso-America.—In recent years this term has been applied to that part of Mexico lying south of about the 21st parallel plus Guatemala, British Honduras, El Salvador, and parts of Honduras and Nicaragua. This is the land of the famous Mayas and Aztecs, who have been compared to the Greeks and Romans. The Mayas were the intellectuals who invented a place number system to record important dates on monuments and devised a remarkably accurate calendar, parts of which still survive today in the area. The Aztecs were the conquerors and politicians who dominated most of the peoples in southern Mexico when Cortés first set foot on Mexican soil. They compelled all the peoples they conquered to pay them tribute at regular intervals, and it is from similar tribute lists compiled by the early sixteenth-century Spaniards that much of our best data on population, settlement patterns, and political organization are obtained. The population of Meso-America in 1520 was greater than that of all the other culture areas combined, according to the best estimates. This large population was made possible by intensive farming with large irrigation systems and well-organized totalitarian governments to regiment all available labor. Although we may not approve of this kind of government today, the peoples of this area achieved a much more complex and sophisticated civilization than that of any other area. The Aztecs and Mayas stemmed from humble Indian ancestors and, with the help of their Indian neighbors, developed their remarkable culture with practically no assistance from Europe and Asia.

This completes the identification of the culture areas which serve as a framework for organizing information in the chapters that follow. Most of this book describes Indian cultures as they were before they were disturbed by European colonization, but because the Indians left no written records other than the difficult to decipher pictographs and glyphs of Meso-America, this must be done from the writings of early missionaries, army officers, traders, and colonial officials.

Anthropologists employ a wide variety of terms to indicate time periods. Pre-Columbian, pre-European, precontact, prehistoric, native, aboriginal, and indigenous all refer to the culture of the Indians before its disturbance by Europeans. Post-Columbian, post-European, post-White, post-contact, historic, modern, and recent all refer to the period after A.D. 1492, or after whatever later date contact between Indians and Whites in a given locality first took place.

For Spanish America the record begins in the early sixteenth century, for the eastern United States not until the seventeenth, for other less accessible areas not until the eighteenth, and for most Indians in the western United States and Canada not until the nineteenth century. Because much of the information on Indians refers to the nineteenth century, when changes due to European contact has already taken place, no claim is made that everything said about them in this book represents pure Indian culture. However, such things as iron tools, which are certain to be of European origin, have been weeded out, and Indian life has been reconstructed as carefully as possible. Because some tribes became extinct, as a result of European colonization, before others were discovered, most of the maps in this volume do not refer to a single century. They telescope information from the sixteenth to the nineteenth centuries. Sometimes the map itself depicts temporal changes where they are well known, but more often the time element is mentioned in the text. Now and then the findings of archeology have added historical depth; where the evidence overwhelmingly points to one conclusion, some historical speculation has been admitted.

REFERENCES

DRIVER AND MASSEY, 1957; KROEBER, 1939; WISSLER, 1938.

3

Language

EVERY time someone asks an anthropologist or linguist if he knows the Indian language, he is voicing again the common assumption that there was only one Indian language. The truth of the matter could hardly be more different. Estimates of the total number of American Indian languages on both continents at first contact with Europeans vary from 1,000 (C. F. Voegelin, personal communication) to 2,000 (Beals and Hoijer, 1965: 613). This means that there were between 1,000 and 2,000 distinct forms of speech, each mutually unintelligible with every other. A thousand languages, when combined in every combination of two at a time, would yield about half a million pairs of unintelligible forms of speech, and 2,000 languages would produce about two million such pairs. Fortunately, the speakers of one language were never confronted with speakers of all the other languages, and most Indians knew so little about their own linguistic diversity that it was not regarded as a serious problem. There were bilingual and even trilingual persons within each social group who could translate when the occasion required. The number of languages listed and classified by the Voegelins below in Table 1, is only 221 for North America because that is all that are well enough known to classify.

Reports by traders, missionaries, soldiers, colonial officials, and others untrained in linguistics have sometimes described Indian languages as being made up of strange animal-like sounds combined into only a few hundred sloppily pronounced words bolstered by signs. There is no evidence that such rudimentary languages have existed anywhere in the world since the beginning of the Upper Old Stone Age, although they must be postulated as an early stage in the evolution of language. It is generally agreed that by the time man became physically Homo sapiens he was probably using fully developed languages with thousands of words and precise systems of pronunciation and grammar. The first immigrants to the New World

25

were indisputably Homo sapiens and must have possessed well-developed languages. Relatively few dictionaries of Indian languages have been compiled, but one published in 1890 on the Dakota (Sioux) language lists about 19,000 words. Some linguists believe that this is about the minimum number of words in any language, and that most dictionaries of Indian languages are far from exhaustive. Languages of culturally more advanced peoples, such as the Meso-Americans, had much richer vocabularies.

PHONOLOGY

Because the Indian languages encountered by Europeans were totally unintelligible to them at first contact, the notion was common that they were composed of strange sounds of a very different character from those used in European languages. A handful of scholarly missionaries knew better, but they had little influence on the rank and file of the colonists, and the belief in the exotic character of Indian speech sounds persists to this day. When Indian speech is analyzed into the distinct elements of sound of which it is composed, called phonemes, even the strangest of these to our ears is paralleled in the languages of Europe and Asia. None is unique to the American Indian. Each phoneme in Indian languages, and for that matter in all languages, should be indicated by a single letter in an alphabet. Linguists employ principally the Roman alphabet, but bolster it with a few Greek letters, special signs, and numerous diacritical marks over, under, and on both sides of the letters. Thus a single, international alphabet of about one hundred symbols can record with sufficient accuracy the speech of all languages, including those of Indians.

A recent inventory of all the consonant phonemes in 176 representative Indian languages (Pierce, 1957) employs sixty-one different symbols. Thus there were only sixty-one essential consonant sounds in this large sample of Indian languages, and the addition of vowel sounds would not have increased the total number beyond about eighty.

A common misconception about phonology is that the ability to pronounce syllables, words, and phrases in an exotic language is determined by the form or shape of the speaker's vocal equipment. Some educated Europeans in Africa today believe that the thick lips of the Negro are necessary for the pronunciation of some of the sounds in African languages, and many persons in the Americas believe that some anatomical peculiarity of Indian speech organs must account for some of the strange noises emitted. It is interesting to note that Indian informants are often as naïve as linguistically unschooled Europeans in respect to the acquisition of the ability to pronounce their language. Some believe that an anthropologist or linguist who can pronounce their words correctly must have some Indian ancestry in his family tree. Every normal human being in the world, however, can learn to speak any language in the world like a native if exposed to the language in infancy or early childhood or patiently taught the language at a later date by a trained and skilled linguist. No one inherits the specific content of any language. In short, babies are interchangeable from one language environment to another; each will learn correctly the language of the society in which he is reared. Every Indian child can learn English, or any other European written language, as effectively as children of European ancestry if given equal opportunity.

Still another misconception is the notion that Indians and other nonliterates speak in a more slovenly manner than those whose languages have been taught them in schools with the aid of writing. On the whole, Indian languages are probably spoken more precisely and with less individual variation among speakers than the languages of Europe. Uniformity of speech is partly a function of the size of the language-bearing group and the closeness of contact among its members. In small, compact societies in which everyone is able to converse with every other person in the group, a high degree of uniformity of speech is the rule. In large language groups spread over large territories or made up of isolated pockets of people, each of whom may be exposed to a different language of a neighboring people, considerable variation in speech is likely to exist, and conditions are right for separate dialects to emerge. Such variation in speech is normal for language and should not be equated with the slovenly or substandard speech of a few subnormal persons. At the same time, some individual variation in speech is normal, as our recognition of voices of acquaintances over the telephone indicates. Such speech peculiarities of individuals, as long as they fall within the normal range, are called idiolects. Everyone has his own idiolect. In fact, if you can imitate the speech of another closely enough to be mistaken for him, you are considered clever and a potential entertainer. Each Indian speaker likewise spoke his own idiolect.

Even though most phonemes in Indian languages have parallels in European languages, the presence of a few kinds of sounds totally absent or rare in European languages makes it very difficult for a European to speak some Indian languages. In about one-third of the American Indian languages, the stops *p*, *t*, or *k* are sometimes pronounced with the breath held at the glottis. This is so rare in European languages that few untrained Europeans are able to pronounce Indian words with such glottalized consonants. A skilled linguist can teach an apt pupil to pronounce these sounds in about an hour, but few adults ever learn to do it on their own. Another impediment to the amateur is phonemic tone. When the meaning of a word can be altered by changing only the pitch of one vowel, then the language is said to possess phonemic tone. The minimum number of tones is two, Mandarin Chinese has four, and a few languages of Southeast Asia possess about a dozen. Phonemic tone is less common in American Indian languages than it is in the languages of Southeast Asia or of Africa, but at the same time it is more common in Indian languages than in those of Europe. Unless a European has had training in tone languages or in music, he is likely to fail to learn the tones of an Indian language. Voiceless or whispered vowels have phonemic value in a number of Indian languages and are likely to be observed only by trained linguists.

The isolated phonemes of an Indian language and a European language may closely match one another, and yet be combined in different sequences and in different positions in words. In English the sounds *tl* occur in that sequence in the terminal or medial position, as in bottling, but never in the initial position. For this reason the pronunciation of Indian words with *tl* in the initial position, as in anglicized *Tlingit*, is difficult for an English speaker. Another illustration is the *ts* combination, which occurs in the terminal position in the plural forms of all English nouns ending in *t*, and also frequently in the medial position, as in "catsup"; but it never occurs in the initial position in English. In Indian languages it frequently occurs in the initial position, where it is difficult for an English speaker to pronounce. When three or more consonants are combined into strange consonant clusters, the difficulty for an English speaker is increased. For instance, persons who have no difficulty at all with the phrase "cat's pajamas" find it almost impossible to pronounce without the first two letters. The manner in which phonemes are combined and located in words is therefore as important to both speakers and hearers of a language as the nature of each in isolation. Because amateurs do not isolate phonemes of foreign languages, it is generally the combinations of phonemes which produce syllables and words that seem impossible to imitate. And finally, the number of combinations and permutations of phonemes taken two, three, four, or more at a time, as they appear in words, is so enormous that two languages could conceivably have identical sets of phonemes and yet share not a single word or phrase in common.

GRAMMAR

The grammars of Indian languages show greater differences from European languages and more variation from one Indian language to another than do phonologies. So complex and variable are Indian grammatical structures that no comprehensive summary can be given in the space of one chapter, but a few illustrations can suggest how different these grammars are from those of the languages of Europe. For instance, inflections of verb forms outnumber those of nouns in most European languages and make the learning of verb forms in Spanish, French, and German more difficult than noun forms for a native English speaker. In some Indian languages, on the contrary, noun forms are complex, as in the following words for "aunt" in the tongue of the Chichimeca-Jonaz of Northeast Mexico.

These terms translate as follows:

	Singular	*Dual*	*Plural*
First person	natü	natüs	natün
Second person	utü	utüs	utün
Third person	erü	erüs	butün

	Singular	*Dual*	*Plural*
First person	my aunt	the aunt of us two	the aunt of us three or more
Second person	your aunt	the aunt of you two	the aunt of you three or more
Third person	his or her aunt	the aunt of those two	the aunt of those three or more

A glance at the native terms above is enough to reveal that pronouns are combined with nouns and that the form for "aunt" changes with each person. With the change in number, however, the stem remains the same, except in the third person plural, while the ending changes. The dual is formed by suffixing *s* to the singular, as in English, and the plural is formed by adding *n* to the singular, as in German (and in some English words). So far the noun has been held constant and the pronoun varied; but the noun may also be varied by introducing dual and plural "aunts." Each would yield nine more forms, making a total of twenty-seven. The terminal *n* in many Chichimeca-Jonaz words is unvoiced, but it may be detected by placing a small piece of paper in front of the speaker's nostrils and observing the deflection of the paper by the air exhaled through the nose. Such voiceless nasals occur in a number of other Indian languages and also in Welsh.

In the Chichimeca-Jonaz language it is impossible to express an unpossessed or unrelated noun concept. There is no way of saying "aunt" without saying whose aunt it is. Likewise, there is no way of saying "earth," "air," or "water" without indicating personal relation or possession. The Chichimeca-Jonaz word for "earth" has the same range of meaning as in English; it means anything from a handful of earth to the entire world. If one wishes to talk about the entire world without suggesting possession, the nearest he can come is "the world of those three or more," translated freely as "their world," or more freely as "world."

Those who believe in a close relationship between language and culture might infer from this language that property concepts were elaborately developed among these people. Such is not the case; in fact, the opposite is true. These people, at the time of the first Spanish contact, were nomads roaming daily in search of wild foods. They moved about constantly, carrying everything they owned on their . backs or in their hands. Their material culture was among the simplest in all of North America, and the landscape was not owned by individuals or kinship groups but was open territory to all. Incorporeal property concepts seem to have been as poorly developed as those governing ownership of material possessions, yet the language demands a possession marker for every noun spoken. On the other hand, a culture with an elaborate development of property rights could not exist without an adequate method of expressing possession in its language. Therefore, possession markers in language are necessary for the functioning of a property-minded culture, but are not sufficient to cause every culture that has them to develop complex property concepts.

The Yana language of California is peculiar because of the presence of distinct "male" and "female" forms for most words. These have nothing to do with sex gender, which is lacking in the language. Men use the "male" forms when speaking to men. "Female" forms are used for all other combinations of the sexes in conversation: by men speaking to women, women speaking to men, and women speaking to women. A few examples follow.

	Male	Female
deer	ba-na	ba'
grizzly bear	t'en'-na	t'et'
moon	wak!āra	wak!ar^a
person	yā-na	ya'
man	īsi	is^i
woman	mari'mi	mare'm^i

The raised terminal vowels in the "female" forms are pronounced softly or whispered. Inspection of the examples above shows that the "female" forms are reductions of the "male" forms, either by eliminating the last syllable or by giving it less stress. Although Yana culture is not well described, there is no evidence to support the view that this linguistic feature is related to any trait or pattern of personality or culture.

Word length shows tremendous variation in Indian languages. Although linguists have not produced a satisfactory definition of a word that is applicable to all languages, it is possible to count empirically the number of phonemes in the words in published texts. For instance, a modest sample of Shawnee yielded an average of ten phonemes per word. This is significantly longer than the words in most English texts. It is perhaps better to label it a phrase, or call it by a compound term, word-phrase.

An unusually long word or phrase from the Southern Paiute language is this: *wii-to-kuchum-punku-rügani-yugwi-va-ntü-m(ü)*. In free translation, it means "they who are going to sit and cut up with a knife a black cow (or bull) buffalo." In more literal translation in the order of the Indian elements, it means "knife-black-buffalo-pet-cut-up-sit (plural)-future-participle-animate plural." In the language of the grammarian, this compound word or phrase is the plural of the future participle of a compound verb "to sit and cut up." The four grammatical elements at the end cannot stand alone, but must be joined to elements that precede them.

This single compound Paiute word, about which Sapir (1921:

30–32) has written two pages of analysis, should be enough to illustrate how grammatically complex some Indian languages can be. It takes years for a brilliant linguist to become fluent enough in such a language to understand every utterance by native speakers and to obtain a full description of the culture exclusively in the native language. Those who have known only a lightly inflected language, such as English, have great difficulty in mastering all the inflections in a more heavily inflected language; and where inflections are modest in number, a strange word order may create difficulties.

In English and other European languages, most words fall into two classes: nouns and verbs. On the whole, verbs denote events of temporary or short duration, while nouns are used to label events or things that are long-lasting and stable; verbs denote processes of change; nouns, the steady state. But English fails to distinguish consistently between the two classes on the continuum of experience. For example, "lightning," "wave," "flame," "storm," and "cycle" are nouns, although they represent both temporary events and processes of change. In contrast, "keep," "adhere," "continue," and "dwell" are verbs, yet they describe long-lasting conditions or steady states. Therefore English arbitrarily tosses many of its words into one category or the other without adherence to any logical scheme.

The Hopi Indians do it better. They classify "lightning," "wave," "flame," "storm," and other things of short duration as verbs and consistently place experiences of longer duration and more steady character in a noun class. The Nootka, in contrast to both English and Hopi, do not make a basic distinction between nouns and verbs. They take a monistic view of the continuum of length of duration of experience.

Although the Hopi carefully distinguish nouns and verbs, their verbs have no tense—no past, present, or future. Instead, their verbs are distinguished according to aspects, validity forms, and clause-linkage forms. Aspect refers to the relative length of time an event lasts. Validity forms are of three kinds; the first denotes that the speaker is reporting a completed or an on-going action or event; the second indicates that the speaker expects that an action or event will take place; the third means that from his experience he knows the action or event is a regular or predictable occurrence. Clause-linkage forms relate the temporal characteristics of two or more verbs; they indicate which action is earlier, later, or going on simultaneously with respect to another one or more verbs.

It should be clear from these illustrations of grammar that a linguist cannot describe Indian languages in terms of Latin grammar, as some have tried in the past. Each Indian language has its own grammar, which differs more or less from the grammars of other languages. Types of Indian grammar are not randomly distributed over the language map of native North America, but tend to cluster in adjacent areas, as will be suggested below in the section on language classification.

LANGUAGE AND CULTURE

The concept that has attracted the most attention in discussions and writings on the relations of language and culture is the Sapir-Whorf hypothesis, named after the two men who pioneered its development in modern American linguistics. The following paragraph from the pen of Edward Sapir ably presented its essentials in 1929.

Language is a guide to "social reality." Though language is not ordinarily thought of as of essential interest to the students of social science, it powerfully conditions all our thinking about social problems and processes. Human beings do not live in the objective world alone, nor alone in the world of social activity as ordinarily understood, but are very much at the mercy of the particular language which has become the medium of expression for their society. It is quite an illusion to imagine that one adjusts to reality essentially without the use of language and that language is merely an incidental means of solving specific problems of communication or reflection. The fact of the matter is that the "real world" is to a large extent unconsciously built up on the language habits of the group. No two languages are ever sufficiently similar to be considered as representing the same social reality. The worlds in which different societies live are distinct worlds, not merely the same world with different labels attached. (*In* Mandelbaum, 1949: 162.)

Translation from one language to another with a high degree of fidelity is easiest for the so-called material culture and the technological processes of its manufacture and manipulation. This is because the objects and the techniques have an objective existence apart from the semantic categories of any of the languages that may be used to describe them. In fact, scientists and engineers have coined many special terms to increase the precision of technical communication in European languages, and many non-European languages have adopted these in wholesale groups, such as the taxonomical nomenclature of biology. Translation becomes more difficult in the field of social organization—for example, for kinship terminology—as will be apparent in the chapter on kinship terminology below. However, here again the experts have devised special abbreviations and special algebras to increase the precision of communication in the field of kinship, and the basic framework of biological relationship lends itself to this precise treatment. Translation is most difficult and at times impossible in religion and mythology, where the ideas have no existence whatsoever except in the imaginations of the speakers and listeners. No scientist or engineer can devise an equivalent of the table of chemical elements for concepts of the soul in a hundred or more languages. This is because such concepts have no objective existence and are ill defined, subjective, and highly charged with emotion. Therefore, the difficulty of translation increases from the most objective to the most subjective domains of verbalization. Sapir's statement applies most accurately to the subjective end of the continuum.

If we try to translate the English phrases "his horse" and "their horses" into Navaho, we run into difficulty on two counts: Navaho lacks a distinction between "his," "her," "its," and "their"; and it lacks a distinction between singular and plural for nouns, in this case between "horse" and "horses." The nearest short equivalent in Navaho *bilį́ⁿ ?*, which is translated according to context as "his," "her," "its," or "their horse" or "horses." By rephrasing "his horse" to "one horse of one man," the following Navaho phrase suffices: *diné-là-bilį́ⁿ ?-là ?*. This means literally "man-one-his-horse-one." Because horses were a symbol of prestige, it is certain that every Navaho knew how many horses he owned as well as the number owned by his close relatives and friends. The failure of the language to include this information in its shortest grammatical forms does not mean that Navahos do not know who own the horses in their neighborhoods.

Another example is words for colors. Everyone who has had a physics course knows that color varies continuously from red to violet. The difference between the various colors along this continuum is a matter of the length of the light waves. There are almost as many ways of dividing up the color spectrum as there are languages which do it. The Navaho have only five principal terms for colors, which may be translated freely as "white," two kinds of "black," "red," and "blue or green." In color-matching tests the Navaho would be able to match fine gradations of blues and greens as accurately as we do, and we would be able to differentiate blacks and grays as carefully as they do.

Perception is equally precise among members of both groups regardless of the arbitrary semantic categories of the languages, and no painter in either language group is handicapped by color semantics. However, recent experiments with color semantics show that most people habitually communicate with the primary color categories of their language, even though all are capable of making finer distinctions. Although language may shape perceptions and thought, it does not limit its users to the conventional semantic categories when an occasion calling for finer distinctions arises.

Also, many grammatical patterns in language are dead with respect to any real function in the thinking of the language users. A good example of this is the sex gender for inanimate objects in German and French. Thus the word for "sun" in German, *Sonne*, is feminine, while that in French, *soleil*, is masculine. For "moon" the genders are reversed: *Mond* is masculine in German, and *lune* is feminine in French. Neither word has any gender in English. The gender of the sun and moon could not possibly have any effect on the attitude toward the sun and moon of the modern speakers and hearers of these languages. Gender categories for other inanimate objects are likewise nonfunctional today. Although the gender of the sun and moon may have had some influence on Indo-European thinking in the remote past, when religion and mythology regarded the sun and moon as gods, it is no longer functional. At any stage in the history of any language, it contains a considerable quantity of nonfunctional grammatical survivals.

CLASSIFICATION

Languages are classified according to resemblances to one another, and resemblances are of at least four kinds: universal, convergent, diffusional, and genetic. Universals are those features of speech shared by all languages. With respect to phonology, for instance, all languages have stops, fricatives, and vowels, and these are produced by expulsion of the breath from the lungs, glottis, and oral cavity. Most of the meaning categories of the hundred basic words used by glottochronologists, given below, are universal or nearly so.

Convergent resemblances are those which arise independently in two or more languages. Many features of phonology are probably convergences, and a few similar words seem to arise in this manner.

For instance, the word for "wood" in the Wappo Indian language of California is *hol*, resembling the German *Holz*; and the Wappo word for "valley," *tul*, is similar to the German *Tal*. A person fluent in both Wappo and German could surely find many more such convergences. There was no contact between Germans and Wappo Indians before the nineteenth century and not a shred of evidence to suggest common derivation of Wappo and German from a common parent language. The percentage of convergences among such short words (root morphemes) in historically unrelated languages is higher than one might suppose—about 4 per cent on the average (Greenberg, 1953: 270). This figure is admittedly achieved only when a generous interpretation of similarity is employed. A more critical appraisal of resemblances would lower the percentage.

Resemblances brought about by diffusion are those taken over by one language from another. The most obvious examples are so-called loan words, such as tobacco, which spread around the world with the plant and its leaves as they were traded from tribe to tribe and nation to nation. Although there is more than one word for "tobacco" in Indian languages, the number of terms for this plant is much fewer than the number of languages, proving the diffusion of the words beyond all doubt.

A more subtle kind of influence of one language on another is the result of stimulus diffusion. In this case the clusters of sounds (morphemes or words) are not taken over by the alien language, but the categories of meaning are diffused nevertheless. For example, most Athapaskan numeral systems are based on tens, as in English, or on some complicated combination of threes, fours, and fives. Only a few Athapaskan systems are based throughout on fives. Wherever this deviant quinary system occurs, it is adjacent to totally alien languages, such as Eskimo, in which counting is by fives. In this case the principle of counting by fives has been derived from the Eskimo, but the words contain only Athapaskan morphemes. The meanings of other words, such as kinship terms, may also diffuse from one language to another without the morphemes of the donor language. Stimulus diffusion of semantic categories is most likely to be implemented by considerable numbers of bilingual persons who speak both the donor and the recipient language. This would require prolonged contact, intermarriage, and other exchanges of persons.

Genetic resemblances are those resulting from uninterrupted derivation from an earlier language. Thus Spanish is derived from

Latin and may be described as a lineal descendant of Latin, as may also French; the relation of Spanish to French is a collateral one. Linguists often refer to the older language as the mother tongue and to the younger forms of speech as the daughter languages or, in relation to each other, the sister languages. Although the word "genetic" is a twentieth-century biological term, Darwin used comparative philology as an illustration of what he meant by common descent. Therefore the concept may be extended from biology to language without doing much violence to the history of thought.

Genetic classifications of languages are the most meaningful to scholars in general, and especially to those outside the field of linguistics. The cultural anthropologist often uses genetic classification to reconstruct the past history of peoples and thus solve the many puzzles of cross-cultural research. For example, the Crow Indians are the only Plains tribe with matrilineal descent, a pattern which makes no functional sense in an otherwise male-dominated society where hunting and fighting skills carry the most prestige. This apparent anomaly is easily explained by genetic language classification, which places the Crow language nearest to that of the Hidatsa in the Siouan family. In the historic period the Hidatsa lived in North Dakota on the upper Missouri River, where they obtained about half of their sustenance from the farm products raised exclusively by women in plots of land owned entirely by women. If we postulate that the Crow and the Hidatsa both farmed at some time from five hundred to a thousand years ago, when they spoke a single common language, the matrilineal descent of the Crow in the nineteenth century becomes a survival from an earlier period when women were more prominent in the society.

Although all languages are subject to change from elements received from neighboring languages, there is much evidence to suggest that language is more stable than the rest of culture, that its rate of change is slower in most instances. Such being the case, genetic language classification can reveal much information on past history and migrations of peoples that is not obtainable from any other kind of data. Where the results of modern studies in comparative linguistics are supported by documentary evidence dating back thousands of years—in the case for Indo-European languages, about 2,700 years—genetic resemblances can usually be distinguished from similarities brought about by convergence or diffusion. But where practically no written sources appear until the post-Columbian era, as is the case for American Indian languages, it is much more difficult to distinguish these

TABLE 1

CALIFORNIA INDIAN WORDS

	Head/Hair	Eye	Ear	Tongue	Earth	Fire	Water	One	Two
1. Entimbich......	wo	bus	nak	ego	tübop	kŏs	paya	sümü'ü	wahai
2. Woponuch......	wo	bus	nak	ego	tübop	kŏso	paya	sümü'ü	wahai
3. Hodogida.......	wŏ	pus	nak	ego	tibop	kŏs	paya	sümü'ü	wahai
4. Tuhukwadj.....	wo	pus	nak[a]	ego	tibop	kŏs	paya	sümü	wahai
5. Big Pine	wo	busi	nak[a]	ego	tibip	koso	paya	süümu'ʸu	wahai
6. Independence ...	wo	busi	nak[a]	ego	tibip[a]	koso	paya	süümu'ʸu	wahai
7. Koso.........	dzopipa	bui	nagi	ego	sŏgobi	kuna	paa	suut[a]	waat
8. Kawaiisu	tcopiwa	pui	nagabi	egu	tiipü	kunä	po'o	suyu	wahayu
9. Tubatulabal.....	tcompmon	pundz	nang	lal	cuwal	küt	pal	tcĭtc	wo
10. Yauelmani......	ŏto	säsä	tük	talhat	paan	osĭt	ilĭk	yĕt	ponoi
11. Koyeti	ŏto	säsä	tük	talhat	paan	osit	ilĭk	yĕt	ponoi
12. Nutunutu.......	otco	säsä	tuk	talhat	pa'an	osit	moyoxon	yĕĕt	ponoi
13. Paleuyami	ŏto	säsä	tuk	talhats	paan	osit	ilĭk	yĕt	ponoi
14. Yaudanchi......	ŏto	säsä	tük	talhat	paan	osĭt	idĭk	yĕt	pongoi
15. Wukchumni.....	ŏto	sasa	tük	talhats	pa'an	usit	idĭk	yĕt	ponoi

three kinds of resemblances. The picture is further complicated by the fact that convergences or diffusions can occur at any and all periods of time in the history or evolution of languages. A loan word may enter a language as a diffused element, only to be passed on by genetic descent to multiple daughter languages.

The surest way to prove that a group of languages has genetic unity, where documents cannot prove it directly, is to reconstruct the protolanguage or mother tongue from which all members of the family are descended. This is a highly technical and time-consuming task, requiring the formulation of rules of both phonology and grammar, and has been achieved for only a few Indian language families, most completely for Central Algonquian.

A much easier but less exact way to proceed is to compare short lists of words. Table 1 gives a few Indian words from fifteen localities in California (Driver, 1937). Without worrying about how to pronounce these words exactly, a novice can see at a glance that the first six examples of speech are almost identical. They are regarded as one language by linguists, and Indian informants agree that they are all easily mutually intelligible. The next three samples show a progressive departure from the first six, with number 9 being the most deviant. These middle three are classified as separate languages, although 7 and 8 are closer to each other than either is to 9. If we compare the middle three with the top six and the bottom six, it is apparent at once that the middle three are much closer to the top six and, in a twofold division, would be classed with them. This package of nine, along with some others, was originally called the Shoshonean language family. It is now known to be a subfamily of the larger Uto-Aztecan family. Numbers 10 through 15 are all dialects of the Yokuts language, originally regarded as isolated but now accepted as a member of the Penutian phylum.

The first modern genetic classification of North American Indian languages was that of J. W. Powell (1891). Powell's scheme was based principally on word lists, often of no more than a hundred items. The amazing thing about this classification is that none of the families Powell set up has been split apart by further research; all of them are regarded today as having genetic unity. However, most of them have been combined into genetic units of a larger order. At the present time the hierarchy of classes within classes approaches that of biology. Just as the biologist combines races or varieties of plants and animals into species, species into genera, genera into families, families into orders,

orders into classes, and classes into phyla, so the linguists have used as many as seven or eight sizes of classes to construct their genetic classifications. There is no standard terminology for such classificatory units in linguistics or anthropology, but a workable set of labels, starting with the most specific, would be: dialect, language, subfamily, family, superfamily, subphylum, phylum, and superphylum.

In a comparison of the validity of genetic language classification with that of biological taxonomy, language comes out second best. The principal difference is that, once biological forms have diverged enough to be classed as separate genera, they are no longer able to crossbreed. Dogs and cats, for instance, cannot crossbreed, and intermediate fossil forms may be safely regarded as common ancestors, not as hybrid forms. The fact that such intermediate forms are found only in the remote geological past and never in the recent period clinches the argument.

Not so for languages. Any two languages which come into contact may influence each other no matter how far apart they are in classification and history. Convergences may also arise at any time. Therefore it is difficult to distinguish diffused elements and convergences from genetic resemblances without reconstructing the protolanguages for all the language families involved. Because this has not been done for most Indian language families, present genetic classifications are to be regarded as tentative or provisional. In the Americas, where writing was extremely rare and not alphabetic, it is impossible for the archeologist to discover "fossil" languages to prove which intermediate ones are ancestral types and which are hybrids.

About 1950 a new method of classifying languages and estimating how long ago the various daughter languages diverged from ancestral tongues was devised by Morris Swadesh. It is now called glottochronology. Robert B. Lees (1953) compared the documented rates of change of thirteen streams of language, all Indo-European except Coptic and Chinese. He used a list of only about two hundred words, selected in advance for slow rate of change. Lees found that on the average these thirteen languages retained about 80 per cent and lost about 20 per cent of this basic vocabulary per thousand years. In other words, if one begins with a known mother language, such as Latin, he will find that after a thousand years the daughter tongues will retain about 80 per cent of these basic or conservative words and will have lost and replaced the remaining 20 per cent. Because there was relatively little difference in the rates of change of the thirteen languages investigated, Lees made the inference that all languages change at about the same rate.

To derive a universal generalization for 5,000 languages from a sample of thirteen, with all but two from a single language family, breaks the rules of sampling and statistical inference. If one took only thirteen samples of physical type from the same localities in Europe, Africa, and Asia and generalized for all mankind, he would characterize the human race as principally Caucasoid with a dash of Negroid and Mongoloid. If he drew thirteen samples from Africa south of the Sahara or from native Australia, he would think everyone on earth was Negroid or Australoid. If a selected sample of thirteen cases is not likely to give a true picture of physical type over the face of the earth, there is no reason to suppose that it is adequate for linguistics. Lees' inference that all languages change at about the same rate has been shown to be false by a number of studies since 1960—for instance, that of Bergsland and Vogt (1962). Chretien (1962) has shown that extrapolation backward in time to determine how long two cognate languages have been separated is much less accurate than Lees believed. Van der Merwe (1966) gives a new formula for rate of change which is more curvilinear than that of Lees, which means a slower rate of change in the remote past, followed by an accelerated rate of change up to modern times. This matches the rate of culture growth more closely than the Lees formula. In spite of these criticisms, the percentages of cognate words shared by a group of languages still gives a first approximation to their genetic relationships and can serve as a guide to indicate where more intensive study is needed. Most of the recent studies in glottochronology operate with only the following one hundred basic words, which show an average rate of retention of about 86 per cent per thousand years:

I, thou, we, this, that, who, what, not, all, many, one, two, big, long, small, woman, man, person, fish, bird, dog, louse, tree, seed, leaf, root, bark, skin, flesh, blood, bone, grease, egg, horn, tail, feather, hair, head, ear, eye, nose, mouth, tooth, tongue, claw, foot, knee, hand, belly, neck, breasts, heart, liver, drink, eat, bite, see, hear, know, sleep, die, kill, swim, fly, walk, come, lie, sit, stand, give, say, sun, moon, star, water, rain, stone, sand, earth, cloud, smoke, fire, ash, burn, path, mountain, red, green, yellow, white, black, night, hot, cold, full, new, good, round, dry, name.

These words were chosen because experience in comparative linguistics has shown that most of them occur in every language on earth; and they are "culture-free" in the sense that they are associated with simple as well as complex cultures, with literate and nonliterate cultures, and need not change when important innovations revolutionize other vocabulary. For instance, everyone has a head regardless of the cut of his hair, his headgear, or his theory of the location of the center of intelligence in the body. Changes in these three "culture-bound" items would not necessitate a change in the "culture-free" term for head. Similarly, the word "walk" is likely to be retained after horses, automobiles, airplanes, and space ships are introduced because people will still continue to walk. Although no word is entirely "culture-free," much evidence shows that the words in the above list have a much slower rate of change than general vocabulary.

Once lists of words have been collected for a number of Indian languages, any two languages can be compared by determining the number of cognate words shared. Words in two or more languages are said to be cognate when they can be proved to have been derived from a common mother tongue. They are often not identical but must share something in common to indicate divergence from a common ancestral language. Returning to the list of California Indian words (Table 1), it is apparent at once that all words in dialects 10 through 15 form clusters of cognates except the term *moyoxon* for "water," which may be an error. Similarly, all words in dialects 1 through 6 fall into clusters of cognates. Languages 7, 8, and 9 are not so obvious, but a little imagination suggests common origin for all the words for "eye," "ear," "fire," "water," and "two." The word for "tongue" (*lal*) in language 9 appears to be a loan word from dialects 10 through 15, and the speakers of 9 were indeed close neighbors of the speakers of dialects 10 through 15. Without giving any more examples, it should be clear that anyone can spot many cognates in word lists. To do an exhaustive and accurate job, however, requires linguistic training and experience.

Once cognates have been identified, any two languages in a sample may be compared by determining the percentage of cognates shared. Those sharing a high percentage of cognates are said to be linguistically close, while those sharing only a low percentage of cognates are linguistically distant. Experience shows that when twenty or thirty languages or dialects are compared in this manner, they often show a considerable range of linguistic distance.

In exhibiting such a large number of relationships, it is convenient to arrange the figures in a square table identical in form to mileage tables on road maps. Just as one reads the mileage between any two towns or cities on the mileage table, so one may read the linguistic distance between any two dialects or languages on the linguistic table. Continuing our analogy, if the twenty largest cities in California were grouped on the same mileage table, they would fall into geographical clusters, one in the Los Angeles area and the other around San Francisco Bay. The mileage table would show two clusters of low mileages within each of these areas, and a cluster of high mileages between the areas.

Similarly, a linguistic table showing two clusters of languages with close internal relationships within each but distant external relationships between clusters suggests at once a classification into two families. Three or more clusters with close internal relationships and distant external relationships would suggest three or more linguistic classes, and so forth. The systematic determination of linguistic propinquity and distance between hundreds of North American Indian languages in the past ten years has greatly changed and sharpened our classifications. Groups of languages which no one had compared in the past have recently been shown to share at least some cognates.

TABLE 2

GENETIC CLASSIFICATION OF NORTH AMERICAN INDIAN LANGUAGES
(Voegelin and Voegelin, 1966)

AMERICAN ARCTIC-PALEOSIBERIAN PHYLUM I
Ia Eskimo-Aleut Family
   1. Central-Greenlandic Eskimo (Trans-
      Arctic Eskimo)
   2. Alaskan Eskimo (Kuskokwim Eskimo)
   3. Eastern Aleut (Unalaskan)
   4. Western Aleut (Atkan, Attuan)
Ib Chukchi-Kamchatkan Family
    (in Siberia)
NA-DENE PHYLUM II
IIa Athapascan Family
   1. Dogrib-Bear Lake-Hare
   2. Chipewyan-Slave-Yellowknife
   3. Kutchin
   4. Tanana-Koyukon-Han-Tutchone
   5. Sekani-Beaver-Sarsi
   6. Carrier-Chilcotin
   7. Tahltan-Kaska
   8. Tanaina-Ingalik-Nabesna-Ahtena
   9. Eyak
  10. Chasta Costa-Galice-Tututni
  11. Hupa
  12. Kato-Wailaki
  13. Mattole
  14. Tolowa
  15. Navaho
  16. San Carlos Apache
  17. Chiricahua-Mescalero Apache
  18. Jicarilla
  19. Lipan
  20. Kiowa Apache
IIb Tlingit Language Isolate

IIc Haida Language Isolate
MACRO-ALGONQUIAN PHYLUM III
IIIa Algonquian Family
   1. Cree-Montagnais-Naskapi
   2. Menomini
   3. Fox-Sauk-Kickapoo
   4. Shawnee
   5. Potawatomi
   6. Ojibwa-Ottawa-Algonquin-Salteaux
   7. Delaware
   8. Penobscot-Abnaki
   9. Malecite-Passamaquoddy
  10. Micmac
  11. Blackfoot-Piegan-Blood
  12. Cheyenne
  13. Arapaho-Atsina-Nawathinehena
IIIb Yurok Language Isolate
IIIc Wiyot Language Isolate
IIId Muskogean Family
   1. Choctaw-Chickasaw
   2. Alabama-Koasati
   3. Mikasuki-Hitchiti
   4. Muskogee (Creek)-Seminole
IIIe Natchez Language Isolate
IIIf Atakapa Language Isolate
IIIg Chitimacha Language Isolate
IIIh Tunica Language Isolate
IIIi Tonkawa Language Isolate
MACRO-SIOUAN PHYLUM IV
IVa Siouan Family
   1. Crow
   2. Hidatsa

TABLE 2—*Continued*

GENETIC CLASSIFICATION OF NORTH AMERICAN INDIAN LANGUAGES
(Voegelin and Voegelin, 1966)

3. Winnebago
4. Mandan
5. Iowa-Oto
6. Omaha-Osage-Ponca-Quapaw-Kansa
7. Dakota
IVb Catawba Language Isolate
IVc Iroquoian Family
1. Seneca-Cayuga-Onondaga
2. Mohawk
3. Oneida
4. Wyandot (Huron)
. 5. Tuscarora
6. Cherokee
IVd Caddoan Family
1. Caddo
2. Wichita
3. Pawnee-Arikara
IVe Yuchi Language Isolate
HOKAN PHYLUM V
Va Yuman Family
1. Upland Yuman (Walapai-Havasupai-Yavapai)
2. Up River Yuman (Mohave-[Maricopa-Kavelchadom-Halchidom]-Yuma)
3. Delta River Yuman (Cocopa-Kohuana-Halyikwamai)
4. Southern and Baja California Yuman (Diegueno-Kamia-Akwa'ala-Kiliwa-Nyakipa)
Vb Seri Language Isolate
Vc Pomo Family
1. Coast Pomo
2. Northeast Pomo
3. Western Clear Lake
4. Southeast Clear Lake
Vd Palaihnihan Family
1. Achumawi
2. Atsugewi
Ve Shastan Family
Vf Yanan Family
Vg Chimariko Language Isolate
Vh Washo Language Isolate
Vi Salinan Family
Vj Karok Language Isolate
Vk Chumashan Family
Vl Comecrudan Family
Vm Coahuiltecan Language Isolate
Vn Esselen Language Isolate
Vo Jicaque Language Isolate
Vp Tlapanecan Family
1. Tlapanec
2. Subtiaba
3. Maribichicoa
Vq Tequistlatecan Family
1. Tluamelula
2. Mountain Tlequistlateco
PENUTIAN PHYLUM VI
VIa Yokuts Family

1. Yokuts, Foothill North
2. Yokuts, Foothill South
3. Yokuts, Valley
VIb Maidu Family
1. Southern Maidu
2. Northwest Maidu
3. Mountain Maidu
4. Valley Maidu
VIc Wintun Family
1. Patwin
2. Wintun
VId Miwok-Costanoan Family
1. Sierra Miwok
2. Coast-Lake Miwok
3. Costanoan
VIe Klamath-Modoc Language Isolate
VIf Sahaptin-Nez Perce Family
1. Nez Perce
2. Sahaptin
VIg Cayuse Language Isolate
VIh Molale Language Isolate
VIi Coos Family
VIj Yakonan Family
1. Alsea
2. Siuslaw-Lower Umpqua
VIk Takelma Language Isolate
VII Kalapuya Family
1. Santiam-Mackenzie
2. Yonkalla
VIm Chinookan Family
1. Upper Chinook
2. Lower Chinook
VIn Tsimshian Language Isolate
VIo Zuni Language Isolate
VIp Mixe-Zoque (Zoquean) Family
1. Mixe
2. Zoque
3. Sierra Popoluca
4. Texixtepec
5. Sayula
6. Oluta
VIq Mayan Family
1. Huasteco
2. Chontal of Tabasco
3. Chol
4. Chorti
5. Punctunc
6. Moianec
7. Tzeltal
8. Tzotzil
9. Tojolabal
10. Chuh
11. Jacaltec
12. Kanjobal
13. Solomec
14. Motozintleco
15. Mam
16. Aquacatec
17. Ixil

TABLE 2—*Continued*

GENETIC CLASSIFICATION OF NORTH AMERICAN INDIAN LANGUAGES
(Voegelin and Voegelin, 1966)

18. Tacaneco
19. Tlatiman
20. Taquial
21. Tupancal
22. Tutuapa
23. Coyotin
24. Quiche
25. Cakchiquel
26. Tzutujil
27. Rabinal
28. Kekchi
29. Pokonchi (Pocomchi)
30. Pokomam
31. Maya
VIr Chipaya-Uru Family (in Bolivia)
VIs Totonacan Family
　1. Totonac
　2. Tepehua
VIt Huave Language Isolate
AZTEC-TANOAN PHYLUM VII
VIIa Kiowa-Tanoan Family
　1. Tiwa (Taos-Picuris)-(Isleta-Sandia)
　2. Tewa (San Juan-Santa Clara-San
　　　Ildefonso-Tesuque-Nambe-Hano)
　3. Towa (Jemez)
　4. Kiowa
VIIb Uto-Aztecan Family
　1. Mono
　2. Northern Paiute (Paviotso)-Bannock-
　　　Snake
　3. Shoshone-Gosiute-Wind River-
　　　Panamint-Comanche
　4. Southern Paiute-Ute-Chemehuevi-
　　　Kawaiisu
　5. Hopi
　6. Tubatulabal
　7. Luiseno
　8. Cahuilla
　9. Cupeno
　10. Serrano
　11. Pima-Papago
　12. Pima Bajo
　13. Yaqui-Mayo
　14. Tarahumara
　15. Cora
　16. Huichol
　17. Tepehuan
　18. Nahuatl
　19. Nahuat
　20. Mecayapan
　21. Pipil
　22. Pochutla
　23. Tamaulipeco
LANGUAGE ISOLATES AND FAMILIES WITH
　UNDETERMINED PHYLUM AFFILICATIONS VIII
VIIIa Keres Language Isolate
VIIIb Yuki Family
　1. Yuki
　2. Wappo

VIIIc Beothuk Language Isolate
VIIId Kutenai Language Isolate
VIIIe Karankawa Language Isolate
VIIIf Chimakuan Family
　1. Quileute
　2. Chimakum
VIIIg Salish Family
　1. Lillooet
　2. Shuswap
　3. Thompson
　4. Okanagon-Sanpoil-Coville-Lake
　5. Flathead-Pend d'Oreille-Kalispel-
　　　Spokan
　6. Coeur d'Alene
　7. Middle Columbia-Wenatchi
　8. Tillamook
　9. Twana
　10. Upper Chehalis-Cowlitz-Lower
　　　Chehalis-Quinault
　11. Snoqualmi-Duamish-Nisqualli
　12. Lummi-Songish-Clallam
　13. Halkomelem
　14. Squamish
　15. Comox-Sishiatl
　16. Bella Coola
VIIIh Wakashan Family
　1. Nootka
　2. Nitinat
　3. Makah
　4. Kwakiutl
　5. Bella Bella-Heiltsuk
　6. Kitamat-Haisla
VIIIi Timucua Language Isolate
VIIIj Tarascan Language Isolate
OTO-MANGUEAN PHYLUM IX
IXa Manguean (Chorotegan) Family
　1. Mangue
　2. Chiapaneco
IXb Otomian (Otomi-Pame) Family
　1. Otomi
　2. Mazahua
　3. Ocuiltec
　4. Matlatzinca
　5. Chichimeca-Jonaz
　6. Pame
IXc Popolocan Family
　1. Popoloc
　2. Chocho
　3. Ixcateco
　4. Mazateco
IXd Mixtecan Family
　1. Mixtec
　2. Trique
　3. Cuicateco
　4. Amuzgo
IXe Chinantecan Family
IXf Zapotecan Family
　1. Zapotec
　2. Chatino

The classification of North American Indian languages in Table 2 is that of Voegelin and Voegelin (1966). It is divided into three levels: phylum, family, and language. The phyla are designated by capital Roman numerals, the families by capital Roman numerals plus a lower-case Roman letter, and the languages by Arabic numerals. When there is only one language to represent a family, it is called a language isolate. Hyphenated phrases give the principal tribes or dialects within each single language. Altogether there are nine phyla, counting the one for the families and languages of undetermined phylum affiliation, forty-two families with two or more members each, thirty-one language isolates, and 190 languages within the families with two or more members. The total number of mutually unintelligible languages is 221 when language isolates are included. The little-known languages in the uncolored corridor, on the Voegelins' (1966) map, running north and south in Mexico are not included.

The definition of a language as a form of speech mutually intelligible to all the speakers has been stretched a bit here and there in this classification where chains or meshes of intelligibility occur. For example Central-Greenlandic Eskimo (Ia 1), stretching from the mouth of the Yukon River in Alaska to east Greenland, is listed and mapped as one language. Rasmussen, a native speaker of both Danish and Central-Greenlandic Eskimo, traveled all the way from Greenland to Alaska over a period of years, making many stops along the way to gather ethnographic information in the Eskimo language. His comment was that, while changes in speech did occur from east to west, he had no trouble making the adjustment until he reached southern Alaska, where an abrupt break occurred and he could not converse at all with the speakers of Alaskan Eskimo (Ia 2). Although adjacent dialects in the long chain of Central-Greenlandic Eskimo (Ia 1) dialects were all mutually intelligible, the dialect at one end was not mutually intelligible with that at the other end.

Two other well-known chains of dialects are Cree-Montagnais-Naskapi (IIIa 1) and Ojibwa-Ottawa-Algonkin-Salteaux (IIIa 6). Some of the other hyphenated phrases in the classification are also chains of dialects, every member of which is not necessarily mutually intelligible with every other member. Thus the amount of mutual unintelligibility in native North America was greater than the number of languages shows.

Map 37 gives the geographical distributions of the more widespread language families. The phyla have not been mapped for two reasons:

the Voegelins have already mapped them in colors; the families are of shorter time depth and more likely to show significant correlations with cultural data than are the phyla.

From about 1850 to 1950, linguists agreed that the principal process of linguistic change and the formation of new languages was one of diversification and rediversification from ancestral languages. Convergences and diffused elements were recognized but were assigned a minor role in linguistic change. It was assumed that every language fell definitely into one family and not into another. Since that time this view has been challenged more and more. Swadesh (1959a) uses the phrase "mesh principle" to describe the complicated relationships which glottochronology and other kinds of comparative research are bringing to light. This recent work shows that many languages and language families are linked to many others by combinations of genetic and diffused resemblances which cannot be adequately described by family tree diagrams or by classes within classes, as in the classification given above in this book. These more complicated relationships between languages and language families must be expressed on language distance tables, mentioned above. Although such tables are two-dimensional on paper, the variation of the distances in them may be multidimensional. The "mesh principle" does not demolish all order in linguistic classification. It merely requires a more sophisticated technique to express the more complicated kind of order that exists.

LANGUAGE AREAS AND CULTURE AREAS

A comparison of Maps 2 and 37 shows the geographical relations between culture areas and language family areas. Beginning in the north, the Eskimo-Aleut language family coincides exactly with the Arctic culture areas. Although the Arctic has been divided into two culture areas, the difference between the two is slight as compared to the difference of either from all other culture areas. Therefore the correlation between language family and culture area is nearly perfect in this instance. This correlation may be explained by several factors: the relative uniformity of geographical environment throughout the Arctic; the relatively rapid migration of the Eskimo from west to east; and the considerable isolation from neighbors. A single Eskimo language is spoken from the Yukon River in Alaska to eastern Greenland and Labrador. No other language in native North America was as widespread. The Polar Eskimo, who are estimated to have been isolated from other Eskimo as well as from all other peoples for at least five hundred years, spoke a dialect which was still mostly intelligible to Eskimo guides from other localities when John Ross discovered them in 1818. Ross (1819: 1: 167–68) lists thirty-seven words commonly used, about half of which were nouns associated with material objects such as weapons: twenty-four terms were said to have been identical, seven were different but appear to be cognate forms, four are extremely different and appear to be noncognates, and the remaining two are different but difficult to classify.

No other language areas and culture areas match as closely as do those in the Arctic, but a number elsewhere exhibit a significant degree of correlation. For example, the Iroquoians and Muskogeans are both confined within the East culture area. If the East is divided into Northeast and Southeast, as it sometimes is, the correlations will be much higher. The Siouan languages are most numerous on the Prairies, with a little overflow in the East and a more recent expansion onto the northern Plains. The Caddoan group falls principally on the Prairies but also is found in the Southeast. Similarly, the Sahaptin group is confined to the Plateau area, which it shares with the Salish family, while the latter also appears on the adjacent Northwest Coast. The position of the Mayan family is similar; it is wholly confined to Meso-America but shares this area with other language families.

The distribution of the Athapaskan languages is curious because they are found in the Yukon and Mackenzie Sub-Arctic, on the North Pacific Coast, in the Southwest, and Northeast Mexico. Two or three thousand years ago there seems to have been only a single Athapaskan language or a close-knit mesh of dialects, each mutually intelligible to at least some of the others in the group. From this small area, presumably somewhere in the Yukon or Mackenzie Sub-Arctic, a series of southward migrations began. They did not cease until California was reached on the Pacific Coast and Mexico in the Southwest. As the various bands of Athapaskans moved southward, they adopted much of the cultures of the peoples they contacted, partly because of necessity in new geographical environments and partly by preference. The end result of these migrations and acculturations, first observed in the nineteenth century, was three distinct types of culture so different from each other that without the linguistic evidence no one would have suspected a common origin for the bearers of these cultures.

The Athapaskans in the north remained wholly Sub-Arctic in

culture and personality as well. Those who reached California became so highly acculturated in their material goods that museum curators cannot distinguish the objects of the Athapaskan Hupa from the Ritwan-speaking Yurok or the Hokan-speaking Karok. Personality and ethos exhibit just as complete an acculturation; the Hupa are obsessed with the desire for wealth and social prestige, as are all other North Pacific Coast peoples. The Navaho and Apache of the Southwest showing varying degrees of acculturation to the Pueblo peoples and other earlier residents of that area. The Navaho have acquired horticulture, matrilineal descent, and much of their religious ritual from the Pueblos. In some respects they have even excelled the Pueblos in these acquired pursuits—for instance, in their more elaborate sand paintings. The conclusion derived from Athapaskan history is that language is much more stable than culture; the languages changed much less than the cultures in these extensive migrations.

An even more startling example of the greater stability of language over culture is that of the Uto-Aztecans. These languages are thought to have been a single mother tongue about five thousand years ago. There is no agreement on the exact location of the homeland, but it may have been in southern California or the western Southwest. The presence of only three closely related languages in the Great Basin suggests relatively recent occupation of that area, probably during the Christian era. The Comanche migrated from what is now Wyoming to Texas about A.D. 1700. The Aztecs arrived in the Valley of Mexico from the northwest only about three and a half centuries before the Spanish Conquest.

When the culture of the western Shoshoni in the Great Basin is compared with that of the Aztec in Meso-America, the range of complexity is as great as can be found anywhere on the continent. It seems likely that the Shoshoni experienced some deculturation in their postulated migration from southern California to the even more inhospitable deserts of Nevada and Utah. The Aztecs, on the other hand, seem to have experienced a rapid acculturation in the direction of the more complex cultures which preceded them in the Valley of Mexico. In spite of these extremes of deculturation and acculturation, the languages remained close enough to the ancestral form to be identified as members of the same language family, and linguists have made progress in reconstructing a protolanguage for the entire group.

The geographical distributions of all the language families on Map 37 are explained by migrations. Loan words and other isolatable parts of language may spread by diffusion from one people to another, but whole languages of nonliterates spread only by migration of the speakers of the languages. However, not all the migrations will show on such a map because some languages have become extinct. There are instances from the historic period of the speakers of a language being reduced in numbers by war or disease and finally joining another society and acquiring its language. There must have been many cases of this kind in the thousands of years of Indian prehistory. Nevertheless, the evidence of migration given by language classification is indeed impressive.

A comparison of Maps 2 and 37 also has bearing on the Sapir-Whorf hypothesis. If the relation of language and culture were as close as these linguists suggest, then language areas and culture areas should match each other more closely. The fact that they do not is evidence that culture can be altered drastically while language is undergoing only a moderate amount of change and, conversely, that language may sometimes change more rapidly than culture.

WRITING

The Olmecs, Mayas, and Zapotecs were the only peoples in the New World to develop forms of true writing. They wrote with ideographic glyphs comparable to those of the ancient Egyptians and Chinese but totally unrelated historically. The Mayan glyphs, which are the best known, are formed by a main element plus affixes, with prefixes to the left and above and suffixes to the right and below. They were used principally to record sacred texts associated with astronomy, the calendar, and the many songs and incantations in religious ceremonies. The Mayas produced paper books, known as codices, on a single long sheet of paper folded like a screen (Plate XXIV). The largest to survive the book burnings of the Spanish is the Madrid Codex, twenty-three feet long, with fifty-six leaves each nine by five inches. This contained horoscopes for divination by priests. Unfortunately, only about 150 of the 400 or more Mayan glyphs have been deciphered; so such manuscripts can be read only in part. The Mayas also wrote a number of historical codices giving the history of separate political units. These were written soon after the Conquest, in the Mayan language, but in a Spanish-devised alphabetic script, making translation virtually complete.

The Mayan numeral system is remarkable in its use of a number of symbols for zero, which made a place-numeral system possible. This was never achieved by the Greeks or Romans; our modern Arabic system was derived, in the Middle Ages, from the Arabic people who, in turn, got it from India. The Mayas used dots for units from 1 through 4, a bar for 5, and added combinations of bars and dots together up to 19. One dot above a symbol for zero represented 20. One dot with two zeros below stood for 400, not 100. In addition to numbers, the Mayas had twenty symbols for days, nineteen for "months," nine other symbols for longer time periods, and symbols for astronomical bodies and signs of the zodiac. With these symbols they wrote dates, accurate to the day, on manuscripts and also carved them on stone monuments.

The Aztec system of writing was less abstract and has been called a pictographic form of rebus writing. It was little more than an elaborate mnemonic device, but much more of it than that of the Mayan has been preserved. In addition to religious subjects the Aztecs have left us historical annals, records of contemporary events, daily diaries, year counts, amounts of tribute paid by various towns, lines of descent of important kin groups, landownership records, and other things important to the operation of their large capital city and their loose-jointed military and economic "empire."

The Aztecs drew conventionalized pictures to represent important trade goods, such as bags of cochineal dye, bags of cacao (chocolate) beans, bales of raw cotton, cotton blankets, jars of cactus honey, and bundles of copal resin used as incense. The quantity of each commodity was indicated by numeral signs: a dot for each unit up to 19; a flag for 20; a tree-like sign denoting hairs for 400; and a bag of cacao beans for 8000. The number 8421 would be indicated by one bag, one hair sign, one flag, and one dot. The number 8848 would be represented by one bag, two hair signs, two flags, and eight dots. These numeral symbols were drawn on top of the commodity symbols mentioned above, and the tax records for each subject town were kept in this manner. The Spanish also devised a Roman-type alphabet for the Aztec language, and the oral utterances which the sight of the pictographic symbols evoked were written down at great length in this alphabet, thus making accurate "translation" of the pictographs possible. Soon after the Spanish arrived the Aztecs began adding symbols for syllabic sounds, but a complete syllabary for all the syllables in the language was not achieved before written Spanish became the official form of writing.

REFERENCES

BERGSLAND AND VOGT, 1962; CHRETIEN, 1962; DRIVER, 1937; GREENBERG, 1953; HOIJER, 1954; HYMES, 1959, 1960, 1964; LEES, 1953; MANDELBAUM, 1949; PIERCE, 1957; POWELL, 1891; SAPIR, 1921; SWADESH, 1959*a*, 1959*b*, 1960; VAN DER MERWE, 1966; VOEGELIN AND VOEGELIN, 1966.

4

Subsistence Patterns

Most of the food consumed in the modern world is derived from cultivated plants; smaller amounts are produced by milking and slaughtering domesticated animals and by fishing; only a very small amount of the modern diet is obtained from wild animals and wild plants. Indians of North America also depended principally upon domesticated plants; wild animals, wild plants, and fish were of secondary importance, while domesticated animals probably provided less than 1 per cent of the total diet. This chapter will offer a classification of the principal ways in which Indians obtained food, as well as a description of the major subsistence activities in each culture area.

Cultivated plants supplied nearly all the dietary in Meso-America, where population was greater than in all the other cultures areas combined. The domestication of the llama, alpaca, and guinea pig in the Andean region of South America supplemented the predominantly vegetable diet of that area from about 1000 B.C., but these animals were absent in North America and the dog, which was widely distributed on both continents, was only rarely eaten.

In the Americas farming probably began a little later than in the Old World. The earliest certain dates for farming in the Old World are about 9000 B.C. in the Middle East, though some specialists believe that peoples of southeastern Asia farmed at a still earlier period. In Chapter 1 we cited 7000 B.C. as the earliest date for farming in the Americas. Because there was probably no trade or traffic between the two hemispheres at that early time, except across Bering Strait, where none of the domesticated plants can grow, and because the earliest genera and species of plants are different in the two hemispheres, except for the gourd, the only conclusion to draw is that the American Indian independently invented farming. In other words, he had the same amount of intelligence or inventive genius as the first farmers in the Old World. Furthermore, most anthropologists believe that the first farmers in both hemispheres were women, not men. While this point cannot be proved, women almost everywhere in the world gather more wild plant foods than do men, and women are more often the farmers among those primitive peoples whose agriculture is little developed.

What determines the kind of food economy that a given people will follow? This depends on many things which, however, may be divided into two classes of factors: availability of the raw material in the environment, and knowledge of how to obtain the raw material and how to prepare it for food. Few foods are eaten without any preparation whatsoever. Because our knowledge of agriculture today far surpasses that of the American Indians, we can and do raise many foods in the United States which were totally unknown to them. Most of these were brought over by the colonists from Europe, and many came ultimately from the Middle East or southeastern Asia.

Nonetheless, many of the plants first domesticated by the American Indians were imported into the Old World, after the discovery of America, and continue to play an important part in the diet of Europeans, Asians, and Africans. Of these, maize is probably the most widespread. As we shall see later, in the section on food preparation and preservation, a number of foods eaten by Indians contained poisons which had to be extracted before they could be consumed. The amount of experimentation necessary to acquire the vast knowledge of plants and animals that they possessed was enormous. This took many millenia, because knowledge came slowly to peoples without writing or other adequate means of keeping records or conveying information other than by word of mouth.

The inhabited regions of North America were the same in A.D. 1492 as they are today. They extended from the home of the Polar Eskimo in northwest Greenland to Panama. Within this vast area there are sharp differences in topography, soils, climate, fauna, and flora, which in turn have greatly influenced native subsistence patterns and their geographical distributions. These patterns may be classified in terms of the dominance in the diet of fish, game, wild plants, or cultivated plants (Map 3). Fish was the staple food on the Northwest Coast, part of Alaska, and in a number of smaller areas shown on Map 3. Game predominated in a huge triangular area which includes most of the Arctic, Sub-Arctic, Plains, and Prairies. Wild plants were the principal article of diet in California, the Great Basin, and probably Northeast Mexico. Cultivated plants predominated in the East, sporadically on the Prairies, in the Southwest area, Meso-America, and on to Panama.

Two areas in the West were difficult to classify and were finally assigned to a category of their own labeled "balance of animal and wild plant foods." These include a portion of the Plateau and Great Basin in the Far West and most of the Apache territory in the Southwest.

The five categories of Map 3 may be further subdivided into the twelve shown on Map 4. These twelve units are of a magnitude more comparable to that of the culture areas on Map 2. They do not correspond exactly to the culture areas because no single aspect of culture ever matches culture areas exactly. Culture areas are composite units based on all major aspects of culture, and each separate aspect of culture, as represented by the various chapters in this book, fits the culture areas to a greater or lesser degree. In some regions the dependence was mainly on a single species of animal, such as the buffalo, while in others there was a great variety of food resources used. A description of the subsistence patterns of each of the culture areas in turn follows.

AREAL SURVEY

Arctic.—Beginning in the north, we see that almost the entire Arctic Coast, from the Alaska Peninsula on the west to Greenland and Newfoundland on the east, depended mainly on sea mammals for food. The only exception to this generalization is the small area at the mouths of the Yukon and Kuskokwim rivers, on the Bering Sea, where fish predominated. The inhabitants of this vast sea mammal area were all Eskimos except for the Aleuts on the Alaska Peninsula and the Aleutian Islands. Second in importance to sea mammals was probably the caribou, hunted during the summer, while fish of various kinds were perhaps third. This seems to have been true of most of the sea mammal area, but would have to be reversed in some localities, such as Alaska, where fish were more important than caribou.

Of the various kinds of sea mammals and their importance in the diet, seals would certainly be first, with walruses second and whales third. This rank varies inversely with the size of the animals partly because of the fact that walruses and whales did not inhabit the shallow, land-locked waters of the central area west from Hudson Bay to Coronation Gulf. Here the seal was the only one available.

Because the Eskimos ate at least half of their meat raw, and included the fat and internal organs as well as the muscle meat, the diet contained every vitamin and mineral salt necessary for human nutrition plus an abundance of protein, which is insufficient in the diets of many more civilized peoples. It was only in times of scarcity that malnutrition occurred.

Sub-Arctic.—The people of the Sub-Arctic area, from interior Alaska on the west to the Atlantic Ocean on the east, subsisted primarily on caribou and moose meat. While both animals are found together in many localities, caribou predominates in the north and moose in the south. The nine species of caribou are likewise often divided into the barren ground types occupying the treeless tundra in the summer and the woodland types confined all year round to the forested area farther south. Other animals which were commonly hunted for food were bear, beaver, porcupine, deer, and rabbit.

Second only to mammals in this area were fish, which were the primary food in the Yukon drainage and a few scattered localities; but they were of secondary importance over the remainder of the Sub-Arctic. On the Atlantic Coast shellfish were eaten everywhere. Birds were obtained in many localities, especially in the summer, but constituted only a minor part of the diet. Plant foods were very limited, with berries outranking greens, roots, and seeds, all of which were occasionally eaten.

Northwest Coast.—Salmon of five different species was the chief article of diet from the Eel and Klamath rivers of northern California to the mouth of the Yukon.

A dozen species of salt-water fish were also important. People living on islands or peninsulas whose streams were too small to attract large numbers of salmon depended more on halibut, cod, and sea mammals. This was true of the Haida of the Queen Charlotte Islands, the Kwakiutl and Nootka of Vancouver Island, and the Makah of Cape Flattery. The candlefish, so oily that it will burn like a candle when a wick is inserted, was the most common source of oil, which was used as a sauce to go with meat and fish.

With the various species of shellfish and the sea mammals which were obtained everywhere along the coast, it is easy to see that salt-water dwellers had a more bountiful supply of aquatic products than the peoples on the inland streams. The coastal peoples also gathered sea plants, which were dried and pressed into cakes for future use. That land plants were not neglected is shown by an exhaustive list of 60 species used for food in western Washington (Gunther, 1945). Salal berries, blueberries, and camas roots were commonly eaten throughout this area.

This diet was entirely adequate, both qualitatively and quantitatively; there are no reports of famines among coastal dwellers. The fish, shellfish, and mammal components in the diet furnished an excess of protein and an abundance of fat, the roots provided starch, and the berries sugar. Recent biochemical analyses of these foods show that the drying methods universal in the area do not appreciably diminish vitamin content, and that while vitamins A and D vary from species to species, their amounts in some of the fish oils approach those of cod liver oil, which has long been a standard source of these nutritive elements in our culture. One species of berries, Saskatoons, was found to contain three times as much iron and copper as prunes and raisins.

Plateau.—The subsistence pattern of the Plateau area was mixed. In the north, it was similar to that of the Sub-Arctic, with chief dependence on moose and other large game. In the west, fishing dominated all other food-getting activities, as it did on the Northwest Coast. In the east, a number of large animals, such as the moose, elk, and deer, combined to make meat the staple diet. And in the corridor running south through Oregon to California, wild plant foods seem to have furnished about as much nourishment as meat and fish combined. The Plateau peoples of Washington and Idaho also ate considerable quantities of wild plants, especially the camas, a close relative of the hyacinth. The roots of the camas were the most important food furnished by any single plant species on the Plateau.

Plains.—On the Great Plains of North America, which extend from the north Saskatchewan River in Alberta nearly to the Gulf of Mexico in Texas and from the Rocky Mountains on the west to about the 100th meridian on the east, the buffalo was the principal source of food. This extreme specialization was accentuated by the acquisition, in historic times, of the horse, which greatly facilitated buffalo hunting. Buffalo were supplemented by elk, antelope, bear, and occasionally smaller game. The only plant food eaten in any quantity was berries, which were a standard ingredient in the pemmican made by all the tribes. A few roots were obtained by women with the aid of a pointed digging stick. Tribes adjacent to the agricultural areas to the east and to the southwest sometimes obtained a little corn in trade or in predatory raids on their more sedentary neighbors.

As long as the buffalo lasted, Plains diet was adequate, as the superb physiques of the people proved. Until this animal was exterminated, food was seldom a serious problem. Fish were to be found in all the streams on the Plains but were not eaten, more often because they were considered not worth bothering with than as the result of a definite taboo.

Prairies.—In a relatively large part of this area, hunting was dominant, with farming definitely secondary. Agriculture certainly furnished less than half the diet in most of this area, and in many localities a fourth would be a better estimate. Maize, beans, squashes, and a few sunflowers were the crops raised. In the early nineteenth century, most tribes as far east as Lake Michigan traveled westward on annual hunting excursions for buffalo. In the seventeenth century, one observer in Illinois stated that buffalo were obtained in greater numbers locally than any other species of large game. Tribes adjacent to the buffalo area depended as much or more on that animal than they did on agriculture, and those farther east spent most of the year hunting other large game, of which the deer was the most frequently taken. Wild rice was more important than maize in a small area in Wisconsin and was perhaps the first-ranking food for the Menomini. Around the Great Lakes in general, fishing rivaled hunting for first place in food economy.

Farming was more important than hunting for a few tribes on the southern edge of the Prairies area, and this may also have been the case on the western edge of this area before the horse was acquired in large enough numbers to shift the economy toward buffalo hunting. By the nineteenth century, the western tribes were depending for about half of their food on the maize, beans, and squashes they raised. But, with fewer horses in the eighteenth century, they could not have obtained as many buffalo.

East.—In the Eastern United States, it is difficult to say whether agriculture furnished even half of the diet. At any rate, early historical observers report larger and more permanent towns with greater maize acreage than in the Middle West. In the Southeast, men as well as women were compelled by the chief and other public officials to work in the town fields. That hunting was still far from a lost art, however, is shown by the fact that many of these Eastern tribes fled their villages when attacked by superior forces and managed to get a living from the woods after their supplies of corn, beans, and squashes had been appropriated or destroyed. Wild plant foods, especially nuts, were of tertiary significance in the Eastern United States but were used more than is generally known. Fish were caught in considerable numbers everywhere east of the Mississippi, but were no more important in this area than wild plant foods except on the coast and in the Great Lakes region. Shellfish were much in demand along the coasts, and archeologists have found them in huge quantities on a number of inland rivers, where they date from some time before agriculture was known. The diet of the East satisfied every nutritional need, and famines were rare because there were enough wild foods to fall back on when crops failed or were destroyed by enemies.

California.—In most of California, the acorn was the staple article of diet. It was ground into a meal, from which the tannic acid was leached out with water, and then it was boiled to make mush or baked into an unleavened bread. A wide variety of smaller seeds was prepared similarly after first being parched. Secondary to plants in the diet, small game, such as rodents and birds, plus a number of such invertebrates as earthworms, grasshoppers, and caterpillars, probably furnished more food the year round than did deer and other large game. On the coast, seafood of all kinds formed the staple diet wherever sufficient quantities were obtainable. Fish were evidently of tertiary significance in the interior except in the Sacramento and San Joaquin drainages. The wide variety of food resources and the mild winters made California relatively free of famines.

Great Basin.—In the southern Great Basin, wild plant foods predominated over animal foods. The piñon, from which pine nuts were obtained, was the most common single species used for food, but seeds of many other plants were also eaten, and a few roots were obtained with the aid of the digging stick. Deer inhabited the mountains of the Great Basin, where they were probably the most common large animal, and mountain sheep were to be found on the higher crags and summits over most of the area. Antelope became more frequent toward the north and, because they lived in open country in large herds, were usually hunted communally. Compared with other areas, however, large game was scarce and probably furnished a smaller part of the year-round diet than did rodents, reptiles, and insects. Rabbits in particular were hunted in communal drives. Famines were common in the Great Basin and people were hungry much of the time, according to old Indian informants.

Northeast Mexico and Baja California.—In Northeast Mexico, there was emphasis on mesquite pods and cactus fruits although many other plants were also eaten. Mesquite is a tree which bears a pod full of seeds resembling our string beans. These were eaten green or were gathered when dry, ground in mortars, and boiled. Several parts of the cactus were consumed: the fruit was eaten fresh or dried for preservation; the seeds were dried or roasted and then ground; the leaves and the pulp of the stalk were also edible; and the juice was drunk. Other food plants utilized in this area include the mescal or agave, yucca, tule (cattail), and the piñon. Large game was about as scarce as in the Great Basin; rodents, reptiles, and insects were eaten more often than the deer. On the Gulf Coast, fish and shellfish were eaten in quantities. Hunger was a chronic condition, famine a constant threat, and malnutrition widespread in the interior of Northeast Mexico.

On the peninsula of Baja California and in southern California, at inland localities, such desert plants as the agave, mesquite, and, in the south, pitahaya (a cactus) were the staples, with rabbits and deer furnishing supplementary diet; on the coast seafood, ranging from shellfish to stranded whales, was the main bill of fare. Hunger must have been common, but access to seafood made it far less serious than in the Great Basin and the interior of Northeast Mexico.

Southwest.—All of the Southwest peoples farmed, but in varying degrees. Intensive agriculture was the pattern of the Pueblos, who lived on the Colorado Plateau in northern Arizona and New Mexico. One author has estimated that maize constituted 80 per cent of the diet. If this is true, agricultural products as a whole must have accounted for 85 or 90 per cent of their food, because beans, squashes, and sunflowers were also raised in aboriginal times. Wild plants were much less important than agricultural ones, but a great many species were eaten. Since game was scarce, meat was seldom obtainable and formed as small a fraction of the diet as did wild plants. The rabbit was the most common single species eaten. A few fish were obtained in the Rio Grande, but they were a negligible factor in the diet and were not eaten at the other pueblos. Famines were a real threat to the pueblos, where drought seriously affected population density and movements. Diet was also probably deficient in protein, although the bean offset this to some extent.

The Navaho acquired agriculture from the Pueblo people, probably in the eighteenth century, and by the nineteenth century were relying more on maize and other crops than on hunting or wild plant gathering. The Apaches of the nineteenth century seem to have relied almost equally on game and wild plants, with farm crops of tertiary rank.

As for the River Yumans, farm crops furnished about half of the total diet of the Mohave, perhaps 40 per cent for the Yuma, 30 per cent for the Cocopa, and less for the Maricopa. Wild plants were of first rank for the latter two tribes. The Desert Yumans relied principally on wild plants, with game second and farming third. Fish were generally scarce in the Southwest but were eaten by all of the River Yumans, who lived on the Colorado and Gila rivers.

Meso-America.—Southward down the west coast of Mexico, the role of agriculture in the subsistence pattern increased, until in central and southern Mexico it was more intensive than among the Pueblos of the Southwest. While maize was by far the most important single species in both areas, southern Mexico cultivated a much greater number of other species, as we will see in the next chapter. Wild plants, wild game, and domesticated animals (dogs, turkeys, geese, ducks, quail, bees, maguey slugs) competed with each other for second place, each achieving secondary importance in restricted areas. Many parts of Meso-America were capable of supporting a large and varied assortment of animals, but, with the increase of human population accompanying the development of maize agriculture, game was reduced to a fraction of its former density. Hunting was a sport reserved for the nobility among the Aztecs. Fish and other seafood certainly outranked land game on the coasts, but were every bit as inconsequential as game in most localities in the interior. Fish was also an important trade item for coastal peoples. Famines were rare, but it seems likely that the diet was deficient in protein, although the bean bolstered this nutritional element to some extent.

NATURAL VEGETATION AREAS

Natural vegetation areas provide a good summary of total geographic environment because plants reflect rainfall, humidity, temperature, soils, and other essentials of geography. Without citing every detail of agreement or disagreement between culture areas (Map 2) and natural vegetation areas (Map 5), one can see at a glance that the correspondence is close. Therefore culture, at the development level achieved by North American Indians, is heavily dependent on geographical environment, although nowhere near wholly determined by geography. The poorest match is in Meso-America, where four natural vegetation zones occur. This reflects the generalization that as culture becomes more and more complex, it becomes less and less geared to geography. Irrigation canals make farming on deserts possible, and extensive trade makes products available many miles from where nature provides the materials from which they are made.

As civilization advances, man gains more and more control over nature and becomes less and less dependent on the raw materials nature provides; he constructs more and more of his environment as his knowledge of how to do so increases. The Meso-Americans were far in advance of the peoples of any other culture area in North America and had managed to adjust their culture to several geographical environments.

Subsistence areas (Map 4) also show a substantial, though far from perfect, agreement with natural vegetation areas (Map 5). Again, the correspondence is poorest in Meso-America and also in the Southwest. In other words, in areas where farming was most intensive, man's way of life was least dependent on what nature provided. He had learned to maneuver nature to his own advantage.

DOMESTICATED ANIMALS

Domesticated animals provided only a very small percentage of the diet and were much less a part of the North American Indian bill of fare than they were in the Old World. Turkeys were domesticated in the Southwest and Meso-America, where they were actually bred in captivity. The chief use of the bird in Meso-America was for food, although the Mixe in southern Mexico confined the eating in recent times to ceremonial occasions. In the Southwest, on the other hand, the turkey was kept principally for its feathers, which formed a part of sacred costumes and other ritual objects.

Dogs were raised for eating in the Eastern United States, in the central Plains, in California, and in Meso-America (Driver and Massey, 1957: Map 6), but were eaten only on special occasions or in ceremonies. Horses were eaten by many Indian tribes when first obtained, but on the Plains their greater utility for hunting and transportation soon removed them from the dietary.

Bees were kept for their honey by a few Meso-American tribes, and quail and maguey slugs were raised for eating in some localities. Ducks and geese are reported for the Aztecs, at least. The ducks seem to have been derived from Peru in early historic times, while the origin of the geese is still more problematical. Fish were impounded by the Aztecs. Several of these instances are to be regarded as borderline domestication, if indeed the fish impounding can be regarded as domestication at all. None of these animals made any significant contribution to the diet. The stocking of small streams with salmon by depositing their eggs near the headwaters, as was practiced on the Northwest Coast, is certainly closer to domestication than is mere impounding.

POPULATION

Estimates of the Indian population in A.D. 1492 vary enormously because the first censuses were usually taken decades or even centuries after the first European contact. By this time warfare, famine, and disease had taken a heavy toll of Indian lives. The lowest estimate for the North American continent (not counting Costa Rica and Panama), that by Kroeber (1934, 1939: 166), gives a total of 4,200,000. The highest estimate, that of Dobyns (1966), gives about 60,000,000. Since Kroeber's pioneer effort, there have been many intensive studies in restricted regions, all of which have produced figures larger than Kroeber's. The greatest difference has occurred in the area of the densest Indian population, Meso-America.

Dobyns' method is, first, to determine the nadir population figure for an area after European contact had taken its maximum toll of lives and, then, to multiply this figure by 20 or 25 to obtain a reconstructed zenith population before White contact. In the areas where population was densest and decline greatest, this technique probably yields estimates somewhere near the truth; but in the regions where population was thinner and subsistence was entirely on wild plants and animals, the multiplication of the nadir population by 20 or 25 would seem to yield too great a number. In the United States except for Alaska and Hawaii, Dobyns' nadir population of 332,000 in 1930 is too large and too late. Driver (1968) obtained a nadir of 250,000 in 1890 for the same area. If this were multiplied by 10, it would yield an aboriginal figure of 2,500,000, which seems more plausible than a larger number. In Canada, Alaska, and Greenland, where Indian population was still sparser and numbers of Whites far fewer, a multiplication of the nadir population by a factor of about 5 would probably be more correct, and an aboriginal figure of 1,000,000 would seem to be a generous estimate.

Dobyns' estimate of 30,000,000 to 37,500,000 for aboriginal Mexico also seems too high. The population of Mexico in 1940 was only 19,654,000, and its increase in the next 20 years to 35,000,000 in 1960 must be explained in part by the introduction of modern medicine as well as by improved agricultural methods and land tenure reforms. Because the aboriginal Mexican cultures were less efficient in medicine, if not in land distribution and food production, it seems unlikely that aboriginal population was anywhere near the 1960 figure. If we cut Dobyns' aboriginal Mexican estimate to about the 1940 figure, say 20,000,000, it would be much more plausible. For Central America, Dobyns' estimate of from 10,800,000 to 13,500,000 might better be halved, to yield about 6,000,000.

These revised estimates added together give a total of about 30,000,000 for the entire continent, only half of Dobyns' estimate.

From the cultural point of view, the interesting thing is the correlation of population with types of subsistence and other aspects of culture. The relative density of native population is shown on Map 6. Even though the absolute figures are uncertain, the relative density can reflect the essential facts. Several generalizations are apparent at once: population was heavier in the south than in the north, heavier on the coast than in the interior, and heavier on the Pacific Coast than on the Atlantic Coast. Although areas where farming was practiced generally show a denser population than areas where farming was unknown, it is interesting to note that the nonfarming regions of the Pacific Coast were more heavily populated than the farming areas of the Eastern United States. Kroeber has estimated that Eastern Indians cultivated less than 1 per cent of the available land suitable for horticulture by modern standards. Nowhere in the East did cultivated plants seem to have furnished much over half of the total diet, and on the Prairies they provided less than half. On the North Pacific Coast, fish and marine mammals supported a denser population than occurred anywhere on the eastern coast of the United States, and even in California, where food resources were less specialized than in most other parts of North America, population density topped that of the East.

The difficult conditions of human habitation are reflected in the population figures of the Arctic, Sub-Arctic, and parts of the Great Basin and Northeast Mexico. Although many nonfarming tribes in the deserts of the Great Basin and Northeast Mexico must have been familiar with the farming of their neighbors in bordering areas, the environment checked the diffusion of domesticated plants. It is noteworthy that these same areas remain sparsely populated to this day. The modern population picture differs from the aboriginal one most strikingly in the Eastern United States, where, first, intensive plow farming and, later, industrialization have brought about the heaviest population on the continent. In Mexico and Central America, areas which held the greatest population densities in North America in aboriginal times, the situation has changed only slightly. The uplands of central Mexico still dominate the population picture, but recently there have been significant increases in population in northern Mexico as agriculture with irrigation and industries has increased.

REFERENCES

DOBYNS, 1966; DRIVER AND MASSEY, 1957; GUNTHER, 1945; KROEBER, 1934, 1939; ROSTLUND, 1952; SAUER, 1935, 1939; STEWARD, 1938; SWANTON, 1946; WISSLER, 1938; YANOVSKY, 1936; YANOVSKY AND KINGSBURY, 1938.

5

Horticulture

THE importance of farming can scarcely be overestimated. Although the total area where farming was practiced constituted less than half of the entire North American continent (Map 7), the native population (Map 6) was much heavier in those regions. In relation to total Indian population and total diet, horticultural products probably furnished about 75 per cent of all the food consumed by North American aborigines. The greatest culture development, which occurred in Meso-America, was made possible in part by the increased food production in this area of intensive cultivation.

Before considering the field practices, techniques, and tools used in agricultural North America, we shall discuss the important crops, their uses, history, and distribution in pre-Columbian times.

MAIZE

Indian corn or maize (*Zea mays*) was the most important and widespread cultivated food plant in the entire New World (Map 7). It probably provided more food than all other cultivated plants combined at the time of the first European contact, and still does in Mexico, where over half of all crop land is used to raise maize. In 1965, Mexico produced 8,865,000 metric tons of maize, as compared with 2,088,000 metric tons of wheat, the second largest Mexican grain crop, introduced by the Spanish in the sixteenth century (*Statistical Yearbook of the United Nations, 1966*). Aboriginally, maize was grown from the upper Missouri River in North Dakota and the lower St. Lawrence River region, 47° north latitude, to Chiloé Island in Chile, 43° south latitude. This span is roughly the middle 90 degrees of the 180 between poles. With the possible exception of Northwest Coast tobacco, no other plant was raised by Indians beyond these limits—certainly no other food plant. In the Andean region of South America maize was grown from sea level to 12,700 feet above sea level at Lake Titicaca in the Peruvian Andes, the difference in altitude here causing as much variation in climate as is found at sea level along the entire latitudinal range from Chiloé to the St. Lawrence.

Maize was probably first domesticated in southern Mexico. The oldest maize so far discovered that may have been cultivated is that from southern Puebla, Mexico, and it has been dated at about 4000 B.C.; but pollen of wild maize goes back to 80,000 B.C. By 3000 B.C. cultivated maize had spread to other localities in Mexico and north to Bat Cave, New Mexico. This most ancient maize is a popcorn with each kernel inclosed in a little separate pod, so that it may also be called a pod corn. This same type of maize has also been found in Romero's Cave, in southwest Tamaulipas, Mexico; the date there is 2770 B.C. Since no wild close relatives of maize have ever been found in New Mexico, we may assume that this pod-popcorn at Bat Cave was introduced as a cultivated plant, no doubt from Mexico. At later levels in Bat Cave, corn showing evidences of crossing with teosinte (*Euchlena mexicana*) appeared. Teosinte is a "cousin" of maize which grows wild in southern Mexico and Central America. Actually it is intermediate between maize and *Tripsacum*, a wild "second cousin" of maize. *Tripsacum* flourishes in the most tropical regions in Central America and Colombia, and extends as far north as the state of Indiana in the United States. Most forms of maize grown today exhibit relationship to *Tripsacum* or teosinte. Maize and *Tripsacum* have been crossbred in laboratory experiments, and maize and teosinte cross in nature.

Many varieties of maize are to be found in Mexico. Research on Mexican maize has resulted in the collection of thousands of specimens and a classification of all the variants into 25 "races." Like the races of man, which are all regarded as belonging to a single species, the 25 races of corn belong to *Zea mays*. These races of corn do not exist as pure races anywhere, because there is considerable variation within each race, and boundaries between races are not always clearly defined. They do serve, however, to induce some order in what would otherwise approach chaos. Once a large number of specimens is available for experimentation, it is possible to crossbreed them in many combinations and eventually to work out the history of the domesticated corn plant. This is what botanists are doing.

The races of maize in Mexico may be divided into four main groups: Ancient Indigenous, Pre-Columbian Exotic, Prehistoric Mestizos, and Modern Incipient.

Ancient Indigenous races are those believed to have originated in Mexico from the kind of primitive pod-popcorn found in Puebla. There are four races in this group, all popcorns, with two of them showing weak development of pods. The earliest corn from South America also seems to belong to this group.

The Pre-Columbian Exotic races are believed to have spread by diffusion from Central or South America to Mexico in prehistoric times. All four of the races in this second group have South American counterparts, and all but one (*maíz dulce*) have been the parents of later hybrid races.

The Prehistoric Mestizos are races which are believed to have resulted from the crossing of Ancient Indigenous with Pre-Columbian Exotic races, plus hybridization with teosinte. Thirteen races of this type have been identified so far. Some of these are related to the dent corns found in the Eastern United States.

The Modern Incipient races consist of four types which are definitely post-Columbian, some less than a century old, and all somewhat unstabilized.

North of Mexico less is known about races of maize, and varieties from these areas cannot always be equated with those from Mexico. Nevertheless, it is clear that Indian corn in the Southwest is of four kinds which have as many distinct origins. The oldest is the pod-popcorn of about 3000 B.C., mentioned above. The second oldest is a flour variety which diffused up the west coast of Mexico to Arizona as early as 200–100 B.C. It is called Hohokam–Basket Maker after the archeological cultures with which it is found. It is probably derived from the Mexican Pre-Columbian Exotic group, which, in turn, stems from South America. It survives today among the Pima, Papago, and River Yumans. In northern Arizona, among prehistoric Basket Maker peoples, this type of corn was modified from A.D. 200 to 1200 in the direction of that from the Mexican Plateau, creating a third kind. Between A.D. 1200 and 1300, the third variety developed into a fourth as the result of hybridization with flint corn, so called because of the hardness of its grain. This flint corn was derived from the Eastern United States.

On the Prairies and in the East there were at least four major varieties of maize grown by Indians. The first is popcorn, which may be presumed to be the oldest in these areas. Even though its priority is definitely established in the Southwest, it could have diffused to the Southeast from either the Southwest or Mexico at a much later date.

The second oldest variety is apparently flint corn, which is characterized by a full-bodied and hard kernel. This is the only kind of corn
found archeologically in the East, and it is also common in archeological sites on the northern half of the Prairies. The oldest sites date
from the first millennium of the Christian era. The source of this flint
corn is not positively known, but because flint corns farther south
center in the Circum-Caribbean area, this is a possible derivation for
these kinds in the United States.

The third variety to appear on the scene is closely related to the
Basket Maker corn from the Southwest, and presumably spread from
there to the Prairie area in the first millennium of the Christian era.

The fourth and apparently latest major variety to appear on the
Prairies and in the East is a kind called dent corn because of the dents
in the tops of the kernels. This flour variety has been found in prehistoric and protohistoric archeological sites on the Prairies but not
in the East. The earliest reference to dent corn in the East is in Bever-
ley's *History of Virginia*, published in 1705. The dent corns therefore
appear to have arrived in the Southeast from the Prairies in historic
times. They are closely related to the dents of Mexico, which belong
to the Prehistoric Mestizo group. The relatively late appearance of

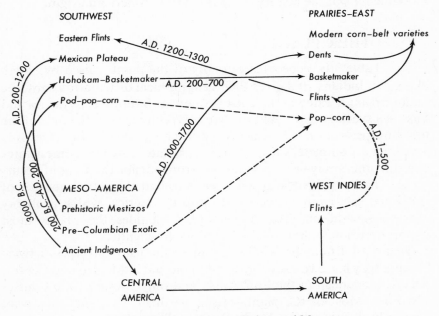

FIG. 1. Diffusion of maize. Driver and Massey

this group in Mexico explains the even later appearance of its derivatives in the United States. The Mexican Plateau influence on Basket Maker corn, A.D. 200–1200, resulted in an increase in denting, among other changes. The modern commercial corn raised in the corn belt of the United States is a cross between Indian flints and dents.

Figure 1 summarizes our historical reconstruction of the diffusion of maize in North America. If more were known about it, the picture would probably be much more complicated, but, as it is, it conveys some idea of the intricacies of maize history. Thus the Southwest received at least three waves of diffusion from Mexico and at least one from the Prairies. The Prairies and East apparently received influences from the West Indies, Mexico, and the Southwest. Diffusion was multiple with respect to a single direction and also was multidirectional. For more detail on Central and South America, see Wellhausen *et al.* (1957), Brieger *et al.* (1958), and Grobman *et al.* (1961). These studies clearly show that varietal variation in maize exceeds that of any other cultivated species.

Carl Sauer (1960) believes that maize reached Europe before A.D. 1492, and George Carter (1963) gives an argument for pre-Columbian maize in Africa. Even if accepted, these views do not change the fundamentals of the history of maize and its American origin.

OTHER PLANTS

Table 3 is a checklist of many of the plants raised by North American Indians, and gives their geographical distribution for three major areas: Mexico and Central America; Southwest; Prairies and East. All species are thought to have been cultivated at the time of the first European contact but, because early historical botanical records are far from complete, some plants may be later endemic domesticates and still others may be later diffusions from outside the areas of occurrence. The list probably gives fewer than half the actual number of cultivated species in Mexico and Central America, which probably runs to several hundred. However, it includes the plants most important to the Indians and best known to scientists.

Of the total number of 155 species in the list (four appear twice because they had two uses each), 151 are found in Mexico and Central America, eighteen in the Southwest, and only twelve in the Prairies and East. Most of the plants raised north of Meso-America were derived by diffusion from Meso-America. The only plant of any consequence which was probably first domesticated in what is now the United States and later diffused southward to Meso-America is the sunflower (*Helianthus annus*). The other four species found only in the United States are too trivial to call more than bare attention to, and there is no archeological evidence to show that any of them were cultivated earlier than maize, beans, or squashes. The latter three staples were first domesticated in Mexico, Central America, or South America, and diffused northward at later dates. After farming was established north of Meso-America by the introduction of these foreign plants, a few endemic species were domesticated or semi-domesticated. In terms of contribution to the diet, maize dominated other domesticates in the Southwest, Prairies, and East as much as it did in Meso-America.

Beans (*Phaseolus*) of one species or another were grown almost everywhere that maize was raised (Map 7), usually in the same field, and in most localities were the second most important plant. The runner bean (*P. coccineus*) makes the earliest appearance, at 7000–5000 B.C., in Tamaulipas, Mexico. Its absence in archeological sites in South America indicates that it was most probably first domesticated in Meso-America. The lima bean (*P. lunatus*) was probably first domesticated in South America; it appears as early as 5800 B.C. in Peru, but not in Meso-America until 300–500 B.C. (Heiser 1965: 936). The tepary bean (*P. acutifolius*) is found wild only in a continuous area in the Southwest and northwestern Meso-America. Since this is also the region where it is cultivated, its domestication must have taken place here. The nearest wild relatives of the common bean (*P. vulgaris*) range all the way from Mexico to Argentina, but the archeological date in Mexico, 5000–3000 B.C., is much earlier than that for South America, 400 B.C., suggesting first domestication in Mexico and subsequent diffusion southward.

The squashes (*Cucurbita*) are equally complex. The pumpkin and summer squash (*C. Pepo*) appears in Mexico from 7000–5000 B.C., but is absent in Peru and the rest of South America. It seems clearly to have been first domesticated in Meso-America. The Cushaw squash (*C. moschata*) first appears at about the same time in Puebla, Mexico, 5000–3400 B.C., and in Peru, 3000 B.C. If the earlier squash from Puebla, 7000–5000 B.C. is *moschata* rather than *mixta*, this would seem to give Mexico the priority. Independent domestication in Mexico and Peru is further suggested by sharp differences in the varieties in the two areas. The walnut squash (*C. mixta*) never reached Peru, and if the early (7000–5000 B.C.) squash in Puebla is *mixta*, it is not only a Mexican domesticate but also an old one. *C. ficifolia* is found in the highlands from Mexico to Chile. Its name "mexicana" in most of the Andes suggests Mexican origin, but its absence in Mexican archeological sites and its presence in Peru at about 2000 B.C. suggest an Andean origin of its domestication.

It is clear from the above examples that, once agriculture became established, there was a considerable exchange of species and varieties by means of diffusion from one area to another in the Americas. The past 20 years, however, have witnessed a greater emphasis on independent origins of domestications, even for a single species, and less emphasis on wholesale diffusion. Scholars have become more and more skeptical of the intentional spread of cultivated plants across the Pacific by men in canoes or on rafts. Earlier and earlier archeological appearances of a number of plants in the Americas have greatly lessened the probability of their being carried across oceans by people.

Research on cotton (*Gossypium*) has shown beyond all doubt that the two principal New World domesticates, *G. hirsutum* and *G. barbadense*, are each crosses between New World and Old World wild forms. When first discovered, this evidence was interpreted as proof that men had intentionally hybridized the Old World and New World species in the New World after first bringing cotton samples to America from the Old World. When cotton (*G. barbadense*) was found in Peru from as early as 2000 B.C., doubts arose about the diffusion of one of its ancestors by people at a date when Polynesia was totally uninhabited. Then when MacNeish (Smith and MacNeish, 1964) discovered cotton (*G. hirsutum*) in his Puebla excavation with a date of 5800 B.C., this eliminated transoceanic diffusion by men as an explanation of the hybridization. The fact that the Puebla cotton was probably wild further increased the likelihood that nature, not man, produced the hybrid *hirsutum*. It therefore seems likely that nature — including birds, which have been known to carry seeds for 14 days without destroying their fertility (Proctor, 1968) — was the disperser of the many forms of cotton over the two hemispheres at an early period before man entered the picture at all.

The gourd (*Lagenaria*) has also undergone a change of interpretation. It was once thought to have been first domesticated in Southeast Asia and later carried intentionally by men in boats to the New World. But if the plant rinds from sites in the New World as early as 7000–5000 B.C. are correctly identified as *Lagenaria*, this is much too early

TABLE 3

CULTIVATED PLANTS OF NATIVE NORTH AMERICA
(Principally after Meighan *et al.* 1958, Mangelsdorf *et al.* 1964*a*, Kelly and Palerm 1952)

Common Name	Genus and Species	Mexico, Central America	Southwest	Prairies, East
EDIBLE SEEDS				
Amaranth	*Amaranthus cruentus*	×		
Amaranth	*Amaranthus leucocarpus*	×	×	
Amaranth	*Amaranthus paniculatus*	×		×
Barnyard grass	*Echinochla crusgalli*	×	×	
Bean, common	*Phaseolus vulgaris*	×	×	×
Bean, jack	*Canavalia ensiformis*	×	×	
Bean, lima*	*Phaseolus lunatus*	×	×	×
Bean, runner	*Phaseolus coccineus*	×		
Bean, scarlet runner	*Phaseolus multiflorus*	×		
Bean, tepary	*Phaseolus acutifolius*	×	×	
Bean, yellow	*Phaseolus calcaratus*	×		
Chia	*Salvia hispanica*	×		
Chia grande	*Hyptis suaveoleus*	×		
Jicama	*Pachyrhizus* sp.	×		
Jerusalem artichoke	*Helianthus tuberosus*		×	×
Long bean	*Vigna unguiculata*	×		
Maize (corn)	*Zea mays*	×	×	×
Marsh elder	*Iva ciliata*		×	×
Mesquite, pod	*Prosopis edulis*	×		
Panic grass	*Panicum hirticaule*	×	×	
Panic grass	*Panicum maximum*	×		
Panic grass	*Panicum sonorum*	×	×	
Peanut*	*Arachis hypogaea*	×		
	Phaloris sp.		×	
Pigweed, Goosefoot, Apozote	*Chenopodium nuttalliae*	×		×
Ragweed*	*Ambrosia trifida*		×	×
Sunflower*	*Helianthus annus*	×	×	×
Tree legume	*Inga feuillei*	×		
EDIBLE ROOTS, TUBERS, UNDERGROUND STEMS				
Arrowroot*	*Maranta arundinacea*	×		
Cacomite	*Tigridia pavonia*	×		
	Colathica allonia	×		
Coyolxóchitl	*Bomarea edulis*	×		
Manioc*	*Manihot esculenta*	×		
Manioc*	*Manihot dulcis*	×		
Pisís*	*Xanthosoma* sp.	×		
Potato*	*Solanum tuberosum*	×		
Sweet potato*	*Ipomoea batatas*	×		
Yam bean	*Pachyrrhizus erosus*	×		
Yautia*	*Xanthosoma saggitifolium*	×		
EDIBLE GOURDLIKE FRUITS				
Chayote, chocho	*Sechium edule*	×		
Squash	*Cucurbita ficifolia*	×		
Squash, cushaw	*Cucurbita moschata*	×	×	
Squash, summer, pumpkin	*Cucurbita pepo*	×	×	×
Squash, walnut	*Cucurbita mixta*	×		

TABLE 3—*Continued*

Common Name	Genus and Species	Mexico, Central America	Southwest	Prairies, East
OTHER EDIBLE FRUITS				
Anona	*Annona purpurea*	×		
Anona	*Annona glabra*	×		
Avocado	*Persea americana*	×		
Avocado	*Persea gratissima*	×		
Avocado	*Persea schiedeana*	×		
Banana†	*Musa paradisiaca*	×		
Bullock's heart	*Annona reticulata*	×		
Cachichin	*Oecopetalum mexicanum*	×		
Caimito, star apple	*Chrysophyllum caimito*	×		
Capulin cherry	*Prunus serotina*	×		
Cashew*	*Anacardium occidentale*	×		
Caujilote	*Parmentiera edulis*	×		
Chalahuite	*Inga paterno*	×		
Cherimoya*	*Annona cherimoila*	×		
Chocho	*Sechium edule*	×		
Coconut†	*Cocos nucifera*	×		
Cuayote	*Gonoglobis edulis*	×		
Elderberry	*Sambucus mexicana*	×		
Guava	*Psidium guajava*	×		
Guayabilla	*Psidium sartorianum*	×		
Gurupillo	*Couepia dodecandra*	×		
Hog plum	*Spondias mombin*	×		
Ilama	*Annona diversifolia*	×		
Jocote	*Spondias purpurea*	×		
Lelekes	*Leucaena glauca*	×		
Mamey	*Mammea americana*	×		
Matasano	*Casimiroa sapota*	×		
Nance	*Byrsonima crassifolia*	×		
Papaya	*Carica papaya*	×		
Peachpalm	*Guilielma utilis*	×		
Pejibaye	*Guilielma gasipaes*	×		
Pepino hueco	*Cyclanthera explodens*	×		
Pineapple*	*Ananas comosus*	×		
Pitahaya	*Hylocereus undatus*	×		
Prickly pear	*Opuntia ficus-indica*	×		
Prickly pear	*Opuntia megacantha*	×		
Prickly pear	*Opuntia streptacantha*	×		
Ramon	*Brosimum alicastrum*	×		
Sapodilla	*Manilkara zapotilla*	×		
Sapote, black	*Diospyros ebenaster*	×		
Sapote	*Calocarpum mammosum*	×		
Sapote, green	*Calocarpum viride*	×		
Sapote, mamey	*Calocarpum sapota*	×		
Sapote, white	*Casimiroa edulis*	×		
Sapote, yellow	*Lucuma salicifolia*	×		
Sapote, yellow	*Pouteria campechiana*	×		
Soursop	*Annona muricata*	×		
Sweetsop	*Annona squamosa*	×		
Tejocote	*Crataegus pubescens*	×		
Tree tomato	*Cyphomandra betacea*	×		
POT HERBS AND OTHER VEGETABLES				
Calahi (spinach)	*Phytolacca decandra*	×		
Chaya	*Cnidosculus chayamansa*	×		
Chayote	*Chayote edulis*	×		

TABLE 3—*Continued*

Common Name	Genus and Species	Mexico, Central America	Southwest	Prairies, East
Chipilín	*Crotalaria longirostrata*	×		
Coral bean (blossoms)	*Erythrina edulis*	×		
Pacaya	*Chamaedorea wenlandiana*	×		
Tepejilote	*Chamaedorea tepejilote*	×		
Tomato	*Lycopersicon esculentum*	×		
Tomato, husk	*Physalis ixocarpa*	×		
Tree fern (buds)	*Cyathea arborea*	×		
Yucca	*Yucca elephantipes*	×		

STIMULANTS, NARCOTICS, MEDICINES

Albahaca	*Ocimum micranthum*	×		
Aquau	*Bixa orellana*	×		
Cacao	*Theobroma angustifolium*	×		
Cacao	*Theobroma bicolor*	×		
Cacao	*Theobroma cacao*	×		
Campana	*Datura candida*	×		
Chicasquil	*Jatropha acomtifolia*	×		
Coca*	*Erythroxylon coca*	×		
Flor de mechuda	*Caesalpina* sp.	×		
Frangipani	*Plumeria rubra*	×		
Maguey	*Agave atrovireus*	×		
Maguey	*Agave latissima*	×		
Maguey	*Agave mapisaga*	×		
Physic nut	*Jatropha curcas*	×		
Tobacco*	*Nicotiana rustica*	×		×
Tobacco*	*Nicotiana tabacum*	×		

CONDIMENTS AND OTHER FLAVORING

Chili pepper	*Capsicum annum*	×		
Chili pepper	*Capsicum frutescens*	×		
Vanilla	*Vanilla planifolia*	×		

FIBER PLANTS

Cotton	*Gossypium hirsutum*	×	×	
Cotton*	*Gossypium barbadense*	×		
Henequen	*Agave fourcroydes*	×		
Maguey	*Agave atrovirens*	×		
Maguey	*Agave tequilana*	×		
Sisal	*Agave sisalana*	×		

DYE PLANTS

Achiote*	*Bixa orellana*	×		
Indigo	*Indigofera suffruticosa*	×		

RESIN USED AS INCENSE

Copal	*Protium copal*	×		

HOSTS FOR WAX AND COCHINEAL INSECTS

Piñoncillo	*Jatropha curcas*	×		
Cochineal cactus	*Nopalea cochenillifera*	×		

TABLE 3—*Continued*

Common Name	Genus and Species	Mexico, Central America	Southwest	Prairies, East
	FRUITS USED AS UTENSILS			
Bottle Gourd	*Lagenaria siceraria*	×	×	×
Calabash	*Crescentia cujete*	×		
	LIVING FENCES AND HEDGES			
Cereus	*Cereus* sp.	×		
Dahlia	*Dahlia lehmannii*	×		
Muite	*Gliricidia sepium*	×		
Piñoncillo	*Jatropha curcas*	×		
Pinula	*Bromelia pinguin*	×		
Pitayo	*Pachycereus emarginatus*	×		
Yucca	*Yucca elephantipes*	×		
	ORNAMENTAL PLANTS			
Chanacol	*Bombax ellipticum*	×		
Cypress	*Taxodium mucronatum*	×		
Dahlia	*Dahlia coccinea*	×		
Dahlia	*Dahlia excelsa*	×		
Dahlia	*Dahlia lehmannii*	×		
Dahlia	*Dahlia pinnata*	×		
Galán	*Brunfelsia americana*	×		
Jazmin	*Bourreria huanita*	×		
Marigold	*Tagetes erecta*	×		
Marigold	*Tagetes patula*	×		
Mechuda	*Caesalpinia pulcherrima*	×		
Mirasol	*Cochlosperum vitifolium*	×		
Mirasol	*Tithonia diversifolia*	×		
Tiger flower	*Tigridia pavonia*	×		
Tuberose	*Polianthes tuberosa*	×		
TOTAL NUMBER OF SPECIES		151	18	12

*Probably not native to Meso-America, but of American origin.
†Probably not native to the Americas, of Old World origin.

for transoceanic boat travel. It now seems likely that the gourd too may have been dispersed by nature before man arrived in the New World, even though it no longer grows wild in the New World.

The strongest case for trans-Pacific diffusion in pre-Columbian times is that for the sweet potato (*Ipomoea batatas*). It is unquestionably of New World origin somewhere in Latin America. Before A.D. 1492 it was carried by raft or boat to all parts of Polynesia, where many varieties of it were found by the first South Pacific explorers. Some of the Polynesian words for "sweet potato" can be shown to be cognate with those of Indian languages, thus clinching the argument for diffusion by man. After A.D. 1492 it was carried by ships of Spain and other European nations to Melanesia, Indonesia, Asia, Europe, and Africa.

The banana (*Musa paradisica*) and the coconut (*Cocos nucifera*) are both natives of Southeast Asia or neighboring islands, and were once thought by some scholars to have been carried by men across the Pacific to the Americas before A.D. 1492. Because neither has been found in archeological sites certainly dating from pre-Columbian times, they are best regarded as imports in European ships in the early post-Columbian period.

From the evidence above, it is clear that the Indians began to cultivate plants on their own volition thousands of years before they had any contact with Old World farmers. At present there is no generally accepted evidence of any pre-Columbian cultivated plant having been brought by people from the Old World (including Polynesia) to the New World before A.D. 1492. In the other direction, the strongest case for diffusion by people from the New to the Old World is that of the sweet potato from South America to Polynesia, where it became a major source of food.

TOOLS AND TECHNIQUES OF FARMING

The plow was totally unknown in the New World until it was introduced by Europeans, and draft animals were not used in farming. Cultivation with hand tools, as was done by the Indians, is frequently called horticulture (garden cultivation). All the farming tribes used a straight pointed stick for some part of the routine. This was shaped like the digging stick used to obtain wild roots and bulbs, and often the same individual implement was used for both purposes. The pointed stick was used most frequently to make a hole for planting the grains of corn, beans, or squashes, although it might also be used to break up the ground for planting. In areas where precipitation was adequate, a hole a few inches deep would suffice, but in the dry Southwest area the planter sometimes made a hole as much as eighteen inches deep. The stub of a forking branch was left on the stick by the Pueblos and Navahos to serve as a footrest and thus facilitate the making of the deep holes which the dry soil demanded.

A number of tribes used an end-bladed implement made of a single piece of wood. In the Northwest this tool resembled a modern spade with a footrest on one side, but, because it was reported by Champlain, it appears to have been aboriginal. This tool was not always distinguished from a swordlike weeding tool which was limited to the Southwest. Throughout that area the end-bladed wooden implement lacked a footrest, and this difference suggests that the end-bladed feature in the two areas is best explained by independent histories.

The northern Missouri River tribes employed a rake of wood or antler to handle brush when clearing land, and in the Southwest the Hopi, at least, used a similar wooden tool. Whether either or both instances are aboriginal or modern is unknown, but it is certain that there was no direct contact between the two areas.

Hoes were probably universal on the Prairies and in the East. They seem to have been used much less frequently in the Southwest and Meso-America. One of the most common materials for the blade was animal bone, most often the shoulder blade. On the Prairies this was invariably derived from the buffalo, but in the East deer and perhaos other Cervidae furnished the material for the blade. Hoes with wooden blades were also common, especially where the buffalo shoulder blade was not available. Hoes with copper blades are reported only for the central Mexican area of Meso-America, where wooden ones were also used, and do not seem to have been common there. Hoes with shell, stone, and fishbone blades were common in the East, where they have been unearthed in quantity by archeologists. It is quite apparent that the hoes of the Prairies and East stem from a single origin, and possibly those in the Southwest are derived from them. Those in Mexico, however, may even be post-Columbian. Hoes were most often used to hill up the soil around the growing corn, but sometimes they were used to clear land or to dig holes for planting.

Irrigation was limited to Meso-America and the Southwest. Complete irrigation systems with ditches were fairly common in the Southwest, one of the oldest being at Snaketown, on the Gila drainage, A.D. 800–900. The largest and longest canals were in that part of southern Arizona; those on the Colorado and Rio Grande drainages to the north were less pretentious. The huge irrigation canals and dikes in the Valley of Mexico were the largest irrigation operation in all of North America. The dense population of central Mexico was made possible by the intensive farming which demanded irrigation.

In the Southwest, the custom of planting in soils which were naturally irrigated by floods of overflowing streams was widely distributed. This floodplain agriculture was important to the Yuman tribes of the lower Colorado River and to the Cáhita tribes of the lower

Yaqui, Fuerte, and Mayo rivers in Sinaloa. The overflow, which was the key to Cáhita economy, usually occurred in winter and summer, making possible two crops a year. The Indians planted in the rich alluvial mud deposited by the streams. Any other kind of farming would have been impractical because the annual rainfall is only about five inches. In other parts of the Southwest, where large streams were absent, crops were planted at the foot of mesas or in washes where the runoff from an occasional shower provided the precious moisture. Here and there wing fences, dikes, or dams were constructed to control this natural runoff. In one locality in Nevada, some sort of irrigation without ditches was practiced on wild plants, but details and time of origin are unknown.

Grass, brush, and trees were cleared from farm land by burning in most localities where agriculture was practiced in aboriginal North America. The purpose was threefold: to get rid of the vegetation, to fertilize the soil, and to make the soil more friable. The northern Missouri River farmers spread brush evenly over the entire plot, including barren spots, before burning, because the ashes loosened the soil and made it more workable. In areas of heaviest rainfall, in southeastern Mexico and Central America, the soil possessed only the minimum of essential minerals because these were continually leached out by the torrential rains. Some of this land was so poor that it had to be abandoned after a single crop. In one Maya locality, land was cultivated only one or two years out of seven. In more favorable localities, it might be farmed for several years in a row. Among some Cáhita groups living in mountain basins, fields were abandoned every one to three years, in contrast to conditions of floodplain agriculture where continual replanting was possible. Among the Iroquois of New York state, a town was moved about twice in a generation because of exhaustion of the soil, scarcity of firewood and timber for building, and depletion of game. For the Prairie-East area as a whole, about ten years constituted the maximum length of time a plot could be continuously farmed in any locality.

In the tropical forest, farming was done in the woods because the entire landscape was overgrown with vegetation and there was no other choice. On the Prairies and in the East, however, farming was done in the woods even where open meadows or prairies were available. This held also for the Indians living in the savanna lands of Central and South America. The meager tools used by the Indians and the absence of the plow and draft animals made the softer soils in the woods more attractive. The prairies of Iowa, which constitute the best land for corn today, could not have been worked with the pointed sticks and hoes of the Indians. These implements could not have broken up the tough sod which the heavy grasses produced. It was therefore more profitable to clear woods than to till the tough soils of open country. Large trees were not felled, but were simply girdled by pounding with a stone ax. This treatment was sufficient to kill the tree and permit the sun to shine through its bare branches. Another way was to pile brush around the trunk and set it afire. Burning to produce a better wild crop the next season was practiced over a large area in the Great Basin and California. This treatment was applied to grasses and to such small plants as tarweed and wild tobacco. This method is especially effective for perennials because the roots beneath the surface are unharmed and the elimination of surface coverage gives the new sprouting crop the maximum of sunlight and the minimum of competition from other species. Wild seeds were sown in a few localities, but this is hardly to be called farming because the varieties sown were identical with endemic wild forms. In the area from Lake Winnipeg to Lake Superior, wild rice (*Zizania aquatica*) was sometimes sown in the swamps. In California, Nevada, Utah, and northern Mexico, a few wild grasses were occasionally planted. It was on the Colorado and Gila rivers, however, that this activity attained its greatest importance. A recent analysis by Martínez del Río of the historical documentation on the Laguneros of northern Mexico indicates that reports of agriculture among those people refer to the possible cultivation of seeds which were probably wild.

Fertilizers, other than the ashes from burned-over land, were probably not employed. Although fish heads and ground shell were applied to corn hills in New England and Virginia, the former were used in Europe and were probably introduced into America by Europeans. The references to manure among the Seneca and Arikara also may be questioned in regard to aboriginality. The same is true of the use of manure by the Zapotecs and the mountain Maya. Informants from many other tribes on the Prairies and in the East emphatically deny the use of manure. In the areas where fertilizers were most needed—the tropics—there was no adequate source available, and soil exhaustion has often been mentioned as a partial explanation of the fluid political fortunes of these peoples.

The sexual division of labor for farming activities presents a clear picture (Map 8). Women did most of the farm work everywhere in the

Prairie-East area except among the Ojibwa and a few tribes in Maine and New Brunswick. These exceptions to the rule were on the northern periphery of horticulture, and these people may have adopted the White pattern by the time their customs were recorded. The men of the Prairie-East normally helped with the clearing of the new land and also with the harvest, although on the western Prairies, where buffalo hunting was important, young and active men might disdain farming entirely. In the Southeast the men did all the planting and cultivating of the "town" fields outside the town, but the women cultivated their own garden plots inside the town. Women also bore the brunt of farming among the Apaches of the Southwest. This pattern seems to stem from the Plains, through which some of the Apaches had passed on their migration southward a short time before White contact and where some of them lived in the early historical period. Both sexes among the Jicarilla farmed, at least in the nineteenth century, but among the Navaho the men have done most of the horticultural labor as far back as the record goes. This is not surprising, because, of all the Athapaskans, the Navaho have become most acculturated to Pueblo ways.

Among the Pueblos, the men everywhere did most of the farming, although early accounts mention the help of women more often than recent reports do. Men also dominated horticulture among most of the Yuman-Uto-Aztecan peoples in the Southwest and on down the west coast of Mexico to Meso-America.

To sum up, in the areas most intensively farmed—the Southwest and Meso-America—men were the principal farmers. In areas where farming was secondary in importance to some other subsistence activity (Map 4), women were the principal farmers. In the Prairies and East there are local exceptions to this rule, but we must remember that although farming seems to have dominated subsistence, it is problematical whether it provided over half the total food supply in much of this area. Therefore we may say that for North America as a whole there is a positive correlation between the importance of farm products in the dietary and the amount of time men devote to farming.

CONCLUSIONS

By the time Columbus discovered America, maize was being raised about as far north and west in North America as climate permitted (Map 7). In Canada, except for a narrow strip along the St.

Lawrence, the frost-free season is too short to raise a good crop of maize. The western boundary of the maize area in the Plains states is at about the 100th meridian, which is also the approximate boundary between regions with more than twenty inches of average rainfall and those with less than twenty inches. West of this line there is less than twenty inches of rain, which is too little rain for maize unless it is irrigated or grown in the best-watered spots. In the Great Basin region, maize was formerly grown about as far west and north as Great Salt Lake, but the abandonment of this region by the farmers long before America was discovered by Europeans is probably an indication that the climate was not very favorable for agriculture. In the Southwest, the area west of the Colorado River in California is desert, averaging only a couple of inches of rain each year. This served as a barrier to the spread of maize into California, but even where rainfall in that state is adequate in quantity, it comes at the wrong season for maize. Maize demands summer rains during its growing season, but in California most of the moisture falls in the winter months. The absence of maize in Northeast Mexico is also to be explained partly by climate. Here it was also too dry to grow a good crop consistently. Geography was therefore an important limiting factor in the distribution of both maize and other plants.

The origin of North American plant domestication in Meso-America, rather than in the Southwest or the eastern United States, is no mystery when the quantities of wild plants provided by nature in these areas are compared. The number of wild plant species in El Salvador, the smallest Central American nation, is as great as the number in the United States (including Alaska), Canada, and Greenland combined. Because the area of El Salvador is less than 1 per cent as large as that of the nations north of Mexico, the number of plant species in El Salvador is more than 100 times as dense as in the northern area. With so many plants available, the probability of the Indians finding suitable domesticates in the tropics is over 100 times greater than in Temperate, Sub-Arctic, and Arctic zones.

In the past, scholars have agreed on a minimum of two independent origins of plant cultivation in the Americas: one in lowland South America for root crops, such as manioc and the sweet potato; another in Meso-America for seed crops, such as maize, beans, and amaranth. As more and more becomes known about the botany, geography, and archeology of American domesticates, the greater becomes the number of postulated independent origins. The former belief that a single species is likely to be domesticated only once, and that multiple occurrences of the cultivated species over the map must always be explained by intentional diffusion by man from this one center of origin, is now obsolete. Where a close wild ancestor of a single domesticated species is widespread over a large area, and there are two or more distinct varieties or races of the domesticate concentrated in two or more subareas separated by wide geographical and cultural gaps, it is more reasonable to postulate two or more origins of domestication than one.

Although cultivated plants alone are not sufficient to produce an advanced civilization, their history in both the Old World and the New World shows that they are a necessary part of such a development. No great civilization has ever arisen in the world without a well-developed domesticated plant syndrome, which reduced the proportion of time necessary to acquire food and made possible the large permanent settlements and the elaborate divisions of labor that are features of civilization.

REFERENCES

BRIEGER *et al.*, 1958; BROWN AND ANDERSON, 1947, 1948; CARTER, 1945, 1963; CARTER AND ANDERSON, 1945; CASTETTER AND BELL, 1942, 1951; DRIVER AND DRIVER, 1967; GRIFFIN, 1967; GROBMAN *et al.*, 1961; HEISER, 1951, 1965; HO, 1955; KELLY AND PALERM, 1952; KROEBER, 1939; MANGELSDORF *et al.*, 1964a, 1964b; MEIGHAN *et al.*, 1958; SAUER, 1950, 1952, 1959, 1960; SMITH AND MACNEISH, 1964; WELLHAUSEN *et al.*, 1952, 1957; WHITAKER AND CARTER, 1954; WHITAKER, CUTLER, AND MACNEISH, 1957; WHITAKER AND DAVIS, 1962; WILLEY, 1966.

6

Other Aspects of Subsistence

THE earliest dates of archeological sites where actual remains of domesticated plants or animals have been found are 9000 B.C. in the Old World (Wright, 1968) and 7000 B.C. in the New World. This seems a long time ago, but man hunted, fished, and gathered wild plants for several millions of years before he learned to farm. The first Indian immigrants to the New World knew nothing of farming and could not have raised crops in the Arctic climate of Siberia and Alaska if they had wanted to. These peoples lived solely on the wild animals, fish, and wild plants that nature provided. The abundance of spear points in the early archeological levels, mentioned in Chapter 1, is mute but incontestable evidence that the earliest immigrants to North America were hunters.

In over half the area of aboriginal North America at the time of European contact, the Indians did not farm but lived exclusively by hunting, fishing, or gathering wild plants. Complete inventories of all species of animals, fishes, and plants consumed as food by the Indians of North America have never been compiled, but they would probably total more than 2,500 species. This suggests tremendous knowledge of the habits of the animals and fishes and an equally vast acquaintance with the nutritional qualities of the plants. Such knowledge could be acquired only by thousands of years of experimenting and some casualties from sickness or death. As we shall see below, some of the plants eaten contain poisons in their raw condition and must be cooked or otherwise treated before they can be consumed by human beings.

HUNTING

We saw in Chapter 4 that hunting was the dominant means of obtaining a livelihood in seven out of seventeen culture areas. The hunting regions cover at least half of the total area of the continent: nearly all of Canada and Alaska, and the middle half of the United

States (Map 3). This area is wedge-shaped, with the point of the wedge in southern Texas. It falls almost entirely to the east of the Continental Divide, and the near-linear character of its western boundary is determined by this Great Divide. Hunting of wild game was also practiced to some extent in all other areas of North America, even in those regions where farming supplied 80 per cent or more of the diet.

Sea mammal hunting.—Sea mammals were hunted chiefly with the harpoon, which consisted of a detachable head with retrieving line attached, a foreshaft, and a main shaft. The significant feature of the harpoon is that the head remains in the hide or flesh of the animal, which is then played like a fish. The flexible line absorbs the swiveling and thrashing about of the animal, whereas a shaft with a fixed point would break in two. Inflated floats and drags were indispensable in whaling, because the boats used were too small to withstand the pull of a diving whale and would have been submerged if the line had been attached to them; but floats were also used for capturing smaller sea mammals. The seals were small enough to be played with a hand line if the hunters wore mittens for protection from rope burns or the loss of a finger.

Land animal hunting.—Land animal hunting methods show almost endless variation in details from locality to locality and from species to species. The bow and arrow was almost everywhere the chief weapon used. The thrusting lance was likewise nearly universal. The sling, which could be effective only against small game, is reported for about half the North American tribes. The spear-thrower is reported by European observers only in the far north and extreme south with a huge gap in the middle, and the blowgun is found only in the south. The javelin, hurled with the hand without a spear-thrower, was extremely rare. Clubs of some kind were fairly common but were used more in warfare than in hunting.

Cooperative drives involving a number of hunters were almost universal, being absent only in restricted localities where artiodactyls (split-hoofed animals) and rodents were absent, or nearly absent, in the environment. The driving of land mammals into water or the pursuit of them in water is most characteristic of the Arctic and Sub-Arctic areas, where it is most often associated with the hunting of caribou and moose. Driving game with fire was probably practiced almost everywhere in the United States in aboriginal times, but was rare in other parts of North America. The surround appears to have been most common in the Prairies, Plains, Great Basin, and Southwest, although it is reported from other areas as well. After the acquisition of the horse by the Plains tribes, the surround became much easier and replaced such other methods as driving over cliffs or into man-made enclosures. Driving animals along a fence or barrier, or between a converging pair of them into a corral made of timber, was common in the northern two-thirds of North America. Another variant of the fence and enclosure was the long flat net—like a tennis net, but higher. Nets were used to catch deer and elk in British Columbia, and farther south deer or antelope were occasionally caught in them, but most often in the west they were employed in rabbit drives.

Pitfalls, concealed traps into which animals may fall, are reported from every major area of North America but not for every tribe. Deadfalls appear to have been known to about three-fourths of the tribes, being absent, little used, or not reported in the southeastern quarter of the continent. A deadfall is any sort of trap with a triggered weight which falls when sprung by the victim, pinning it fast or killing it instantly. Snares or nooses were almost universal, but were probably absent among most of the Plains tribes, where the dominance of buffalo hunting and the dearth of trees made them impractical.

Deceptive techniques were common in hunting and may be divided into visual disguises and auditory decoys. Visual disguises, consisting of the horns, head, and sometimes the entire hide of an animal, were worn by the hunter, who stalked his quarry from the down-wind direction, so that he would not be detected by his body odor until he was within bow shot. A considerable variety of auditory decoys were employed by North American Indians. The conical bark trumpet was used to imitate the call of the moose, and smaller models of the same type for caribou as well. The blowing on a leaf or piece of grass held in the hands employs the principle of the ribbon reed. It was used more often for deer than for any other game and imitated the cry of a fawn which might attract a doe. Whistles used as auditory decoys were fairly widespread but seldom described in detail. A number of tribes struck antlers together to imitate the sound of fighting bucks in the rutting season, or rubbed a scapula against a tree to produce a noise like a female in heat rubbing her horns to call a buck. The Shoshoni of the Great Basin struck stones or sticks together to produce a sound like the clashing together of mountain sheep horns. Hunters in the Sub-Arctic in the rutting season sometimes poured water out of a container, held a few feet above a stream or lake, to imitate the sound of a urinating female moose in order to attract a male.

Dogs were probably used in hunting by the majority of North American tribes, but on the Plains, Prairies, in the Great Basin, and in Meso-America only a minority of peoples seem to have followed this practice. In general, it appears that dogs were of little utility for large animals running in herds, which were easy for man to locate, but were of greater utility in hunting animals which were solitary or lived in small social groups and were therefore more difficult to find.

FISHING

Although fishing as a dominant subsistence activity was the rule mainly on the Northwest Coast, it was an important source of food in several other areas which total about half of the continent. The rank of fishing in the native production economy depended of course on the quantity of fish available, the fishing skills, equipment, and knowledge possessed by the Indian, and on the other kinds of food resources available in the area. The mere presence of quantities of fish in nature is insufficient to bring about their extensive utilization as food by man.

Fish were obtained by Indians in every major manner known to modern commercial fishermen: by means of weirs and traps, nets, spears, and hooks. They were also poisoned, shot with the bow, snared, and raked in.

The net is one of the most generalized of fishing devices, and all species of fish are obtainable with it. At the same time it is among the most efficient of devices to operate, although it may take many hours to manufacture. Small hand nets, dip nets, and scoop nets were widely used in native North America, but seines and gill nets were of more limited distribution.

A weir is any sort of fence or barrier sufficient to block a fish yet permit the passage of water. The majority of weirs were built in streams, but some were built on the tidelands of the coasts to impound fish when the tide ebbed and flowed. They consisted normally of stakes or posts, driven into the bottom of the stream or tideland, with cross members attached to form a fish-proof latticework. In areas where wood was scarce or absent, such as the Arctic, weirs were made of stones; sometimes both wood and stones were used. Although nets were highly efficient fish-taking devices, weirs and traps probably caught more fish per year than any other method. Weirs and traps were especially effective for migrating fish such as salmon and shad.

On the Northwest Coast, where fishing most completely dominated all other subsistence pursuits, more salmon were taken with these devices than with any other.

Fish spears were used in all regions except of course the deserts and semideserts, where streams and lakes were few and fish scarce. Harpoons were less common. Fish spearing and harpooning are most effective in relatively shallow water which is clear or heavily stocked with fish. Attracting fish by means of a torchlight or a bonfire on the prow of a boat or raft is associated with spearing, and was known in both eastern and western North America but not in the Arctic or most of the Sub-Arctic. This method is so efficient that it is forbidden by law in most civilized areas lest the numbers of fish become seriously depleted.

On the whole, fishhooks were much less effective than nets, weirs, and spears. Many species of fish will not take bait at all, and others, such as salmon and shad, will not do so when ascending rivers to spawn. The fact that civilized nations today generally limit freshwater fishing to hook and line, in order to conserve their fish resources, is conclusive evidence of the relative ineffectiveness of hooks.

Catching fish with poisons was limited to the Plateau, Great Basin, California, Baja California, the Mexican part of the Southwest, Meso-America, and the East. For the continent as a whole, this method was much less important than angling. Optimum conditions for fish poisoning, in addition to the presence of poisonous plants, include sluggish streams and a high concentration of fish.

It is significant to note that fresh-water streams and lakes in North America constitute only about 5 per cent of the surface of the continent, but the quantity of fish obtained shows that fishing was more productive per acre than hunting or wild plant gathering. It was second only to agriculture in this respect. The relatively sedentary way of life on the Northwest Coast was made possible by the abundance of food available within a small territory (Rostlund, 1952).

WILD PLANT FOODS

Wild plants dominated subsistence in California, the Great Basin, Northeast Mexico, and a small part of the Southwest (Map 3). Before the time of agriculture, they were probably either dominant or much more important in the areas which later became agricultural. A combined list of both wild and domesticated native American plants north of Mexico, dating from 1936, gives 120 families, 444 genera, and 1,112 species (Yanovsky, 1936). About 2 per cent of these species were cultivated plants; the other 98 per cent were wild. Because considerable work in ethnobotany has been done since 1936, the above figures on numbers of families, genera, and species are too low. Also, if Mexico and Central America had been included, the list would contain the 134 domesticated species grown only south of the Mexican border (Table 3), plus a number of wild species, bringing the total to perhaps 1,500 species.

The dominance of wild vegetable foods in California, the Great Basin, and Northeast Mexico was largely conditioned by geographical environment. The flora of these areas was richer than the fauna at the level of exploitation known to the Indian. While agriculture supplanted wild plants in parts of the Southwest, its spread into Northeast Mexico, the Great Basin, or California was limited by climate and other environmental factors. It is notable that the population in California, where only wild plant foods were utilized, was denser than that of the Prairies and East, which were farming areas (Maps 4, 6).

FOOD PREPARATION AND PRESERVATION

Every Indian tribe prepared and preserved its food in some way and stored some of it for future use. Recipes are well reported in many localities and run into the thousands. For the Kwakiutl alone there are 150 recipes on record. We have already noted that about 1,500 species of plants were eaten, and if we add to this the lists of mammals, birds, fishes, and invertebrates consumed by Indians, the total might exceed 2,500 species. Now if we combine these by twos, and threes, into food recipes, we get an enormous number of dishes. No attempt will be made to give even an abbreviated list here; instead, a description of some of the widespread ways of preparing and preserving food follows.

Boiling.—Indians boiled food in all culture areas except possibly in Northeast Mexico and Baja California, where boiling is not mentioned in early sources. Boiling techniques are of two major kinds: direct-fire boiling, or placing a vessel containing liquid near a fire; and stone boiling, or immersing heated stones in the liquid. Both methods were known to Indians, and each is about equally widespread. Direct-fire boiling was almost the exclusive method in the Arctic, where stone vessels were the rule, and in the Prairie, East, Southwest, and Meso-

America, where pottery vessels were known. Stone boiling was the dominant type in the western Sub-Arctic, Northwest Coast, Plateau, and California, where only burnable vessels of wood, bark, basketry, or hide were used. In the middle regions there were huge areas where both types were known and used, especially on the Plains, in the Great Basin, and in the Eastern Sub-Arctic. Because the early Indian immigrants into the Americas were without pottery and do not seem to have had other adequate containers for direct-fire boiling, it is almost certain that stone boiling was once a general practice, except in the Arctic and possibly part of the Sub-Arctic. As pottery became more and more common it tended to replace stone boiling with direct-fire boiling because the latter required less labor on the part of the housewife. But the change was slow, and stone boiling continued to be used on certain occasions. For example, when hunters were a long way from home and had nothing to cook in except the body of the animal they had slain, they stone-boiled in the paunch, hide, or thorax. Although pottery in North America was more widespread than farming, it was little used in areas which lacked farming, except in Alaska. It is only the sedentary peoples that can make full use of pottery, because pottery is difficult to transport without breakage.

Earth oven.—The earth oven, a kind of Indian fireless cooker, was known to some tribes in all culture areas except the Arctic. It was simply a hole in the ground into which hot stones and food were placed. It was covered with the earth from the hole so that the heat and steam would be confined long enough to cook the food, normally overnight. The food was wrapped in leaves, bark, and other handy materials to keep it clean. In most areas both animal and plant foods were cooked in the earth oven, but plant foods certainly more often.

Broiling and roasting.—Although meat was boiled in vessels and baked in the earth oven, it was broiled or roasted more frequently in areas with little or no pottery and only the laborious stone-boiling technique. In areas where pottery vessels occurred, on the other hand, meat was most commonly boiled. This was certainly true of the Prairies and the East, where the Indians boiled most of their meat, often mixed with plant foods, which were also cooked chiefly by boiling. The Arctic is the only nonfarming area where meat was usually boiled, when it was cooked at all; boiling was the only practical method in this area, where firewood was lacking and all cooking had to be done over the small flame of an animal-oil lamp. In other areas, meat was broiled on single sticks stuck into the ground and inclined toward a wood fire and on horizontal frames over the fire, or it was roasted on hot stones beside the fire or in the ashes. Small animals, from mice to porcupines, were most often roasted, unskinned and whole, in ashes.

Acorn preparation.—Many foods are indigestible or poisonous in their raw condition and must be processed before they can be eaten in quantity. One of the best-known examples is the acorn, which is normally unpalatable without special preparation. It was probably of greater importance in the Indian diet before the Christian era, when farming was less known than it was later, when almost half of the tribes farmed. There are some sixty species of oaks in North America, most of which are grouped under a single genus, *Quercus*. Of these, acorns from twenty-seven species are known to have been eaten by Indians. Acorns from all these species are known to contain tannic acid in varying amounts. The majority contain enough of this acid so that large quantities cannot be eaten unless at least some of it is removed. The main nutritive elements of acorns are starches and fats, with the former predominating in most species.

Although acorns were eaten by at least half the Indian tribes in the United States, they were a staple food only in California, where they were eaten in greater quantity than any other food product, animal or vegetable. The acorns were first cracked open with the aid of a small elongated stone for a hammer and a heavy flat slab of stone for an anvil. The nut meats were then ground with a mortar and pestle. When the meal was ground sufficiently fine, it was taken to the bank of a stream for the leaching process. Most frequently the meal was placed directly on the sand in a shallow depression or basin which had been prepared for the purpose. Then water was dipped from the stream and poured over and through the meal in the manner of making drip coffee. This leaching process was repeated until the bitter taste of the tannic acid was eliminated. The meal was then ready for cooking (Driver, 1953*a*).

Grinding and pounding.—Many foods, both animal and vegetable, were prepared for eating by grinding, pounding, pulverizing, mechanical tenderizing, hulling, and shelling. Vegetable foods were more consistently treated in this manner than animal foods, and seeds more often than any other part of the plant. Equipment used for grinding and related processes is generally divided into mortars, which are operated by pounding, and milling stones, to which a rubbing motion is applied. A mortar is usually hollowed out like a vessel, but also may be a flat slab. A milling stone is usually flat, but may also be grooved or troughed. Mortars and the pounding technique were used to pulverize and tenderize meat as well as to grind plant foods, but milling stones and the rubbing technique were usually limited to plant products. Our definitions are therefore based as much on how the mortar or milling stone was used as on its appearance in a museum showcase. Furthermore, milling stones and their hand stones often served a double purpose. Although designed for the grinding of seeds with a rubbing motion, they were also used to crack nuts or to tenderize meat by pounding. The mortar and pestle was less versatile, but might be used to mash berries or fruits as well as to grind or hull nuts and grains. Grinding equipment of all kinds was little used or absent in much of the Arctic, Sub-Arctic, Northwest Coast, and Plains. This emphasizes its primary association with plant products.

For both North and South America there is an east-west contrast in climate which affects both wild and cultivated plant ecologies. West of the Continental Divide, the climate is drier and frequent deserts and semideserts are found. The edible wild plants in deserts must be drought-resistant and able to subsist on a minimum of moisture. Seeds from such plants tend to be hard and dry, and require the thorough grinding which is possible with stone and a rubbing technique. East of the Continental Divide, except for the Plains near the Rockies and Northeast Mexico, climates are much more moist, and seeds tend to be replaced by fruits, nuts, and tubers which are fuller-bodied and softer. These may be adequately ground with wood and a pounding technique. Therefore it appears likely that these two contrasting grinding patterns were somewhat differentiated before cultivated plants were known. Milling stones date from 9000 B.C. at Danger Cave in the Great Basin (Jennings, 1957: 212), and outnumbered projectile points in the Cochise Culture in the Southwest by 5800 B.C. (Wormington, 1957: 169–73). Mortars are probably of equal age.

Smoking and drying.—The majority of peoples north of Mexico fire-dried or smoked meat. The fire and the smoke not only hastened the drying process but also kept away flies and other insect pests. The majority probably also dried meat in the sun and wind when the weather permitted, but as an exclusive method this would have been inadequate for most of the continent. It was only in parts of the Plains, Great Basin, California, and Southwest that meat was exclusively sun- and wind-dried. These climates were dry the year round and hot in summer, making a fire necessary. The term "jerky" is derived from the South American Indian word *charqui*, which means "dried meat." Jerky was merely dried, not jerked.

Dried meat on the Plains and in parts of neighboring areas was pounded with the stone-headed maul to make pemmican. The dried meat was first softened by holding it over a fire, then pulverized, mixed with melted fat and marrow and, finally, with berry or fruit paste to give it the desired taste and texture. The whole mess was then packed in a folded rawhide container called a parfleche. With proper care such pemmican would keep for years, although most of it was consumed within a single year.

Fish were also preserved in a number of ways. They were sun- and air-dried exclusively in most of the Arctic, Plateau, Great Basin, California, and probably Meso-America. Fish were buried in pits and allowed to decay in the Arctic, on the North Pacific Coast, and less frequently on the Plateau. In the East, the Micmac, Huron, and Iroquois Indians suspended fish and allowed the flesh to decompose partially. Possibly the action of microorganisms on the fish produces some ingredient beneficial to human nutrition, because European explorers in the Arctic grow fond of rotten fish.

The smoking of fish is mentioned less often than the smoking of meat. The former is reported consistently only on the Northwest Coast, in the Sub-Arctic, northern Prairies, and East, although it has been noted sporadically in other regions.

Fish was pulverized after drying in California, on the Northwest Coast south of the Columbia River, on the Plateau, sporadically in the Sub-Arctic, and in a small area in the East among the Iroquois and their neighbors. Meriwether Lewis and William Clark estimated that about 30,000 pounds of dried and pulverized salmon were prepared annually for the Indian trade in the area of The Dalles on the Columbia River. The addition of berries, the storage in hide bags, and the sealing of the bags with fat—all suggest a common origin with the making of pemmican on the Plains.

A great variety of vegetable foods, both wild and domesticated, was preserved by drying. The only area where plant foods were not dried was the Arctic, where practically no plant foods were eaten. In the areas where plant foods predominated, including agricultural areas, their drying for winter use was indispensable. In the United States west of the Rockies, occasionally east of the Rockies, and south through Meso-America, seeds, including those of maize where cultivated, were dried and cooked by parching. In Mexico, parched and ground corn is known as *pinole*. The popping of corn is primarily a cooking rather than a preserving technique, but is obviously related to parching and was done in a pottery vessel heated to the necessary temperature. Ordinary corn will not pop in an open vessel, but the Indians of the Southwest, Meso-America, and the Southeast raised popcorn and cooked it this way.

Ordinary varieties of maize dried sufficiently in the sun and air in the Southwest and highland Meso-America, and required no other drying method; but in the Prairies, East, and lowland tropics, the humidity was sufficient, in many localities, to necessitate drying on a scaffold over a fire.

Salt.—Sodium chloride is a biological necessity without which a human being cannot live. Vegetable foods contain a high concentration of potassium, which tends to replace sodium in the blood. In order to overcome this sodium deficiency, vegetarians require additional sodium chloride. Meat eaters, on the other hand, get adequate amounts of mineral salts of all kinds from the meat and blood of the animals they eat. The amount of salt required by a human being is further determined by the amount he loses in perspiration. Therefore dwellers in warm climates need more salt than those in cool climates.

The distribution of the intentional eating of sodium chloride is given on Map 9. A comparison with Map 4 shows a close correspondence between the predominance of vegetable food, whether wild or domesticated, and the eating of salt. Thus in California, the Great Basin, Southwest, parts of the Prairies and East, Meso-America, and the Circum-Caribbean areas, salt was eaten. In Northeast Mexico, refined sodium chloride was lacking except near the Meso-American border, where a little was obtained in trade. However, the Northeast Mexicans ate crude salts obtained from dry lake beds and such natural sources. Salt was eaten by a few tribes which relied mainly on fish or meat, but in all cases these areas of salt eating were minor extensions from adjacent regions where vegetable fare predominated.

The correlation between salt eating and temperature is also apparent. Salt-eating peoples are those in the southern half of the continent. The chief exception to this generalization is the salt-free corridor in the southern Plains and Northeast Mexico. The predominance of hunting in the southern Plains accounts for the discrepancy in that area, but Northeast Mexico is again anomalous. Possibly salt was eaten more often than is reported there.

In the Southeast and Meso-America, salt was obtained principally by evaporating salt water. In the Great Basin, by contrast, most of the salt was obtained dry from the surface of the land in and around dry lake beds. Indians in California and the Southwest employed both methods; they gathered it in dry form on the surface or from shallow mines, and also evaporated the moisture from salt water.

Salt was an important trade article in the Southeast, Southwest, California, and Meso-America. In Mexico, it approached the status of a currency and, with cotton, was the major trade item. In the Southwest, salt was obtained in the greatest quantity by tribes living near the source of supply and traded to those at a distance, although long journeys were also made to obtain it. In the Southeast, salt was widely traded, especially on the Mississippi, where de Soto's men obtained it from the natives. In California, it was traded from the east side of the Sierra, where it was plentiful, to the west side, where it was less common; in one area, a dispute over a salt deposit was the cause of a local war.

In the Southwest and Meso-America, salt played a prominent role in religion, mythology, and ceremonies. The Southwest peoples engaged in elaborate salt-gathering expeditions, for which the choice of leaders, dietary restrictions, sexual continence, and the precise manner of gathering and refining salt were all prescribed by ritual. This was done to propitiate a female deity who was supposed to be the guardian of the salt supply. The Aztecs of Mexico had a still more elaborate ceremony in honor of their salt goddess, who was described as having golden ears, and wearing yellow vestments, an iridescent green plumed miter, a wave-shaped embroidered bodice, a fishnet skirt, and woven cotton sandals. This goddess was impersonated in the ceremony by a maiden who was sacrificed as the climax of the ten-day rite (Hunter, 1940).

NUTRITION

The meat and fish eaten by Indians contained an abundance of protein, fat, mineral salts, and vitamins, including ascorbic acid in raw meat and blood. In the areas where hunting and fishing dominated the subsistence picture, the Indians were well nourished except when fish and game were scarce. An analysis of the nutritional ingredients in sixty-six species of wild plants eaten by Indians (Yanovsky and Kingsbury, 1938) showed an average of only 8 per cent protein by dry weight.

Modern corn (maize) in the United States averages about 12 per cent protein, but some varieties consumed by Indians averaged a little higher. Squashes (*Cucurbita*) average only about 10 per cent, but beans contain around 25 per cent. In the areas that depended heavily on wild plants—the Great Basin, Northeast Mexico, and parts of California and the Southwest—the diet lacked sufficient protein. This was also true of the areas of most intensive farming—Meso-America and parts of the Southwest—although beans raised the amount of protein a little. Intensive analyses of Indian bones and teeth found in archeological excavations in the Prairies and East show that those peoples who depended principally on wild foods were healthier than those who lived mainly by farming. The teeth of the farmers, who ate a great deal of maize, showed many more cavities than those of the wild-food eaters. However, in Meso-America, where the corn was soaked in lime water, this extra calcium produced better teeth. Mexican children today, on a diet that is substandard in many respects, have better teeth than most children in the United States.

SOCIAL AND RELIGIOUS ASPECTS

Man throughout the world lives in social groups which range in size from a single family to the huge cities and nations of modern times. He is everywhere a participant in a cooperative economic venture, even though the unit may include only two persons—a man and wife. Such a unit nowhere exists independendently of other such units. More remote kindred are everywhere recognized, and couples everywhere have social obligations and privileges which involve food. Food is hedged by religion in all cultures, probably more so among so-called primitives than among civilized peoples. Spirits and magical forces everywhere are thought to determine one's success in one's food-getting venture whether it is hunting, fishing, gathering, farming, or stock breeding. One must propitiate these spirits or forces in the proper way and at the proper time if one is to be a successful provider. Although primitive man's knowledge of ethnobotany and zoology is often impressive, it is invariably linked with a maze of religious notions which almost defy analysis.

One example of the way the mind may work will suffice. A generation ago an anthropologist was cruising down a Canadian river in a canoe with some Indians. Half a mile or so downstream they saw an object that they all thought was a bear. It went out of sight as they rounded a bend in the stream; when it reappeared at much closer range, the anthropologist saw that it was only a stump and remarked about his mistaken perception. Not so for one of the Indians, who insisted that it had been a bear in the beginning and had somehow been changed into a stump while out of sight. Indian religion bristles with notions of this kind which pyramid onto one another in a manner hard for us to understand.

A few simple generalizations on sexual division of labor will be offered here. Almost all hunting was done by men. Women, however, occasionally hunted birds or small game, and frequently helped butcher and bring home game. They also participated in communal drives in some areas. While fishing was likewise chiefly a man's job, women generally did more fishing than hunting. The gathering of wild plant foods was largely a task for women, but men helped in areas where plants were indispensable or where tree climbing was required (Map 36). For horticulture, there is a distinct cleavage between east and west: on the Prairie and in the East, farming was mainly the work of women, with men concentrating on hunting, fishing, and fighting; in the Southwest and Meso-America, farming was mainly the work of men, who did relatively little hunting, less fishing, and not much fighting (Map 8). Women normally did the cooking in all areas and also the bulk of the processing of food short of cooking. Other aspects of economics, such as trade and property concepts, will be discussed in later chapters.

Hunting.—Although a hunter sometimes hunted alone, he normally shared his kill at least with the members of his family. While he generally made his own weapons, his wife usually had a hand in making his clothing. In the Arctic where a wife prepared all the hides and made all the clothing, a man could not have hunted at all without the cooperation of his wife.

Boys in all areas were given toy weapons with which to play until they were old enough to hunt small game. Each received constant instruction from an older relative, usually his father, in the habits of game, the use of weapons, the manufacture of weapons and traps, and in the ever present religious aspects of hunting. The average North American Indian boy progressed through a series of stages of learning, beginning first with birds and small game and then gradually working up to the more elusive, more dangerous, but also more valuable large animals, such as the seal, caribou, deer, bear, or buffalo. Each time the boy killed his first of a new species, he had to carry his game back to camp and stand by while the others of the family or band cooked it and ate it. He was not allowed to eat a single bite. His reward came in the form of direct praise and the social recognition of his enhanced status in the community. It was not until after he had demonstrated his ability to obtain a major game animal that he could even consider getting married. Some form of special attention to a youth's first game was probably a universal practice in areas where hunting was of importance.

Even when a mature hunter went out alone and brought home game unassisted, he usually shared it with other families in the community if they were in need. While such families were often related by blood or marriage, unrelated members of the same community were treated in the same way. Furthermore, whenever a visitor made a social call, he was always offered food. A good hunter could therefore expect plenty of visitors in time of need, and in all hunting areas there was a tendency for mediocre men to attach themselves to a more skilled individual. This was the lowest level of leadership and political organization.

For a group of hunters going out together, there was invariably a series of rules governing the disposition of the meat. The one who killed the game usually got the lion's share, but he who was first to touch a fallen animal often got a sizable portion. Under these conditions, a man who was a poor shot with the bow, or who was unskilled in stalking or locating game, could profit by being alert when a more capable person dropped an animal.

The belief in animal souls was probably universal among North American Indians. This in no way interfered with the parallel belief in human souls, which was likewise found everywhere. Animals and human beings were spiritually equated by the Indian as they are physically equated by biologists today. Every animal, then, since it had a soul which survived after its death, was able to report on the manner in which it had been killed, butchered, and consumed, and on the disposal of the inedible parts. If the hunter did not follow the proper procedure, he offended the spirit of the slain animal, which did not hesitate to inform other animal souls of its indecent treatment. Souls of living game, as well as of dead ones, heard of such cases and refused to allow their bodies to be slain by such an unkind hunter, who therefore failed to get any more game.

The taboos surrounding hunting have never been catalogued or classified for the whole continent, but it is certain that they run into the hundreds. Some were shared by many tribes, and others by only a few. One of the most widespread beliefs was that menstruating women were offensive to game animals. When a hunter's wife was menstruating, he often must not hunt at all, or he must at least take care that she did not touch any of his hunting gear or drop any menstrual fluid on the meat of previously slain game. In northwestern California, meat was taken into the house by removing a wall board instead of through the normal entrance, for fear that a menstruating woman had dripped fluid in the entrance way. A hunter usually abstained from sexual intercourse for one or more nights before a hunt.

Anyone who was ill or associated with illness was thought to be potentially dangerous to hunting luck, and was required to refrain from eating meat, particularly fresh meat. This applied to menstruating women, medicine men acquiring power or practicing their arts, warriors who had slain an enemy, and mourners for a recently deceased kinsman. In some areas, a hunter who had killed a major animal, such as a whale, had to go into mourning the same as he would for a dead relative. An entire Eskimo community occasionally starved to death because of the rule forbidding anyone to hunt until several days after the death of a member of the community. When one of a number of persons on the verge of starvation died, the others got no food for several days, which was sufficient to cause the death of another, and so on until all were dead.

Fishing.—The social aspects of fishing resemble those of hunting in that one normally shared one's catch with others and, in turn, obtained a share of another's fish. The fishing education of a boy also closely resembled that for hunting, including special attention to the first fish he caught. Because the best fishing places were small areas at the falls of streams, these were more often owned by kin groups than were hunting territories. Furthermore, fishing was hedged with less ceremonialism than hunting. The reason is probably twofold: fish were less important in the diet for the continent as a whole; fish are farther removed from man biologically than mammals, and resemble man much less in both appearance and behavior. Nevertheless, the first salmon ceremony on the Northwest Coast and the Plateau was an elaborate affair which surpassed all other subsistence rituals in these areas. It is no accident that such was the case here, because these were the two areas which relied most heavily on fish for food, and the salmon was the most frequent fish.

The psychological attitude of the Indians included the belief that the salmon had a soul, and that if the first one was caught, killed, and eaten in the most formal and correct manner, its soul would tell other salmon about the event and they would swarm up the stream to be caught and eaten in the same respectful manner. The first fish was usually thought to be a leader whose word was a command to others. The major first-fish ceremonies of the Pacific drainage suggest that many of the beliefs and practices spread from one tribe to another from a single point of origin somewhere in the area (Gunther, 1928).

Gathering of wild plants.—The gathering of wild plants was principally the work of women. While a woman sometimes gathered alone, she was more often accompanied by other women, who were either relatives or friends residing in the same camp or village. Women seem to have gathered in groups more consistently than men hunted in groups, probably for mutual protection against intruders from hostile tribes. At any rate, the woman gatherer shared her plant produce with the other women of the group and, in the form of prepared food, with the other members of her family. Husbands probably contributed less to wives' gathering ventures than did wives to husbands' hunting forays. Nevertheless, the manufacturing of the digging stick and gathering poles was usually the work of men. Seed beaters and basketry containers, however, were made by women, as were most other articles of basketry.

A girl was almost always taught plant lore, gathering techniques, and food preparation by her mother. Special attention was given to the first plant products gathered by a girl much less often than to a boy's first game. The theory behind a girl's rite was the same as for that of a boy: she should be encouraged to be a good provider by the praise and publicity she acquired at this time. She also was not allowed to eat any of her first gatherings. The plant products to which the rite applied varied according to the locality: berries in the north, berries or roots on the Plateau, seeds in the Great Basin.

Rites for the first plant food of the season were much more frequent. They were characteristic of the Northwest Coast, Plateau, California, Southwest, Meso-America, Prairies, and East. On the whole, first-fruits ceremonies were found in areas where other kinds of public ceremonies were well developed. In the West, first-fruits ceremonies were distributed in close conformity to major first-fish rites. In the rest of the first-fruits area, they conformed closely to the distribution of maize. These facts suggest that all these subsistence ceremonies were interrelated, that one had been stimulated by another. As a matter of actual fact, some tribes combined all of their subsistence rites into a single major ceremony. This was true in the East among the Creek, was common in the Southwest and Meso-America, and occurred in northwestern California in the form of World Renewal Ceremonies. Tribes with first-fruits rites belonged to the more sedentary half of those on the entire continent. Those leading a more nomadic life seldom found time for such cultural elaboration. To say that tribes with elaborate public subsistence ceremonies possessed them because their anxiety over food was greater than that of tribes which lacked them is certainly missing the mark. Anxiety over food was universal in native North America. The areas where population was thinner because starvation was more frequent were the very ones which lacked such major ceremonies. While some sort of psychological necessity must be present to give rise to such rituals, it is far from sufficient to produce them. Many other factors must be taken into account.

Horticulture.—Farming was a highly socialized activity with a myriad of rules and regulations. Two reasons for this were: the great importance of agriculture in the economy, and the relatively small amount of acreage devoted to it for each family. When a large amount of a person's time and effort was concentrated in a few acres of land, he was bound to be concerned about the rules of tenure and of consumption of the products of his handiwork. Farm plots were usually assigned to a family or an individual by a leader of a larger social unit, such as a sib or a community. A family or individual normally kept a plot for years or even a lifetime, except in the Prairies, East, and lowland tropics, where the clearing of new land was a necessity. At any rate, if land was not used or if the owner died, it reverted to the sib or tribe. Normally it would be reallocated to an heir of the deceased, but in native theory farm land belonged to the group, not to the individual.

Girls were taught to farm by their mothers on the Prairies and in the East, and boys most often by their fathers in the Southwest and Meso-America. There was nothing in farming rites comparable to the first-game rite for a boy or the first-wild-plant ceremony for a girl. Such minor rituals associated with a child's education seem to have been submerged by the huge public ceremonies which lasted for days.

In the Southeast, there were special public fields, called either town fields or the chief's fields. While there were a few tribes whose chief was in complete authority, among the majority of Eastern Indians he was more like an elected official subject to impeachment. He or his lieutenants gave orders for all able-bodied men and women to work in the public fields, and criers walked through the towns and villages to call out the workers. The produce from these fields did not become the personal property of the chief, but was stored in a public granary. While the chief's immediate family subsisted on the results of this community enterprise and did no physical labor themselves, they were also obligated to feed foreign guests as well as needy local families from the public stores. Food for public ceremonies also came from the same storehouses. The role of the chief, then, was that of a custodian of a public reserve of food.

In the agricultural areas, there was more ritual associated with maize than with all other cultivated plants combined. There were planting rites, Green Corn rites, and harvest rites. Such rituals were more complicated and formalized in densely settled Meso-America, where ceremonies were in the hands of the priesthoods. Local village observances were also important there, just as they are today. Ceremonial emphasis varied in the agricultural cycle; in the Southwest and Meso-America, planting and rain rituals were preeminent; in the Prairies and the East, the Green Corn harvest ceremony was the greatest ritual occasion and was frequently in the nature of a new year celebration. In the much drier regions of the Southwest and Meso-America, where periodic droughts sometimes brought actual starvation, the most elaborate group rituals were concerned with rain-making, which was the most recurrent theme in all public ceremonies. Prominent in the rituals of both Aztecs and Mayas were vigils and ceremonies honoring the rain gods. The Aztec Tlaloc controlled the rain so necessary for Indian survival. Similarly the Chacs, rain gods of the Mayas, received offerings of *balche* (fermented honey) and child and bird sacrifices. For both peoples, as elsewhere in the Southwest and Meso-America, imitative magic was an essential aspect of the ritual; this included ceremonial weeping, bloodletting, and attention to such associated phenomena as thunder, lightning, and the croaking of frogs. The sacred numbers 7, 9, and 13 play important parts in all of these ceremonies. Rain ceremonialism must be ancient throughout these areas. This is to be expected where agriculture furnished a very large part of the annual diet, and where at least all adults had experienced severe droughts at some time in their lives. Environment can therefore be a partial determinant of religion and ceremony.

CONCLUSIONS

Some generic hunting techniques, such as harpoons for sea mammals, driving animals over a cliff, pitfalls, deadfalls, snares, animal-head disguises, and auditory decoys, were probably known in Paleolithic times and therefore known to the first Indian immigrants to the New World. Although the American Indian probably did not invent these major hunting methods, a more detailed analysis of them would reveal many minor details which were absent in the Old World and which were therefore invented by the Indian. The same is true of fishing; the generic techniques were probably brought from the Old World, but specific details were invented in the New World. Because the earliest immigrants to the New World came by way of Siberia into Alaska, they could not have survived in that region without expert knowledge of hunting and fishing.

In wild plants, the picture is different. There are few edible wild plants in the Arctic, and the knowledge of wild plants in more southern latitudes in the Old World would have been lost in the slow trek of centuries through the Arctic made by all early immigrants to the New World. Therefore practically all American Indian knowledge of the more than 1,000 species of wild plants eaten by them was acquired after they arrived in the New World. This demonstrates that the early Indians were capable of patient experimentation with plants, and were able to pass on this knowledge to future generations.

Techniques of preparing and preserving food must be divided into those associated with animals and fish, wild plants, and domesticated plants. Methods of processing meat and fish must have been known, at least in part, to the earliest immigrants to the New World, because they lived principally on these foods. Ways of preparing and preserving wild plants, in contrast, must have been invented after immigrants reached the regions where edible wild plants were common. The processing of domesticated plants was likewise developed independently by the Indians. Religious ceremonies associated with hunting and fishing must have existed in some form when the first immigrants appeared in the Americas, because they lived almost wholly by those means. Therefore at least parts of such Indian ceremonies are of Old World origin. Plant ceremonies, in contrast, originated in the areas in the New World where food plants were plentiful. They could not have been derived from Siberia, because nearly all American food plants were absent in Siberia.

REFERENCES

BARTLETT, 1933, 1936; BEALS, 1932*a*; BIRKET-SMITH, 1929, 1945, 1953, 1959; BIRKET-SMITH AND DE LAGUNA, 1938; BONNERJEA, 1934; COOPER, 1938; DRIVER 1953*a*; EWERS, 1955*a*; KENT FLANNERY, 1965; REGINA FLANNERY, 1939, 1946; GODDARD, 1945; GUNTHER, 1928; HEIZER, 1953; HILL, 1938; HUNTER, 1940; JENNESS, 1932; JENNINGS, 1957; KROEBER, 1925, 1939, 1941; LANTIS, 1938, 1947; LOWIE, 1954; MENDIZÁBAL, 1930; PARSONS, 1939; PETTITT, 1946; ROE, 1952; ROSTLUND, 1952; SAUER, 1939; SPECK, 1935; SPECK AND EISELEY, 1939; STEWARD, 1938; SWANTON, 1946; UNDERHILL, 1948, n.d.; VAILLANT, 1941; WEYER, 1932; WILLEY, 1966; WISSLER, 1938, 1941; WITTHOFT, 1949; WRIGHT, 1968; YANOVSKY, 1936; YANOVSKY AND KINGSBURY, 1938.

7

Narcotics and Stimulants

NARCOTICS and stimulants were common in the New World before 1492. South America was well in advance of North America in this respect, the total list of drugs and the frequency of use in the southern continent far exceeding that of the northern continent. Nevertheless, drugs were used to a considerable extent by North American natives in what is now Mexico and the United States, although they were not used in the Arctic and Sub-Arctic. Some of the North American substances, particularly tobacco, are known to have originated in South America; and others common to both continents, whose places of origin are veiled in mystery, may also stem from South America. The principal narcotics and stimulants used in aboriginal North America were tobacco, peyote, Jimsonweed, and alcoholic beverages. Probably all were used as medicines. Many modern drugs —for example, cocaine and quinine—are derived from South American Indian narcotics and medicines.

TOBACCO

Our word "tobacco" comes from the Spanish *tabaco*, which in turn is derived directly from the Arawak term for "cigar." Christopher Columbus brought the first knowledge of tobacco to Europe. Members of his crew observed natives on Cuba or Hispaniola smoking huge cigars. The Indians claimed that it comforted the limbs, made them sleepy, and lessened their weariness. Other European explorers found tobacco being used by Indians almost everywhere except in the Arctic, Sub-Arctic, and part of the Northwest Coast.

From America, tobacco was taken to Europe: to Portugal in 1558; from Portugal to France in 1560; from Portugal to Italy in 1561; to Spain, probably directly from the New World, at about the same time; and to England, directly from the West Indies, in 1565. By 1600, it was grown and widely used in Europe. European colonists in the eighteenth century took tobacco to the Arctic and Sub-Arctic, where it could not be raised and had been unknown aboriginally: the Danes, to Greenland; the British and French, to most of the Sub-Arctic; the Russians, to Alaska. By the end of the nineteenth century it had penetrated almost everywhere in North America.

Tobacco has been much studied by botanists, who have found over a dozen species, almost all of which are native to the New World (Map 10). At least two forms are cultigens, plants which have been modified by man by selection or hybridization, and which are cultivated by man in areas where the wild ancestors are absent. The cultigen tobaccos are *Nicotiana tabacum* and *Nicotiana rustica*. *Tabacum* was taken to Europe and spread by Europeans over the world. *N. tabacum* has been found to be a hybrid of two wild forms: *N. tomentosum* and *N. sylvestris*. The wild *N. tomentosum* is found in Peru and Bolivia, the wild *N. sylvestris* in northern Argentina. After its origin in one of these localities, *N. tabacum* seems to have spread by diffusion or migration north to the West Indies, where it was discovered by Columbus. *N. rustica* is also a hybrid, having been derived from two wild species growing on the west side of the Andes near the border of Ecuador and Peru (Goodspeed, 1954). *N. rustica* spread by diffusion and migration over a much larger territory than did *N. tabacum*—south to the limits of agriculture at Chiloé Island off the coast of Chile, and north to the limits of agriculture in New Brunswick. Its distribution in North America (Map 10) closely follows that of maize (Map 7).

It is unusual to be able to determine a species of tobacco archeologically, but pipes give us a clue to the first appearance of tobacco. The proof is not final, because we are seldom able to determine conclusively what was smoked in the pipes and because some pipes were not used for smoking. However, in area after area and site after site, pipes appeared at about the same time as maize agriculture. This temporal correlation, when combined with the spatial one just cited, yields overwhelming evidence that *N. rustica* spread from south to north in North America along with other cultivated plants. Because its wild ancestors do not exist in North America, it could not possibly have originated there. Its absence in the West Indies makes it highly probable that the Eastern United States Indians received the plant from Mexico. The *N. tabacum* of the West Indies did not reach North America until post-Columbian times, when the British began raising it on their Virginia plantations. Here it soon superseded the local *N. rustica*, which was the first species to be raised commercially there.

The next most widely distributed species is *N. attenuata*, which grows wild in the Great Basin, the Southwest, and the southern Plains. It was used by Indians in these areas, both as a wild plant and as a cultivated one, and extended north as a cultivated plant into western Canada (Map 10).

Tobaccos of the *bigelovii* group (*bigelovii, quadrivalvus, multivalvus*) have a curious distribution (Map 10). They are native to the West, where they are also sometimes cultivated; *quadrivalvus* seems to have been introduced from the West into the northern Plains as a cultivated plant in pre-Columbian times. The same native term, *op* or *ope*, is found all the way from southern California to Montana and North Dakota.

A majority of North America Indians mixed other plants with their tobacco. This was done partly for economy among tribes which had little tobacco, partly to improve the flavor, and partly to dilute the strength of the tobacco. It is agreed that *N. tabacum* is much the mildest species, and that all the others have a much more pronounced narcotic effect. Tobacco mixtures in the Eastern United States and Canada were called *kinnikinnik* from an Algonquian word meaning "that which is mixed." Two common adulterants in this area were sumac leaves and the inner bark of a species of dogwood.

Tobacco was cultivated more widely than most other North American plants (Map 11). It was raised nearly everywhere that maize was grown and, in addition, on the northern Plains, in California, on the Oregon coast, and on the northern Northwest Coast. The species grown outside the maize area are all indigenous to western North America.

Tobacco was smoked everywhere it was known in North America except on the northern Northwest Coast, where it was only chewed with lime. There the leaves were pulverized, mixed with shell lime, and made into pellets which were allowed to dissolve in the mouth. A similar practice, better labeled eating, was followed in California and Nevada. Tobacco leaves were ground in a stone mortar with lime and water and the concoction licked off the pestle; the tobacco was less often eaten straight, or was mixed with an infusion of *Datura* and drunk. Sometimes the stupefying effect was all that was desired, while on other occasions the mixture served as an emetic. In the Southeast, tobacco was eaten with lime from mollusk shells; among the Creek, it was an ingredient of the famous "black drink," which was definitely a ceremonial emetic. The Aztecs ate the tobacco leaves, apparently not in combination with other narcotics, and also snuffed. Because tobacco was not smoked in the areas of South America where *N. tabacum* and *N. rustica* originated by hybridization, chewing or snuffing is likely to have been indulged in earlier than smoking.

Cigarettes with corn husk wrappings predominated in Meso-America and the Southwest. We are not certain that they are aboriginal in the Southwest, because the earliest Spanish settlers may have brought them north from central Mexico. At any rate, they have been the common smoking device in the Southwest in the historic period. Cigarettes or pipes made by filling short pieces of cane with tobacco do date, however, from Basket Maker times in the American Southwest. True pipes predominated in all other areas where tobacco was smoked.

Tobacco was used religiously as well as secularly. Most shamans used tobacco, both to establish rapport with their spirit helpers and to drive away disease from a patient's body. Tobacco was a part of almost every public religious ceremony, whether the occasion was a puberty rite, funeral, war expedition, or harvest festival. Not all tobacco used for religious purposes was smoked, chewed, or snuffed. A considerable amount was burned as incense, was cast into the air or on the ground, or was buried.

On the Plains, Prairies, and in the East, tobacco was an important part of the culture. Medicine bundles nearly always contained a pipe and tobacco. The pipe was smoked as a part of the bundle ritual whenever the bundle was unwrapped and put to its religious use. The most famous term for "pipe" in early American records is "calumet," which centered in the Prairies. The name itself is not Indian, but is derived from a Norman-French word meaning "reed" or "tube." However, all calumets in early historical times consisted of a hollow tube of reed or wood to which an elbowed stone bowl had been attached. Except for the unusual length of stem, it was a typical elbow pipe. It was employed in many ways: by ambassadors and other travelers as a passport; to secure favorable weather for journeys; to bring needed rain; in ceremonies designed to placate foes and hostile tribes; to ratify alliances between friendly tribes; and to make binding any sort of contract or treaty. A breach of such a contract or agreement was thought to bring the wrath of the gods down on the violator. Its most important use was in peace ceremonies in which representatives of both sides smoked the pipe of peace amidst the singing and dancing of a formal character in keeping with the gravity of the occasion.

ALCOHOLIC BEVERAGES

The distribution of alcoholic beverages (Map 12) falls almost wholly within the bounds of horticulture (Map 7). However, there was a sizable area in Northeast Mexico which was without agriculture and where wine was made from wild plants. For the world as a whole, there is a definite correlation between alcoholic beverages and agriculture, although negative instances can also be found in the Old World. The explanation is a simple one—the liquors were made principally from domesticated plants. It is commonly assumed either that knowledge of the fermenting of these plants spread with the plants or that the making of the liquor from the plant could spread only as far as the plant was known. There are also a number of examples of alcoholic beverages having been made only from wild plants in an area where agriculture was known, for example, the persimmon wine of the Southeast.

Agave and Dasylirion.—Two distinct plants, *Agave* (maguey) and *Dasylirion* (sotol), were widely used in the Southwest, Meso-America, and Northeast Mexico for the production of alcoholic beverages. They were even more widely used as food. It has been conjectured that before the time when agriculture was common, say, in the second or third millennium B.C., these plants were a staple food or even *the* staple food of a large part of this region. In the Southwest, the wine was usually made from the cooked juice of the agave, not from the fresh juice as in Meso-America.

In Meso-America, when the agave plant is ready to sprout a flower shoot, the heart of the plant is cut out and the juices which collect in the hole are removed. The juice is removed from the same plant every day for a few months until the plant is exhausted. A large specimen will produce from four to seven quarts of sap daily for from three to six months, totaling over 1,000 quarts. The principal nutritional element is a sucrose sugar. When this juice is allowed to stand a few days, it ferments and, in this condition, is called pulque. The alcoholic content is only 3 or 4 per cent. Besides containing sugar and gums, pulque is a rich source of vitamin B_1 and has considerable quantities of vitamin C. Its 88 per cent of water makes it a significant source of comparatively safe liquid in areas where drinking water is scarce or contaminated.

Cacti.—Other wines were made from the fruit of cacti, such as the saguaro, pitahaya, and nopal. The Pima and Papago cactus wine was made once a year and played an integral role in the rainmaking ceremony, which was the most important ritual occasion, held on their

New Year's Day. Everyone drank, believing that as men saturated themselves with the liquor so the earth would be saturated with rain.

Maize.—Maize beer was made in the Southwest south of the Mexican border and in Meso-America. There were two principal varieties: that made from sprouted maize grains, and that made from the stalks. Sprouted maize beer, *tesgüino* of the Tarahumara, was characteristic of western Mexico; cornstalk beer was most common in Meso-America.

Mesquite and screwbeans.—The alcoholic beverage made from mesquite and screwbeans was prepared simply by mixing the dried or baked cakes, or the flour, with water and allowing the mixture to ferment. The production of alcohol obviously stemmed directly from the production of food and did not require any special technical knowledge. This drink was widely used in the Southwest and Northeast Mexico.

Persimmons.—A kind of wine made from persimmons seems to have been enjoyed by a few Southeastern tribes. It is mentioned by Captain John Smith, which indicates that it was of Indian origin. Corn liquor is mentioned for a number of tribes in this area; but all the references are from the eighteenth century or later, and so it may be the result of European influence. Many other fruits were used in the making of alcoholic beverages in colonial times in the Southeast by both Indians and Whites, but, like corn, the aboriginality of their use for alcohol is not established.

Other alcoholic beverages.—The wide variety of plants used for liquors in Mexico is amazing. Bruman (MS) describes 40 distinct alcoholic beverages made by the Indians there. Fermented honey, *balche*, was found particularly among the Mayan-speaking peoples. Wine from the sap of the wine palm was made among Central American groups, the Aztecs, and the Chinantecs at least. Other common sources of drinks in Meso-America include wild plums, pineapple, mamey, and the sarsaparilla root.

Functions.—Alcoholic drinks played only an informal and secular role in the Southeast and among the Yumans, Apaches, and Zuñi of the Southwest; but from the Pima and Papago southward, they were also associated with religion and ceremony. A number of Mexican sources tell us that the women hid the weapons of the men during these drunken orgies to avoid trouble. In other localities, half of the men remained sober so that they could maintain order when the other half became intoxicated. The dreams and emotions associated with intoxication in Mexico were thought to have supernatural potency and to be necessary to success in meeting the many problems of daily life. An example is the Papago belief, mentioned above, that getting drunk would bring rain. However, among the Aztecs, drunkenness was regarded as the root of most evils. Public drunkenness on the part of students, nobles, or priests was punished with death. A commoner would receive only a beating for the first offense, but would be killed if found drunk a second time. Few cultures in the world have placed such a heavy penalty on inebration. However, on a few ceremonial occasions, old persons were allowed to get drunk without penalty.

MAJOR NARCOTICS

Peyote.—The plant peyote, known botanically as *Lophophora williamsii*, belongs to the cactus family. It is unique among the cacti in having no spines. It ranges from carrotlike to turniplike in size and shape, and grows mostly below ground. The rounded top surface, which alone appears above the ground, is cut off, dried, and becomes the peyote "button," which is the part eaten. Chemical analyses of the plant reveal as many as nine alkaloids which fall into two classes: strychnine-like, which are stimulants; morphine-like, which are sedatives. The most studied of these alkaloids is mescaline. The considerable variation in the amounts of these two kinds of drugs in peyote apparently accounts for the wide range of reactions to it.

The effect of peyote on the individual is difficult to isolate from its varying cultural contexts. Its many cultural associations may be divided into ritual and nonritual uses. It was used nonritually by natives in all parts of its area of distribution (Map 13) for many purposes. It was taken to allay hunger, thirst, and fatigue in strenuous tasks; to find lost or stolen articles; to detect the approach of the enemy; and to predict the outcome of a battle. Prediction of the weather was another one of its virtues. When worn on the body, it was thought to ward off disease and all manner of danger. Shamans performed magical tricks under its influence. Perhaps its most frequent function was in the curing of disease.

Its ritual uses can be classified into two main areal types: northern Mexican and Plains. In northern Mexico, the ceremony was participated in by the whole community, and was for the benefit of all; on the Plains, it was confined to a society of more restricted membership. The Mexican rite served to allay anxieties associated principally with the food quest: hunting, gathering, and especially agriculture, where the emphasis was on rainmaking. The Plains rite, in the beginning at least, revolved around success in warfare. Dancing was a conspicuous part of the Mexican performance, but was totally lacking in the Plains rite. The Mexican rite was seasonal because of its association with the food quest, but the Plains tribes held their peyote meetings the year round. Both men and women participated in Mexico, but the Plains ceremony was originally limited to men. The Mexican affair was held outdoors; that of the Plains in a tipi. Ritual racing and ball games were associated features in Mexico, but were absent from the Plains ceremony. Ceremonial drunkenness was an indispensable part of the Mexican affair, but was unheard of on the Plains. Christian elements were rare in northern Mexico, in spite of centuries of contact with the Spanish monks, but were common in the Plains ritual after European contact.

The history of peyote is fairly well known, especially in the United States. The geographical range of the plant, which was never domesticated, is limited to the Rio Grande Valley in the United States and to Mexico (Map 13). Its aboriginal use in Mexico is beyond question since it is mentioned by a number of observers in the sixteenth century. By the early seventeenth century in Mexico, it was so obtrusively employed in native religious ceremonies that the Spanish officials in charge of the Mexican Inquisition attempted to stamp it out. That they failed is demonstrated by the many reports of it from later dates.

The diffusion of peyote in the United States is shown schematically on Map 13, and peyote ceremonies are still being held by most tribes shown on the map. Their organized Peyote religion is called the Native American Church, and is described more fully in Chapter 27.

Anthropologists are not in complete agreement on the reasons why peyote spread where and when it did. However, one explanation recurs again and again in the literature. During the past hundred years in the United States, the Indians have been fighting a losing battle against the encroachment of our culture. Anxieties have multiplied to the point of despair. A new drug, associated with a new religion which promised to improve the individual's plight, had strong appeal.

Why was peyote received so enthusiastically by Plains tribes and not by the Pueblos? Plains tribes suffered greater shock from their complete defeat by Whites in the last half of the nineteenth century than did the Pueblos in any period of equal length in their history. The change from the free hunting Plains way of life to the confinement of the reservation was severe indeed. The Pueblos had been farmers for centuries before the Spanish arrived. Although most were forced by various pressures to abandon their homes, they fled only a short distance away and continued to farm and otherwise carry on much as they had in the past. Furthermore, the Pueblo Indian, by culture rather than nature, was a more introverted and conservative personality than the Plains Indian. Pueblo religion was highly socialized; every act of ritual was for the benefit of the entire community, and most of the ceremony was in the hands of societies whose members performed as a group. Personal experiences were almost completely submerged in group activities. Not so on the Plains. There religion centered in the individual vision quest. Those who experienced new illusions and hallucinations were regarded as at least minor prophets. The Plains area was therefore a much more fertile field for a new religion based primarily on individual emotional experience. After the 1890 Ghost Dance movement played out, it was replaced by peyote cults in many cases.

The spread of peyote westward was checked by the presence of another narcotic, the Jimsonweed. A comparison of the distribution of peyote (Map 13) with that of the Jimsonweed (Map 14) shows that the two are almost mutually exclusive in the United States. Actual testimony from recent Indian informants in the Great Basin reveals the fact that Jimsonweed users did not want to take up peyote and did not want the competition of peyote to move in on them. If this is true of Great Basin tribes, it probably applies also to other Jimsonweed users, although the occurrence of the two drugs together in a few localities proves that this principle cannot account for every single instance.

The role of the individual in the spread of the peyote religion was obtrusive when a person with exceptional powers of persuasion became a proselyter. What were the rewards which the individual received for his efforts? That there were "spiritual" rewards in the form of feelings of satisfaction at having furthered a noble cause cannot be denied. At the same time, there were mundane rewards in the form of money: cash from the sale of peyote buttons; fees for curing the sick; cash from taking up collections, as in European religions; and even a charge for a handshake with a prophet.

Jimsonweed.—Plants of the genus *Datura*, called Jimsonweed or Jamestown weed in English, and *toloache* (from the Aztec *toloatzin*) in Spanish, were taken for their narcotic effect by a considerable number of tribes (Map 14). The name Jamestown weed is derived from the fact that a troop of soldiers stationed at Jamestown in 1676 cooked and ate the leaves of the plant without anticipating its effect. The results were startling enough to be reported in the historical record. There is no proof that the plant was eaten or drunk by Indians in that area, or for that matter in any part of the eastern United States.

Datura was used intensively in aboriginal California. The leaves, stems, and sometimes even the roots of the plant were pounded and soaked in water to make a concoction which was drunk. The drug produced visions and dreams which were thought to foretell the future or to make supernatural beings visible. Clairvoyance was also believed to result; a person was able to see things hidden from ordinary view, events happening at a distance or in the future. The acquisition of a personal spirit helper, so important to the Indian, was facilitated by drinking *Datura*. In California, the drug was usually taken at the age of puberty or later by a group of young persons under the supervision of elders. In the Southwest, it was most often taken individually and for a number of reasons: to bring success on a deer hunt, to alleviate vomiting and dizziness, to induce the drinker to utter prophecies, or simply for the pleasure derived from the accompanying dreams and visions.

Although *Datura* was widely used and known in Mexico, our fullest information is for the Aztecs, who used the drug for both religious and medicinal purposes. Here again, it was regarded as holy. There were special officials who took *Datura*, along with peyote, to discover cures for illness, lost or stolen property, and the cause of chronic illness due to witchcraft. Sometimes the patient was given the drug instead. *Datura* was also one of the ingredients in an ointment made of venomous insects, burned to ashes, and tobacco. The priests who were anointed with this salve were said to have lost all fear and to have become bold and cruel enough to kill their sacrificial victims. This ointment was also used to cure the sick who came from all parts of the land to be treated by the priests. *Datura* was used in Mexico, the Southwest, and California as an anesthetic to be used when setting fractured bones or performing surgery.

MINOR NARCOTICS

A narcotic mushroom, *teonanácatl* (*Paneolus campanulatus*), has been used in central Meso-America since before the time of the Conquest (Map 14). When eaten, the *teonanácatl* produces a sensation of euphoria and well-being very similar to that resulting from peyote. Aztecs present at the ceremonies surrounding the coronation of

Montezuma II were said to have intoxicated themselves with the mushrooms. The modern Mazatec medicine men find lost objects and divine the future under the intoxication of *teonanácatl*.

The seeds of another narcotic plant, *ololiuqui* (*Rivea corymbosa*), are widely used in the same area (Map 14) for divining purposes and as a "truth drug." Although the plant was known to the Maya, they were unaware of its narcotic effects.

The "mescal bean," *Sophora secundiflora*, grows wild in Mexico from Coahuila to San Luis Potosí, and in the United States in western Texas and southern New Mexico. It is a member of the bean family, *Fabaceae*, and is not to be confused with the term *mescal* used to designate the genus *Agave*, which belongs to the amaryllis family. The mescal bean contains a highly toxic alkaloid, called sophorine, which resembles nicotine in its physiological action. At least a dozen tribes had organized cults centering in the eating of the bean in a group ritual. It was acquired earlier than peyote by tribes in the United States, but never attained as wide an appeal as did peyote. Troike (1962) adds the Arikara, Caddo, Coahuiltecans, and Jumano to the tribes given on Map 14.

The leaves of the tree *Ilex cassine* were the principal ingredient in the "black drink" of the Southeast (Map 14). This drink produced immediate vomiting. It was most often used as a form of ritual purification before setting out on a war expedition. The Creek, however, drank the concoction before important council meetings and in connection with most sacred ceremonies.

REFERENCES

ABERLE, 1966; ABERLE AND STEWART, 1957; ARISS, 1939; BEALS, 1932a; BELL AND CASTETTER, 1937; BENNETT AND ZINGG, 1935; BRANT, 1950; BRUMAN, MS; CARR, 1947; CASTETTER, 1935, 1943; CASTETTER AND BELL, 1937a, 1937b, 1938; FLANNERY, 1939; GAYTON, MS; GOODSPEED, 1954; GUERRA AND OLIVERA, 1954; HEIZER, 1940; HOWARD, 1957; JONES, 1944; JONES AND MORRIS, 1960; LABARRE, 1938a, 1938b, 1960; LEONARD, 1942; LINTON, 1924a; LOWIE, 1954; MCGUIRE, 1897; MARTÍNEZ, 1936; MASON, 1924, 1948; PORTER, 1948; ROJAS, 1942; SAFFORD, 1917; SAUER, 1950; SCHULTES, 1940; SETCHELL, 1921; SLOTKIN, 1952, 1955, 1956; SOUSTELLE, 1956; STEWART, 1944; SWANTON, 1946; THOMPSON, 1954; TROIKE, 1962; WEST, 1934.

8

Housing and Architecture

EVERY tribe of North American Indians constructed some form of dwelling. Caves were used temporarily for habitations, and travelers sometimes slept outdoors, but everyone occupied a house at least part of the year. Many tribes used more than one kind of dwelling, the particular type at any given time depending on the season of the year, the building materials available, and sometimes on the amount of wealth of the occupant family. For example, a number of tribes along the Missouri River lived in large multifamily earth-covered lodges arranged in villages about half the year during the farming season, but when hunting buffalo they changed to hide-covered conical tipis. Some of these same tribes occupied bark-covered dome-shaped wigwams part of the time, in emulation of their Algonquian neighbors to the east and north, where this kind of house was more common. A detailed description of each type of dwelling possessed by every tribe would fill several volumes. In order to simplify this vast amount of information, we have selected a single representative variety for each tribe. The kind of dwelling used by the largest part of the population or for the greatest part of the year has been chosen as the type. The geographical distributions of these structures are shown on Map 15.

DOMINANT HOUSE TYPES

Arctic.—The domed dwelling built of snow blocks was the typical house of the central Eskimo, although it was used to a lesser extent by almost all the Eskimos (Fig. 2). The builder, working from the inside, piled up the snow blocks in a continuous spiral which was less likely than separate rows to collapse during the process of construction. This is the only type of dome known to architecture which can be constructed out of blocks without first building a scaffold to support it. When the last block was put in place at the top, the builder

116

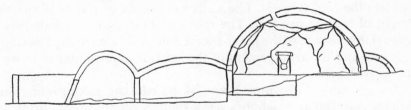

FIG. 2. Domed snow house (Eskimo). Driver and Massey

cut a hole for an entrance and exit and let himself out. To complete the house, he constructed a low passageway or tunnel of snow in front of the entrance. This tunnel had to be negotiated on hands and knees. A double door consisting of two suspended hides kept out the cold.

A snow platform was made or left at the rear half of the floor plan as well as on both sides. The family slept on the rear platform, which was amply provided with hides to serve as mattresses and bedding. On the side platforms the women of the house cooked and sewed. A small hole was left in the top of the roof, and an ice window was sometimes placed in the front wall over the passageway. Snow houses were normally occupied by single families, but sometimes two or more families might live in an unusually large one.

The dwelling of the eastern Eskimo is labeled domoid, or domelike, because its ground plan frequently had rounded "corners," which made it transitional between circular and rectangular shapes, and its walls usually rose almost vertically and then turned in rather abruptly

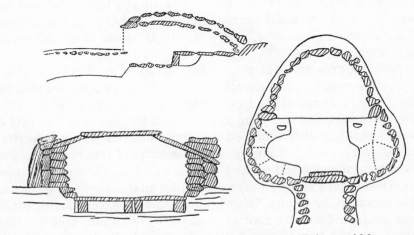

FIG. 3. Domoid stone-earth-whalebone house (Eskimo). Driver and Massey

to form the roof (Fig. 3). The walls were made of sod or stones to a height of four or five feet. The roof was bridged with whale ribs or large slabs of stone in the manner of a crude corbeled arch. The tunnel entrance and the arrangement of the interior were similar to those of the snow house.

The permanent or winter house of the Alaskan Eskimos and their Athapaskan Indian neighbors was a shallow pit house consisting of a rectangular framework of horizontal logs, about five feet high, over which was a four-pitched pyramid roof of logs (Fig. 4). The entire

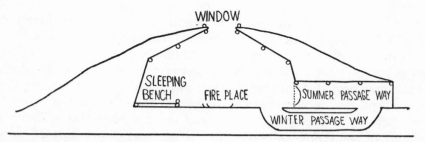

FIG. 4. Rectangloid earth-covered Alaskan house (Eskimo). Driver and Massey

structure and its passageway were covered over with several feet of earth from the pit, which made it almost airtight and insulated it from the cold. Raised log platforms a foot or less in height occupied three sides of the room. These were sat on by day and slept on at night. Commonly three families occupied such a house, each appropriating one of the platforms. On the earth floor directly under the roof hole was the fireplace, which served for cooking, heating, and lighting. Fuel consisted of wood or, where wood was scarce, of seal oil burned in a lamp.

Northwest Coast.—The large plank houses of the Northwest Coast were supported by a framework of logs to which planks were attached vertically or horizontally to complete the structure (Fig. 5). These dwellings varied in size from about fifteen by twenty feet to fifty by sixty feet. They were occupied by several families which collectively made up an extended family. Each constituent family had its own allotment of space and cooked over its own fire, although obtaining food was often a group enterprise in which all the families participated and shared in the results. These houses had a gabled end facing the sea and in this end was the doorway, consisting of an oval hole in a large plank. On the inside around the walls were built platforms of poles

FIG. 5. Rectangular plank house (Kwakiutl). Driver and Massey

and planks on which to sit and sleep; the same effect was sometimes achieved by excavating the center of the house and leaving one or two terraces around the edges. All floors and terraces were covered with planks.

A number of peoples in the center of the area built houses with a one-pitch roof, the so-called shed-roof type. One such house in the historic period was 520 feet in length, although most were within the

FIG. 6. Crude conical tipi (Ojibwa). Driver and Massey

range of the gabled houses described above. In the extreme southern part of this area, in northwest California, a few peoples built a house having a roof with three pitches.

Sub-Arctic.—The dominant house in this area was a crude conical tipi covered with hide or bark (Fig. 6). Both kinds of covering were sometimes used together on the same structure, and hides were never sewn together as on the Plains in the nineteenth century. Additional poles laid on top of the many pieces of bark or hide held the covering in place in windy weather. Smoke escaped through a hole at the apex, and the covering was left loose in one place for a doorway. These houses were only about half as large in linear dimension as the Plains tipis of the nineteenth century.

In a part of the western Sub-Arctic, double lean-tos with gables at the ends appear to have been the most common type of habitation (Fig. 7). Single lean-tos were also used but were inadequate for permanent winter occupancy. These lean-tos were made of a framework of

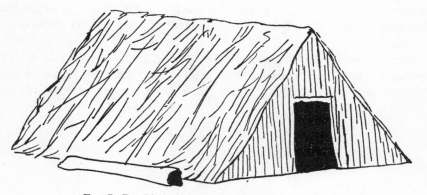

FIG. 7. Double lean-to (Slave). Driver and Massey

poles covered with bark, hides, or brush. The double lean-to was occupied by a single family or an extended family, depending on its size or the type of family which built it. There were no bed platforms or other furnishings.

Plateau.—The most typical dwelling consisted of a circular pit, four or five feet deep, over which a conical or pyramidal roof was built (Fig. 8). The roof was supported by from one to four posts erected near the center of the pit, and was covered with the earth from the pit. The smoke hole, usually at the top center, served also as entrance and exit, and was reached by means of a notched log ladder. These houses

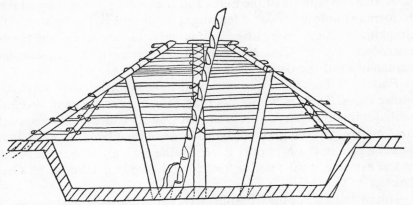

FIG. 8. Semisubterranean Plateau house (Thompson). Driver and Massey

were occupied by one or by several families, according to size and to local or individual preference.

Plains.—The conical tipi of the Plains was a carefully constructed portable dwelling with a tailored buffalo hide cover (Fig. 9). The fire was built near the center, and the beds were placed on the ground around the circle except in front of the doorway. Nineteenth-century tipis were often ten or twelve feet high, twelve or fifteen feet in diameter, and were covered with fifteen or twenty buffalo hides. The erection and dismantling of the tipi were the work of the women, as

FIG. 9. Plains tipi (Crow). Driver and Massey

were also the tanning of the hides and the cutting and sewing of them to form the tailored cover. Men might obtain the poles, however. The dragging of the poles by dogs, and later by horses, which the treeless character of the Plains made necessary, seems to be an adequate explanation of the origin of the travois.

Prairies.—This area was one of the most mixed with respect to house types. There were no less than four distinct kinds of dwelling, each dominant in part of the area: the Dakota tribes lived most of the time in hide-covered tipis similar to those of the Plains; an earth lodge was the rule in the Missouri River drainage; a grass-thatched house in the extreme south; and a low domed dwelling around the Great Lakes.

The earth lodge of the Missouri River area consisted essentially of a cylindrical base on which rested a conical roof and from which projected a tunnel-like entrance passage (Fig. 10). The whole structure

FIG. 10. Prairie-Southeast earth lodge (Pawnee). Driver and Massey

was covered over with earth; hence the name earth lodge. These dwellings, by inside measurement, varied from thirty to forty feet in diameter, from ten to fifteen feet in height in the center, and from five to seven feet high at the eaves. The ground was often dug down a foot or more in order to find compact earth to serve as a good floor. In the center of the earthen floor a round hole was dug for a fireplace. A low platform of poles around the outer wall served as a bed by night and a bench by day. A number of families of related persons, collectively making up an extended family, occupied a single such dwelling.

The thatched house with Gothic dome is found among the Caddo, Wichita, and their neighbors on the southern Prairies (Fig. 11). The fireplace, as usual, was in the center, and the smoke found its way out through the thatch without the aid of a smoke hole. Bed platforms were placed around the sides. These houses were occupied by a number of families, which collectively formed an extended family. They were larger than the nineteenth-century tipi, averaging about fifteen feet in height and perhaps a little more in diameter.

FIG. 11. Gothic dome thatched house (Wichita). Driver and Massey

The domed houses around the western Great Lakes were called "wigwam" in the Algonquian languages (Fig. 12). They were covered with woven or sewn mats, pieces of bark, and sometimes hides. Single families occupied small domed structures of this type which were approximately round in ground plan; extended families lived in elongated houses which were elliptical in ground plan.

FIG. 12. Domed bark, mat, thatch, or hide house (Ojibwa). Driver and Massey

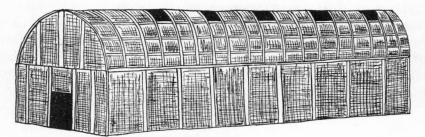

Fig. 13. Rectangular barrel-roofed house (Iroquois). Driver and Massey

East.—The famous longhouse of the Iroquois Indians of New York state dominated the northern part of this area (Fig. 13). These averaged sixty feet in length, eighteen feet in width, and eighteen feet in height. The entire frame was covered with bark, most often elm bark, which was perforated and sewed on in overlapping layers like shingles. A central hallway from six to ten feet wide ran the length of the interior. On both sides was a series of booths, each occupied by a separate family. They were on platforms about eighteen inches high, from five to six feet wide, and from six to twelve feet long. A second level of platform around the sides of each booth served as a bed, and a third level about seven feet above the ground was used for storage. Down the center of the hallway was a series of fireplaces, each shared by pairs of families in opposite pairs of booths. These families were related, the whole constituting an extended family.

Dominant house types on the Atlantic Coast from Cape Cod to the Savannah River were of the same essential variety as those of the Iroquois except that they were smaller.

Summer houses of the Southeastern tribes were similar in shape to those of the Iroquois except that the roof was two-pitched and gabled instead of barrel-shaped (Fig. 14). They were rectangular, with four vertical walls of poles plastered over with mud to form mud wattle or of a pole frame covered with thatch. The fire was built in the middle of the earthen floor, and bed platforms were placed around the walls. Such dwellings were normally occupied by a single family, but those of a number of related families were built close together in extended family clusters. The eaves were a little higher than a man's head, the length fifteen or twenty feet, and the width somewhat less.

The winter house of the Southeast was a semisubterranean earth-covered structure with a tunnel entrance, identical in its essential features to the earth lodge of the Prairies.

FIG. 14. Rectangular gabled house, thatched (Middle Mississippi). Driver and Massey

California.—In this area the most common type was the domed house, made with a framework of poles bent and tied in the proper shape over which was placed a thatch of grass, tules, or other plant materials. The second most popular dwelling was a crude conical tipi covered with slabs of bark or with thatch. Semisubterranean earth-covered structures with tunnel entrances were also to be found, but usually functioned as men's sweathouses or as religious assembly houses rather than as family dwellings.

Great Basin.—In this arid region the dominant dwelling was a conical tipi covered most often with thatch held down by pole binders, but sometimes the covering was of hide or bark. This structure was much smaller than the nineteenth-century Plains tipi. The second most popular house was domed and covered with thatch or brush. Many Basin houses were crude, hastily assembled and soon abandoned in the wandering in search of food.

Southwest.—There were six kinds of houses in the Southwest, each dominant in its special area. The Pueblo peoples lived in rectangular, flat-roofed rooms, built flush against one another to form a continuous large village unit comparable to an apartment house (Fig. 15). The western Pueblos built principally of stone, while those on the Rio Grande in the east generally used adobe (clay); but because the western peoples plastered over their stone walls, the appearance of the houses in the two localities is very much the same. In aboriginal times lower-story rooms had no doorways or windows but were entered by means of notched log ladders through a hatchway in the roof. Pueblo rooms were about twelve feet square and were grouped together in apartment houses of from one to five stories which accommodated several hundred people. Each family lived mainly in a single room, although it might possess other rooms used for storage and sacred rites. Furnishings were few; the most conspicuous article was a built-in bench of logs or stone along one or two walls. Wall niches served as cupboards. The boxed-in milling stones occupied one side of the room, and the fireplace the center, with the smoke going out through the hatchway.

FIG. 15. Rectangular flat-roofed house (Zuñi). Driver and Massey

The Colorado River Yumans had a distinct kind of house, called Mohave type, after one of the tribes. It had a frame of logs and poles, a thatch of arrow weed and a covering of sand (Fig. 16). The ground plan was rectangular and nearly square, dimensions averaging about 20 by 25 feet. The door was in the middle of one side and always faced south. The roof was nearly flat, sloping only about 10 degrees, and had four pitches. Sand covered the roof and three sides, so that the house itself was visible only from the front. The fireplace was near the door, perhaps because there was no smoke hole, but also because the warm climate made heat unnecessary during most of the year. Such habitations were built and occupied by a number of related families which formed an extended family.

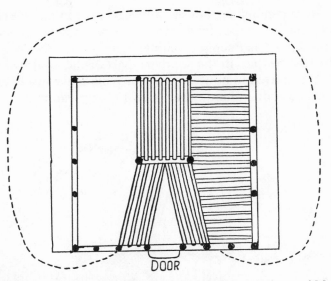

FIG. 16. Mohave type four-pitch roof house (Mohave). Driver and Massey

The non-Pueblo peoples of the northern and eastern part of the Southwest lived in a crude form of conical tipi, made of poles leaned together and covered with thatch, brush, or slabs of bark or wood and sometimes with earth piled as high up on the sides as possible. The Navaho hogan was originally such a structure, but today it is a hexagonal structure with walls of horizontal logs.

Other non-Pueblo peoples in the Southwest occupied domed huts covered most often with thatch but sometimes with other materials. In a few localities the domed hut became blended with the rectangular house to produce a halfbreed type consisting of four rectangular walls covered with a domed roof (Fig. 17).

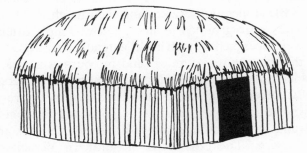

FIG. 17. Rectangular domed-roof house (Opata). Driver and Massey

There were rectangular houses with flat roofs in the Mexican part of the Southwest, but they tended to be set apart and not clustered into apartment houses as Pueblo dwellings were.

Finally, the peoples in the southern part of the Southwest nearest Meso-America lived in houses with four rectangular walls topped by a four-pitched roof, either hipped (Fig. 18) or pyramidal.

FIG. 18. Pyramidal or hip-roof rectangloid house (Guaymi). Driver and Massey

Northeast Mexico.—The Chichimecs of this area probably lived in crude domed huts or double lean-tos in pre-Columbian times, but they slept in the open so much when traveling that more than one Spanish priest thought they had no houses at all.

Meso-America.—This complex region had at least three major types of houses. The rectangular flat-roofed house was the dominant variety in western Mexico and highland central Mexico. Its walls were of stone cemented together with adobe, of adobe plastered against poles (mud wattle), adobe supported between walls of poles, or adobe mixed with little stones. The Aztecs and their neighbors lived in such dwellings. They were grouped in small clusters, most often had one story, and were occupied by patrilocal extended families.

Among the many house types found in Meso-America, the rectangular gabled house was particularly common among peoples along the Gulf of Campeche and among the Lacandones. In pre-Conquest times most of the commoners among the Totonac lived in such houses with pole walls and thatch or grass roofs; similar houses are general in the area today. The Popolocas of southern Veracruz and the Lacandones of the Guatemalan lowlands have such houses. The rectangular, gabled house was probably an alternate form among neighboring peoples. Today in Mexico this house type is widespread, but its dispersal was due to Spanish influence.

The hip roof (Fig. 18) or pyramidal roof of the rectangular house of Meso-America and Central America was invariably thatched, but the walls were more varied; they consisted of poles or canes without adobe, of mud wattle, of adobe bricks or puddled adobe, and sometimes of stone, especially at the base. The four pitches of the roof were relatively steep, the better to shed the downpours to which much of the area was subject. Sometimes the ends of such houses were rounded. Doorways were rectangular openings in the end or side, and the floor was of earth. Some of these houses were large enough to accommodate extended families. Wooden platforms, carved stools, and sleeping mats were common, although there were regional variations in the household furniture.

COMPARATIVE ANALYSIS

Ground plans.—Houses with round or oval ground plans are almost universal in North America, although they were not the dominant type everywhere. The distribution of those of conical shape is shown on Map 16. Domed shapes are even more widespread, because the water vapor sweathouse (Map 20) was nearly everywhere of this shape. Only in Mexico and Guatemala was it consistently rectangular. In many areas where other shapes were dominant, domed houses were used as temporary or secondary dwellings. Because the round ground plan is so nearly universal, its distribution does not give us any historical clues.

Not so for rectangular ground plans, which were definitely limited in distribution. They occurred in the western Arctic, Yukon Sub-Arctic, Northwest Coast, and adjacent parts of the Mackenzie Sub-Arctic and Plateau. They are also found in the United States east of the Mississippi, and continuously from the northern Southwest to Panama and the West Indies. The Northwestern rectangular houses were probably derived from Asia. They show a generic similarity to dwellings in Siberia, China, and Japan, although there is argument about the details. They appeared in the Old Bering Sea Culture, about A.D. 100 to 500, and also in the early Aleut Culture about 100 B.C. to A.D. 500.

Houses with rectangular ground plans east of the Mississippi, in the

Southwest and Meso-America, were closely correlated with agriculture (Map 7). Temporally, the relationship also holds. Both traits appeared together at about the same time in both the Southwest and the Southeast. Because maize and other domesticated plants were diffused from south to north, it seems very likely that rectangular houses in farming areas have the same history.

It is therefore evident that rectangular houses in North America have a dual origin and history: those in the Northwest seem to have been derived from Asia, those in other areas apparently from Meso-America.

Conical and subconical houses.—The term "subconical" is introduced to account for shapes which were intermediate between conical and domed forms and which sometimes had projecting entrance passages and other features which departed from a true cone. Conical dwellings may be classified according to the number of poles tied together and erected as the foundation against which the remaining poles were leaned (Map 16). Because four poles were more frequent in the West, and three in the East, there is some indication that diffusion within each of these major areas had taken place. Some of the irregularities can, however, be explained in terms of migrations. For example, the Comanches who lived in Wyoming and Colorado in A.D. 1600 were indistinguishable from the other northeastern Shoshonis. About A.D. 1700 they migrated southward to the southern Plains, retaining the four-pole tipi foundation of the northeastern Shoshonis. It is probably significant that the area of most elaborate development of the tipi, the Plains, was one in which the number of foundation poles was most consistently patterned. Conical dwellings were distributed continuously across northern Eurasia to Lapland, and occurred as far south as Tibet. They were rare or absent in Africa, southern Eurasia, Oceania, and South America. These facts suggest a single origin in the north, more likely in Asia than in North America, because the bulk of cultural features shared by these two continents seem to have originated in Asia.

Semisubterranean houses and tunneled entrances.—The majority of the houses covered over with unprocessed earth were semisubterranean or had tunnel entrances, and about half had both (Map 17). Although the correlation of these three elements is not perfect, it suggests that these features were of northern origin. Alaskan houses consistently had all three. In other areas, one or the other is occasionally absent. Nevertheless, when these distributions are viewed from an overall point of view, the compactness of the North American data is overwhelming. These elements of house construction were found to be associated also in Eurasia, but were apparently absent as a complex everywhere else in the world. Eurasia and North America therefore constitute a single area for these features of house building, with a single origin somewhere in Eurasia.

Early evidence for semisubterranean houses dates from the early Upper Paleolithic period (Gravettian, Aurignacian) in southern Russia (Daifuku, 1952). Their age has been estimated at about 25,000 years. These were oval in ground plan, and varied from 18 feet to 108 feet in greatest diameter. The larger ones were obviously multifamily dwellings, as the nine to eleven fire hearths of each house indicate. In the same area but in late Upper Paleolithic (Magdalenian) times, the oval shape of the earlier semisubterranean houses changed to rectangular, the entrance passageway appeared, and the stone lamp replaced the wood-burning hearth.

Small semisubterranean rectangular huts with entrance passage have been found near Lake Baikal in Siberia. These are also dated as early Upper Paleolithic. This type persisted with little change down to modern times, as finds in the Ob River drainage dated in the second millennium B.C. and the first millennium A.D. indicate. Modern Paleo-Asiatic peoples of northeast Siberia still occupy essentially the same kind of dwelling, as do the neighboring Alaskan Eskimos.

The semisubterranean, earth-covered, tunnel-entranced structures of the Southeast were called the winter house or "hot house." They were round in ground plan, and were occupied mainly in cold weather. The men's council house, which was located in the center of the town, was of the same construction but much larger. The largest of these reported was said to have accommodated several hundred men and to have had forty-seven posts supporting the roof. In the Southwest, houses with the same three features date from Basket Maker II period, A.D. 100–500. They ultimately developed into the ceremonial men's house called the kiva, which abandoned the entrance passageway and flattened the roof but retained the circular ground plan.

Multifamily dwellings.—Large houses occupied by two or more families were widespread in North America (Map 18). The more sedentary peoples tended to have multifamily houses, the more nomadic tribes to live in single-family structures. Before the appearance of the horse it was impossible for the nomadic Indians to transport a large dwelling. The earliest reported multifamily dwellings are those of the early Upper Paleolithic in Russia, mentioned above. They were semisubterranean structures which may be ancestral to houses of similar construction in northern North America.

Division of labor.—Map 19 shows the areas in which each sex dominated the bulk of the most indispensable tasks connected with building the dominant types of houses shown on Map 15. In general, the women erected and dismantled the conical and dome-shaped portable structures of the Sub-Arctic, Prairies, and Plains. Large dwellings supported by heavy timbers were usually constructed by both sexes, but the men performed the most indispensable task—the cutting and erecting of the timbers. Houses of stone or adobe were built principally by men.

SWEATHOUSES

Special sweathouses were used by the vast majority of North American aborigines (Map 20), except the central and eastern Eskimos, a few tribes in the southern Great Basin, the Yumans (except Diegueño) and Pimans, and the northern Mexican peoples. Sweating was induced in two ways: by direct exposure to a fire and confinement inside a building with the fire; by first heating stones in a fire, then pitching a portable structure over them or rolling the stones inside a nearby structure, and pouring water on the hot stones to produce water vapor.

The buildings used for these two sweating techniques differ considerably. The direct-fire sweathouse of Alaska was a semisubterranean earth-covered log house with tunnel entrance, very much like the Alaskan dwelling. It served as a men's clubhouse in which bachelors or male travelers might sleep and in which married men might spend considerable time. It was owned collectively by all men of the village. The direct-fire sweathouses of California are surprisingly similar. The majority of these were also semisubterranean, earth-covered, and with tunnel entrance. They differed in being round in ground plan, while those of Alaska were rectangular. In both Alaska and California, sweating was a daily group affair, indulged in simply to "feel good" more often than for a specific reason. Archeological evidence from Alaska indicates that the earliest dwellings there were round in ground plan. Like the dwellings mentioned above, all of these men's houses seem to have stemmed from a common ancestral house of round ground plan in northern Asia.

Water-vapor sweathouses were of a very different character. They were almost invariably small, domed structures with round ground plans. Although they were sometimes permanent structures, the majority were hastily assembled for a particular occasion and not used daily. They consisted of a light framework of poles or withes over which hides, pieces of bark, or mats were thrown to confine the water vapor. Often they were so low that the occupant had to stoop to enter. They were used most often for a purification rite by those seeking supernatural power or by the sick seeking relief from infirmities. Usually only a single person sweated in such a structure, whereas in the direct-fire type all the men of a village might join together in a contest to see who could withstand the most heat. Women were usually permitted to sweat by the water-vapor method, but almost never by the direct-fire one. Lopatin (1960) claims that the American water-vapor bath was derived from northwestern Europe by diffusion across the North Atlantic. I prefer an Asian origin.

In the Southeast, the winter dwellings, called hothouses, were reminiscent of direct-fire sweathouses. Men, women, and children slept together in them with a fire burning all night, arose together in the morning dripping with perspiration, and rushed out the door to the nearest stream for a cold bath. Among the Delaware, each village apparently had an earth-covered sweathouse entered through a hole in the roof, and a crier invited the entire populace to come and sweat.

ARCHITECTURE

Although some would like to dignify the building skill of the Pueblo Indians with the label "architecture," the term is here reserved for the much more spectacular achievements of the peoples of Meso-America. At least a hundred centers of population were large enough to be called cities. They differed from our modern cities in being less compact and less congested. They were scattered over a wider area, which was more suburban than urban, with its garden plots intermingled with dwellings. In the centers of these cities were courts and plazas around which public buildings, such as temples, sanctuaries, palaces, pyramids, monasteries, ball courts, dance platforms, and astronomical observatories, were assembled (Fig. 19). Near these public buildings were the houses of the nobles, priests, and the wealthy, while on the outskirts of the town were the dwellings of the lowest and poorest class. Public buildings were made of—or at least faced with—stone and, although the Spanish wrecked untold numbers of them to

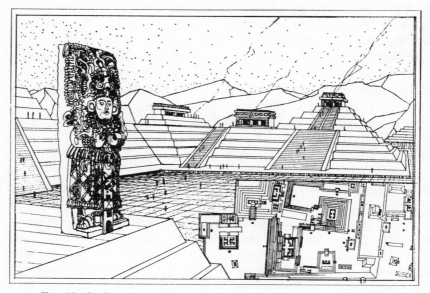

FIG. 19. Sculpture, ground plan, and elevation from Copan, Honduras

obtain the stones for their Christian churches, a large number still survive as ruins.

The true arch is generally regarded as absent in the New World, although the domes of the Eskimo snow house and the Meso-American sweathouse (Clavigero, 1945: 348) could be regarded as examples of the true arch. Ekholm (1964) describes a single example of the true arch in a Maya building at La Muñeca in southeastern Campeche. This building belongs to the late classic period, A.D. 600 to 900. I much prefer to interpret it as an independent invention rather than as a diffusion from overseas. The corbeled arch, on the other hand, was much used by the Maya and their neighbors for public buildings, and has been found by archeologists to date as early as A.D. 317. Because of the limitations of this arch, there were no large rooms in which hundreds of people might assemble. The total volume of the walls of such buildings about equaled the room space within. Flat roofs of lime-concrete or adobe supported by logs were probably more common than the corbeled arch. They were similar in all essentials to the flat roofs of dwellings.

The principle of the post-and-beam is involved with the flat roofs supported by logs but becomes more conspicuous in doorways or on the façades of buildings. Columns were both round and square and were normally of several blocks of stone, but those employed for mere decoration on the front of the structure were sometimes in the half-round.

Most public buildings in Mexico were built on substructures which varied from terraces a few feet high to the huge pyramid of Cholula which is 1,150 feet square at the base and rises to a height of over 210 feet. Although this pyramid is less than half as high as the tallest in ancient Egypt, its greater base gives it a volume 15 per cent greater. A pyramid of smaller volume but with the greatest height in the New World is that of the Mayas of Tikal, Guatemala, which rises to 228 feet. These structures were ascended by broad, steep stairways on one or more sides.

Buildings in the early centuries of the Christian era were almost devoid of decoration, but those erected after about A.D. 1000 were embellished with elaborate sculptures. Although geometric designs were common, conventionalized figures of men and animals also abounded. One of the most frequently represented characters was the feathered serpent, Quetzalcoatl, who was a prominent member of the pantheon. He was first a part of the decoration on the temples and pyramids at Teotihuacán, and was later incorporated into Aztec, and Maya architecture. Sculptures consisted of carvings in stone and of modeled figures in baked clay.

On the whole, the architecture of aboriginal Meso-America is impressive because of its massiveness and elaborate sculpturing. Some compare it with the massive and ornate architecture of Hindu origin in Southeast Asia at such famous sites as Angkor Wat and Borobudur, but few believe there is any historical connection between the two.

REFERENCES

ARREOLA, 1920; BEALS, 1932a; BEALS, CARRASCO AND McCORKLE, 1944; BIRKET-SMITH, 1929, 1936, 1945; BIRKET-SMITH AND DE LAGUNA, 1938; BUSHNELL, 1919, 1922; CLAVIGERO, 1945; CRESSON, 1938; DAIFUKU, 1952; DOUGLAS, 1932; FAIRBANKS, 1946; FLANNERY, 1939; JUDD, 1948; KRICKEBERG, 1939; KROEBER, 1925; LINTON, 1924b; LOWIE, 1954; MARQUINA, 1951; MORGAN, 1881; OLSON, 1927; POLLOCK, 1936; RAY, 1939; SANFORD, 1947; SATTERTHWAITE, 1952; SMITH, 1940; SWANTON, 1946; VAILLANT, 1941; WATERMAN, 1924; WISSLER, 1908, 1938, 1941.

9

Clothing

CLOTHING in aboriginal North America exhibits a wide variety of styles and materials which are definitely correlated with geographical environment. The sharp contrasts between the cold of the Arctic, the heat of the tropics, the dampness of the rain forests, and the dryness of the deserts have all had their effect on dress. At the same time, these correlations are far from perfect, because fashion also played a part. Styles and materials changed with the times, and fashions spread from one tribe to another. Clothing was also dependent on other facets of culture, for example, subsistence economy. If a tribe subsisted mainly on the flesh of large mammals, it was likely to make its clothing out of hides, which were readily available. The acquisition of the horse increased the efficiency of hunting and encouraged the spread of hide clothing to areas where it had been less common formerly. On the other hand, in areas where people lived mainly on agricultural products, seldom were there sufficient hides from which to manufacture clothing for everybody. They more often made clothing of plant materials.

MAJOR STYLES

Arctic.—The principal clothing material of the Eskimo was caribou hide, which is warmer, lighter, and more flexible than sealskin. The winter upper garment of both men and women was and is the well-known parka, which consists of two hides sewn together at the sides, with sleeves and hood (Fig. 20); it must be pulled on and off over the head. The length varies, according to locality, from the hips to below the knees. The woman's parka differs from the man's in being cut much fuller so that the infant may be carried inside it or inside the wider hood, and in being longer in back to provide insulation from the cold when sitting. Most of the time the child rides naked, except for its cap, in a hide sling on the mother's naked back.

Both sexes wore fur trousers, which seem to have originated by sewing together two leggings. They were made of two pieces with the joining seam running down the middle in front, between the legs, and up the middle in the rear, exactly like modern men's trousers, which are derived from the same Asian source. Both sexes also wore inner garments in winter similar in cut to the outer ones but made of lighter fur. In the summer only these inner garments were worn.

On the feet and lower legs both sexes wore fur stockings and fur

FIG. 20. Arctic clothing

boots, the stocking being of lighter material than the boot. Grass was sometimes stuffed into the boots for added warmth, either with or without the fur stocking. The sole of the boot was a separate and heavier piece than the upper, which extended nearly to the knee. Mittens with thumb stalls were worn everywhere by both sexes, and were necessary to protect the hunter's hands from rope burns and more serious injury from the sealskin thongs used to land sea mammals, as well as against the cold. Gloves with separate finger stalls were unknown aboriginally.

A combination suit sewed together in one piece like modern coveralls was worn by Greenland whalers. It was made of waterproof sealskin, had parka, mittens, and boots attached, and was put on by means of a round hole in the front. A similar combination suit was worn by men in Alaska and by children over most of the Arctic.

Snow goggles of wood, or more rarely ivory, with one or two slits for the eyes, were used everywhere to prevent snow blindness. Eye shades were also used by men in kayaks in the Hudson Strait region, in Greenland, and in Alaska.

Clothing was made entirely by the women. The thread was of split sinew, the eyed needle of bone, the thimble of thick animal skin worn on the index finger, and the sewing direction from left to right. Animal skins were colored only in Greenland, where they were dyed red by immersing them in a concoction of driftwood bark, but in other areas banded designs were made by using skins of contrasting natural colors.

Women consistently allowed their hair to grow full length, but were careful to do it up close to the head or to part it in the middle and braid it. Men, on the other hand, always cut their hair in some manner, usually leaving bangs in the front even though the back might be full length; it was not braided and seldom tied up. Tattooing was practiced by all groups and nearly everywhere confined to the faces of women.

Northwest Coast.—The clothing of this area is illustrated in Figure 21. Men sometimes went entirely naked in summer, but might wear tunics of woven plant fiber. In winter and on ceremonial occasions a rectangular robe of animal skins or woven plant fiber extending to the knees was worn. The fur most highly prized by Indians and Europeans alike was that of the sea otter, which was nearly exterminated in the first century of European contact. As protection against rain, conical hats of woven plant fiber were worn on the head, and waterproof mats of woven or sewn plant materials cut like a poncho were worn on the body. Moccasins and leggings were known but were worn only occasionally when the Indians were traveling to the interior.

Women never went naked in public, except on rare ceremonial occasions, but wore a plant fiber skirt. The upper part of the body, including both shoulders, was covered with a robe of the same material. A woman of rank or wealth might wear a fur robe, but such garments were more often the exclusive possession of the men. Rain hats were sometimes worn by women, but less often than by men

Fig. 21. Northwest Coast clothing

because women spent more time indoors. Footgear was also worn less often by women than by men because the women traveled less.

A wide variety of bodily ornamentation characterized both sexes. Necklaces, belts, and arm bands and leg bands of shells, teeth, and claws were commonly worn. The ears of both sexes were pierced, and the same articles were worn as earrings. Only men pierced the nasal septum and attached ornaments to it. Both sexes were tattooed on the face, chest, front of legs, or back of arms. The designs were often inherited crests which only the owners could use. Paint of red, black, and white pigments mixed with grease was applied to the bodies of both sexes on gala occasions, and might also depict the inherited crests. Men plucked their beards, and women their eyebrows. Intentional head deformation was practiced in the central part of the area.

Northern Plains.—The styles of clothing worn on the Northern Plains at White contact also extended over much of the Sub-Arctic. The Plains is chosen as the type merely because it is better known (Fig. 22).

FIG. 22. Northern Plains clothing

Two articles of clothing represented the minimum costume for a Plains man: the breechcloth, and moccasins. When a man was at home in the summertime, he might wear only these items. However, he always kept a buffalo robe on hand to wear when appearing in public or in cold weather. When traveling, a man wore full-length leggings tied at the top to his belt. The breechcloth, leggings, and moccasins combined covered practically all the body from the waist down, and gave the appearance of trousers from a distance. A buckskin shirt, with flaps for sleeves, was worn on the upper part of the body in winter or on gala occasions. This was normally made of two deerskins. The head was left bare most of the time, but a fur cap might be worn or the robe pulled over the head in winter.

Plains women wore more clothing than the men. The main garment was a dress made of two deer or elk hides sewn together with the tail ends up. The tails of the animals and part of the skin of the hind legs folded downward to form a yoke. Such dresses reached to the calf and were fringed at the bottom. Women's leggings reached only to the knee; their moccasins were of the same type as those of the men. Fur robes were worn primarily by men, but women sometimes wore them in winter.

Both sexes wore the hair in two braids. Men wore feathers in the hair aboriginally, and these culminated in the nineteenth-century war bonnet familiar to every schoolboy. Claws, teeth, and shells were worn as beads around the neck or as ear ornaments. There was little tattooing, and noses were seldom pierced. The hair on the face and parts of the body was plucked with small tweezers. A porcupine tail was used for a hairbrush.

Southeast.—The clothing of this area is illustrated in Figure 23. The one indispensable article of clothing for men was the buckskin breechcloth, which went between the legs. They also wore untailored robes or mantles over the upper part of their bodies in winter or on formal occasions. These were made of furs—either of a whole hide of a large animal, such as the buffalo, or of a patchwork of small animal hides—of feathers thatched on a netted foundation, or of woven inner bark. When traveling, men wore full-length leggings, fastened to the belt, and moccasins.

Women in the Southeast wore a wrap-around skirt reaching from the waist to the knees. It was of buckskin, woven inner bark, or woven bison hair. In winter and on special occasions, they wore robes of the same materials and in the same manner as the men. Women's leggings were only half-length, and were fastened by a garter just below the knee. The wealthier women sometimes wore moccasins, but not regularly.

Neither sex habitually wore any form of headgear, although priests and officials decorated their heads with symbols of their supernatural powers and offices. Women allowed their hair to grow full length; they parted and braided it, or put it up on top of the head. Men shaved their hair, except for a scalp lock from the crown, or allowed enough to grow to form a longitudinal ruff which stood up like a crew haircut. Both sexes plucked all body hair with tweezers of clam shells.

Both men and women pierced their ears and wore ear ornaments of shiny stones, pieces of shell, or feathers—all of which were later replaced by trade metal. Men, at least, pierced the nasal septum and wore similar kinds of ornaments in the nose. Both sexes were tattooed

FIG. 23. Southeastern clothing

by pricking the skin and rubbing in soot. The most elaborate designs were worn by warriors and chiefs, who recorded their valorous deeds in this symbolism. Face, trunk, arms, and legs were all tattooed. The head was intentionally deformed by the pressure of a bag of sand or a buckskin-covered block of wood applied to the heads of infants.

Painting in a wide variety of colors and designs all over the body was used for war, mourning, ball games, and other ceremonial occasions, mostly by men. A great variety of necklaces, arm bands, leg bands, and belts were also worn—strings of pearls and manufactured beads of bone, stone, or shell, for instance. Garters and belts of woven bison and opossum hair were also common. Women wore turtle shells containing pebbles and bunches of deer hooves on their legs to produce a rhythmic rattle when dancing.

Although sharply defined social classes did not occur everywhere, differences in rank were reflected in dress. The quantity and quality of clothing were some indication of rank, whether acquired by noble deeds or by amassing wealth. Chiefs' families were consistently better dressed than the average citizen.

Southwest.—The Pueblo Indians of Arizona and New Mexico were the only Indians living wholly within what is now the United States who wore garments made of cotton cloth in pre-Columbian times. Skins were also used for clothing, but cotton predominated. Pueblo clothing is illustrated in Figure 24.

The men wore between the legs a piece of cotton cloth which was held in place by passing the ends over a belt. A second piece of the same material was wrapped around the waist to form a kilt, and a sash of braided cotton cords was worn on top of the kilt. A cotton shirt, which was nothing more than a rectangular piece of cloth with a woven-in hole for the head in the middle, was sometimes worn. It was tied at the sides rather than sewn, and sometimes smaller rectangular pieces of the same material were tied on at the shoulders to form half-length flaps or sleeves. Moccasins had a separate stiff piece of buffalo hide for the sole, but the upper, which covered the ankle or reached halfway to the knee, was of buckskin. Blankets woven of twisted strips of rabbit fur were thrown over the upper part of the body in cold weather, and a garment of feathers thatched on a net foundation was sometimes worn in the same manner.

Women wore a kind of dress which was nothing more than a rectangular piece of cotton cloth worn under the left arm and tied over the right shoulder. It was not sewn together or fastened at the right side except by a belt of the same material. On the feet and lower half of the leg a combination moccasin and legging was worn. The sole was of buffalo hide, to which was sewn a piece of buckskin large enough to fold over the toe and instep. A strip of buckskin three or four feet long was wound around the moccasin proper and on up the leg to just below the knee, where it was tied. The legging part resembled a First World War puttee.

Both sexes cut their hair just above the eyes in front, just below the ears at the sides, but allowed it to grow full length in back. Men wore most of the jewelry, which consisted of beads of turquoise and other

FIG. 24. Pueblo clothing

precious stones as well as shells. These were worn as necklaces and ear ornaments.

Meso-America.—There is no doubt that in this area clothing attained a greater degree of elaboration and distinction than elsewhere on the continent. The descriptions from the Conquest, native codices, and murals, as at Bonampak, all attest to the colorful and varied nature of the costumes (Fig. 25).

FIG. 25. Meso-American clothing

The preferred clothing material was woven cotton cloth; in many parts of the area, as among the Aztecs and the Mixtecs, only the nobility could use this material. Commoners wore clothing woven of *ixtle* (maguey fiber). Prohibitive laws enforced this class distinction. Dog hair was the only form of wool and, because of its scarcity, was used more for decoration than for the body of any cloth. Mantles of feathers, attached to a cloth base by threads or by paste, were also worn. The lesser ones were covered with feathers of the domesticated turkey, but the finer were overlaid with the multihued and brilliant plumage of tropical wild birds.

The common man wore sandals of hide or woven agave fiber (*cactli*) on the feet, a woven breechcloth (*maxtlatl*) between the legs and around the waist, with the ends hanging down the front, back, or both, and a knee-length cloth mantle tied over a shoulder and running under the opposite arm. In cold weather a man might add a sleeveless tunic (*xicolli*), which was naturally worn under the robe. Men banged their hair at the forehead, allowed locks resembling sideburns to extend down the sides of the face, and cut the hair behind the ears to shoulder length.

Women wore a wrap-around skirt (*cueitl*) of cloth from waist to calf and, on the upper part of the body, a sleeveless blouse which was similar to the tunic worn less often by men. There were two distinct types of these blouses. In the south and west of Meso-America, the *huipil*, a straight sleeveless blouse, was worn; in the north and east of the area, the *quesquemitl*, a capelike blouse, predominated. Women went barefoot a greater part of the time than did men, but might don sandals for a special occasion or a long walk. Women's hair was cut like that of men in front and at the sides, but was allowed to grow full length in the back.

Both sexes pierced the ears and wore conspicuous cylindrical plugs in them, but only the men pierced the nasal septum and the lower lip and wore ornaments in these orifices.

Clothes reflected social status among the Meso-Americans. Costumes of renowned warriors, priests, and chiefs bristled with symbols of their offices. They were decorated with copper, gold, silver, jade, turquoise, emeralds, and opals. Elaborate headdresses of the colored feathers of wild tropical birds and body painting in half a dozen hues added to the glamour of these important personages.

GEOGRAPHICAL DISTRIBUTIONS

Dominant clothing materials.—Hide was almost the exclusive clothing material in the huge area which included the Arctic, Sub-Arctic, Plains, Prairies, and the Northeastern United States (Map 21). This area corresponds closely to that in which hunting was the dominant subsistence economy (Map 3). The relation of the two is obvious. The severe winters of the Arctic and Sub-Arctic also made fur clothing a necessity for hunters, who spent most of their time in the open in pursuit of game.

Hide, fur, and wild plant materials were used jointly on the Northwest Coast, the Plateau, in California, the Great Basin, Northeast Mexico, part of the Southwest, and in the East as far north as Cape Cod (Map 21). Bast (inner bark) was probably the most important plant material. It was woven on the North Pacific Coast, in the Southeast, and to a lesser extent in other parts of this large area. So fine was the weave and so white the color of the mantles of this material in the Southeast that the Spanish mistook it for cotton. Unwoven grasses, mosses, rushes, and leaves were also widely used for clothing, especially by women.

Cotton was the dominant or preferred clothing material in much of the Southwest and most of Meso-America (Map 21). Where it was not raised, it was obtained as woven cloth in trade. Its distribution in these areas closely follows that of other cultivated plants (Map 3). It was not raised at all in the present-day cotton belt of the Southeastern United States. Although the area of cotton dominance or preference is smaller than the other two areas shown on Map 21, its population was much larger, so that cotton clothed considerable numbers of people. In Meso-America, the poorer classes often wove their cloth for garments out of the fiber of the agave, which was both a wild and a domesticated plant. Because the poor outnumbered the rich, this fiber clothed greater numbers of people than any other material in aboriginal North America.

Fur-strip clothing.—Furs of small animals were often sewn together to form a patchwork robe large enough to cover the human figure. For example, furs of the sea otter were combined in this manner on the Northwest Coast to produce the most valuable single article of clothing known to that culture. Another technique, most often applied to rabbit skins, was also widely used. Strips of fur were joined together at the ends and twisted or braided to form a fur rope, which was finally woven, netted, or sewn into a rectangular or circular shape. The resulting blanket was used for bedding or worn as a mantle. This technique was common in the Sub-Arctic, Plateau, California, Great Basin, and Southwest, and was practiced by the Aztecs, at least, in Meso-America. It was probably more common in these areas than the patchwork technique before the appearance of trade needles.

Feather clothing.—Feathers were thatched onto a foundation of netting or cloth, working from the bottom upward. The result was a garment which was water-repellent, less warm than fur, and, above all, decorative when made from brightly colored feathers. Such garments were common in California, Meso-America, and the East. This is the familiar reversed Y distribution, suggesting a southern origin.

Aboriginal uses of wool or hair.—Large garments of woven wool or hair were characteristic of only three areas: the Northwest Coast, Prairies, and Southeast. On the Northwest Coast, the hair of the wild mountain goat was most frequently used in the northern half of the area; the hair of a domesticated dog was also used among the Salish tribes farther south. Wild mountain sheep hair was used to a lesser extent here and there, as was the inner bark of the cedar, which was combined with wool to form the warp elements. In the north, members of the Chilkat tribelet, a subdivision of the Tlingit, were the most industrious weavers, and traded their blankets to many other tribes. Woolen garments consisted entirely of rectangular blankets, which were draped around the body. There was no tailoring.

On the Prairies and in the Southeast, the most common animal fiber was buffalo hair, although opossum hair was also used to some extent. As on the Northwest Coast, these garments had only the rectangular shape of the woven material itself, but they seem to have been made in more sizes; some are called kilts instead of blankets. In addition, a number of small articles of wearing apparel, such as bands worn around the head, neck, waist, arms, and legs, were also woven of buffalo and opossum hair.

In a vast area across the Sub-Arctic, probably stretching continuously from Bering Sea to New England, moose hair was embroidered on hide clothing. It was often dyed several colors, so that the effect produced was superficially similar to that of dyed porcupine quills. In Meso-America, the hair of the domesticated dog and of wild rats and rabbits was occasionally used for embroidery on cotton clothing.

Other clothing materials.—Porcupine quill decoration on hide clothing was widespread in aboriginal North America and, except for its absence in the Arctic, conformed closely in distribution to the area where hunting was the dominant food pursuit (Map 3). The quills were dyed a variety of colors and were sewn onto buckskin with sinews. In historic times, quills were largely replaced by glass trade beads. Many of the elaborate designs so plentiful in nineteenth-century beadwork were formerly made with porcupine quills.

Unwoven bark cloth competed with cotton in Central America and adjacent Mexico as a clothing material, but seems to have been less used than cotton. Pieces of inner bark were beaten with a wooden mallet into pieces of material large enough for breechcloths or wrap-around skirts. The place of origin of bark cloth is undoubtedly South America, where it was more extensively used. Inner bark was also used for paper making in Mexico.

Tailored hide clothing.—Strictly tailored clothing, with hood attached to the upper garment, full-length sleeves, trousers, moccasins, and mittens, was limited to the Eskimos and their immediate Indian neighbors in Alaska and on the Labrador Peninsula. In the historic period, many imitations of European clothing were worn in the Sub-Arctic and East.

The history of tailored clothing is an interesting one. It probably goes back to Upper Paleolithic times, when the eyed needle first appeared. Tailored clothing was probably first used in the middle latitudes in Eurasia, and spread north and east as the glaciers retreated. Because Eskimo culture in North America dates back only about 4,000 years, we can be quite certain that the Eskimos derived their tailored clothing from Siberia.

Semitailored clothing, like that described above for the northern Plains, was also worn in most of the Sub-Arctic. Leggings were cut to fit, and moccasins were sometimes sewn to them. Sleeves, however, usually consisted of half-length flaps, except in the Eastern Sub-Arctic, where separate fur sleeves were worn. The upper garments of men and the dresses of women were slightly cut to conform to the human body, although the shape of the hide of the animal was still discernible. No close counterpart of this style of clothing is reported for Asia. It either has been replaced by more modern garments in Asia or originated in North America. In the historic period, the Plains type of clothing spread south to the Apaches on the Mexican border, east to the Iroquoians, southeast to the Chickasaw and the Natchez in Mississippi, and west to the Pacific Coast. At the present time, Plains-type clothing has replaced most other kinds of Indian clothing for occasions in which Indians appear in costume.

In much of the Sub-Arctic, tailored fur coats with an opening in front, like European garments, were made in imitation of European models.

Headgear and haircutting.—Headgear was continuously worn outdoors only by the Eskimos in winter; in summer, these people often removed the parka hood from the head. In other areas, utilitarian headgear was confined to winter or to the rainy season. Fur caps, separate from the upper garment, were sometimes worn by the Eskimos, but were more characteristic of Sub-Arctic, Plateau, and northern Plains peoples. Buckskin caps were worn on the Plains, in the East, in the Great Basin, and in the Southwest, but mainly as war bonnets. They served as foundations to which feathers and other showy articles might be attached. Women seldom wore fur caps in northern areas but never the buckskin caps of the more southern latitudes.

In the Far West, utilitarian hats and caps, woven like basketry from plant materials, were regularly worn. On the North Pacific Coast, from Kodiak Island to the Columbia River, broad-brimmed rain hats were worn by both sexes in rainy weather. These are surprisingly similar to the "straw" hats of China and Japan. On the Plateau, in the Great Basin, California, and Baja California, a smaller-brimmed or completely brimless basketry cap was worn, principally by women, to protect the forehead from the carrying strap, but here and there was worn almost continuously.

Hairdressing shows a great deal of variation from tribe to tribe and area to area. Nevertheless, a few generalizations are possible. Over much of North America, both sexes allowed the hair to grow full length. Exceptions were the Eskimo men, who cut their hair in some manner; the men of the Southwest and Meso-America, who wore a long bob; and the men of the Prairies and East, who shaved their heads so that the remaining hair formed a pattern, the most common of which was a longitudinal roach or ruff. At present, the aboriginal manner of head shaving is not practiced, but many of those who participate in costumed dances or ceremonies wear a roached headdress of deer hair dyed red.

Stockings and leggings.—Almost all the Eskimos wore hide stockings or grass socks inside their boots, and about half the Sub-Arctic peoples either wore hide stockings or sewed their moccasins to the bottoms of leggings or breeches. Thigh-length leggings were worn by men throughout most of the continent north of Mexico, although many of the instances west of the Rockies and a number in the East are probably historic. Long leggings were everywhere associated with the breechcloth; when the two were combined, they approached the completeness of trousers. In the Far West, men wore only knee-length leggings or none at all, and a few instances of knee-length leggings are reported from other areas. Because men traveled more, leggings were more common among them than among women.

Moccasins.—There were as many kinds of moccasins in North America as there were tribes wearing them. Fortunately, the fundamental construction of the moccasin falls into two major types: the soft-soled, made from a single and continuous piece of buckskin for both sole and upper; and the hard-soled, consisting of a buckskin upper sewn to a heavier and stiffer piece of hide for the sole. The hard-soled variety predominated in the Arctic, the Great Basin, the Southwest, and Plains (Map 22). In the areas depicted as having both types, the hard-soled seems to have been more frequently worn. The soft-soled type was characteristic of the Sub-Arctic, Plateau, northern Prairies, and East. The soft-soled type is generally regarded as more efficient for use with snowshoes, and the area of its exclusive occurrence correlates fairly well with the distribution of snowshoes. However, the soft-soled moccasin has spread all the way to the Gulf in the Southeast and to the Mexican border in the Southwest, far beyond the limits of snowshoes.

The distribution of the hard-soled moccasin is more difficult to explain. A hard and stiff sole is good protection from the thorns and stones of the deserts and plains of the West. The hard- and separate-soled Eskimo boots appear to have developed independently of the hard-soled forms of footgear to the south. The Eskimo boot is apparently of Asian origin, and may even be historically related to the riding boots of Asia.

Sandals.—Sandals have a peculiar distribution. Those worn by the Central and Eastern Eskimo and Chipewyan were usually pieces of fur tied on over the regular boot to give added traction on slippery ice or make it possible for a hunter to tread silently from one seal breathing hole to another. The hide sandals used by the Lillooet and Shuswap on the Plateau were worn only by those so poor that they did not have enough hide for a moccasin. The true hide sandals of the south were made from dehaired skins and were associated with a hot, dry climate, as they are in the Old World. They are characteristic only of the area from Mexico to Chile in the New World. Sandals made of plant fibers were also worn in the same areas, but extended farther north into the Southwest and Great Basin in the United States. The Arctic and Plateau "sandals" are surely historically independent of those in the south.

Footgear frequency.—Footgear was worn most of the time in a huge area which corresponds closely with that of the dominance of hide and fur for clothing (Map 21). It is also significant for the continent as a whole that moccasins were the kind of footgear which was worn daily. Warmth, as well as protection, was a factor, especially in the north. Sandals were worn less regularly, and seem often to have been reserved for trips or gala occasions. Because they provided no warmth, there were no marked seasonal differences in their frequency of use. In the Southeast, both the heavier rainfall and the warmer climate discouraged the daily wearing of moccasins, and, even when traveling, a group of men would often stop to take off their moccasins when it began to rain.

Hand and arm covering.—Mittens with thumb stalls were regularly worn in winter in the Arctic, Sub-Arctic, Plateau, and northern Plains. They kept the fingers warm enough to permit accurate shooting of the bow and arrow and the manipulation of other weapons as well. In the Western United States—more specifically in California, the Great Basin, and the Southwest—hunters carried a fur muff in winter to keep their hands warm enough to shoot the bow effectively. In the Eastern Sub-Arctic and the adjacent northern fringes of the Plains, Prairies, and East, detachable sleeves of fur were worn in cold weather, especially by women.

DIVISION OF LABOR

The sexual division of labor in clothing manufacture depended partly on the materials from which the clothing was made. For most of North America north of Mexico, where hide material predominated, women made most of the clothing. In California and the Great Basin, where both hide and plant materials were used, no definite division of labor prevailed. In the northwestern Southwest, men made most of the clothing, although it consisted of both hide and woven plant materials. In Meso-America, women made most of the clothing out of the cloth they wove; but in urban centers, men specialists sometimes wove textiles and fashioned them into clothing.

REFERENCES

BEALS, 1932*a*; BIRKET-SMITH, 1929, 1936, 1945; BIRKET-SMITH AND DE LAGUNA, 1938; CARR, 1897; CONN, MS; DEMBO AND IMBELLONI, 1938; DIENES, 1947; DINGWALL, 1931; FARABEE, 1921; FLANNERY, 1939; GODDARD, 1945; HATT, 1916; JACOBSON, 1952; JENNESS, 1932; JOHNSON, 1953; KINIETZ, 1940; KRIEGER, 1929; KROEBER, 1925; MARTIN, QUIMBY AND COLLIER, 1947; ORCHARD, 1929; ROEDIGER, 1941; SINCLAIR, 1909; SOLIER, 1950; SPECK, 1911, 1928; SWANTON, 1946; UNDERHILL, n.d.; WISSLER, 1916, 1926, 1938, 1941.

10

Crafts

THERE was much variation in crafts from one area to another, as in other aspects of Indian culture. The crafts to be described in this chapter have been selected on the basis of widespread occurrence, except for metallurgy, which was confined to Meso-America. There is a high correlation between the number of distinct crafts practiced by a people and their general level of cultural achievement. Meso-America attained by far the highest standards of craftsmanship, and is universally regarded as having possessed the most advanced total culture in North America; indeed, it ranks as an equal with Incan Peru. At the same time, areas of modest general achievement might become expert in single crafts. For example, the basketry of the California Indians is ranked among the finest in the world.

As an introduction to basketry and pottery, let us first discuss containers in general. In Chapter 6, we gave descriptions of the more common kinds of boiling vessels. The dominant forms of containers used for other purposes are shown on Map 23. Thus the Eskimo used hide containers for water pails, for storing and transporting meat, and for many other purposes about the household. The dominance of hunting in the subsistence economy provided an ample supply of hides for every use. Dishes were carved out of wood, but, because of its scarcity in most of the Eskimo territory, wood was used less often for containers than was hide.

The other area where hide predominated was the Plains. One of the most common articles of hide there was the parfleche, which was simply a piece of rawhide folded together like an envelope to form a container. Food especially was carried in the parfleche, but other articles might also be included. In historic times, a horse carried two parfleches, one on each side. Other common hide containers were quivers, tobacco pouches, berry mashers, cases for sacred objects, and medicine bundles. As among the Eskimos, hunting was the basis of subsistence.

Bark, especially birch bark, was the dominant material for containers in the entire Sub-Arctic from Alaska to Nova Scotia. The bark was curved or bent into the desired shape and sewn where necessary with strands made from roots. Such vessels served as water pails, carrying containers, food storage receptacles, berrying baskets, dishes, trays for winnowing wild rice, and troughs for making maple sugar. They could be made much more rapidly than woven basketry, but wore out sooner.

Wooden containers predominated on the Northwest Coast in Canada and Alaska. They were of two main types: dugouts and boxes. The dugouts were made by hollowing out a solid chunk of wood. Dishes, ladles, and oil storage vessels were commonly made in this manner. Box containers were made by bending and sewing boards together. They were thinner-walled and lighter than dugouts, and were used for water pails and as storage containers for a wide variety of things from food to sacred objects and even as coffins. The North-Coast was the area where woodwork reached its highest development.

Woven basketry containers predominated on the Plateau, the Northwest Coast of the United States, in California, the Great Basin, Northeast Mexico, part of the Southwest, a small fraction of the Prairies, and in the East. Baskets were put to dozens of uses in these areas. They were used by women for gathering plant foods, for carrying loads on the back, as water pails and dishes, and as storage containers for all materials stored in and around the house. Special shapes were used for winnowing, sifting, gambling, and even for housing rattlesnakes. In the western half of this basketry area, pottery was absent or scarce. In the deserts of the Great Basin, drinking water was carried in a jug-shaped woven container, plastered on the outside with pitch to make it completely waterproof. In the eastern half of the basketry area, on the other hand, pottery was universal and served for water pails as well as for cooking vessels. There was no point in making baskets watertight, and, indeed, they were far from it. As we shall see later, the weaves and materials also differed in the East and the West.

Pottery vessels were the dominant noncooking (as well as cooking) containers among the more sedentary tribes of the Southwest and in Meso-America. Basketry was also known, but was less common about the household. Besides their use as cooking pots, pottery vessels were used for dishes, water jars, storage of food, incense burners, and even for burial urns. The total number of uses would probably exceed that for basketry. The area of pottery dominance corresponds closely to that of the greatest dependence on agriculture and the most sedentary mode of life.

WEAVING

Basketry, bags, and matting.—Basketry, bags, and matting are treated as a unit because the technique of manufacture is often the same. Mats were used most commonly as floor coverings, house coverings, mattresses, and raincoats. Baskets were made in a wide variety of three-dimensional shapes, and the number of different uses to which they were put was as great as the number of shapes. Bags are more flexible than basketry and more finely woven than mats. The artistic embellishment of basketry far exceeded that of matting and probably also that of bags. Most of the basketry made by North American Indians was decorated in some way, with design elements running into the thousands. Because the weaves in basketry, bags, and matting are fewer in number than the shapes, uses, and decorations, this brief survey will be restricted to weaving techniques.

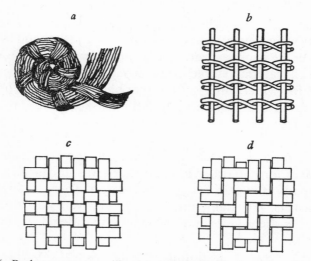

FIG. 26. Basketry weaves, coiling (*a*), twining (*b*), checker (*c*), and twill (*d*)

There are three major kinds of basketry weaves: coiling, twining, and plaiting (Fig. 26). Although each, in turn, may be further divided into a number of varieties, the three categories are mutually exclusive. Even when two are employed in the manufacture of a single basket, it is easy to see where one weave ends and the other begins. In coiling, the warp or foundation element is horizontal and its coils are sewn together with a flexible vertical weft element; in twining, the vertical warp elements are fastened together with pairs of horizontal wefts, which are twisted between each adjacent pair of warps; in plaiting, there is no distinction between warp and weft, because both elements are of equal size, shape, flexibility, and activity in the weaving process. The two principal kinds of plaiting are checker and twill.

Mats were commonly twined or plaited, but rarely, if ever, coiled. Mats of whole plant stems were also held together by sewing: piercing each stem at intervals with needle or awl and inserting cords to bind the stems in a parallel row. This sewing was of course not true weaving. Bags also were normally twined or plaited, rarely coiled.

The geographical distributions of coiling and twining are given on Map 24. Coiling was the dominant basketry technique in the Arctic, although baskets there were rare or unimportant in most localities. Mats and bags were still less numerous. Coiling was the exclusive technique in the Plains area, where it was limited to gambling trays. In a third area in the Western Sub-Arctic, from the Han tribe to the Carrier, coiling was the only technique known. Here, woven baskets were more numerous and more important than among the Eskimos, but they still seem to have been dominated by birch-bark vessels. The other area of exclusive coiling was Baja California, where basketry was the dominant type of container.

Twining reached its maximum development on the North Pacific Coast, where basketry rivaled wooden containers in importance in the culture. Coiling and twining occurred together in Alaska, where coiling was the more frequent, and again in a much larger area farther south which includes the Plateau, Great Basin, Southwest, and most of California. In all of these latter areas except the Great Basin, coiling was more frequent than twining.

Baskets used for stone-boiling were either twined or coiled. Both techniques employed fine materials which were woven so tightly that when wet they would swell enough to make the basket practically watertight. Coiled baskets were almost always tightly woven, but the twining technique was well adapted to both close work and open work. As a result, baskets used to carry or store coarse materials were more often twined than coiled in areas where both techniques were known. Basketry fish traps, most characteristic of the Pacific Coast, were also twined.

The twining on the Prairies is confined to buffalo-hair bags and mats of whole plant stems, and that in the East to mats. The stems were laid parallel to one another and fastened together with pairs of cords which were twined around each stem at intervals of about one foot.

Plaiting is the dominant basketry, bag, and matting technique in the East, the Mexican part of the Southwest, and Meso-America (Map 25), but is a minor method in all other areas of its occurrence. It is significant that its greatest development occurred in areas where cooking vessels and water containers were consistently made of pottery.

Women made most of the baskets, bags, and mats in all areas north of Mexico. The exceptions consisted of fishing baskets and other types used exclusively by men and of baby cradles, which men sometimes made. In Meso-America, by way of contrast, baskets and mats were often made by male specialists who devoted a considerable portion of their time to this craft. In historic times in the Eastern United States, splint basketry for the White trade was often made by men; but in pre-Columbian times, women seem to have made all the basketry and matting.

Twining and plaiting are both found at the earliest levels of the Ocampo Caves in southwest Tamaulipas, Mexico, where the time range is about 7000–5500 B.C. (Whitaker, Cutler, and MacNeish, 1957). Another early date for twining is about 7500 B.C. at Danger Cave, Utah (Jennings, 1957: 93, 257). Coiling is at least as old. It appears in the earliest farming levels in both Tamaulipas and Puebla, 7000–5000 B.C. Plaiting is the dominant technique in most of South America and covers a continuous area with the North American data presented on Map 25. It seems likely that plaiting in the Eastern United States, Meso-America, and the Circum-Caribbean area had an origin common with that in South America.

Splint basketry in the Eastern United States is known to have been diffused to the northernmost areas of its occurrence in very recent times. The Abnaki of Maine received it about 1890, and the Micmac of New Brunswick and Nova Scotia as late as 1900. The Lake St. John Montagnais learned this craft at about the same time. It has gained ground against birch-bark containers among these tribes (Speck, 1920a). On the other hand, splint basketry is known to have been pre-Columbian in the Middle West at least as far north as Wisconsin, where it has been found there by archeologists.

Knotless netting.—A curious technique analogous to weaving is knotless netting or knitting. In the Sub-Arctic, this technique was employed in the manufacture of rabbit-skin blankets from twisted strips of fur. The Yavapai of the Southwest was the only tribe outside the Sub-Arctic which is known to have made rabbit-skin blankets in this manner. Bags or nets for carrying were made with knotless netting technique in all major areas. More restricted uses to which this technique was put included the manufacture of caps, leggings, and sandals in California and the Southwest. Archeological specimens conclusively establish the indigenous character of the North American knotless netting.

Spindle whorl.—Spinning is known to nearly all peoples in the world. The rolling of fibers between the palm and thigh is a very widespread and presumably old method of spinning. This was done by many American Indian tribes to make cordage for a variety of purposes short of weaving. Some weaving peoples still clung to the old palm-and-thigh method of spinning—for example, the Tlingit of the Northwest Coast, and a large number of tribes east of the Rockies who spun and wove buffalo hair. However, most peoples who spin and weave cotton and wool extensively use a spinning device called the spindle whorl. It consists of a shaft over which is slipped a perforated disk of wood, stone, or clay which acts as a flywheel to keep the spinning shaft in motion longer. The weighted end of the spindle whorl is commonly placed on the ground, and from the other end the instrument is twirled, either vertically between the fingers or horizontally along the thigh. The free hand of the spinner manipulates the cotton or wool, which, when spun, is wound around the spindle. In North America, the spindle whorl was used on the Northwest Coast and the adjacent part of the Plateau, by the Illinois and Cherokee, and generally in the Southwest and Meso-America. Spindle whorls received their greatest elaboration in Meso-America, where pottery whorls were decorated with stamped and incised designs. They are frequently found in archeological excavations in this area.

Weaving frames and looms.—The number of weaving techniques is so great, especially in Meso-America, that no attempt will be made to list them all. Instead, we shall rest content with a brief treatment of frames and looms. The weaving of flexible material is differentiated from basketry by the use of a support of some kind. A few North American tribes (Aleut, Tlingit, Haida, Virginia Indians) wove twined baskets upside down, with the basket suspended from a stake. This represents a transition between basketry and true weaving. Another group, consisting of the central Algonquians and southern Siouans of the Prairies, suspended the radial warps of twined buffalo-hair bags from a stake in similar fashion to facilitate weaving.

A still more advanced technique is the suspension of warps in a linear arrangement from a cord or bar (Map 26). This was character-istic of the Northwest Coast of Canada and Alaska, of the Algonquians of the Prairies, and of doubtless many others for which we have no information. The weaver twined with her fingers from top to bottom in a manner as time-consuming as that for basketry, except that the materials employed for the mats and blankets made in this fashion were generally coarser than those used for twined baskets. The famous Chilkat blankets of the Northwest Coast, made princi-pally of mountain goat wool and beautifully decorated, were made in this crude manner, as were also mats of the inner bark of the cedar. Inner bark seems to have been the chief material thus woven on the Prairies. A single California tribe is reported to have twined together rabbit-skin blankets in this manner.

The next step toward loom weaving was the attachment of both ends of the warp to a two-bar frame. Frames of this kind were used on the Northwest Coast and the adjacent part of the Plateau, in Cali-fornia, the Great Basin, the Southwest, and the Southeast (Map 26). All such frames on the Northwest Coast and the adjacent strip of the Plateau were upright; one bar was directly above the other, and the fixed warp ran vertically. Weaving was done with the fingers and from top to bottom.

In California, a number of interesting variants of the two-bar frame were to be found. In some cases, the bars consisted of two vertical stakes around which the continuous warp was wound, resulting in a warp which was horizontal but a weft which was vertical. In other instances, both bars were attached to stakes close to the ground, so that both warp and weft were horizontal and parallel to the ground. In the Great Basin and the Southwest, the majority of heddleless frames were of this latter variety. They were used chiefly to weave rabbit-skin blankets. In the Southeast, the same type of horizontal frame supported by stakes in the ground is reported for the Creek. Such weaving frames which hold the warp rigid are a necessary step in the development of the loom, because without them the heddle would have been impossible.

The bow "loom" (Map 26) is a curious variant found principally in the Sub-Arctic. It was used to weave bands worn on the body. These were decorated with porcupine quill and moose hair embroidery. The warp elements were held rigid by the tension of the flexed bow.

The true loom may be defined as a two-bar, fixed-warp weaving frame to which heddles have been added. A heddle is simply a stick to which only a part of the warp strands are attached. If the weaver desires a checker weave, she attaches each alternate warp strand to the heddle, so that a single pull on the stick will separate every other warp strand from the remainder. She is then able to thrust a ball of weft in a single motion all the way across the material being woven. By releasing the tension on the heddle after the weft ball has traversed its course, a checker weave results. A second heddle, attached to the remaining warp strands, separates them for the return journey of the ball. Thus, with the aid of the heddle, the worker can weave a row many times faster than by working the weft with the fingers over and under each alternate warp. Modern machine weaving is made possible by the principle of the heddle.

Two-bar frames with heddles are indigenous in the Southwest and Meso-America (Map 26). True shuttles seem to have been unknown. Weaving was always from bottom to top when the looms were upright. Two other weaving tools commonly associated with these looms are the comb and the batten, both of which were used to beat down the weft elements in order to increase the closeness of the weave.

The warp threads of true looms may run horizontally, diagonally, or vertically. The diagonal or slanting position is associated with the waist or belt loom, so called because one bar is attached to a house

Fig. 27. The true loom

post or tree several feet off the ground, and the other bar to a belt around the waist or hips of the weaver (Fig. 27). The waist loom was used among the Pueblos of the Southwest and in Meso-America. The vertical loom also is definitely known to have been used among the Pueblos. For this we have archeological evidence—holes in dwellings and kivas (sacred men's houses) for the insertion of weaving bars. Cloth too wide to have been woven on a waist loom has also been interpreted as evidence of the vertical loom, but it could just as easily have been woven on the horizontal loom, which is also known to have been used by the Pueblos. Horizontal looms are, in addition, to be found in the Southwest area from the Pima to the Huichol, and sporadically in Meso-America.

In the Southwest and Meso-America, men sometimes did the weaving. In all other areas, women were the weavers. This is another example of the adaptation to sedentary and urban life which characterizes these southern areas. Men in these areas were not predominantly hunters and warriors, but were farmers, craftsmen, and tradesmen instead.

The indigenous character of true looms in the Southeast (Map 26) is problematical. Descriptions of looms for the Creek, Cherokee, and Chickasaw date from the last half of the eighteenth century, and that for the Osage from the first half of the nineteenth. On the other hand, the inner-bark mantles observed by the de Soto expedition in 1540 were woven so finely that they were sometimes mistaken for cotton. Work of such high quality suggests the true loom.

POTTERY

Pottery has already been mentioned in Chapter 6 and in the beginning of the present chapter (Map 23). Its combined ethnological and archeological distribution is presented on Map 27. The pottery in the Eastern United States shows influences from both Asia and Meso-America, suggesting that the two historically independent developments met and fused in this area. It is notable that the earliest pottery in this area predates plant cultivation by about 1,000 years (Willey 1966: 256–257). In the Southwest and Meso-America, the reverse is true: farming is earlier than pottery.

Pottery making.—There were only three major methods of manufacturing pottery in aboriginal North America: coiling, modeling, and molding. Probably more pots were made by coiling than by any other method. The potter shaped the base of the pot in her hands and then built up the sides by adding coils of ropelike pieces of clay made by rolling a lump of clay between the palms. After each additional coil, the potter kneaded the point of contact of the new coil with the previous one to insure a complete fusing of the two. She might also slap with a paddle the outside of the pot, which was prevented from collapsing by an "anvil" held by hand against the inner wall of the pot.

In modeling, the entire pot was shaped in the hands without coiling. The base was made in the same manner as for coiling, but the sides were built up with slablike sections of clay which were pinched or patted into place with the hands. A paddle was sometimes used to manipulate the clay, as in coiling.

In molding, the clay, was shaped around a previously constructed mold of some kind, such as a fired pot, a basket, the end of a log, a hole in the ground, or a specially constructed mold of fired pottery made exclusively for the manufacturing of vessels.

Coiling was dominant in the southern half of the North American continent. Because it was also the most common method of making pottery in South America, there is good reason to believe that coiling had a single origin in the region from Mexico to Peru and subsequently diffused to other areas. Coiling apparently replaced other pottery-making techniques in some localities as it spread north. For example, the earliest pottery in the Southeast was definitely modeled.

Modeling and molding were the principal pottery-making techniques in the northern half of the continent, and extended southward in the Plains and Prairie areas in the familiar wedge-shaped distribution so commonly assumed by predominantly northern culture elements. The only exception is a small Eskimo area on the Bering Sea where coiling prevailed, but this was a recent diffusion from Asia (Oswalt, 1953).

In Meso-America, pottery was apparently sometimes made by both molding and modeling. The simplest form of mold was a previously made pot, which was turned upside down and plastered over with fresh clay to form the new pot. It then had to be removed from the mold and completed by coiling or modeling. Fired clay molds, in the shape of a mushroom, were also employed in making pottery in this area. In a smaller number of localities, pots were molded in two vertically bisected halves, which were then fused by kneading and rubbing before the pot was fired. Small pots were sometimes made exclusively by modeling, but more often the handles, legs, and decorations were modeled on after the body of the pot had been made by coiling, molding, or by a combination of the two.

The paddle-and-anvil technique, employed to produce a complete fusing of the separate pieces of clay used to build up a pot, was most highly developed among the Yumans and Uto-Aztecans of the Southwest in association with coiling. Their anvils were made of pottery, and resemble the pottery molds of southern Mexico so closely that there can be little doubt that they were derived from Mexico. Paddles and anvils were lacking among the Pueblos and Athapaskans, who joined their coils by kneading and rubbing. Paddles and anvils seem also to have been widely used in the Prairies and East, although much of the evidence is indirect.

Potter's wheel.—The true potter's wheel, rotated on a pivot, was unknown in the New World in pre-Columbian times, but was adopted from the Spanish by a few Latin American Indians. It was most enthusiastically received by those peoples who molded pottery, because it offered a quick method for completing the upper section of the vessel. However, a number of twentieth-century observers have reported the making of pots on rotating bases without pivots in Meso-America. Such bases are often wooden cylinders or disks rotated on a baseboard by the feet as well as the hands. Sometimes the rotating base is made of pottery. In one locality in Oaxaca, the rotating platform on which the pot is shaped is spun at speeds as great as those of European-derived true wheels, from sixty to ninety revolutions per minute. It seems likely that slowly rotating bases are pre-Columbian, but that rotation at speeds of from 60 to 90 revolutions per minute is post-Columbian.

The sexual division of labor in pottery making corresponds to that in many other crafts. North of Mexico, it was exclusively the task of women; but in central Mexico, it was also the work of men who were specialists in the craft.

SKIN DRESSING

True tanning by means of tannic acid was unknown to the American Indians, in spite of the fact that a large number of tribes ate acorns, which contain the acid. Skin dressing by other means, however, met the needs of all peoples, including the Eskimos, whose lives depended on the quality of their clothing.

In order to dress a hide in any manner, it must be held stationary in some way. In the central and eastern Arctic, where trees were scarce, large hides were most often laid on the ground or snow and held in place by stakes driven through holes near the edge. Buffalo hides were staked down also on the Plains. The use of ground support was characteristic of only these two areas, although it was practiced occasionally elsewhere. There is no reason to suppose that the Plains Indians learned it from the Eskimos or vice versa, because there was no direct contact between the two areas. It was probably independently invented in the two areas as an adaptation to a treeless environment.

In other areas, hides were fastened to a rectangular frame of poles by means of thongs run through holes around the periphery. The frame was most often placed in an upright position so that the worker could stand up at her task. This kind of support was characteristic of the Alaskan Arctic, the entire Sub-Arctic, the Northwest Coast, Plateau, Prairies, and East. It was used especially for large hides. Small hides might simply be laid on a log or plank.

Small hides were fleshed, dehaired, and softened by being pulled back and forth over the upper end of a post or stake in the ground. This end was often sharpened, so that the post actually constituted an end-bladed tool. This device is reported in all major areas except the Arctic and Meso-America.

The scraping of the flesh off the inside of the hide with an end-bladed tool was characteristic of all areas north of Mexico except California, the Great Basin, and the Yuman-Uto-Aztecan Southwest, where edge-bladed fleshers predominated. On the Plains and Prairies, as well as among a few tribes in neighboring areas, the end-bladed tool had an elbowed handle. It was used something like a hoe. In the Arctic and among a few neighboring tribes in the Sub-Arctic, hides were fleshed with the woman's semicircular stone knife called *ulo* by the Eskimo.

After the hide had been fleshed, and dehaired if this was desired, it was treated with a skin-dressing agent which perhaps acted chemically as well as physically on it. By far the most common agent was animal brains, normally those of the same animal which furnished the hide. They were apparently rubbed into hides in all areas north of Mexico except in the Arctic. The second most widespread skin-dressing agent was human urine, in which the hide was soaked for a time. This practice was limited to the Arctic and Northwest Coast except for one tribe in the Alaskan Sub-Arctic; it dissolved the excess grease on sea mammal hides. Other agents less commonly used in North America were the spinal cord, liver, and marrow of animals; ashes; vegetable materials; and, in modern times, eggs.

Two other kinds of physical manipulation may be barely mentioned: the chewing of the hide by the Eskimos; the pulling of the hide back and forth across a rope of sinews on the Plains. Both practices were localized within their respective culture areas.

Skins were sometimes smoked over a wood fire in all major areas except the Arctic, where the oil lamp was the only kind of fire available. Bark of a certain kind was usually thrown on the fire to give the skin the desired color. In the Arctic, skins were occasionally colored with vegetable or mineral dyes.

Among the vast majority of tribes, women prepared the hides. Since men did practically all the hunting, and fighting as well, this was equitable enough. There is a fairly close correlation between the dominance of hunting in the subsistence pattern (Maps 3 and 4) and the dressing of hides by women. Only in California, the Southwest, and Meso-America were hides characteristically dressed by men.

The dressing of hides by women in the northern Plains played a prominent role in the change of family structure in the first half of the nineteenth century. At that time, the demand for buffalo hides was at its peak. Because women prepared the hides, the more wives a man had, the richer he became. A single hunter, with the aid of the horse and gun, could kill enough buffalo to keep many women busy. As a result of this combination of factors, the maximum number of wives possessed by one man skyrocketed from five or six to as many as twenty or even thirty.

METALLURGY

In most of aboriginal North America, true metallurgy was unknown; the majority of Indians merely cold-hammered chunks of native copper produced in almost pure form by nature. There were no true mines with underground tunnels and subterranean caverns north of Mexico. Copper used by Indians in this area was obtained on the surface or from shallow pits dug to recover metal which had been seen from the surface. The largest deposits of native copper were on the southern shore of Lake Superior, and from this locality the metal and the objects made from it were traded over hundreds of miles. Farther north, the source of copper centered in two regions: southeast Alaska, and the central Arctic on the Coppermine River, which flows into the

Arctic Ocean. There were many other local deposits of less magnitude.

Early observers have left us many accounts from many localities of indigenes beating, with nothing more than a stone, lumps of copper into desired shapes. One enterprising museum curator demonstrated conclusively that all of the types of copper objects from the Eastern United States could be made in this crude manner (Cushing, 1894). However, some specialists believe that Indians north of Mexico might have used an additional technique known as annealing. This is merely heating the metal to the point where some of the brittleness produced by the pounding is eliminated.

The majority of objects made from native copper north of Mexico were body ornaments: beads, ear ornaments, head and breast plates, necklaces, bracelets, anklets, and even embroidery on hide clothing. At the same time, a fair number of tools were made of native copper: knives, ax blades, adz blades, spear points, arrowheads, chisels, hooks, ice picks, needles, and drinking cups. On the Northwest Coast, a large copper plate of stylized shape and design became an object of great value and a symbol of great prestige attainable only by chiefs and rich men.

A single band of Eskimos—the Polar—who are the northernmost people on earth, hammered out meteoric iron, obtained locally, into spear points and knives. Arrowheads were made of the same material after the bow was reintroduced to them in the nineteenth century. In the historic period, natives on all coasts eagerly sought timbers from wrecked European ships for the iron bolts and nails which could be easily extracted by burning the planks. Such iron was worked principally by cold hammering.

A few copper objects have been mentioned by early observers and found by archeologists in the Southwest. They consist mostly of body ornaments, which were much less numerous than those in the Prairies and East and first appeared at a later date. The most complex type of copper object was a "sleigh" type of bell of thin-walled copper with slits and a copper pellet inside. All of these objects except the bells seem to have been made by cold hammering. The bells, on the other hand, are regarded by experts as having been cast by the lost-wax method. It is generally thought that they were obtained in trade from Mexico and not made locally. The earliest of these date from A.D. 900–1100, but they were not common until the thirteenth and fourteenth centuries (Haury, 1947). They have been found all along the west coast route from southern Mexico to northern New Mexico.

Meso-American metallurgy was a combination of practices from Peru, Colombia, and Central America plus a few Mexican inventions. True metallurgy was unknown in Mexico until the Toltec period, about A.D. 800. A copper-lead alloy, unknown to South Americans, was invented by the Mexicans, but bronze was never achieved by them. The Mexicans were also familiar with the gilding of copper. Copper and gold were cast into bells and ornaments by the lost-wax method. The shape of the casting was modeled in clay, over which was dusted finely ground charcoal, followed by an even layer of wax. This wax coating was also dusted with charcoal, and then the whole object was encased in clay, which was perforated at top and bottom. The entire mold was then heated to the point that the wax melted and ran out and the clay became sufficiently hardened. Then the bottom hole was plugged and the molten metal poured in at the top. When the metal cooled, the mold was broken and the finished casting was removed. The metal filled the space previously occupied by the wax. Although Mexican metallurgy stemmed from South America, the best work of the Mexicans is generally regarded as superior.

Nearly all of the metal objects produced in Mexico were ornamental in character, but a few were utilitarian. Copper axes, picks, blow pipes, chisels, helmets, and needles are mentioned by the chroniclers and have been found in excavations. Metal tools and weapons failed to make much headway among the Aztecs not only because copper was soft but also because there was an abundant supply of obsidian, from which razor-sharp blades and points could be manufactured.

Compared to Old World metallurgy, which began thousands of years earlier, New World metal working was in its infancy. Bellows in any form were unknown. The heat necessary for smelting and casting was generated by nothing more than the human breath blown through a reed or copper tube into a charcoal fire. This could not have produced enough heat to smelt or cast iron. Whether the American Indian would ever have invented an adequate bellows and discovered the superior properties of iron, if the Spanish had not arrived with their iron weapons to end forever his freedom of action, will always remain a mystery.

DIVISION OF LABOR

Division of labor according to age was universal in North America, as in the rest of the world. Children were incapable of performing the tasks of adults, and the older adults often worked at different occupations from the younger. Where sedentary crafts were highly valued, old age meant little or no diminution in status; where sedentary crafts were few, as in the Arctic, and much strenuous out-door activity was demanded of men, they either died young or suffered a definite loss of rank in old age.

Sexual division of labor is also practiced by all human societies. The classic picture of the lazy Indian brave and the industrious squaw, however, applies only to certain culture areas, and even there demands considerable qualification. In regions where hunting and warfare loomed large, as on the Plains, the Prairies, and in the East, a man performed his most strenuous duties away from home. Partly because of the violent nature of these activities and partly because of the religious fasting which usually accompanied both, a man often arrived home exhausted and needed a few days of leisure in which to recu-perate. Most of the early historical observers in those areas saw only village life, where the women were actually doing most of the work. The result was a distorted picture.

Not so among the Meso-Americans. Here both men and women labored almost constantly, although perhaps at a more leisurely rate than our present-day workers on a forty-hour week. Men did most of the farming, and sometimes engaged in such crafts as pottery making, basket making, and even weaving. They marketed their products in neighboring towns. Women stayed in their home village. The grinding of maize alone, as fine as the culture demanded, might take as much as six hours a day when the family was large. Add to this the cooking, weaving, child care, and other household tasks, and women probably worked as long as men. Although the tasks assigned to the sexes differed, both sexes spent practically all of their waking hours working at the prescribed occupations.

If we had enough quantitive information, we might scale other cultures along an imaginary work line between the Meso-Americans and the peoples of the Plains, Prairies, and East. For example, the Pueblos of the Southwest would fall rather close to the Meso-Americans. Peoples of California and the Great Basin might be intermediate. Those of the Arctic, Sub-Arctic, and Plateau might be a little closer to the Plains, Prairies, and East. The Northwest Coast would be difficult to classify, but would probably fall into the inter-mediate group.

In other parts of this volume, the sexual division of labor has been discussed comparatively for the following topics: horticulture, Map 8, pages 80–81; house building, Map 19, page 132; clothing manufacture, page 152; basket making, page 158; weaving, page 162; pottery making, page 164; skin dressing, page 166. A few additional generalizations will be attempted here.

Where hunting was the chief source of subsistence (Map 3), men devoted considerable energy to it; women tended to perform all the other tasks listed in the paragraph above if these were present in the culture. In the area where fishing was most dominant, the Northwest Coast, women relinquished the building of the huge plank houses to men, shared skin dressing with them, but otherwise did all the other jobs except pottery making, which was absent in the area. In the East, where horticulture dominated subsistence, women were the principal workers in the fields, but men bore the brunt of building the large frame houses and sometimes helped with skin dressing; women performed all the other jobs. Among the Pueblos of the Southwest, where horticulture was even more important, men did not only most of the work in the field but also most of the house building, clothing manufacturing, weaving, and skin dressing. In Meso-America, where horticulture was most dominant, men might share all other, non-agricultural, tasks with women or become specialists in them and perform them to produce goods for the market.

In areas where wild plants formed the mainstay of the diet (California and the Great Basin), the sexual division of labor was less sharp than in the rest of the continent. Although women may have gathered most of the food, they had considerable help from men. House building was done principally by men or shared by both sexes; clothing manufacture was rather evenly divided; and skin dressing was mainly the work of men or was shared by both sexes. Basket making, pottery making, and weaving were exclusively feminine tasks, however.

It seems likely that, before horticulture was known in the Southwest and Meso-America, the main reliance was on wild plant foods. The sexual division of labor was presumably somewhat flexible, like that of California and the Great Basin. After horticulture arrived and improved the efficiency of the subsistence pattern, more time was available for greater specialization in crafts. Because men were already working at crafts which would have been disdained in hunting societies, it was entirely consistent for them to take up more of the tasks formerly limited to women.

What would have happened in the East if European contact had not put an end to its Indian history is by no means obvious. However, the prehorticultural basis of subsistence seems to have been hunting, and, with the great emphasis placed on warfare, the male was an ultra-masculine type who took little interest in crafts, which he considered to be feminine. Probably horticulture began as a woman's occupation, and it remained largely so up to the time of White contact. If horti-culture in Meso-America and the Southwest was originally women's work, the shift to men had been accomplished in most localities by the time of European contact.

Specialization of labor.—Specialization of labor is less fully known than sexual division of labor. Nevertheless, craft specialization on the part of individuals of the same sex is of vital importance in the growth of culture as we know it today in Europe and America. It is one of the measuring sticks which may be applied to a culture to determine its degree of complexity. Another, perhaps still more advanced, criterion is the amount of craft specialization by community. If one commu-nity specializes in pottery making and exports considerable quan-tities of the ware to other communities, and each community, in turn, pursues its own speciality, the total economic system differs decidedly from one in which every community makes practically everything it uses.

An impressionistic summary of craft specialization is offered in Map 28. In the Arctic, Sub-Arctic, about half the Great Basin and Northeast Mexico, and a few smaller areas, there was either no craft specialization or only a few part-time specialists. A man in these cultures tended to be a jack-of-all-trades, and a woman had to be just as versatile. Often a single family functioned as a complete economic unit for a considerable length of time. While it is true that shamans and headmen among the Eskimos were sometimes distin-guished from other men, their special activities were concerned with the supernatural and with group leadership, which can hardly be called crafts. Probably the nearest approach to a craft specialist in this culture was the whale harpooner. Furthermore, there were some raw materials, such as copper and soapstone, which could be obtained only in limited localities. The fact that these were traded great distances is proof that the individuals who first obtained them from nature had acquired a surplus, which, in turn, implies at least a minimum of specialization.

The Sub-Arctic is about as devoid of craft specialists as the Arctic. No doubt hunters who were thought to be able to locate game or attract it by supernatural means were somewhat in a class by themselves. From a western tribe in this region, the Ingalik, we learn that wooden dishes and bowls were sometimes manufactured for trade to other individuals. This indicates some specialization.

The Great Basin presents a comparable picture. Antelope shamans, thought to be able to attract antelope by supernatural means, were held in high esteem but can hardly be called craft specialists. In a few instances certain men may have produced extra bows and arrows which were traded to others, or certain women a few extra baskets to be disposed of in the same way, but there were no regular surpluses and no regular trade channels in most of the Great Basin. Northeast Mexico and the other smaller regions shown in fine stippling on Map 28 are less well known, but seem to have functioned in about the same way.

Definite part-time specialists are reported for about half of the continent (Map 28). Beginning with the Plains-Prairie area, we find men specializing in the manufacture of pipes, bows, arrows, and lariats. A few women specialized in house building. Unusual skill was required to cut the buffalo skins for the tipi cover and to sew them together so that they would take the shape of a cone when fastened around the tipi frame. Women specialists also directed the building of the earth lodge, even though men obtained the heavier logs and lifted them into place. Sacred objects used in ceremonies were always made by specialists familiar with the rules of manufacture and usually thought to be in rapport with the supernatural.

Specialization was probably more advanced in the East, although it is less often reported in the literature. The rich and variegated material culture of a tribe like the Iroquois is proof of craft specialization. The lively trade which occurred in pre-Columbian times and continued after Europeans settled America is further evidence of specialization. In the Southeast, salt was a common article of trade, and the persons connected with its making by evaporation in pottery salt pans were most certainly specialists.

On the Plateau, there was probably less specialization than on the Plains, Prairies, and in the East, but it was present. Men made all articles of stone, bone, and wood; and those most skilled in the manufacture of a single article, such as a canoe or bow and arrows, traded some of their surplus to other men. The definitely documented intertribal trade in parfleches, buffalo robes, shells and beads, rope, and baskets is indirect evidence of individual specialization.

In central California, part-time specialists were associated with a wide variety of tasks: hunting, fishing, bow making, arrowhead making, pipe making, bead making, salt making, fire making, and the making of ceremonial regalia. Often esoteric knowledge of the supernatural was thought to be required for success in these activities, so that a young man would not attempt to engage in them without adequate instruction from a successful older man. With respect to a single tribe, the Patwin, it is reported that such activities were professional monopolies which ran in lineages from father to son. While this has not been confirmed elsewhere, it at least demonstrates the considerable amount of specialization in the area.

The Northwest Coast was characterized by part-time specialists and perhaps even an occasional full-time specialist. House building and canoe building were largely under the supervision of acknowledged experts, even though every man knew enough to assist in the operation. The carving of totem poles and less conspicuous wooden objects likewise fell to the more skilled individuals. Hunting, of both land and sea mammals, and fighting were specialities of men in some localities. The considerable amount of trade reported on the Northwest Coast also is evidence of surplus goods and, in turn, of some degree of specialization on the part of the makers. One of the most highly specialized professions was that of whale harpooner. Basketry and weaving were the most common specialities of women.

Among the Pueblos of the Southwest, there were also some part-time specialists, even though every individual could perform most of the tasks assigned to his sex. Men tended to specialize in skin dressing, weaving, turquoise work, and, in the historic period, in silver work. Women sometimes specialized in the making of pottery and basketry. The expert was fed by his employer while on the job, and received an additional gift of food when the article was completed. The hiring or commissioning of experts seems to have been more common in the Southwest than in other culture areas north of Mexico. However, the great amount of specialization in things pertaining to the supernatural far exceeds that in purely economic tasks.

In Meso-America, the picture changes. Here we encounter cities with populations up to 300,000, ruled over by nobility and graced with elaborate public architecture. Many full-time craftsmen were required to construct and maintain the quarters of the nobility alone, and large numbers of others found it profitable to specialize in a single craft and sell their goods or services to others. Besides doing farming, hunting, and fishing, men worked full time at manufacturing such things as stone tools, pottery, jewelry, featherwork, and woven textiles; they also engaged in masonry, sculpture, painting, mining, metallurgy, woodworking, and weapon making. Women specialized in spinning, weaving, and featherwork, but did not work full time at such occupations after marriage.

Specialization of labor on the part of whole communities was probably more common than the ethnographic record shows. The most conclusive proof of specialization consists of the wealth of information on trade, some of which will be presented in Chapter 13. Community specialization reached its greatest development in Meso-America, where dozens of products were made locally in sufficient quantities for export. Export often consisted of nothing more than the maker back-packing his wares to the market of a neighboring town. Specialists who made and marketed articles for export were always men; the household duties of women kept them near home. Certain villages specialized in pottery, others in basketry, still others in obsidian points and knives, textiles, cochineal dyes, and almost every other commodity that was widely traded. In such circumstances, the beginnings of mass production were realized. Pottery was made with the aid of molds, textiles with true looms, and buildings were constructed with quantities of adobe brick and faced with pieces of stone of uniform size and shape. For better or for worse, the signs of an industrial age were beginning to be manifested. The vast difference between the total economy of Meso-America and that of the rest of North America is reflected in the size of the population, which was greater in Meso-America than in all other culture areas combined.

REFERENCES

AGUILAR, 1946; AMSDEN, 1932; BEAGLEHOLE, 1937; BEALS, 1932a; BIRKET-SMITH, 1929, 1936, 1945; BIRKET-SMITH AND DE LAGUNA, 1938; CUSHING, 1894; DAVIDSON, 1935; FEWKES, 1944; FLANNERY, 1939; FOSTER, 1948, 1955, 1959; GIFFEN, 1930; GIFFORD, 1928; GOGGIN, 1949; GRIFFIN, 1935; GRIFFIN AND KRIEGER, 1947; HAURY, 1947; HERSKOVITS, 1952; KELLY, 1943; KING, MS; KROEBER, 1925; DE LAGUNA, 1940; LINTON, 1944; LOTHROP, 1952; LOWIE, 1954; MACNEISH, 1955; MARTIN, QUIMBY AND COLLIER, 1947; MASON, 1891, 1904; MENDIZÁBAL, 1942; MILLER, 1950; NELSON, 1899;

OSWALT, 1953; RICKARD, 1934; RIVET AND ARSANDAUX, 1946; SAVILLE, 1920; SPECK, 1920*a*, 1931, 1937; SWANTON, 1946; TAX, 1953; UNDERHILL, 1939; VAILLANT, 1941; WELT-FISH, 1930; WHITAKER, CUTLER AND MACNEISH, 1957; WILLEY, 1966; WILSON, 1917, 1924, 1934; WINTENBERG, 1942; WISSLER, 1938, 1941.

11

Art

THERE are dozens of different Indian art traditions, past and present. Each of these must be judged by its own standards within its own dimensions of variation. Most examples of Indian art, with tribal labels removed, cannot be assigned by art experts to single tribes because they share a tradition common to a number of neighboring tribes. However, art objects can be allocated to areas, comparable to culture areas in size and time depth. The line between arts and crafts is also impossible to draw from observation of examples alone, and, even with knowledge of the individual who made an object and his intentions, this distinction is often impossible to make.

Most Indian art was functional: it decorated a utilitarian object, such as a cooking vessel, tool, weapon, or costume; on ritual objects and costumes, the designs were actually thought to produce the magic or religious quality that distinguished sacred from secular objects. Before White contact, a few areas—Meso-America, the Northwest Coast, and probably the Southeast—had full-time artists who produced works of art for wealthy patrons, priests, and rulers. These were admired as fine examples of technique, form, and color independent of their functions. After White contact, some artistic expression was slanted toward the trade with Whites, thus producing objects that had little or no function within Indian cultures.

On the whole, men produced more art than did women, although the latter decorated the things they made, such as baskets, pottery vessels, textiles, and clothing. Women produced mostly folk art, while men executed the larger and more elaborate carvings and paintings displayed in prominent places by the rich and powerful. Thus men made the conspicuous stone carvings on and around the temples and palaces of Meso-America and the bold wood carving and painting on the houses and canoes of the Northwest Coast.

AREAL SURVEY

Arctic.—Eskimo art shows considerable variation from east to west. That in Alaska is the most showy because of the greater amount of wood carving, which is often accented with paint. The art of the Greenland Eskimo is second in complexity to that of Alaska, while examples from the central Arctic are fewer in number as well as more modest in appearance.

The art of the Eskimo consisted almost entirely of carving and engraving in wood, bone, horn, and ivory. The only exceptions would be the decoration of clothing with borders of hide and fur of different color or shade from the rest of the garment, the moderate amount of tattooing on the face, and the painting of masks in Alaska and Greenland. Because work in wood, bone, horn, and ivory was done exclusively by men, practically all art was produced by men. Few examples were executed wholly to satisfy the aesthetic impulse and without any other utility. Most art consisted of the decoration of a primarily utilitarian article, such as a knife handle or a harpoon head. Some Eskimo art was naturalistic; it depicted human beings, animals, boats, sleds, houses, and other natural and cultural objects. But it was just as often geometric, consisting of designs made up of a variety of lines and abstract two-dimensional figures which were not supposed to represent anything in nature or culture. Sometimes the two styles were combined on a single object (Plate I).

Animal carvings in the round are known from all archeological and nearly all contemporary Eskimo cultures; the whale, walrus, seal, bear, dog, and bird are the most common animals represented (Plate II). Human figures in the round are less frequent, but probably occurred everywhere. Animal engravings on flattish objects were common, and included the caribou in addition to the animals listed above. These engravings were invariably in silhouette, and the internal space was filled with parallel or cross-hatching or in solid black or brown. Carved and painted Eskimo masks, made mostly of wood, were worn in spirit-impersonating ceremonies. They were made only in Alaska and Greenland. Those in Alaska show influence from the Northwest Coast, as do the religious cults with which they were associated. Masks were the largest art objects produced by the Eskimo. The art displayed on small surfaces, such as that on implements used in daily life, was neat, precise, and able to convey meaning with a minimum number of lines. What was lacking in size was made up for in liveliness, humor, and fidelity.

Northwest Coast.—The Northwest Coast area from the Columbia
River north to the Arctic was characterized by a single major art style
which is easily recognisable in museums today. Figures of animals,
mythical monsters, and human beings were carved or painted on
totem poles, house fronts, canoes, wooden boxes, and other objects

FIG. 28. Northwest Coast (Kwakiutl) house front depicting a thunderbird lifting a
whale. Boas, 1897

(Fig. 28). Carving was in the round, in high relief, and in low relief;
painting was applied in red and black to all forms of carving as well as
to smooth surfaces. The animal, monster, or human forms depicted
represented supernatural beings who had revealed themselves to the
ancestors of those persons permitted to carve, paint, or display them at
a later date. All art was thus geared to religion and social organization,
and the production, ownership, and display of objects of art were proof
of the noble descent of an individual as well as of his rapport with the
supernatural. These art motifs have sometimes been called crests because of their universal association with particular lineages, sibs, and
extended families. They were marks of status, rank, wealth, and social
class, as were the crests of Europe in the past. The same art motifs
were occasionally carved in stone, bone, horn, and ivory, cold-
hammered into copper plates, painted on hide, or woven into baskets

and blankets; but decorated wooden objects probably outnumbered all other kinds of art objects combined.

Artists were always men, but not all men were artists. Although women were nowhere regarded as artists, they sometimes wove art motifs into baskets (especially hats), blankets, and dance costumes. However, it was the male artist who designed the pattern board which the female craftsman followed in weaving a Chilkat blanket.

Northwest Coast art may be divided into two major stylistic divisions: the Tlingit, Haida, and Tsimshian in the north; the Kwakiutl, Nootka, and Salish in the central part of the area. The art of the northern division was the most distinctive and the most highly stylized, and may be characterized by the following features. It was essentially an applied art. Practically all of the work of the artist was the decoration of utilitarian objects, such as houses, canoes, boxes, backrests, cradles, rattles, cups, ladles, and clothing. Even the appurtenances of the medicine man and the totem poles had utility or function other than as ways of displaying artistic achievement. The artist had to adapt his figure to the cylindrical form of the totem pole, the flat surface of a house front, the round flat surface of a plate, or the curved line of a ladle or paddle. Naturalism was forced to give way to conventionalization in the northern area. There was a passion for lateral symmetry. This was accomplished on flat surfaces by "splitting" the animal figure longitudinally and exhibiting two profiles instead of one (Fig. 28). On a round surface, such as that of a dish, two profiles were shown, wrapped around the outside of the dish, so to speak. Certain features of each species of animal served as markers to distinguish it from all other species, and mythical monsters were sometimes identified by combinations of features from two or more species. Thus the bear was characterized by a short snout, large teeth, and protruding tongue, while the wolf was depicted with a long snout and large teeth. The beaver was given protruding upper incisor teeth, a wide flat tail marked with cross-hatching, and was always shown holding a stick in its forepaws. There was a strong tendency to fill all available space, approaching an artistic agoraphobia. The naturally rounded lines of an animal figure were squared to fit a rectangular surface (Plate III), or they were forced into a cylindrical shape to fit a section of a totem pole or handle of some implement.

The art of the Kwakiutl, Nootka, and Salish exhibits enough difference from that of the northern peoples to make most examples of the two styles distinguishable. Figures of the central peoples were more naturalistic and less conventionalized. For three-dimensional carvings, this was accomplished by cutting deeper into the log, to the point that the statue approached naturalistic proportions, rather than a high relief carving on the cylindrical shape of the natural log, as was done in the north. A closer approach to naturalism was also achieved by adding appendages to a figure carved from a single piece of wood (Plate V). On a Kwakiutl dance costume depicting an eagle, cedar wood slats were used to represent feathers on the wings and upper legs, and overlapping pieces of caribou hide served the same purpose on the upper body and lower legs (Plate IV). The elaborate masks, which reached their peak of development among the Kwakiutl, were decorated with feathers when they represented bird spirits, and with vegetable fiber hair when a human figure was portrayed (Plate V).

The absence of strictly unilateral organization in the form of lineages and sibs, the greater premium placed upon direct rapport with the supernatural in visions, and the generally more individualistic ethos of the culture of the Kwakiutl and their neighbors—all were reflected in the boldness, vigor, and greater individualism of their art. However, the art of the Tlingit, Haida, and Tsimshian remains the most distinctive for the Northwest Coast as a whole, and represents the most specialized achievement of that area in the graphic and plastic arts. The sheer size of carvings and paintings on houses, canoes, and totem poles produces a dramatic effect not equaled by any other art style north of Mexico.

Plains.—Plains art may also be characterized as a decorative or applied art because all objects on which it was displayed had use or function in the culture other than for the exhibition of the art itself. Almost all Plains artwork was applied to hide, which was the most common material available in this hunting culture where the buffalo was the principal animal taken. Of the two techniques of hide decoration—painting and porcupine quill embroidery—painting was the more frequent. Glass bead embroidery became increasingly more common after trade beads were obtained from Europeans in the nineteenth century, and today has almost replaced the pre-Columbian quillwork. In addition to the decoration of objects made of hide, the Plains Indians decorated stone pipes, rattles, and other wooden ceremonial objects with painting and by attaching feathers, quills, and beads.

Painting and embroidery were applied to buffalo robes, men's shirts, women's gowns, moccasins, tipi covers, tipi linings, rawhide containers (parfleches), drums, medicine cases, quivers, and shields. All of these objects were made wholly or principally of hide, and the decoration was always applied to the hide part of compound objects such as drums and shields. The colors used in painting were brown, red, yellow, black, blue, and green. Most of them were obtained from clays, but charcoal was a ready source of black.

There were two distinct styles of painting associated to some extent with the sexes. Men generally painted naturalistic figures of horses, men, buffalo, and, more rarely, other animals (Plate VI). Women painted only geometric figures and designs (Plate VII). The two styles were kept separate for the most part on buffalo hide robes, but occasionally both appeared on the same robe when painted by a man.

The naturalistic forms of men, animals, and objects were usually painted in profile, in flat color and without background. Horses and men were the most frequent figures depicted, appearing together on 90 per cent of the painted hides. Perspective was lacking; there were no highlights and shadows, and a more distant figure was placed partly behind or above a closer one without any reduction in size. Composition was limited to small scenes, such as a pair of men engaged in combat or a single man riding home with stolen horses. The painting on a single hide showed a number of such scenes as well as a number of scattered isolated figures.

Porcupine quill embroidery was the only kind known before glass beads of European manufacture were received in trade in the nineteenth century. As might be anticipated, it was the work of women. The quills were softened with water, flattened, and dyed a variety of colors. After they were sewn onto dressed hide, they presented a smooth, glossy surface like that of straw. Angular geometric designs predominated in quill embroidery among the older specimens (Plate VIII). More naturalistic floral designs and human and animal figures became more common after European contact. Beadwork reached its maximum florescence at the end of the nineteenth century after the Plains Indians had been rounded up and confined to reservations (Hunt, 1951).

Southwest.—Pueblo art manifested itself on pottery, basketry, woven cloth, jewelry of shell and stone, walls of religious structures, ceremonial objects, and in sand paintings. No one material dominated the art as did wood on the Northwest Coast and hide on the Plains. Because of the dry climate and intensive archeological investigation in the Southwest, our knowledge of the pre-Columbian art

there is much more certain and fuller than that for any other area
north of Mexico. Since women made the basketry and pottery, they
executed the decoration on these receptacles. Men created almost all
other objects of art.

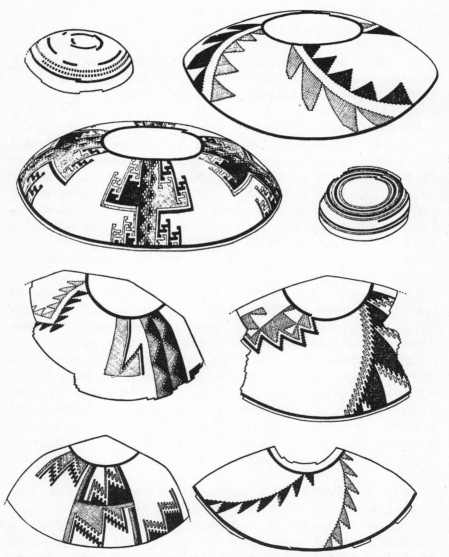

FIG. 29. Pueblo basket designs (Basket Maker III). Earl H. Morris and Robert E.
Burgh, 1941. Courtesy of the Carnegie Institution of Washington

Basketry was most often decorated by staining some of the materials black or red before weaving them into the basket. Basketry designs were overwhelmingly geometrical, but a few suggested animals, birds, and possibly the human figure. Symmetry, repetition, and contrast were established early in basket decoration, and continued as fundamental principles of Pueblo art down to the nineteenth century (Fig. 29).

The art displayed on Pueblo pre-Columbian woven cotton textiles is richer than that on baskets, as might be anticipated, but it remained entirely geometrical and seems to have been derived in part from basketry designs. Although weaving did not appear until A.D. 700, five hundred years after basket making, textile art reached its florescence at the same time as that of basketry, in the Pueblo III period, A.D. 1000–1300 (Kent, 1957). A type of decoration limited in the pre-Columbian Southwest to the Pueblo people is the stripe twill, in which the primary pattern consists of transverse stripes extending the entire width of the cloth. Patterns on tapestry are more complex because none extends the entire width of the material. Designs on cloth were also made by a technique called tie dyeing. The cloth was folded in a prescribed way at certain points and tied firmly with string. When it was dipped momentarily in dye, the dye did not penetrate the tied areas, which formed a white pattern against a colored background.

Cloth was also decorated by painting designs on it after the weaving was completed. The Pueblo artist did not fail to take advantage of the greater freedom which painting permitted and to employ curved design elements similar to those painted on pottery. Colors used on pre-Columbian cotton fabrics were predominantly inorganic kinds made from minerals, and were largely limited to three colors: red, from iron oxide; yellow, from yellow ocher; and blue-green, from copper sulfate. Organic dyes from plants were used for black, dark brown, and light blue. Modern Pueblo textile designs are a blend of pre-Columbian designs from all over the Southwest area, as well as a retention of those from the Pueblo III period.

Pueblo pottery decoration is principally geometric. However, a few conventionalized natural forms and occasional truly naturalistic forms were employed (Fig. 30, Plate IX). As might be anticipated, curves are common in pottery designs, in contrast to the straight lines and angles which the basketry and weaving techniques impose upon the artist. Practically all the pottery was decorated in some way. In the "golden age," Pueblo III, the most common decoration was black

FIG. 30. Pueblo "Rain Bird" design on pottery (Tsia). Harry P. Mera, 1937. Courtesy of the Laboratory of Anthropology, Santa Fe, New Mexico

lines and other geometric elements on a whitish background. In later prehistoric times, the variety of colors and design motifs increased. Three colors on the same vessel became common, and occasionally four were used together. Negative painting—the background painted and the design left in the original color of the pot—was also known. Along with this increase in number of colors came an increase in naturalistic forms, especially conventionalized bird and feather symbols, which originated among the Hopi and Zuñi Indians of the West. Designs on basketry, textiles, and pottery are predominantly geometric but not necessarily lacking in symbolism.

Mural paintings on the inside walls of underground religious structures, called kivas, reached a florescence in late prehistoric and early historic times. They are almost certain to have been parts of altars around which religious ceremony rallied, because most of the nineteenth-century Pueblo peoples painted murals for their altars. The two most famous examples of Pueblo murals are those in the Jeddito Valley of northern Arizona and those at the pueblo of Kuaua, near Albuquerque, New Mexico. The subjects represented in these murals include people, animals, and inanimate objects, and a great variety of colors was used. This unusual art seems to have evolved from simpler drawings and paintings on kiva walls and to have been wholly of Indian origin (Tanner, 1957:9–15, facing p. 8).

The art of sand painting is the most distinctive form of Pueblo art because it is restricted to the Southwest and a small region in southern California. Sand paintings were part of the sacred altars in the kivas, and were executed on the floor in front of the fetishes and wall paintings associated with the altars. Sand or ocher of various colors, corn pollen, pulverized flower petals, and pulverized green leaves were employed as dry pigments in "painting" the religious symbols. Handfuls of the dry material were carefully sprinkled from between the thumb and forefinger to form the lined and solid figures of the painting. These figures were conventionalized representations of the sun, moon, stars, earth, mountain lion, snake, and kachina; or of something associated with spirits, such as clouds, a cornfield, and the house of the sun or of a kachina. The purpose of these sand paintings was to influence the spirits to bring rain, plentiful crops, good health, and other beneficial things to man. Although the Navaho learned the art of sand painting from the Pueblo, the finest and most elaborate examples today are made by the Navaho (Covarrubias, 1954: pp. 231–34 and plate facing p. 248).

Another aspect of Pueblo art is the ceremonial costumes which are worn in the great religious dramas valued above all else by the Indians. Practically all colors of the spectrum are represented in these elaborate costumes, especially after the acquisition of sheep and wool from the Spanish and, later, modern dyes from the United States. Colors are associated with the six cardinal directions: yellow with north, turquoise with west, red with south, white with east, many colors with the zenith, and black with the nadir. The most important color is turquoise, made from blue-green copper ore.

Pueblo art may be divided into two major varieties: the modest geometric designs that predominate on basketry, textiles, and pottery; the more naturalistic motifs that characterize the religious art in murals, sand paintings, fetishes, and ceremonial costumes. The latter variety ranges from truly naturalistic figures to conventionalizations of naturalistic forms which may appear geometric to the naïve viewer unfamiliar with Pueblo symbolism. Nevertheless, every element of religious art is symbolic and thought to be of benefit to the society producing and displaying this art in the manner prescribed by the spirits.

Parallels between Pueblo art and that of neighboring culture areas point principally to Meso-America to the south, although the number of similarities suggesting a common origin of art motifs in the two areas is not great.

East.—The art of the Southeastern United States was probably as rich and varied as that of the Southwest, but European contact disturbed the Southeast peoples much more, and most of their art vanished before it was described or collected by literate observers.

A considerable range of artistic endeavor was involved in the ornamentation of the human body. Objects made of wood, stone, shell, pearls, and copper were worn on the body as head bands, bracelets, necklaces, and so on. Paint was applied to the bodies of men for all public occasions and in preparing for ball games and war. The most common colors, in order of mention, were red, black, yellow, white, and blue. Figures were geometric but, at the same time, probably symbolic. The most famous warriors were tattooed from head to foot with mementos of their successful war exploits (Fig. 23). The most decorated article of clothing was the cloak, which was worn principally in winter.

The canoes which de Soto's expedition encountered on the Mississippi were said to have been painted in a variety of colors. The front posts of the council buildings in town squares were carved to represent snakes, alligators, and garfish, and the walls of such structures were painted with a great variety of animal, bird, and human figures some of which had animal heads and human bodies or vice versa. While some of these may have had totemic significance, others, like the opossum, were not venerated.

Wood carvings in the round of humans, animals, and birds were common in, on, and around the buildings in the central area of the towns, including the winter council house, the ossuary, and the four structures forming the square. Birds, especially the eagle, were perched on the tops of the buildings like weather cocks and were also housed inside. Human figures, life size or even larger, stood impressively at attention, some bearing arms. Alligators, serpents, and frogs were also carved in the round. Images were made even in stone, but averaged much smaller, probably owing to the difficulty of working that material. Many of these figures were not representations of gods or other important religious personalities, but seem to have been art for art's sake. Almost none of these carvings and paintings have survived to find their place in museums. The above descriptions are all from literary sources.

The one art which has survived into the twentieth century with comparatively little change is that of basket decoration. This was most elaborate on the lower Mississippi, and a number of specimens made by women of the Chitimacha tribe have found their way into museums. Baskets were decorated by plaiting and twilling in elements previously colored black, yellow, or red by vegetable dyes. Designs were all geometric but included a few curves along with the more common angled motifs. Some design elements bore unimaginative names, such as dots, crosses, and plaits, while others were given animal names.

Much Southeast pottery seems to have been undecorated, but decoration increased from about the beginning of the Christian era to the time of European contact. This was due in part to influence from Meso-America, which reached its peak at the time of European contact. The most common technique of pottery decoration was incising the soft surface before firing or engraving the hard surface of the finished pot after firing. Second to incising and engraving was the impressing of the unfired soft clay with a stamp on which the design had already been produced in the negative.

Effigies of people, animals, and even plants were commonly modeled on pottery vessels or pottery pipes, and sometimes non-utilitarian works of art took the form of effigies modeled in clay. Human beings appeared more often than any other figure in these effigies, but birds, mammals, reptiles, fishes, invertebrates' shells, gourds, and squashes were also used as motifs. Only a few of the pottery vessels recovered by archeologists in the Southeast were painted. Red seems to have been a common color; it was frequently associated with white, and was sometimes used against a buff background. Black on white was also employed, and all-black or all-brown vessels were not uncommon. Even the technique of negative painting was used.

Designs made by stamps, punches, and textiles were always geometric, but those incised or engraved on pots were occasionally naturalistic or at least recognizable conventionalizations of life forms. Painted designs were likewise predominantly geometric and only rarely naturalistic. Modeled effigies were either naturalistic forms or easily recognizable conventionalizations of naturalistic forms. Sometimes the head of an animal appeared at one end of an oval bowl, the tail at the other, while the profile appeared twice, once on each of the sides. A large number of vessels with long bottle necks have been found in the Southeast as well as a few pots possessing three legs or a stirrup neck. All three of these features are reminiscent of Meso-American forms. Geometric pottery designs in the Southeast exhibit many more curves than those in the Southwest, although curves are not lacking in the latter area. What the Southeast lacked in color, as compared to the Southwest, it made up for in its intricately engraved scrolls and other curvilinear designs (Griffin, 1952).

Sculpture in stone was much more developed in the Southeast than in the Southwest. Effigies of many kinds of animals, as well as humans, appeared on stone pipe bowls, beautifully wrought and polished to perfection. Stone statuettes of men up to two feet in height have been unearthed by archeologists in a few localities. The best examples of Southeast stone carving in the round compare favorably with those from Meso-America (Plates X–XIII) (Dockstader, 1966: Plates 19–54).

Elaborately engraved shell disks a few inches in diameter were worn on the body as chest ornaments. The combinations of life figures and geometric designs strongly suggest Meso-America again. A number of these ornaments depict a warrior with a knife in one hand and a severed enemy head in the other (Plate XIV), and eagles and snakes are common. Ornaments made from sheets of copper and mica are common in the graves of chiefs and other important persons (Kelemen, 1956: Plate 193). These reflect the same fundamental art style as other objects described above. The cold-hammering of copper, which was the only technique applied to this metal, is the highest achievement in metals north of Mexico.

Meso-America.—Meso-American art easily surpasses that of all other culture areas in both quality and quantity. With a population that exceeded that of all other culture areas combined, and with a large number of full-time artists and craftsmen, the quantity of art objects produced may have exceeded that of all other areas combined. Meso-American art was displayed in basketry, textiles, pottery, metal work, sculpture in stone and stucco, carving in jade and other precious stones, and in murals and manuscripts.

Weaving seems to have been a well-developed art, but few examples

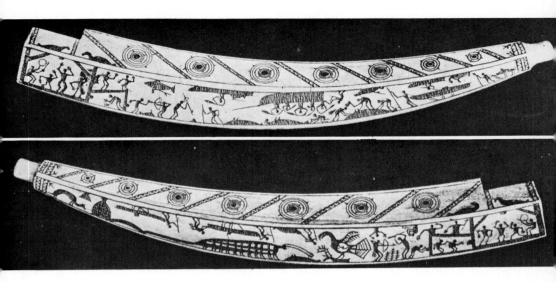

Plate I.—Eskimo ivory pipe stem. After W. J. Hoffman, 1897. Courtesy of the Smithsonian Institution, U.S. National Museum.

Plate II.—Eskimo ivory seal carved by the "Mystery People," buried city of Ipiutak, Alaska. Courtesy of the American Museum of Natural History.

Plate III.—Northwest Coast carved and painted wooden chest (Haida). Courtesy of the Washington State Museum (photo by Carroll Burroughs).

Plate IV.—Northwest Coast dance costume (Kwakiutl) representing an eagle. Courtesy of the Museum of the American Indian, Heye Foundation.

Plate V.—Northwest Coast mask (Kwakiutl) depicting a sculpin. The wearer covers his head with the hide at the bottom. Courtesy of the Washington State Museum.

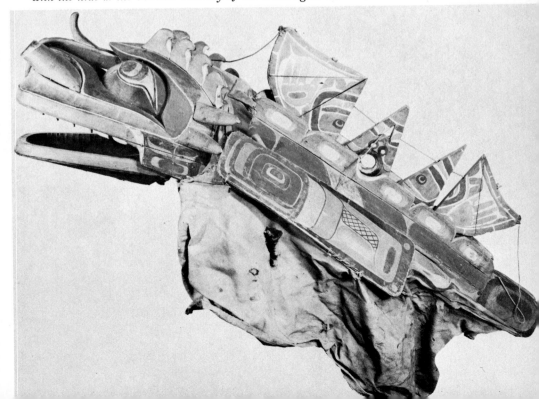

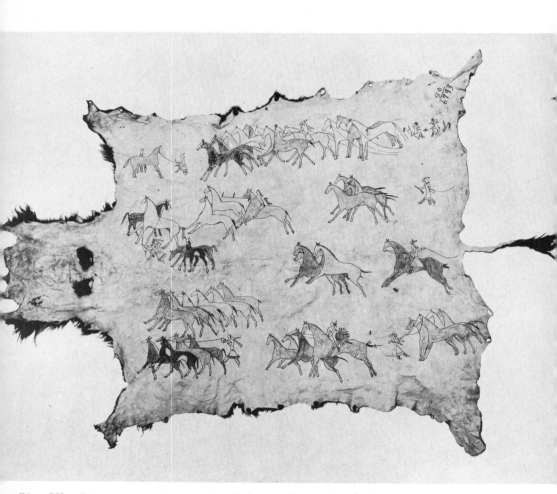

Plate VI.—Plains man's painting on buffalo robe (Oglala Sioux). Courtesy of the American Museum of Natural History.

Plate VII.—Plains woman's painting on buffalo robe (Dakota). Courtesy of the American Museum of Natural History.

Plate VIII.—Plains quill-decorated band for a man's blanket or robe (Blackfoot). Courtesy of the American Museum of Natural History.

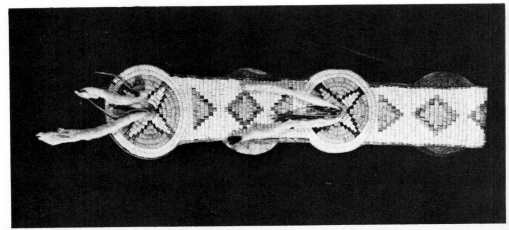

Plate IX.—Pueblo pottery vessels; left, *Tularosa black-on-white jar* (ca. A.D. *1100–1200*); right, *Reserve black-on-white duck effigy* (ca. A.D. *1000–1100*). *Courtesy of Paul S. Martin and the Chicago Natural History Museum.*

Plate X.—Eastern stone pipe from the Tremper Mound, Ohio. ($3\frac{7}{8}$ *inches long, $2\frac{1}{2}$ inches high.*) *Courtesy of the Ohio State Museum.*

Plate XI.—Eastern fluorspar figurine from Angel Mounds, Indiana. ($8\frac{3}{4}$ inches high.) Courtesy of Glenn A. Black and the Indiana Historical Society.

Plate XII.—Eastern stone pipe from the Adena Mound, southern Ohio. (8 inches high.) Courtesy of the Ohio State Museum.

Plate XIV.—Eastern shell gorget from Sumner County, Tennessee. (3⅞ inches in diameter.) Courtesy of the Museum of the American Indian, Heye Foundation.

Plate XV.—Meso-American naturalistic weaving designs. Modern Huipil from San Pedro Sacatepéquez, Guatemala. Photograph by Hilda Schmidt de Delgado; courtesy of the Museo Nacional de Etnología.

Plate XVI.—Meso-American sculptured pottery jar from San Augustin, Acasaguastlán, Guatemala. (7¼ inches high.) Courtesy of the Museum of the American Indian, Heye Foundation.

Plate XVII.—Meso-American pottery head from Vera Cruz, Mexico. (11 1/16 inches high, 10⅜ inches wide.) Courtesy of the Cleveland Museum of Art, I. H. Wade Collection.

Plate XVIII.—Meso-American pottery head from Vera Cruz, Mexico. (6 inches high.) Courtesy of the American Museum of Natural History.

Plate XIX.—Meso-American seated clay figure from Vera Cruz, Mexico. (13½ inches high.) Courtesy of the American Museum of Natural History.

Plate XX.—Meso-American baked clay figure from Chiapas, Mexico. (About 6 inches high.) Courtesy of the American Museum of Natural History.

Plate XXI.—Meso-American baked clay group of dancing women (Tarascan). (About 9 inches high.) Courtesy of Instituto Nacional de Antropología e Historia.

Plate XXII.—Meso-American sculpture in stone. Mayan stela from Copan, Honduras. Courtesy of the American Museum of Natural History.

Plate XXIII.—Meso-American metal work. Mixtec cast gold chest ornament depicting Jaguar-Knight as God of Death, from Monte Alban, Oaxaca, Mexico. ($4\frac{1}{2}$ inches high.) Courtesy of Instituto Nacional de Antropología e Historia.

Plate XXIV.—Meso-American manuscripts. Courtesy of Pál Kelemen.

Plate XXV.—Meso-American painting. Scene from Mayan temple at Bonampak, Chiapas, Mexico. Courtesy of Instituto Nacional de Antropología e Historia.

from pre-Columbian times exist today. Modern Guatemalan weaving designs are both stylizations of living forms and abstractions unrecognizable as life forms. In addition, the weaver often includes his own signature, initials, or other identifying trade mark. In O'Neale's (1945) illustrations of design motifs, abstract forms slightly outnumber conventionalized life forms. Abstract forms are mostly geometric, and some may be stylizations of former natural figures and therefore may possess symbolism. Bird representations are the most frequent and varied class of naturalistic designs, but figures of humans, other mammals, and plants are also numerous (Plate XV). The colors employed in decorative designs are more varied than in pre-Columbian times because of the wool and aniline dyes introduced since the Spanish Conquest; but the blood of the cochineal insect has been the chief source of red up until the past few decades.

Meso-American pottery easily surpasses that of any other North American area in its variety of shape and decoration. Polychrome painting, handles, legs, lids, and effigy forms burst forth in great profusion. What appear to be purely geometric patterns are present, but conventionalized symbols and definitely naturalistic forms are more frequent than in the Southwest and Southeast. The Maya made fresco vases on which they painted important personages clothed in the garments and decorated with the symbols of high rank. Some are seated on thrones, some ride in litters, and others walk or stand. Glyphs often accompany such pictures, presumably to explain what life drama is being enacted. In addition to painting, pottery vessels were decorated by incising, by engraving, and by relief which is deep enough to be called sculpture. Many naturalistic forms were modeled on vessels, often to represent important mythological deities, such as the eagle, the jaguar, and the plumed serpent; but the human figure, particularly the head, was the most common (Plate XVI). In addition to the many human figures appearing on pottery vessels as appendages, there were many human heads and statuettes made of baked clay and untold thousands of figurines of the same material (Plates XVII–XXI). The baked clay human figures of the Olmecs are the largest, sometimes attaining life size. The variety in posture and dress of these human figures is indeed great, and those which seem a bit crude, when compared to the treatment of the human body in the classical art of the Old World, may still possess a bold quality that commands attention. Meso-American pottery is amply illustrated in Kelemen's excellent work (1956: Plates 110–49).

Meso-American sculpture in stone is the most impressive work of its kind in the entire New World. It varied in size from figurines small enough to be held in the palm of the hand to the huge stone heads of the Olmecs which, without any body, are up to seven or eight feet in height and thirty tons in weight. Like the stone statues of the ancient Greeks, those of the Aztecs, Mayas, and their neighbors were lavishly painted in many colors, and, in association with architecture, created a striking spectacle. Kelemen (1956: 106–7) believes that none of these statues and relief carvings can be regarded as portraits of particular individuals; there is too much stylization and not enough attention to idiosyncratic detail for actual portraiture. But the fact that portraiture was not achieved does not mean it was not attempted. At any rate, the Maya sculptors featured the high-bridged convex nose, the receding chin, and the sloping forehead achieved in life by binding the head. The art styles approximated the different physical types in the various areas.

On Maya stelae, as on painted pottery, human and other figures carved in relief or modeled with stucco are often accompanied by glyphs, which give the date and apparently other explanatory data about the historic event being depicted. The dates are the only parts of the glyph writing that can be translated with any degree of certainty. In addition to the glyphs, other conventionalized designs were crowded around the principal figure or figures to fill all available space (Plate XXII). These huge monoliths, up to a height of thirty-five feet and a weight of fifty tons, were erected periodically to commemorate important dates and events associated with the ceremonial calendar. Each portrays the figure of a religious or political leader, well adorned with the regalia of his high office and surrounded with glyphs.

The metal work of Meso-America is known, from the archeological record, to have been largely derived from that of South America; yet the metal jewelry made by the Mixtecs and Zapotecs of Oaxaca is the most elaborate in the pre-Columbian New World. Therefore it developed its own idioms of expression. Jewelry, in the form of finger rings, bracelets, necklaces, lip plugs, chest ornaments, and masks, was beautifully designed and wrought (Plate XXIII).

A number of semiprecious stones were worked by Meso-American artists. The principal ones were jade, turquoise, rock crystal, serpentine, amber, onyx, jasper, and agate. Of these stones, jade was the most valuable in the eyes of the Meso-Americans, and their finest stonework was done with jade. When Montezuma saw how delighted the greedy Spaniards were with his gifts of gold, he promised them even more valuable presents the next day; he brought forth some of his best jade, only to find them disappointed with the "green stones." Jade jewelry was worn only by the nobility, in the form of bracelets, anklets, masks, figurines, and other ornaments, some of which were regarded as amulets possessing supernatural power. Jade was carved in the round and in relief, both in about equal proportions (Kelemen, 1956: Plates 253–54). The human figure, or some part of it, predominates over all other subjects.

The Meso-Americans also possessed books, or codices, in the making of which they displayed their art. The covers were of wood or hide, and the "pages" of dressed hide, inner bark, or paper made from the maguey plant. The "pages" were a continuous sheet of material, as much as 34 feet long, folded like a screen. The human figures, glyphs, and other symbols were painted in the same style as similar compositions on pottery, murals, and stone carvings. The profusion of color was great, Aztec glyphs alone being painted in red, blue, green, black, white, yellow, orange, brown, and purple. These books contained all the official codified religious lore of the societies they served. From them the tremendous round of ritual, all geared to the calendar, was taught to young men dedicated by their parents to the celibate life of the priest. Those outside the priesthood were not allowed to see these sacred books, and would have been unable to read them (Plate XXIV).

Similar human figures, glyphs, and other symbols were painted on the inside walls of temples and palaces, and were viewed only by the priests, their students dedicated to the priesthood, and the nobility. Some of the most famous of these murals were found at Bonampak ("painted walls") in Chiapas, Mexico, near the border of Guatemala. There, the inner walls of a Mayan temple are covered with a series of murals depicting a raid for prisoners and the subsequent sacrificial ceremony. Among these is a dramatic scene showing the arraignment of a group of captives before a group of chieftains standing above them on a platform (Plate XXV). The chieftains are elaborately arrayed in headdresses crowned with the heads of animals, including the jaguar; the highest-ranking chief, standing in the center, is wearing quetzal feathers on his head. This central figure is about 4 feet tall, including his plumes. The bodies of the chiefs are clothed in the skins of the jaguar or in body armor decorated according to their rank. In addition, all the chiefs carry weapons in their hands. Each of these chiefly figures differs in some details from all the others, emphasizing their individualities, which the artist does not submerge by exact repetition of costume or body posture. The captives, in contrast, crouch on a terrace below, wearing nothing but breechcloths. Some show blood dripping from their fingers, and in the left foreground are a head, a leg, and an arm from a dismembered body. Several of the captives crouch with upturned palms and eyes directed toward the head chief as if begging for mercy. The central captive, half reclining and with eyes closed, is painted with an unusual degree of naturalness and grace of line. Various chiefs and attendants occupy the lowest terrace. Although the figures of the chiefs above and in the rear are not reduced in size, one nevertheless gets some feeling of depth in this remarkable mural. On the whole the figures are less stiff and distorted than others produced by the Meso-Americans.

The wood of utilitarian objects, such as suits of armor, helmets, shields, canoe prows, lintels over doors, and the large cylindrical drums, was normally decorated by carving. Since wood decays rapidly in soil, few examples of wood carving are preserved in museums. Their quality and style, however, compare favorably with those of carvings in stone.

Stone mosaics, consisting of small pieces of precious stones set in wood or stone, were also made by Meso-Americans. A beautiful mosaic plaque composed of more than 3,000 bits of stone was found in the Temple of the Warriors at the famous Mayan site, Chichén Itzá, in Yucatán. The most common material used in mosaics was turquoise; but jade, other semiprecious stones, and shell were also employed.

An inventory of Meso-American art must include mention of the feather mosaics overlaid on cloaks, shields, and decorative objects. Feathers on cloaks were fastened to a cloth base, while those on shields were attached to the hide covering. Four different kinds and colors of feathers are arranged in horizontal bands around the neck and shoulders of a royal cloak, while on a shield the figure of a coyote is done principally in turquoise blue, with the belly, feet, and facial features set off in purple against a red background (Kelemen, 1956: Plates 286–87). Both the cloak and the shield were given by Montezuma to the king of Spain.

Although the art of the Aztecs, Mayas, Toltecs, Mixtecs, and Zapotecs is better known, that of the earlier Olmecs is, on the whole, subtler, gentler, freer, and more naturalistic than that of the others.

GENERAL REMARKS ON VISUAL ART

In this survey of American Indian art we have omitted entirely the curvilinear floral motifs incised, painted, and stamped on the birch bark of the Sub-Arctic, the unsymbolic but intricate basketry designs of California and the Great Basin, and other more localized art styles of aboriginal North America. Nevertheless, our inventory of the artistic achievement of the American Indian reveals a great variety of techniques and styles of expression. Although the innovation of the individual artist obtrudes here and there, most work in the visual arts conforms to localized styles which the specialist can recognize at a glance and allocate to the proper place or time level. Innovations are more often in small details than in totally new conceptions. Where we have the most archeological documentation, in the Southwest, we find a definite continuity between the art of adjacent time periods and of neighboring localities.

Until the past few decades, American Indian art has been given little attention by the art critics and connoisseurs of Europe and its derivative cultures. This has been due more to ignorance of native American art than to the culture-bound snobbery of some members of this group. Most examples of Indian art were destroyed by the Spanish and other European invaders. It was only after archeology came of age and implemented a program of field investigation that enough exciting specimens appeared in museums to attract modern artists and their camp followers. Although researchers on the American Indian are pleased at the present stampede of interest toward this art, they hope that most of the great and inimitable artistic achievements of the Indian will find their way into universities and public museums, where they can be seen by every interested person and studied by all qualified scholars.

REFERENCES

BUSHNELL, 1908; COVARRUBIAS, 1954; DOCKSTADER, 1964, 1966; DOUGLAS AND D'HARNONCOURT, 1941; DRUCKER, 1955; EWERS, 1939; GRIFFIN, 1952; HOFFMAN, 1897; HUNT, 1951; INVERARITY, 1950; KELEMEN, 1956; KENT, 1957; DE LAGUNA, 1932–33; LORM, 1945; LOWIE, 1954; MERA, 1937, 1939; MORRIS AND BURGH, 1941; O'NEALE, 1945; ROEDIGER, 1941; RUPPERT, THOMPSON, AND PROSKOURIAKOFF, 1955; STEVENSON, 1904; SWANTON, 1909, 1911; TANNER, 1957.

12

Music and Dance
By Wilhelmine Driver

Nᴏʀᴛʜ American Indian music, like other aspects of Indian culture, exhibits great variety. It is far from conforming to the usual stereotype in the mind of the general reader. The average intelligent listener, if asked to describe American Indian music, would mention the prevalence of drums and rattles and the harshness of the singing tone. A student of ethnomusicology would go into more detail concerning musical instruments. He might also describe the technique of voice production in terms of great tension in the vocal organs, strong accents, and pulsations of intensity on the longer notes. If he attempted to analyze the actual melodies, he might characterize them as predominantly descending from higher to lower pitch, either in a gradual progression or "terraced" or "cascading" downward.

All of these features were formerly thought to make up the general type of North American Indian music, following the analysis by E. M. von Hornbostel. They can, in fact, be found in a number of areas, but only in the Plains, Prairies, and Southwest are all of them present in the majority of songs. Early collectors obtained more music from these areas than elsewhere, and scholars like Hornbostel assumed that these samples were representative of the whole continent.

Nowadays, on the basis of wider and more thorough research, it is possible to make more valid generalizations about North American Indian music as a whole. It consists, for the most part, of songs, which may last (including repetitions) from about twenty seconds to about three minutes. Larger forms, where they exist, are produced by stringing together a series of brief songs. In most areas, the range of the melodies lies between a fifth (e.g., C to G) and a twelfth (e.g., C to G an octave higher). Melodic patterns vary, but among the most common are pentatonic tunes and melodies consisting of chains of major and/or minor thirds. Most of the intervals of the samples studied by Nettl (1954) approximate, he says, those of the Western tempered scale. This resemblance may, however, be partially due to European influences in the music which has been recorded or to faulty notation. Nearly all songs are monophonic, consisting of only a single melody—that is, at a given moment only one pitch is sounded. In some areas, women sing along with the men, but in the higher octave. Melodic polyphony (the simultaneous singing of two or more rather independent melodic lines) is practically absent, except for some occurrance of the "drone" type, in which a melody is accompanied by sustained notes on a single pitch. Harmony is absent, except in modern hymns sung by Christian congregations.

Consistent measure or bar lengths are apparently less common than uneven bar lengths and asymmetrical rhythmic patterns. Rhythms are, in general, relatively complex. Songs in most areas are strophic. A strophe consists of between two and twelve separate sections or phrases; these last several seconds each and are often of unequal length within an individual song, tending also to become longer toward the end of the song.

Song texts very frequently consist entirely or partly of meaningless syllables. Texts may also include archaic words or phrases, loanwords, or special phonetic alterations. These devices, in certain areas, make the song text style rather different from the spoken prose style, and tend to obscure the meaning.

Instruments are used mainly as rhythmic accompaniment to singing; there is very little purely instrumental music. Before European contact, chordophones (stringed instruments) were unknown, with the possible exception of a hunting bow used as a rhythm instrument. In most of the continent, the only melodic instruments were flutes or flageolets, usually played by young men for courting or love charms. Flute melodies might also be sung, but simultaneous combination of two or more flutes, or of flute and voice, was unknown. Other aerophones (wind instruments) include whistles and, in a few areas, simple trumpets or reed instruments. Most widely distributed are the percussion instruments. Of these, the idiophones are represented by several varieties of rattles, musical rasps, sticks beaten together, and beaten planks, rods, and slit drums. Membranophones (drums with skin heads) are also widely used.

American Indian music is, for the most part, functional—that is, used as an integral part of other, nonmusical activities. It is indispensable to all rituals and ceremonies. Since most of these are performed by men, it is men who predominate in music making. Men lead the singing, and compose or learn the ritual songs; they also make and play the instruments. The fact that women in North America are relegated mainly to a passive role in ritual may account, to some extent, for the lack of polyphonic music. Songs are also interspersed in tales, though true narrative songs are rare. There are special gambling songs and songs for other games as well. Dances of all sorts are accompanied by singing and percussion instruments. Marching songs, however, were absent in North America, except possibly in Meso-America, before the Spanish Conquest. Work songs lighten such labor as rowing, farming, or corn-grinding. Women sing various types of songs, including of course lullabies. Both group and solo singing are common everywhere. In some areas, certain songs are individually owned as property which can be inherited or even sold. Songs may also be used for lovemaking, for ridicule, or for boasting.

Music is valued principally for its magical or personal power rather than for its aesthetic component. If well performed, it is "good" rather than beautiful. Not all music, however, is functional; some of it is produced simply for the pleasure of making music, individually or in groups.

Music has attained its most complex development on the Northwest Coast, in the Southwest, Meso-America, and possibly the Southeast. It is in these areas that we find the most complex musical styles and forms, theories about types and origins of songs, some musical instruction, and musical specialists or semiprofessionals.

The comparative study of North American Indian music is not yet advanced enough to permit a satisfactory division of the entire continent into musical areas. Three significant attempts have been published so far: the first a brief survey by George Herzog in 1928; the second, stressing the distribution of musical instruments, by Helen Roberts in 1936; the most recent, based on technical aspects of musical style, by Bruno Nettl in 1954. Since none of these presents a comprehensive picture, we shall rest content in this volume with a brief nontechnical description of the music of several of the major culture areas. More detailed discussion of such technical matters as melodic contour, intervals, and rhythmic patterns may be found in the sources listed in the references at the end of this chapter.

Dancing, with vocal and instrumental accompaniment, plays an essential role in religious, agricultural, hunting, war and curing ceremonies; life cycle rituals, such as puberty and funeral rites; and many other cultural and social activities. For ceremonial dances, symbolic costumes, headdresses, masks, and other accessories, as well as face and body painting, are often required.

Styles in men's dancing vary widely according to area, and dance areas do not always coincide with those of music. For group dancing, choreographic ground plans and steps show three principal types which can be mapped. One region, following roughly the areas of aboriginal farming, extends over a lopsided Y shape, with its stem in Meso-America, the shorter arm in the Southwest, and the longer arm through the Eastern Woodland and north to Labrador. In this region, the dancers form an open-ended circle or ellipse, and proceed counter-clockwise, usually facing forward, though occasionally facing a focal object or person in the center. Spirals and serpentine lines are also seen. Though some leaping dances occur, especially in Meso-America and the Southwest, the usual step is an earthbound stomp with the right foot, followed by the left pulling up beside it. A second region, of clockwise motion in a closed circle, with the dancers more often facing the center, occupies the Plains and much of the Great Basin and Plateau. It also overlaps the former region as far east as Lake Michigan and spills over into some of the Southwest. Many of the dances are light-footed, with dynamic bodily motion, arm waving, and often virtuoso leaps. In earthbound dances, the left foot leads. A third type, dancing in single or parallel straight lines, occurs mainly in the western Plains, Great Basin, and Plateau, extending also to the Navaho, Apache, and a few other Southwestern tribes, but appears sporadically in other areas. In "back and forth" dancing, parallel lines face each other, the two lines alternately meeting and receding. All three ground plans are found in California.

Women take part in many of the group dances, though they are excluded from some special male ritual dances; they also have dances for their own female societies and rites. Their dancing shows less areal variation than the men's. They usually share in the quieter communal dances, and their style is decorous, with small steps and arms close to the body. In traditional Indian dances, men and women rarely dance together in couples. Some solo dances are found everywhere. They are at least as common as group dances in the Plains and westward, and are dominant on the Northwest Coast and in the Arctic.

Arctic.—The Eskimo singing technique is characterized by considerable vocal tension and rhythmic pulsations on the longer notes. Accents and stressed grace notes are common. In most of the Arctic, however, these features are less intense than in Plains or Southwest

music. Melodies are undulating in contour. Antiphonal singing, with
alternation of solo and chorus, occurs, but melodic polyphony is
unknown.

Eskimo songs are usually in slow tempo. Rhythms tend to be asymmetrical and complex. Most of the songs are accompanied by the beating of drums or of a part of the body. In some areas, this is in indefinite
rhythmic patterns, producing a complex rhythmic polyphony between
voice and accompaniment. The drums are of the tambourine type, a
single hide stretched over a hoop—that is, a disk-shaped variety of
single-headed drum. This type of drum was probably derived from
Asia. Rattles, flutes, and whistles are absent in the Arctic.

Music in the Arctic serves chiefly religious purposes. Shamans deliver incantations to the spirits for good weather, success in hunting,
health, and the like. Individuals own, inherit and buy charms, including magical songs. Disputes are sometimes conducted in song. Two
men, instead of fighting, may compete with each other in songs of ridicule, with the audience acting as an informal court. There are no professional music specialists, though shamans approach that status.
Certain individuals, however, are considered particularly good
singers, and some of these evince great love of music and devotion to
their art.

Eskimo dances are of two kinds: ceremonial and pantomime. The
first are performed in a prescribed manner, with the men jumping
violently, and the women merely swaying gracefully. Pantomime
dances can be improvised, and the principal actor is often accompanied by a chorus of men, women, or both. Many dances involve animal or bird impersonations, and some, especially of shamans, spirit
possession.

Northwest Coast.—The musical style of the Northwest Coast is
more complex than that of the Arctic, and includes both tense and
relaxed vocal techniques. Melodic contours are undulating or descending. Here, in addition to some antiphonal singing, we find a few
instances of the drone type of melodic polyphony, one voice sustaining
a single tone while another sings a moving melody. Rhythmic polyphony between the melody and the percussion accompaniment is
often intricate.

Percussion instruments include clappers made of split sticks, "foot
drums" consisting of a plank over a pit in the floor, and rattles. The
rattles are of the container type, filled with small pebbles, and are
made chiefly of wood, often carved in bird or animal form. Logs,

planks, or boxes are beaten. The tambourine was acquired in the nineteenth century. Here we also find wind instruments. True flutes are rare, but single-note whistles occur. The Northwest Coast is one of the few areas in which reed instruments, on the order of very simple clarinets and oboes, were played by some tribes. They reached their most elaborate development in this area, and included tubes with single, multiple, or ribbon reeds, but without finger holes. These instruments may have been derived, in part, from Asia in recent times.

Here also the principal function of music is religious. Individuals, both men and women, own songs as property which may be inherited or sold, and many of these songs are correlated with their individual spirit dances. There are no strictly professional musicians, but music is taught and rehearsed and musical errors may be punished. A fairly well-developed musical terminology exists here.

In Northwest Coast winter ceremonies, individuals of either sex, one at a time, dance around a central fire. The dancer, first singing his personal song, soon accompanied by a group of musicians, enters a trancelike state, and then proceeds to imitate the actions of the spirit by whom he is "possessed." Mimetic animal and bird dances, with appropriate masks and costumes, were common in the past.

Great Basin.—Among the simplest musical styles on the continent are those of this area and of the Modoc and Klamath on the Oregon-California border. The singing technique is smooth, without vocal tension or pulsation. The range of the melodies is usually small. Many of the songs are performed without any percussive accompaniment.

Percussion instruments include drums, rattles, and musical rasps. The only kind of drum was the tambourine, which was derived from the Plains and Plateau area in the nineteenth century. Both container rattles, made of rawhide filled with pebbles, and jingler rattles, usually made of deer hooves, were common. The musical rasp, a notched stick a couple of feet long, rubbed back and forth with a smaller stick, was much used in the Great Basin. In the twentieth century, two instruments have spread to this area from the Plains with the Peyote religion: the gourd rattle and the kettledrum. The latter consists of a hide stretched over a pottery vessel partly filled with water.

Other instruments include whistles, true flutes capable of producing a melody, and the musical bow. The last-named is the only stringed instrument which may possibly be pre-Columbian in North America. In its simplest form, it consists merely of a hunting bow, of which one end is held between the teeth; the string is struck with a stick. The pitch and quality of the sound are varied by the player's changing the shape of his mouth, which serves as a resonator. The tone is feeble and the range so limited that the instrument sounds more percussive than tonal. It is used more often for musical doodling than for a more serious effort.

Music has both religious and nonreligious uses in the Great Basin area. Because the peoples of the Great Basin and the Plateau lacked organized religious societies, formal cult dances did not occur in these areas. A few of the nonreligious uses of music include songs in animal tales, songs connected with gambling games, and lullabies. For these three purposes, very simple music is widespread, and is thought by Herzog to represent archaic layers in North American Indian music.

California.—Little research has been done on the music of this area, but, except for that of a few of the northern California groups, it seems to be best represented by that of the Yuman-speaking peoples of Arizona and California. The vocal technique is smooth and relaxed, like that of the Great Basin. The Yuman melodies contain a section of higher pitch, called the "rise", somewhere in the body of the song. Percussion instruments provide a brief introduction and conclusion for the song as well as rhythmic accompaniment. In the "rise" section, the instruments often play tremolo.

Rhythm instruments in California include foot drums, baskets beaten or scraped, split-stick clappers, musical rasps, and rattles. The tambourine was introduced here in the nineteenth century. Container rattles are made of gourds, turtle shells, or cocoons filled with pebbles. Deer-hoof jingler rattles are also common. Wind instruments include flutes, tubes with reeds, and whistles. Two whistles are sometimes bound together to produce a two-tone instrument. Most of the Yuman songs are organized into long series with a set order of songs. The religious function of music is important in California, as elsewhere in North America. Dance styles are eclectic, including features from neighboring areas. Some formal cult dances formerly occurred, especially in connection with puberty rites; individual spirit-impersonation dances, resembling those of the Northwest Coast, have been reported for northern California.

Plains-Prairies.—This musical area includes the Plains, the Prairies, and the western Great Lakes region. Its singing technique is characterized by loudness, great vocal tension, strong accents, glissandos, and heavy pulsation on the long tones. These vocal practices tend to produce fluctuating pitch or intonation. Melodies cover an average range of a tenth, but may even exceed two octaves. Melodic contours are mainly descending, of the terraced or cascading type, in which each section is lower in pitch than the preceding section. Song rhythms are usually complex and asymmetrical. The most common rhythmic accompaniment, however, consists of regular pulse beating. Songs are usually introduced and concluded by drum beats or rattle tremolos. The great majority of songs have instrumental accompaniment.

Percussive instruments include the tambourine and a few double-headed hide drums which may be of modern introduction. The pottery kettledrum spread through this area with the Peyote religion in the late nineteenth and twentieth centuries. Pieces of rawhide were sometimes scraped to provide rhythmic accompaniment, and musical rasps made of wood and, less often, of bone were also used. Rattles include animal-hoof jingler rattles and container rattles made of rawhide filled with pebbles. Gourd rattles probably diffused to the Plains from the adjoining farming areas. The musical bow is absent in this area. Wind instruments include one-note whistles, flageolets, and true flutes. The latter are played principally by youths courting their ladyloves, and are not used in ceremonies.

Most of the Plains music is functional, and a large proportion of it is connected with dancing. Men's war and hunting dances are conspicuous in this area, and their eagle-feather ritual warbonnets have spread to many other tribes in recent times. Both performers and audience are predominantly masculine, since much music serves such male activities as religious ritual, cult societies, warfare, military and other sodalities, curing ceremonies, gambling, the vision quest, and serenading. Women's sodalities, however, also have music. Music is also used for entertainment, in social dancing, games, and storytelling, and for education in the form of story-songs. Women of course sing lullabies to their children.

There are no professional musicians, but there is some informal specialization. In large group activities, usually a few individuals—medicine men or song leaders—perform the music while the others listen. Plains Indians have few theories about music and little musical terminology. However, boys' vision-quest songs are thought to be given by the spirits.

Songs may be owned, sold, or inherited. They may be individual property, such as those pertaining to a medicine bundle, or may be owned by a social group, such as a sodality.

Throughout the Plains, four types of music differ radically, in both singing and instruments, from the characteristic Plains style. Two of these result from diffusion in modern times: the 1890 Ghost Dance music from the Great Basin, and the Peyote cult music from the south and southwest. The third type—for lullabies, animal-tale songs, and some gambling songs—is of the archaic style mentioned above. The fourth—for love songs—is probably also the result of diffusion.

Southwest.—In this area, we find three principal musical styles, represented here by the Pueblos, the Pima-Papagos, and the Navahos. In the Pueblo style, the vocal technique resembles closely that of the Plains, except that many of the Pueblo Kachina songs begin at a very low pitch. Melodies are also of the Plains style, though much more complex and of greater range. Rhythmic accompaniments range from steady beats to definite rhythmic designs coordinated with those of the melody. Pueblo musical style is the most complex in North America in post-Columbian times.

Pima-Papago musical style combines Pueblo with California-Yuman musical traits. The singing technique is smooth and relaxed. Melodies seldom exceed an octave in range. Rhythms and melodic patterns are comparatively simple. Melodies are mainly descending, but the terraced or cascading contours of the Plains and Pueblo songs are not common. The Pima-Papago style appears among the Pueblos in the women's corn-grinding songs.

Much of the Navaho ritual music has been learned, with the rituals, from the Pueblos. However, the basic musical style of the Navahos and their linguistic relatives, the Apaches, seems to be connected with that of areas farther northwest. The vocal technique resembles that of the Pueblos and Plains. Melodies cover a fairly wide range, and are often arc-shaped in contour. Large intervals, with almost acrobatic jumps from low to high notes, sometimes occur and phrases in falsetto and normal male voice may alternate. Rhythms are simpler than those of Pueblo music, and the accompaniments are usually even, pulsating beats. The songs of the Peyote cult, wherever it is found in the United States, are somewhat similar in musical style to those of the Navahos and Apaches. Peyote songs have usually, however, a smoother singing technique, more like that of the Great Basin or of European folk singing.

In the Southwest as a whole, a wide variety of instruments is used. Drums include double-headed hide drums, which may be comparatively modern, pottery kettledrums, and "foot drums" consisting of a plank over a pit. Baskets are also beaten, and musical rasps are used. Rattles made from the domesticated gourd, filled with pebbles or seeds, are used here, as in all other farming areas. Other container rattles include turtle shells and sections of hollow horn. Handled pottery rattles contain stones, seeds, or clay pellets. Rattling material was also built into hollow parts of pottery vessels, and a few "sleigh bells" of pottery with rattling pottery pellets have been reported. These "sleigh bells" may have been imitations of the copper ones which were traded to the Southwest from Meso-America. Animal-hoof jingler rattles are also used. In the Southwest, the musical bow is employed in some religious rituals, a usage unique to this area. Whistles are common, and tubes with ribbon reeds are found in some tribes. True flutes are played not only for lovemaking but also in sacred ceremonies.

All of the uses of music on the Plains, by individuals and by groups, have their parallels in the Southwest. In addition, there are work songs—the corn-grinding songs of the Pueblos. Southwestern music is, however, predominantly religious. Even the gambling songs of the Navaho are used to contact spiritual power. The most striking difference in musical function between the two major areas, however, reflects the contrasts between the natures of the sodalities. Whereas the social groups of the Plains are usually loosely organized and are formed for a variety of purposes, some being merely social clubs for entertainment, those of the Pueblos consist of permanent cult groups with complex religious ceremonial. Ritual music must of course meet the needs of these ceremonies. Therefore songs are organized into set, invariable series, from short suites of a few songs to elaborate song cycles to accompany ceremonies lasting several days.

Such song series are usual also among the Pima-Papagos, as, for instance, in the harvest festival, and in Navaho curing ceremonies, such as the Night Chant or the Enemy Way. Since any mistake or omission in performance may invalidate the entire ceremony, the ritual leaders may have to spend months in learning a single song cycle. Certain cult group officials are, therefore, also music specialists. Among the Navaho, where permanent cult organizations are lacking and where groups are formed for specific curing ceremonies, we find semiprofessional singers. A young Navaho Singer pays a tuition fee to the older Singer who teaches him the text and music of one of the longer ceremonial song cycles as well as all the accompanying lore of the ceremony. To learn and be able to perform several such cycles is the accomplishment of a lifetime.

The texts of these chants are often obscure to the audience, though better understood by the performers and by the older men. Among the Pima-Papago, phonemes may undergo changes from speech to song, *b* becoming *m* or *mw*, *d* becoming *n*, and so on. Archaic religious words, or words borrowed from another language, are frequent and are sometimes described as "old language."

In the Southwest, there is little interest in theories about music. The Pima-Papagos, however, distinguish between "picked-up" songs learned from other tribes or from White people, "dreamt" songs obtained from the spirits, and songs "given in the beginning"—that is, dating from the creation of the earth. To the Navaho, on the contrary, all songs were "given in the beginning," even those which they are known to have learned from the Pueblos.

Among the Pueblo farmers of the arid Southwest, rain-making ceremonies are of prime importance. As many as two hundred dancers, bedecked with turquoise and silver jewelry, handsome costumes, and pine boughs, participate in dances lasting several days. Of these ceremonies, the Hopi Snake Dances are particularly famous. War dances are absent among the Hopi and the Pima-Papago, who consider killing criminal, even in war. Navaho dances include both Pueblo and Plains features, and function nowadays mainly in curing ceremonies. Apache ceremonial dances center on girls' puberty rites.

East.—Information about the music of this culture area is derived partially from recordings in the past fifty or sixty years and partially from descriptions by early writers and travelers. The modern musical style is fairly consistent throughout the area. Its singing technique has a moderate amount of vocal tension and pulsations. Melodic contours are mainly undulating and gradually descending. Song series consist of 6 or 8 or fewer songs performed in fixed cycles. Rhythms are fairly simple. Rhythmic accompaniment, when present, is usually a steady beat, though rattle tremolos are also used. The most distinctive feature of this area is antiphonal singing, between two individuals or between leader and group. This, by overlapping the end of one phrase with the beginning of the next, may give rise to some rudimentary polyphony. Early writers reported polyphony of the round or canon type as well as drone polyphony.

Percussion instruments include the tambourine, the double-headed hide drum (which may be modern), and pottery and wooden kettledrums. Container rattles were made of gourds, turtle shells, hollow horn, or—around the Great Lakes—of cylinders of bark. Deer-hoof jingler rattles were also common. Musical rasps were used, but the musical bow is not reported for the area. Whistles were common, and some tribes played tubes with reeds.

True flutes were used on official occasions and in sacred ceremonies. For instance, de Soto encountered chiefs and other high-ranking officials in Florida playing cane flutes as a sign of peace and goodwill on greeting him. In the Southeast, trumpets like those of Meso-America and the Caribbean, made of marine conch shells, were used as bugles in war. The presence of music specialists seems likely on the Southeastern coastal plain, where hereditary kings and full-time priests were the rule in the most complex societies. The music associated with religious ceremonies was an important part of the knowledge of these priests, who taught it to the students in the schools for priests.

Outstanding in the Eastern Woodland are calendrical, first-fruits, and agricultural dances, especially those of the Green Corn ceremony. Ritual dances among the Iroquois serve to give thanks to the gods, animals, and plants for their generosity to mankind. Women represent corn, beans, and squash in group dances. Notable also are the Iroquois men's Buffalo, Eagle, and other mimetic animal dances, and the masks used by the Falseface societies.

Meso-America.—Most of the aboriginal music of this area was destroyed by the conquering Spaniards, who were fully aware of its powerful religious influence. The Spanish priests, in Mexico at least, immediately taught their converts the ritual of the Catholic Church, and soon the Latin singing of some of the Indian choirs compared favorably with that of Spain. Indians also adopted Spanish popular songs and dances and the use of the mandolin, guitar, and other European instruments. It is therefore impossible to know much about the native folk music of Meso-America. Mexican musicologists and composers, exploring remote areas in search of native music, have recovered only traces of aboriginal melodies and instruments.

Considerable historical evidence is available, however, for the music of the Aztec ruling class. Powerful chiefs employed singers to compose ballads about their military exploits, and Montezuma had an orchestra play at all his meals. Most of the Aztec music was, however, connected with religious ceremonies. All official and ritual music was performed by members of a professional caste, which was highly trained because perfect performance was required; since any error was thought to disturb the cosmic order, mistakes might incur the penalty of death. Musical notation was lacking, so that musicians needed prodigious memories. Special pieces were composed and carefully rehearsed for each of the 260 days of the religious cycle, and creativity in composition was prized. Since most Aztec music was concerted rather than solo, names of individual musicians were not recorded, though the expert singers and players had high social prestige.

The Aztecs used a wide variety of instruments, many of them unknown north of Mexico. They had tubular trumpets, often more than two feet long, made of clay, wood, or cane, sometimes with a gourd added as resonator. Conch-shell trumpets, on which could easily be played the third, fourth, fifth, sixth, or eighth harmonics—that is, the components of a major chord—functioned as war bugles. Flutes, of bone, reed, or clay, had up to five holes, and played an important part in official and religious ceremonies. Among the many sorts of idiophones were several which could produce melodies. A musical rasp, of notched bone, furnished funeral music which even the Spanish conquerors considered "very doleful." A barrel-shaped wooden slit-drum, the *teponaztli*, played with rubber-tipped mallets, had from two to five tongues, each producing a different pitch. By using two or more *teponaztli*, elaborate melodies could be performed. Membranophones (true drums) were also carefully tuned. The Aztec orchestra must have provided considerable melodic, and perhaps even harmonic, display. Panpipes, which occurred farther south in Meso-America, were probably lacking in Aztec music.

In the great Aztec ceremonies and secular festivals, thousands of dancers participated. These were accompanied by singing, often antiphonal, and the full orchestral array. Costumes, especially of the principal dancers, were brilliantly colored and richly ornamented with gold, jewels, feathers, and flowers. Special dances were performed by groups of priests, nobles, merchants, sacrificial victims and their attendants, actors, buffoons, and acrobats. The *volador*, a "flying" dance performed by men attached by ropes to a pole, survives today, but was formerly associated with shooting arrows at a crucified victim.

Mayan dances, known to us from statues, frescoes, and early Spanish descriptions, were equally elaborate, and included highly stylized body and hand positions unknown farther north. Though very little information exists about ancient Mayan music, we may assume that it had attained a complexity commensurate with that of other aspects of Mayan artistic development.

REFERENCES

BARBEAU, n.d.; DENSMORE, 1926; DRIVER, 1953*b*; DRIVER AND RIESENBERG, 1950; HERZOG, 1928*a*, 1928*b*, 1934, 1935*a*, 1935*b*, 1936, 1938, 1949; IZIKOWITZ, 1935; KURATH, 1953, 1966, 1968; KURATH AND MARTÍ, 1964; MCALLESTER, 1954; MERRIAM, 1964, 1967; NETTL, 1954; ROBERTS, 1936; SAHAGÚN (ANDERSON AND DIBBLE), 1950–58; ROBERT STEVENSON, 1952.

13

Exchange and Trade

IN the discussion of craft specialization in Chapter 10, it was pointed out that such specialization must be accompanied by the exchange of surplus goods, at least within a single community. If each family lived in isolation, there would be no point in producing a surplus, because there would be nobody else with whom to exchange it for some other desirable product. Probably every family in aboriginal North America exchanged something of value with another family at least a few times a year. There is no record of any culture in which the nuclear family, consisting of parents and children, was the only social group. Each family had some contact with other families and was combined in some way to form a larger social grouping at some season of the year.

GIFT AND CEREMONIAL EXCHANGE

The process of distribution in nonindustrial societies may be inextricably blended with facets of culture ordinarily not regarded as economic. There is a wide range of exchange behavior, varying all the way from informal giving to a friend to elaborately stylized reciprocal exchange by large groups of kindred. Practically every major North American Indian ceremony is accompanied by feasting, which is a form of distribution. For example, the rites performed for an individual at birth, puberty, marriage, and death are often of this character. There is usually a host group, consisting of the relatives of thc individual for whom the rite is performed, as well as a guest group of nonrelatives who have been invited to attend the celebration. The hosts provide the guests with food as long as the ceremony lasts, which may be for days. Then at some later date the roles are reversed — the guests become hosts, and the hosts become guests.

Probably the one occasion on which gifts were most often exchanged was that of marriage. Among the majority of North American tribes, the families of the bride and groom exchanged gifts. While it is true that the amount of goods "paid" by the groom's relatives for the bride was sometimes negotiated in a businesslike way, this practice was characteristic only of the Northwest Coast, although occurrences in other areas have been reported. Even on the Northwest Coast, the bride's family was expected to make reciprocal gifts. The strong bride-purchase ideas of the northern Plains in the nineteenth century were at least partly the result of White contact and the fur trade, which placed a premium on women skin dressers.

The most elaborate ceremonial exchange of economic goods was that of the famous potlatch of the Northwest Coast Indians of British Columbia and southeastern Alaska. A potlatch could be given only by a chief and the people of his local group, who acted as hosts to another chief and his following. Sometimes the guests consisted of multiple chiefs and their followings. The potlatch proper was the formal distribution of gifts from the host to the guests, but it was always preceded by a feast. The purpose of both the feast and the potlatch was to announce a change of status of an individual. This might be the birth of a future heir to a high position, the marriage of an important person, the formal assumption of an important position by an heir at his maturity, or the restoration of a person to free status by paying a ransom after he had been enslaved by an enemy tribelet. An heir to an important position could not exercise the authority of the position, enact the associated rituals, sing the songs, or wear the crests on his clothing until his right to exercise these privileges was validated by a potlatch. The gifts at the potlatch were distributed by the host chief but in the name of the person, normally a relative, whose status was being established. Privileges validated at potlatches included the right to manage a household or village and the productive real estate where food and other necessities were obtained by the occupants, who were also a kinship group. The authority to exercise control over the entire wealth of the society had to be validated by potlatches, which included long speeches reciting the mythical or actual origin of ownership or property, both corporeal and incorporeal.

When two men were equally eligible to inherit a prominent position from a deceased ancestor, a series of rivalry potlatches might result. One man would give the first potlatch, with a long speech about his claim, and later the other would give another to assert his rival claim. These were more frequent after White contact, and included destruction of material property by breaking and burning and, before Whites put a stop to it, even the killing of a slave. Each man was trying to "break" his rival financially.

It is important to distinguish a person's formal status, which was hereditary and could not be enhanced by lavish gift giving, from his reputation as a party giver, which was subject to rise and fall. Thus in native theory, heredity was more important than material wealth, even though the latter was also highly valued. While a guest chief was obligated to reciprocate in the future by giving a return gift of equal or a little greater value to the host chief when their roles were reversed, there was no fixed rate of "interest" and the gifts were not regarded as commercial loans. When commercial loans were made—and they were common in the historic period—interest up to 100 per cent might be charged for a long-term loan of several years; but such a transaction was independent of the potlatch, except that the leader had the right to demand repayment if he was planning to give a potlatch in the near future.

In order of their rank, the host seated his guests, served them food, and presented them with gifts to take home. The value of the gift was also correlated with rank; the more important one's rank, the more expensive the gift he received. The result was that every time a potlatch was given, all who attended were ranked in a series from high to low and everyone saw exactly how everyone else was rated by the host.

The potlatch of the Kwakiutl Indians of British Columbia was probably the most ostentatious and dramatic of all in the historic period, and has been studied in most detail. There were altogether 658 titles or positions in all the 13 local subdivisions of the Kwakiutl. The translations of the names of some of these positions are: "creating trouble all around," "giving wealth," "throwing away property," "about whose property people talk," "envied," "satiating," "getting too great."

Kwakiutl material possessions did show a phenomenal increase in the historic period, which surpassed anything of the kind in pre-European times, and made possible the giving away of large quantities of goods. The maximum number of each material item exchanged at any single Kwakiutl potlatch from 1729 to 1936 will give an idea of the immensity of some of these affairs: 6 slaves, 54 dressed elk skins, 8 canoes, 3 coppers, 2,000 silver bracelets, 7,000 brass bracelets, 33,000 blankets. As many as 50 seals were eaten at the accompanying feast.

Anthropologists in the past have attempted to justify the potlatch by saying that it was a legitimate form of investment analogous to life insurance. A more recent and convincing justification, however, is that it became a substitute for physical violence. Disputes or rivalries which would have led to feuds a century or more ago were settled by potlatching in later times. This change was due in part to the firm stand of the Canadian government, which on one occasion burned an entire village as punishment for the killing of a war captive in connection with a winter ceremonial. Regardless of the cause of the change, the destruction of property is to be preferred to the loss of lives, and the outlet for aggressions provided by the potlatch made it desirable, at least in the stage of transition from aboriginal to Canadian culture.

TRADE

Trade was engaged in to some extent by all but one North American local group or tribe. This exception is the Polar Eskimos, who had no contact with other tribes and who thought they were the only people on earth when discovered by John Ross in 1818. Every tribe but this one possessed at least some objects which could not be obtained locally but which had to be obtained in trade from the outside. Data on trade are of theoretical importance because they demonstrate the process of diffusion, which is so powerful a determiner of cultural growth. We need not speculate how customs or ideas traveled from one tribe to another when we realize that every locality had some contact with the outside through trade.

Transportation was a daily problem for all Indians, whether it involved a group of men with trade goods to be taken hundreds of miles or a single woman carrying home the food she had gathered within a few miles' radius during a single day. The greatest amount of tonnage was carried on the backs of human beings, mainly because of the absence of suitable beasts of burden. Back packing was universal in aboriginal North America, and was the principal method known to the most heavily populated area, Meso-America. Although dugout canoes and balsas were also known in this area, they dominated human carrying only on lakes and on the coasts. In the Southwest, Northeast Mexico, and the Great Basin, the picture is about the same, with the human back being relieved only occasionally by balsas and log rafts, which were makeshift structures hastily assembled from whatever materials were at hand and abandoned as soon as a stream was crossed. Women consistently carried heavier loads than men, except in Meso-America, where specialized male craftsmen usually carried their own wares to market. While this may seem inequitable, it must be remembered that much travel was in search of food and that a man had to be prepared at any moment to pursue game as well as to defend his family against enemies. Therefore, he traveled lightly laden but heavily armed.

The wheel was never put to any practical purpose by the Indians. It has appeared only on a few wheeled pottery toys which were unearthed by archeologists in Mexico. There was no wheeled vehicle of any kind; nor was the true wheel used in making pottery. Both of these revolutionary inventions were made in the Middle East of the Old World about 4000 B.C. which means that in this respect the New World lagged behind 5,500 years by the time of the European Conquest. Indian methods of land transportation were inferior to those of the Old World because of the absence of the wheel. The importance of the wheel in our own machine age can scarcely be overestimated.

Arctic.—The Copper Eskimos obtained copper from the Coppermine River, which empties into the Arctic Ocean in their territory, and traded it both west and east. They also possessed the largest supply of soapstone in the entire Arctic. Neighboring Eskimo bands sometimes traveled hundreds of miles to mine this soapstone. Those at greater distances, as far west as Alaska and east to Labrador, obtained finished lamps and pots in trade. The Copper Eskimos and their closest eastern neighbors made journeys south to obtain wood. This was a valuable article of trade as far east as Baffinland, because driftwood was extremely scarce in the central Arctic. Wood was more valuable than ivory in much of this territory, because it was the best material for sleds and was indispensable for boat frames.

Giddings (1960: 128, 133) mentions a brisk trade across Bering Strait in hide boats by the Eskimo of the Seward Peninsula in the historic period. The Alaskan peoples traded furs and fur clothing, ivory, nets, sausage, objects of jade and copper, wooden vessels, rawhide line, and oil to Siberian peoples; they received in exchange mostly trade objects manufactured in Europe or Asia, such as iron knives, metal kettles, metal bells, glass beads, lances, liquor, and tobacco. There were annual trade fairs on both sides of the strait. Archeological evidence points to prehistoric trade at least as early as 1000 B.C. and probably earlier. This does not change the statement in Chapter 1 that the earliest immigrant to the New World probably had no boats of hide or any other material and most likely crossed on a land bridge.

Northwest Coast and Plateau.—On the Northwest Coast, the Plateau, and the adjacent Sub-Arctic, there was a lively trade in pre-European times. Dentalia shells, obtained principally on the west coast of Vancouver Island, were widely traded, and served as a medium of exchange over a considerable part of the area where they were known. At White contact, they were found in the western Arctic as far east as the Mackenzie Delta, in the Yukon Sub-Arctic, on the Northwest Coast and the Plateau, on the northern Plains as far east as the village tribes on the upper Missouri in the Dakotas, and among the northernmost tribes of central California. Copper, from the Copper River in southern Alaska, was traded as far south as the Columbia River.

The trade articles brought by European ships, as well as the demand for furs by the European traders from about 1775 on, greatly stimulated Northwest Coast trade. In the south, the Chinooks soon dominated the Columbia River route and exacted a toll from other tribes who paddled their wares up or down the river. At The Dalles, where huge falls make portaging necessary, the aboriginal trading center grew to great proportions. A trade language called Chinook jargon was used in this region as far north as Alaska and as far south as northern California. It was composed of about 90 per cent Chinook words, the remainder being divided between English and French.

Farther north, the coastal tribes became the middlemen in the exchange of furs from the interior for European and American goods on the coast. At trading rendezvous near the coast, the buyers and sellers spent days in feasting, singing, dancing, and otherwise enjoying themselves, much as our modern businessmen do at a convention. Some of the interior tradesmen who had become wealthy could afford to "buy" wives from the coast people. As a result of such intermarriages, some features of the coast social organization spread to the interior.

The social repercussions on the coast were equally revolutionary. Surpluses of blankets and metal utensils soon arose as a result of the unprecedented amount of goods pouring into Indian hands. There was plenty to give away at potlatches, which became larger, more frequent, more competitive, and more destructive of physical property. The carefully graduated scale of social rank began to disintegrate. Energetic young men who had acquired a few sea otter furs or had worked a while on a fishing schooner could save enough to give an impressive potlatch. Furthermore, a considerable number of titles went begging because of the decline in population caused by such European diseases as measles and scarlet fever, to which the Indian lacked immunity. The result was that new social climbers appropriated the unclaimed titles.

Southwest.—Marine shells, worn as beads and pendants, were derived from two sources: the coast of southern California in the vicinity of Los Angeles and the Gulf of California (64 species); the Gulf of Mexico (9 species). Pacific Coast shells were traded as far north as southwestern Colorado and as far east as the Texas panhandle. Pacific Coast shells reached the Southwest over two principal trade routes: from the Gulf of California to the middle of the Gila, thence north and east; from the vicinity of Los Angeles across the Mohave Desert to northern Arizona. The Mohave were the middlemen along the second trade route across the Mohave Desert. On the Pacific Coast, they obtained shells, fishhook blanks, beads, and other manufactured shell objects from the Angelinos and traded them to Pueblo Indians in Arizona for pottery and textiles.

Fine cotton textiles and cast copper "sleigh bells" reached the Southwest from Meso-America. Cotton textiles were also woven locally, but it does not seem likely that the Indians of the Southwest were familiar with the lost-wax technique by which the bells were almost certainly cast. An extraordinary trade item from Mexico was macaws, which were apparently transported alive the entire 1,200 miles from their nearest habitat in Mexico to northern Arizona and New Mexico. They seem to have been highly valued, which was fortunate because their careful burial preserved their bones for archeologists.

In historic times, Plains Indians visited the eastern Pueblos to trade buffalo hides and jerked meat for corn and other farm products. The Navaho in early historic times, and the Apache well into the nineteenth century, traded products of the chase for those of the farm with all the Pueblos at one time or another.

Plains and Prairies.—On the Plains and Prairies, trade consisted mostly of the exchange of products of the chase by the hunting tribes for the agricultural products of the farming tribes. The nomads offered horses, dried meat, fat, prairie-turnip flour, dressed hides, tipis, buffalo robes, other furs, shirts and leggings of buckskin decorated with quillwork, and moccasins. The sedentary village tribes offered in return corn, beans, pumpkins, and tobacco. After trade goods began to arrive from Europe and the Atlantic Coast of America, it was the agricultural tribes which first received the most articles. After about

1800, these agricultural peoples were trading quantities of guns, powder, bullets, metal kettles, axes, knives, awls, glass beads, and mirrors to the nomads.

The way of life of the Plains Indians was changed a great deal by the acquisition of the horse, which they obtained from the Spanish colonists in northern Mexico and New Mexico. The horse fitted in ideally with their roving, predatory way of life, and those tribes who first acquired it had a tremendous advantage, in both the chase and warfare, over their neighbors who lacked it.

The Indian demand for horses skyrocketed to unbelievable dimensions. They were stolen at every opportunity, not only from the Spanish but from other Indians. The horse rapidly became an important motive behind the perpetual raids which the Plains tribes made on each other. By the nineteenth century, stealing a picketed horse from within the camp of an enemy became one of the highest-ranking war deeds. Probably a hundred times as many horses changed owners by theft as by trade. Horses as far north as the Canadian border often bore Spanish brands. Members of the Blackfoot and other northern Plains tribes journeyed all the way south to Santa Fe to obtain horses. By 1800, all the Plains tribes were fully horsed.

The great demand for furs had a decided effect on the marriage structure of the northern Plains. Although a man actually killed the buffalo, the sexual division of labor ruled that his wife should dress the hide and dry the meat. As the demand for furs grew, men who were successful hunters purchased more and more wives to do the skin dressing and meat jerking for them. The maximum number of wives possessed by one man of the Blackfoot tribe rose from 6 in 1787 to 20, or possibly 30, by 1840. Because wives were purchased with horses and horses were essential to the buffalo economy, this extreme form of polygyny could not have arisen without large numbers of horses. Therefore, it arrived late, and came to an abrupt end when the buffalo became practically extinct in 1880.

Effects of the fur trade on material culture were less startling but numerous. Tipis grew from small structures covered by half a dozen buffalo hides, and accommodating as many people, to huge structures requiring 20 skins for covering. Pottery was abandoned early in favor of the metal trade kettle, which was not subject to breakage. Trade tobacco replaced the native tobacco which had been raised by some of the nomadic tribes. Woven rabbit-skin robes and basketry became extinct, being replaced by buffalo robes and trade dishes.

The policy of the Hudson's Bay Company was to trade with chiefs. As long as this company had a monopoly of trade, the authority of chiefs increased, but when other trading firms or independent tradesmen arrived, business was done directly with any Indian. The chief, who had served as a middleman, was no longer necessary and his authority declined.

Even religion was affected by the fur trade. The wealth brought by the fur trade encouraged men to buy, as an investment, medicine bundles which might later be sold at a profit or kept as symbols of prestige. Bundles changed hands oftener, became more numerous, and sold for higher prices.

Along with the fur trade came the gun and the horse. Guns reached the Plains from the Northeast, and horses from the Southwest. Those tribes who acquired one or the other had an advantage in warfare over those who had neither, but those who got both were superior. After horses and guns arrived, casualties increased, war parties became smaller, war chiefs disappeared, and the element of surprise often determined the outcome.

Trade on the Plains was facilitated by the famous sign language, which was the most elaborate means of silent communication in the New World. The multiplicity of languages would have made trade difficult, if not impossible, without this lingua franca.

Northeast.—There were well-established water routes in the Northeast along which the Indians, in birch-bark canoes, plied their trade. The copper from the southern shore of Lake Superior found its way east, where it was exchanged for tobacco and wampum. One tribe specialized in raising tobacco and trading it to neighbors in quantities sufficient for it to be labeled the Tobacco tribe. Brown pipestone from the Chippewa River and red pipestone from Minnesota were taken east on the Great Lakes as far as the Iroquois country in New York state and thence north into Canada. Flint from Ontario traveled west and north in unfinished "blanks" to Saskatchewan and Alberta. Obsidian from the Rocky Mountains, in the form of raw material and in finished points and knives, has been found in Hopewell mounds in Ohio in amounts of up to several hundred pounds.

From the beginning of European contact, the Hurons had a monopoly on trade with the French at Montreal. The Hurons acquired the entire crops of maize, tobacco, and hemp raised by two weaker tribes, the Tobacco and the Neutral, and traded the crops to nonagricultural tribes for furs and fish. The furs were passed on to the French. The

Hurons traveled nearly as far as James Bay to the north and to the mouth of the Saguenay River in the Gulf of St. Lawrence on the east. Although the Hurons obtained beaver furs in their home territory around 1600, these resources were exhausted by 1635, and they were forced to acquire them from tribes to the north and west.

The strongest rivals of the Hurons in the first half of the seventeenth century were the Iroquois, who dominated the trade with the Dutch in New York state. By 1641, the Iroquois were in a predicament. Their own beaver supply h⸢ ⸥ the Dutch had passed legislation forbidding the sale ⸢ ⸥dians. This left the Iroquois without the two mo⸢ ⸥ the Euro-Indian trade. It was at this time that the⸢ ⸥-laden canoes of their Huron rivals on the St. La⸢ ⸥ty of one thousand Mohawks and Senecas attacl⸢ ⸥ge at night. As the village was almost without g⸢ ⸥s swift; before sunrise they attacked a second ⸢ ⸥rmed and fired by 9:00 A.M. Panic seized the ⸢ ⸥urned their 15 remaining villages and fled, i⸢ ⸥ousand and eight thousand, to an unproduc⸢ ⸥e sole virtue of being easily defended. Durin⸢ ⸥f the Hurons on the island starved. By th⸢ ⸥t five hundred were left; they made their fir⸢ ⸥e their descendants remain to this day. Wit⸢ ⸥roquois found excuses to attack and an⸢ ⸥hbors, the Tobacco, Neutral, and Erie. The trade w⸢ ⸥ eagerly sought never materialized. After the defeat of the Hurons, the Ottawas seized most of the trade along their river and many tribes feared the Iroquois so much that they refused to trade with them.

Southeast.—Trade in the Southeast was principally between contrasting geographical environments: coast with interior; uplands with lowlands. The Mississippi River became a trade artery in historic times and probably served in that capacity in prehistoric times as well. Perhaps the most important single trade item was salt, which was peddled by itinerant merchants throughout the area but especially in the Mississippi drainage. Most of it was made by evaporating saturated solutions, obtained at salt licks, in shallow pottery pans over a fire. West of the Mississippi, at least, salt was made into cakes of 2 or 3 pounds each, as in Meso-America. Copper obtained in the Appalachians, and possibly a little from the south shore of Lake Superior, was also a common article of trade and was used mainly for ornaments. Catlinite pipes from the same area penetrated the Southeast in historic times, much later than the feathered stem and wand called calumet.

Fairs or markets were held periodically, and drew people from towns within a radius of 50 or 60 miles. Although they were reported as late as the eighteenth century, there is no reason to doubt their occurrence in earlier times.

The fur trade had its ultimately disastrous effects here as elsewhere. The acquisition of the gun made hunting so easy that large numbers of animals were killed just for the hides, the meat being left to rot or to be devoured by carnivores. Game eventually became scarce, and dependence on corn increased. As in other areas, European and American trade goods rapidly replaced many Indian articles.

Meso-America.—Meso-America differed from areas to the north in having a greater amount of community craft specialization and along with it a greater amount of intercommunity trade. One town might have access to a source of superior clay and be able to make better pottery than its neighbors. Another might be close to a supply of obsidian, which was the preferred material for points of weapons and tools and for knives. A third might be near deposits of metal which could be cast into ornaments in quantity. As technical knowledge grew, specialization and trade increased and markets grew in number and in size. Women normally went to market only in their hometowns, but men sometimes back-packed their wares a hundred miles. Markets in small villages were held at regular intervals, while those in large towns and cities were often daily affairs. Those in the great commercial centers were attended by merchants from distant nations who brought their wares to be exchanged.

Barter was the only means of exchange, and scarcity affected price. True money did not exist, but the chocolate bean was used in making "change" and approached the status of money. The beans were of fairly uniform size, were scarce enough not to be subject to damaging inflation, were portable, and had universal utility as food. In the more sophisticated cities, quills of gold dust and copper knives were sometimes used as mediums of exchange. Jade, being worth much more than gold, was the most precious substance among the Aztecs.

Differences in geographical zone had their effect on trade here as elsewhere. The Aztecs of the temperate highlands obtained chocolate, vanilla, pineapples, rubber, and bitumen from the tropical lowlands of Veracruz; serpentine, porphyry, and jade also had to be imported from the southeast. In exchange, they offered obsidian, cloth, salt, jewelry, pottery, and rope from the Valley of Mexico. Shells from both oceans found their way to inland cities. The extension of the Aztec "empire" can largely be understood in economic terms, as this people sought to control the source areas of both necessities and luxuries. The Spanish conquerors moved along Aztec trade trails.

The Aztecs sponsored a class of itinerant merchants, called *pochteca*, whose members traveled widely in armed bands over Meso-America, exchanging their goods for foreign products. They had their own god, trappings, and insignia, and lived in a special quarter (*barrio*) in the cities. Like fifth-column agents of modern governments, they served as spies and made estimates of the amount of tribute a given town could pay if conquered. They also passed on secret information about its military establishments. Their security of body and property, which at first had been preserved because of the desirability of their wares, later became guaranteed by the force of arms of the Aztec government. They ultimately grew to be a sort of commercial corporation which controlled the entire trade of the country. They had their own laws and courts of justice and, with this protection, became a threat to the nobility. Full-time professional traders are also reported for the Otomí, Zapotec, Popoloca, Zoque, and Maya, but they were less organized among these tribes than with the Aztec.

Maya trade in general was as well developed as that of the Aztecs, and probably more in sea trade. Maya trade was also handled by a class of professional merchants who often traveled with their goods. There was no competition with the nobility here because these merchants belonged to the nobility. The chocolate bean was a medium of exchange all the way from the Valley of Mexico to Nicaragua, although stone beads, copper bells, copper axes, and shell beads approached the same status.

Christopher Columbus encountered, at the Bay Islands in the Gulf of Honduras, a huge Indian trading canoe, with a crew of twenty-five paddlers, transporting colored cotton blankets, shirts and breechcloths, obsidian-edged wooden swords, copper axes, copper bells and ornaments, crucibles for melting copper, and many chocolate beans used as money. No one knows the nationality of the sailors or the destination of the canoe. However, other sources mention regular sea trade on the Caribbean side of Mexico and Central America.

In Meso-America, where trade reached its highest development, most trade goods fell into the hands of a wealthy minority. The average individual continued to consume principally local products and to produce many of them himself.

CONCLUSIONS

The above summaries on trade have been given to demonstrate the tremendous amount of contact between the many distinct tribes of native North America. Some trade objects traveled only a few miles, but others were traded hundreds and occasionally thousands of miles from point of origin. What was the mechanism of their dispersal?

Corn was not carried from its point of origin in the tropics all the way to the St. Lawrence River by a single trader or by a single trading expedition. It was relayed from one locality to the next, and the time it took to negotiate this great distance ran into thousands of years. Because corn does not survive in nature but must be cared for by man, each people who received corn kernels for seed for the first time had to have learned how to farm in advance. This meant some exchange of personnel between the donor and recipient peoples. As this process was continued, corn became consciously or unconsciously selected for the cooler climate and shorter growing season in the north. The development of special varieties of corn, adapted to the many environments in which the plant was raised by A.D. 1492, took a great deal of time.

Many trade objects moved much faster than corn, but they were normally dispersed by the same relay process, called "diffusion" by anthropologists. It is true that a few trading expeditions traveled some hundreds of miles, but these were the exceptions rather than the rule. A man with a surplus traded most often with one of his immediate neighbors, who in turn might relay some of the goods received to another neighbor a little farther away.

After European contact, there was a tremendous increase in trade and in the number of full-time professional traders, many of whom were Europeans. Individuals and expeditions traveled greater distances than were negotiated in pre-Columbian times. This marked increase in trade was accompanied by an equal increase in the diffusion of elements of culture other than trade goods, with the result that the contemporary historian of culture is able to reconstruct the pre-European picture only with difficulty. Nevertheless, we can be sure each pre-Columbian Indian society made regular contacts with other societies which were independent politically and spoke different languages.

There was no true money in the Americas, but there were a number of articles used as media of exchange in as many areas. Dentalia shells were a standard of value on the Northwest Coast, clamshell disk beads in California, beaver furs in the Sub-Arctic, marine-shell tubular beads (wampum) in the Northeastern United States, and chocolate (*cacao*) beans in Meso-America. Most trade goods, however, were exchanged by barter and were not carefully priced in terms of some other medium of exchange.

REFERENCES

ACOSTA, 1945; ALEXANDER, 1939; BARNETT, 1968; BEALS, 1932a; CHARD, 1950; CODERE, 1951; COLTON, 1941; DEN-HARDT, 1948; DRIVER AND MASSEY, 1957; DRUCKER, 1965; DRUCKER AND HEIZER, 1967; EWERS, 1955b; HAINES, 1938a, 1938b; HAURY, 1947; HERSKOVITS, 1952; HUNT, 1940; JAB-LOW, 1951; LEWIS, 1942; LOWIE, 1954; MARTIN, QUIMBY, AND COLLIER, 1947; OLSON, 1927; QUIMBY, 1948; RAY, 1939; ROE, 1939, 1955; ROYS, 1943; SLOTKIN AND SCHMIDT, 1949; SPECK, 1919; STEWARD, 1938; SWANTON, 1946; VAILLANT, 1941; WILLEY, 1966; WILSON, 1924; WISSLER, 1914, 1938, 1941.

14

Marriage and the Family

NORTH American Indians exhibit an amazing variety of ways to acquire a mate, of forms of marriage such as polygamy, of incest taboos, of postnuptial residence customs, of parent-in-law relations, and of family structure. In fact, almost all of the principal variants of these phenomena known to the entire world are found in North America alone. By comparison, European marriage and family practices were almost uniform. This wide range of variation indicates great historical depth as well as meticulous adaptation to natural and cultural environments.

The sex act itself may be called mating, whether done within or without wedlock. Marriage, on the other hand, is usually defined as both an economic and a sexual union known to other members of the society, accepted by them, and considered to be permanent. The secret marriage of today, made legal by a marriage license and ceremony obtained without publicity, was unheard of in Indian societies. In the absence of written records, every marriage had to be known to everyone in the community; otherwise, there would be no adequate regulation of sexual activity.

Another point which cannot be overemphasized is that the parents and other elder relatives of a bride or groom normally had more to do with the selection of a marriage partner than did either of the principals. Marriage among most nonliterate peoples is regarded as a contract between two groups of kin rather than between two individuals. In general, a bride and groom had more voice in the matter among the economically less-advanced tribes such as those in the Arctic, Sub-Arctic, Great Basin, and Northeast Mexico. Those areas which were economically more advanced or possessed sib systems tended to give more weight to the opinions of elders.

INFANT OR CHILD BETROTHAL

The authority of the parents in choosing a mate for their off-spring is reflected in the custom of betrothing an infant or a child. This practice might seem to belong in cultures of considerable economic and social stability, but such is not always the case. The Eskimo commonly betrothed infants or children, even though the vicissitudes of their way of life often made consummation of these agreements impossible. Among the central Eskimos, where the incidence of female infanticide was greatest, it was said that only betrothed female infants were spared. Whether or not this is literally true, it emphasizes the importance of infant betrothal in this culture.

Infant or child betrothal is reported from some tribes on the Northwest coast, Plateau, in the Western Sub-Arctic, California, Great Basin, Southwest, East and Meso-America. On the Northwest Coast, at least, a partial payment of the bride price was made at this time. Elsewhere some gift exchange may have taken place at the time of betrothal, but it should hardly be labeled bride price.

PREMARITAL MATING

Mating prior to marriage was tolerated in the majority of North American Indian societies although it was far from universal. Even where condoned or taken for granted, there might still be a premium placed on virginity. Thus among Plains tribes, where unchastity was everywhere condoned except among the Cheyenne, we find the higher-ranking families attempting to instill standards of virtue in their daughters. With the Crow, a certain ceremonial role could be performed only by a woman who had been a virgin bride and remained faithful to her husband, which proves that premarital chastity was valued. On the Northwest Coast, young women were sometimes confined in a boarded-off room in the house from the time of first menstruation until marriage, so that their virginity plus an unusually light skin would not only command a higher bride price but would also facilitate a union with a higher-ranking family.

By and large, premarital sexual relations were less a problem in Indian societies than in our own, partly because of the younger age at which marriage took place. Young women were normally considered marriageable after first menstruation, which might take place at twelve or thirteen years of age (we have no adequate figures on the average age). Men tended to be older, but probably married at less than twenty years of age on the average. Carefully compiled modern statistics tell us that young women near the age of first menstruation are much less fertile than they will be even a few years later. Illegitimate pregnancies must have been less common in Indian societies than in societies with later marriage age. This fact, coupled with the more permissive attitude taken by some Indians, contrived to make premarital intercourse a somewhat less traumatic experience than in our society today.

In the Southeast, attitudes about sex were especially liberal. Both young men and women were allowed premarital sexual experience, which was taken for granted and was nothing to be ashamed of or kept secret. The only restriction was that they should not violate the rules regarding incest, exogamy, or adultery. Premarital pregnancies were fairly common, and the children were reared by the mother's family, extended family, or sib as a matter of course. While the child was apparently always kept within its mother's sib, it might be adopted by some family other than the mother's; or, if the unwed mother preferred, she had a right to put her infant to death within one month after birth. There was little or no stigma attached to the mother or the offspring of a premarital sexual union.

WAYS OF ACQUIRING A SPOUSE

Most of the ways and means of acquiring a bride reported for primitive man the world over are also known for aboriginal North America. One of these is called marriage by purchase or by bride price. Such purchase does not give the right to dispose of the bride either by sale to another or by renting her out as a prostitute. Neither does it carry the right to injure or to kill her. All the husband purchases is the right to share with her the type of sexual and economic life permitted and approved by the society in which he lives. Furthermore, the bride's family often repays or makes return gifts to the groom's family of a value equal to that of the gifts received. Because of these qualifications, many anthropologists prefer the phrase "bride wealth" to "bride price." Where bride wealth was obtrusive in the culture, as on the Northwest Coast, the social prestige of a woman, and that of her offspring and husband as well, was positively correlated with the amount "paid" for her. In this same area, the bride price was often negotiated as in a business transaction. In spite of this bargaining feature, the return payments or gifts from the bride's family to that of the groom were commonly of a value equal to that of the bride price. Therefore it is best to regard this whole process of exchange of wealth at marriage as a means of establishing social rank and position rather than as a business transaction.

Bride service or suitor service was another way in which a man could qualify as a husband. The prospective groom went to live with his future bride's parent, and worked for and with her father. If, after a year or so, he had demonstrated his ability to hunt and otherwise earn a living in the way prescribed by the culture, he was given the daughter as a bride. This custom often resulted in a temporary matrilocal residence for a year or so after the couple was married, or until the first child was born. At that time the marriage was regarded as fully consummated, and the groom often took the bride to his own community to live.

In general, it may be said that the concept of bride price or "purchase" was strongest on the Plains, Prairies, and Northwest Coast. Bride service was most dominant in the Sub-Arctic and Great Basin areas. A mixture or balance between bride price and bride service characterized all other areas. For example, among the Creek Indians of the Southeast, gifts of about equal value were exchanged by the families of the bride and groom, and the groom often helped his wife's relatives farm, or built the house on their land which he and his bride were to occupy in the near future. For the Aztecs of Mexico, no bride service is mentioned, but the wealth exchanged by the families of the principals was of about equal value.

Marriage was sometimes effected by two families exchanging daughters, each of whom became a wife of the other family's son. This is called "interfamilial exchange marriage." It eliminated bride wealth and suitor service. This rare custom is reported mainly in areas where formalities were at the minimum, such as the Great Basin and Sub-Arctic.

The majority of tribes sometimes captured women in warfare and kept them as wives. On the Northwest Coast, however, women were enslaved rather than married when they were taken in a raid. Some tribes in Mexico and Central America enacted a mock capture as part of the marriage ceremony, and a few abducted a minority of brides against their will. On the whole, however, the percentage of wives acquired in this fashion was small and had little effect on the customary marriage practices.

Still another means of acquiring a spouse is called "adoptive marriage." Where patrilocal or patrilineal families lacked a son to inherit the family property and perpetuate the line of descent, they sometimes adopted a young man to marry one of their daughters. The third generation inherited from him in the same manner that they would have from a true member of the line. This custom was practised in the Eastern Sub-Arctic, the Prairies, the patrilocal part of the Northwest Coast, and no doubt in other patrilocal or patrilineal areas. Matrilocal and matrilineal societies seem to have adopted daughters less often, although among the Haisla on the Northwest Coast a man who had no sister's son adopted his own daughter to inherit his title. Among the Mandan of the upper Missouri River, a family without a daughter adopted a daughter-in-law to carry on the line. Some maternal lineages and sibs among the western Pueblos have become extinct because the lack of female heirs, which is evidence that adoption was absent or at least rare in that area.

Elopement was practiced now and then by almost all North American tribes, but was rarely the approved method of acquiring a bride. A man without the usual family connections, having difficulty in raising an adequate bride price alone, might resolve his predicament by elopement. If a love match was frowned upon by ambitious elders trying to arrange an economically or socially advantageous marriage, the lovers might settle matters by elopement. When this happened in the Southeast, a posse of the bride's relatives often pursued the couple with an eye to breaking up the affair. If, however, the eloping pair were able to hide in the woods until the annual harvest ceremony, all they had to do was to appear as man and wife at this public ritual in order to win approval of the society. All offenses short of murder were annually forgiven by this culture at this time, and elopement was less serious than many other wrongs.

INCEST TABOOS AND EXOGAMY

Mating with any person regarded as a genetic (cognatic, blood) relative is called "incest." Incest was universally tabooed in Indian North America. Nowhere was mating or marriage tolerated between father and daughter, mother and son, or brother and sister. Marriage with certain first cousins was permitted and even preferred among a small number of tribes, but, as we shall see later, these cousins were not regarded as genetic relatives.

Incest taboos were often automatically extended by the meaning of the terms for kin in the many Indian languages. For example, if the word for "sister" included all of a man's female cousins, as it actually did for many tribes, marriage with cousins would normally be forbidden by extension of the incest taboo from sister to cousin. The same principle applies to other relationships. Where sibs exist, an individual has a large number of fictitious or traditional relatives who may actually be unrelated to him. Nevertheless, such traditional relationships are a bar to marriage, and a man must look for a mate outside his sib. The rule requiring a person to marry outside a defined social group is called "exogamy."

Where does the incest taboo leave off and exogamy begin? There is no agreement among anthropologists on the limits of these two terms. A simple rule of thumb is to designate the ban on marriage or mating with actual genetic relatives as the incest taboo, and to reserve the term "exogamy" for the prohibition of sexual relations within the larger kin group which recognizes traditional relationship. Exogamy may also apply to a locality; a man may be compelled to seek a mate outside the locality or community in which he lives. This is called "local exogamy." Normally this rule is applied only to small communities in which most members are genetically related or are so considered by tradition.

COUSIN MARRIAGE

First-cousin marriage was permitted or preferred by a small minority of peoples. Before describing particular areas or tribes, we must first consider the different kinds of first cousins commonly distinguished by Indians. From the point of view of a man looking for a wife, there are four kinds of female cousins: his father's brother's daughters; his father's sisters daughters; his mother's brother's daughters; his mother's sister's daughters. The first and the last types of cousins are sometimes grouped together by Indians as well as by anthropologists and, by the latter, are called "parallel cousins." This refers to the fact that the sex of the two connecting relatives in the parental generation is the same. The second and third types are called "cross-cousins" because the sex of the two connecting relatives in the parental generation is different.

On the northern Northwest Coast, cross-cousin marriage was the preferred kind of union. If no first cross-cousin was available to a man, he chose a more remote cousin designated by the same word in the language. Among the Haida, a boy of ten years of age ideally went to live with his mother's brother, who gave him his education in the lore of the sib as well as in practical matters. When the boy reached marriageable age, he ideally married his mother's brother's daughter and continued to live in the house of his mother's brother. When the latter died, the boy, who was now the deceased's son-in-law and also his sister's son, inherited his house, land, and chattels as well as his social position and prestige. If no mother's brother's daughter was available to a young man, he might substitute a father's sister's daughter, who was designated by the same kinship term in the language. As we shall see later on, one's cross-cousins always belong to a different sib or moiety than oneself, and because of this fact, are sometimes regarded as nonrelatives for marriage purposes.

Among the Kaska, inland from the Northwest Coast, the only first cousin a man was permitted to marry was his mother's brother's daughter. This was the preferred marriage, although many men had to be content with cousins further removed or with unrelated wives. At Lake Teslin, between the Kaska and the coast, and among the Chipewyans farther east, a man could marry only his father's sister's daughter.

Proceeding farther east to the Cree and Ojibwa, we find a different picture. Although marriages with both kinds of first cross-cousins were permitted, they were less frequent than those with more remote cousins. Double cross-cousin marriage sometimes occurred; a man married a woman who was both his mother's brother's daughter and his father's sister's daughter at the same time. This could happen only when two men in the older generation had exchanged their sisters, each marrying the other's sister. The offspring from these unions would be double cross-cousins. Figures on the frequency of single cross-cousin marriage show that the mother's brother's daughter was married more often than the father's sister's daughter. The pattern of the Montagnais-Naskapi of the Labrador Peninsula was similar to that of the Cree and Ojibwa.

In California and Oregon, cross-cousin marriage was permitted or preferred only by a small minority of tribelets, and in every case the mother's brother's daughter was singled out. In the Great Basin, cross-cousin marriage was permitted in a minority of localities but was nowhere the preferred form. In the Southwest, only the Walapai permitted a man to marry either variety of cross-cousin. The Maya of

Yucatán appear to have had both kinds of cross-cousin marriage at the time of first Spanish contact, although the evidence is indirect.

North American instances of cross-cousin marriage are remarkable for the wide variety of other social traits associated with them. Thus descent may be patrilineal, matrilineal, or bilateral; postnuptial residence may be patrilocal, matrilocal, avunculocal, or bilocal; kinship terminology may be Crow, Omaha, Iroquois, Hawaiian, or Eskimo. These facts, added to the scattered appearance of the geographical distribution of cross-cousin marriage, suggest a multiple origin of the phenomenon as well as a multiple causality.

If everyone married his cross-cousin, it would not be necessary to have any kinship terms for in-laws because they would also be genetic (blood) relatives. Such is actually the case in most of the Eastern Sub-Arctic. Special terms for in-laws do not exist in the language. Wherever in-laws are thus lumped with genetic relatives, we may suspect marriage or former marriage of genetic relatives. All the kinship terminologies of the Algonquians of the Plains have features suggesting cross-cousin marriage. The same is true of the Santee and Teton Dakota. All of these tribes seem to have had cross-cousin marriage at some time in the past when they were living farther east, where their territories probably adjoined those of the Ojibwa and Cree, who have continued to marry cross-cousins down to the present time.

Parallel cousin marriage was tolerated in a very few localities, but was nowhere a preferred form. Because parallel cousins were most often designated by the same terms used for brothers and sisters, marriage with such relatives would not be anticipated.

AFFINAL MARRIAGE

There are two major kinds of relatives: genetic or "blood" relatives; affinal or relatives by marriage. Affinal relatives include all the genetic relatives of one's wife or husband, commonly designated as in-laws. Any marriage with an in-law is an affinal marriage. Affinal marriages are always secondary marriages, because there are no in-laws before a first marriage.

The marriage of a woman to her deceased husband's brother is called "levirate." This form of marriage was found among most tribes of North America; at least there are few reports of its being forbidden. Each party to such a marriage may be regarded as an asset or a liability by the other according to circumstances. A widow with children to support would be in need of a husband, and an attractive younger brother of her deceased husband would definitely be an asset. If, on the other hand, he was an unattractive person, or was already married, so that the widow became a second wife who took orders from his first wife, then he might appear to be a liability. A widow was generally obligated to accept her husband's unmarried brother as a mate, and the latter was equally obligated to care for his sister-in-law and her children. This custom reflects the attitude that a marriage is a contract between two families or lines of descent, and not binding merely to the two principals.

The marriage of a man to his deceased wife's sister is called "sororate." As in the case of the levirate, there was an obligation as well as a benefit involved for both parties. The sororate was also practiced and approved by a large majority of tribes.

The levirate and sororate were often extended to relatives of the deceased more remote than a brother or sister, in cases where the latter were unavailable. For example, a man might marry his deceased wife's cousin or niece if she had no sister. Similarly, a woman might marry a more remote relative of her deceased husband if he did not have a brother. Such extensions are the rule in primitive cultures and may be taken for granted except where they are specifically denied.

POLYGAMY

Any marriage with multiple husbands or wives is called "polygamy." It may take two forms: polygyny, the marriage of one husband to two or more wives simultaneously; polyandry, the marriage of one wife to two or more husbands simultaneously.

The vast majority of North American peoples practiced polygyny. It was probably most frequent in the northern part of the Plains and Prairie areas. We have already mentioned the prodigious increase in numbers of wives on the Plains in the nineteenth century as a result of the fur trade. This could have happened only in an area where the institution was well established in early times. Actual figures obtained from the records of priests among the Crees and Ojibwas indicate an incidence of polygyny in former times well over 20 per cent. Another area of common occurrence was the Northwest Coast. Although polygyny was limited to the wealthier class in this area, mainly because of the great amount of the bride price, it seems to have exceeded 20 per cent in many localities.

Exclusive monogamy was the rule among the Iroquois and a few of their neighbors. This is to be expected in cultures in which matrilineal descent and matrilocal residence were coupled with female ownership and control of agricultural land and houses, not to mention the unusual authority of women in political affairs. Here the men literally moved in with their wives, who could divorce them merely by tossing their personal effects out of the door of the longhouse. Even sororal polygyny, which was the only form conceivable under these conditions, was lacking.

The only other area where female dominance approached this level was that of the western Pueblos in the Southwest. Here the picture was similar, and exclusive monogamy prevailed. The other instances of exclusive monogamy were scattered and occurred in both bilateral and patrilineal societies. They do not lend themselves to any ready explanation.

Sororal polygyny—that is, the marriage of a man to two wives who were sisters—probably occurred wherever polygyny was to be found. A number of Plains tribes had no other form. A man in this society was especially anxious to acquire an eldest sister as a first mate, with an eye on acquiring her younger sisters if and when he could afford them. Although it is not the purpose of this volume to justify Indian behavior, it is easy to see that polygyny had more utility in societies where male mortality in hunting and warfare was high. The Plains was one of these areas. Among the Eskimos, where a man had more difficulty in supporting multiple wives, the extremely high male mortality was offset by female infanticide. This partially explains the more modest amount of polygyny present in the Arctic.

Polyandry as a preferred form of marriage is extremely rare in the world, and its existence in North America may be questioned. It was nowhere the preferred kind of union, was never lifelong, and is best regarded as an expedient solution to the male sexual problem.

It has been argued that female infanticide has been a cause of polyandry among the Eskimos, that the killing of too many girl babies has produced a sex ratio of more males than females. Population figures available for the Eskimo show that forty-two communities out of seventy-six (55 per cent) had fewer women than men. Because male mortality was higher than female mortality among all the Eskimos, these figures appear to reflect female infanticide. Where female infanticide eliminated half the girl babies, as it did near the magnetic pole in the central Arctic, it definitely encouraged polyandry; but where the sex ratios showed only slightly fewer females, infanticide alone was hardly a sufficient cause. The other factor was polygyny. The strongest and most capable men appropriated more than their share of wives. Polygyny, polyandry, and of course monogamy—all existed side by side. Monogamy was much the most frequent, but polygyny was the form of marriage preferred by men and was generally more common than polyandry. Polygyny may therefore be regarded as a partial cause of polyandry.

POSTNUPTIAL RESIDENCE

When a couple married, they had to decide where they were going to live, whether with or near the groom's relatives or the bride's relatives or somewhere else. "Patrilocal residence" means living with or near the groom's parents; it is also called "virilocal." "Matrilocal" refers to residence with or near the bride's parents; it is also called "uxorilocal." "Avunculocal" is applied to residence with the groom's mother's brother's family; "neolocal" to residence in a new house or locality where neither the groom's nor the bride's parents are present; "bilocal" ("ambilocal") to residence with either the groom's or the bride's parents or a shifting back and forth from one to the other. Sometimes the same couple followed one residence pattern for a time and then changed to another, and in some societies a shift from one form to another was followed by many if not most couples. These changes have been ignored, and only the final or more permanent form of residence is shown on Map 31. Where the rule for community residence differed from that for the house, the map gives the community. Thus the Apaches in the Southwest were neolocal with respect to house, but matrilocal with respect to community; they are mapped as matrilocal.

Patrilocal residence is the most widespread type—the dominant form in the Arctic, Eastern Sub-Arctic, northern Prairies, northern Plains, Plateau, southern Northwest Coast, California, the Mexican Southwest, and Meso-America. Matrilocal residence is characteristic of the East, central Plains, Ute, Southwest Athapaskans, western Pueblos, and the western part of the Athapaskan Sub-Arctic. Bilocal residence is the most frequent form in the Great Basin and the Mackenzie Sub-Arctic. Neolocal residence occurs only sporadically, and may be partly the result of European contact. Avunculocal residence is limited to the Northwest Coast, perhaps extending all the way to the Aleut.

THE FAMILY

Before describing the different family units of aboriginal North America, let us first review the general terminology of family structure. The family is a social group consisting of adults of both sexes, at least two of whom maintain a socially approved sexual relationship, and one or more children produced by this relationship or adopted by the adults. It is also characterized by common residence, economic cooperation, and responsibility for the education of children. According to Murdock, families may be classified into three major types: the nuclear family, consisting of parents and offspring; the polygamous family, which is an aggregate of two or more nuclear families brought about by plural marriages; the extended family, which is also an aggregate of two or more nuclear families but is produced by joining three or more generations of genetic relatives.

Family structure can best be described with the aid of diagrams. In anthropological genealogies it is customary to use triangles to represent males and circles to represent females. Marriage is indicated by double horizontal lines which connect the two principals in midsection, brother-sister relationships by a single horizontal line which connects these relatives by means of a short vertical line from above. Relationship must always be reckoned from a single individual called the "ego" or "I."

Figure 31 illustrates the simplest kind of family, called the "nuclear

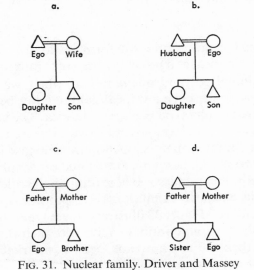

Fig. 31. Nuclear family. Driver and Massey

family," from the point of view of the husband and father, *a*, the wife and mother, *b*, the daughter, *c*, and the son, *d*. There may of course be a larger number of children, but it is necessary to indicate only one of each sex.

Figure 32 represents the polygynous family in which the wives are unrelated, *a*, and the polygynous family where the wives are sisters, *b*, as well as a polyandrous family in which the husbands are unrelated,

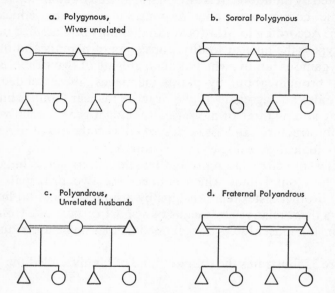

FIG. 32. Polygamous families. Driver and Massey

c. As an accepted and permanent form of family, type *c* does not exist in North America, and possibly not in the entire world. Figure 32 shows the fraternal polyandrous family, *d*, which was accepted as a temporary arrangement in a few localities but never became a permanent or preferred family type in North America. The various kinds of polygamous families are composed of two or more nuclear families which share a common member. All more complex types of family structure may be said to be aggregates of nuclear families.

Extended families are classified according to the rule of postnuptial residence. Thus extended families may be patrilocal, matrilocal, bilocal, or avunculocal. Figure 33 illustrates these types. In the patrilocal extended family, the sons continue to live with their fathers and bring their wives to their father's house or locality; married daughters live elsewhere, but unmarried daughters belong to this group. For the matrilocal type, it is the daughters who stay at home; their husbands must come to live with them. In the bilocal variety either sons or daughters may stay at home, or either may go to live with the spouse's family. We have diagramed it arbitrarily to show one son and one daughter remaining under the family roof. For the avunculocal extended family, the groom takes his bride to live with his mother's brother, and the son of the next generation stays with his father until

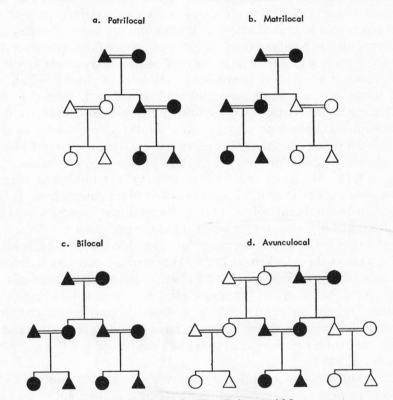

Fig. 33. Extended families. Driver and Massey

he is about ten years of age or until he marries. The minimum number of relatives required to define each type has been shown, but in actual practice there were often four generations and about fifty persons in all.

Because nuclear families were combined to form polygamous and extended families, and also occurred where these more complex forms were absent, they were universal in North America. Because polygyny probably nowhere constituted more than a minority of cases in a given locality, less than half the families in any society were polygynous. Polyandrous families were never permanent social units in any North American culture and probably nowhere reached even 10 per cent. They were everywhere dominated by monogamy.

Extended families would appear to be widespread if we noted low frequencies. Practically every tribe had at least a few three-generation groups of relatives living together at a given time. While we do not have adequate statistical evidence to prove this statement, the abundant references to grandparents and grandchildren in biography and folklore indicate plenty of three-generation propinquity. However, the history of such a group of relatives may be necessary to classify it. If each younger generation continues to reside with older generations, and forms a functioning economic and social unit, then the term "extended family" would seem to be applicable. But when younger generations set up independent households and economies which they operate for years, and take in the older generations only after the latter are unable to care for themselves, this is not properly termed an extended family. Extended family organization implies a certain amount of authority and leadership in the older generations. It can be said to be dominant only where it is the preferred form as well as the form actually achieved by the majority of the population.

The extended family is the dominant type for the western Eskimo as far east as the Mackenzie Delta. Where residence was patrilocal and inheritance of real estate and chattels patrilineal, there can be little doubt that many of the house groups were patrilocal extended families. Where the residence rule was bilocal and inheritance less definite, the household unit seems to have been the bilocal extended family, as Robert F. Spencer (1959) has confirmed for the northern Alaskan Eskimos.

Proceeding to the central and eastern Eskimos, we find the independent nuclear family the predominant house unit except in the part of the central region where the independent polygynous family is indicated. Houses were smaller than in the west, and nomadism more pronounced. However, married men ideally resided in the same settlement with their fathers, thus forming patrilocal extended families.

The Sub-Arctic offers many difficulties of classification. Perhaps the most controversial part of this area is the east, where the family hunting territory system prevailed. Although these family groups in one area averaged only six persons, and 70 per cent of them had only a single hunter and trapper, the land tended to pass from father to son. The patrilocal extended family existed potentially. In another locality, where families averaged fifteen persons, including three hunters and trappers, there is little question about the reality of the patrilocal extended family. Partly on the assumption that White contact and the fur trade, with its emphasis on individualism, tended to reduce the size of families as well as the tracts of land they occupied, it is safe to assume that the patrilocal extended family was formerly the rule in most localities. In the Mackenzie Sub-Arctic, the bilocal extended family was common; in the Yukon Sub-Arctic, the picture is too complicated to permit any simple generalizations.

On the Northwest Coast, we find definite extended families with clear-cut functions, especially in the north where avuncular residence and matrilineal descent prevailed. To the south, the pattern shifts to the patrilocal extended family, which shows little variation all the way to California. This patrilocal area was bilateral in descent, and the residence rule was much less strict than in the north. Some of these extended families owned or used productive sites jointly, engaged in trade, and accumulated chattels for the potlatch.

In central and southern California, patrilocal extended families were again the rule. These families sometimes were housed in a single structure but, more often than not, seem to have occupied several adjacent small structures, each with its nuclear family. Life was a little more nomadic than on the Northwest Coast, especially in southern California. The larger extended families merge into patriclans over a part of the area. Productive sites were exploited by either extended families or patriclans, or by both, indicating that these social groups were important economically. In the Southwest, the Pima-Papago pattern differed only in detail; in addition to sites productive of wild foods, their patrilocal extended families also owned farm land, and the members formed work parties to accomplish the most necessary economic tasks. The Colorado and Gila River Yumans conform to the same general pattern but again differ in details. Here it was only farm land which was owned by individuals or families and worked jointly by family members, with the products shared within the families. The substantial house of the River Yumans, called Mohave type in the chapter on housing, sheltered several nuclear families related most often through males, thus constituting a patrilocal extended family.

In the Great Basin, the independent nuclear family was the most characteristic type. Although these were often aggregated into larger units possessing some of the earmarks of bilocal extended families, these larger units were of such a temporary and unstable nature that they have never been so labeled. The extended family was the most common family unit among the northeastern Shoshoni after the acquisition of the horse, when Plains influence penetrated this region.

The Plateau is difficult to classify. Three types of families occurred in different parts of the area: patrilocal extended, bilocal extended, and independent polygynous. The extended families here seem to have had a looser integration than those on the Northwest Coast. The frequency of polygynous families certainly increased after White contact, as on the Plains, so that they may reflect as late a time period as that for the northeastern Shoshoni.

On the northern Plains, it is difficult to choose between independent polygynous and patrilocal extended families. Both were present among all tribes, and any differences among them can at best be a matter of emphasis. Probably the larger unit was more typical before the horse, and later gave way to the more individualistic polygynous unit when the fur trade changed many features of the sociopolitical organization. The Cheyennes and Arapahos possessed matrilocal extended families which dated from the time when they lived farther east, on the Prairies, and farmed. Comanche culture was dominated by the independent polygynous family. The Kiowa family type was probably bilocal extended because of that trend in the residence pattern.

On the Prairies, the most widespread and dominant family type was the patrilocal extended family, which correlated with the patrilineal descent of the area. The men of these families cooperated in hunting and other essential economic activities. The picture is complicated by the fact that most of these tribes also farmed and that women did most of the farming. Among the Omaha, matrilocal extended family organization seems to have prevailed during the farming season, when everyone lived in the large earth lodges. During the rest of the year, when hunting dominated subsistence, tipis were the universal house type and these were grouped according to patrilocal and patrilineal alignment. This may have been true of other tribes which occupied both types of dwellings. One gets the impression that the matrilocal bias may have been more obtrusive at an earlier date, and that the shift has been toward the patrilocal, perhaps again aided by the fur trade, the horse, and the buffalo.

Matrilocal extended families were dominant among tribes on the extreme western edge of the Prairie area: Hidatsa, Mandan, Arikara, Pawnee, and Wichita. All of these peoples lived in permanent houses large enough to accommodate an entire extended family. The first three tribes occupied these structures almost all the year round, while the last two spent more time in tipis. Besides the house, these families owned, in common, farm land, and such chattels as mortars and pestles and dogs—but not horses, which belonged to individual men. Because polygyny was principally, if not wholly, sororal, it fitted into the matrilocal picture.

Among the Iroquois in the Northeast, the matrilocal extended family also prevailed. It occupied a longhouse, with each constituent nuclear family partitioned off in a room by itself but sharing its fire with the nuclear family opposite it. Leadership was vested in the oldest matron, who directed farm work, kept peace within, and appointed a man in the same maternal line to represent the group in council. Husbands were expected to hunt and thus provide meat for their families, but had little to say about management of the household. Compared to the extended family, the nuclear family amounted to little. Although monogamy was the only form of marriage tolerated, the practice was highly elastic because of the high mortality of men in warfare and the ease with which a disgruntled wife could divorce a husband. The nuclear family was therefore unstable and, aside from reproduction, performed no important functions that could not be more effectively handled by the extended family. Individuals came and went, were born and died, but maternal lineage segments, which formed the core of the extended family, went on indefinitely.

The same matrilocal extended family organization prevailed in the Southeast, although by the time literate observers arrived, it was already on its way out. Nonsororal polygyny was one of the disruptive factors. A man could not reside matrilocally with two wives who were unrelated and hence from two different families. He had to break the residence rule and set up an independent establishment of his own. The fact that the chiefs and other officers were all selected by a male council is evidence of the weaker authority of women as compared to Iroquois women.

The western Pueblos in the Southwest possessed a matrilocal extended family organization which approached that of the Iroquois in its importance. It was the maternal lineage segment which constituted the core of the extended family, owned the farm land and houses, and functioned as a stabilizing force in the society. As among the Iroquois, monogamy was insisted upon, and strict matrilocal residence was formerly observed. Because everyone in a pueblo shared a large apartment house with everyone else in the community, separate housing for extended families did not exist. However, nuclear families commonly occupied separate rooms, and those which collectively made up a matrilocal extended family lived in adjoining rooms. Female members often worked together, especially when grinding maize. The extended family section was also a center for ritual activities, not of the husbands but of the brothers and mother's brothers of the women. This was really a lineage or sib function, but the location was in the household.

All the Athapaskan-speaking peoples of the Southwest had matrilocal extended families. The Navaho family structure was most like that of the western Pueblos, with that of the western Apache next nearest the western Pueblo model, and that of the other Apaches still further removed. Modern Navaho hogans are larger than the earlier and more widespread southern Athapaskan house types; yet they continue to shelter only a single nuclear family, as did earlier hogans. Such dwellings were grouped in clusters to form the extended family unit. The functions of these extended families were mainly economic; the women worked together at sheep raising and farming, and the men at hunting and raiding.

The patrilocal extended families of the Aztecs of Mexico occupied walled courtyards, within which there were several separate houses for as many constituent nuclear families. Although farm land nominally belonged to the tribe, it was parceled out by officials to families, and the use of a certain plot often passed from father to son, thus staying within the extended family as well as within the lineage. Such family units probably manufactured some surplus goods to be exchanged at markets or traded to distant towns. The picture for the Maya is similar but somewhat looser because of the geographical environment. The heavy rainfall in most of the Maya territory leached out minerals from the soil, resulting in land of inferior quality. A field could be used for only two or three seasons, after which it was allowed to be reclaimed by the jungle; then a new field was cleared. This constant shifting of farm plots discouraged strict inheritance. Patrilocal extended families had similar economic functions among other Meso-American peoples.

George Peter Murdock, in his book *Social Structure* (1949), stresses the role of the nuclear family when he says, "Whatever larger familial forms may exist, and to whatever extent the greater unit may assume some of the burdens of the lesser, the nuclear family is always recognizable and always has its distinctive and vital functions—sexual, economic, reproductive, and educational . . ." (p. 3). In contrast, Ralph Linton, in his book *The Study of Man* (1936), says that the nuclear family plays "an insignificant rôle in the lives of many societies" (p. 153). In an attempt to evaluate North American family structure in the light of these opposing statements, the extended family may be regarded as playing a socially more important role than the nuclear family among about half the tribes of the continent. The matrilocal extended families of the western Pueblos, Hidatsa-Mandans, and Iroquois played an especially dominant role. The position of women was particularly strong in these societies where women owned the houses and farm land and were the sex through which descent was traced. In these same cultures, the position of the husband in the nuclear family was consistently weak; he had little to say, had little control over his own children, and could be divorced at the drop of his hat outside the dwelling door. The average man or woman in these cultures had been a member of three or four different nuclear families in his lifetime, as a result of death, divorce, and remarriage, but membership among the core of women in the extended family had remained stable. The sexual and reproductive roles of the males were absolutely necessary to biological and cultural survival, but one individual was readily replaced by another. In such matrilineal societies, the nuclear family was relatively insignificant.

REFERENCES

DAMAS, 1963; DRUCKER, 1939; EGGAN, 1950, 1955; GAYTON, 1945; GIFFORD, 1916, 1926, 1944; GOLDSCHMIDT, 1948; GRABURN, 1964; HALLOWELL, 1937, 1949; HELM, 1965; 1969; HELM AND DAMAS, 1963; HOEBEL, 1939, 1966; KELLY, 1942; LEACOCK, n.d., 1955; LEWIS, 1942; LINTON, 1936; LOWIE, 1948, 1954; MICKEY, 1955; MURDOCK, 1949, 1957; SPECK, 1915, 1917, 1918, 1920b; SPECK AND EISELEY, 1939; SPENCER, 1959; STEWARD, 1938; STRONG, 1929; SWANTON, 1946; WEYER, 1932.

15

Larger Kin Groups, Kin Terms

I N addition to the family units described in the preceding chapter, there were six other kinds of kinship groups known to North American natives: lineages, sibs, moieties, phratries, clans, and demes. All except the lineage were normally larger than the extended family. All are generally regarded as kin groups, but relationship in all but the first might rest partly on tradition; moiety affiliation was sometimes determined by factors other than kinship.

LINEAGES, SIBS, MOIETIES, PHRATRIES

The extended family groups described in the preceding chapter were residential groups; all the members resided together in a single dwelling or in several small dwellings close together. They all included husbands and wives and unmarried children. The kinship bonds which linked the members were in part genetic and in part affinal. In contrast to families, lineages were bound together exclusively by genetic ties. Lineages as functioning kinship units do not exist in the United States among Whites, but our patrilineal (agnatic) inheritance of surnames is undoubtedly a vestige of a former lineage system in Europe.

Lineage structure may be illustrated by the following hypothetical example. Suppose that all women in the United States retained their maiden surnames after marriage and that everyone was compelled to marry a person with a different surname. Assigning the name "Smith" to the senior male, his patrilineal descendants inheriting the same name would be: son, daughter, son's son, son's daughter, son's son's son, son's son's daughter, and so forth. These relatives are shown in Figure 34a. They constitute a paternal (agnatic) lineage, or patrilineage, and all members are genetically related to each other. Brothers and sisters always belong to the same lineage, but husbands and wives never do, because the rule of exogamy requires everyone to marry outside of his own name group. A lineage is therefore not a residential group (except for a few deviant peoples in the Old World). Brothers and sisters reside together only in childhood; they part company at marriage.

A maternal (uterine) lineage may be illustrated by a hypothetical example in which everyone inherits his surname, "Jones," from his mother instead of his father. If everyone is required to marry a person with a different surname and women retain their maiden surnames, as above, those who possess the name "Jones" are aligned as in Figure 34*b*. These genetic relatives form a maternal lineage—or matrilineage, for short.

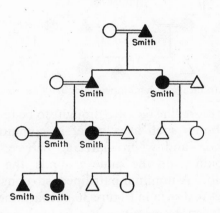

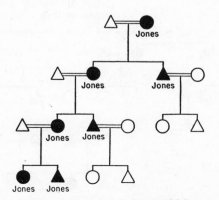

FIG. 34. Lineages. After Driver and Massey

In actual life, multiple sons and daughters frequently appear in the same generation, so that in succeeding generations cousins belong to the same lineage. A patrilineage with multiple males in all but the first generation is illustrated in Figure 35. In the third generation, the two males belonging to the lineage are first cousins; in the fourth generation, they are second cousins. A matrilineage may also be ramified by the presence of multiple females in any or all of its generations.

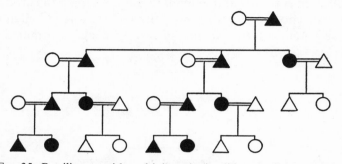

FIG. 35. Patrilineage with multiple males in all but the first generation

When two or more lineages are thought to be related by a fictitious or traditional bond, such as a belief in common descent from a mythical ancestor, and when marriage between persons in these lineages is forbidden on the same grounds, the group of lineages constitutes a "sib." A minimal patrilineal sib consisting of two minimal patrilineages is shown in Figure 36. A matrilineal sib is formed by combining two or more matrilineages according to a principle which prohibits marriage between the member matrilineages.

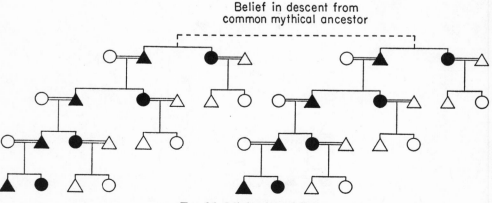

FIG. 36. Minimal patrisib

Historically, lineages probably arose before sibs, and sibs appear to have been formed most often by a lineage forking and reforking, as in Figure 35, until the cousins were so remote that it was impossible to trace their ancestry back to a real progenitor. In the absence of written records, this might occur in as few as six or seven generations. Sibs are normally larger than lineages, although a sib recently decimated by war or disease might be smaller than a lineage which escaped these ravages. The largest sibs in native North America probably had about a thousand members, although some of those of the Maya may have been larger. North of Mexico, there were few towns with populations as high as a thousand, so that when sib membership approached this figure, the members usually were distributed among a number of villages or towns. For example, the Creek Indians of Alabama and Georgia possessed about forty sibs, fifty villages, and a population of about 18,000. Although the sibs averaged about 450 members, some were much larger than others and may have had a thousand members. Each village, on the average, was occupied by people from half a dozen different sibs. Rules of sib exogamy were extended to all of the fifty

Maternal lineage   ━ ━ ━ ━ ━
Matrilocal extended family   •••••••••

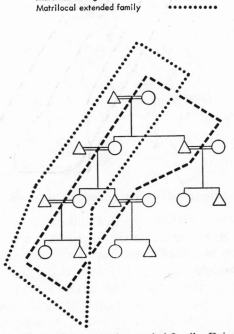

Fɪɢ. 37. Matricentered lineage and extended family. Driver and Massey

villages: for example, a man of the deer sib could not marry a women of the same sib, even though she lived in another Creek village more than a hundred miles distant from his place of residence.

The difference between an extended family and a lineage is further illustrated in Figure 37, where a matrilocal extended family and a maternal lineage are shown together. Note that immature children in the last generation belong to both. When the boy marries, however, he will go to live with his bride's family and will no longer be a member of the family in which he was born.

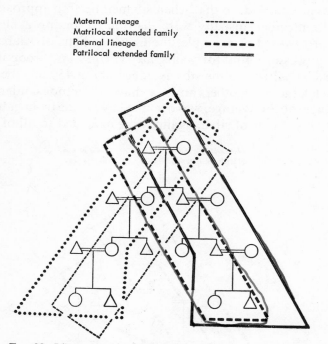

Maternal lineage	-----------
Matrilocal extended family	••••••••••
Paternal lineage	-------
Patrilocal extended family	▬▬▬▬▬

FIG. 38. Lineages and extended families. Driver and Massey

Figure 38 illustrates all four types of unilocal extended families and lineages in one figure: the maternal lineage; the matrilocal extended family; the paternal lineage; the patrilocal extended family. The opposed patrilocal and matrilocal systems could not exist in the same society; but there are a few societies in the Old World where both kinds of descent, but in respect to different attributes, coexist. Again, it should be pointed out that large numbers of children can increase such kin groups to several times the size indicated on the diagram.

When either lineages or sibs, or both, exist in a society, the society is said to possess "unilineal," "unilinear," or "unilateral" descent. These three terms are synonymous in anthropology, and the thing that descends is affiliation in a kinship group. Such descent may be marked by a name or crest and reinforced by mythology. When lineages and sibs are absent, descent is said to be "bilateral," "ambilineal," or "cognatic." The term "bilineal" is rarely used for this concept, and "bilinear" has been assigned to double descent systems by Murdock (1949). The term "multilateral" or "multilineal" is occasionally used to describe descent in nonunilineal societies, because the number of one's actual genetic ancestors doubles with each ascending generation. One has two parents, four grandparents, eight great grandparents, and so on. Where unilineal descent prevails, only one person in each of these generations is singled out as the significant ancestor, although the others of course are known to exist. It is possible to have lineages without sibs, but not sibs without lineages. Where both exist together, native terminology sometimes recognizes one without the other, designates both by the same term, or has a separate word for each.

Map 32 gives the geographical distributions of the three major kinds of descent. Matrilineal descent was found in a large area in the northwest, which includes part of the Sub-Arctic as well as the Northwest Coast. It appeared again in a small part of the Southwest, and among three tribes on the northern Plains and Prairies; it covered almost the entire East. Patrilineal descent and patrilineages were present in California and adjacent Baja California and Southwest, were of rare occurrence in southwest Mexico, apparently universal for the Mayas of southeast Mexico, and general on the Prairies and the adjacent part of the Sub-Arctic occupied by the Ojibwa. Almost all the remaining territory of aboriginal North America lacked lineages and sibs and traced descent bilaterally.

A term related to lineage and sib is "moiety," from the French; it means simply "half," Applied to social structure, it refers to one of two organizations into which a tribe or community is divided. Moieties may be unilineal and exogamous kin groups, or unilineal but not always exogamous kin groups. They may be patrilineal and consist entirely of male members. They may not be kinship groups at all, but membership may be determined in some other way, as will be shown below. When only two sibs exist, they may be called "sibs," "moieties," or "moiety-sibs." However, some anthropologists designate all twofold kinship groups "moieties," and reserve the term "sib" for three or more. The former usage will be followed here.

Another related term is "phratry." A phratry is two or more sibs which are linked in some way. When a man cannot marry a woman of a certain other sib, the two sibs which form the exogamous unit may be said to constitute a phratry. Phratries may contain three or even more sibs. When there are only two phratries, they are the equivalent of moieties and may be so labeled. Phratries occureed among a majority of tribes on the Prairies and in the East, and also on the northern Northwest Coast.

A large majority of North American Indians with unilineal descent had multiple (three or more) sib systems. Exceptions to this generalization are the following: the Bering Sea Eskimo had only lineages; most of the Sub-Arctic Athapaskans with matrilineal descent had only two moiety-sibs; lineages were the largest unilateral unit on the Oregon coast and in most of California except on the Colorado River. All, or nearly all, other unilateral North American tribes possessed three or more sibs. Some idea of the wide variation in numbers of sibs can be gathered from Map 34. The range of reported sibs is from three to sixty. In most cases of large numbers of sibs, they were not all present in the same community. Thus the sixty sibs of the Western Apache were a summation of the sibs in each of the five subdivisions and, within these smaller territorial units, each sib was not present in every band. This great variation in numbers of sibs suggests local independent history and considerable fluidity for the sib as a social unit. Some of the sibs consisted of only one lineage, and some were extinct by the time the anthropologist arrived. There is no areal patterning in the number of multiple sibs; each of the three major areas, Northwest, Southwest, and Prairies-East, shows much internal variation.

Information on moieties has been assembled on Map 34. In the Northwest, the matrilineal exogamous moieties were most often called Wolf and Raven. They were further subdivided into sibs on the coast, but the interior tribes possessed only the two units. The moieties of the neighboring Haisla were nonunilineal and nonexogamous. They were nothing more than boys' rivalry groups in which membership was determined by place of residence in the village. The nearby Mackenzie Eskimo possessed two informal moieties called Raven and Crane. Everybody could join one of the groups—children usually chose that of their father—but they had no function other than rivalry in jesting and hurling derogatory remarks at one another. The name "Raven" suggests derivation from matrilineal exogamous moieties to the southwest, although the history of the name may be independent of that of the kin alignment and functions.

The patrilineal exogamous moieties of California were made up of constituent lineages, but sibs were lacking in most localities. The moieties functioned in practically every ceremony known to these cultures, and were especially obtrusive at death rites. The Pomo and their neighbors possessed patrilineal but agamous moieties, which did not regulate marriage but functioned in the competitive group sweating of men, in men's athletic games, and in public ceremonies participated in by both sexes, including the Kuksu cycle. Social groups are called "agamous" when marriage is random with respect to one's in-group and out-groups; agamous groups are neither exogamous nor endogamous. The Washo moieties were similar to those of the Pomo, functioning in men's athletic games and, with slight modification, in ceremonies of both sexes. The dual organization of the western Mono and eastern Yokuts was also patrilineal and agamous, and had like functions: games, feasts, ceremonies. All of these peripheral systems seem to have had a common origin with the more central patrilineal exogamous systems.

In the Southwest, exogamous moieties were absent. The patrilineal, agamous, twofold divisions of the Pima and Papago functioned in ceremonies and athletic games and influenced a man's dreaming and choice of guardian spirit. Those of the eastern Pueblos showed much internal variation, but were generally agamous and nonunilineal, but with some patrilineal leaning. Multiple kivas (religious organizations) were divided into two moietal groups; political officers were dual, one set for each moiety; and moieties functioned in racing and dancing at public ceremonies.

A considerably variety of moieties occurred in the Prairies and East. Among the Prairie Sioux, multiple sibs were grouped into two moiety-phratries which functioned in athletic games, tribal councils, and religious ceremonies. Those of the Pawnee were unique: the endogamous demes were divided into north and south divisions for the chief's council, the camp circle, and the ceremonial circle of practically all ceremonies. With the Hidatsas and Mandans, moieties owned game pits and served as units for the division of the products of the hunt. In the Southeast, the Chickasaws and Choctaws had moieties which were dedicated to peace versus war but which also buried each other's dead. The Creek possessed two sets of moieties: phratry-moieties and town-moieties. Both sets were called "peace" (white) and "war" (red).

The phratry-moieties divided the sibs nearly evenly between them, and both were present in every town. The town-moieties divided the towns into two groups, there being thirty-one peace towns and eighteen war towns among the forty-nine for which moiety affiliation is known. There was only one town-moiety in each town, because the whole town belonged to it. The phratry-moieties tended to be exogamous, the town-moieties endogamous. Among the Iroquois, multiple sibs were grouped into two moiety-phratries which opposed each other in athletic games. Around the Great Lakes, a number of tribes had non-unilinear agamous moieties, in which membership in some cases was determined by order of birth or season of birth. These units competed in athletic contests.

The eastern Eskimo had weak moieties, the membership in which was determined by season of birth. Those born in the winter belonged to one; those born in the summer to the other. The men competed in a tug-of-war at a public festival in late autumn.

Many aboriginal Mexican towns were divided into two or more sections which are known in the source material by the Spanish term *barrio*. Wherever two such divisions exist, they may be called moieties. Among the Mixe, membership in the moiety-barrios was inherited from the father. The town was divided into two halves by an imaginary line through the plaza. As regards marriage, these moieties were agamous, but a woman joined that of her husband at marriage if her father had belonged to the opposite one from her husband. The highest officials in the town, the major and judge, had to be of opposite moieties, and each year each office rotated to a man of the opposite moiety. The police force also had to be chosen from the two moieties, and its leadership rotated weekly from one moiety to the other. All of this strongly suggests the town organization of the eastern Pueblos.

This cursory survey of moiety organization shows amazing variety. In general, it may be said that the distribution of moieties conforms fairly closely to the distribution of unilateral descent, whether the moieties are unilateral or not. This intimates some historical relationship between the two, as Olson (1933) has suggested.

CLANS AND DEMES

The term "clan" has been used in anthropology for about a century, but a new meaning, which is used here, has been assigned to it (Murdock, 1949). The new meaning introduces a new concept, which clears up earlier confusion and fills a vacuum left in previous systems of kinship structure. We have seen that families are residential groups and that exogamous lineages, sibs, moieties, and phratries are unilineal genetic (blood) groups. The clan has been called a compromise kin group because it is both residential and unilineal. It is composed of persons of one sex who are members of the same sib, the unmarried members of the opposite sex, and the spouses of the married members. Thus a "matriclan" consists of the women of a matrisib, their unmarried sons, and their husbands. A "patriclan" is made up of the men of a patrisib, their unmarried daughters, and their wives. An "avunculan" is composed of the men of a matrisib, their unmarried sons and daughters, their married daughters where cross-cousin

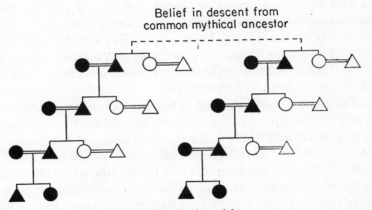

FIG. 39. Minimal patriclan

marriage prevails, their sisters' sons, and their wives. Each clan which is also a village apart from other clans may be called a "clan community," whereas a clan which comprises a section of a town or city is called a "clan barrio."

The clan is made up of two or more unilocal extended families, and also must be associated with a formalized rule of unilineal descent with sib exogamy. A patriclan is illustrated in Figure 39; it consists of two patrilocal extended families joined by a traditional bond of unilineal descent connecting the males. Unilocal extended families may exist with or without strict unilineal descent, but clans occur only where unilineal descent is present. Not every society with unilineal descent has clans, however, because it is possible to have a number of lineages or sibs in the same village or section of a town. Avunculans were found on the northern Northwest Coast, where avunculocal residence and matrilineal descent prevailed. Most of these clans were separate villages, hence they are properly called "avunculocal clan communities." Each was a land owning unit, a political unit, and a warring unit against other clans.

Patrilocal clan communities or extended family communities are found among almost half the tribes in California. Each normally had a separate territory and was a separate entity. Here and there they were aggregated into larger political units. In the Southwest, the Navahos and Western Apaches had matriclans which formerly owned farm land which was worked by both sexes, with men doing more than women in recent years. There is no conclusive evidence for matriclans among the Hidatsas of the upper Missouri River, but for the Mandans it is said that there was a tendency for related families to select adjacent quarters in the village and, in another passage, that lineages were closely associated with lodge groups. These statements may refer to clans. The Prairie tribes with patrilineal descent may have possessed patrilocal clan communities in the early historical period. It is difficult to prove their existence, however, because of the disruptions caused by White contact. When the Deghia Siouan tribes assembled considerable numbers of their members, each clan camped in a certain part of the camp circle and became, for the time being, a clan barrio. These units were ceremonial rather than economic, however.

In the East, both the Iroquois and the Southeastern tribes seem to have possessed matriclans. Among the Iroquois, in historic times these seem to have been principally clan barrios in villages up to 3,000 persons. The Mohawks, however, are reported to have had three villages, each a matriclan community. In the Southeast, there were both matrilocal clan communities and matrilocal clan barrios. The former predominated among the Chickasaws; the latter among the Creeks. The matrilocal clan communities, at least, were farm landowning units and political entities. The matrilocal clan barrios were politically part of a town unit. Whether they had separate fields is uncertain, but it seems likely in light of what we know of extended family organization.

In Mexico, patrilocal clan barrios seem to have occurred on the western coast of Nayarit and Colima. Patrilocal clan communities may also have been present among other Meso-American groups. The paucity of information makes it impossible to give a complete distribution.

Another territorial and political kinship unit is the "deme." Demes may be endogamous or exogamous. Seldom do we find 100 per cent endogamy or exogamy. The endogamous deme is a community (village or band) which is not further segmented by unilineal descent and which is small enough so that all members are aware of their bilateral genetic relationship to all or most other members of the group. Such genetic relationship is often not traceable in cultures that do not have writing; but if the members regard themselves as being genetically interrelated, that is sufficient to label their group a deme. Marriage within the endogamous deme is the rule, providing the bride and groom are not too closely related.

Exogamous demes fall into two classes, according to rule of residence: patrilocal and matrilocal. These may be abbreviated to "patridemes" and "matridemes." Patridemes are communities in which residence is mainly patrilocal and in which most of the marriages may be locally exogamous, but actual data show that this seldom happens. Complete exogamy is associated with unilineal kin groups, such as lineages and sibs. If a patrideme were completely exogamous, its structure would be identical with that of a patriclan. It would differ only in lacking a formalized rule of exogamy and a belief in common descent from a mythical ancestor. If the broken line at the top of Figure 39 were eliminated, it would depict a patrideme. Patridemes, however, are usually regulated by looser rules of behavior. Matridemes are communities in which residence is principally matrilocal and in which most of the marriages are locally exogamous. The majority of the population are genetically related through females. If there were 100 per cent conformity to these rules, the matrideme would be identical in composition to the matriclan, except for the unilineal traditional tie at the top.

Demes tend to be clustered near areas of unilateral descent rather than randomly scattered. This suggests that the kind of geographic and cultural environment conducive to lineages and sibs, or the contact with lineages and sibs, encourages demes. Although Murdock (1967: 49) has dropped the concept of the exogamous deme, recognition of such social units on the border between unilateral and bilateral descent is needed in order to fill out the descriptive picture as well as to show transitional stages for both the acquisition and the loss of full-blown unilateral descent systems. I regard the exogamous demes of Murdock (1949) and the first edition of the present book as satisfactory concepts of this nature. Such terms as "quasi-lineage" or "quasi-sib" are satisfactory for borderline descent groups, but "quasi-clan" would be nearer the earlier concept of the exogamous deme.

KINSHIP TERMINOLOGY

Kinship terminologies from foreign languages are sometimes confusing if one has an insufficient knowledge of English kinship terms. Therefore, we shall begin this discussion with English terms. Figure 40 assembles the basic English words. It is noted immediately that some of the terms, such as "cousin," appear more than once in the diagram. As anthropologists, we need a more specific term for each of the relatives not distinguished by English words. If we begin with English terms for primary relatives, that is, the relatives closest to oneself, we can string these together with apostrophes to designate more remote relatives. Thus "mother's brother" refers to an uncle, and "mother's brother's daughter" to a cousin. The length of these terms can be obviated by using the following two-letter abbreviations: *Fa*, father; *Mo*, mother; *Si*, sister; *Br*, brother; *So*, son; *Da*, daughter; *Hu*, husband; *Wi*, wife. To express a more remote relationship, these abbreviations may be strung together without apostrophes. For example, *MoBrDa* may be used to signify one's mother's brother's daughter.

Figure 41 presents the same relatives as Figure 40, but gives them a more precise set of labels in terms of these abbreviations. If we list the terms in both diagrams for comparison, as in Table 4, we find that there are twenty-three basic English terms which designate forty-six specific relatives which anthropologists keep separate in their thinking. On the average, each English term accounts for two relationships. In more detail, we find that: ten basic English words include only one relative; another ten include two relatives each; two others include four relatives each; and one basic word, "cousin," includes eight relatives. The twenty-three basic English terms may also be divided into fifteen words for genetic relatives and eight for affinal relatives.

In addition to the twenty-three basic English terms, there are a number of others in common use: parent, child, grandparent, grandchild, stepfather, stepmother, stepson, stepdaughter, stepparent, stepchild, stepbrother, stepsister, half brother, half sister; and, in cases of adoption, foster father, foster mother, foster son, foster daughter, foster parent, foster child.

Every language not only has its own words to designate kin but it normally employs a classification of kin specifically different from that of every other language and culture. The result is a bewildering amount of detail which anthropologists have not succeeded in analyzing completely. However, by narrowing down to a few relatives and to a few principles of classification, it is possible to exhaust the data. Let us first consider terms for genetic aunts and their relation to terms for mother. Altogether there are three relationships involved: mother, mother's sister, and father's sister. In English we designate "mother" by one term, but we lump "mother's sister" and "father's sister" under

TABLE 4

BASIC ENGLISH KINSHIP TERMS, WITH
ANTHROPOLOGICAL MEANINGS

Aunt	FaSi, FaBrWi, MoSi, MoBrWi
Brother	Br
Brother-in-law	SiHu, WiBr
Cousin	FaBrDa, FaBrSo, FaSiDa, FaSiSo, MoBrDa, MoBrSo, MoSiDa, MoSiSo
Daughter	Da
Daughter-in-law	SoWi
Father	Fa
Father-in-law	HuFa, WiFa
Granddaughter	DaDa, SoDa
Grandfather	FaFa, MoFa
Grandmother	FaMo, MoMo
Grandson	DaSo, SoSo
Husband	Hu
Mother	Mo
Mother-in-law	HuMo, WiMo
Nephew	BrSo, SiSo
Niece	BrDa, SiDa
Sister	Si
Sister-in-law	BrWi, WiSi
Son	So
Son-in-law	DaHu
Uncle	FaBr, FaSiHu, MoBr, MoSiHu
Wife	Wi

a second term—"aunt." This is called *lineal* terminology because the lineal relative (mother) is distinguished from the collateral relatives (aunts). In some languages, there is only one word for all three of these relatives; this is called *generation* terminology. In still other languages, there are three separate terms for each of the relatives; this is labeled *bifurcate collateral* terminology, to emphasize the fact that the two forks of one's ancestry are distinguished as well as the lineal from the collateral. In still other languages, there is one word for both "mother" and "mother's sister," and a second word for "father's sister"; this is called *bifurcate merging*, because it distinguishes both ancestral forks but merges the mother and the mother's sister on one fork. Figure 42

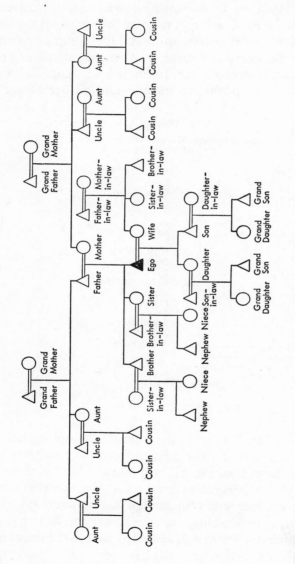

Fig. 40. Basic English kinship terminology. Driver and Massey

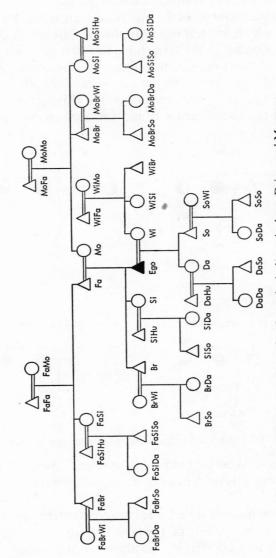

FIG. 41. English abbreviations of anthropological terminology. Driver and Massey

illustrates these four types of mother-aunt terminology. Each different shade stands for a different word in the language.

A considerable number of North American tribes have pairs of kinship terms which are not exact duplicates but which overlap. An example from English is the term for one's first cousin's child. This relative is called "first-cousin-once-removed" by some persons, and "second cousin" by others. The phrase "second cousin" may also be applied to one's parent's first cousin's child. This sort of confusion is to be found in the classification of mother-aunt terms among North

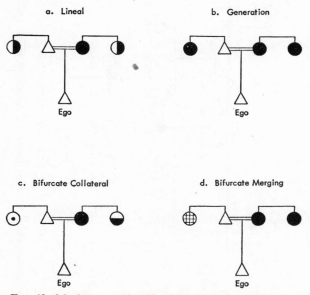

Fig. 42. Mother-aunt classifications. Driver and Massey

American Indians. Wherever two ways to refer to these relatives occur for the same tribe, this evidence has been plotted with overlapping or special symbols.

The distinction must also be made between the term used to address a relative when he is present and the term used to refer to him when he is absent. The vast majority of kinship terms are employed in both address and reference, in Indian languages as well as in our own, but a minority are limited to one or the other usage. For example, in English, we refer to our spouse's mother as "mother-in-law," but we address her as "mother." In address, we classify her with our true mother; in reference, we put her in a class by herself. In general, experience has shown that terms of reference are more specific than terms of address. For this reason, terms of reference have been selected over those of address wherever they differed.

Map 35 gives the geographical distributions of the four ways of classifying mothers and aunts for terms of reference. It can be seen at a glance that bifurcate collateral is the most frequent for the continent as a whole. It is the dominant type in the Eastern Sub-Arctic, on the Plateau, in California, the Great Basin, and the Southwest. It coexists with bifurcate merging on the northern Northwest Coast, in the Southeast, and among isolated tribes in other areas. It is positively correlated with bilateral descent (Map 32) in conformity with functional theory, although there are a fair number of instances where it is associated with either matrilineal or patrilineal descent. In the majority of these unilineal instances, bifurcate collateral classification coexists with bifurcate merging. The inference naturally drawn from these facts is that bifurcate collateral is probably the oldest type of mother-aunt classification in aboriginal North America, or at least older than bifurcate merging. After unilocal residence and unilateral descent arose, bifurcate collateral seems to have lost ground to bifurcate merging. The process of change, however, was not abrupt; on the contrary, both systems coexisted for a time during the transitional period. After White contact, the process was reversed; bifurcate merging lost ground to bifurcate collateral. The fairly common coexistence of the two systems among a number of tribes, as shown on Map 35, is to be explained in this historical manner.

Lineal mother-aunt terminology is much more restricted than bifurcate collateral, and overlaps it in only one instance. Nevertheless, lineal is also positively correlated with bilateral descent (Map 32). Lineal and bifurcate collateral combined, however, yield a higher correlation with bilateral descent than either alone. Furthermore, lineal shows much less overlap with bifurcate merging than does bifurcate collateral. Bifurcate merging and bifurcate collateral both incorporate the principle of bifurcation, which tends to tie them together conceptually.

Bifurcate merging mother-aunt terms (Map 35) exhibit a definite positive correlation with unilateral descent (Map 32), although this correlation is far from perfect. Murdock (1949) has previously established this and the other correlations from his worldwide sample of 250 tribes. The explanation is a simple one. In a system of unilateral descent with exogamy, one's mother's sister is always in the same lineage and sib as one's mother, while one's father's sister always belongs to a different lineage and sib. This is true regardless of whether descent is matrilineal or patrilineal.

The Plains area bristles with negative instances. Here most tribes have bilateral descent along with bifurcate merging mother-aunt terms. A possible explanation of this discrepancy is that most of the Plains tribes formerly possessed unilateral descent or cross-cousin marriage when they lived farther east and were more sedentary, but that they lost one or both when they adopted the nomadic life of the Plains. Linguistic evidence favors Eastern origin for all the Plains tribes known to have had bifurcate merging terminology, except the Sarsi, Wind River Shoshoni, and Comanche.

Generation mother-aunt classification is much the rarest of the four, and overlaps each of the other three in at least one instance. It coexists with patrilineal, matrilineal, and bilateral descent—all three. It is too rare, however, to be satisfactorily explained by correlation theory.

What about correlations with language? It is generally agreed that any possible correlations which might exist between kinship classification and systems of phonology and morphology would prove no causal relationships. The aspect of language that is relevant to kinship problems is the historical relationships revealed by language family classification based primarily on vocabulary. Map 37 gives distributions of the language families of native North America. A comparison of major language units with mother-aunt terminologies reveals no startling high correlations. However, there are a few language families in which all or nearly all the member languages possess the same mother-aunt classifications. Thus the Yuman languages of the Southwest are all bifurcate collateral; the Salish of the Northwest are predominantly lineal; the Plains-Prairie Sioux are all bifurcate merging. In spite of the fact that all three of these mother-aunt classifications occur among languages in many other families, their near universality within these particular language families would yield a significant positive correlation between them and the language family. This suggests that these ways of classifying mothers and aunts may possess considerable antiquity. While they may not go back to the time when each language family consisted of only a single mother tongue, they may date from a time when there was much less linguistic differentiation within these families. If such is the case, the present uniformity or near uniformity of mother-aunt categories within each of these families may be *partially* explained as a linguistic heritage—*partially* explained (with emphasis on the *partially*) because, unless the social structure remained fairly stable, we should not expect the kinship classification to remain stable.

Another example of a correlation between language family and mother-aunt terminology is that of the Algonquians, most of whom have bifurcate collateral terminology. Only those who are neighbors of the Sioux and the Iroquois employ bifurcate merging terminology. The historical inference from these facts is that the older variant among the Algonquians is bifurcate collateral, and that those tribes which later contacted Sioux and Iroquois acquired a more sedentary economy, unilateral descent, or some other cultural feature which encouraged the shift to bifurcate merging terminology. In such cases, the classification for mothers and aunts may be acquired by contact with languages of another family, even though the words themselves are not transferred. This is called "stimulus diffusion" (Kroeber, 1940: 1–20). The acquired culture, which goes with the new verbal classification, seems to be the principal cause of the change. Language classification gives us clues to historical priority and direction of change.

An exhaustive study of the relationship of kinship terminology to language and culture demands analysis of the words themselves used to designate kin. Demitri Shimkin has done this for Uto-Aztecan languages. After making a careful reconstruction of the original Uto-Aztecan terms for relatives, he found that, on the average, each language retained about half of the list. The origin of the new terms, which replaced the half that was lost, is still uncertain. In order to show that words from neighboring language families were acquired by the Uto-Aztecans, it would be necessary to reconstruct prototypes of the kinship terminologies of these language families. This has not been done completely. In regard to the mere classification of kin, only about one-third of the original classificatory elements seems to have been lost. Classificatory categories are, therefore, more stable than the words used to label them in this language family. When we look to neighboring language families for possible sources of classificatory categories, the search is rewarding. Those tribes which have had most contact with alien language families have not only lost the most Uto-Aztecan elements but have replaced them with the largest number of foreign elements. The processes of change have also involved shifts in economy and social organization, often facilitated by intermarriage.

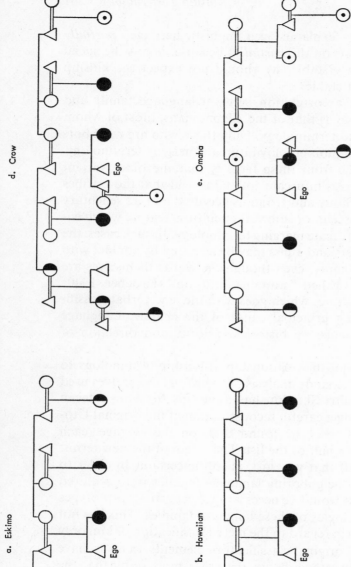

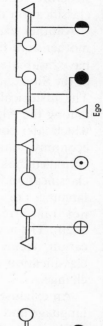

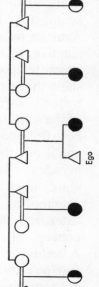

Fig. 43. Sister-cousin classifications. Driver and Massey

a. Eskimo

b. Hawaiian

c. Iroquois

d. Crow

e. Omaha

f. Sudanese (Quiche Maya)

Ego

Language and culture therefore changed together; one did not cause the other to change.

Kinship terminologies for sisters and female cousins are a little more complicated. There are six principal ways of classifying sisters and cousins in native North America, as shown in Figure 43. The Eskimo or lineal type has one word for all female cousins but a separate term for "sister." The Hawaiian or generation type uses a single term for "sister" and for all female cousins as well. The Iroquois type designates "sister" and female parallel cousins by one word and female cross-cousins by a second word. The Omaha type merges "sister" and female parallel cousins under a single term, calls MoBrDa and MoSi by a second term, and FaSiDa and SiDa by a third term. The Crow type follows suit by merging "sister" with female parallel cousins, but calls MoBrDa and BrDa by a second term and FaSiDa and FaSi by a third term. The Descriptive (Sudanese) type uses separate descriptive terms for MoBrDa and FaSiDa, and for each of the parallel cousins as well, in the few instances reported for North America. In Figure 43d, Crow type, we have added an extra generation on the left side to bring out the fact that FaSi, FaSiDa, and FaSiDaDa are all referred to by the same word. These relatives form a maternal lineage which may be extended in a descending direction indefinitely. The significant point about the Crow kinship system is that persons of the same sex in certain maternal lineages are designated by a single kinship term. For the Omaha type, Figure 43e, a paternal lineage may be observed on the right side of the diagram. The Omaha type agrees with the Crow in being a lineage system; but it features the paternal line, while the Crow stresses the maternal line. Geographical distribution of types of classification of sisters and female cousins have been given by Driver and Massey (1957: Map 161).

THE ORIGIN OF UNILATERAL DESCENT

The origin of unilateral descent has been a favorite topic for speculation by anthropologists from the time of Lewis H. Morgan (1871, 1877) down to the present. There are two extreme points of view which may be regarded as the poles between which all others range. The first is the extreme diffusionist explanation of Morgan and others. All of this group have argued for a single origin and subsequent worldwide diffusion of unilateral descent, or a dual origin with patrilineal and matrilineal descent originating independently of each other and subsequently spreading over the world. The second extreme point of view is that of certain evolutionists who do not always deny diffusion but who stress the repeated independent origin of unilateral descent from certain relatively uniform antecedent conditions. The most recurrent evolutionary sequence begins with a unisexual division of labor in subsistence pursuits, from which unilocal residence is derived, and proceeds from unilocal residence to unilateral descent. No evolutionist has argued, however, that there are as many separate origins of sibs as there are tribes known to have possessed them. Evolutionary hypotheses have, therefore, not been pushed to the extreme that marks some of the diffusionist explanations. Almost all of the evolutionists have also recognized the role of diffusion or acculturation.

Because Murdock's discussion of evolution versus diffusion in *Social Structure* is among the most comprehensive, we can use a quote from him as a point of departure:

> The evidence from our 250 societies supports the contention of the American historical anthropologists, against the evolutionists, that there is no inevitable sequence of social forms nor any necessary association between particular rules of residence or descent or particular types of kin groups or kinship terms and levels of culture, types of economy, or forms of government or class structure. On the other hand it supports the evolutionists, against the several schools of historical anthropology, in the conclusion that parallelism or independent invention is relatively easy and common in the field of social organization, and that any structural form can be developed anywhere if conditions are propitious (p. 200).

It should be emphasized that evolutionary and diffusionist interpretations are not necessarily mutually exclusive, even with reference to a single society. For example, agriculture may diffuse to a hunting and gathering economy and initiate a sequence of evolutionary changes. It may also carry some social correlatives along with it, for example, a unisexual division of labor and a unisexual property concept. Where diffusion is facilitated by intermarriage, involving an introduction of foreign personnel, it is conceivable that changes in economy, residence, and descent might all get a foothold at about the same time and gain ground in the new home at about the same rate. Finally, no matter how extreme the diffusionist point of view, it does not explain how unilateral descent arose in the first place. The diffusionist needs the economic determinist to account for the first instance of unilateral descent, even though he believes that all subsequent instances are derived from it by diffusion.

Detailed information on subsistence has already been presented in Chapters 4–6. Here we are interested only in the dominant sexual division of labor in obtaining food. The sexual division of labor for subsistence pursuits behaves consistently for three out of four of our major activities. Hunting and fishing were nearly everywhere chiefly the work of men. Wild plant gathering, in contrast, fell mainly to women, with men assisting most often in obtaining tree crops such as acorns and pine nuts.

It is only for agriculture that an areal difference in sexual division of labor is marked. In the eastern half of the United States, women consistently did most of the farming, with men cooperating by clearing new land or by helping with the planting and harvest. In the Southeast, men were required to work in the community fields along with women, but this also appears to have been confined to planting and harvesting. Even where such public fields existed, each woman usually cultivated a separate allotment of her own and, in addition, farmed a small plot near her dwelling.

In the Southwest and Meso-America, men did most of the farming, although women frequently helped. Beals (1932*b*: 100) says that the division of labor in agriculture in north Mexico was "more or less equal," but his table heading for the localized information (1932*b*: 160) reads "women help in fields." Perhaps women helped more in the sixteenth and seventeenth centuries than in the nineteenth, from which most of our information comes. It is true that women among some of the Apaches of the Southwest did most of the farming, but agriculture was of tertiary significance in the diet of most of these tribes. They depended more heavily on wild plants and game. Among the Colorado River Yumans, where agriculture was of more importance, there was no clear sexual division of labor, the whole family of men, women, and children sometimes working together.

The results of an attempt to determine sexual dominance in subsistence pursuits are shown on Map 36. The selection of subsistence activity is limited to the actual procurement of food, thereby eliminating cooking and all other kinds of food processing between the delivery of food to the dwelling and its final consumption. This seems to be the kind of thing the economic determinists have in mind, or at at least it has the virtue of being specific enough to provide an answer of sorts from the source material. Any attempt to decide which sex did the most total labor in each culture would be likely to result in endless controversy.

Men seem to have procured more food than women among the vast majority of North American tribes. Thus men dominated food-getting activities in all hunting and fishing areas, as well as in the intensive farming areas of the Southwest and Meso-America. Women seem to have obtained more food than men in the East, among a few tribes on the Prairies, in the deserts of the Great Basin and part of the Southwest. In a considerable area in the western United States, there was no very clear sexual difference. Where there was a balance in rank between animal foods and wild plant foods, no sexual dominance would be anticipated. However, in most of California, where almost every authority agrees that wild plants dominated animal foods, the division of labor was still not precise. Men everywhere climbed oaks and pines to knock down acorns and pine cones to their women below, and sometimes helped carry home the gatherings or assisted in the hulling of acorns or the burning of pine cones to get at the nuts.

Although men assisted in gathering pine nuts in the Great Basin and parts of the Southwest, they certainly did not use the seed beater and conical basket to help gather wild seeds. Among the Papagos, men gathered no wild plant foods of any kind (Underhill, 1939: 99); because wild plants probably provided more food the year round than agriculture and hunting combined, we have characterized this tribe as female-dominated. Game was scarce in all of the desert areas, and supplied a much smaller fraction of the diet than did vegetal products.

The areas depicted as patridominant are perhaps less controversial. Where hunting and fishing furnished most of the diet and agriculture was absent, there is no question about the greater contribution of men to the dietary. Where agriculture was present, but secondary to hunting, the picture is more complicated; because men helped a little in agriculture, their dominant role in the total subsistence pattern can scarcely be questioned for the areas so indicated on Map 36.

When the areas for sexual dominance in subsistence pursuits (Map 36), postnuptial residence (Map 31), descent (Map 32), and kinship terminology (Map 35; Driver and Massey: Map 161) are compared by correlation method (Driver and Massey: 425–34), a threefold classification tends to emerge. Societies in which women dominate subsistence tend to have matrilocal residence, matrilineal descent, and Crow kinship classification. Societies in which there is a balance of men's and women's subsistence activities tend to have bilocal residence, bilateral descent, and Hawaiian kinship terminology. Societies in which men dominate subsistence tend to have patrilocal residence, patrilineal descent, and Omaha kinship terminology. This evidence lends support to the theory of economic determinism of descent. However, although the relevant correlations are significant, most of them are low. This means that there are many exceptions to the three general trends. Therefore there must be other causes involved in addition to the dominance of one sex over the other in the procuring of food.

Changes in economy and social organization may come about in at least three major ways. The first is innovation within a single society without direct stimulus from neighboring peoples. The second is the introduction of new culture elements from the outside. For example, the introduction of the maize plant with women doing the farming might bring about matrilocal residence and initiate an evolution toward matrilineal descent and Crow kinship terminology. This may well have been the case in parts of the Southwest, Prairies, and East. The third major cause of change is the migration of a people from one geographical environment to another, necessitating a change in economy. For example, the Crow Indians probably lived and farmed on the Missouri River in North or South Dakota several centuries ago. When they moved west to Montana, they were forced to abandon farming because of geographical factors and to concentrate on buffalo hunting. The dominant subsistence activity changed from farming by women to buffalo hunting by men. Residence followed suit, and became predominantly patrilocal. Descent and kinship terminology, however, were slower to change, and remained matrilineal. Thus the Crow Indians seem to have gone halfway through the cycle of change from dominant division of labor to kinship terminology by the time the ethnographer arrived to describe their way of life.

The second and third classes of causes of change, introduction of new culture elements or patterns from the outside, and migration to a new geographical environment, are accompanied by contact with alien peoples. This contact may be brief, and may involve the exchange of only a modest amount of the total cultural inventory; in this case, the word "diffusion" may be applicable. Such contact may also be prolonged and continuous, and, by means of intermarriage and other exchange of personnel, may engender the transfer of a relatively large amount of the cultural inventory. In this case, the term "acculturation" would be more appropriate. Diffusion and acculturation seem to have been neglected in favor of internal factors confined to single tribes or peoples in most theories of social change.

On the other hand, diffusion and acculturation should not be viewed as mechanical processes which proceed everywhere at a uniform rate. Both are highly selective. Although all societies are exposed to the different ways of life of neighboring peoples, they acquire only the culture elements or patterns which have value to them and which can be fitted into their own manner of living. If all societies rapidly acquired every alien cultural feature to which they were exposed, Indian cultures would be much more uniform than the many maps and descriptions in this volume show them to be.

REFERENCES

BEALS, 1932a, 1932b; DORSEY, 1897; DRIVER AND MASSEY, 1957; EGGAN, 1950, 1955; FOSTER, 1949; GIFFORD, 1944; GOLDMAN, 1941; GOLDSCHMIDT, 1948; HALLOWELL, 1937; HOIJER, 1956a, 1956b; HYMES, 1957; KELLY, 1942; KROEBER, 1937, 1940; LEACOCK, n.d., 1955; LID, 1948; MORGAN, 1871, 1877; MURDOCK, 1949, 1957, 1967; OLSON, 1933; PASSIN, 1944; SHIMKIN, 1941; SPECK, 1917, 1918, 1920b, 1938; SPIER, 1925; SPOEHR, 1947; STRONG, 1929; UNDERHILL, 1939.

16

Property and Inheritance

ALL peoples in the world have some concept of property rights, and the North American Indians are no exception. Their aboriginal ideas on this subject differed considerably from those of the European colonists, and showed great variation from one tribe to another. To begin with, property might be owned by a single individual, two or more individuals, an entire community, or a tribal group. The number of joint owners might vary all the way from two persons to thousands. Joint owners were seldom randomly chosen; they normally belonged to a definite social group, such as a family, clan, deme, lineage, sib, phratry, or moiety.

Property may also be fixed (real estate), or it may be movable (chattels). In our culture, buildings on real estate are usually considered to be part of the real estate, and the sale of a plot of land usually includes the buildings on it. Dwellings of Indians were seldom bought and sold, but where they were immovable, they also were regarded as belonging to the land and were therefore real estate. Where dwellings were portable, they were regarded as movable property or chattels. Thus the Plains Indian recognized individual or family ownership of tipis but not of the land on which they were pitched.

Property may also be divided into corporeal and incorporeal forms. Both real estate and chattels are usually regarded as corporeal property, while patents and copyrights are examples in our culture of incorporeal property. Indian cultures abounded in examples of incorporeal property. Songs, dances, family or clan crests, curing rites, and many other intangibles were owned and exclusively used by certain individuals or groups of individuals.

Property might be transferred in a variety of ways: by gift, barter, sale, inheritance, appropriation; or it might be inalienable. Many examples of transfer were given in Chapter 13; others will be discussed in this chapter. The method of transference was often correlated with other aspects of ownership. Thus, chattels were frequently individu-

269

ally owned, and tended to be disposable by gift, barter, or sale. Real estate, in contrast, was often owned or used by a tribe or a kin group, and might be inherited by succeeding generations of kin without being disposable by sale or barter. Land which had not been used for some years might be appropriated by anyone who chose to use it, or might be reapportioned by a tribal or sib official.

At the outset, we should also keep in mind the difference between nominal ownership—that is, ownership in name or speech—and use ownership, or usufruct, as it is technically called. Often a single person was said to own a dwelling or a tract of land, but he was normally compelled to share it with certain kin, such as the members of his immediate family. He could not dispose of it or refuse to share it with his relatives. Land was often said to belong to the tribe, yet in practice it might be used exclusively by a single family or lineage segment.

In discussing land tenure, it is important to separate the various uses to which land may be put and also to distinguish between productive sites and continuous tracts of land. As we shall see below, different uses of land were shared, inherited, or transferred in different ways, just as we may sell mineral rights to land without relinquishing title to other rights.

The variation in property rights which surrounded a single person's activity might be great. Thus a man might own his weapons individually, own a fishing station jointly with relatives, share hunting territory with the whole tribe, share the meat he obtained with other families in his community, share the fish he caught with only his own household, and earn the right to sing a bear song at a public ceremony by having slain a bear.

Ownership may also be regarded as having three main aspects: privilege of use, privilege of disposal, and privilege of destruction. These represent a scale of increasing control over the property in question. For example, a slave among the Yuroks could be used in the sense that he could be compelled to perform work for his master but he could not be bought or sold, or killed. Farther north, a slave could be used for labor, could be bought or sold, but could not be killed. Among the Kwakiutl, the slave was completely owned, because he could be compelled to work at labor, could be bought and sold, and could also be killed. For North America as a whole, however, this privilege of destruction was rare. Privileges of use were certainly most frequent, privileges of disposal next, and privileges of destruction least common.

LAND TENURE

Land tenure in aboriginal North America shows much variation from tribe to tribe and area to area, depending not only on the kind of exploitation of the land, but also on the political and social organization associated with it (Map 29). One of the most obtrusive features is the differentiation of land tenure rules for the various uses of land within a single tribe. For purposes of this summary, we shall distinguish between unimproved hunting land, improved hunting sites, fishing sites, wild-plant-gathering tracts, and farm plots. Improved hunting sites are those at which game fences, traps, pitfalls, and any other devices to facilitate the taking of game have been constructed.

A great deal of discussion has arisen over nominal ownership and use ownership. If the nominal owner was a specific individual, sib, or official in a culture, this distinction is of some significance; but if the nominal owner was the whole tribe, this does not tell us much. More often than not, land was used by smaller groups of individuals who cooperated in its exploitation and shared in its products. The relationship of the members of these work parties to one another had important bearing on social organization.

The kinship relations among groups of owners or users and modes of inheritance of land are often poorly described. I have, therefore, created a few broad terms to designate certain fundamental distinctions. By "patricentered" I mean that a tract of land or site is owned or used by a group of persons residing together patrilocally or belonging to the same patrilineal descent group, or that it is owned or used by a single individual who will pass it on at his death to another individual belonging to his patriresidential or patrilineal group. The term "matricentered" applies likewise to matrilocal and matrilineal groups of kinsmen. It is important to remember that in matrilineal societies land may be exploited by males and inherited from mother's brother to sister's son. To the best of our knowledge, there are no instances in patrilineal societies of land being shared or inherited by father's sisters and brother's daughters. "Bicentered" refers to the same concept applied to bilocal or bilateral groups of kin. "Kincentered" is used for those cases in which it is known only that a group of relatives owned, used, or controlled a tract or site, without knowing whether the group was patricentered, matricentered, or bicentered. There are still other instances of improved sites owned by the person or persons who improved them, but there is no information about the relationship of the joint owners or about the disposal of the property at death or abandonment by one or more of the owners. These cases have been placed in a residual category of their own.

Where residence was patrilocal and descent patrilineal, it was a common occurrence for title to land to be vested in the oldest male or all the mature males in the paternal lineage, lineage segment, or patrilineal sib, but for the land or its products to be used by patrilocal extended families or patriclans. The lineage or sib was never the land-using unit, because it would require married brothers and sisters to use the same land. The patrilocal residence rule and the rule of lineage or sib exogamy demanded that the sisters marry men from the outside and go elsewhere to live with them. The men who belonged to the lineage or sib stayed at home and, after acquiring wives on the outside, brought the wives home with them. The land-using unit was therefore composed of the male members of the paternal lineage or patrilineal sib plus their wives. Such units are called patrilocal extended families and patriclans.

Where residence was matrilocal and descent matrilineal, the title to land was likewise often vested in the oldest female or all the mature female members of the maternal lineage, lineage segment, or matrilineal sib. The land was used, however, or the products were almost always shared by these women and their husbands, who constituted matrilocal extended families and matriclans. In similar fashion, where avunculocal residence and matrilineal descent were paired, the title might be vested in the males of the maternal lineage or matrilineal sib, but the land was used by avunculocal extended families and avunculocanal families and avunculocal extended families and avunculoclans. Most ethnographers have failed to distinguish adequately between the family-clan type of unit and the lineage-sib concept. Because of the garbled nature of most of the source material, the loose terms "patricentered," "matricentered," and "bicentered" have been coined as a matter of expediency.

Land and productive sites might be owned or used by individuals (at least nominally), by a group of kin, by a group of unrelated persons, by a community consisting of two or more groups of kin, by a tribelet or tribe consisting of two or more communities, and by any and everyone who comes along. This last unit is the equivalent of our international one to which the oceans in the modern world have been allocated. In the Prairie and East areas, where tribal organization was well developed in the historic period, most of these land-owning units might exist even in the same tribal area. In the Far West, where true tribal organization was lacking, the largest land-holding unit was often the kin group, the band, or the village community. In a considerable number of localities, the kin group was the largest territorial unit; it was not aggregated into larger units. Statements about communal ownership of land have little meaning unless we know the size and sociopolitical structure of the community unit.

A summary of the facts is given on Map 29. Here every instance of even a tendency for land to be used and inherited by the various kinds of kin groups is shown. In the detailed descriptions to follow, the products of these tracts or sites, as controlled by kin groups, and their importance in the total subsistence or economic picture will be discussed.

Arctic.—Among the central Eskimos, both the landscape and the seascape approached an international status. Any central Eskimo could hunt sea or land animals anywhere he chose. The Eskimo "tribes" shown on our maps were mere aggregations of people at various localities. They had no real political organization and no conception of boundaries between "tribes." When Eskimos and Indians met in the summer, they sometimes fought, but always over the particular product they were seeking at the time, never over boundaries. It was only when a caribou fence or a trap of some sort had been built that any group of individuals claimed hunting land, and this was only for a short time or, at most, a season. Whoever got there first the next season could appropriate the spot.

In the Western Arctic, the most productive places for setting salmon nets were regarded as personal property and handed down from father to son. If an outsider put a net in one of these places, the owner removed it and put his own in its place. Sometimes these sites were rented for a fixed sum, but more often on a percentage basis, the renter giving the owner half his catch. The best spots to set seal nets were also owned and operated by patricentered groups of relatives, and inland hunting tracts or sites were controlled in the same manner.

In Greenland, seal breathing holes and favorable places to set seal nets were owned and operated by families. The mode of inheritance, if any, is unknown.

Sub-Arctic.—The Algonquians of the Eastern Sub-Arctic recognized ownership of hunting and trapping territories by patricentered families. This system was remarkably uniform all the way from near Lake Winnipeg to Labrador and Nova Scotia (Map 29). Such tracts were delimited by natural boundaries, such as rivers, lakes, forests, and mountains, and, in historic times, by ax marks on trees. Trepass might be punished with death or, more commonly, witchcraft. Permission might be given to a man to hunt in the territory of another family if he and his family were badly in need of food, but the hides were always given to the owner of the tract. Such permission was always reciprocated. Not only was each family territory carefully guarded from without, but game was consistently preserved from within. Pregnant female animals or those with young were spared, and the number of other animals taken was regulated, so as to prevent depletion. Although inheritance was not sharply crystallized, it usually followed the male line.

One of the remarkable features of this system is the smallness of the land-holding unit. In one region, these families averaged only six persons, and in one of the more favorable areas, only fifteen (Hallowell, 1949). In former times, such families spent every winter in isolation except for an occasional visit to or from a neighbor. When the spring thaw came, however, each family left its winter hunting territory and congregated with others at fishing places on lakes and rivers. Then when winter came again, everyone returned to winter quarters.

There has been much discussion in anthropological writings about the aboriginality of these family-owned hunting territories. Most authors believe that they were an adaptation to the European demand for furs. In keeping with the latter view is the fact that rules regarding fur-bearing animals, particularly the beaver, are more strict than those applying to meat-producing species, such as the caribou. However, small animals, of which the beaver is again typical, tend to restrict their movements to small areas, moose move around more, and caribou migrate. Conservation of small animals in a small area would have direct bearing on the numbers available in future years, while the same principle applied to large animals would be ineffective because they might be killed if they wandered into another man's territory.

Knight (1965) argues that forest fires over much of the Labrador Peninsula in the nineteenth century destroyed not only the forests but also the lichen and moss carpets on the surface of the land. Because caribou feed principally on these lichen and moss carpets, their numbers were seriously depleted by such fires. The moose, in contrast, benefited from the forest fires because they feed mainly on shrub foliage and grassy weeds which replaced the former forests. Estimates of the numbers of game in the past hundred years show a consistent decrease in caribou and an increase in moose. The strong herd instincts of the caribou makes their hunting by groups of men with a driving technique the most profitable. Moose, in contrast, tend to be solitary, and a single hunter or, at most, two hunters can trail and stalk a moose as effectively as a larger hunting party. Knight believes that the change in numbers of these most important sources of food changed the human social groups from bands hunting caribou to families hunting moose. He does not deny that the demand for beaver furs also encouraged the "atomization" of the society, but thinks that the primary cause of this "atomization" was the change in the numbers of caribou and moose. To him, the food supply is a more powerful determiner of the size of human groups in the Eastern Sub-Arctic than the price of furs. I accept Knight's thesis as having some truth in it, but prefer to regard it as something to be added to the fur-trade explanation rather than as an independent interpretation to be substituted for the fur trade. There is no conflict between the two explanations; combined, they make a better explanation than either does singly.

When we compare the Western Sub-Arctic, where the environment is similar but European contact later, we find several examples of tribes adopting the concept of individual- or family-owned trapping territories in the historic period. Adaptation to the European fur trade is thus established by documentary evidence in the west. It appears likely that the family hunting territory system of the northeast Algonquians, as observed in the nineteenth century, is a post-contact development. Leacock (n.d. and 1955) elaborates this view of the facts, and even goes so far as to say that these cultures were originally bicentered and that whatever patricentering they achieved was a result of European contact. However, the European fur trade in the Northwest did not consistently produce patricentered concepts of land tenure; a number of societies there retained their matricentered or avuncucentered systems. This suggests that patricentered rules would not have arisen in the Northeast if the culture had not already had a bias in that direction. Therefore, it seems clear that the Eastern Sub-Arctic possessed a patricentered bias aboriginally, and that this became crystallized into small hunting territories as a result of the fur trade and the trend from caribou to moose. The system was most rigid in the southern part of the territory nearest European colonists.

In the Mackenzie Sub-Arctic, most territorial rights were controlled by loose and fluid bands rather than by individuals or families. The kinship structure of these bands was bilocal and bilateral, and they also included members from a number of unrelated families. Trap lines, however, were owned and operated by individuals and families in the western part of the area. Both matrilocal and patrilocal residence occurred, with a corresponding tendency toward matrilineal and patrilineal inheritance of the trap lines. The patricentered system seems to be the older, with the matricentered pattern a later derivation from the Tlingit and Tsimshian on the Northwest Coast.

In the Yukon Sub-Arctic, kinship groups owned fishing places as well as trap lines. Such ownership was patricentered in the north and matricentered in the south, where the amount of contact with the Tlingit was greatest. The hunting of the caribou and other animals for food was controlled by the band in some localities, while the concept of open territory for all prevailed elsewhere in the area. It seems likely that in the Mackenzie and Yukon Sub-Arctic the kinship control of trap lines was largely a post-European development, as it was in the Eastern Sub-Arctic.

Northwest Coast.—On the Northwest Coast and, to some extent, elsewhere, it was seldom the entire landscape which was parceled out to groups of kindred but only the most favored sites. These were nominally owned by rich men, each of whom granted permission to his house or village mates, most of whom were his relatives, to exploit the land. That such permission was never refused proves that the use of the land belonged to the entire group of kindred rather than to a single individual. What at first appears to be individual ownership turns out to be a sort of stewardship—the right to direct the economic exploitation of the tract by the local group. Over most of the area, from the Wiyot to the Bella Coola, such usufruct was patricentered; but in the north, from the Haisla north to the Tlingit, it was matricentered. Such private ownership applied to fishing, hunting, trapping, and wild-plant-gathering rights.

Rules and regulations surrounding fishing sites were strictest on the Northwest Coast, where the rich man held title to the weir but could not refuse permission to members of his household or village to fish there. Sometimes sharing was accompanied by dividing up the twenty-four-hour period so that the weir was used by different men at different times. Where this system prevailed, the nominal owner managed to retain the time period which was likely to yield the most fish. At the southernmost extension of the Northwest Coast culture area, among the Yuroks, fishing stations were owned by individual men, sometimes jointly with a nonrelative, and they were rented to outsiders for a share of the catch. Rights in such locations might also be bought or sold. At a man's death, his fishing rights passed to his son. In addition to those privately owned fishing stations, there were communally owned weirs, which were constructed annually at certain places in the river. Rights to fish at certain sections of these weirs were privately owned, however.

Although some of the land was free to hunt over, the best places for snaring and trapping land animals were owned in the same manner as places to gather roots and berries—that is, nominally, by rich men who could not refuse to grant permission to their house and village mates to exploit these tracts.

Plateau.—On the Plateau, the large weirs at the most profitable fishing places were owned or shared by everyone in a community, and even outsiders who chanced along were commonly given a share of the catch. It was only the small weirs or scaffolds, built and operated by single men or small groups of relatives, which may be said to have been patricentered. In the minority of cases, where postnuptial residence was reported as bilocal, the ownership of small fishing stations should likewise be regarded as bicentered. Traps, pitfalls, game fences, and other improvements at hunting sites were owned by the builders; but the relationship of the builders is vague or unknown, and the duration in time of their tenure equally obscure.

Plains.—On the Plains, where band and tribal organization existed, hunting territory was controlled by the band or tribe. The boundaries between bands or tribes are difficult to establish, and neighboring tribes often shared a large territory. It was only when enemies were encountered that disputes arose, and these were less concerned with boundaries than with establishing dominance (in the prehistoric period) or eliminating competition (in the historic period). Vague as knowledge of tribal or band territories is, we know for sure that no individual or small group of individuals within a Plains tribe owned any hunting land.

Prairies.—On the Prairies, control of hunting lands was similar to that on the Plains, with tribal, village, or band ownership the rule. Individuals or kinship groups did not own unimproved hunting territory, and if traps, fences, or pounds were so owned, other than for a season, it has not been reported except for eagle pits. Such pits were owned by maternal lineages and lineage segments among the Hidatsa and Mandan, and probably by other kinds of kinship groups elsewhere on the Prairies. In the wild-rice area around the western Great Lakes, each family gathered the rice in its own tract, which was marked by tying the plants in a particular manner. Apparently the same spot was returned to year after year, the family making its camp nearby. Most of this wild-rice area is labeled patricentered because residence was preponderantly patrilocal and descent mostly patrilineal.

Turning to farming, we find the Hidatsas and Mandans on the Missouri River divided into maternal lineages, lineage segments, and matrilocal extended families, the women of which owned their own farm plots. There was a tendency for the same field to be cultivated by these maternal kin groups year after year, although exhaustion of the soil necessitated some changing about. When a woman died, her female relatives did not work her garden for a couple of years, but, after letting it lie fallow for that length of time, a sister or a daughter would cultivate it the following year. Although title to a particular plot might technically be vested in an individual, it was normally cultivated by work parties of matrilineally related women, who worked each other's gardens in a group.

East.—In the East, restricted ownership of hunting land is reported only for the Delawares and Powhatan. Among the Delawares, hunting land was owned by a matricentered kin group of some sort. Although such land was hunted on principally in winter, ownership seems not to have been seasonal but permanent. Individual Powhatan men were the nominal owners of tracts of land, as among the northeastern Algonquians; we may assume that these were shared by kin or inherited in some manner, but this practice may be modern. For the better-known tribes, such as the Iroquois and Creek, the emphasis is always on the tribal ownership of hunting territory. However, if we accept the matriclan as an aboriginal social unit, we may assume that it was associated with its own hunting territory at some time in its history.

Ownership of fishing sites by kinship groups is reported for the Powhatan and Iroquois. Fishing as well as hunting rights were included in the ownership of tracts of land by individual men among the Powhatan. Details about the Iroquois system are few, but apparently some of the best places to fish were owned by maternal lineages and sibs in the same way that farm land was.

Among the Iroquoians, cultivated lands were parceled out to maternal lineages, or lineage segments, and the women members occupied a single longhouse with their husbands and children. The oldest woman, who was the lineage head, directed the work party of women members. Some individual women may have had the individual right to cultivate a certain part of the plot and to control its produce, but most of the ownership and operation were on the lineage-segment level. When the fertility of the land waned and firewood became scarce, the whole village moved. At a new village site, plots of fresh land were allocated to each household.

The picture in the Southeast is essentially the same, except that there were also fields nominally owned by the chief—more properly called town fields—which were worked by everyone and from which some or all of the produce was kept in a public storehouse to be served to out-of-town guests or to be doled out to the needy. Even men were required to help with the planting and harvesting of these fields, although women seem to have done most of the cultivating, weeding, and watching. We do not know for sure whether maternal families or lineage segments were assigned separate plots in the town fields, or whether each kin group cleared land of its own, or whether both systems prevailed.

California.—California exhibits a few instances of hunting land being owned privately. Among the various clans of the Chumash, unimproved hunting land was divided, as well as among the equally small but less definable local units of the Owens Valley Paiute. With the Yokuts, pigeon-snaring blinds were owned by individual men and probably passed on to sons or brothers. Outsiders had to ask permission to use such blinds, but apparently the permission was usually granted. Farther north, we find that certain Maidu families erected fences for deer drives in certain favored spots and controlled their operation. Among the neighboring Nomlaki, all land of any productive value was divided among the various villages, and the chiefs were the nominal owners of such tracts. These village communities seem to have been patrilocal extended families and patriclans. In the northern part of the state, the patricentered ownership of the Northwest Coast appears.

In California, about half the peoples seem to have recognized ownership of wild plant tracts by groups of relatives. Most of these were patricentered, but a few were bicentered or even matricentered. The small area with stippled pattern in central California (Map 29) refers to an interesting incipient matricentered system which never fully matured because of conflict with other facets of the culture. Among some local groups, a newly married daughter continued to gather wild plant products from fields owned or exclusively used by her mother. This might continue for a year or two, which was the

normal length of the initial and temporary matrilocal residence pre-
valent in the area. If, when the couple later joined the groom's parents,
the distance was too great for the bride to continue gathering on her
mother's land, she stayed at home and did the housework for her
mother-in-law and unmarried or newly married sisters-in-law while
they gathered in their own family wild plant plots. Because of the
preponderance of final and more or less permanent patrilocal residence and the dominance of men in sociopolitico-religious affairs, this
incipient matrilineal succession to tracts of land never developed into
permanent matrilocal residence, much less matrilineal descent. It is
significant that this matricentered system coexisted in the same locality
with the patrilineal use and inheritance of pigeon-snaring booths.

Great Basin.—In this desert region, we find no ownership of hunting
territory by individuals or groups of kin, except for eagle nests, which
were owned by individual men. Eagles were not eaten but were caught
for their feathers, which were considered sacred. A few bands recognized ownership of wild plant tracts by vague groups of bicentered
relatives, but this was not the general rule. The few fishing sites were
apparently not owned by kinship groups.

Northeast Mexico.—What little we know about this area suggests
that there was no ownership of natural resources by kinship groups.
As in the Great Basin, there was much wandering by families in search
of the uneven natural food supply.

Southwest.—For the most of the Southwest area, the ownership of
hunting tracts by kin groups was apparently lacking. Among the
Chiricahua Apache, however, all land was controlled by bands which
were endogamous demes. Although the membership was somewhat
fluid, most members of a single band were related in a vague bilateral
manner. This may also have been true of the Mescalero. The Walapai
and Papago had a patricentered system of land tenure in which the
patrideme was the territorial unit. While the system was not rigid, the
patrilocal residence practiced by the majority kept together lines of
males who hunted over the same territory generation after generation.
The clans of the Navaho and Western Apache suggest separate hunting territories at an earlier time, but the literature does not state the
fact specifically. As for the Pueblos, hunting land was either international or controlled by an entire pueblo, which was an autonomous
political unit. Such pueblos consisted of a considerable number of kin
groups, each of which owned agricultural land separately but never
hunting land. This is explained in part by the fact that the most efficient

way to hunt rabbits, which were the most important single species of game, was for all the men of the pueblo to join in a great drive. Smaller groups of relatives, limited to a fraction of the territory, would have accomplished little.

Farm plots in the Southwest were limited to the small fraction of the total area which received sufficient water, and were therefore cultivated for an indefinite period of time. Among the Hopi, the matrilineal sib was the most important land-controlling agent. Within the sib, fields were assigned to lineage segments, which lived in separate households; these, in turn, were divided so that each woman had her own plot. She had the right of usufruct and also the right of disposal subject to the veto of the sib expressed either by mass opinion or as a decision of the sib mother. In spite of the fact that women held title to farm plots, their husbands did most of the agricultural work. Women's title to the land is believed by many anthropologists to be evidence of former dominance of women in farm work.

The Navaho system was more individualistic, and lacked control over the land by sibs or community officials. Farm land was formerly inherited matrilineally, however, although at present inheritance is often patrilineal. The first person to farm a plot, whether man or woman, automatically acquired and subsequently retained possession of the plot. Ownership applied only to the agricultural products raised on the land; wild shrubs or trees, roots or berries, and springs were free to everyone, and the entering of a field to obtain these natural resources was not considered trespass. Only trees which were planted were privately owned. Apache concepts of farm land tenure were looser, and are characterized as matricentered and bicentered.

Among the Yumans of the Colorado River, farm lands were restricted to the bottoms which were annually flooded. Plots were marked by boundaries and were inherited patrilineally. They were also bought and sold, a successful warrior often purchasing land with the spoils of victory. If a man wanted more land, he could obtain it by clearing the natural vegetation which grew thickly near the river. Boundary disputes not settled by arbitration were settled by force: first by a pushing contest, but, if the results of this did not satisfy both parties, then by a battle with sticks and staves. Land was normally inherited from father to son, the theoretical claims of daughters being waived when they married and went to live on their husbands' land. A widow had a right to some of her deceased husband's land, which was cultivated for her by her nearest male relatives.

Meso-America.—In Meso-America, where agriculture dominated subsistence, hunting territory seems to have been international or controlled by the tribe or state. An exception to this was the control which chiefs and kings, such as Montezuma, exercised over hunting preserves which were set aside for royalty. The common man, however, never belonged to a kinship group which owned hunting land.

Caso (1963) gives the best description to date of Aztec land tenure. He distinguishes six kinds of lands, three of which were under public domain and the remaining three under private domain. Lands under public domain were: palace lands owned by the king and worked by the servants of appointed officials (*tecalec*), commoners (*macehualtin*), and conquered peoples who paid tribute; sacred lands owned by the temples and worked by serfs (*mayeques*), commoners, and conquered peoples who paid tribute; lands of the shield owned by the army and worked by conquered peoples who paid tribute. Lands under private domain were: patrimonial lands owned by the king and worked by serfs; lands owned by nobles (*pipiltin*) and knighted commoners and worked by serfs; lands owned by the demes (*calpulli*) and worked by commoners, who had the right of usufruct but could not sell or give away the land. The agricultural products of lands under private domain could be consumed or sold by the owner, after he had given a fair share to the workers. The king and the nobles could thus increase their personal wealth by the efficient management of their private lands. The commoners had less opportunity to accumulate wealth, but were likewise free to consume or exchange what they raised. The owners of public lands, in contrast, were only nominal owners in that the food produced on these lands was used to support public officials, priests, and military personnel. Even the king was required to distinguish between his private and public lands. Slaves might also work the land of their masters but were not permanently attached to it as were serfs.

An outstanding fact about land tenure in general is the consistency with which a single tribe was patricentered, matricentered, or bicentered with regard to two or more uses of land. With few exceptions, the same alignment of relatives controlled multiple uses of land when these used were controlled by groups of relatives in any way. For example, on the Northwest Coast, hunting, fishing, and wild plant sites were all three matricentered in the north and patricentered in the remainder of the area. The fact that men exploited the first two kinds of sites and women the third did not interfere with a consistent matrilineal or patrilineal bias. Sexual division of labor did not cause ownership to descend in two different lines.

OWNERSHIP AND INHERITANCE OF DWELLINGS

A sample of facts on the ownership and inheritance of dwellings has been assembled on Map 30. Houses were occupied by kinship groups and inherited within these groups in the Western Arctic, Western Sub-Arctic, North Pacific Coast, East, Meso-America, and parts of the Plains, Prairies, and Southwest. In general, dwellings which were large or substantially built to last a number of years tended to be inherited rather than destroyed at the death of an inmate or owner. These dwellings were usually occupied by a number of related families (Map 18). Small, hastily constructed houses, in contrast, were normally destroyed or abandoned at death, so that there was nothing left to inherit.

The social structure of the groups of relatives occupying large permanent houses and the inheritance of such dwellings conforms closely to the rules of land tenure. In other words, housing functions like other real estate. Where land was owned tribally or internationally, dwellings were portable, in keeping with the nomadic way of life. Such dwellings were often destroyed at the death of an inmate, or at least torn down and moved. The parts which were movable (poles, hides, mats, bark) are best regarded as chattels. The large, sewn hide tipis of the Plains in the nineteenth century were not consistently destroyed at a death, and in this respect conform to the pattern of large, permanent housing.

A comparison of Map 30, on the ownership and inheritance of dwellings, with Map 31, on postnuptial residence, shows substantial agreement between the corresponding traits when the cases where houses were destroyed at death are eliminated. On the other hand, correspondence between the dominant house-building sexual division of labor (Map 19) and ownership and inheritance of dwellings (Map 30) is low. One noticeable difference is on the northern Northwest Coast and adjacent interior, where men dominated house building and ownership was matricentered. However, this discrepancy is only apparent: men were the nominal owners and title passed from a man to his sister's son on the coast. Among the Kaskas of the interior, title passed from a man to his son-in-law, who might not be a genetic relative. We have labeled this "matricentered" also because title was held nominally by the husbands of a maternal lineage segment. Another area where a difference appears consistently is the East. Here the men did most of the work of house building, but the women owned the houses and inherited them matrilineally. The same was also true in part of the Southwest. The female ownership of houses constructed by men is a common feature of matrilineal societies in other parts of the world, and demands no special explanation in North America. These are examples where the sex of the maker and sex of the user and owner of material possessions do not correspond.

OWNERSHIP AND INHERITANCE OF CHATTELS

Movable property of all sorts is called chattels, a term which has the same root as the word "cattle." Chattels were often owned by single individuals, although canoes and other things requiring a crew for operation might be jointly owned by the whole crew or several of its members. Tools, weapons, household articles, and any other objects used exclusively or nearly exclusively by a single individual were generally regarded as the property of that individual with the right of disposal and destruction. Ethnologists purchasing museum specimens from Indians have often found a husband refusing to sell anything belonging to his wife. Even children owned a few things which their elders would not dispose of. At death the chattels of the deceased were often buried with the corpse or burned sometimes so extensively that there was nothing left to inherit. In other societies, only a part of a person's chattels was destroyed or buried at death, the remainder being inherited in some fashion. Disposal of property before death by willing it to certain individuals was also known to some North American Indian societies, but seems to have been less common than inheritance.

Movable property might be divided according to sex. A comparison of the rules of inheritance for men's chattels shows high correlations with the corresponding modes of inheritance for land (Map 29). In the same areas where land tenure was matricentered, men inherited chattels matrilineally—that is, from a man to his sister's son. Likewise, where land tenure was patricentered, inheritance of chattels tended to be patrilineal; where land was bicentered, chattels were bilateral.

Women's chattels show a striking difference; inheritance was either matrilineal or bilateral, never patrilineal. Not a single instance of women's chattels' being inherited from a woman to her brother's daughter was found. This was anticipated in patrilineal societies but never appeared. A significant point is the fact that women's household articles, clothing, and the like were commonly inherited from mother to daughter in societies where most other kinds of property descended from father to son. It shows that there were conflicting lines of inheritance coexisting in single societies. The type of lineage or sib descent which a society subscribed to apparently depended on which line of descent received the most emphasis in that society as a whole.

INCORPOREAL PROPERTY

Incorporeal property, such as songs, dances, magic formulas, myths, crests, and membership in sibs and sodalities, was universally recognized by North American natives. Such material has never been systematized, but a few examples will suffice here. Medicine men often possessed magic formulas or songs which were owned and used by individual practitioners in curing the sick. A fee was charged for their use on a patient, and they were sometimes bought and sold. On the northern Plains, medicine bundles, which were a combination of corporeal and incorporeal property, were normally bought and sold. Along with the sale went the teaching of the songs and ritual, without which the bundle would have been ineffective. These bundles were not the exclusive property of a class of medicine men but were owned by every man of any importance.

Membership in sibs involved a number of incorporeal rights, such as the right to participate in sib ceremonies, to wear sib insignia, and to be protected legally by one's sib mates. In fact, the whole sib system is an outstanding example of ownership and inheritance of a wide range of intangibles by the membership. The fact that sibs might also own corporeal property should not obscure the fundamentally incorporeal nature of these unilateral institutions.

The area of greatest elaboration of incorporeal property concepts was probably Meso-America, although the Northwest Coast was not far behind. Other examples of such ownership may be found in Chapters 19, 20, and 23.

REFERENCES

Caso, 1963; Cooper, 1939; Drucker, 1939; Eggan, 1950; Flannery, 1939; Goldschmidt and Haas, 1946; Hallowell, 1949; Herskovits, 1952; Hickerson, 1966, 1967; Kroeber, 1925; Leacock, n.d., 1955; Linton, 1942; Lowie, 1948; Murdock, 1949; Roys, 1943; Speck, 1915; Speck and Eiseley, 1939; Swanton, 1946.

17

Government and Social Controls

POLITICAL organization is generally regarded as synonymous with territorial organization, and is concerned with the manner in which those people who occupy a particular territory are integrated internally with respect to each other and, at the same time, are organized to present a united front to the outside. Although the territorial tie has been stressed in all discussions of government, the territory may be a shifting one, as among Plains Indians. At a given time, however, the members of a nomadic band or tribe are occupying a common territory, even though the precise locality may change from week to week or month to month.

Each political unit always includes a number of families, and sometimes is made up of a number of larger residential kinship groups. In the chapters on marriage, family, and kinship, above, we distinguished two kinds of kinship groups: genetic ("blood," consanguineal) and residential (territorial). Residential kin groups, such as families, clans, and demes, always bring together husbands and wives but usually not married brothers and sisters. Residential kin groups reside in separate territories or in distinct subdivisions of villages and towns, but they are generally dependent on their neighbors for wives or husbands, the only exception to this rule being the endogamous deme. Because clans and demes can be enlarged to include hundreds of members by the extension of fictional or traditional bonds of kinship, there is no universally accepted line of demarcation between kinship organization and political organization. However, for our purposes it is best to draw the line between residential kin groups, within which all the members are bound together by actual or traditional bonds of kinship, and larger residential entities, united by other common ties and concepts. Societies which have no territorial organization larger than the residential kin group will be classed as lacking true political organization, while those with territorial ties based on nonkinship factors will be classed as possessing it.

AREAS WITHOUT TRUE POLITICAL ORGANIZATION

Most peoples in the Arctic, Great Basin, Northeast Mexico, and Baja California lacked true political organization at the time of first European contact. In these areas, the largest permanent unit was generally the family. Clans and demes were absent, unreported, or rare; population was sparse (Map 6); and band organization was weak and fluid. These areas were the least productive economically at the level of exploitation known to the Indian inhabitants, and even today they are thinly populated and underdeveloped. None of these Indians farmed (Map 4); they were all nomads on the move almost daily in search of a meager living. Their failure to develop political organization is generally attributed to the impossibility of maintaining a permanent local group of sufficient size in the face of such adversities.

Arctic.—Among most of the Eskimo, the nearest approach to a permanent residential unit was the nuclear family, but even this was frequently broken by the high mortality and by wife exchange. Polygynous and polyandrous families also existed but were less common than the nuclear family. In the west, a bilocal or patrilocal extended family occupied the larger and more permanent log houses which were owned by the occupants and returned to each winter. In the Central and Eastern Arctic, the snow houses melted entirely in the summer, and even the place of residence might be obliterated. Where walls of earth, stone, or whalebone remained, they could be appropriated by the first family who came along when the icy blasts of winter drove them indoors; ownership of dwellings was only seasonal. Nevertheless, the Eskimo family lived in a larger group most of the time, especially in winter. Ideally, a young married man lived in the same village as his father, but the patrilocal extended family was better characterized as incipient rather than as achieved because the mortality of males especially was very high, and this tended to break up patrilocal groupings. These winter settlements averaged less than a hundred persons for the Eskimo as a whole and less than fifty for those in the central region. The composition of these settlements was fluid because the same families did not return to the same locality every winter. In spite of such instability, most settlements enjoyed a minimum of leadership by a headman and a shaman.

The headman was the best hunter and most capable individual in the village, as translations of epithets applied to him show: "he who thinks"; "the one to whom all listen"; "he who knows everything best." His status was achieved wholly by his performance; there was not a trace of hereditary transmission of this position, nor was there any mechanism for election or appointment to it. As the first among equals, he continued to be the acknowledged leader in the relentless pursuit of game animals. What the headman gained from this relationship was the manpower at his disposal when he wanted to go whaling or walrus hunting in the big *umiak* boat or to attack the ferocious polar bear.

The Eskimo shaman also enjoyed a role of leadership because he was thought to be able to locate or to attract game animals in time of need, and it was also his responsibility to ferret out confessions from those who had broken taboos and thus jeopardized the hunting luck of the entire group. For instance, if a person ate caribou and seal meat at the same meal, he was thought to have insulted the sensitive souls of both species, which would then retaliate against the entire settlement by no longer permitting themselves to be taken in the chase. The shaman, who had the power to prescribe penance to such an individual, ranked along with the headman in authority.

Great Basin.—In the deserts of the Great Basin in Nevada and Utah, man struggled against the heat instead of the cold and against the drought instead of angry seas, but the margin of life over death was just as narrow. Among the western Shoshoni and many of their Northern Paiute and Southern Paiute neighbors, the largest permanent residential unit was the family. This was nearly always the nuclear family, but there were also a few polygynous families and fewer polyandrous families. These families often wandered about independently in search of food in the summer, but tended to group themselves into small villages in the winter. These winter villages ranged from two to ten families and probably averaged less than fifty persons. The larger of these villages, at least, had a headman, called a "talker." He gave periodic orations to the group, telling them about the ripening of plant foods in various localities, planning the trip to these productive areas, and allocating to each person or family a particular spot in which to obtain food. He had little actual authority, and any family so inclined might leave the group and wander off on its own.

Organization larger than the village was only temporary among the western Shoshoni and their neighbors. The most common occasion for the assemblage of the members of several villages was the rabbit or antelope drive, which rarely lasted more than two or three weeks and was normally held only once a year. One group of a hundred persons could round up more game per capita than, say, five groups of twenty operating independently. Such drives were led by skilled hunters thought to possess supernatural power and to be able to attract rabbits and antelopes. There was enough time and energy left over from necessary tasks to permit a little dancing and singing under the direction of a dance specialist.

Northeast Mexico and Baja California.—Northeast Mexico is less known than the Great Basin, but seems to have been as devoid of true political organization. Because winters were milder, there was less tendency to settle in winter villages, and family groups continued to wander about in search of food at all seasons. Band affiliation was fluid and temporary except along the southern border, where there was contact with Meso-America. Baja California is even less known, but probably had no permanent social unit larger than the family.

AREAS WITH BORDERLINE AND MIXED SYSTEMS

The Sub-Arctic, Northwest Coast, Plateau, California, and Southwest areas exhibit borderline and mixed systems of territorial organization which range all the way from family groups to true tribes of several thousand.

Sub-Arctic.—In the Sub-Arctic of eastern Canada among Algonquian-speaking Indians, we find, in the nineteenth century, a twofold system geared to the two principal environments: barren grounds and forest. On the barren grounds in the northern part of this region, the people were grouped into bands with more or less mutually exclusive territories. They relied chiefly on the caribou for sustenance. The caribou herds could be more effectively taken by a number of hunters than by a single individual. It was only when caribou were scarce that those bands split up, with each family reduced to hunting smaller game on its own. In the forest, on the other hand, each family occupied its own trapping and hunting territory in the winter and subsisted to a greater extent on the beaver and other small animals taken principally with traps. Such families congregated during the short summer season at lakes and streams, where fish were available in quantity, or joined one another in a communal caribou or moose hunt. Thus the barren-ground families lived most of the time with the band, while the forest families lived most of the year alone, each isolated on its own tract of land. The forest pattern of ecology is largely a post-European development, as mentioned in the section on land tenure in the preceding chapter.

The first extensive figures on band size in this area date from 1857, when H. Y. Hind (1863: 336) estimated 3,910 persons in twenty-four bands, averaging 163 persons per band. Each band had a headman who was an excellent hunter and a man of high ethical standards willing to lead and help his fellow bandsmen. It was he who did most of the bargaining when his group traded at the summer rendezvous, both with other bands and with the Hudson's Bay Company. It was ideal for a son to succeed his father as headman, but ability was stressed much more than heredity. The headman was sometimes aided by an informal council of the older men. There was no mechanism for enforcing the headman's wishes or those of the informal council, which was consulted when a serious problem arose, except in the case of murder; but other offenders were brought to justice by being ostracized from society if they refused to conform. If a murderer was not killed or seriously injured by the relatives of the person he had killed, he was tried before the headman and council. If found guilty, he would be told to leave camp and would be followed by armed members of the council. At a given signal the three or four men chosen in advance as executioners would shoot him in the back.

The shaman also enjoyed a position of authority in the Eastern Sub-Arctic, especially in the forested areas where the family trapping territories prevailed. If a man came to him with a complaint over infringement of territorial rights, he would accept a gift from the plaintiff and, after the latter had gone, would investigate the details of the case. If the shaman thought the plaintiff had been wronged, he would warn the offender, either in person or by supernatural means. Warning by the shaman therefore helped to maintain the social order.

Helm (1965) gives a scheme for the Mackenzie Sub-Arctic in the twentieth century with four levels of social grouping. From smallest to largest, these are: task group, local band, regional band, and tribe. The task group is a temporary arrangement for hunting, fishing, or some other activity where a group is more efficient than an individual. The local band is a bilocal group held together by both genetic and affinal kinship ties. Genetic ties through males are about as numerous as genetic ties through females. A husband and wife may join the local band of either the husband's or the wife's genetic relatives. The regional band is a larger bilocal and bilateral group made up of two or more local bands who are tied together also by both genetic and affinal relationship. The tribe is a still larger territorial group with a common language, a name, and an awareness of common affiliation by the members; but it had no tribal organization with a chief and a formal council, and the members never assembled all at one time and place. Helm reasons that the unpredictable habits of game and the unpredictable weather caused so many deaths by starvation that unilineal inheritance or affiliation could not possibly have been maintained. Since there were no rules of either endogamy or exogamy, these groups were all bilocal and bilateral. Because the tribe had so few functions, it seems best to use the term "band" for the dominant social groups of this area.

The Yukon Sub-Arctic presents a somewhat different picture because of contact with the Northwest Coast. Bands had a little more cohesion, and their leaders tended to inherit their positions patrilineally, in spite of the presence of matrilineal moieties in most localities. Leadership was also associated with the prestige acquired from success in predatory raids against outside groups. Such raids brought material possessions, which increased a man's wealth, gave him extra wives, and provided proof of physical superiority.

Northwest Coast.—Population in this area was much more dense than in the Sub-Arctic (Map 6), and life depended mostly on fishing (Map 3). Therefore the population was concentrated at the mouths of streams, where fishing was best, in villages of hundreds of persons at the maximum. Before European contact there was probably no territorial unit that exceeded a thousand souls. Some villages were clans or demes, but some were aggregations of a number of clans and demes. Sometimes the villages were combined into larger territorial units, which might be called tribelets, but the population of such tribelets was often no larger than that of one of the larger autonomous villages in another locality. After European trading vessels arrived and trading posts were established, there was an increasing trend toward larger villages at or near these trading centers and also wider territorial organization. Everywhere on the North Pacific Coast, headmen and chiefs were men of wealth. They were the nominal owners of houses, canoes, lands, and a vast assortment of social and religious statuses more highly valued than material goods.

Among the matrilineal and avunculocal peoples in the north (Maps 31, 32), there was a hierarchy of residential units: from the single plank house inhabited by an avunculocal extended family, to a village representing an avunculocal clan community, to a larger village with a number of avuncuclans, and, finally, to a tribelet comprising a number of villages. The headmen or chiefs in these societies inherited their positions matrilineally from their mother's brothers.

The Tlingit, for instance, are estimated to have numbered 10,000 at European contact, and in the late nineteenth century were divided into fourteen named territorial districts or tribelets averaging about 700 persons each. Each district possessed from one to eight villages, which may formerly have been distinct avuncuclans. While the people in each district were aware of common mutual interests and cooperated occasionally to repel invaders or to conduct an offensive campaign against them, there was no district chief or any other form of district government. Each clan had its own headman, exclusively exploited its own lands, and was under no compulsion to cooperate in any way with other clans. There is no instance in the historical record of all fourteen of the districts ever uniting for any purpose.

The relation of kinship units to political units is well illustrated by the Haida, who lived on the Queen Charlotte Islands directly south of the Tlingit. Each nuclear family was a part of an avunculocal extended family which occupied an entire plank house. This was the unit of use of chattels, such as canoes, hunting and fishing gear, and the household articles used in common by the women. Each house had a male leader, who inherited his authority from his mother's brother—not from his father—and directed the economic activities of his following. Most houses were grouped in villages which were avunculocal clans, each with a headman who also inherited his position matrilineally. The clan was the real-estate-using unit; each clan had title to, and exclusive use of, its share of the more productive areas in the neighborhood, both on land and in the sea for several miles from shore. The clan and the multiclan village were the unit of warfare against outsiders. The multiclan villages, however, had no distinct form of government; the headman of the largest or highest-ranking clan tended to assume the leadership when an occasion demanded concerted action.

The Nootka of Vancouver Island had a system as complex as that of the peoples just described, except that it lacked strict unilateral descent. Nuclear families were combined into extended families in the large plank house, and the houses were aggregated into villages which appear to have been patridemes. These villages were named, and each was led by a headman who inherited his position. Each owned land, houses, and many incorporeal privileges as well. Each village was formally united with several others nearby, and all lived together in a larger, named winter village in which the headmen of the smaller member villages were ranked in order of wealth and prestige. This unit we shall call a "tribelet." These tribelets were sometimes still further combined into a third unit, which we shall call a "tribe." The tribe possessed a still larger town on the ocean, where all the member tribelets might assemble in the summer for the taking of salt-water fish and sea mammals. Such towns were named, and the headmen or chiefs who assembled there were carefully ranked as in smaller territorial units. There was a very real feeling of solidarity within these tribes, which were united in war as well as in peaceful ceremonies. Wars between factions within these tribes were almost unheard of, although one or two are reported in old traditions. The total population of the Nootka has been estimated at 6,000, suggesting that the tribal unit may have embraced 1,500 or even 2,000 persons. In light of the fact that most of the Nootka data were obtained from informants in the 1930's, the tribe may be a post-European development, and may not alter the generalization so often made that true tribes were lacking on the Northwest Coast.

The Yurok of northwest California, who fall within the Northwest Coast culture area, were totally devoid of true political organization, as were their neighbors. The largest residential unit was the patrilocal extended family which occupied a plank house. A number of such extended families normally lived close together in what superficially appeared to be a village, and a census taken in 1852 shows that these villages ranged from under fifty to a maximum of 165 inhabitants. However, there was not a shred of village organization. All property, both real estate and chattels, belonged to the extended families, nominally to the single headman of the family. All wrongs were against individuals, and when disputes arose, it was the extended families who quarreled, fought, paid compensation, and made peace. However, many extended families would join each other for the great annual religious festival called the World Renewal Ceremony. There was, then, some feeling of solidarity as well as a common language, but there was no true political organization.

Plateau.—A small minority of peoples in this area possessed only village organization, almost half were grouped in tribelets or aggregations of villages with slight tribal tendency, and the remainder acquired tribal organization from the Plains area in the historic period.

The village unit was probably predominant before European contact and was rather small, those of the Sanpoil averaging only seventy-five persons. Fishing rights on rivers were jealously guarded, but the hunting territory between streams was normally shared by neighboring villages. After the eastern peoples acquired tribal organization, they tended to exclude speakers of foreign languages from their entire territories.

The office of headman or chief over most of the Plateau was passed on from father to son if the son also had the personal qualifications. Among the peoples with the greatest amount of Plains influence, however, the premium was placed on war record, not on heredity. Over most of the Plateau, where loose heredity prevailed for civil chiefs, the war leader was a separate officer. The majority of peoples in this area also had councils of men to support the chief, and, in a few localities in the central region, women occupied seats on councils.

California.—This area offers two distinct types of territorial organization. The smallest unit was the extended family, which possessed its own territory, a small winter village, and a headman. Over more than half of the California culture area, however, these extended families were combined in groups of two to perhaps six to form tribelets. The tribelets sometimes had definite territories, a rallying point at the largest village, and chiefs with limited authority. Patrilineal inheritance of chieftainship was the general rule. Occasionally these tribelets defended their territories against outsiders. Those peoples with no organization larger than the extended family lacked true political integration, while the tribelets had achieved the rudiments of government.

The Miwok formerly possessed no territorial unit larger than the patrilocal extended family, but each of these families had its own territory and a headman. The aggregation of several such families into tribelets seems to have been the result of Spanish pressure in the historic period.

The Yokuts, however, possessed the most definite tribelet organization of any people in the California culture area. With a total population of about 50,000, they were divided into about fifty tribelets, averaging 1,000 persons each. Most tribelets possessed a single permanent village and several more transient ones of smaller size. Each tribelet had a number of male officers: a chief, a chief's messenger, a ceremonial leader, and a village crier. Each of these offices was confined to a single lineage, was inherited patrilineally, and functioned principally at social and religious ceremonies. Most tribelets were on friendly terms with some of their neighbors and mutually shared each other's territories, but they also had Yokuts enemies, whom they repelled by force of arms when the latter poached on their lands. Marriages might be either exogamous or endogamous with respect to tribelet, but the former predominated. Each tribelet also had a name, which was a pure ethnic term with no other meaning in the language.

Southwest.—This area exhibits every kind of organization from small weak bands to true tribes. The desert-dwelling Yumans were grouped in loose bands which averaged about 135 persons each, but part of the year these broke up into extended families of about twenty-five persons each. The bands were led by headmen who had good war records and were bold enough to speak to the others and advise them about economic and military matters. This organization was little more stable than that of the western Shoshoni and is, therefore, at the borderline between absence and presence of government.

The Athapaskans, both Navahos and Apaches, never attained political units larger than bands until they were forced onto reservations by the United States government. The matrilocal extended family was the basic residential unit shared by all the Athapaskans, and these were combined into bands of from perhaps one hundred to several hundred persons. From late-nineteenth-century figures for the Western Apaches, the bands of this group averaged about 200 persons each, but this was after they had been somewhat reduced by warfare with the United States.

Basehart's (1960) description of Mescalero bands indicates that each band was named after its leader, and that the membership rallied around such a man because he was a good leader in the raids on other peoples. In the eighteenth and nineteenth centuries, these bands numbered nearer 100 than 200 persons on the average. The Navaho also had bands named after leaders, and, in addition, might have a special war leader chosen for his ritual attainment.

The Pueblo peoples, who live in the compact apartment-house villages, never achieved any unity beyond that of the village with a population numbered usually in the hundreds. The most populous pueblo at Spanish contact was Acoma, which was reported to have had 3,000 inhabitants; in 1960, Zuñi, with about 3,000 persons, was the largest. A Spanish system of officials can be found today at all pueblos except those of the Hopi, which lie farthest west. At the same time all the pueblos still retain a second set of pre-Conquest officials.

Because the pre-Conquest system is so closely geared to religion, it is frequently called a theocracy. Every pueblo had a number of religious organizations, comparable to our churches, lodges, fraternities, and faith-healing groups. Each chapter of each type of religious society had its own officers. These positions tended to be inherited, although which one of a man's sister's sons or own sons would succeed him depended on the interest the young man took in religious affairs and his ability to learn and perform the ritual correctly. All—or nearly all —such officers in a particular pueblo sat on its council, the number of council members varying from ten to about thirty among the various pueblos. The council was the highest authority in the pueblo, and functioned principally as a judiciary body. It decided the fate of citizens accused of such crimes as witchcraft, betrayal of religious secrets, and disloyalty to the pueblo. Theft, adultery, and even homicide were regarded as torts by Pueblo standards, and did not reach the council unless they became too violent to be handled by the proper officials. Tort-handling officials were the leaders of the warrior society, present in some form among all the Pueblos, and the members of this society served as police within the pueblo as well as an army without. On most Pueblo councils there were two individuals who served as executive officers. They may be called the civil priest and the war priest, and their orders were enforced, if necessary, by the warrior society led by the war priest or his lieutenant. Most of the concern of the council centered on deciding what course of action would be most in harmony with the supernatural, from which all blessings flowed. It is clear from this brief description that the Pueblos possessed true political organization at the village level.

Hoebel (1960) stresses the roles of individual officers or society members in enforcing the wishes of the council and, derivatively, of a large majority in the pueblo. Every pueblo had individuals empowered to whip, hang by the thumbs, and ultimately kill offenders. There is every reason to believe that every pueblo officially put to death its most flagrant deviants, including those who served as informants to anthropologists and revealed information regarded as sacred and secret. There was also a great deal more litigation and debate going on than has been generally reported. For instance, Frank Cushing, who served as a Zuñi bow priest in the 1880's, mentioned having attended two or three hundred councils and lawsuits.

The Yumans living on the Colorado and Gila rivers were organized into tribes of from two thousand to three thousand persons each. Each had multiple chiefs, who supposedly controlled as many areal sub-divisions, but these smaller territories have never been mapped. The chief was a versatile man who kept peace within his following, led them in economic pursuits and religious festivals, and often inherited his position from a paternal relative. Warfare was the national sport for these River Yumans, and again and again tribes fought with tradi-tional enemies, most often other Yumans. Sometimes two or three of the tribes formed an alliance against another group, but national identities were never confused and warriors normally returned to home territory after the campaign. Each tribe spoke a different lan-guage or dialect, and each had a distinct name. In spite of a fairly heavy concentration of population on the rivers, most of the Yumans did not live in definite towns of known size but, rather, on little farms scattered about on the floodplain of the river.

In the Southwest on the Mexican side of the border, towns became larger as one proceeded southward. These towns differed from those of the Pueblos not only in the greater size of their populations but also in the absence of apartmentlike clusters; they were more spread out and had more space between houses. Sixteenth- and seventeenth-century writers mention towns ranging in size from one hundred to six hundred houses. The populations of these towns averaged larger than those of the Pueblos of the United States, and the largest towns must have had several thousand inhabitants. The political unit was at least as large as the town, which makes it larger than that of any people discussed so far in this chapter except the River Yumans. Possibly several towns were united at times. All the towns had chiefs, who most often inherited their positions patrilineally, although the particular individual chosen from a lineage also had to have sufficient ability. In the very southernmost part of the Southwest area, there were regular markets, nobility, the collecting of tribute by large towns from small, and other manifestations of Meso-American culture, but these are not typical of the Southwest.

AREAS WITH TRIBAL ORGANIZATION IN THE HISTORIC PERIOD

On the Plains, Prairies, and in the East, some Indians—but not all—had tribal organization in the historic period, although it seems probable that band and village organization was much more common before White contact. The populations of the historic tribes ran into the thousands, and all tribes had chiefs and other officers. These are the classic tribes mentioned most often in United States history. The number of political units does not, however, always correspond to the linguistic names on the large map at the end of this book. The Crow and the Shawnee, for example, were divided into three and five subdivisions respectively, each of which was a separate political unit. These subdivisions were, however, of sufficient size and possessed enough integration to be labeled tribes.

The distinction between civil chiefs and war leaders was general throughout these areas. A man could not be both a civil chief and a war leader at the same time. All young men went to war to obtain scalps and other war honors which were necessary before they could be accepted as full citizens in the society. Only after success in war was a man likely to be selected for membership on the council and from there to civil chieftainship. Civil chiefs were obligated to stress peace within their own societies, as well as to discourage hotheaded young men from stirring up too much trouble with other tribes, and they had to resign their positions as chiefs before they could go on the warpath. Because chiefs were generally mature or old men, this was seldom done, but there are enough cases on record to establish the principle involved.

Plains.—Most of these peoples achieved tribal organization in the historic period, but a few, such as the Shoshoni-speaking Comanche, never got beyond the band stage. The Plains tribes occupied fairly well-defined territories which, although sometimes shared with friendly neighbors, were at the same time defended against enemy tribes. Each tribe assembled at least once a year, and sometimes oftener, for a communal buffalo hunt; each was further integrated by tribal religious ritual and beliefs. Each also was led by chiefs, and the will of the leaders was enforced by a police group. Chieftainship was acquired by achievement, particularly in warfare; but, once having gained this high status, the chief became a peacemaker within his own society, and often advocated a peaceful course of action in disputes with other tribes.

Wilson's attempt (1963: 376) to explain the lack of tribal organization among the Comanche on ecological grounds gets nowhere. The ethnohistory of the Comanche provides a very simple answer. They and the Wind River and Ute are all Uto-Aztecan speakers whose ancestors formerly lived in the Great Basin area. They brought no tribal organization with them when they first arrived on the Plains, and never acquired or developed any there. The Siouans, Caddoans, and, to a lesser extent, the Algonquians were farmers in the Prairies area before they moved out on the Plains and brought with them the tribal superstructure they already possessed, modifying it of course to suit the new conditions encountered. This historical explanation is far better than Wilson's ecological one to explain why some Plains peoples had tribal organization and some did not.

The political structure of the Cheyenne, who numbered about 4,000, has been more completely described than that of any other Plains tribe. The Cheyenne were governed by a civil council of forty-four chiefs, divided into five priestly chiefs, two doormen, and thirty-seven others. The priestly chiefs, who outranked the others, conducted tribal rituals, including the chief-renewal ritual performed every year when the group assembled. One of the five priestly chiefs presided at the meetings of the council of forty-four chiefs and manipulated the sacred medicines in the chief's medicine bundle; he was called the Prophet, and represented the mythical culture hero. The doormen were sometimes called upon to sum up the essence of the discussion and to render a decision for the group. When one of the five priestly chiefs retired, he chose his successor from the remaining thirty-nine members of the group; if he died so suddenly that he could not choose his successor, the surviving four priestly chiefs chose one for him. A priestly chief, on retirement, stepped down only to the rank of the undifferentiated thirty-seven chiefs; he did not have to leave the council. If an undifferentiated chief died without choosing his successor, the entire council chose one for him. Each ordinary chief could serve only ten years, which explains why the rules of succession are so complicated. New chiefs were chosen on the basis of merit, and it was considered bad taste for a man to choose his own son. The personal qualities which constituted merit were control of temper and generosity.

None of the forty-four chiefs ever exerted any force to carry out the will of the civil council. Force was applied by the members of one of the six men's societies which the council selected on two important occasions: moving camp, and the tribal buffalo hunt. Moving camp was a military venture because there was always some danger of encountering an enemy. The tribal buffalo hunt was the most important occasion of the year, and teamwork was necessary to kill the maximum number of buffalo.

The two headmen and the two doormen of each of the men's

societies formed a council of twenty-four war chiefs. A man could not be both a civil chief and a war chief. If a war chief was chosen as a civil chief, he must first resign his position of war chief before accepting that of civil chief. The council of war chiefs chose the war leader for each military raid; but, once the campaign was ended, his authority terminated.

Prairies.—Some of the Siouan tribes of this area had intricate systems of government in the historic period comparable to that of the Cheyenne, who were a Prairie tribe before abandoning farming and moving farther west onto the Plains in the early nineteenth century. The Algonquians, on the other hand, tended to be less well integrated. A most interesting account of Fox government illustrates how elusive and tenuous the role of leadership can be without actually being absent.

Fox concepts of power in religion and government were closely related. Supernatural power, called *manitu*, was impersonal, like atomic energy, but had to be possessed by both human beings and spiritual beings if they were to achieve any outstanding success. The possession of *manitu* was thought to be temporary and contingent on many things, so that the only proof that one person possessed more power than another was successful performance at a given time and place, such as success in battle. Since supernatural power was temporary and contingent, success in one venture did not insure success in the next, so that success in one battle, or even in several, did not tend to raise a man to a permanent position of success and leadership. Because religious power was dangerous, it was considered both hazardous and immoral for one individual to exercise much control over another. Individualism was extreme in comparison with other Prairie tribes.

There were three principal leaders in Fox society: the civil or "peace" chief, the war leader, and the ceremonial leader. The civil chieftainship was a permanent position, inherited patrilineally by a member of the Bear lineage. This chief was supposed to encourage harmonious relations within the group and to act as arbiter in the event of dissension in council meetings. The war leader's position was the result of *manitu* acquired in a vision and was limited to a single campaign. Any warrior in the tribe who, according to his own testimony, had acquired supernatural power in this manner could become the leader of a war expedition. As is general for the Plains, Prairies, and East, membership in a war party was voluntary, the number and

ability of the volunteers being correlated with the amount of incitement which the relating of the vision brought. The war leader therefore
merely suggested what the group should do, and, if the majority
dissented, he might be forced to come up with a fresh suggestion. The
ceremonial leader was anyone who had memorized one or more of the
many religious rituals of the Fox.

In addition to these three kinds of weak leaders, there was a village
council composed of the headmen of each of the extended family
groupings. This was presided over by the civil chief. No action was
taken unless the decision of the council was unanimous. Public
opinion was therefore almost automatically followed because every
family was represented on the council. Any person not an actual
member of the council might attend a meeting and plead any cause he
chose. On the whole, Fox government was a weak village system, and
did not attain the level of true tribal organization. This was true of
other Prairie Algonquians.

East.—In the East, the League of the Iroquois, embracing a population of from 10,000 to 17,000, was the largest and best-organized
political unit; yet its lack of cohesion is easily shown by its part in the
Revolutionary War, when the Oneida and half of the Tuscarora sided
with the colonists while the others took the side of the British. This was
the strongest confederacy north of Mexico at the time of European
contact, soon after 1600, and the traditional date of its founding was
about 1570. Others probably existed before Europeans arrived, and
still others came and went at later dates as Indians and Whites clashed
in the contact period.

There was a limited strip of territory along the coastal plain extending from Louisiana to Florida, thence north up the Atlantic Coast to
Virginia, where the political units were true tribes and the rulers had
absolute authority, including the power of life and death, over their
subjects. This is the only area north of Mexico where such absolute
power existed. The best-known examples of this system are the
Natchez and the Powhatan, whose populations are estimated at
4,500 and 9,000, respectively, in the seventeenth century. Among the
Natchez, the chief was regarded as a descendant of the sun god and
traveled in a litter, the bearers running in relays and changing over
without slackening their pace. His subjects were required to keep at
least four paces away from his person and to speak to him with
reverence. When the chief died, his wives and servants were killed to
serve him in the afterlife, and his body was disemboweled and laid to

rest in a temple near those of his predecessors. This reminds us of the Incas of Peru and the Circum-Caribbean peoples.

Matrilineal descent was the prevailing form in the East, and leadership in all its forms tended to be inherited matrilineally. The clan and sib organizations were the units which made up the towns and tribes, and normally both religious and political offices were confined to particular lineages and sibs, which were matrilineal.

Since the League of the Iroquois has been described so often in books, let us choose the government of the Creek Indians of Alabama and Georgia as our typical example for this area. The territorial unit among the Creeks was the village, of which there were about fifty among a total population of about 40,000, averaging about 800 persons per village. Some villages or towns, as they were often called, were much larger than others, the largest single one having 500 houses, according to Garcilaso de la Vega. The highest officer in the town was the chief, and each of the fifty towns had its own chief. The position was not strictly hereditary because the chief was chosen by the town council, but normally the council selected the chief from a single sib, such as the Bear sib. It was thus hereditary within the sib. Chiefs of Red ("war") towns were usually chosen from one of the Red sibs, and chiefs of White ("peace") towns from one of the White sibs. The council might also impeach a chief any time they felt he was unsatisfactory, and there are actual cases of this on record. The chief's duties were many: he was in charge of the public area in the center of the town, including the public granary which stored part of the harvest from the town fields, and, after a successful hunt in which he participated, he might invite the whole town to a feast followed by an all-night dance; he presided over council discussions, maneuvering the members so as to reach a decision; he designated the time for the annual harvest ceremony, distributing invitation sticks to heads of families; he received embassies from other towns and tribes and represented his town in foreign affairs. Chiefs were all called "peace" chiefs, meaning civil chiefs, even though some were from "war" sibs and served "war" towns. Policing of the town and actual warfare were in the charge of officers and members of a warrior group, to be described below.

Each Creek town also had a second, or vice-chief who might be nominated by the chief but also had to be approved by the council. Another official, who was a spokesman for the chief, sat beside the chief in council and orated the latter's wishes. There was in addition a group of officials whom we shall designate as "cabinet members." They directed the planting, cultivating, and harvesting of the town fields, as well as the gathering of leaves for the black drink, which was the emetic and purge used on all ceremonial occasions. Another similar group was that of the "beloved men," the ceremonial leaders who actually conducted the harvest ceremony. They were veteran warriors, too old to go to war but held in high esteem.

There were three classes of warriors, who had a certain amount of political authority. Their statuses were achieved entirely by valorous deeds of war. The highest class served as town police, punishing those who acted contrary to the will of the council or who failed to attend the harvest ceremony. There was also an official, called the "war speaker," chosen by the warriors from their highest class. He was the chief of police, orator for the cause of war, and announcer of a war campaign to the public.

All of the above officials and classes of officials, except possibly the lowest class of warriors, were members of the town council. While we are not always told so, it seems certain that every officer, including the "peace" ones, got his start up the ladder of fame as a warrior. Once he had attained one of the more modest civil offices, he could progress to higher ones on the basis of oratorical ability, knowledge of tribal lore and law, administrative ability, and other such civil qualifications. It also seems likely that every officer could be impeached by the council.

The existence of any sort of Creek confederacy in de Soto's time or earlier is doubtful. White pressure in the eighteenth century encouraged the Creeks to attempt centralization for mutual protection.

THE STATE

Meso-America.—The Aztecs, Tarascans, and Totonacs, at least, were organized into political units with populations of more than 100,000, and the Aztec confederation had some control over millions. The Mayas of Yucatán were divided into at least a dozen territorial units with as many separate governments in the early sixteenth century. With a total population of 250,000 in 1549, these small Mayan states averaged about 20,000 persons each, but they were surely considerably more populous before Spanish contact. The Mixtecs' political unit was generally the town, but one ambitious ruler con-

quered a stretch of Pacific coastline 120 miles in length and subjected
the entire population of this territory to his rule. Since the total population of the Mixtecs has been estimated at an even million in 1520,
this largest Mixtec state may have reached 100,000.

Because the Aztec system of government was dominant in Meso-
America when the Spanish arrived, it will be described in more detail.
Every individual was a member of a patrilocal extended family and a
deme (*calpulli*). Each deme had three principal officers: a secretary-
treasurer, who was in charge of economic affairs; a war leader or
sheriff, who maintained order within the deme in time of peace and
led the deme's military force in time of war; and a speaker, who represented his deme on the council of state, which, in turn, controlled the
entire nation. There were twenty demes in Tenochtitlán (Mexico City)
and apparently the same number in the other large towns and cities of
the Aztecs. The officers of the deme were selected by the deme council,
composed of heads of extended families and other elder male citizens.
There was no formal ballot, voice vote, or standing vote; all selections
of officers and other decisions as well were, in theory, unanimous. In
addition to the three principal officers, there were many petty positions
open to men who had distinguished themselves in civil, religious, and
martial affairs. These include those who policed the markets, members
of tribunals to settle disputes within demes, teachers of young men,
and the keepers of the records of tribute and wealth in the deme's
storehouses.

The speakers from each of the twenty demes formed the council of
state, which, in turn, selected four officials from among its twenty
members. Each of these officers represented one of the quarters into
which a city was divided and, derivatively, five of the demes. Their
duties were generally to lead the military forces and to settle disputes
between demes. Two were concerned principally with judicial affairs,
a third was an executioner, and the fourth served as a liaison officer
between civil and military affairs. A "chief of men" was chosen by the
four officers just described. He represented the nation in foreign
affairs involving war and alliances; when Cortés arrived, it was
Montezuma who held this position. A second official who shared top
honors with the chief of men was the "snake woman," who was a man
in charge of the internal affairs of the nation. All of these officials
selected by the council of state or the four special councilors could be
impeached by action of the council and removed from authority. In
practice, however, the council tended to choose successive chiefs of

men from a single lineage, so that the office came to be inherited within the lineage.

These top officials were of royal blood and were descendants of a Toltec prince. Caso (1963) calls the chief of men a "king," which is an appropriate term because this chief was so treated. If any lesser chief wished to speak to him, he approached with downcast eyes, barefoot, and wearing the clothing of a commoner. Montezuma was carried on a litter borne on the shoulders of four chiefs, and under no circumstances were his feet allowed to touch the earth. Four additional chiefs held above the litter a canopy of green feathers fringed with gold, silver, pearls, and jade. At home, Montezuma was served food seated behind a screen so that no one could watch him eat. Even his closest relatives approached him in humble manner and remained standing in his presence. His palace had a hundred rooms and a hundred baths and, with attached buildings, was large enough to accommodate the more than 2,000 soldiers of Cortés and his Tlaxcalan allies.

About a century before Cortés arrived, the Aztecs of Tenochtitlán formed a triple alliance with two other city-states in the Valley of Mexico. They soon dominated the alliance, and continued to do so until the Spanish conquest. It was during this period that they conquered most of the important peoples in central Mexico and even some as far away as Guatemala. They collected tribute from all these subject peoples, occasionally by force of arms, but never welded them into a single "empire" or nation. Small, insignificant, and poor minority groups within this huge territory were sometimes bypassed. The state organization of the Aztecs never became larger than the city of Tenochtitlán, but with a population estimated at 300,000, this was easily the greatest political achievement of aboriginal North America.

SUMMARY AND CONCLUSIONS

Our survey has shown that the family was the largest permanent residential unit over most of the Arctic, Great Basin, and Northeast Mexican areas. The Sub-Arctic, with its weak bands of a hundred or two, was only slightly more integrated politically. On the North Pacific Coast and in California, the territorial unit was generally the village or tribelet, with population numbered in the hundreds. The Plateau formerly seems to have had only village and tribelet organization throughout, but in the eighteenth and nineteenth centuries Plains influence brought true tribes to the eastern part of this area. In the Southwest, we found all degrees from small bands of less than a hundred to true tribes numbering several thousand. On the Plains, Prairies, and in the East, integrations of a thousand or more persons into tribes were common in the historic period. In Meso-America, we found much larger territorial units, which we labeled "states," with populations in the tens and hundreds of thousands.

How are these differences to be explained? The largest political entities were in the areas where farming was the principal source of food: Meso-America, Southwest, and East (Map 3). The Plains tribes are an exception to this rule, but, because most of them formerly lived farther east and farmed, their government can easily be demonstrated to be of Eastern derivation. The size of the political unit is also correlated with population density (Map 6), although this relationship too is far from perfect. It was in Meso-America, with more people than in all the other culture areas combined, that large states developed. In the areas of sparsest population, the Arctic, Sub-Arctic, Great Basin, and Northeast Mexico, political integration was either absent or at the minimum. In areas of intermediate population density, however, we found our relationship reversed. On the Northwest Coast and in California, population was generally more dense than on the Plains, Prairies, and even in the East; yet the political units in the former areas were generally smaller than those in the latter.

At this point we must again introduce the historical factor. The tribes in the Southeastern United States unquestionably derived some of their social and political organization from Meso-America, as Kroeber long ago (1928: 392–96) pointed out. The Natchez, Powhatan, Timucua, and other Southeastern peoples show a great deal of similarity in their entire sociopolitical structure to the peoples of Meso-America. It therefore appears that most of the Indians in the United States east of the Rocky Mountains were exposed to forms of government originally derived from Meso-America. Why the Southwest peoples failed to acquire more of this interest in political organization is not obvious. Population per square mile in the Pueblo part of the Southwest was greater than that of the East, and presumably it would have been no more difficult to form a permanent federation among the Rio Grande Pueblos than among the five or six Iroquois tribes. But the fact remains that it was never done. Thus, there appear to be differences of a subtle nature, perhaps in personality, which determine in part how far a given people will proceed in the direction of a larger governmental integration.

REFERENCES

BASEHART, 1960; BEALS, 1932*a*; BIRKET-SMITH, 1936; DAHL-
GREN DE JORDAN, 1954; DRIVER AND DRIVER, 1963; FISHER,
1939; GIFFORD, 1932, 1936; GOODWIN, 1942; HIND, 1863;
KROEBER, 1925, 1928, 1935, 1939, 1955; LIPS, 1947; LLEWEL-
LYN AND HOEBEL, 1941; LOWIE, 1951, 1954; MILLER, 1955;
MURDOCK, 1957; OPLER, 1941; OSGOOD, 1936, 1937; RAY,
1939; ROYS, 1957; SPECK AND EISELEY, 1942; SPIER, 1928;
STEWARD, 1938; THOMPSON, 1940; VAILLANT, 1941; WEYER,
1932.

18

Violence, Feuds, Raids, War

FEW INDIGENOUS peoples in the world at the same level of culture have fought so valiantly against European intruders as did the Indians east of the Rocky Mountains in the United States. Man for man, bow for bow, and gun for gun, they were a match for the best troops sent against them and were overwhelmed only because of the greater numbers and superior armament of the English and French colonizers. The more civilized and settled peoples of Meso-America and around the Caribbean fell an easy prey to the Spanish for a number of reasons, among them the fact that the rank and file were so overregimented that it never occurred to them to resist after their leaders were slain or captured.

The arrival of Europeans in the Americas produced many indirect changes in Indian ways of life, largely in the nature of adaptations to the changing conditions. Without these changes the end of the Indians as independent cultures would have come much sooner. Patterns of warfare were no exception to this rule. In pre-Columbian times, war parties in the area that is now the United States were smaller, just as the political units they represented were smaller. After the European invasions, small villages or bands tended to unite with one another to form tribes and ultimately confederations. Although the cohesiveness of these larger political entities left something to be desired and many were only temporary, they were able to offer more resistance to the Whites collectively than individually. The pressure of White settlement on the East Coast pushed the Eastern Indians toward the west and stirred up a host of conflicts between them and those tribes already located in the new land. Although the Indians did not use their land as intensively as did the colonists, the forcing of two tribes onto land formerly occupied by one stirred up trouble between them. Competition for beaver and other fur-bearing animals became extreme. Probably as many Indians were killed fighting each other after White contact as were killed in wars with the Whites.

The weapons of war will be mentioned only incidentally here, except for the gun. The first trade guns from Europe were so deficient technically that their superiority over the bow and arrow was debatable. As late as our own Revolutionary War, George Washington and other military leaders had considerable discussion on whether the bow and arrow should be a part of the armament of the thirteen colonies. Washington had been present at Braddock's defeat and had seen with his own eyes what the Indians could do with the bow and arrow. While an English soldier was reloading, with powder and shot, through the muzzle, an Indian could shoot at least half a dozen arrows; sometimes the flint failed to produce a spark, or the powder became too wet to fire. When breech-loading guns and ammunition in cartridges appeared, however, the superiority of the gun became obvious, and this improved weapon was a factor in the final defeat of the Indians.

"Violence" is the broadest word in the title of this chapter. It refers to bodily injury or killing whether resulting from an encounter between two persons, two families, two bands, two lineages, two sibs, two tribes, two confederacies, or any other social and territorial units. It may terminate with the death or injury of one party, continue in a series of reprisals, or go on indefinitely. "Feuds," on the other hand, is limited to conflicts between two families, lineages, clans, sibs, or other kinship groups. "Feuds" also suggests a protracted series of reprisals without any mechanism for settling the dispute, but, because concepts of law and order show much variation, one cannot always draw a sharp line between feud and law. The term "raid" will be used to designate a single small military engagement of short duration. "War," on the other hand, will be reserved for conflicts between two factions with true political organization, each of which possesses definite leadership, some kind of military tactics, and at least the hope of being able to weather a series of battles.

ABSENCE OF TRUE WARFARE

Because we have defined war as a military encounter between two political units, those areas which lacked true political organization lacked true warfare. Therefore, most of the peoples of the Arctic, Great Basin, Northeast Mexico, and probably Baja California lacked true warfare before European contact. None of these had any permanent military organization, special fighting regalia, or associated public ceremonies. However, violence occurred in these areas in the form of duels and raids by small groups, and feuds were common.

Arctic.—Murder apparently occurred from time to time in every Eskimo settlement. Disputes over women were the most common immediate cause of murder. One anthropologist carefully canvassed every Eskimo man in a certain settlement in northern Canada on this question and found that every mature man of about thirty or older had killed at least one Eskimo man at some time in his life. A man's status in the society was enhanced by an occasional murder of another; it was only when he killed too many men too close together in time that he was socially disapproved of and in danger of losing his own life at the hands of a group of vigilantes. Feuds were also present among the Eskimo. For example, an anthropologist's chief informant among the Caribou Eskimo had killed his wife's entire family when he appropriated her, because they disapproved of him. If he had left a single man or boy alive, the latter might have taken revenge on him at a later date.

Sometimes, however, the community might rise up to enforce justice. A series of unprovoked murders might be punished by a group of able-bodied men who banded together and killed the offender. One who was reputed to kill by sorcery might also be disposed of in this way. Such groups of justice dispensers were not appointed or elected in any way, nor had they any leader. Even when the desire to acquire a woman was not the cause of a murder, the murderer was nonetheless expected to provide for the murdered man's wife and children. This meant that a man normally reared the son of a murdered victim, a boy who might later exact blood vengeance upon his foster father. Revenge was more often accomplished by a surprise attack on the unsuspecting victim, but might take the form of an open challenge to a wrestling match with the loser forfeiting his life.

When small bands of Eskimo met their Indian neighbors to the south, as they sometimes did in the summer, they often fought them over the hunting and fishing rights at a particular locality. These were not planned punitive expeditions, and did not involve large enough, permanent enough, or sufficiently well-integrated social groups, to be labeled "war." Nevertheless, it is significant that intergroup encounters on this scale happened much more often with Athapaskan and Algonquian bands than with other Eskimo bands.

The Alaskan Eskimo carried on a series of raids and feuds with their Athapaskan neighbors. The motivations included the desire to appropriate the material possessions and young women of the vanquished as well as to avenge an injury or death from an earlier engagement. The prestige of the victor was always enhanced also.

Great Basin.—The western Shoshoni and their neighbors in the heart of the Great Basin lacked definite warfare. With the family the largest permanent residential unit, there was no government to carry on a true war. Violence, raids, and feuds were not totally lacking, however, although they were normally carried on without any special organization, regalia, or ritual. Such hostilities were more frequent between speakers of different languages: Shoshoni versus Northern Paiute, Southern Paiute, Ute, or even Mohave. Woman stealing is the most frequently reported motivation for such attacks, although economic motives were not lacking. "Legal" procedure for settling disputes within a band seems to have been totally lacking or at least is unreported. The western Shoshoni therefore appear to have had less law even than the peoples of the Arctic and Sub-Arctic.

Northeast Mexico.—The Chichimecs of this area apparently lacked true warfare in pre-Columbian times except in the south, where they made contact with the peoples of Meso-America. Later, when the Spanish invaded their territory in the middle of the sixteenth century to mine silver, the Chichimecs became very aggressive against the intruders and formed bands for mutual defense. However, the temporary and expedient nature of these bands is shown by the fact that after winning a victory, they sometimes fought among themselves over the spoils. Although the aboriginal Chichimecs lacked the political organization to carry on true wars, their geographical position between Meso-America on the south and the Plains-Prairies-East on the north and northeast gave them a number of traits which they share in common with these more advanced cultures. For instance, they took scalps, tortured prisoners, mutilated corpses, ate the flesh of slain enemies, and each man kept a record of the number of his victims by carving a notch for each on the bone of a human arm or leg.

WEAK OR MIXED PATTERNS OF WARFARE

In the Sub-Arctic, Northwest Coast, Plateau, California, and Southwest, at least some of the peoples possessed a more definite form of warlike behavior. Territorial units were a little larger, and those with true political organization tended also to have more military organization. At the same time, all these areas included some peoples with little in the way of violence, raids, or feuds, and no hostilities pretentious enough to be labeled war.

Sub-Arctic.—Among the Naskapi of the Labrador Peninsula,

murders sometimes occurred but were not common. Murder in self-defense went unpunished, but an unprovoked murder brought re-taliation from the male relatives of the slain man. If these relatives failed to act, the band chief might remind them that they had a social obligation to do so. If a murder occurred at the summer rendezvous with the band chief and informal council present, the chief would call a hearing. If the majority of the old men of the council thought the murderer guilty, the chief would pronounce the death sentence. The condemned man would start walking away, with the armed council members following. When they reached an appropriate spot, three or four men, previously designated as executioners by the chief, shot the offender in the back. His corpse was left to lie where it fell without burial.

Among the northern Ojibwa just east of Lake Winnipeg, murder by physical encounter is unheard of. Wrongs are avenged by witchcraft, sometimes performed by the injured man, but also by a shaman employed for the purpose. These people occasionally fight when drunk, but are normally completely nonviolent. Witchcraft serves as a substitute for physical violence and is thought to be capable of killing a person or of making him severely ill. The widespread occurrence of the belief in the Windigo mythical cannibal and the psychosis associated with it in the Eastern Sub-Arctic suggests that murder and cannibalism may have happened more often in periods of starvation in the past than Indian informants in the twentieth century are aware of (Ray, 1960).

Peoples of the Eastern Sub-Arctic who had contact with the Eskimo occasionally fought with them, but there is no record of an entire band of Montagnais, Naskapi, or Cree fighting against another speaking the same language. The southernmost Montagnais, who contacted the Iroquois, learned some of the tricks of organized warfare from the latter, but it was generally the Iroquois who were both the aggressors and the victors. When the Cree moved west in the early nineteenth century, they often fought with the more timid Athapaskans and stole their material possessions and women.

In the Mackenzie Sub-Arctic, the Athapaskan bands sometimes fought each other as well as the Eskimo. The Chipewyans, Slaves, Dogribs, Yellowknives, Kaskas, and Beavers fought one another regularly, more often for material goods and women than for any other reason, although revenge was also a motive. There were also raids and feuds between bands speaking the same language, although these seem to have been less common than interlingual disputes.

In the Yukon Sub-Arctic, the Athapaskans fought principally with the Eskimo. Here the economic prestige motives loomed larger than elsewhere in the Sub-Arctic because of contact with the Northwest Coast, but revenge was also a factor. The spoils that went to the victor were weapons, boats, clothing, hides, and any other goods of value, as well as women. The proof of physical superiority, added to the gain in personal wealth, raised the prestige of the winner in his society. As elsewhere in the Sub-Arctic, these encounters were in the nature of small raids, or occasionally feuds, initiated by any individual.

Northwest Coast.—In this area, kinship was of much greater importance than in the areas described in the sections above, and all the more productive pieces of real estate were owned and used by kin groups, such as extended families, lineages, sibs, clans, and demes. Competition and rivalry in the accumulation of wealth and prestige were keen, along with an almost paranoid sensitivity to criticism and slander. Under these circumstances, disputes between kin groups were common enough to have been reported for almost all the peoples on the entire Northwest Coast.

After a physical injury or a killing, the relatives of the victim sometimes retaliated by injuring or killing a member of the kin group which had initiated the violence. If the retaliation succeeded, the two sides were even, but the affair did not stop there. Each side demanded compensation from the other in tangible goods or "money." Sometimes there was no retaliation and the original wrong was settled by an indemnity. Regardless of the number of casualties involved, each victim had to be paid for by the kin group of the person who had committed the violence. The amount of damage was negotiated by an intermediary, who was not a member of either of the disputing groups. In northwest California among the Yurok and their neighbors, the valuation placed on a life was exactly the amount of the bride price that had been paid for the victim's mother. Elsewhere in the area, the price for a life was not fixed in any manner, and often the aim was to demand enough wergild to embarrass and humble the opponents. Sometimes among the Tlingit, when the amount of compensation for a life could not be agreed upon, the headman or chief of the slayer's kin group would give his own life to keep the peace. The Kwakiutl and Nootka were more openly aggressive, and defended their aggressions with a renewal of hostilities if necessary.

Should this system be labeled "feud"? The fact that physical retaliation for an injury or life was common suggests the concept of the feud, but the further fact that compensation had to be paid eventually for every injury or life is evidence that there was a mechanism for settling such disputes. The system therefore stands astride both law and feud, with some of the aspects of both.

The Northwest Coast peoples of British Columbia and Alaska also carried on campaigns aimed at robbing, driving out, or annihilating another group in order to appropriate its lands and movable possessions. Although these were not usually disputes between true political units, the economic motivation is clear and the aggression just as deadly. Most of such economic conquests were between groups speaking different languages. Among the Nootka, however, these economy-motivated raids of extermination took place between speakers of the same language. Here, there was true political organization, at least in the historic period, so that the larger encounters of this nature involving this people may be labeled "war."

Slaves were a further reason for conducting a raid or, rather, they were another kind of movable property to be acquired along with canoes, furs, food, and clothing. Most of the peoples on the Northwest Coast from Alaska to the Columbia River and then southward inland to the Klamath of southern Oregon captured persons, as well as movable property, in raids. Some of these persons may already have been slaves, but most were freemen, who were sold or kept as slaves after being captured. Sometimes they were ransomed later by relatives, but often the stigma attached to the slave status was so marked that the relatives did not want to have a freed slave in their midst and therefore took no steps to recover their kinsman. Children of slaves, if any, became slaves. This is the only area in North America where slavery was sometimes hereditary.

Heads were taken by most of the Northwest Coast peoples in Canada and Alaska, but scalping was done only by the Tlingit—on their way home, at leisure, from the previously acquired whole head. The heads were mounted on tall poles erected in front of the village.

With all this fighting there was no separate military organization. The same wealthy men who were the headmen and chiefs of their kinship groups, tribelets, and tribes normally accompanied the fighting force and claimed the lion's share of the spoils. Supernatural sanction was required of at least the leader of a raiding expedition among the Salish-speaking peoples of southern British Columbia, Washington, and Oregon, as well as others in Oregon and northern

California. This usually took the form of a vision or a dream which the visionary interpreted as support from the supernatural. On the Oregon and northern California coasts, this was coupled with a dance of incitement before the raid. There was also a connection between aggressiveness and other psychological states. A man who had lost a relative by death, including natural death, or one who had been defeated in a potlatch or suffered some other kind of economic misfortune, would often go to war to even the score.

Plateau.—The raids, feuds, and wars on the Plateau have been much influenced by the practices of neighboring culture areas in the historic period. What appears to have been formerly the predominant pattern is most in evidence in the center of the area in the state of Washington. Hostilities were limited to raids and occasional small-scale feuds in this region. The principal motives for raids seem to have been plunder, adventure, and revenge. When captives were taken, they were regarded as slaves in the beginning but might later become free citizens, often by marrying a member of the group that had captured them. Raiding parties were small, normally two or three canoes full of men representing only their own selfish interests. Volunteers made up the entire party, and anyone who wished could lead a party. Headmen and chiefs of villages and bands disapproved of such raids and went to great lengths to maintain peace, sometimes risking their lives in negotiations with hostile outsiders. Feuds between kin groups were known but not common, and chiefs served as arbiters of such disputes, which were often settled by blood money. The rudiments of a legal mechanism were therefore present.

Hostilities among the Salish-speaking peoples on the Canadian side of the Plateau area were more pronounced. Here raiding parties numbered all the way from five or six individuals to several hundred. Although participation was voluntary, a man who refused to join such expeditions lost the respect of his fellows. The motives were, therefore, multiple: plunder, adventure, revenge, and prestige. Such parties were made up of men from a single village, or at most a band, never from all the speakers of a given language. However, they more frequently raided a village where a different language was spoken, as elsewhere in North America. These expeditions were led by a war leader who acquired his position by his proficiency as a warrior and who was often the one initiating the enterprise. There were also blood feuds between kinship groups. The most trivial quarrels and insults often precipitated hostilities, and no man went unarmed. Such disputes were sometimes settled by blood money, again demonstrating the presence of the germ of law and order.

The Plateau peoples with the most Plains influence acquired the Plains pattern of warfare in the eighteenth and nineteenth centuries. It will be described below in the section on the Plains.

California.—On the whole, these Indians were among the most mild-tempered and peace-loving on the entire North American continent. Most hostilities were between small parties representing a kinship group or a village, but tribelets also clashed at times, and because these conflicts were between political units, they may be labeled "war." Motives were multiple, as the following list in order of frequency of reporting shows: revenge of witchcraft; revenge of violence; disputes over economic rights in productive areas; retaliation when women and girls were kidnapped. As compared with other areas, witchcraft loomed large but, because witchcraft was probably universal for the whole continent, this impression may have resulted from unevenness of reporting. On the other hand, witchcraft could be met with counter-witchcraft, and if the California Indians met it more often with physical aggression than did peoples of other culture areas, this was a significant difference. Land grabbing was not a common thing; yet boundary disputes between tribelets were fairly common, and in a few instances the aggressor took land by force and held it permanently. Some of the intralingual conflicts were feuds between kinship groups, but because these were often settled by blood money in the northern half of the area, at least, the germ of law was there.

Southwest.—The Pueblo peoples have been characterized as unemotional, cooperative, and peaceful by Ruth Benedict in her famous book *Patterns of Culture*, but she has overstated her case. While the Pueblos were less warlike than their neighbors, they could not have survived without military activity. All of the Pueblo villages had a war priest, who was ranked with the head civil priest in executive authority, and the two were responsible to a council whose unanimous decision controlled the affairs of the pueblo. In some pueblos, the war priest led the fighting force; in others, they were led by his lieutenant. The warrior sodality served as a police force within the pueblo and a military force without. Participation in offensive hostilities was determined by membership in this sodality, not by the voluntary action of the individual as in the areas discussed so far in this chapter. The war priest and the warriors' sodality formed a permanent group ready to cope with violence at any time. Each pueblo embraced people from a number of internally related but externally unrelated kinship groups, so that conflicts between pueblos can scarcely be called "feuds." In size, they fit the term "raid," yet their organization suggests the term "war."

The Spanish put a stop to interpueblo warfare at an early date, but there is good evidence to indicate that all the Pueblos at one time or another fought with other Pueblos as well as with Navahos, Apaches, and Utes. Sometimes two or more pueblos would unite to make war on a third, and, under the yoke of the Spanish in 1680, nearly all joined together and succeeded in driving out the Spanish. When the latter returned in 1693, however, the confederation had come apart at the seams and was further split asunder over the issue of loyalty to the new Spanish regime.

Fear of witchcraft was sometimes a cause of hostilities between pueblos. However, reprisals against raids initiated by enemies probably accounted for more Pueblo forays than any other motivation. The weakness of the Pueblo military position, as compared to that of the Navahos and Apaches, was that the Pueblos usually waited until they were attacked before they fought. They were like sitting ducks for the mobile Athapaskans, who were mounted on horses for the most part after Spanish contact. The Pueblos possessed a great deal more material wealth, including food, than the Navahos and Apaches and were repeatedly preyed upon by the latter. The Athapaskans stole anything they could lay their hands on and run off with: food, clothing, jewelery, livestock, and women and children, who were adopted into the band. The war leader was sometimes a different individual from the civil leader, and attained his position solely on the basis of his achievement as a fighter. The informal band council and civil leader had to approve an offensive foray of any size before it could be undertaken; but any man could initiate the raid, and participation in it was voluntary. A shaman usually accompanied the expedition to maintain contact with the supernatural at all times. If a raid was successful, a victory celebration, with women participating, was held when the party reached home.

The desert Yumans lived in smaller family groups or bands than the Athapaskans, were more timid, and lacked horses. Their raids were smaller and less frequent. The Yuman tribes on the Colorado and Gila rivers were more warlike than other Southwest peoples on the United States side of the border, and fighting took on some of the character of an international sport. They fought principally among themselves, that is, with other River Yuman tribes, only occasionally raiding one of the weaker desert peoples. There is one instance in the historical record of a River Yuman tribe being defeated and driven out of its territory, but the intent of the aggressors was to win in a fair fight with this tribe, not to cause them to flee. Plunder and captives were sometimes taken but were never a major incentive to fight. Warfare was an obsession among the young men of these tribes, and war power was acquired in dreams, which were interpreted as contact with spiritual personalities who conferred upon the dreamer the supernatural power to insure success in war. Any River Yuman man who had acquired war power in this fashion could lead a small raiding party of a dozen or so men, but the larger campaigns involving hundreds of participants were planned by the war chief, who was a permanent officer of the tribe. The warriors were divided into two groups according to weapons: those with bows, who projected their arrows from a distance; those with short clubs, used in hand-to-hand fighting.

The River Yuman emphasis on war is reminiscent of the Plains region, to be described below. Two details, not described so far, link the River Yumans with the Plains Indians: the round shield of hide; and the feathered stave, planted in the ground and defended at all costs. Only a very brave man carried one of the feathered staves, but once he plunged it into the ground, he was pledged not to retreat from his position but to defend it with his life. However, because there was no direct contact between the River Yumans and the Plains peoples, and these traits were also found in Mexico, the River Yuman and Plains tribes probably derived them from Mexico, not from each other.

In the Southwest area in Mexico, the political units were comparable to the tribes of the River Yumans, and the pattern of warfare also shows resemblances, although it is much less fully reported. Armies were larger than any reported for the areas described so far in this chapter, were divided into definite squadrons with a commander for each, and fought pitched battles. Beals (1932a: 190) lists two squadrons for the Pima Bajo; 1,000 men in four squadrons on the Rio Fuerte; some 400 or 500 men in three squadrons for the Ocoroni; definite squadrons in Sinaloa and among the Chiametla; 3,000 men under a chief at Tepic (according to one writer); and from eight to ten squadrons of men in an army at the same town (according to a second writer). Some of these armies apparently maintained their ranks on the march as well as in battle formation. With some allowance for exaggeration of the numbers of fighting men, these armies were still much larger than any fighting force north of Mexico at the earliest White contact. The round hide shields and feathered staves, which were stuck in the ground and defended to the death, link these peoples with the River Yumans and the Plains Indians.

WELL-DEVELOPED WARFARE

On the Plains, Prairies, and in the East, warfare was a more integral part of the total culture than in any other region of equal size north of Mexico. Features shared by all three areas will be described first.

Although tribal organization was common in all three areas, fights between whole tribes seem to have been rare before White contact. Small raiding parties of from four or five to fifty men were far more common than larger "armies." And even when numbers were large, as in an engagement of Cree and Blackfoot versus Shoshoni about 1725, when 800 men took part, casualties were few. After White settlement on the East Coast, clashes of both Whites against Indians and Indians against Indians became much larger and more deadly. The largest war parties in the seventeenth century were probably those of the Iroquois, which ran as high as about 1,000 fighting men. If we define "war" as a clash between territorial units with true political organization, war was less frequent throughout the Plains, Prairies, and East before White contact, because political organization also was less frequent in the pre-White period. White contact stirred up the Indians in many ways and brought about many irreversible trends in their cultures. The European demand for trade goods, especially furs, created a general economic competition which, when added to previous causes of fighting, vastly increased the number and size of armed conflicts. The economic motive was therefore paramount in this area in the historic period.

In all these areas, fighting was a means of acquiring prestige for the individual. No young man ever thought of getting married or of being accepted as an adult citizen until he had slain an enemy and brought back a scalp to prove it. So important was this achievement to the individual that when war parties failed to contact the enemy and to obtain the necessary scalps, they sometimes killed members of their own tribe, whom they accidentally encountered on their way home, rather than return empty-handed and in disgrace.

Motives for violence were, therefore, always multiple and mixed. The individual wished to enhance his personal prestige in the social hierarchy, and the band, village, or tribe wished to maintain its unity and independence as well as to improve its economic position. In addition to these general motives, desire for revenge was always present, and mere adventure should not be ruled out entirely. Although plunder in the form of weapons, food, clothing, furs, and other movables was generally taken in raids, this was not a major cause of hostilities, except possibly on the Plains, where horse stealing was general. On the Prairies and in the East, where villages were the rule, more movable goods seem to have been destroyed by fire and other means than were carried away by the victors. The taking of captives was common in the East but was never a major cause of conflicts.

Armed clashes were more common between speakers of different languages than between speakers of the same language, but the latter were far from lacking, for there was emphasis in the tribal and confederational councils on keeping the peace within such linguistic units.

Anyone could lead a raiding party, and membership in the party was on a voluntary basis. Some peoples insisted that a raiding expedition must be approved by the band, village, or tribal council, but others had no mechanism for preventing a raid against an enemy. A permanent war chief to lead war activities is reported for the Prairies and East, but this official always coexisted with lay leaders and probably did not exist before White contact in these areas. Supernatural sanction for at least the leader or a shaman, obtained through dreams, was necessary before even the smallest raid would be undertaken. The authority of the lay leader, little as it was, ceased when the raid was over.

Probably all war parties of any size employed scouts and sentries in these areas. They communicated with signs, such as animal cries and smoke signals. The men were not divided neatly into squadrons, as in Mexico, nor was armament definitely divided, as among the River Yumans. The premium was placed on individual fighting with full use of the natural protection afforded by trees and rocks. The close formation of the colonial armies, as in Braddock's defeat, made them an easy prey to the individualism and open fighting of these Indians. The greater mobility of the Indian, both on foot and on horseback, and his ability to live off the country and to go for long periods without food and water made him a formidable foe for colonial, or later United States, troops. Fasting, before and during a fight, was the general rule for Indians, and they were psychologically hardened to discomfort to a degree never attained by our soldiers. As elsewhere north of Mexico, the surprise attack was the preferred method of the aggressors. Pitched battles were fought only when forces were large and when deception had failed.

Ceremonies before departing on a raid, and victory celebrations after returning, were general throughout all three areas. Women took part in the victory celebrations, sometimes dancing with or around scalps or other trophies.

Those who were mourning the death of a relative or close friend often helped promote, or joined, a war expedition. Often the motive was to avenge a life lost in a previous encounter at the expense of the particular enemy group involved; but deaths from disease and other natural causes sometimes gave rise to punitive expeditions directed at the first enemy group encountered. Because material possessions of the relatives, as well as those of the deceased, were often destroyed at a death, the raid was also a chance to even the economic score with a little stealing from the vanquished. When a victorious war party returned, the scalps were often given to mourners, especially to women, to dry their tears, both literally with the hair and psychologically with the feeling that revenge had been achieved.

Although the civil chief and most other officers were committed to a policy of peace, they would never have been selected for these high positions without successful war records. It was only by demonstrated worth as a warrior that one was regarded as qualified to smooth ruffled tempers, settle disputes between litigants, and decide whether war or peace was to be chosen for the group when a crisis arose. The brash and ambitious young men would never have taken the advice of an old man who had had no experience in the thick of battle. A successful war experience was also an occasion for bestowing a new name, reminiscent of the brave deed, on the warrior.

Plains.—Many writers on the Plains Indians of the nineteenth century have described their warfare as a game, but while this was a prominent aspect of it, it was not the whole story. Many men were killed, and whole war parties were sometimes wiped out by superior numbers. As the buffalo became progressively scarcer, the competition for good hunting territory, horses, and guns became keener; and as European trade goods came more and more to be used, the desire for these modern conveniences, obtained in exchange for buffalo hides, drove men to greater efforts.

All the Plains tribes had a set of graded war honors, such as coups, killing, scalping, stealing a fine horse from inside an enemy camp, or stealing a gun or magic shield. A coup meant merely touching an enemy without harming him, but was done at the risk of one's own life. It is interesting to note that this harmless act often rated higher than killing or scalping. At the scalp dance following the return of a victorious war party, each warrior who had performed one of the honorific deeds told about it in public. This is called "counting coup." Thereafter, as a young man accumulated new war honors, he would recount the old ones on appropriate public occasions. It was only the old men, with well-known records of past war honors and no new ones to add, who refrained from recounting coup again and again in public. In the absence of newspapers, radio, and television, this was the only way to keep the public informed about its great men. If a man lied about his war achievements, he could be challenged by anyone who had been on war parties with him.

Horse stealing was a part of most raids on the Plains, and war parties frequently set out on foot to give themselves a greater incentive to steal enemy horses. Probably a hundred times as many horses were stolen on the Plains as were obtained in legitimate trade. Horses with Spanish brands were observed as far north as the Canadian border. In the nineteenth century, the horse became the principal symbol of wealth and prestige and was the most common commodity traded for a wife.

East.—The war between the Iroquois and the Huron over the fur trade has already been described above (Chapter 13). Economic causes were paramount here, the death toll amounted to thousands of lives, and the Huron were eliminated as an independent tribe. This war took place in 1649, less than half a century after European contact. This suggests that, even though White contact was an incontestable contributing factor to the catastrophe, the Indians in this area already possessed the political and martial mechanism to make such a war possible. It could not have happened on the Pacific Coast so soon after Europeans settled there.

The Iroquoians and their neighbors settled disputes between kin groups, and even between tribes, with blood money in the form of the shell beads called "wampum." Champlain recorded such a settlement between a Huron and an Algonquian band as early as 1615–18 (Champlain, 1619: 101–3). At meetings of the council of the League of the Iroquois, much emphasis was placed upon the cessation of strife within the league in order to present a united front to the outside, and wampum was one of the principal means of arriving at peace within the league. Although blood money was probably known here and there on the Plains and Prairies, it seems to have attained its greatest development in the East.

The most distinctive feature of the warfare pattern in the East as compared with other areas north of Mexico was the emphasis on the torture of prisoners. Most instances of torture on the Plains and Prairies seem to have been derived from the East in the historic period. Generally the prisoner was tied to a stake, frame, or platform, and tortured with fire, blows, mutilation, stabbing, shooting with arrows, or dismemberment while still alive. Such orgies lasted from a few hours to a few days, and the remains of the victim were often eaten in a cannibalistic feast. The prisoner might also be required to run the gauntlet. Two parallel rows of warriors lined up with clubs and sticks and beat the captive as he ran between them. If he survived this ordeal, he might be given his freedom. Men, women, and children were taken as prisoners, but normally only men were tortured, at least in the large public spectacles. Because the terrific mortality from warfare left many widows, a young man captive might be taken as a husband and eventually adopted into the tribe. Older men prisoners were likely to be tortured to death, especially if the tattooing on their bodies suggested many successful war exploits, as it did in the Southeast. Women and children seem generally not to have been mutilated, but they were treated as slaves until married or until they were formally adopted into the tribe.

HUMAN SACRIFICE

Southeastern coastal plain.—Along the Gulf from Louisiana to Florida and then up the Atlantic Coast to Virginia, chiefs had absolute authority over their subjects, including the power of life and death. In this area, men were compelled to serve in the armed forces; they had no choice in the matter. The war leader was the chief himself or a lieutenant appointed by him. Scalps or heads taken in battle were treated primarily as sacrificial offerings by the tribe to the supernatural rather than as appeasers of individual grief or as symbols of individual war achievement. They were kept in or near temples. It also seems likely that true slavery existed in this area and that war prisoners were sometimes kept as slaves for the remainder of their lives. The tendons in the feet of captives were sometimes cut so that they could not run fast enough to escape.

Human sacrifice of members of the in-group, as well as the sacrifice of war prisoners, has also been reported for this region. Wives and slaves were also killed at the death of a chief so that they might accompany him to the afterworld. Such sacrifice was also thought to appease the wrath of powerful spirits. Men sacrificed their own children at public spectacles to gain the favor of the chief and be raised to the rank of nobility. These sacrifices were generally independent of the fortunes of war; they were held annually by some tribes, but only when castrophe struck among others. They were more closely associated with religion than with war, although the two were interrelated. Sacrificial victims were not tortured, but were killed quickly and efficiently; nor was cannibalism practiced on their remains.

The Pawnee Indians of Nebraska were the only other people north of Mexico to practice human sacrifice. Although they were located outside the Southeastern coastal plain in the historic period, they spoke a language related to that of the Hasinai (the westernmost member of the coastal plain peoples) and showed other evidences of having formerly lived in the Southeast. They used to sacrifice a maiden of their own tribe by tying her to a rectangular frame and shooting her with arrows.

ECONOMIC CONQUEST AND HUMAN SACRIFICE

Meso-America.—This area, with a population greater than that of all other culture areas combined and with states with citizens numbered in the tens and hundreds of thousands, possessed huge armies divided into a hierarchy of subdivisions and carried on military campaigns of far greater magnitude than those of any other area. Two motives for warfare stand out above all others: to enhance the national economy by exacting tribute from the conquered peoples; to obtain prisoners for sacrifices to the gods. An individual's rank and wealth in the society were determined principally by the number of captives he took in battle, although as he grew older other qualifications played some part. Insults to or ill-treatment of the Aztec itinerant merchants (see p. 219) was a frequent precipitator of hostilities. Because the Aztecs were the dominant military power at the time the Spanish appeared, their war machine is subject to more detailed description.

Every able-bodied male over fifteen years of age, except civil officials and priests, was technically a member of the army, although it is not likely that the entire male population was ever mobilized at one time. They were all subject to call, like our national guard or officer's reserve units. At an early age every boy was taught the use of the bow and arrow and the spear thrower. At fifteen years of age, all boys, except those training for the priesthoods, went to live in boarding schools, called "houses of youth," where they were taught the art of war along with other subjects. There were twenty such schools in Tenochtitlán (Mexico City), one for each deme. Every twenty days there occurred a religious festival in which the warriors appeared in full costume and engaged in sham battles. The youths were required to attend such performances to learn all they could about war.

Weapons were kept in arsenals called "houses of darts," the dart thrower and dart being the principal weapon of the army. Stewards in charge of these arsenals handed out the weapons for sham battles and target practice as well as for actual warfare. In addition to the dart thrower and darts, the bow and arrow and the sling were used to launch projectiles. The obsidian-edged sword and clubs were used for hand-to-hand fighting. For defense, every warrior carried a shield made of quilted cotton over a cane frame and wore a tunic of quilted cotton on his body. Warriors of rank wore wooden helmets carved to represent such ferocious beasts as jaguars, wolves, and rattlesnakes, and the highest military officers added brilliant feathers to the tops of their helmets. Rank was indicated by the style of haircut as well as by the regalia and insignia worn on the body.

The army was subdivided into a hierarchy of units of varying sizes, like modern armies. The largest subdivision, called the "brigade" by us, included the entire fighting force of one of the four quarters of Tenochtitlán. Each brigade was divided into regiments, called "minor quarters," and each minor quarter was divided into companies of from 200 to 400 men, each company in turn into platoons of twenty men; on the eve of the battle, the platoons were further divided into squads of from four to six men. Some of these smaller units were made up from kin groups, such as demes and patrilocal extended families. Each military unit was distinguished from the others by the color of the feather overlay on the tunics or by some other conspicuous mark.

There were two main classes of officers: the war chiefs and the lesser officers. The former commanded entire armies, brigades, and regiments; the latter led companies, platoons, and squads. The chiefs were elected by the junior officers or the social units they represented, while the lesser officers won their positions by capturing the enemy in battle.

It seems likely, however, that the chiefs were usually of noble birth. Both classes of officers were apparently divided into three grades each, corresponding to the different sizes of units they commanded, making a total of about six grades of officers and six sizes of military units. The chiefs apparently did not fight regularly in the ranks, but the lesser officers, like our lieutenants, sergeants, and corporals, led their men in the thick of the fight. These fighting lesser officers were called "fierce cutters" or "beasts of prey," "strong eagles" or "old eagles," and "wandering arrows."

When a dispute arose between the Aztecs and a neighboring nation, the former sent a foreign minister (comparable to the secretary of state in the United States) and other delegates to the neighboring nation to negotiate the amount of tribute to be paid. If the other nation agreed to the demands of the Aztecs, the delegates returned home laden with gifts and all was well. If the nation refused to pay the tribute requested, the Aztec delegates stepped up to the commander in chief of the enemy army, anointed his arms with white paint, placed feathers on his head, and gave him a shield and a sword. This was a formal declaration of war. After war was declared, the Aztecs notified their allies to muster troops and meet the Aztec army at certain localities and then advanced against the foe. Sometimes, however, the Aztecs made surprise attacks without formal declaration of war.

Although the Aztecs possessed by far the most formidable military organization in North America at the time of the Spanish Conquest of Mexico, they fell an easy prey to the Spaniards. The reasons for this are multiple. The purely military shortcomings of the Aztecs were their failure to concentrate sufficient numbers of men at a critical spot in a battle, their inability to sustain an assault by sending in fresh troops when needed, and an armament inferior to that of the Spanish, who employed crossbows with iron-pointed arrows, guns, and even cannon. Perhaps more important were the fear and awe which the Spanish inspired in the Aztecs. Their myths of White gods prevented them from understanding the true motives of the Spaniards, and their belief, in the beginning, that a man on a horse was a two-headed monster struck terror in their hearts. They had never before witnessed anything like the amount of slaughter that the Spanish inflicted on them. In their own system of warfare, the taking of a prisoner far outranked killing him in battle, and casualties seem to have been light. And when Cortés' men killed Montezuma and other high-ranking leaders, there was no ready mechanism for replacing them. Men accustomed to obey did not suddenly begin to command. We must remember that the Spanish had been fighting the Moors almost continuously from A.D. 711 to 1492. Almost 800 years of military experience with the best armament and competition in the world at that time had made the Spanish a formidable foe for any force. The Aztecs were no match for them.

CONCLUSIONS

There is no connection between the size of military operations and the percentage of human suffering and mortality from violence. Mortality by violence was apparently as high among the Eskimo as anywhere, and human suffering under torture was rampant among the simple Chichimecs. Both of these peoples lacked true political organization, and their fights, raids, and feuds can scarcely be labeled "war." The huge war machine of the Aztecs probably inflicted no more pain and death per capita than the duels of the simplest cultures, even though 20,000 captives are said to have been sacrificed at the dedication of a single Aztec temple.

Population density (Map 6) shows some association with the size of the war operation. Areas with dense population had larger armies and bigger battles than those with sparse populations. However, for the areas north of Mexico, the Pacific Coast was more densely populated than the Atlantic Coast, and yet the size of the military machine was less on the Pacific Coast than on the Atlantic Coast. This was also true of the size of the political unit, as was pointed out in the preceding chapter.

Of the motives behind violence, raids, and wars, the economic factor seems to be more important than some text writers in anthropology admit. In order to call the attention of the reader to the game aspect of war, the function of war as a ranker of men and creator of social solidarity within the political unit, and the religious functions of war, some anthropologists have disparaged the economic aspect. Economic motives were probably most important in Meso-America and on the Northwest Coast, but they can also be found in most other areas. The desire for material wealth north of Mexico was stepped up by trade with Europeans, but the response to the new opportunity would not have been so rapid if the Indian cultures had not already possessed a considerable interest in acquiring possessions. Even the least competitive individuals, bands, and tribes were forced to acquire steel traps, guns, or horses in order to survive at all in the new system.

Motives for violence and war seem normally to have been multiple and mixed. Although one or two appear to dominate the others in this or that area, the others were also present.

The pattern of warfare in a particular region is partly determined by contacts with peoples on the outside and by the ideas and values derived from these contacts. For example, the torture of prisoners, or their sacrifice to the supernatural, and cannibalism, occur in a continuous area from the Iroquoians in the Northeast to the Gulf tribes in the Southeast, thence south through Northeast Mexico to Meso-America and the Caribbean. For instance, both the Iroquois and the Aztecs adopted a prisoner before killing him, sometimes calling him by a kinship term. The methods of killing, as summarized by Knowles (1940), show much in common between the East and Meso-America. It is true that the Aztec sacrificial victim sometimes impersonated a god and lived in luxury before his death, but the religious facet of torture in the East was by no means lacking.

There is no reason to believe that the warfare syndrome of the Meso-Americans or, for that matter, of the Incas of Peru was derived from the Old World before A.D. 1492. Although there was a little trans-Pacific contact between South America and Oceania, a few boatloads of people would not be likely to exert much influence on the political organization and warfare systems of the New World. Therefore it seems likely that war could and did arise independently in the Old and New Worlds. However, the greed, cupidity, deceit, and utter disregard of Indian life on the part of most of the European conquerors surpassed anything of the kind that the Indian cultures had been able to produce on their own in their thousands of years of almost complete independence from the Old World.

REFERENCES

BANDELIER, 1877; BEALS, 1932a; CHAMPLAIN, 1619; CODERE, 1951; COOK, 1946; DRUCKER, 1955; ELLIS, 1951; FARMER, 1957; HADLOCK, 1947; HOEBEL, 1940, 1941, 1960; HONIGMAN, 1946; HUNT, 1940; JENNESS, 1932; KNOWLES, 1940; KROEBER, 1925, 1932; LINTON, 1944; LIPS, 1947; LOWIE, 1940, 1954; NADEAU, 1944; NEUMANN, 1940; NEWCOMB, 1950; OSGOOD, 1936, 1937; RAY, 1939, 1960; SAHAGÚN (ANDERSON AND DIBBLE), 1950–58; SALAS, 1947; SECOY, 1953; MARIAN W. SMITH, 1938, 1951; SNYDERMAN, 1948; STEWARD, 1938; STEWART, 1947; SWANTON, 1946.

19

Rank and Social Classes

ALTHOUGH American Indian societies were more democratic on the whole than those of Africa and Oceania, there were, nevertheless, marked differences in status and rank in some areas and true social classes in a smaller number. All societies in the world recognize the simple fact that some people can perform a certain task better than others, that one man is a better hunter than another, or that one woman is a better weaver than another. American Indians were no exception to this rule, and were well aware of individual differences within societies.

The term "status" refers to the social position of an individual with respect to other members of his society. It may be based on a single attribute, on several attributes, or on all the attributes of which a particular society is aware. Statuses may or may not be ranked from high to low. Among some Indian societies, statuses tended to be unranked, while in others they were very meticulously ranked from highest to lowest. The basis of rank might be proficiency, wealth, social heredity, supernatural sanction, or some combination of a number of such criteria.

Social classes are said to exist in a society when the entire population can be grouped, according to statuses and rank, into a limited number of units, such as nobles, commoners, and slaves. A society with social classes, then, must possess an explicit number of criteria for pigeonholing individuals, and there must be breaks somewhere in the continuum where boundaries can be drawn between one class and another. Ideally, all statuses present in a particular society should be employed in allocating a given individual to one social class or another, but, in practice, a few tend to be emphasized more than others. There must be a minimum of two social classes in a class society; a one-class system would not differentiate the members.

MINIMAL DEVELOPMENTS OF STATUS AND RANK

In several culture areas in native North America, differences in status, other than those based on sex and age, and differences in rank were at the minimum. These areas are Central and Eastern Arctic, Mackenzie and Eastern Sub-Arctic, Great Basin, and Northeast Mexico. These are the now familiar areas where life was hardest, the land least productive, and population (Map 6) sparsest. None of these peoples farmed. These areas also possessed no, or few, part-time craft specialists (Map 28) and certainly no full-time craft specialists. In these regions, a man was a jack of nearly all masculine trades, and a woman was equally experienced in nearly all feminine tasks. These areas also lacked true political organization and organized warfare.

At the same time, differences of ability within each sex were recognized; some men were regarded as better hunters than others, and some women were admitted to be better at household tasks than others, but there was not the slightest notion that such aptitudes were hereditary. Leadership, weak as it was, tended to be vested in the most capable man, regardless of ancestry, and this man was followed only as long as he continued to demonstrate his superior skills and judgement. Social classes could not possibly develop in regions with so little differentiation in status and rank, and, as might be anticipated, they were completely absent.

NORTHWEST COAST SYSTEM

All the peoples on the Northwest Coast shared a system of rank based on a combination of wealth and heredity. As pointed out in Chapter 16, the most productive parts of both the land and the sea were owned nominally by individuals but were exploited by kinship groups. On the death of the nominal owner, the title to the real estate always went to a surviving kinsman, and the same kinship group continued to use it in the same manner as it had done before the death of the first nominal owner. Much movable property was also owned and used by kinship groups in the same way. Incorporeal property, in all its forms, was likewise shared and inherited. Social position, then, was based on the value of the corporeal and incorporeal forms of wealth and the hereditary titles that went with them.

Two distinct social classes were to be found everywhere on the Northwest Coast: freemen and slaves. The following account of the status of slaves refers to the dominant pattern over most of the coast, but does not apply to a small area in northwest California and southwest Oregon. Slaves were obtained by taking prisoners in raids, but, once slave status was established, the slave could be bought or sold, either from one society to another or from one freeman to another within the same society. The owner had the power of life and death over his slave, and slaves were sometimes killed on the following occasions: at the death of the owner; at a potlatch, as destruction of wealth to show that the owner could afford it; at the building of a new house, in the form of a foundation sacrifice; and at performances of the cannibal society of some of the British Columbia peoples, who actually ate part of the corpse. Slave killing was much more common in Alaska and British Columbia than in Washington and Oregon, and was totally lacking in California. However, slaves were sometimes freed at the death of an owner in the same areas where killing was permitted, showing variation within societies in this respect. Slaves were released for ransom if their kinsmen could raise the price, although in a few localities the stigma attached to slavery was so great that even the slave's closest relatives did not want him after he had been for a time in this lowest status, and they refused to redeem him. In the north, where matrilineal descent prevailed and kinship ties were strongest, slaves were generally ransomed by kinsmen and the stigma removed by a purification ceremony.

Slaves were treated almost as well as the lowest-ranking freemen in some localities, but in others they were compelled to do the most menial work, to eat inferior food, and at death were denied normal burial by being cast into the sea. Slaves were allowed to marry each other in most localities, but their children usually remained slaves, thus showing that slavery was hereditary. Debt slaves are also reported sporadically all along the Northwest Coast. Inability to repay a loan, as well as gambling debts, was sufficient to relegate a person to this status. As elsewhere, the debt slave was normally ransomed by relatives, and was never equated to the true slave described in detail above.

In respect to differences in rank of freemen, all anthropologists agree that most freemen were carefully ranked from highest to lowest according to wealth and heredity. The two always went hand in hand because the most valuable kinds of property were inherited. Freemen were carefully scaled according to rank at potlatch feasts in four ways: they were seated, served, and given presents to take home in order of rank; and the value of the present was correlated with the order of rank. Because the same persons attended many potlatches, this carefully calibrated order of rank was confirmed publicly again and again.

The most productive parts of the landscape and seascape were all owned by kinship groups and nominally by individuals, so that there was no easy way to increase one's wealth and position. However, a man who was an unusually skilled canoe maker, mask carver, or warrior might be given a title and its associated privileges by his chief. Such privileges might include a title of "war chief," the right to use a special crest, or the exclusive right to some good fishing place. Sometimes the chief would give the title and privileges directly to a man's heirs. A man might also acquire titled status more directly by capturing real estate or by killing a titled man in a raid, by accepting a title as repayment on a debt, or by receiving a title as repayment of a bride price.

After White contact, mobility in rank increased through two principal causes: increased economic opportunities, which made the acquisition of wealth easier; and a sharp decline in population by death from European diseases, alcohol, and firearms. The value of sea otter fur skyrocketed to previously unheard of figures, and later the furs of land animals showed a parallel increase, with the result that an industrious man could get rich in a few years as an independent businessman or as a hired hand on a sealing schooner. Because titles had been vacated by the sharp increase in mortality, it was easier to find a title and to validate it at a potlatch feast.

At the present time, anthropologists disagree on the question of the existence or nonexistence of social classes among freemen on the Northwest Coast. This confusion is the result both of variation from one village or tribelet to another and of changes after White contact. Within some tribelets, all free individuals seem to have possessed at least minor titles and privileges of some sort, so that no line can be drawn on this basis. However, there were other tribelets whose members formed two distinguishable classes: nobles, those who had titles; and commoners, those who did not.

In British Columbia and in southeastern Alaska, there were secret societies of limited membership which divided freemen into members and nonmembers. Those of highest rank in the potlatch system were of highest rank in the secret society system. It seems clear that these native cultures drew a line of demarcation between freemen who were members and freemen who were nonmembers of these secret societies, and that the members were the ranking group. However, unless the wives and children were classed with their husbands, a system of social classes would not exist. Further, every high-ranking person also had his share of poor relations, thus showing that kinship groups as wholes could not be ranked or placed in classes.

SYSTEMS ADJACENT TO NORTHWEST COAST

Plateau.—Most peoples on the Plateau took prisoners in war, but these were few in number and were more often women and children than men. Such so-called slaves lived like the poorer classes in these societies and were normally adopted or assimilated into the tribelet in due course. Women especially could gain full status quickly by marrying their captors, bearing children, and otherwise playing the role of a wife. However, the peoples from near the Columbia River south to the Klamath and Modoc on the Oregon-California border engaged in captive-motivated raids for the express purpose of obtaining prisoners to sell at the slave market at The Dalles. The Dalles is a fifteen-mile stretch of rapids on the Columbia River which blocks navigation in both directions and therefore became a trading center for all kinds of movable property. Some of these Oregon peoples got their first horses by exchanging slaves for them. Slaves sold at The Dalles were resold later to peoples living as far north as the Canadian border. Trade slaves were held in lower esteem than those captured in war, but they were rarely abused or killed and could still be ransomed by relatives. A trade slave was often exchanged for a wife, a good slave being regarded as of equal value to a wife. Slavery on the Plateau was therefore of a borderline variety which gave rise to a separate social class only in the part of the region where slaves were traded. The system was obviously derived from the Northwest Coast, and most of it was probably post-European.

Distinctions in rank and wealth among freemen were marked only in the western part of the Plateau adjacent to the Northwest Coast, and the evidence points also to the recency of such notions. On the whole, the Plateau was as democratic as any culture area in native North America, and nothing like social classes existed there. The eastern peoples likewise acquired in recent times the ranking system, based on war record, of the Plains tribes, but whatever status of this kind the individual acquired was not passed on to his descendants, and nothing remotely approaching social classes developed there. A more detailed description of the Plains system will be given below.

Yukon Sub-Arctic.—Only those peoples closest to the Northwest Coast possessed true slaves, which were obtained from the coast in trade. They were few in number but were sometimes sacrificed at the death of their owner, and their children tended to remain slaves. War captives were mostly women and children, who were assimilated into the society of their captors, but occasionally young men were also taken in raids and treated as menials until their loyalty to their captors was demonstrated by participation in a later armed clash on the side of their masters. As mentioned above in Chapter 18, plunder was a more prominent motive for raids than in the Mackenzie or Eastern Sub-Arctic, and the tendency to rank all men according to wealth was also stronger. This interest in wealth and rank was obviously derived from contact with Northwest Coast peoples. However, freemen were nowhere differentiated into social classes.

Western Arctic.—These Eskimo were strongly influenced by Northwest Coast cultures, and shared with them considerable emphasis on wealth and rank. They captured women and children in raids but assimilated them into the society of the captors. Enemy men were killed, not enslaved, and trade slaves were unknown.

California.—In the California culture area, there was a weak and vague ranking of men according to wealth, from the border of the Northwest Coast area south at least to the Yokuts. There was a little debt slavery in the extreme northwest, and those peoples nearest the Klamath and Modoc were captured by them and taken north for sale at The Dalles, but these exceptions were the result of border contacts and did not amount to a system of slavery for the California area. In Chapter 17, we mentioned that all the Yokuts tribelets had several officers including that of chief, each of which was confined to a lineage. In other words, these were hereditary offices which passed from an incumbent to some lineage mate, normally a younger brother or a son. Those who belonged to one of these lineages enjoyed a little more prestige than those who did not, especially in the case of the chief's lineage. The word for "chief," *tiya*, was applied not only to the chief but also to all the mature members of his lineage, sometimes including even women. Thus there was a correlation between authority, prestige, heredity, and wealth, but it was much weaker than on the Northwest Coast.

It is obvious from these brief descriptions of status and rank in the areas adjacent to the Northwest Coast that the tremendous emphasis on rank in that coastal area fades out rapidly in all directions as one leaves the area. In the Mackenzie Sub-Arctic, the central Plateau, and the Great Basin, it disappears entirely in favor of a sweeping egalitarianism. Another center of rank and prestige, which seems to have been totally independent of that on the north Pacific Coast, is found in Meso-America.

COMPLEX SYSTEMS OF MESO-AMERICA

In Meso-America, a number of native states possessed complex systems of social rank based on multiple kinds of achievement and, to a lesser extent, on heredity. The early Spanish chroniclers, saturated as they were with knowledge of the hereditary classes of Europe, described these systems with the same terms they applied to European class structure. Although hereditary monarchs and the royal lineages from which they stemmed emerge with some clarity, the hereditary character of the lower ranks is open to doubt. The acquisition of rank by achievement, especially in warfare, is much more frequently mentioned in the literature than are descriptions of hereditarily tight compartments ascribed to the individual at birth. Although modern scholars may be divided over the precise number of social classes, they agree that the Meso-American systems of status and rank were based on many more criteria and were otherwise much more complex than those of any other culture area in native North America. The Aztecs, Huastecs, Totonacs, Zapotecs, and Mayas all possessed complicated systems of rank and social classes, and the Tarascans and Mixtecs had at least three social classes each. Because material on the Aztecs is fullest, they will provide the basis of description here, following Caso (1963).

The king (*tlatoani* or *tlacatecuhtli*).—The king was a descendant of the Toltec prince Acamapichtli, who came from Tula, the Toltec capital city. The prince was, in turn, regarded as a descendant of Quetzalcoatl, the principal god of the Toltecs. Acamapichtli came to Tenochtitlán (Mexico City) at the request of the Aztecs to found their royal line. He was given twenty wives (probably one from each deme) by the Aztecs, all daughters of chiefs. All Aztec nobles at the time of the Spanish Conquest were descendants of these unions. In addition to the Aztecs, at least six other nations acquired a prince from the Toltecs and initiated a royal line: Tlaxcalans, Tarascans, Mixtecans, Huastecans, a nation in Morelos, and the Quiches and Cakchiqueles of Guatemala. Caso suggests that such royal lineages may go back as far as the ancient civilizations at Teotihuacán and Monte Albán.

Nobles (*pipiltin*).—All nobles were descendants of the Toltec prince Acamapichtli. They held the highest administrative, judicial, military, and religious offices, but not all of them held such offices. Some had no employment or authority, and others worked as palace servants or skilled craftsmen.

Knights (*caballeros pardos*).—Knights were commoners who had been knighted by the king for distinguished service, usually in war.

Commoners or *plebeians* (*macehualtin*).—Each man worked his land held in usufruct. He could not sell the land because it belonged to the deme (*calpulli*), but he was free to consume or exchange the crops raised on it. He worked for himself, not for an overlord, but he had to pay taxes. He could also move to another deme (ward) if the deme leaders agreed. If he did not work his land for two consecutive years, he could lose his right of usufruct. He might rise as high as the chief of his deme and, in authority, outrank a noble without an official position.

Serfs (*mayeques*).—Serfs could not leave the lands to which they were attached; they received a share of the crops for their own sustenance. They were obliged to render menial services to their masters: to construct houses, carry water and firewood, plant and harvest crops, and (the women) grind maize dough and make tortillas. In case of sale or succession of ownership, they went with the land. They did not pay taxes to the king or any other government official, as did commoners, but they could be drafted as soldiers in the army. Many serfs were the descendants of the commoners of the nations conquered by the Aztecs. During the colonial period, the status of serf was preferred to that of commoner because serfs paid no taxes, and many commoners tried to pass as serfs.

Slaves.—Slaves could be transferred from any job to any other job according to the will of their masters, but the master owned only the services of the slave, not his life. This status was not hereditary, and was often for a limited period of time rather than a lifetime. That this was not typical slavery is brought out clearly by the fact that a slave could himself own the services of another slave. Slaves normally owned their own homes and could not be sold to another master without their consent.

Propertyless proletariat.—We need to add a propertyless proletariat to round out the scheme. These people had no land, as did commoners and serfs, and no masters, as did slaves. They worked as servants, porters, craftsmen, and as day laborers at many menial tasks. In general, their economic status, at least, was more precarious than that of serfs or slaves because they were not attached to a person of higher rank who was obligated to provide for at least their biological needs or to a plot of ground on which they could raise food for themselves.

The Aztecs thus appear to have had a system of seven major social classes, with some mobility possible in either direction, at the time of the Spanish Conquest. They acquired their system partly from contact with earlier peoples in Meso-America, such as the Toltecs, rather than wholly from internal factors in Aztec society.

SYSTEMS DERIVED IN PART FROM MESO-AMERICA

Southwest.—There may have been marked differences in rank and even social classes in the southern part of this area nearest Meso-America, as the size of political units, the magnitude and organization of warfare, the presence of markets, and the collecting of tribute from subjugated peoples seem to indicate. However, this system is obviously derived from the Tarascans or other Meso-American peoples and is not typical of the Southwest as a whole. Nevertheless, some of this Meso-American interest in warfare and the rank achieved by it extends as far north as the River Yumans, but with considerable attenuation. The peoples of Arizona and New Mexico were unusually democratic as compared with those south of the Mexican border, and, although differences in rank were recognized, they were based generally on merit, not heredity. There was some tendency for chieftainship to be inherited, but the chief was always chosen from a lineage, so that it was possible to select from among the lineage group a man with some desirable qualifications. Just as frequently, chieftainship was nonhereditary or was almost devoid of authority, which remained vested in a council. Among the Pueblos, seats on the council were hereditary because they were filled by the leaders of the many religious societies in which offices tended to be filled from within a certain lineage. However, no hereditary official or chief in Arizona or New Mexico was regarded as a member of a higher class. Slaves were totally lacking in most localities, and, in the few places where they are said to have occurred, they were war captives who were eventually assimilated into the society as freemen if they were cooperative.

Ruth Benedict, in her *Patterns of Culture*, has given the egalitarianism and sobriety of the Zuñi Indians a great deal of publicity. Although later writers have challenged some of the ideas in her Zuñi pattern, this part of her characterization has withstood the criticisms of the years. These people, and the other Pueblos as well, were—and are today— as devoid of class structure as any people in the world; differences of rank were at the minimum, depending almost wholly on achievement in civil and religious affairs, and not at all on material wealth. All officials dressed in the same manner as other citizens and worked at least part time at farming and at the same crafts as the rest of the population. In council meetings, it was considered bad form to become self-assertive and vociferous, and those who did so almost never gained the assent of the council to their proposals. Although many important features of the economic culture in the Southwest, such as domesticated plants, houses, and clothing, unite it with Meso-America, its social organization and ethos were very different. The democratic village government, minimization of war, and almost complete absence of differences in rank among the Pueblos offer the sharpest possible contrast with the societies of Meso-America.

East.—A caste system is reported for the Chitimacha (Swanton, 1911: 348–49). The chief and his descendants were regarded as nobles and were addressed with special terms of respect by the commoners. Apparently the noble caste was endogamous; if a noble married a commoner, he would have to live with the common people, and for that reason many refused to marry at all when no women of noble caste were available and thus hastened the extinction of the tribe. If this account is true, we seem to have a caste system among the Chitimacha. However, the statement that when a noble married a commoner he lived with the common people probably refers to nothing more strange than matrilocal residence, whereby the noble husband would have to live in his commoner wife's home.

No book on North American Indians would be complete without reference to the Natchez system of so-called social classes. As originally diagramed by Swanton (1911) from French sources, this is the scheme:

	Suns: Children of Sun mothers and Stinkard fathers.
Nobility	Nobles: Children of Noble mothers and Stinkard fathers, or of Sun fathers and Stinkard mothers.
	Honored People: Children of Honored women and Stinkard fathers, or of Noble fathers and Stinkard mothers.
Stinkards:	Children of Stinkard mothers and Honored men, or of Stinkard fathers and Stinkard mothers.

If this scheme is correct, there were three ranked groups of nobility and a single group of commoners called "Stinkards." Everyone in all three nobility groups had to marry a Stinkard, making these groups exogamous. Only Stinkards were allowed to marry within their own social group. The Suns were royalty, and this status descended by strict matrilineal inheritance. One observer reports only seventeen Suns in A.D. 1700, and another only eleven Suns in A.D. 1730, after two wars with the French. It is probable from these small figures that the Suns were a single royal lineage. They had absolute authority over all other citizens, and women as well as men Suns could order the death of any person of lower rank, including Stinkard husbands, who would in any case be strangled to death at the demise of their Sun wives. The Nobles were a more numerous group, and from them were drawn war chiefs and other officials.

Hart (1943) has pointed out that, because the three upper groups must marry only Stinkards, the population would eventually lose all its Stinkards to the three upper ranks and could not function indefinitely. Quimby (1946) has shown that, to meet this calamity, the Natchez regularly replenished the Stinkard class by assimilation of remnants of neighboring peoples whose ethnic independence had been destroyed by defeat in war. Fischer (1964) gives several numerical models to show how the Natchez system could have functioned, but it is difficult to determine which model is nearest the actual one of the Natchez. Tooker (1963) interprets the system as one of matrilineal descent in a royal sib that outranked all other sibs without bothering to cite my parallel view in the paragraph above, first published in 1961.

The Natchez system, in sum, appears to consist of a royal lineage, two collateral lineages or groups of lineages ranked according to distance from the royal lineage, and a fourth group too remotely related to royalty to possess any rank, as well as a sprinkling of outsiders. These four ranked groups may be called social classes but most certainly not castes.

Although nothing exactly like the Natchez system has been reported for other peoples on the Southeastern coastal plain, royal lineages with matrilineal descent were the rule in this region, and war captives seem to have been kept frequently as slaves. The mutilation of the feet of male prisoners of war, so that they could not run fast enough to escape, is evidence that their prolonged captivity was desired. Slavery, however, does not seem to have been hereditary, so that the existence of a slave class is problematical. At any rate, royalty and commoners were distinguished everywhere in this area, so that a minimum of two classes existed, and this seems to have been the point of departure for the Natchez system.

The Creek of Alabama and Georgia recognized marked differences in rank, but did not have definite social classes. As mentioned in Chapter 17, the chief was always selected by the council from a single lineage, and individual merit was what gave one lineage member the edge over another. Some of the other civil officers and advisers of the chief belonged to the same lineage or to the same sib. There was, then, a tendency to rank lineages and sibs, but it was not carried far enough to produce social classes. Warriors were divided into three grades, but these statuses were based entirely on war record, not on heredity. The ceremonial leaders, called "beloved men," were also of high rank, but their position was achieved only after learning the long and complex rituals of the tribe. Therefore the Creeks had a rather well-defined system of rank, based primarily on achievement and only secondarily on heredity, but there were no definite social classes.

Among the Iroquoians, the principal civil and religious offices were kept within maternal lineages, and the various lineages of a sib were ranked according to the offices they possessed. However, each officer was nominated by the matriarch or by a group of dominant women in the lineage, and he could be impeached any time his conduct displeased the women. Achievement was therefore necessary not only to become a chief or priest but also to maintain an extended tenure of office. This system applied even to the fifty sachems who sat on the council of the league. Shamans, especially those organized in societies, also enjoyed high rank. Although men, women, and children were taken prisoner in warfare, a slave class never materialized. On the whole, the Iroquois standards of status and rank were close to those of the Creek, with perhaps less marked differences in rank and more premium placed upon merit. There were no true social classes.

Plains and Prairies.—The peoples of these areas differed little from the Creeks and Iroquois with respect to rank and social classes. There were definite differences in rank, but these were not hereditary and seldom crystallized into social classes. As in all other areas where distinctions of rank occurred, the children of distinguished men enjoyed certain advantages. Their goals tended to be higher, and their education in the ways and means of acquiring rank was better. In regions where public offices belonged to particular lineages and sibs, these social units tended to outrank the others, but the power of the officers was so limited that the advantage was slight.

All of the Plains and most of the Prairie tribes carefully graded war deeds and encouraged successful warriors to recount their military exploits on public occasions. But success in raids was, in turn, dependent on the sanction of the supernatural. This was realized in a dream or vision, which was as likely to come to a man of low rank as to one of high. This individual religious experience therefore opened the road of success to all comers.

Wealth was also a means of grading men, especially after the appearance of the horse and European-inspired economic competition. Horses were the most common property exchanged for a bride on the Plains, and the giving away of wealth on other occasions was topped only by the Northwest Coast peoples. Next to the war record, generosity to the poor was the basis for high social standing among the Plains tribes. Medicine bundles, which aided the establishment of rapport with the supernatural, were privately owned among many tribes in these areas and were bought and sold. A man of means was therefore likely to be in possession of one or more powerful medicine bundles, which gave him an edge over the poor man in dealings with the supernatural.

I am willing to concede that most Plains tribes in the nineteenth century did have a tendency toward class structure, but the exact number of classes and the amount of mobility from one to the other is vague or unknown. I do not go as far as Wilson (1963), Mishkin (1940), or even Ewers (1955) in this respect. My view is intermediate between theirs and that of Lowie (1954), who stresses the absence of hereditary class structure.

CONCLUSIONS

The area with the most complex systems of status, rank, and social classes is most certainly Meso-America. It is no accident that this area also possessed the most efficient food production with its intensive farming and irrigation (Maps 3, 4) as well as the greatest concentration of population (Map 6), the most ramified specialization of labor (Map 28), the largest political units, the largest armies, and the most complicated religious organization. In sharp contrast, the Arctic, Sub-Arctic, Great Basin, and Northeast Mexico possessed the minimum of differentiation in status and rank and no social classes at all. These areas also had the least efficient methods of food production, lowest population density, practically no specialization of labor, no true political organization, no true war, and the minimum of religious organization.

In what is now the United States, there is little doubt that the development of distinctions of rank and social classes in the East, Prairies, and Plains owes some of its inspiration to the peoples of Meso-America. This comes out most clearly in the tribes of the Southeastern coastal plain, but some influences appear to have reached most peoples in these areas. The similarities in patterns of government and warfare and the derivation from Meso-America of most of the plants raised by Prairies and Eastern Indians have been pointed out in earlier chapters. It is no accident, then, that the fundamentals of economy, government, war, and society all match. The resemblance is far from perfect, and details tend to disappear as one proceeds north and west of the Southeastern coastal plain, but this is normal where diffusion is involved. After White contact, economic factors in rank and warfare became considerably augmented in these areas, as well as others, and have partly obliterated the earlier aboriginal patterns.

The Southwestern patterns of status, rank, and social classes show much variation. The southernmost part of this area shares much with Meso-America, and a little of this pattern, as related to government and war, extends as far north as the River Yumans. But the other Southwest peoples, in Arizona and New Mexico, were as strongly egalitarian as any in North America. In spite of the derivation of domesticated plants, housing, clothing, and many other material things from Meso-America, the fundamental drives of these cultures were very different from those of Meso-America or, for that matter, those of the Plains, Prairies, and East. The Southeastern Indians, especially, show a much closer relationship to Meso-America with respect to government, war, rank, and social classes than do the Pueblo, Navaho, and Apache of the Southwest.

The Northwest Coast stands apart from other areas with definite systems of rank and social classes. Here, geographical environment provided a supply of fish and sea mammals that was inexhaustible by the techniques the Indians employed in taking them. The surplus of food, obtainable in favored spots as productive per acre as the best farms, made possible a relatively sedentary economy and an accumulation of a surplus of other material and nonmaterial possessions. Population was as concentrated as in any other area of equal size north of Mexico, and specialization of labor may have been more developed than Map 28 shows. Although political units remained small, raids motivated by economy were common, and in a few localities land was actually taken by force. Religious organization, with its secret societies, was also relatively advanced. Distinctions of status and rank, based on a combination of wealth and heredity, were more marked on the Northwest Coast than in any area north of Meso-America, except possibly on the coastal plain of the Southeast. The slave class on the Northwest Coast was more clearly differentiated than in any other North American area, and has been estimated to have varied from 10 per cent to 30 per cent of the population. Distinct classes among freemen are difficult to demonstrate, however, and controversy over the matter exists at the present time. All areas bordering on the Northwest Coast share some of its interest in rank based on wealth and heredity, but this fades away rapidly as one proceeds away from the coast. The historical as well as geographical independence of the Northwest Coast, as compared with Meso-America, is conceded by most anthropologists today. Its system of rank and at least two social classes seems to have developed on the spot in response to a bountiful geographical environment and an economy advanced enough to exploit it efficiently.

REFERENCES

BARNETT, 1938, 1968; CASO, 1963; CODERE, 1957; DRUCKER, 1939, 1955; EDMONSON, 1958; EWERS, 1955b; FISCHER, 1964; NANCY P. HICKERSON, MS; LOWIE, 1954; MISHKIN, 1940; MURDOCK, 1957; OSGOOD, 1936, 1937; RAY, 1939; SAHAGÚN (ANDERSON AND DIBBLE), 1950–58; SUTTLES, 1958; SWANTON, 1911, 1946; THOMPSON, 1940; TOOKER, 1963; VAILLANT, 1941; WILSON, 1963.

20

Sodalities and Their Ceremonies

IN CHAPTERS 14 and 15 genetic kin groups and residential kin groups were distinguished, and, in Chapter 17, larger residential subdivisions into which some societies are divided were described. Societies may be further divided into subgroups not primarily determined either by kinship or by coresidence. Such subdivisions are called "sodalities," from the Latin *sodalis*, meaning "comrade," "companion," "friend," "associate" (Lowie: 1948, 14; 294–316). Some examples from modern life are churches, lodges, fraternities, sororities, service clubs, social clubs, professional associations, boys' and girls' clubs, and political organizations. In all of these, membership is generally voluntary, although one's older relatives may exert a certain amount of pressure to persuade him to join what they consider to be the proper one. At least it can be said that membership in such social units is not irrèvocably ascribed to every individual at birth, as is membership in kinship groups and in most coresidential units.

The type of sodality embracing the largest part of a band, tribelet, tribe, or state, is the so-called tribal sodality. In its most typical form, it includes all mature males in a society, but excludes children of both sexes and women. Every young man at about the age of puberty undergoes an initiation ceremony which he enters as a boy and from which he emerges as a man. He generally receives some formal education at this time in the lore of the society; and religious secrets, known only to mature men, are also revealed to him. More rarely there are parallel initiations for pubescent females, all of whom must participate in the system, and the resulting group of mature women may also be called a sodality. Membership in tribal sodalities is not voluntary, but compulsory, yet where there are multiple chapters in a single locality, the initiate is often allowed to choose the particular chapter he wishes to join.

The term "restricted sodality" applies to an organization with membership restricted to only a part of the mature males, mature females, or some mixture of both short of the totality. Restricted sodalities may also have initiation ceremonies, as well as other rituals, with content and meaning unknown to the nonmembers in the remainder of the population.

A club is a more informal sodality of restricted membership without any secrets. Age classes are another type of sodality; these include any division of a population into organized age groups of a more or less permanent nature. Because a single society often possesses more than one kind of sodality and the relations of the two or three types may be close, they will be described for each culture area in turn.

INCONSEQUENTIAL SODALITY ORGANIZATION

Most of the peoples in the Arctic, Sub-Arctic, Plateau, Great Basin, and Northeast Mexico lacked all kinds of sodalities. Where such organizations occurred, they were invariably in the parts of these areas closest to a culture area supporting a sodality system. This suggests that the rare occurrences of sodalities in these areas are to be explained in part by influences from the outside.

There were no sodalities anywhere in the Arctic except in Alaska south of Bering Strait. These Alaskan Eskimo seem to have possessed a men's tribal secret sodality which included all mature males in these societies. Women and children were definitely excluded. The center of sodality activities was in the semisubterranean men's house, where the men and boys slept. Women never entered this men's house except to deliver food and other necessities to their husbands or when they were allowed to witness the dramas produced by the men. These dramas, centered in spirit impersonations, were enacted by a number of men, disguised by masks and grotesque costumes representing spirits, who would sing and dance in the manner associated with each "devil" or "giant."

One part of the performance is reminiscent of the secret sodalities of Northwest Coast peoples. At a ceremony given to appease the wrath of evil spirits, two men impersonating the spirits pretended to cut open the abdomen of a third actor and eat his intestines. What they actually did was to cut open a seal's stomach, previously filled with seal's blood, and to pretend to eat the seal's intestines. Blood flowed freely over the reclining third party and created a horrible spectacle sufficient to chill the spines of the innocents in the audience. Later in the ritual the third party, supposedly killed, was brought back to life again by the powerful skills of other members of the sodality. This death and resurrection theme is common to many primitive religions as well as to modern faiths.

In the Sub-Arctic, sodalities occurred only among the Ojibwa and Cree, and they were almost identical with those of their neighbors to the south. No sodalities of any kind have been reported for the Plateau, Great Basin, and Northeast Mexico, but they occurred in all other culture areas.

RELATIVELY IMPORTANT SODALITIES

Northwest Coast.—Most of the Northwest Coast peoples from the panhandle of Alaska to the mouth of the Columbia River possessed secret sodalities of restricted membership. Membership in these sodalities and participation in their dramas were limited to those persons of high rank who had inherited the right to play the various roles. Although kinship played a part, the restriction of the membership to those of high social position justifies the use of the term "sodality" for these organizations. Each drama reenacted an ancestor's encounter with a spirit, who kidnapped him, whisked him away into the woods, bestowed supernatural power on him, and then returned him to his village, where he demonstrated his newly acquired power to the people. The public was sometimes allowed to witness such ceremonies, but the knowledge of the religious secrets and the privilege of playing a role were limited to members.

Such rituals were most elaborately developed by the Kwakiutl-speaking peoples of British Columbia. Here as many as three separate secret sodalities flourished at the same time: the Shamans' Sodality, the Ones-Returned-from-Heaven, and the Nutlam (untranslatable). Each sodality possessed its own cycle of secret rituals, which could be witnessed only by its members. Persons who were active participants in one sodality were barred from membership in the other two. Within each of these sodalities, all members and participants were not equal, and the dances each performed were graded from high to low. Tribelets south of the Kwakiutl on Vancouver Island and on the mainland of British Columbia and Washington state possessed only a single secret sodality, modeled on those of the Kwakiutl. Tribelets north of the Kwakiutl had one or two such sodalities, but not all three.

The principal actor in one of these spirit-seeking dramas might reenact the myth in a variety of ways. He might slip quietly away from his village and hide in the woods, or he might be seized bodily by a few men disguised as spirit monsters and bundled off to a secluded spot. After hiding out for the proper length of time, he would return alone, or in the company of his abductors, so filled with spiritual power that he would be in a state of frenzy and likely to harm his fellow villagers. In this condition, it was necessary to capture and restrain him. After the edge of his supernatural experience had worn off a bit, he would demonstrate the powers he had acquired from his ancestral spirit helper to the members of a sodality or to the public. Sometimes he might pretend to be struck dead by a spirit and to be resurrected in a public ritual.

The Kwakiutl, especially, had a full bag of tricks comparable to those of our own vaudeville magicians. These were always performed by the dim light of the fire at night, when visual illusions were easy to put across. The elaborate costumes of the performers made good hiding places for stomachs or bladders of animals filled with animal blood, which could be brought forth and pierced when a person was supposed to be stabbed. Spirit impersonators were disguised by carved and painted wooden masks which resemble, to us, the conventionalized heads of animals and birds. Sometimes a second wooden mask would be hidden inside the first, so that the performer could open up the outer one by pulling strings, revealing only the inner one. This stunt was interpreted by the naïve as a metamorphosis on the part of the spirit.

The houses in which these seances were held were rigged in advance for the occasions. Actors and puppets swung from ropes suspended from the roof to give the illusion of flying through the air. Tunnels with trap doors were dug in the floor so that the performers could miraculously disappear and reappear. Hollow kelp stems were joined and buried under the floor to serve as speaking tubes so that the voices of spirits could be heard from unexpected places, such as under the fireplace, where it was too hot for a mere human being to survive.

Perhaps the most shocking illusion of all was the eating of a human corpse by the cannibal dancer, who was supposed to be so completely possessed by the cannibal spirit that he could not restrain himself from eating human beings. To prevent him from murdering his fellow tribesmen, he was supposed to be fed on a diet of human corpses. A small black bear, or some other animal of proper size, was smoked to resemble a well-dried human body and masked to make its face look human. In the dim light of the fire, the cannibal impersonsonator ate a portion of such an animal. Sometimes he would dash among the spectators, biting or cutting off a piece of skin from someone's arm before his handlers could restrain him. Those he bit or cut were chosen for their roles in advance and were paid with special gifts for their cooperation.

These sodalities provided a mechanism for an individual to acquire supernatural power and at the same time to acquire high rank for himself and to maintain the high position of his extended family in the social hierarchy. The religious dramas sometimes went on almost continuously for several months. Such devotion to ritual was possible only in a society with a large surplus of food and other necessities to consume during this period when little work was done. The peoples of the Northwest Coast enjoyed by far the greatest economic surplus of any hunting, gathering, or fishing area, and in this respect compared favorably with those of Meso-America.

California.—The Indians of central California possessed three kinds of sodalities: tribal sodalities for all men, restricted sodalities for a limited number of men, and restricted sodalities for a limited number of women. Some tribelets had a second restricted sodality for men in place of that for women. Twentieth-century Indian informants refer to the initiation ceremonies of these sodalities as schools, comparing the tribal initiation to elementary school and the more restricted initiation to high school. This is a meaningful analogy, because the young were taught cosmology and general religious lore in all such initiations, and, in those restricted to the more talented offspring of the higher-ranking families, they were taught the art of curing the sick by supernatural means. The pupils in the elementary school were ten or twelve years of age, while those in the high school were a little older. These schools lasted from four days to about six months. The students were usually housed in the permanent religious structure, which, in this area, was semisubterranean and earth-covered. Such initiations were annual events in some localities, while in other places they might be held at intervals as far apart as seven years. Frequency apparently depended on the number of eligible initiates as much as on a fixed calendar of events. All of these sodalities in central California are called Kuksu Cults, after one of the principal spirits impersonated.

The central core of the Kuksu initiations was the acquisition of supernatural power and knowledge by direct contact with spiritual personalities. When elderly Wappo Indian informants were asked if their religious leaders dressed up in masks and special costumes to impersonate spirits, they replied in the affirmative but hastened to add that real spirits also attended these ceremonies and helped instruct the younger generation. Such seems to have been the general belief. The initiates thought in the beginning that all characters in the drama were genuine spirits, but gradually learned that persons of their acquaintance possessed the regalia and wore them to impersonate spirits. Edwin Loeb (1933: Table 1) lists a total of twenty-five spirits impersonated for all the tribelets with Kuksu Cults. In addition to these twenty-five spirits, there were four gods: the creator, the culture hero, thunder, and coyote. These four figured more prominently in the mythology of the area and were held in higher esteem than the others.

In southern California, there were very different religious sodalities, called collectively the Chungichnish Cults, after the name of the highest-ranking god in the area. These seem to have been tribal sodalities in some localities, because all boys were initiated, while in other tribelets participation in the rites was voluntary and seems not to have included all boys. Like those of northern California, the principal ceremonies of these cults were initiations, but the impersonation of spirits by masked dancers was totally lacking; the central theme was the obtaining of contact with the supernatural through the medium of a narcotic plant, the Jamestown weed or Jimson weed, genus *Datura*. The roots of this plant were crushed in a sacred mortar reserved for the purpose, and a concoction was made by adding hot water. Each of the initiates, boys of adolescent or preadolescent age, drank some of the drug directly from the mortar in which it was made. The potion was a powerful one that invariably produced hallucinations and sometimes resulted in a fatality. The hallucinations consisted principally of visions of animals, which often taught the initiate a song or dance. Such animals became the lifelong spirit helpers of the boys, and were regarded as essential to success as a hunter, ritualist, shaman, or in any other male activity. Each boy was guided through the ceremony by his individual sponsor, who instructed him in the religious lore of the tribelet and in various sacred songs and dances. Southern California peoples also had women's tribal sodalities, in which membership was achieved by undergoing an initiation similar to the one for boys.

The Cochimi of Baja California had ceremonies in which both a man from the sky coming to benefit the earth and the ghosts of the dead were impersonated (Kroeber, 1932: 414–15). Only the men knew that the characters in the drama were masked and disguised human beings; the women and children thought they were spirits. While little is known of these ceremonies, they seem very similar to the sodality initiation rituals of central California.

Southwest.—The Pueblo peoples in the northern Southwest possessed the largest number and most elaborate system of sodalities of any group described so far. All the Pueblos initiated all their youths into tribal sodalities called "Kachina Cults." The Kachina Cults of each village were independent in organization of those of every other village, and there were as many as six such distinct cults within a single village. These can be compared to six different Protestant churches in a town in the United States today. They shared much in common but at the same time had separate sets of officers and assembled in separate sacred structures called "kivas." In addition to the Kachina Cults, which embraced all the mature males, there were men's sodalities restricted to only a part of the mature males, sodalities restricted to only a part of the mature women in most of the villages, and also restricted sodalities with both men and women members. In the west, among the Hopi and Zuñi, about half the adults belonged to at least one restricted sodality in addition to the men's "tribal" Kachina Cults. Farther eastward on the Rio Grande, the numbers included in the restricted sodalities diminish to a small minority of the total population. In the Hopi villages and at Zuñi, the number of members in each restricted sodality ranged from about thirty to sixty, while on the Rio Grande, it was nearer six to twelve. Another difference between east and west was the greater emphasis on kinship in the west, where all or most sodality offices were matrilineally inherited.

Boys were usually initiated into the Kachina Cults at ten or twelve years of age. Up to that time they, along with the women and girls, were supposed to believe that the masked dancers were indeed supernatural visitors from the village of the spirits. Revelation of this and other secrets of the cults was formerly punished in some localities with death. The boys were severely whipped by the kachina spirit-impersonating priests to impress them with the gravity of the occasion, to inspire awe of the supernatural, and to remove sickness and contamination from their persons. Then they were told that they were the ones who would wear the masked costumes in the future, thus making it clear that the dancers were human beings in disguise.

Perhaps the most distinctive characteristic of Pueblo sodalities was their dedication to the welfare of the entire society of which they were a part rather than to the selfish interests of the members. We saw above that the sodalities on the Northwest Coast were principally concerned with maintaining or enhancing the high rank of the members, in some cases by advertising their shamanistic powers which, in turn, brought in fees for curing the sick. In California, the tribal sodalities brought no special prestige because all boys, and less often all girls, were initiated into them, but sodalities of restricted membership were principally concerned with the training of shamans, who also enjoyed a position of high rank as well as a superior income from curing fees. Among the Pueblos, members of restricted sodalities enjoyed none of these economic advantages, although both civil and religious prestige were associated with membership and the holding of sodality office. Rain making was the most recurrent motivation behind sodality ceremonies; yet, when the rain came, it fell on the fields of members and nonmembers alike. The curing fraternities of the Pueblos performed cures on all comers, not just their members, and in most cases being cured of an ailment by the fraternity was requisite to membership in it. Likewise the Warriors' Sodality fought for the benefit of an entire village, not just its own members. As noted above in Chapter 17, the village council, which was the seat of sovereignty among the Pueblo peoples, was composed of the head priests of the various sodalities. Sodalities therefore have important political functions.

Other Southwest peoples on the United States side of the border seemed to have lacked sodalities, but they appear again on the Mexican side in more than one locality. Beals (1943: 69–70) postulates a men's tribal sodality, several men's restricted sodalities, and one or more women's restricted sodalities for the Cáhita of Sonora and Sinaloa. So far as the scanty information goes, these sodalities were more like those of the Pueblo peoples than those of any of the other areas described so far. It seems likely that the Acaxee of Sinaloa and Durango and other peoples to the south also possessed sodalities.

Plains and Prairies.—These two areas shared a system of sodalities which were indisputable geographic and historical units as compared with those of neighboring areas. Because these were largely confined to men, and because all men were warriors, they may be called men's sodalities, military sodalities, or police sodalities. They were more secular, informal, and less secret than the sodalities of the Northwest Coast, California, and Southwest described above. Membership was limited to men with good war records, was voluntary, and was not required of all males of a certain age, although in the early nineteenth century most men belonged to one such sodality. These organizations therefore were restricted—not tribal—sodalities, and may simply be called "clubs."

There were two principal types: graded and ungraded. The ungraded clubs of the Crow Indians are typical of that variety. When the death of a member caused a vacancy in the ranks, the club usually took the initiative in filling it by offering gifts to one of the relatives of the departed. Or, if a man distinguished himself in war, he would be given gifts and asked to join one of these men's clubs. At the same time, a nonmember could take the initiative by expressing his desire to join. There were no initiations or entrance fees.

Five tribes—the Hidatsa, Mandan, Blackfoot, Gros Ventre, and Arapaho—had a system of clubs graded roughly according to the ages of the members, with the oldest group being of highest rank. Boys at play would imitate the songs and dances of these clubs and, when old enough to have acquired some material possessions of value, such as hides, parfleches, and arrows, would buy the costumes, dances, and songs of the club with the youngest membership. The sellers did not remain without club affiliation, but jointly bought out the next club and stayed together without change in membership but with a new set of costumes, dances, and songs. The second group of sellers, in turn, jointly bought out the next older age group, and this exchange of club identification continued until the oldest group sold out entirely and retired from the system. Then, after a few years, another group of young men would enter the system by buying out the youngest club, and the turnover in regalia, songs, and dances would again continue until the oldest club had retired. Some tribes had as many as ten such graded clubs, suggesting that each covered about a four-year span of age. The names of the Hidatsa clubs, as recorded by Prince Maximilian of Wied in 1833, were as follows: Stone Hammers, Lumpwoods, Crow Indians, Kit-Foxes, Little Dogs, Dogs, Halfshaved Heads, Enemies (Black Mouths), Bulls and Ravens.

There was no difference in the functions of the graded and ungraded clubs in their relation to the tribes of which they were a part. To the individual member, his sodality served as a club, and at its lodge he could lounge, sleep, eat, dance, sing, and otherwise enjoy the company of his fellow members much as in fraternities elsewhere. Upon occasion, these clubs paraded in public dressed in their best finery on their prancing horses, or put on a dance outdoors for all to see. But, at the same time, a club might be called upon to perform serious public duties associated exclusively with it, with all such clubs, or with each in rotation. There was variation in this matter from tribe to tribe. The most important of these duties was policing other members of the tribe on the collective buffalo hunt, on the march, or in camp on such important occasions as the Sun Dance. Wrongdoers were punished by a severe beating, in which bones were sometimes broken, and by the destruction of their horses, tipis, and weapons. Punishment was especially severe for a man who rode out against orders and frightened off a buffalo herd, leaving everyone without food for a time.

Among the Hidatsa, Mandan, and Arikara, on the upper Missouri River, there were several women's societies which had collective purchase features like those of the men but lacked of course the military and police duties. One such group, called the Goose Women, performed ceremonies to insure a good corn crop and also to attract the buffalo. Another women's club, called the White Buffalo Cow Women, also had a ritual to lure a buffalo herd within range of the hunters. Cheyenne women who had embroidered thirty buffalo robes with porcupine quills were eligible to join a club of robe quillers.

Prairies and Eastern Sub-Arctic.—There was a secret sodality, called the Grand Medicine Society or Midewiwin, among the Indians of the northern Prairies and the adjacent part of the Eastern Sub-Arctic area. This sodality appears to have originated among the Algonquian-speaking peoples and to have spread from them to the speakers of Siouan languages. Because membership was on a voluntary basis, and not everyone in a community belonged to it, at least in the past, it is best labeled a "restricted" sodality. The Ojibwa form of this sodality is well documented and typical of the area.

Secret meetings in a special elongated lodge built for the purpose were held at least once a year among the Ojibwa. The initiation of new members was the principal activity, although old members also renewed their contact with the supernatural at this time. The ceremonies were conducted by priests, who instructed the candidates in the religious meaning of the rites as well as in the proper behavior during the initiation. In the old days, initiation fees were high and candidates carefully screened; membership was small and limited to men. At the present time, almost anyone can join, rites are no longer secret except to prying outsiders (including anthropologists), and the organization as a whole differs little from that of a church, which is the label the Indians give to it. In earlier days, the purpose of the cult was strictly generalized; it was thought to insure a long and successful life for the members, and at the same time to constitute a thanksgiving for benefits already received from the supernatural. A candidate normally had to have a proper dream interpretable as a visitation of a spirit before he was eligible for initiation. Today, anyone who is ill may be initiated, in the hope of curing his ailment. This narrowing of purpose, from a panacea to take care of all life's problems to a mere cure for a specific ailment, has been going on for about a century.

The sodality was generally divided into four grades, each with its separate initiation rite and its associated myths, songs, herbal remedies, and Midewiwin bags. The essentials of each initiation ceremony were recorded in line drawings on bark scrolls. The animal and human characters on the scrolls were engraved with a bone stylus, and the indentations filled in with vermilion. One writer compares these scrolls to the trestle board of the Masonic lodge, which is printed and available to a nonmember but is so esoteric that it does not convey any real meaning to the uninitiated. It serves essentially as a mnemonic device for those informed about its meaning, as do the Midewiwin scrolls of the Great Lakes Indians. Each candidate for membership is instructed from these scrolls by a member thoroughly familiar with their meanings.

A separate initiation fee is paid to the priests in charge of the rite for each of the four grades, the amount increasing as one progresses through the grades. A member's rank in the system is shown by the design painted on his face and by the animal or bird skin out of which his Mide bag is made. Common materials for bags were weasel skins, mink skins, the skin from the paw of a wildcat or bear, the skin of a rattlesnake, and the skins of owls and hawks. Each material denoted one of the four grades.

Hickerson (1963) shows that the Midewiwin arose just after first White contact partly in response to the changed historical conditions, but it was not the conventional nativistic movement launched after a tribe had suffered defeat in war, loss of land, and other deprivations. The Midewiwin belongs to a period of increased prosperity due largely to the fur trade. It also served as a rallying point for the newly formed multiple clan villages, because there was one such sodality for each village. This sodality organization overlaid and bound together the clans which had earlier been localized clans without any external cohesion to a large social unit.

East.—Tribal initiations for youths occurred in the Southeast among the Virginia Algonquians, the Siouans of the Carolinas, the Chitimacha at the mouth of the Mississippi, and probably elsewhere along the coast. The Siouans, at least, had a separate tribal initiation for adolescent girls. The Chitimacha shut their youths up in the ceremonial house and forced them to dance and fast for six days. The Algonquians of Virginia kept their males of ten to fifteen years of age isolated in a special structure in the wilderness for nine months, not allowing them to speak with anyone during the entire period. They were instructed in religious lore by religious leaders at this time, and later some of them became "priests and conjurers." The fullest account from the Southeast, however, is that of John Lawson, on the Siouan peoples, with whom he lived from 1701 to about 1711.

You must know, that most commonly, once a year, at farthest, once in two years, these people take up so many of their young men, as they think are able to undergo it, and husquenaugh them, which is to make them obedient and respective to their superiors, and as they say, is the same to them as it is to us to send our children to school, to be taught good breeding and letters. This house of correction is a large, strong cabin, made on purpose for the reception of the young men and boys, that have not passed the graduation already; and it is always at christmas that they husquenaugh their youth, which is by bringing them into this house and keeping them dark all the time, where they more than half starve them. Besides, they give the pellitory bark, and several intoxicating plants, that make them go raving mad as ever were any people in the world; and you may hear them make the most dismal and hellish cries and howlings that ever human creatures expressed; all which continues about five or six weeks, and the little meat they eat, is the nastiest, loathsome stuff, and mixt with all manner of filth it is possible to get. After the time is expired, they are brought out of the cabin, which never is in the town, but always a distance off, and guarded by a jailor or two, who watch by turn. Now when they first come out, they are as poor as ever any creatures were; for you must know several die under the diabolical purgation. . . . They play this prank with girls as well as boys, and I believe it a miserable life they endure, because I have known several of them run away at that time to avoid it. Now the savages say if it were not for this, they could never keep their youth in subjection, besides that it hardens them ever after to the fatigues of war, hunting, and all manner of hardship, which their way of living exposes them to. Beside, they add, that it carries off those infirm weak bodies, that would have been only a burden and disgrace to their nation, and saves the victuals and clothing for better people that would have been expended on such useless creatures. (Lawson, 1860: 380–82.)

The loss of life in such initiations is emphasized even more in William Strachey's report on the Virginia Algonquians. Because the initiates in these rites later became "priests," these organizations appear to have been restricted sodalities. The Carolina Siouans, on the other hand, may have had tribal sodalities, because young people seem to have had difficulty in escaping the initiations. At any rate, the harsh character of the initiation ceremony comes out clearly in both localities. To the best of our knowledge, no other ceremonies of this character have been reported anywhere else in Anglo-America east of the Pueblos in New Mexico.

The Iroquois Indians of New York state and their neighbors speaking related languages possessed elaborate systems of sodalities whose activities centered in the curing of the sick. As elsewhere, illness was thought to be caused by the supernatural; therefore, it could be cured by appeasing the wrath of malevolent spirits or by soliciting the aid of benevolent ones, and also by maneuvering impersonal supernatural forces by magical means. These so-called medicine societies numbered eleven among the Seneca (Fenton, 1936) and nineteen among the Cayuga of Ontario (Speck, 1945). Because neither all the men nor all the women were compelled to join these sodalities, they were restricted in membership, but each had both men and women members. Among the Cayuga, eleven out of nineteen sodalities permitted anyone who wished to join by taking part in the curing ceremonies. The attitude was that an increased number of participants, each wanting the recovery of the patient, would augment the force of the appeal to the spirit helpers of the sodality. For the remaining eight Cayuga medicine sodalities, membership was limited to those who had had the proper dream or visionary experience or who had been cured of their own illness by the sodality. These organizations were somewhat secret, while those open to everyone who wished to join were not secret at all. All sodalities performed publicly in the longhouse at one time or another, and in these ceremonies the freedom of the entire town or tribe from disease and misfortune was sought. These sodalities therefore were concerned with the welfare of the entire town or tribe as well as that of the individual they might be trying to cure or that of their own membership.

The best-known Iroquois sodality is that of the False Faces. This name refers to the carved and painted wooden masks worn by all participants in the curing rituals of this organization. Each mask represented a benevolent spirit who was invariably ugly, apparently the better to frighten away the evil spirits causing disease among the people. The carving of a new mask was begun on the trunk of a living tree to keep within it the spirit of the tree, and later it was removed from the tree to receive its finishing touches. It was painted red or black, according to whether the carver began work in the morning or the afternoon, and fibers made from inner bark (or horse hair in historical times) were fastened to the top to represent hair. In addition to the masks worn over the face, performers shook hand-held hollow rattles made of turtle shells.

Probably all the tribes in what is now the Southeastern United States had men's sodalities of restricted membership. The Creek, for instance, had schools with three grades for the training of medicine men; graduates of these schools shared a common secret knowledge of the healing art and therefore constituted a sodality. The peoples of the coastal plain from the Natchez to the Powhatan had priests who were in charge of temples and ossuaries. Such men necessarily received considerable training and joined each other in religious ceremonies.

GREATEST ELABORATION OF SODALITIES

Probably all the peoples of Meso-America had sodalities of one kind or another. Where the record is fullest, among the Aztecs, the number and importance of sodalities far exceeded those of any people in any other area.

At fifteen years of age all Aztec boys left their homes and went to live in one of two types of boarding schools. The first were the *Telpuchcalli*, or "houses of youth," which were maintained by the demes, each deme educating its own youths. There were twenty houses of youth in Tenochtitlán because there were twenty demes in that city. Young men were given instruction in farming, in arts and crafts, in the bearing of arms, in the history and religion of their people, and in the duties of citizenship. In addition to receiving formal instruction, the young men formed work parties to cultivate public lands and to build public buildings and irrigation works. They also served in the army, making up the bulk of the fighting force. The second type was the *Calmecac*, a school for priests, which was attended by a restricted number of youths, drawn principally from the upper classes. These schools were only six in number, were located near the temples of important gods, and concentrated on the elaborate rituals which the pupils studied with the aid of pictographic writing in books. Both types of schools are described in more detail at the end of Chapter 22.

Still other boarding schools trained a smaller group of young women to become priestesses. Their training and work were limited for the most part to weaving the priestly costumes and embroidering them with feathers. There were thus three kinds of sodalities dedicated to the education of the youth. There were also three additional sodalities restricted to men with outstanding military records who served as the lesser officers in the army. These military orders were called the Eagle, the Ocelot, and the Arrow.

In addition to the sodalities mentioned above, there was a host of religious cults of more restricted membership, each centering in the worship of a single deity. Vaillant (1941: 182–84) lists sixty-three Aztec gods, not to mention lesser spirits, and each of these gods had its special priests who joined one another in ceremonies propitiating their patron deity. Each of these sixty-odd groups of priests was a sodality dedicated to the service of its god, and young men were constantly being educated and initiated into the secret lore of each of these religious cults.

The organization of the priesthood converged with that of the government at the top. In Tenochtitlán, a man called the "snake woman," one of the two top political officials, was in charge of the temples and the entire organization of the priesthood. Directly beneath him were two high priests who directed the worship respectively of the two highest gods, the war god and the rain god. Next in rank was a third priest who supervised the religious activities of conquered towns as well as acted as a deputy in Tenochtitlán for the higher-ranking priests. Below all of these officials were the sixty-odd priests in charge of the temple, worship, ritual, and sacrifice connected with each specific god. It was these priests who wore the dress of their patron divinities and impersonated them in the elaborate religious dramas which topped all others in native North America. It has been estimated that there were 5,000 priests in Tenochtitlán alone.

The priesthood was the fountainhead from which the most highly valued knowledge flowed. The priests were the ones who understood the complicated calendar system which was the core of the religion. There were twenty named days, twenty named "weeks" of thirteen days each, and eighteen named "months" of twenty days each; each day, "week," and "month" was associated with a particular god or goddess. There were, in addition, thirteen "hours" of daytime and nine "hours" of nighttime, each with one of the same deities assigned to it. Each ritual for each god had to be performed on the proper "hour," day, "week," or "month," or it would bring harm instead of good. It would have been impossible to carry on such an elaborate ceremonial cycle without a system of writing. Much of Aztec writing was a series of mnemonic symbols, each associated with an oral tradition which was not only memorized but also chanted, the better to make it stick in the mind. All of such knowledge was lodged in the persons of the priests, who spent a considerable portion of their time imparting it to the less-informed members of the cults as well as to new initiates.

The human sacrifices of war captives were carried on by these priestly sodalities. This so shocked the Spanish that they lost no time in destroying every manifestation of Aztec religion in sight. However, one case history of a sacrificial victim illustrates what must have been the common attitude toward this practice. It seems that a valiant Tlaxcalan chief, who was selected for sacrifice to the sun, fought so well with the inferior weapons given the victim on such occasions that he killed or wounded all his opponents. For this brave exhibition against overwhelming odds he was offered his freedom and a commission (chieftancy) in the army of Tenochtitlán. This he declined, however, because he preferred the greater honor associated with his major role as a sacrificial victim and the high-ranking position it assured him in the afterlife.

SUMMARY AND CONCLUSIONS

Our survey indicates that there were no sodalities of any kind on the Plateau, in the Great Basin, or in Northeast Mexico. In the Arctic, sodalities occurred only in Alaska south of Bering Strait, where contact with the Northwest Coast was most pronounced. In the Sub-Arctic, they were to be found only among the Cree and Ojibwa. The latter had considerable contact with the Iroquoians to the east as well as with Algonquians and Siouans to the south. Thus we see that the areas of poorest geographical environment, lowest population density, simplest division of labor, crudest material culture, lack of true political organization, and smallest differences in rank were the very ones which lacked sodalities entirely or had them only in limited numbers. The area with the greatest number of sodalities was Meso-America, which excelled all other areas in general cultural complexity. On the whole, therefore, there is a strong positive correlation between ramification of sodalities and general cultural complexity.

Tribal sodalities have a rather sporadic distribution. They seem to have occurred in southern Alaska, California, Baja California, Southwest, East, and Meso-America. All of these areas, except possibly Alaska, also had sodalities of more restricted membership. It was only on the Northwest Coast, Plains, and Prairies that restricted sodalities were the only type present.

Most sodalities were closely linked with religion. In fact, religious interests dominated sodalities everywhere except on the Plains, and even here some such organizations possessed religious features. Instruction in mythology and religion and personal contact with the supernatural were the rule in most sodality initiations, which were the nearest approach to formal education among most of the peoples possessing them.

Men's sodalities were much more frequent than those of women, although the latter were found in smaller numbers or with less conspicuous functions in most of the areas where men's sodalities prevailed. In most cases, the women's sodalities appear to have been modeled on, and to have been derived historically from, those of the men. Sodalities of mixed male and female membership are most characteristic of the Iroquoians, although they also occur among the Pueblos. Perhaps the dominance of matrilineal descent in both localities has something to do with the more equal opportunity accorded women in these cultures.

When we compare the sodality systems as wholes for the various culture areas, a number of linkages are apparent which are best explained in terms of contact between areas or by common origin. Thus Kroeber (1932: 408–15) makes out a good case for the common origin of a number of details in the initiation ceremonies of California, Baja California, and the Southwest, and Underhill (1948) extends the idea to other ceremonies.

The Midewiwin rites possibly stemmed from the medicine sodalities of the Iroquois. This is shown directly by the origin legend of the Midewiwin among the Ojibwa, and indirectly by a comparison of ceremonial organization and behavior. Fenton (1953: 208–10) has made out a good case for the Iroquois having derived their Eagle Dance from the Calumet Dance of the Prairies and some of its features from the Buzzard Cult of the Southeast, which, in turn, owed some of its inspiration to Meso-America. From these brief allusions to the diffusion factor, it is clear that while cultures must attain an economic surplus and a certain population density or community size before sodalities are likely to develop, such attainments do not explain the details of a particular sodality system in a particular locality. Such details are normally shared with neighboring tribes, as well as with tribes in other culture areas, and must be accounted for also by contact of peoples, diffusion, acculturation, and other historical processes.

REFERENCES

BEALS, 1943; BOAS, 1897; DENSMORE, 1929; DRIVER, 1936; DRUCKER, 1940, 1955; EGGAN, 1950; FENTON, 1936, 1941*b*, 1953; HICKERSON, 1963; HOFFMAN, 1891; KROEBER, 1925, 1932; LANTIS, 1947; LAWSON, 1860; LOEB, 1932, 1933; LOWIE, 1916, 1948, 1954; MÜLLER, 1954; PARSONS, 1939; SPECK, 1945; STRACHEY, 1849; SWANTON, 1946; UNDERHILL, 1948; VAILLANT, 1941.

21

Life Cycle

THE FOUR principal events in the life cycle of mammals are birth, the attainment of maturity, reproduction, and death. Man is no exception to this sequence, and everywhere in the world he devotes some special attention to these important events. Each is accompanied by anxiety, and, where this is great, a considerable elaboration of special behaviour and belief tends to surround the occasion. However, the emphasis may vary tremendously from one primitive society to another. Puberty may be subjected to the greatest amount of ritual recognition in one culture, while death may be the dominant ceremonial occasion in another. On the whole, birth and marriage receive less attention than the other life crises but are still regarded as important.

The supernatural is thought to be very close to man at the time of these four biological crises, in some cases for the better and in others for the worse. But whether the attitude of supernatural personalities was regarded as benevolent or malevolent, North American Indian peoples prescribed certain acts of behavior and forbade others, in order to attract the good or fend off the evil.

Apparently all American Indians were familiar with the essential facts of sexual reproduction and admitted that sexual intercourse is necessary to initiate conception and pregnancy. Anthropologists have not reported any cases from North America in which knowledge of the connection between sex and conception was denied, as in native Australia and Melanesia. Many persons in Christian nations today believe that God takes a hand in conception, that mere biology is not a sufficient explanation, and most Indians also believed that the supernatural plays a role in such matters.

When a woman realized she was pregnant, she performed certain positive acts thought to be beneficial to her health and that of the child, and avoided doing other things she believed would harm the child and herself. Dietary restrictions, especially the taboo on eating

363

meat, were general at this time. The most common explanation of this is that the souls of the game animals would be offended if a pregnant woman had contact with their flesh and would broadcast the offense to all the game animals, with the result that none would permit themselves to be killed by the housemates of the unfortunate woman. To the meat taboo were often added taboos associated with water, such as the requirement that she must drink only a little water or drink through a special tube provided for the purpose. The pregnant woman was often secluded from the rest of the society in a screened-off part of the house or in a special hut nearby, especially toward the end of her period of gestation. Frequently she could scratch her body only with a stick provided for the purpose, because her hands might give her a skin disease. Even her glance was sometimes thought to be harmful to others, so that she had to glance downward or cover her head when she went outdoors. As the time for birth drew near, such special behaviors increased in intensity and frequency until the blessed event itself took place.

Meso-America was the most deviant area with respect to the generalizations just offered. Here there was no formal seclusion, but only a gradual narrowing of participation in social and public life, somewhat like that of the Victorian era in England and the United States. The expectant mother avoided foods characterized as "cold," but was encouraged to indulge her cravings for other foods because of the belief that such cravings originated with the fetus. Pleasing the unborn child averted illness, miscarriage, or a difficult labor.

Voluntary abortion was practiced in all culture areas and probably by most tribes in every area. Devereux (1955) has assembled information on abortion for ninety North American Indian peoples, but the data are too meager to establish significant differences between culture areas. However, they do permit generalizations for the continent as a whole. The motivations for abortion, listed from most frequent to least frequent, are the following: illegitimacy of the pregnancy; desire to avoid the trouble and work of rearing children; fear of the pain, of injury to the mother's health, or of death at childbirth; poverty of the parents; desire to avoid bringing a child into the modern world with its discrimination against Indians and half-breeds; quarrels between parents and desertion of a pregnant woman by her husband or lover; fear of bringing into the world a child associated with coitus taboos, such as those during pregnancy or during the nursing period of a previous child; desire to avoid producing a child who will become a slave, a prisoner of war, or a person of any other undesirable status; desire to avoid producing offspring from an adulterous union.

The techniques of abortion are equally varied, but most of them fall into three principal categories: mechanical means, strenous exercise, and drugs. These are reported in about equal frequency for North American Indians. The great variety of such techniques suggests that abortion was well known to North American Indians; nowhere was it considered a crime. Although illegitimate pregnancies and births are regarded by most anthropologists as being associated with less stigma among Indians than among modern Western societies, the fact that the most frequently reported motivation for abortion was illegitimacy of the pregnancy suggests that there was greater disapproval than has been generally believed. The effect of abortion on population was probably not great because mortality of children was very high anyway; if no abortions had been performed, more children would have died at a later date from lack of food and other necessities.

Newlyweds normally wanted children, and if none were born after several years of marriage, this was often grounds for divorce. Where polygyny was approved, a younger sister of the barren wife might be taken as a second wife in the hope of producing offspring. Where there was no younger sister or other relative available, the bride price was sometimes returned to the groom and the marriage dissolved. Sterility on the part of the husband does not seem to have been understood by many Indian peoples, because it is conspicuously absent in field reports and documentary data on Indians. Sons were valued more than daughters in areas where patrilineal descent prevailed or where men dominated the culture; but in matrilineal societies, daughters were at a premium because they were the ones to carry on the family name and inherit the real estate.

BIRTH AND INFANCY

Birth took place in a special hut made for the purpose or in a screened-off portion of the house. The position the woman assumed in labor varied from tribe to tribe and area to area, but the most frequent ones for the continent as a whole seem to have been kneeling or squatting. Sitting, however, is more often mentioned for the Northwest Coast, California, and the Southwest. Standing or stooping is less often reported for the continent as a whole than the above postures, and lying flat on the back still less. The woman in labor, in all positions except lying, often supported herself by holding onto one or two stakes in the ground or onto a cord attached to the roof of the dwelling. She was assisted by a midwife in most localities, if one were available or, if not, by a female relative. The husband less often helped at parturition because it was generally taboo for men to be present except for men shamans or other male native physicians supposed to be skilled in obstetrics.

Probably all Indians disposed of the placenta and the umbilical cord in some prescribed manner. The placenta might be buried in the earth floor of the house or otherwise disposed of where carnivores would not eat it; but the umbilical cord, after it had become disengaged from the infant's navel, was normally kept in some safe place in the house for a considerable time. Proper disposal of these objects insured the good health of the baby and sometimes of its mother.

Infanticide was practiced in every culture area, although it has been denied by informants from a number of individual societies and therefore was probably not universal. When the mother died at childbirth, there was no way of feeding the infant unless a wet nurse could be found. In the Arctic, Sub-Arctic, Great Basin, and Northeast Mexico, where population was sparsest and residential units smallest, a wet nurse was least likely to be available and the frequency of infanticide from this cause was greatest. When no wet nurse could be found, the infant was most often buried with its mother. If the father of a newborn infant died suddenly, leaving the mother with several children to care for on her own, she might kill the new arrival in order to free herself to obtain a living for the other children more easily. In areas where the stigma attached to the illegitimate child was greatest, the unwed mother might put her infant to death to spare him and herself from social censure. Deformed infants were frequently killed, especially in the more nomadic areas, where they could not possibly measure up to the demands on children, not to mention those on adults. In the time of famine, infants would more often be killed because their chances of survival, with the mother's milk supply impaired by starvation, was slight.

Infanticide among the Eskimo in the Arctic has received more attention than that of any other region. In this area, girl babies were killed more often than boys because the man was the hunter and more indispensable to survival than the women. The mortality of adult males was about twice as high as that of adult females because men were often killed in hunting or in fights with each other, so that some elimination of female infants was necessary to maintain a workable sex ratio later on in life.

In most North American Indian societies, the parents had the power of life and death over their newborn infant and did not have to consult any higher authority to dispose of it. However, some societies placed a time limit on this power, as in the case of the Creeks, where a mother possessed the option on her baby's life for only one month after its birth. She had to obtain the approval of her lineage or sib to put to death an older child.

Perhaps the harshness of living conditions for mother and child in some areas can best be conveyed to the reader with a quotation from Gonzalo de Las Casas about the Chichimecs of Northeast Mexico in the sixteenth century.

> They bear their children with great distress because, having no houses and roaming constantly, they often give birth while traveling. Even with the placenta hanging and dripping blood, they walk on as if they were sheep or cows. They wash their infants or, if there is no water, cleanse them with herbs. They have nothing to give their children but their own milk; nor do they wrap them in blankets, because they have none. They have no cradles, no houses for shelter, nothing more than a piece of cloth or a rock, and in such harsh conditions they live and rear their children. (Las Casas, 1944 [1574]: 35–36.)

This inventory of birth customs would not be complete without mention of the couvade (from the French *couver*, "to hatch"). This term refers to the participation of the father in birth rites. In its extreme form, the father lies in bed after the birth of his child, complains of labor pains, observes food taboos, and otherwise acts like a woman in confinement. The mother, on the other hand, gets up and assumes her normal household duties as soon as possible after giving birth, sometimes on the same day, and waits on the bedfast father. Thus the roles of the sexes are reversed. Nowhere on the mainland of North America did this extreme form of couvade prevail, but a number of California and Great Basin tribes practiced what might be called a half-couvade, with about equal restrictions on both parents after the birth of their child. Some restrictions on the father following the birth of a child were probably universal in aboriginal North America. California and the Great Basin differ only in the greater emphasis placed on the role of the father as compared with that in most other areas.

Twins were probably as rare among Indians as among Europeans, and were generally regarded or treated in some special manner. The emotional response to them ranged all the way from fear and anxiety to esteem and pleasure. Twins were generally thought to be caused by the supernatural, and, where benevolent spirits were thought to be more numerous or powerful than malevolent ones, twins were welcomed; but where the reverse was true, they were feared. Incomplete information suggests that Indians were about equally divided on this score. Among the Pomo of California, twins were feared, and it was thought that sexual intercourse done lying on the side would prevent the conception of twins. The Quinault Indians of the state of Washington thought that twins should always live together, because separation would cause both to die. The Iroquois of New York state and other peoples in the East believed that twins would grow up to possess supernatural power and would be able to foretell the future; the southern California peoples and the adjacent River Yumans believed that twins went to a special heaven for the highly esteemed. The belief that the death of one twin brings death to the other is most frequently reported on the Plateau and in the Great Basin, but it may also be common in other areas. The killing of one twin at birth has been reported for several culture areas, but seems to have been most frequent in the Arctic, where, when the twins were of both sexes, the girl was usually killed. If someone could be found to adopt one of the twins, however, both might be spared.

When a child was born, the pregnancy taboos surrounding the mother were not waived at once but, on the contrary, were intensified for a period of from a few days to a few months. Dietary restrictions were broadened, seclusion was more severe, and the fear of the supernatural increased. At the end of this period the mother bathed, put on new clothing, and formally presented her child to her relatives or the public at a feast and ceremony. The child was usually given a name at this time. Names were often inherited from a deceased ancestor. Thus, among the Eskimo, not only was an infant given the name of a dead ancestor, but the soul of the ancestor was thought to reincarnate itself in the body of the child. Eskimo parents never slapped their children or otherwise abused them for fear of insulting the soul of the ancestor, which might decide to depart from the body of the baby and take its life away.

Where descent was strictly patrilineal or matrilineal, personal names tended to be inherited in the same unilateral fashion; in bilateral areas where male dominance over females was marked, as in the Sub-Arctic and on the North Pacific Coast from the Kwakiutl southward, patrilineal inheritance was the rule, at least for male names. In Meso-America, however, the personal name, as well as the fate of the individual, was determined by the date of birth. Such a system could prevail only in cultures with well-developed calendars, and was therefore limited to this single area. For other facts about personal names, see the section on names in Chapter 22.

Babies were kept in shallow, open containers of bark, basketry, and wood or were strapped to frames to make it easier for the mother to carry the infant and to anchor it out of reach of harm. These devices are called "cradles" by anthropologists, but none of them had rockers like the conventional European-derived cradle. In the Arctic, the mother carried her baby inside her parka, supported by a hide sling under the baby's buttocks and over her shoulder. Most Indians, however, bound the child to a flat board or framework which could be carried on the mother's back, with the infant facing backward, or could be suspended from a tree or leaned against the house. Such cradles were made of a single board in the Sub-Arctic, East, Prairies, Plains, Plateau, and on part of the Northwest Coast. In other areas, a flat framework was made of small plant stems woven together like basketry, and the baby was strapped to this in the same manner. These areas were the ones where basketry dominated woodwork: California, Great Basin, Southwest, and Meso-America. On the Plains, a thick, stiff piece of rawhide was also used as a cradle "board."

On the Northwest Coast as far south as the Columbia River, babies were kept in containers of two types: a doweled and sewn box made of boards, and a dugout wooden container. Bark containers were used for the same purpose in at least the Yukon Sub-Arctic and the Canadian Plateau. And in northern California and southwestern Oregon, a basketry container, in which the infant sat with his legs hanging out, was the characteristic cradle. Like the flat cradles of the paragraph above, these container cradles were carried on the backs of mothers, suspended from above, leaned against some object, or laid down with the infant lying supine. In the more tropical regions of Meso-America, where it was too hot to wrap up the child, he was carried naked in a woven sling under his buttocks and over the mother's shoulder and was kept in a hammock in the house.

Mortality of infants was high everywhere in aboriginal North America compared with rates in modern civilized countries. It was especially high in the areas with the poorest natural resources and most severe climates: Arctic, Sub-Arctic, Great Basin, and Northeast

Mexico. A study of a modern remnant group of Chichimecs in the last-named area, for the years 1946–55, yielded the following figures: 30 per cent of the infants died in the first year; 50 per cent died in the first two years; and 67 per cent died in the first five years. These figures may have been even higher in pre-Columbian times, and were almost certainly higher in the sixteenth, seventeenth, and eighteenth centuries, when the Chichimecs were at war with the Spanish. They are probably not far from the average mortality for the continent as a whole in pre-Columbian times.

PUBERTY

For both girls and boys, puberty is not an abrupt change but one which extends over a period of years. However, there is one feature of feminine physiology which appears suddenly and makes it possible to say exactly when a girl has reached a stage of maturity—that is, first menstruation. All Indians make note of this event and give the pubescent girl some advice or instruction about the facts of life and the proper behavior of a female at this time. Because there is no generally accepted mark of maturity for the human male, ceremonies for boys cannot be properly called "puberty rites." They have already been discussed in Chapter 20.

First of all, there were tremendous differences in the emphasis placed upon first menstruation from area to area and tribe to tribe. It probably received the least attention in Meso-America, especially when viewed in relation to the other activities and interests of these peoples. In the twentieth century, the Indians of this area take a secretive attitude toward girls' puberty and usually do not explain this fact of life to girls in advance. When a mother learns of her daughter's first menstruation, she explains what she knows about it to the girl and tries to keep it a secret from the men of the house. There are no seclusion, dietary restrictions, or special avoidances, because these would only serve to call attention to the girl's condition. The Catholic priests and other early chroniclers have left so little information on this matter that positive statements are difficult to make about the aboriginal period in Meso-America.

On the Plateau and in the Yukon Sub-Arctic, on the other hand, special behaviour was required of a pubescent girl for a period of one year in most cases, of two years in several instances, and of four years among the Carrier of British Columbia. The fear of the harm that feminine physiology could bring to the girl, her family, and the whole community was intense, and every precaution was taken to see that the girl did not endanger the health and lives of others by breaking the rules.

The greatest publicity given to first menstruation was in northern California and among the Apaches of the Southwest, where the girl's puberty ceremony was the greatest ritual occasion in the entire culture. The ceremony lasted for several days and included much feasting, singing, and dancing far into the night. Everyone in the local community was invited by the parents of the girl, and even outsiders were welcomed and sometimes urged to attend.

Still another example will illustrate the tremendous importance of female physiology to some Indians. In northwestern California, which is a part of the Northwest Coast culture area, elaborate annual rites called World Renewal ceremonies were performed. When the investigators finally got around to asking the Indians what it was that polluted the world and made the ceremony necessary, they said that menstrual fluid was the principal offender. Here we have an example in which the girls' puberty rite itself is of modest proportions and the subsequent menstruations of women are little talked about; yet this aspect of feminine physiology is the center about which the greatest ceremonies of these societies revolve.

Along with the sharp differences just pointed out goes a substratum of beliefs and practices which occurred in every culture area and among a majority of tribes in all areas, except possibly Meso-America. The first is that the menstruant is in a state of close contact with the supernatural, which may harm her or other persons is she does not behave properly. She is generally secluded. She especially avoids contact with hunters, fishermen, gamblers, shamans, and priests, all of whom are especially susceptible to harm at this time. She diets in order to avoid illness or bodily disfigurement, and especially abstains from meat so as not to spoil the hunting success of the men who killed the game. She must not touch her body with her hands, lest she catch a skin disease or lose her hair, but must use a stick provided for the purpose. She is proctored by an older female relative and instructed in the proper behavior of a menstruating woman, in sex, and in her future duties as a wife and mother. It is also generally believed that the conduct of the girl at this time tends to predetermine her behaviour throughout her future life; for example, if she works well at an assigned task, such as gathering firewood, she will grow up to be an industrious woman. At the end of the taboo period, she is bathed and dressed in new clothing. These are the beliefs and practices that are the most widespread in native North America, and it is interesting to note that all of them occur in all other major areas of the primitive world as well. We seem to have here a very old and psychologically deep-seated set of notions surrounding feminine physiology.

Northwest Coast.—The Salish-speaking tribelets in the center of this area possessed the most elaborate public girls' puberty ceremony of the region. The girl was confined for a time in a wooden cubicle within the large plank house. Women who knew the proper songs came daily to see the girl and to sing the songs to insure her a happy and successful future. They were paid for their services by being given an article of the girl's clothing or the products of her weaving during the period of seclusion. There is an interesting case in this century of a father who confined his daughter longer than she or the women of her family thought necessary. The word was passed around to all the women who knew girls' puberty songs, and they came to visit the girl daily, each singing a song. When the matter of the gift for this service arose, each in turn asked the father for a sewing machine. This had by that time become a standard household item and a generous gift to receive for such a service. After the father had given away a dozen or more sewing machines and was approaching financial ruin, he was forced to release his daughter in order to avoid bankruptcy. Thus the women got their way in this matter, and there were no more long puberty confinements in that family.

Southwest.—The Pueblo peoples paid the minimum of attention to puberty, but the Athapaskan-speaking Apaches had a girls' puberty rite that was a large public ceremony. It began as soon after first menstruation as the relatives of the girl could make the arrangements. They were hosts to all visitors, providing food and entertainment consisting of social dancing by both sexes, dancing by men wearing costumes similar to those of the Pueblo kachina dancers and impersonating mountain spirits, and also games and races. The dancing took place at at night by firelight, and the games and races were held in the daytime.

This ceremony was formerly given for each girl singly at her first menstruation, but more recently the relatives of several girls who have come of age within the preceding year give the ceremony jointly from the first to the fifth of July. In the late nineteenth century, United States government officials would not allow the Apaches to hold a public ceremony at any time except once a year on or near the Fourth of July, Independence Day, for fear that they would put on war dances and go on the warpath. This is the reason that all the puberty ceremonies which would have been held throughout the year were telescoped together on a single occasion, the Fourth of July celebration. The earlier games and races are now overshadowed by a roundup, with the men competing for honors in riding, bulldogging, roping, and hog-tying cattle.

A detailed analysis of girls' puberty rites (Driver, 1941) has shown an unexpected number of similarities between the Apache ceremony and that of Northern California and the Northwest Coast. Therefore it is likely that the public ceremonies in these three areas stem from a single origin, probably somewhere in the north, because the Apaches came from the north and arrived in the Southwest about five hundred years ago.

The above examples of the reasons or rationalizations for observing the various taboos at first menstruation suggest that supernatural punishment for wrongdoing was more frequent than reward for right doing. A fairly exhaustive tabulation of 283 rationalizations for the area west of the Rocky Mountains reveals that 81 per cent mention the harm that will befall the girl, other members of her society, or nature if she breaks the rules. Only 19 per cent mention the good things that will happen if the girl faithfully follows all the rules. This illustrates the predominantly negative character of the religious sanctions associated with girls' puberty rites.

Marriage is discussed in Chapter 14. We need only add here that marriage ceremonies are predominantly secular, social, or civil in character rather than religious. Shamans and priests seldom play leading roles, as do our pastors and priests, and the sanction of the supernatural tends to be taken for granted rather than to be sought on this occasion.

DEATH

The causes of death among Indians were as varied as those for modern populations. Most deaths were attributable to disease or to the violence of the chase, wars, and feuds. A smaller number of deaths resulted from infanticide (discussed above, under Birth and Infancy), suicide, and parricide. The emotional disturbances responsible for suicide were caused by such experiences as disappointment in love, family troubles, illness and incapacitating senility, remorse after unintentionally causing the death of another, sorrow after the death of a loved one, fear of revenge after injuring another, fear of being taken captive by an enemy, and loss of rank in cultures which placed a premium on high rank. The techniques of suicide included hanging, drowning, stabbing, shooting, poisoning, and crawling under a deadfall and releasing the trigger. Neither the causes nor the techniques of suicide are well enough known to determine significant differences between areas, but suicide has been reported in some frequency in all culture areas.

Parricide and the killing of invalids are most frequently reported in the Arctic and Sub-Arctic areas. A person too old or too ill to keep up with the hunting party was frequently abandoned to death by freezing and, less often, to the wolves. Sometimes the incapacitated person requested a son to kill him to put him out of his misery, because death at the hands of a nonrelative might start a feud. Parricide or abandonment was also common in the Great Basin and Northeast Mexico, and probably occurred in lower frequency in many other culture areas as well.

In areas where houses were small, temporary, or easily rebuilt, a person close to death might be allowed to die in his house. The house would then be abandoned, burned, or torn down and moved because of fear of the ghost of the deceased. In areas where houses were larger and more permanent, such as those occupied by extended families or in the Arctic, where the extreme cold made it difficult to abandon a house, a dying person was sometimes removed from the house to a special hut in which to die. Another alternative, where fear of ghosts was prominent, was to exorcise the house after the death of an inmate to drive away the ghost. Still another practice was to remove the corpse through a specially made opening in the wall or roof, rather than through the door, so that the returning ghost would find the opening walled up and presumably would not know enough to use the door.

Most of the tribes in the United States killed a horse or a dog at the death of the owner as a sacrifice to the supernatural. On the Northwest Coast, and in the Southeast and Meso-America, human beings were normally sacrificed at the death of an important person. Such sacrificial victims might be slaves, war captives, and, in the two more southern areas, servants, a child of a civic-minded citizen, or the widow of the deceased.

Methods of disposing of the corpse show variation not only from tribe to tribe and area to area but also within single cultures. Chiefs or priests might be buried in special tombs or ossuaries above ground, the rank and file in graves below the surface, and shamans might be cremated. However, in most societies, one practice was more common than the others.

In the Arctic, the dead were most often left on the surface of the ground, because it was impractical to dig a grave in the frozen soil and there were no trees to provide poles for a raised scaffold or wood for a crematory fire. Sometimes the corpse was covered with stones and, with this protection, might later be discovered by the archeologist; in other instances, it was left unprotected, to be devoured by hungry dogs or wolves. Surface burial was common also on the Northwest Coast, but here the dead were generally placed in wooden coffins, in canoes, or in more elaborate surface tombs of wood. Surface deposition in caves and rock shelters was practiced at least in the Arctic, on the Northwest Coast, Plateau, and Plains, and in the Great Basin and Southwest; on the Prairies and in the East, a corpse was sometimes placed in a hollow log or tree.

Cremation was the dominant form of corpse disposal in three disconnected areas: Yukon Sub-Arctic, adjacent parts of the Northwest Coast, and Mackenzie Sub-Arctic; California and adjacent parts of the Plateau, Great Basin and Southwest; Northeast Mexico and among a few peoples of Meso-America. As an alternative form of secondary or tertiary frequency, it has been reported for the Plateau, Great Basin, Plains, Prairies, and East. Because the necessary fuel was available in all areas except the Arctic, the limited distribution of cremation cannot be explained in any simple manner.

The placing of the dead on a scaffold or in a tree is dominant only in the Mackenzie Sub-Arctic, the northern Plains, the northern Prairies, and in the middle part of the Northwest Coast. In the last-named area, a single tree trunk, carved like a totem pole, served as a mortuary column on top of which the wooden coffin was placed. Like other forms of totem poles, these belong to the historic period, after steel tools to carve them had been acquired from European trading ships. Scaffold or tree burial was also the rule in the winter in the Eastern Sub-Arctic, where the ground was frozen too deep to make the digging of a grave practical. However, corpses were buried in the ground in some localities by preference, and some of those placed on scaffolds and in trees in the winter were reburied in the earth in summer. Because Christian missionaries everywhere encouraged burial in the ground, it is difficult to decide how much inhumation in this area is native and how much is European.

Inhumation was the most widespread means of disposing of the dead, and, because it was dominant in the areas of heaviest population, it accounted for more individuals than any of the other three and may possibly have disposed of more corpses than the other three combined. However, Christian influence increased the frequency of burial in the ground in the historic period, so that the data in A.D. 1492 would show less inhumation. Most Indians possessed nothing better for a digging tool than a sharpened stick, and almost half the tribes flexed the legs of the corpse and bound them against the body, so that a grave three feet long would suffice.

Funeral ceremonies for high-ranking persons were elaborate on the Northwest Coast, along the coastal plain of the Southeast, and in Meso-America. These are the areas where distinctions in rank and social class were most highly developed. In areas of simplest general culture level, such as the Arctic, Sub-Arctic, Great Basin, and Northeast Mexico, funerals were small family ceremonies with the minimum of ritual, although all persons residing in the community at the time of a death might have to practice certain taboos for a time. In the remaining culture areas, they were of intermediate magnitude.

In a few areas, large memorial ceremonies were held some months or years after death. The Hurons and some of their neighbors in the northern parts of the Prairies and East held an elaborate feast of the dead at intervals of twelve years. The corpses were retrieved from scaffolds and trees by their relatives and deposited in a huge community burial pit amid wailing, singing, and speech making.

In California, an annual mourning ceremony was held for all those who had died during the previous year. In the second half of the nineteenth century, this was a large public gathering lasting a week; it was attended not only by everyone in the local tribelet sponsoring the event but by outsiders as well. Among a number of tribelets, it was the greatest single ceremony of the culture in terms of duration, numbers in attendance, and the sacred values associated with it.

SUMMARY AND CONCLUSIONS

Taboos surrounding pregnancy and birth were numerous and general in native North America, which proves that these events were taken very seriously by Indians even though they were little publicized. Naming ceremonies for infants were common and, at least in the case of the Northwest Coast potlatches, were sometimes large affairs known to all, even though the attendance was restricted by formal invitation. Abortion and infanticide were general and were not regarded as crimes to be punished by legal authority. An understanding of the conditions of life under which women carried on their reproductive functions should make the reader more tolerant of these practices.

Girls' puberty rites at first menstruation exhibit a wide range of variation, extending all the way from secrecy in Meso-America to elaborate public ceremonies in northern California and among the Apaches of the Southwest which topped all other ritual occasions in those two areas. Public ceremonies for every girl who came of age were lacking in the most impoverished cultures, such as those of the Arctic, Sub-Arctic, Great Basin, and Northeast Mexico, and were also apparently lacking in the most complex cultures of Meso-America. In the Southwest, they seem to have been introduced by the intrusive Apaches from the north. In the Plains, Prairies, and East combined, there were no public puberty rites for an individual girl and only a single instance in the East of a "tribal" initiation ceremony for a group of girls. Therefore, public ceremonies for each girl at first menstruation achieved their greatest development among cultures at a "lower middle" level of general complexity. Such ceremonies occurred only in the western part of the continent, and appear to have stemmed from a single origin.

Suicide and parricide probably occurred in all culture areas, although not necessarily in all individual societies within the areas. Death probably received more attention than any other life crisis for the continent as a whole, just as it does in many civilized nations. Funerals were most elaborate in areas where the general culture was relatively advanced, such as on the Northwest Coast, in the Southeast, and in Meso-America. These were also the areas of greatest distinctions of rank and social class, and the amount of attention an individual received at death was highly correlated with his rank and eminence in the culture. Memorial celebrations, on the other hand, apparently reached their greatest development among cultures of intermediate general level, those in California and in the northern parts of the Prairies and East.

REFERENCES

DAWSON, 1929; DEVEREUX, 1955; DRIVER, 1936, 1941; DRIVER AND DRIVER, 1963; LAS CASAS, 1944 [1574]; LAWSON, 1860; LIBBY, MS; MACLEOD, 1925, 1926, 1933; PAUL AND PAUL, 1952; VOEGELIN, 1944; WISSE, 1933; YARROW, 1880, 1881.

22

Education

THE TERM "education," as used in this chapter, refers to the entire process by which a person learns the way of life of the society into which he is born and reared. It is equivalent to "enculturation," the term coined by Herskovits (1948). As we pointed out in Chapter 20, the amount of formal instruction and actual schooling given Indian children or adolescents was indeed small as compared to education in the literate world. Areas without sodalities had no formal schooling at all, but relied exclusively on the uncontrolled learning of the child by observation and imitation or on teaching by a parent or other older person. Even in areas where sodality initiations were performed at regular intervals, the schooling of the neophytes often lasted for only a few days. Most of the religious lore, deemed so essential for a successful life, was passed on to the next generation by individual tutoring.

Although the quantity of sodality elaboration is positively correlated with the amount of formal education given the young, this relationship is far from perfect. For example, the medicine men of the Navaho Indians were never organized into sodalities; yet it has been estimated that about one-third of the entire time of the Navaho adult male was occupied with religious ceremony of one kind or another. The verbal material in some of the chants performed by the "Singers" continues for many hours a day for several days. To memorize the verbal formulas and music for one chant of average length took months of close association between teacher and pupil. However, it must be remembered that the elaboration of Navaho ritual is to be explained in part by their contact with the Pueblo Indians for more than five hundred years. The Navaho have derived a great amount of ceremonial content from the Pueblos without acquiring the ceremonial organization of the latter. Few peoples without sodalities possess as

This chapter, except for the last section on the Aztecs, is derived almost wholly from the excellent monograph of Pettitt (1946).

much ritual as do the Navaho. Ceremonialism reached its greatest development in Meso-America, where it was carefully geared to the calendar system and an organized priesthood; yet the number of man hours consumed in it may not have been any greater per capita per annum than it was in the Southwest among the Navaho and Pueblo. On the whole, however, those peoples with the most elaborate development of sodalities gave the young the greatest amount of formal education or schooling.

In the section on Social and Religious Aspects in Chapter 6, it was mentioned that a boy learning to hunt was carefully taught by his father or other older relative. Every time he killed his first animal of a different species he was rewarded by praise and by being upgraded a rung on the ladder to manhood, but the principle of generosity was so important for him to learn that he was compelled to give away all the meat, at the same time receiving praise and recognition of achievement from the recipients of the food. The same rules applied in many areas to the first berries, roots, or seeds gathered by a girl. In both instances, the emphasis was on reward rather than on punishment, because children do not seem to have been punished for failure to take an animal or to gather plant foods. Praise for the young seems to have been less common in farming areas, but boys and girls labored in the fields and were carefully taught the techniques of agriculture.

DISCIPLINE

The emphasis on discipline in Europe and its derivative cultures seems to explain in part the frustration theory of Freudian psychologists. In its simplest form, this theory holds that most learning is an adaptation of the child to frustrations imposed upon it by parents or other older persons who care for the child. This seems to be an extreme view, because children learn a great deal from unsupervised imitation of older children and adults. Although frustration is present here, it is of a different character from that consciously imposed on the child in the form of discipline by an adult. On the whole, the North American Indians were very permissive with their children as compared with Europeans. Corporal punishment was far from lacking, but it was generally less frequent and less severe than in European cultures and their derivatives.

The close relationship of the young child to the supernatural served as a deterrent to corporal punishment. This concept is clearest among the Eskimo, who regard the infant's soul as being derived directly from a deceased ancestor. The infant's body provides a haven of refuge for the wandering ancestral soul, and the infant, in turn, benefits from the knowledge and supernatural power possessed by the soul within. It is as unthinkable to slap or speak harshly to an infant as it is to an aged relative. Such mistreatment of a child may cause its soul to depart, bringing death; or, in other cases, may result in vengeance being taken on the parents by the child developing abnormally large ears, bowlegs, or a humpback. This concept is carried so far that adults explain their own limitations of personality or mental shortcomings in terms of rough treatment received in childhood. This is primitive psycho-analysis totally independent of that of Freud.

The notion that ill-treatment of a child may adversely affect its health and personality, and may even cause its death, has been found by Pettitt (1946: 9–11) to occur also in the Sub-Arctic, Northwest Coast, Southwest, Prairies, and East. This concept, in one form or another, has been regarded as universal in native North America. Although this seems to be an overgeneralization, the idea does account for much of the permissiveness that parents exhibit toward their young children.

Pettitt (1946: 9) also cites about a dozen instances of parents who avoid corporal punishment because they want their children to love them and to regard their home as a refuge from harm from the outside. After having physically restrained a disobedient child or finished with a moral lecture on the proper behavior, the parent may apologize for this mild discipline by saying that custom compels him to do his duty or that the child will be punished by the supernatural if he does not mend his ways. Where whipping is required by ritual, the parent or sponsor of the child may shield the child from the blows or submit to being whipped himself to prove that the treatment being administered to the child is meted out to others as well. Such apologetic behavior or shielding of the child from harm has been reported for the Arctic, Sub-Arctic, Plateau, Southwest, Plains, Prairies, and East, and no doubt occurred in other areas as well.

But the parent-child relationship was not universally affable: children were slapped, whipped, beaten, showered with hot coals, or doused with cold water when their behavior failed to satisfy adults. Pettit (1946: 6–7) mentions such punishment for peoples in the Arctic, Northwest Coast, Plateau, Great Basin, California, and Southwest, and suggests that such instances tend to be more numerous as the level of cultural complexity increases. Thus, among the Aztecs, verbal rebuke was the principal disciplinary method up to the eighth year. From that time, a disobedient child was pricked in the hand with a maguey spine, exposed to the cold on a mountain at night, or compelled to lie bound and naked in a mud puddle. The postponement of such harsh measures to the eighth year is in keeping with the mild treatment of young children in native North America as a whole. Discipline was much stricter in the Aztec boarding schools, where youths of from fifteen to twenty-two years of age were severely beaten and even killed for not obeying the rules.

Discipline was frequently administered by a relative more remote than a parent, such as an uncle or aunt. The mother's brother or the father's sister seems more often to have served as disciplinarian, teacher, and sponsor of the child or youth than did the father's brother or mother's sister. Pettitt (1946: 22–24) explains the preference of the cross-uncle or -aunt over the parallel-uncle or -aunt as due to a strong brother-sister tie, plus the fact that the mother's brother or father's sister never becomes a stepfather or stepmother to the child, but remains forever outside the nuclear family. In contrast, the custom of sororate, found among a majority of North American Indian societies, would result in the mother's sister becoming the child's stepmother in the event of the mother's death. Similarly, the equally widespread levirate would shift the father's brother to the role of stepfather if the father died. The mother's brother, because of the universal brother-sister incest taboo, could never marry the mother, nor could the father's sister ever marry the father. Therefore the mother's brother and father's sister relationships were stable ones, and the nearest unalterable ones in the parental generation to the parents themselves.

At the same time, rules of residence and descent also seem to have played a determining part. Most of the instances in which the mother's brother played a prominent role in the disciplining of a child, as cited by Pettitt, were among societies which were either matrilocal or matrilineal. Because most of the sociopolitical and religious offices in matrilineal societies were held by males and descended to a man from his mother's brother, we can be sure that the mother's brother had a great deal more to do with the education and discipline of a youth than did the father. Areas where this pattern prevailed are the northern Northwest Coast, the northern Southwest, and the East. In patrilineal societies, the father may have served as teacher and disciplinarian more often than did the mother's brother, but no one has collected enough instances to establish this point conclusively. Grandparents also sometimes aided in the education and discipline of a child, both as grandparents and as foster parents in cases where the true parents had died.

In Chapter 20, we mentioned the frequent occurrence of spirit impersonations by men masked or painted so as to disguise their identity. Even though such sodalities were usually secret, they normally performed in public upon occasion in full view of children. Most of the spirits represented were supposed to be dangerous, at least if angered, and parents often told a disobedient child that he would be beaten or killed and eaten by such a spirit if he did not behave properly. The initiation rites among peoples with secret sodalities and spirit-impersonations nearly always included some hazing features, such as striking the youth, exposing him to fire, depriving him of food, and frightening him with impersonations of evil spirits. The element of discipline and subordination to authority was prominent in all such initiations.

Whiting, Kluckhohn, and Anthony (1958) have shown a strong tendency for tribal initiations to be associated with cultures that have a strong mother-son tie. By a strong mother-son tie, we mean a long nursing period, a long period when the son sleeps with his mother while the father sleeps in a separate place, and a long taboo on sexual intercourse between parents. Whiting's psychological interpretation of the worldwide correlation between male tribal initiations and a strong mother-son tie is that the isolation of the youth from his mother and the "hazing" he receives from the men during the initiation serves to break the close bond between mother and son, to reduce the hostility toward the father and, by extension, toward other mature males, and thus to insure the identification of the young man with the mature males of the society.

The hazing features of initiations among North American Indians were nearly always administered by persons disguised as supernatural beings, and the neophytes seldom knew the identity of the persons playing these roles. Thus part of the responsibility for the proper behavior of the child was shifted from parent, uncle, and aunt to the supernatural, much as in our culture some of it has been transferred from parent to schoolteacher.

In areas where sodalities were rare or absent—namely, the Arctic, Sub-Arctic, Plateau, and Great Basin—discipline was also referred to the supernatural. Individuals disguised themselves as spirits and went about warning or whipping disobedient children. Parents with problem children would arrange for someone outside their family to dress up like some evil spirit and play the disciplinary role. Such monsters represented owls, snakes, bears, ghosts, cannibal spirits, and other dangerous beings. In localities where there was no sodality organization, such disguised disciplinarians had no function in the culture other than to frighten problem children.

Without a doubt, the referring of discipline to the supernatural helped keep hostility between parents and children, or between more remote older relatives and children, at a low level. But at the same time it sometimes disturbed children to the point that they continued to have nightmares about evil spirits for the remainder of their lives. The relatively permissive relationship between parents and children, which is encouraged so generally by child psychologists today, was frequently negated by the fear that the Indian child felt toward the supernatural.

PRAISE AND RIDICULE

Since corporal punishment was rare or mild in native North America as compared with Europe and Anglo-America in recent times, correction more often took the form of ridicule, which is reported for every culture area. In the juridical song contest of the Eskimo, two disputants ridiculed each other at length in song in public. This was a powerful deterrent to wrongdoing. Ridicule in song was also applied to persons who had done no wrong but who had merely failed to accomplish what was expected of a mature person. For example, delay in getting married at the usual age was subject to ridicule, and even more serious was the failure to produce children after marriage. Both men and women were criticized for barrenness, but wife lending may sometimes have spared a man or woman from this embarrassing predicament.

Ridicule was frequent in the Plains area. Among the Crow Indians, a person was chided by his "joking relative," who was his father's brother's child or his father's male sib mate's child. These "joking relatives" were always in different sibs because descent was matrilineal. In the case of a marriage between a good-looking young man and an old maid, his female joking relative berated him in the following manner: "You had better marry a frog or mouse or some other animal than an old maid. What is an old maid good for?" The man did not reply but just sat laughing at the joke on himself. On the other hand, a man might say to a woman who was his joking relative, "You are not good enough to attract any man; you have never put up a tent; you have never beaded any blankets; you never make moccasins for your husband; you have been kidnapped again and again." The last phrase means that she was a loose woman, because on certain occasions a man was permitted to kidnap any woman with whom he had had sexual relations before her marriage. Although the accusations leveled by joking relatives against each other were sometimes groundless, the threat of one's protagonist finding real holes in the armor of his personality was always present and served as a deterrent to deviant behavior. Other Plains tribes had similar practices.

Among the neighboring Blackfoot, a boy setting out on his first war party was given a derogatory name which stuck with him until he won honor in war by stealing a horse, killing an enemy, or tagging an enemy, "counting coup." Then he was given a new name symbolizing his brave deed. Women and girls, especially a young man's fiancée, took part in ridiculing a man among the Blackfoot, and the same thing is reported in association with cowardice in warfare among the Cree. For the Mandan and Hidatsa, girls who had won distinction in feminine pursuits might berate young men of their own age who had not yet won honors in war.

The difference between socially sanctioned and unsanctioned ridicule is illustrated by the Iroquois. If a mature man critized a young man severely in ordinary conversation, the latter sometimes committed suicide; but if the occasion were during the War Dance, the same criticism would be taken lightly. On this occasion, any spectator could step forward, make a gift to the dancers, and receive their permission to speak his mind for two or three minutes on any subject he chose, including the shortcomings of a particular individual.

It is noteworthy that personal criticism in public was seldom meted out by parents to their offspring, or by members of the same sib to their younger sib mates. The family and sib presented a united front to the outside, and sought to protect and defend their members rather than to ridicule them. We saw above that corporal punishment was often administered by someone outside the family and sib. Thus the two most common forms of punishment were generally administered by persons outside the immediate kin group.

Reward in the form of praise for a deed well done is more common in the literature on Indians than is blame for failure. This was true of all age levels, but applied with greatest force to very young children.

Turning again to the Crow of the Plains, we find that the father was always on hand to praise his son when the latter was engaged in a shooting contest with the bow and arrow. The father also gave his son many feasts, at which friends made laudatory speeches and predicted future success for the lad; and when the boy returned from his first war party, it was the father's sib mates who rallied round to dance and sing his praise. From the Osage and Kansa of the Prairies, we learn that when boys fought informal duels, not only the victor was praised by the men but also the vanquished if he had fought bravely. Praise was also the rule for the Shawnee in the same culture area:

> Children were taught that good conduct would earn a reward and evil conduct would bring sorrow. . . . A few words of praise from a parent or an elder was regarded as the highest prize that could be given for good conduct. A child would strive with all his might to win such praise while he would be indifferent to bodily punishment. One punishment that was always a bitter one to an Indian child was to have some of his faults told to a visitor or a friend. (Alford, 1936: 19–21.)

Among the Natchez of the lower Mississippi, boys practiced shooting arrows at a bundle of grass thrown in the air. Every time a youngster scored a hit he was praised by an old man in charge of the group. The one who consistently shot best was named the young warrior, and the next best the apprentice warrior. On ceremonial occasions, when mature warriors had recounted their war deeds and received applause, boys were encouraged to recount the deeds they expected to perform in the future and were praised just as much as those who had already achieved them.

Other parallel instances are reported from the Southwest. Among the Hopi, parents and other onlookers bestowed loud applause on the youngster who hit the target with bow and arrow. For the Zuñi, we learn that a child was praised for every acceptable action, such as observing the right social etiquette and using the proper terms of greeting when visiting.

On the Northwest Coast among the Nootka, boys frequently imitated famous orators before an audience of old men, who encouraged the lad by predicting that he would do great things in the future.

The Eskimo celebrated the achievements of very young children with feasts, to which neighbors were invited to hear the parents praise their offspring. Such a feast was given for a child when he was compelled to spend the night away from home because the return of his parents was delayed by a storm or when he had worn out his first pair of boots.

When these examples are added to the praise children received for success in the hunt or in wild plant gathering, the total amount of praise received seems to top the total amount of ridicule.

FREE IMITATION AND DIRECTED LEARNING

All children in all cultures learn partly by voluntary imitation of older children or adults without the awareness of those imitated of their passive roles as teachers. At the same time, all children in all cultures on other occasions receive specific instruction from elders in regard to the proper behavior. Indian children probably learned more by free imitation and less by conscious instruction than do children in the modern Western world. Nevertheless, many instances are reported of children being taught both essential tasks and games by parents or other elders. The distinction between work and play was less sharp among Indians than it is in our modern world. This was especially true of those peoples who did not farm but lived entirely by hunting and gathering. Hunting was always a challenging adventure, and even the gathering of wild plant products necessitated travel over a considerable area, with the chance of meeting neighbors and renewing old acquaintances. When an unusual quantity of wild food was obtained, it was always an occasion for festivities to which friends were invited.

For the most part, children played at activities which trained them for the work of adults; boys practiced shooting the bow and arrow, first at targets and later at small game, and girls played with dolls and at household tasks. The child's first weapon or doll was usually made by an elder and given to him. Later the child might voluntarily make his own, with instruction from a parent. As the child matured, his dependence on elders for toys or help in making them was discouraged. In areas where a premium was placed on warfare, boys were taught the art of war in sham battles. The following excerpt is taken from a description of the games of the Mandans.

One of the most pleasing is the sham fight and sham scalp dance of the Mandan boys, which is a part of their regular exercise, and constitutes a material branch of their education. During the pleasant mornings of the summer, the little boys between the ages of seven and fifteen are called out, to the number of several hundred, and being divided into two companies, each of which is headed by some experienced warrior, who leads them on in the character of a teacher; they are led out into the prairies at sunrise, where this curious discipline is taught them. (Catlin, 1841: 131–33.)

After shooting at each other with miniature bows and blunt arrows, the boys returned to the village, where they put on a scalp dance with imitation scalps for an audience of girls. The girls, in turn, acted out their admiration for their young heroes.

Among the neighboring Sioux, a boy was given a small bow and blunt arrows as early as five years of age and instructed in their use. The father was most often the donor and teacher, but a grandfather or other older relative might substitute if the child was fatherless. One man recalled that his first bow was decorated to show the high rank of his father as a hunter and warrior. As the boy grew older and more skilled, the bow became larger, the arrows were pointed, and the stationary target was replaced by small game on the move. Finally, he was given a man's weapons, or taught how to make them, and allowed to accompany the men on a buffalo hunt or raiding party.

Among the Eskimo, there is considerable evidence of the child's play being initiated and directed by parents. Little boys as young as three years of age were given toy bows and arrows, harpoons, bird darts, sleds, and ivory carvings of animals to play with. A father sometimes modeled snow animals for his son to shoot at. Little girls were given dolls and later encouraged to make them and to make clothes for them out of skins. Puppies were even turned over to children, who harnessed them to toy sleds; both the puppies and the children were supposed to learn something of value from this experience. As a boy grew older, he would accompany his father on the hunt and would be allowed to go through the motions of killing the dead animal his father had taken. Similarly, little girls were encouraged to help in skinning and butchering and in distributing meat. Successful participation by children in such useful tasks brought praise, and failure might bring ridicule.

In areas where weaving, pottery making, and other such crafts were important, children received a great deal of instruction from adults. Often a single child was chosen to carry on a craft of a mature member of the family, since one such specialized individual per family was sufficient. In some instances, a younger child denied formal instruction might learn the craft by voluntary imitation of an adult or an older child. Thus, directed learning and free imitation might exist side by side for the same task in the same family.

Throughout North America, free imitation was combined with teaching. Every Indian society engaged in tasks requiring enough skill to demonstrate the advantage of actual instruction over unbridled mimicry. The survival of every society in the competitive Indian world depended in part on the skill with which it acquired its food, manufactured its tools, and defended itself against aggressors. Any people who dispensed with the tutoring of the young in such necessary skills could not have maintained its independent way of life for long. The fact that Indians often serve as hunting and fishing guides to those of European ancestry in the modern world is proof that they still possess marketable knowledge of wild life, a knowledge handed down to them by their Indian ancestors. For further details on education in subsistence activities, see the section on Social and Religious Aspects in Chapter 6.

THE MARKERS OF MATURITY

All Indian languages possessed age-status terms to designate the various stages of the life cycle, and along with them went a series of other markers. In relation to education, the most important transition was from that of child or adolescent in need of further education to that of adult able to assume the responsibilities of the mature individual. The status markers of maturity were the rewards for acquiring the abilities, skills, and knowledge of the adult. In the areas with sodalities, the tribal initiations marked the acquisition of adult status on the part of the youths who were initiated. Tribal initiations were much less frequently conducted for girls, but all peoples recognized first menstruation as a marker of maturity, and a few of them held a public ceremony for each girl as she came of age (see the section on Puberty in Chapter 21).

In addition to the above major indicators of maturity, there were a host of other achievements which helped raise the child to the status of an adult. On the Plains, Prairies, in the East, and in Meso-America, a successful war record was requisite to manhood. No young man could get married, speak in council, or dress like a man until he had gone to war and brought back evidence of having bested an enemy. Probably all the peoples in these areas distinguished warriors by special colors or patterns painted on the body, by the tattoo marks or designs on the body, by a special hair cut, and by special clothing and regalia. Some of the tribes in the remaining culture areas recognized similar signs of military distinction.

In the areas where game furnished the bulk of the diet (Map 3), success in the hunt was invariably prerequisite to marriage and full adult status. No woman would consider marrying a man who could not keep her supplied with game. This standard of success encouraged boys to bend every effort to acquire skill with the bow and arrow and other weapons of the chase and to learn all they could about the habits of game animals and the best means of outwitting them.

As we shall see in more detail below, a successful vision quest often assured success in hunting or warfare, permitted the youth to wear on his person the designs seen in the vision, and freed him from listening to moral lectures and other pearls of wisdom designed for the consumption of children. Participation in public religious ceremonies was often necessary to achieve full adult status. For example, among the Oglala Sioux, a man could not claim the cardinal virtues of bravery, integrity, and generosity unless he had experienced the tortures of the Sun Dance and had scars on his body to prove it.

There were also dietary restrictions on children which were lifted when they were successful in an adult pursuit. Thus, among the Eskimo, a youth was forbidden to eat young seal meat, eggs, entrails, heart, lungs, liver, narwhal, and small game until he had fully demonstrated himself to be an accomplished hunter. In other localities, boys were given only cold food, served last, or not allowed to eat with elders when strangers were present.

These few examples will give some idea of the many ways in which the Indians distinguished the child from the adult. Although many of the rewards were deferred a number of years, they served as a constant incentive to further effort. With the mild amount of corporal punishment and a generally permissive early childhood, the bliss achieved by children was not sufficient to entice them to remain in the status of children indefinitely. Adults rewarded their achievements sufficiently to encourage them to become adults as soon as they were able. Their education included a series of carefully graded tasks to master before it could be considered complete.

PERSONAL NAMES

The use of nicknames of a trivial, ridiculous, or derogatory character was found in every culture area north of Mexico, although not every people in every area followed the practice. Such names were given to children of various ages and were not changed until the child had distinguished himself sufficiently to be given a new name appropriate to his deed of distinction. In some instances, however, a person was addressed by his nickname throughout life or in jest, even though he had acquired new names by achievement and change of status. Examples of nicknames that a child would not want to keep are:

Turned-up Nose; Flat Head; Long Ears; Turtle Anus; Intestines; Hump on Rump; Big Nose; Without Teeth; Beaten into Submission; Ghost. Such names served as an incentive to the child to upgrade himself to the point of receiving a new name for some accomplishment.

The most common occasions on which new names were bestowed were at first menstruation for girls, initiation into a sodality for boys, success in hunting and war for boys, and the acquisition of supernatural power in the vision quest for both sexes but more often for boys. In some instances of hereditary names, a youth could not assume the name of his father until he had achieved a status comparable to that of his father—for example, in warfare. In other cases, the entire community had to approve a new name for a young man before it would be applied to him. Some men acquired a dozen or more names in a lifetime by performing as many successive deeds of distinction. As men became older they turned to civil and religious affairs and were given new names for exceptional achievement in these activities. Examples of names describing achievement are: Warrior Walking; He Who Causes Fear; Two Buffalo Bulls; Wisdom; Brave Chief; Stampedes the Grizzly Bear; Sacred Hawk; Big Medicine; One Who Is Loved.

There was a strong tendency in all culture areas north of Mexico to name a child after a distinguished person, with the hope of transferring the desirable personality of the elder to the younger, and sometimes even before the child had achieved anything of note. The donor was not of necessity an ancestor or collateral older relative of the child, although heredity was an important factor. The conflict between the status ascribed by heredity and that achieved by behavior was sometimes compromised by giving a child an hereditary nickname in the beginning, and later recognizing his accomplishments by bestowing on him a more serious hereditary name, often from the same ancestor. Persons of distinction normally acquired a series of names over a lifetime, so that it was possible to upgrade a young person by conferring such a series of names from a single important ancestor. In Meso-America, where the personal name was determined by the date of birth, this system was lacking. For other information on names, see Chapter 21.

VISION QUEST AND SPIRIT HELPER

Dreams and hallucinations were interpreted as contact with the supernatural in all culture areas, although their importance in the life of the individual differed from area to area. Such personal experiences were of limited value in Meso-America, the Pueblo part of the Southwest, and in other localities where organized cults and priesthoods dominated the religious scene. Visionary experiences were most highly regarded in areas which lacked organized religions, such as the Plateau and Plains. Peoples in still other areas encouraged both individual contact with the supernatural in visions and group contact in organized ritual. All Indians agreed, however, that one's success in life was due not only to his own efforts but in large part to the sanction of the supernatural.

In the process of acquiring the many markers of maturity, no experience was as important as the acquisition of a spirit helper in a vision quest for at least half the culture areas of native North America. Without it, a man would fail in all important undertakings, such as hunting, warfare, and curing the sick. Where visions were absolutely essential, individuals did not wait patiently to be touched by the divine hand, but sought out spirits on a vision quest. Such quests might be begun as early as five years of age, but more often the first quest was undertaken at about puberty. Both boys and girls went on vision quests on the Plateau, where the concept was perhaps most highly developed, but in other areas it was generally limited to boys.

A youth would travel to an isolated spot with a reputation as an abode of spirits, usually a mountain, or a lake, or an uninhabited wood. Here he remained for several days and nights, fasting from both food and water, naked in the cold, mutilating his body, and otherwise denying the desires of the flesh to the point that an hallucination was likely to occur. He prayed by asking a spirit to take pity on him in his condition of deprivation and want, the idea being that the more miserable his condition, the more likely was a spirit to come to his aid. Such "visions" usually took the form of both visual and auditory hallucinations. The neophyte would frequently see an animal spirit, which would speak to him, teach him a song, or show him designs to paint on his body, clothing, or weapons for protection against the enemy. On returning home, the youth would eventually describe his experience to his family or camp mates, sing the songs he had acquired, and paint the designs on his possessions. If his demonstration was convincing, he might later acquire a following on a future hunting or warring expedition. If the knowledge he acquired in the vision was efficacious in curing the sick, he could set himself up as a medicine man. Such vision quests did not always end with an initial success, but were sometimes continued at intervals throughout life in order to renew or supplement the first power acquired in youth.

The function of the vision in education was to instill confidence in a young person so that he would attempt things considered impossible before such a religious experience. With a spirit helper at his beck and call, an insecure adolescent would become more self-sufficient and would take more initiative in such necessary activities as war and the chase. When the odds were against him, he would exert greater effort in the belief that his spirit helper would get him out of his predicament.

Such supernatural experiences were of greatest importance for the religious leaders of the society, who made careers out of their rapport with the divine. Those religious functionaries who are supposed to have had direct individual contact with the spirit world are generally called shamans. In some areas, such as the Plateau, where everyone of any consequence had a vision, there was no definite distinction between shaman and layman. The difference was one of degree; the shaman possessed more spirits or more powerful spirits than did the layman. In other areas, where visions were less universal, the shaman was more clearly distinguished from the layman. The shaman never stopped with a single initial vision obtained in youth, but renewed his contact with the supernatural by going into a trance or some other preoccupied state every time he functioned in his society. This was true regardless of whether he was trying to locate evasive game, find a lost child, make rain, cause a bad storm to cease, or cure the sick. He had visions again and again and, if he was intelligent enough to convince people of his power or to predict the weather in advance, he might rise to a position of leadership.

Religious leaders called priests depended less on visionary experiences as a means of acquiring competence and more on actual instruction by older priests. As mentioned in Chapter 20, prospective priests were sometimes instructed in groups in schools, but north of Mexico individual tutoring was more common.

EDUCATION AMONG THE AZTECS

In the Aztec system of compulsory education, there were two types of schools: the *telpuchcalli* (houses of youth), and the *calmecac* (school for priests). Every Aztec youth entered one or the other; all sons of commoners and some of the sons of nobles entered the houses of youth by fifteen years of age, and other sons of nobles the schools for priests, sometimes at an earlier age. Youths remained in the houses of youth until they were twenty or twenty-two years of age, at which time they married. Those in the school for priests, for the most part, married after graduation and assumed positions of authority in the government, army, or priesthoods (Caso, 1958: 29, 84–90.)

When a boy was born, he was taken by his parents either to one of the twenty houses of youth or to one of the six schools for priests and enrolled as a future pupil. At this time the parents prayed to the patron deity that their child, likened unto a precious jewel or brilliant quetzal feather, might grow up to be a brave warrior or a distinguished priest. When the boy attained the proper age, he was taken by his father to the school to which he had been dedicated in infancy.

In the houses of youth, the duties of the boys were many. They swept the premises, built the fires, and joined with the others in singing and dancing at night. When they were still very young, they were taken to the forests, where they cut logs and carried them back to their headquarters, first only one log, but when older, two at a time. They were also taken into battle at an early age to determine whether they were likely to be distinguished in war. If a youth was successful in such trials, discreet in speech, pure in heart, and had otherwise acquired a degree of maturity, he was promoted to the status of master of youths. If he enjoyed still further success, especially in warfare, he was advanced to the higher rank of a ruler of youths. In this capacity he was in charge of a group of younger youths and meted out justice, in the form of both promotions and punishments, to his underlings. Those who had taken four captives in battle were elevated to the still higher rank of constable and carried staves as symbols of office.

Work parties of young men from the houses of youth also made adobe bricks for walls, cultivated the fields belonging to the organization, and dug canals for the irrigation of the crops. Work always stopped just before sundown, when they returned to the school, bathed, painted, and adorned themselves for the evening festivities. Those of rank were distinguished from the others by special dress. A fire was built after sunset, and they sang and danced until midnight. The higher-ranking and older men slept with their paramours.

Drinking alcoholic beverages was a much more severe offense than unchastity. If a youth was found drunk and singing in a loud voice in public or fallen into a stupor in a conspicuous place, he paid the extreme penalty. He was beaten to death with staves or strangled with a rope in a public place for all to see. However, if he was the son of a nobleman, he was strangled secretly so as not to stigmatize his family.

As the youths grew older they gradually acquired female mates, sometimes by twos and threes. When twenty to twenty-two years of age they were given permission to leave the boarding school, to get married to one woman, and to join the ranks of the mature citizens.

Rules in the school for priests were stricter. All the students slept in the school, arising before dawn to sweep the building. Some got up between midnight and dawn and went to the forest to gather firewood to replenish the perpetual (fifty-two-year) fires. Work parties performed the same tasks as those from the houses of youths, but they left the priests' house before dawn. About sunset they would cease their utilitarian tasks and cut maguey spines. After nightfall the young priests bathed themselves and gathered up their shell trumpets, incense ladles, sacks of incense, and pine torches in preparation for going forth to offer the blood-stained maguey thorns to spirits residing in sacred spots. Each young man would walk from half a league to two leagues to a forest, desert, or lake, where he placed the thorns stained with his blood.

The priests slept well apart without touching one another or being covered with the same blanket. They prepared their own food, and if one received a gift of food from his family, he had to share it with the others. At midnight everyone was supposed to arise and pray. Those who overslept were punished by having blood drawn from their ears, breasts, thighs, or calves of the legs with maguey thorns or sharpened pieces of bone. Those who drank wine or had sexual relations with women were strangled, shot to death with arrows, or cast alive into fire. Small boys who committed minor sins had blood drawn from their ears or were switched with nettles.

At times of fasting, some ate only once a day at noon, while others ate only at midnight. At such times they were forbidden to eat salt and chile or to drink water. Emphasis was placed upon correct speech; those who spoke poorly or failed to address another in the proper manner were punished with bloodletting. All were taught the gods' songs and the calendar system from the book of dreams and the book of years. Mistakes in the oral rendition of such texts also brought corporal punishment.

Thus it is clear that the formal schooling of youths of the Aztecs and their neighbors in Meso-America went far beyond that of any other area. In fact, until recent times, few cultures anywhere in the world had as much formal education. The details of religion and ceremony were so complex that it took many years to master the knowledge necessary to be a head priest devoted to the worship of a single important god; and the time that it took to teach this knowledge to younger men was also great. This explains why the role of priest was a full-time and lifelong position and why it was necessary to have schools to maintain the system.

REFERENCES

ALFORD, 1936; CATLIN, 1841; HERSKOVITS, 1948; LOWIE, 1935; PETTITT, 1946; SAHAGÚN (ANDERSON AND DIBBLE), 1950–58; VAILLANT, 1941; WHITING, KLUCKHOHN, AND ANTHONY, 1958.

23

Religion, Magic, Medicine

IN ALMOST every chapter so far, some reference has been made to religion or magic and its role in the daily lives of the Indians. In comparison with Whites in the United States today, the Indians were at least ten times as religious. Every thought and act was hedged or bolstered by religion or magic, which ranged all the way from an amorphous feeling of reverence to the performance of elaborate rituals where every word and gesture was prescribed in advance. The distinction between natural and supernatural was never sharply drawn by Indians, who tended to blend the two into one harmonious whole. Only after an advanced philosophy of science has developed a well-formulated concept of the natural can this be contrasted with the supernatural. The compound term "natural-supernatural" is so clumsy that it has been reduced to "supernatural" throughout this book, even though a certain amount of practical science often went along with the supplication of the supernatural. For instance, Indian farmers everywhere combined practical science with religion and magic. One without the other was inconceivable.

"Religion" is technically regarded by anthropologists as the relation of man to supernatural personalities with anthropomorphic attributes. It includes "animism," which is defined as the belief in spiritual beings or personalities. There is no generally accepted classification of spiritual personalities in books on primitive religion, but a division into gods, ghosts, and other spirits introduces a little order into the chaos of animism as a whole. "Gods" are important and powerful spirits whose existence and power are recognized by every mature person in a culture. "Ghosts" are the souls of deceased ancestors, which are propritiated principally by their own descendants, but which may also be recognized and supplicated collectively by the society as a whole. "Other spirits" is a residual category for all other spiritual personalities who have neither attained the rank of gods nor formerly lived as human beings on earth. Animism was universal in native North America.

Gods, ghosts, and other spirits are supposed to have intelligence, emotions, and free will comparable to those of man. They may intervene in the affairs of the world and of man in a manner consistent with a system of ethics or according to their whims of the moment. Because of their humanlike emotions, they may experience love, hate, joy, anger, jealousy, fear, courage, and may act according to their emotional state at the time. They may be benevolent, malevolent, or merely unconcerned, but they are generally susceptible to human pleading, and bend an ear to prayers, sacrifices, and other forms of emotional appeal to their egos.

Such spiritual personalities are generally regarded as more intelligent and more powerful than man, although they may be assigned to different statuses and ranks in their own supernatural hierarchy. Their power is sometimes explained by the possession of a large quantity of the impersonal supernatural energy generally called by the Melanesian term "mana." Mana may be compared to electricity or to atomic energy. When properly controlled by rubber gloves, lead shields, and switches, electricity and atomic energy can be extremely beneficial to the possessor, but they can quickly get out of hand and cause harm. So it is with Mana. But because spiritual beings are generally superior to man, they usually exercise greater control over this impersonal supernatural energy than does man. Man may derive benefit from this infinite supply of power by asking a spirit who possesses it to help him. The concept of Mana was also probably universal in native North America.

However, some men are able to maneuver impersonal supernatural power as well as to compel spiritual personalities to do their bidding. Their technique is called "magic." If the proper spell is recited, if the proper manipulation of physical materials and objects is carried out, or if a symbolic pantomime is reenacted, a certain result is destined to follow. A mere human being therefore is able to compel supernatural forces or personalities to fulfill his desires. The magician does not beg with tears in his eyes and a tremor in his voice for aid from a spirit, but goes methodically through the fixed routine which he believes is certain to bring about the desired result, unless someone else possesses a more powerful countermagic. There need be no conflict between religion and magic, or for that matter between either of the two and modern science. Many persons employ all three in their daily lives.

Thus a farmer may select the best hybrid corn seed available (science), plant it under a waxing moon (magic), and pray to God for rain when he goes to church on Sunday (religion). Indians normally employ mixed systems of religion, magic, and practical science which are difficult to analyze even with the aid of terms in native languages.

The term "sorcery" or "witchcraft" is applied to magic used for antisocial purposes. The harming or even the killing of a person by magical technique, when he is regarded by his society as a criminal, is not an antisocial act, because the people may agree that he should be killed. But when evil (black) magic is directed against an innocent person, only then does it become sorcery or witchcraft. It is then a form of unapproved aggression against a fellow member of a society. Magic, good and bad, was likewise universal in Indian America.

Because of its supposed compulsive character and inevitable sequence of cause and effect, magic has been compared to modern science. It resembles science in that specific formulas and techniques, verbal and nonverbal, are expected to produce specific predictable results. However, science possesses a rigid experimental technique which does not exist in the primitive world of magic. Let us take an example from the field of preventive medicine and contrast the Indian attitude with that of science.

In 1909, the anthropologist Alanson Skinner (1911) went on a field trip to the Ojibwa Indians of Canada, where he observed a woman with a cross tattooed on each cheek. When asked the significance of the crosses, she said they were to prevent toothache. She believed there was a cause-and-effect relation between the presence of the crosses on her cheeks and the absence of toothaches. How does modern science test her hypothesis?

The common scientific procedure at the present time would be to select a population of naïve people from another locality who had not yet tattooed their cheeks, divide the population by some random device into two groups—an experimental group and a control group—tattoo crosses on the cheeks of the experimental group, and then, over a period of years, observe the frequency of toothache in the two groups. If the Indian woman's hypothesis is correct, the frequencies of toothache in the nontattooed group should be significantly greater than those in the tattooed group. If her hypothesis is incorrect, there should be no significant difference in the frequencies in the two groups. The scientific determination of significance is based on probability theory, and requires the application of a statistical formula to the frequencies. It is obvious that no Indian culture ever worked out such a formula. The tendency of all naïve persons who believe in such magic is to remember only the positive cases—those persons whose cheeks are tattooed and who are free of toothaches, and those persons whose cheeks are not tattooed and who do have toothaches. The negative instances—those persons with tattooed cheeks who have toothaches and those with neither tattooed cheeks nor toothaches— are usually overlooked or forgotten. The test cases which Indians and other unsophisticated peoples assemble to "prove" the efficacy of their magic never satisfy the criteria of modern science and are comparable to science only in a very superficial way.

If Indian shamans and priests have no adequate tests to demonstrate the efficacy of their arts, how do they build up reputations as religious or magical practitioners? The success of such operators may be explained in a number of ways: for instance, by the possession of fore-knowledge of the outcome of some event which is doubtful to others. Thus the rainmaker may possess real skill in forecasting the weather by the direction of the winds, the appearance of the clouds, or his feeling for relative humidity and atmospheric pressure. Modern orthopedists have shown that changes in barometric pressure can be felt by persons with arthritis. The rainmaker may likewise feel such changes "in his bones" and, if the weather signs are unfavorable, postpone his rainmaking rites to a time when he believes it more likely to rain.

The curing of disease with plant remedies is widespread among Indians, and some of such curatives are known by modern pharmacology to be efficacious. The best-known examples of modern drugs of Indian origin come from South America rather than from North America. Thus the coca plant, which contributes ingredients to our cocaine and Novocain, is used by many Indian medicine men of South America to alleviate pain. Curare, used as arrow and dart poison by the tropical forest Indians of that continent, is now an important adjunct to modern anesthesia. And the bark of the cinchona tree, from which quinine is derived, was used in other medicines of South American Indians. In North America, after twenty-five of Cartier's men had died of scurvy, a band of friendly Iroquois cured the rest by giving them a decoction of pine bark and needles, a source of vitamin C.

Many of the cures effected by Indian medicine men belong to the category of psychotherapy. Psychosomatic or psychogenic disease is— and was—at least as common among Indians as in European societies and their derivatives. The Indian psychotherapist may be just as skilled in helping his patients as the best psychiatrist or analyst in the modern world. Any of the hundreds of kinds of medicine men's cures may be equally as efficacious as modern psychotherapy for those who believe in them.

The mention of psychotherapy leads to the relation of emotions to religion and magic. Everyone agrees that emotional responses are everywhere associated with religion and magic, but so little is known about human emotions that nothing concrete can be said about this relationship. A mere listing of words such as "reverence," "awe," and "fear" tells us little. Perhaps it is more meaningful to say that all human emotions, whatever they are, may be associated with one or another of the many behaviors and beliefs usually subsumed under religion and magic. The emotions will vary from culture to culture, just as do the behaviors, verbal and nonverbal, which characterize each particular "system" of magic and religion. In extreme cases, such emotions may be violent enough to cause death or, on the other side of the ledger, be able to cure a person of a psychosomatic ailment capable of causing death.

Physiologists and psychiatrists do not agree on the precise physiological sequences which a human being experiences when he dies of emotional disturbance, but experiments with emotional stress on laboratory animals and observations of human patients undergoing severe stress from both physical injuries and emotional disturbance have thrown some light on the subject. At least two physiological stages may be distinguished: shock, and resistance to shock. Which comes first depends on the individual as well as on the nature of the stress. Stress which drives one individual to increased effort will cause another to fall into a faint or to cease to live. The person who increases his physiological and physical activity under stress is resisting the stress, while the one who faints is succumbing to the stress and is in a state of shock.

Walter B. Cannon (1942) found that intense fear or anger is characterized by a powerful resistance to shock, with the following effects on physiology: blood pressure is increased by the acceleration of the heart and the contraction of the small arteries; basal metabolism and body temperature rise; increased liberation of sugar into the blood from the liver occurs, and increased liberation of adrenalin into the blood from the adrenal glands follows; increase in blood chlorides also takes place; and dilation of the small bronchial tubes to increase the amount of air to the lungs results, as well as increased rate and depth of breathing. These changes give the mammal, human or subhuman, increased energy, which may be used in a fight with an opponent or in flight from an opponent. If the mammal wins the fight or escapes, these physiological changes return to normal; but if the stress continues or increases without the normal outlet into physical activity by which the mammal escapes the stress, shock and even death may follow.

The symptoms of shock are the opposite of those of resistance to shock. Blood pressure is lowered, not so much by deceleration of the heart as by loss of blood volume. Plasma escapes through the walls of the smaller arteries and veins, and other loss in body liquids is brought about by excessive sweating, vomiting, or diarrhea. This loss in body liquid is generally hastened by primitive medical prescriptions, which frequently forbid a patient to take food or water. At the approach of death from emotional disturbance, the following symptoms should be found in a human being, according to Cannon: rapid but weak pulse; cool and moist skin from perspiration; high cell count of blood due to loss of plasma; high blood sugar; low blood pressure. Then, if the patient dies, the proof that he died of emotional disturbance rather than of organic disease or injury would require a thorough autopsy of his remains. Needless to say, complete scientific proof of Indians dying of emotional disturbance has not yet been obtained, but many hard-headed scientists as well as anthropologists believe this is not only possible but that it has actually occurred over and over again. Deaths attributed to witchcraft may be of this kind, but organic disease may also be a factor in many such cases.

A study by Curt P. Richter (1957) modifies the sympathico-adrenal theory of Cannon, and shows that death from emotional stress can be caused by overstimulation of the parasympathetic nervous sytem. Richter placed rats in glass cylinders filled with water, in which the rat was compelled to swim constantly in order to keep alive. He found that wild rats were much more "frightened" by this experience than were tame rats descended from other laboratory animals. Wild rats would cease swimming, sink to the bottom, and die in a matter of minutes, while tame rats would swim for as much as sixty hours. It was found that death was preceded by a slowing of the heart rate, slowing of respiration rate, and lowering of body temperature—in other words, exclusively by shock symptoms. That the difference in the length of swimming time between wild and tame rats was due to previous emotional conditioning, and not to genetics, was proved when it was found that wild rats could be conditioned to swim for long intervals if they were kept in the water for only very short intervals in the beginning. They could learn that the situation was not hopeless and that they would be rescued by their keepers. Then, when the swimming time was gradually extended, the wild rats would adjust to the longer intervals and eventually swim about as long as the tame rats. This proves conclusively that the sudden death of the unconditioned wild rats was due to emotional disturbance rather than to other factors. Let us return to human beings.

Having prostrated our Indian by the fear of witchcraft and the resulting shock, we need only bring in the priest or shaman with his countertreatment to restore the patient to health. Under these conditions, the Indian medicine man may be more effective than all the statistically confirmed medical science in the books. This point has been recognized by some of our own physicians and surgeons who have worked among Indians.

A prominent abdominal surgeon, the late Dr. Thomas Noble of Indianapolis, began taking vacations in the Southwest in the 1940's. Here he contacted Navaho and Hopi Indians and made many friends among them. Being a surgeon, he was asked to treat the sick from time to time, and cases needing surgery were not lacking. Working in his trailer instead of in an operating room, with only his wife, who was a nurse, to help him, he performed appendectomies and other abdominal operations on Indians. But he never took a case without first obtaining the approval of a local medicine man, who engaged in his curative "chants" both before and after the operation. Dr. Noble believed that the patient's chances of recovery were greater if Indian curing rites were retained. Since that time, physicians employed by our federal government in Indian health programs have joined forces with the local medicine men in the belief that treatment by the latter has psychotherapeutic value and can actually contribute to the saving of lives.

This introduction to Indian religion would not be complete without mention of the social aspects of religion, which include meetings of cults, group ceremonies produced by cults, and public attendance of rites centering on an individual, such as a menstruating girl or a sick person, where the cults were absent. In Chapter 20 we showed that religious organizations were lacking in most of the Arctic, Sub-Arctic, Plateau, Great Basin, and Northeast Mexico. But religious meetings for anyone who cared to attend occurred in all these areas.

All these peoples conducted religious ceremonies of a public nature, whether for the benefit of a single individual or for that of the entire group. All Indian religions therefore are reinforced by group participation.

THE GODS AND PRIESTS OF THE AZTECS

Aztec religion was dominated by an extensive pantheon, carefully ranked in authority and power, and equally numerous orders of priests, each dedicated to the propitiation of one of the gods. The priests were also ranked in a system parallel to that of the gods they served. The higher political officials of the Aztec state were also technically priests, because all had been educated in the school for priests. Thus government and religion converged at the top of the hierarchy. Although religion, with its appeal to the emotions of supernatural personalities, was dominant, magic was also present. Medicine was a combination of religion, magic, and practical science. The many plant remedies (science) were regarded as ineffective without the proper incantations (magic) or prayers (religion). Physicians were sometimes priests but more often appear to have been shamans and herb doctors not associated with the priesthoods.

Aztec gods numbered more than one hundred. Vaillant (1941: 182–84) lists the sixty-three principal ones, each of which had its own officially recognized cult of priests dedicated to its worship. He groups these gods into a number of classes, to which we prefix the number in each class: four creative deities; three great gods; fifteen fertility gods; six gods of rain and moisture; three fire gods; four pulque gods; twelve planetary and stellar gods; six gods of death and earth; six variants of great gods; four other gods.

The universe was divided horizontally and vertically into sections of religious significance. There were five horizontal divisions, the four cardinal directions plus the center; certain gods were assigned to each of these divisions. More significant, however, were the vertical divisions, which reached a maximum of thirteen "heavens" and nine "hells" with all of the gods of the "heavens" being assigned to levels, according to rank, from top to bottom. This illustrates the generalization often made—that cultures possessing ranked social classes or other means of ranking their human members also tend to rank their gods in a parallel fashion. The creative deities were of highest rank, but were considered too remote from human affairs to be extensively

worshiped. It was the second-ranking group—the three great gods—
who intervened most in the affairs of man and were the most
worshiped: Huitzilopochtli, Hummingbird Wizard, War and Sun
God, chief god of Tenochtitlán; Tezcatlipoca, Smoking Mirror, chief
god of the pantheon, solar attributes, chief god of Texcoco; and
Quetzalcoatl, Feathered Serpent, God of Learning and of Priesthood,
chief god of Cholula, frequently shown as Ehecatl, the Wind God.

The routine of worship included the reciting of prayers, the performance of symbolic acts, and, above all, the giving of presents to
the gods to persuade or induce them to operate for the benefit of man
or at least for the people living at the town or city of which the god was
the patron. Of all the many things given to the gods as sacrifices, the
most precious was the human heart and blood. This was the food most
desired by the gods and most nutritious to their beings. In order for
man to win the many contests of the world, he must be aided by strong
gods, who, in turn, wax strongest on human hearts and blood; and,
because the hearts of brave enemies were the most difficult to obtain,
they were the most strength-giving to the gods. This belief led to the
vicious circle of more and more war and more and more human sacrifice, because the greater the success in war, the greater must be the
number of captives sacrificed to satisfy the divine appetite in order to
maintain or augment the quantity of aid from the supernatural, without which victory would have been impossible. The brutality and sad-
ism of some of the rituals of human sacrifice were so shocking to the
participants that drugs, such as tobacco, alcohol, and Jimson weed,
were frequently given to the priests as well as to the victims to steel
their nerves for the terrible ordeal. In justice to the Aztecs, it should be
mentioned that some of their sacrifices were staged with so much dig-
nity and drama that the religious significance transcended the taking
of human life. One such ceremony has been described by Vaillant.

In contrast to the callous brutality of the fire sacrifice, the ceremony in honor of the
god Tezcatlipoca was strikingly dramatic, tinged with the pathos with which we view
the taking of a life. The handsomest and bravest prisoner of war was selected a year before his execution. Priests taught him the manners of a ruler, and as he walked about,
playing divine melodies upon his flute, he received the homage due Tezcatlipoca himself. A month before the day of sacrifice four lovely girls, dressed as goddesses, became
his companions and attended to his every want. On the day of his death he took leave of
his weeping consorts to lead a procession in his honor, marked by jubilation and feasting.
Then he bade farewell to the glittering cortege and left for a small temple, accompanied
by the eight priests who had attended him throughout the year. The priests preceded him

up the steps of the temple, and he followed, breaking at each step a flute which he had played in the happy hours of his incarnation. At the top of the platform the priests turned him over the sacrificial block and wrenched out his heart. In deference to his former godhood his body was carried, not ignominiously flung, down the steps; but his head joined the other skulls spitted on the rack beside the temple. (Vaillant, 1941 : 202–3.)

The Aztecs also believed that the ghosts of the dead lived on in afterworlds for an indefinite period. The ghosts of warriors who had died in battle, or in sacrifice to the gods, went to one of the multiple heavens, where they were accorded great honor amid much luxury. The ghosts of women who had died in childbirth were likewise accorded a place of honor in another special heaven, because they too had made the supreme sacrifice in an attempt to give birth to sons who might become great warriors. The ghosts of those who had died by drowning, by being struck by lightning, or by other means connected with precipitation and water, were likewise accorded a berth in one of the heavens, where there were perpetual summer and plenty to eat and drink. The souls of the rest of the dead went to an underworld, where the Lord of the Dead assigned them to one of the nine subdivisions according to their status and experiences on earth. The underworlds, as compared with the heavens, were dreary and unattractive, but they were not places of perpetual torture like the Christian hell, nor was there any stigma attached to being there. Offerings were made to the ghosts of the dead at regular intervals after death, but there was no cult of the dead or enough formality involved to warrant labeling this practice "ancestor worship."

In addition to gods and ghosts, there was an indefinite number of other spirits associated with fields, mountaintops, springs, and other features of geography. There were also special spirits connected with individuals (personal spirit helpers), families, demes, craft guilds, and the group of itinerant merchant-spies. However, the roles of the gods in Aztec religion dominated the parts played by lesser spirits and ghosts.

At the end of each cycle of fifty-two years, all fires were allowed to go out or were extinguished. All the people destroyed their household furniture, fasted, and wept during the last five portentous days of the old cycle. Temple furnishings were also destroyed. At the exact moment when a certain star reached the meridian on the last night, the priests sacrificed a captive and kindled new fire with a wooden drill and hearth within the breast of the sacrificial victim. Runners lit torches from the new fire and rekindled all the temple fires in the vicinity, whence the people obtained the new fire for the hearths of their homes. The next day everyone set to work renovating and re-furnishing the houses and temples.

The organization of Aztec religion was briefly sketched above in Chapter 20, and need not be repeated here other than to repeat that it was merged with political organization at the top. Montezuma and other high officials were all graduates of the school for priests as well as that for laymen. It was this hierarchy of priests which was respon-sible for the almost perpetual round of religious ceremonies, which, in both numbers of participants and numbers of observers, far ex-ceeded those of any other area. In terms of its total configuration, the religion of the Aztecs, and some of their Meso-American neighbors as well, was far more elaborate than that of any other culture area in native North America.

Native North American medicine probably also reached its highest point among the Aztecs, who had built much of their knowledge on that of the Mayas and other Meso-American peoples. Aztec medicine included, to be sure, many magical and religious elements. Healing was accompanied by charms, astrological symbols, dances, and incant-ations. Many medicinal plants were named after or associated with particular gods. Some remedies were used also as amulets, or chosen according to the principles of sympathetic magic. It represents, none-theless, a significant advance in medicine, with medical and surgical specialization advanced to the point that they foreshadowed scientific experimentation. The emperor Montezuma, who devoted his mag-nificent pleasure gardens to flowers, blossoming fragrant trees, and aromatic or medicinal herbs, ordered his physicians to make experi-ments with the herbs and to employ only those thoroughly known and tested to cure illness in the imperial court. Furthermore, Aztec methods of animal and human sacrifice must have contributed to knowledge, at least by the priesthood, of internal anatomy.

At the time of the Spanish Conquest, the Aztecs distinguished several types of healers. The *ticitl* (diviners) chanted spells and administered charms. The *curanderos* relieved suffering manually or with medicines. The *tepati* were believed to cure disease by means of knowledge and healing powers received from the gods. These three categories were, moreover, divided into specialists for various types of disease and in-juries. In addition, they distinguished *temixiuitiani* (midwives), *papiani* (pharmacists), and *panamacani* (dealers in drugs). Women as well as men were trained in the arts of medicine and divination. The medicinal values of herbs were common knowledge among the people, who concocted many home remedies from their own gardens.

Records of Aztec surgery are comparatively meager. We know, however, that the native doctors were skillful at trephining, castration, suturing facial wounds with hair, lancing boils and swellings, removing growths and white opacities from the eyes, and splicing long bones with slivers of bone or wood. Tumors which did not respond to herbal applications were lanced but not removed. Fractures were not only set but were also encased in plasters made of downy feathers, gum, and resin with an outer coat of a rubberlike gum. Surgical instruments were made of sharpened wood or bone, thorns, obsidian, and probably of gold, silver, or copper. Thorn or bone needles were used for sewing up incisions. Wounds were washed with water, salt solution, urine, or herbal decoctions. Infected wounds or boils were sometimes cauterized with burning oil. Various wound dressings were used, including one of honey and salt.

Diseases were attributed by the Aztecs principally to punishment by the gods, but also to uncleanliness, all forms of personal intemperance, and atmospheric conditions of extreme heat, cold, humidity, wind, or dust. Prophylactic measures, in addition to cleanliness and sanitation, included fumigating with incense. Unpleasant fumes from burning mouse nests, hair, rubber-producing sap, or odoriferous plants were thought to drive away disease or evil. Much of the incense, however, was pleasantly fragrant with oil of cedar, pine, copal, or aromatic herbs. The fragrance of flowers and herbs was used to dispel unpleasant odors and to treat fevers, melancholia, and fatigue. A prescription to relieve the weariness of government officials was made from sweet-smelling flowers and leaves. Other aromatic prescriptions included lotions for tired feet, for the fetid odor of invalids, and, after thorough bathing, to prevent armpit odor. Purificatory treatments included enemas, ear syringing, brushing teeth and removing tartar, cold baths, steam baths, and baths in sulfur springs.

Pharmaceutical remedies were usually complex mixtures of plant extracts, to which mineral and animal ingredients were often added. Pearls, emeralds, and other precious stones, and bezoars from lizards, birds, or mammals were used as medicines and as amulets. Mineral ingredients also included salt, niter, alum, red ocher, and various other earths. Animal constituents included blood, bile, and brains; decoctions of snakes, scorpions, and millipedes; human teeth or bones; ash from burned horn, bone, or excrement; and charcoal prepared from various animals. Most numerous, however, were the ingredients made from plants and trees. These included hundreds of medicinal substances, narcotics, analgesics, and stimulants, administered orally or by enema. Many of them were of practical therapeutic value, as, for instance, a species of *Ephedra*, used by the Aztecs in the treatment of common colds, and several species of *Datura*, containing hyoscyamine, atropine and scopalamine, which were included in various prescriptions to relieve pain.

A typical prescription is the following, for "treatment of the head." The shrubs *xiuhecapahtli*, *yztac ocoxochitl*, *teamoxtli*, and the precious stones *tetlahuitl*, *yztactlalli*, *eztetl*, *tematlatzin*, ground together in cold water and applied to the head, were thought to stop heat in the head and, when ground in hot water, to stop coldness therein. These hot or cold packs were applied three times a day—morning, noon, and evening—and the neck and throat were bound with the sinew of an eagle's foot and neck. One suffering from headache should eat onions in honey, should not sit in the sun, and should not work or enter the baths (Emmart, 1940).

THE MAGIC AND MEDICINE MEN OF THE NAVAHO

Navaho religion, magic, and medicine are a mixture of the primitive shamanism of the Mackenzie Sub-Arctic and the priest-dominated religions of the Pueblo peoples. The acculturation of the Navaho to the Pueblo way of life began between five hundred and one thousand years ago when the former arrived in the Southwest. The Navaho religious leader has the attributes of both priest and shaman. The words of his chants are learned verbatim from an older medicine man, together with the associated tunes. Such a large body of fixed ritual is generally associated with organized priesthoods, but the Navaho medicine men are not organized into cults of any kind, and in no sense are they officials of any governmental unit. Their individuality identifies them with the shaman. Although the chants were formerly employed to aid all human activities, including hunting and warfare, the gradual depletion of game after White contact and the abrupt cessation of warfare in 1864 did away with these uses of chants. At the present time the curative powers of chants dominate Navaho religion, magic, and medicine.

The Navaho classify personalities into two types: the Earth Surface

People, including living human beings and their ghosts after they die; the Holy People, the gods and lesser spirits who travel around on sunbeams, on the rainbow, and on flashes of lightning. Although the Holy People have great powers to help or harm human beings, they are not always superior in knowledge or in power to man, and they perform evil as well as good deeds. They are both supplicated and coerced, but it is coercion that dominates Navaho religion and magic.

Changing Woman is the dominant personality among the Holy People. She was the principal creator of man, and helped teach him how to control and keep in harmony the forces of nature, such as the wind, storms, lightning, and animals. The meeting at which man was permitted to witness the ceremony of the Holy People harmonizing the forces of nature is reenacted by man in the Blessing Way Chant. Second in importance to Changing Woman is her husband the Sun. Sun symbolism penetrates every aspect of Navaho religion and magic. Third in rank are the Hero Twins, Monster Slayer and Child of the Water, who are propitiated in most ceremonies. Of lesser importance are First Man and First Woman. First Man was the creator of the universe. There are several groups of lesser spirits: Failed-To-Speak People, such as Water Sprinkler, Fringed Mouth, Hunchback, who commonly impersonated in the great public Chants; animals and personifications of natural forces, such as Coyote, Big Snake Man, Crooked Snake People, Thunder People, and Wind People; those who help the Holy People and serve as intermediaries between them and man, such as Big Fly and Corn Beetle. Of all these Holy People, only Changing Woman is unchanging in her attitude toward man and always helpful to man. All the others play at times the roles of tricksters, witches, and other harmful beings, and are feared. The ghosts of the dead are feared even more, so that the dominant feature of Navaho religion and magic is the warding off of evil.

The Holy People live in an underworld, as do also the ghosts of the dead. Life after death is neither pleasurable nor painful, but is a bit on the dreary side. Fear of ghosts is intense; no matter how affectionate, helpful, and friendly a person has been while alive, his ghost is always potentially dangerous. Any slip in the complicated burial routine will offend the ghost and cause it to hover around the grave, or the house where it lived while alive, in order to take revenge on the wrongdoer.

Witchcraft has been most thoroughly investigated among the Navaho, who, in their own language, divide it into several distinct categories: Witchery Way or witchcraft proper (*ʔant'i*); Sorcery (several types referred to by the -*nzin* stem); Wizardry (*ʔadagas*); and Frenzy Witchcraft (*ʔazile*). In addition, they mention Disease Witchcraft and Eagle Pit Sorcery, both of which seem to be specialized forms of Sorcery.

The classic Witchery Way technique consists in the administration of "corpse poison," a concoction made from the flesh of corpses, preferably of dead children, that of twins being especially effective. It is ground into powder and may be given in food or cigarettes, blown into the victim's face, spread on his blanket, or dropped into his hogan through the smoke hole. Witches are closely associated with the ghosts of the dead and with incest. Male witches are more numerous than female. Witchery is usually learned from an older relative, and the initiation into Witchery Way is said to include killing a brother or sister. Witches gain wealth by robbing graves or by fee splitting; one witch makes a person ill, and his partner witch cures the patient and collects a fee. Witches are thought to roam at night as were-animals (wolves, coyotes, bears, and owls), to meet in witches' sabbaths to plan and perform rites to kill or injure people, to have intercourse with dead women, to initiate new members, and to practice cannibalism.

Sorcery is considered a branch of witchery in the Navaho scheme. Sorcerers attend the witches' sabbath, but they are considered less violent than witches, and they use a different set of techniques. Sorcery is usually performed by contagious magic and incantation or spell. The sorcerer obtains a bit of the victim's hair, nails, excretions, or clothing, buries it in a grave or with something taken from a grave, and chants a spell over it. He may also make an "evil-wishing" sand painting or—rarely—practice *envoûtement* by molding or carving an image of the victim and injuring it.

Wizardry is, to the Navaho, the practice of shooting "arrows" (foreign particles, such as bits of stone, bone, quill, ashes, and charcoal) into the victim. English-speaking Navaho sometimes call it "bean shooting," though actual beans are not used. Wizards are almost exclusively old men, but they do not become were-animals, nor do they attend the witches' sabbath.

Wizardry is normally cured by Sucking Way, which includes not only sucking but also singing and application of medicaments (dried and powdered blue lizard, "witchcraft plant," and so on) to the wound. The sucker is generally considered by the Navaho to be a wizard himself, or in league with wizards. Victims of Sorcery and Disease Witchcraft may be cured by recovery of the clothes, excrement, or other buried materials and by the smoke of the Game Way ceremony.

Victims of all types of witchcraft, but especially of its most serious form, Witchery Way, may be cured by catching the witch and obtaining his confession. If the witch refuses to confess, he is usually killed. If he confesses, the victim will gradually improve, and the witch will die within the year from the same symptoms which have afflicted the victim. Witchcraft of all sorts may also be counteracted by prayer ceremonials or by chants. Thus Prostitution Way Chant (evil in itself) may be combined with Blessing Way to form a cure for Frenzy Witchcraft.

While the Navaho Indians have a definitely complex philosophy of disease, they also retain many of the primitive ideas shared with more primitive groups. Thus illness may be caused not only by sorcery or witchcraft, but by ghosts, by contact with the dead or things connected with the dead, by dreams of catastrophe or death, or by incompletely buried monsters. Their more complex theories of disease are bound up with the idea of taboo transgression and lack of harmony with the universe. Navaho life is full of restrictions, many of which are disregarded in ordinary circumstances and remembered only when illness or catastrophe strikes the offender. Ignorance is no excuse for transgression. Transgressions may, similarly, offend the spirits, who may retaliate by shooting invisible arrows or by inducing other forms of object, animal, or spirit intrusion. Diagnosis is made by medicine men, who determine the cause of the illness by gazing at the heavenly bodies, by "listening," by "trembling," or by all three combined. The medicine man, guided by his innate supernatural power, sees a symbol of the ceremony which should be used for the cure.

Since all objects, beings, spirits, and events are thought to be in mystic relationship and sympathy, such diverse ceremonies as the Wind Chant, the Male Shooting Chant, the Big Star Chant, the Bead Chant, and the War Ceremony may be used to cure disease. All of these ceremonies are closely connected with Navaho myths of cosmogony and creation. In modern life, many of them, especially the War Ceremony, have lost their former practical utility. Their principal function nowadays is therapeutic.

The Chants or Ways of the Navaho follow, to a large extent, the ceremonial procedures of the Pueblo Indians, whom the Navaho consider their superiors in the arts of the supernatural, and are extremely complex, elaborate, and colorful. The Navaho War

Ceremony, however, suggests a relationship to Plains warfare and ritual. As conducted nowadays by the Navaho, these ceremonies have two principal aims: purification, to get rid of object, creature, or spirit intrusion; identification, to promote mystic harmony between the patient and other elements of the natural or supernatural world. Purification is attained through sweating, emetics, and bathing. Identification is achieved by means of chants, sand paintings, medicine bundles, and the like.

Ceremonies last from one to nine "nights." In the full nine-night ceremonies, the first night consists of an hour or two of singing and simple ritual. The early morning hours of the first four days are taken up with sweat-emetic rites to drive out evil and to purify not only the patient but all participants. The first four afternoons are devoted to the preparation of prayer sticks, which are prayed over and then placed at designated points as a compulsive invitation to the deities to attend the ceremony. At dawn on the fifth day, the contents of the Singer's medicine bundle are laid out on an altar. The Singer prays over each object in turn, and the patient touches each item as it is deposited on the altar.

On each of the next four days, a sand painting is made inside the house. Some of these sand paintings are so elaborate as to require as many as forty assistants working eight or ten hours. When the painting is finished, the patient sits on it, while the Singer applies sand from the various figures of the painting to specified parts of the patient's body and performs other ritualistic acts, all designed to identify the patient with the deities represented in the painting. The eighth day is called "The Day." Early in the morning, the patient, with the aid of his relatives, shampoos his hair and bathes his body in suds made from the yucca (soapweed) root and dries himself with ceremonially ground cornmeal.

During each night the singing continues, becoming longer as the ceremony progresses. The Singer, who must know a vast number of songs, starts the required song and helps the chorus of laymen around him to sing it. On the ninth night, "The Night," the singing lasts until dawn, summarizing all the purification, invocation, attraction of power, and identification of the preceding rites. Throughout the vigil the patient concentrates on all the singing and ritual.

Participants, in addition to the patient, are supposed to be benefited in proportion to their proximity to the ritual. If the patient himself is not cured, failure is attributed to mistaken diagnosis and use of the wrong ceremony. Even minute errors in the proper chant may ruin its therapeutic efficacy. Occasionally, it is thought, a suitable chant may nonetheless injure the patient or the Singer by being "too strong" for his innate powers.

Many cures have been reported, sometimes in cases given up by White physicians, not only by Navaho but by several unprejudiced White observers. Whether any of these can be rationally ascribed to the "chant lotions" and other remedies administered is uncertain. The Navaho, like most other Indian tribes, have an extensive pharmacopoeia, including a number of simples and compounds of real medicinal value. But Navaho ceremonialism functions most efficiently as a form of group psychotherapy, reinforcing the patient's faith in himself and in the moral support of his social group.

THE FORGIVING CREEKS

Perhaps the most distinctive feature of Creek religion and magic was the forgiving of every wrong short of murder at the greatest ceremony of the year, the Green Corn Dance. Offenders sometimes hid out in the woods until the time for this ceremony arrived, when they returned to their villages to be forgiven and reinstated as full citizens. The making of new fire, from which each housewife obtained fire for her hearth, is reminiscent of Meso-America. Like the Navaho, the Creek religious specialists possessed attributes of both priests and shamans. They performed fixed rituals and uttered verbatim prayers at public ceremonies in the temples or council house, and also made direct contact with the supernatural in dreams and hallucinations. Young men were trained to be medicine men in schools, but these were much less formal than those of the Aztecs, although civil officials were chosen from the graduates. Creek medicine is a mixture of religion, magic, and herbalism, like that of so many other Indians, and its distinctive feature, if it has one, would be the emphasis on animals as the causers of disease.

The Creek Indians, formerly of Alabama and Georgia, believed in a supreme deity, who lived in the sky and was associated with, but not identical to, the sun. His representative on earth was the spirit in the Busk fire or other sacred fires, who served as a sort of liaison officer between the supreme deity and man. There were a great number of lesser spirits difficult to classify. Among these were: two other spirits closely connected with the Busk; meteorological phenomena, such as the wind; pygmies or giants in human form who lived in the forest; a host of other animal or animal-like spirits, including water serpents, a horned snake, a monster lizard, eagles, hawks, owls, panthers, bears, deer, all of which were thought to have souls like human beings and to possess human attributes. In addition to this host of spiritual beings, the ghosts of the dead who had been slain by the enemy were thought to hover about the houses of their living relatives until their deaths had been avenged, when they departed to a spiritual world to join the other ghosts.

The earth was believed to be flat and square, and the sky a solid dome on which the supreme deity lived. Eclipses were supposed to be caused by an animal trying to swallow the sun or moon. The various mythological animals living in water were thought to control rain, starting or stopping it at will. Good ghosts went to dwell in the sky, while evil ones went west.

As in other Indian cultures, every important event was hedged by religion. Hunters, warriors, menstruants, parturients, mourners, and young men training to be medicine men secluded themselves, fasted, and observed a host of taboos supposed to protect them from harm or aid them in their undertaking. One White observer was of the opinion that the fasting and other taboos associated with a war expedition were harder on the men than the actual traveling and fighting. There were many omens by which the success or failure of an undertaking was judged in advance and numerous charms and fetishes to ward off evil.

The Green Corn Dance, or Busk, held when the flour corn was in the roasting-ear stage, in July or August, was the most important single ceremony among the Creeks. The Busk was the fourth and culminating ceremony in a series of similar rites which began about April. Up until the time of the Busk, no one was permitted to eat any of the season's corn, on pain of being barred from attending the ceremony. The term "Busk" is a trader's corruption of the word *boskita*, meaning "to fast." This ceremony was a New-Year rite to renew or regenerate the entire world and the plants, animals, and human beings who lived on it. It was believed to have been taught to the Creeks by the supreme deity, and the leading roles were played by the highest-ranking medicine men, who made the new fire and brewed the "black drink." While the selection of the date at the time of corn ripening establishes the fact that the ceremony centered on corn, animal spirits were also sometimes propitiated with an eye to better hunting, and a fresh start in moral matters was instituted by forgiving every offense short of murder. This last point was a remarkable concession for a people steeped in a tradition of blood feuds and "eye for an eye and tooth for a tooth" notions of justice. It meant that a measure of internal peace had been brought to irritable, vengeful personalities. While peace and tranquility were dominant during the Busk ceremony, the cause of war was not entirely omitted. The warriors occupied their graded bed platforms in the town square, were granted new names for distinguished war deeds of the past year, and advanced accordingly in position in the seating arrangement. They also put on a sham battle against enemy effigies.

The New Year's aspect included the manufacturing of new clothing, household articles, tools and weapons, and the destruction of the old articles. Furthermore, all house fires in the town were extinguished on the first day of the Busk and renewed afterward on the fourth day from the sacred Busk fire made anew with the drill on the first day.

The ritual normally occupied four days, but was sometimes repeated for a total of eight. While there was much variation in procedure from town to town, or from one historical source to another, the following is a generalized calendar of main events. On the first day, the town square was cleared and arranged, and a new fire was started. On the second day, a feast on new corn was held. On the third day, there was fasting by all mature men, followed by drinking the emetic called the "black drink," concocted from *Ilex vomitoria*. On the fourth day, a feast of venison seasoned with salt was held. Ball games were played for amusement by young men; a wide variety of dances were given in the evening, largely for the same purpose. In later historic times, the Busk served as a catch-all for almost every fragment of public ceremony left. Sexual continence was observed by everyone during the entire four days, the men sleeping in the town square.

Among a number of minor public ceremonies of a social or religious character, there was a celebration, whenever there had been a successful hunt, in which an entire town would take part in feasting and dancing. During epidemics everyone would fast and drink medicines publicly to counteract the disease. Council meetings were held periodically, and were always preceded by the formal serving of the "black drink," starting first with the chief and proceeding according to rank. Thus each individual's rank was demonstrated by the council seating arrangement and the order in which he was served. When the ball post was erected in the central area of a new town, a tree was felled without being allowed to touch the ground, and a scalp or skull was placed in the bottom of the posthole. There were at least thirty dances with animal names and mimicry which were danced at any time, mostly as entertainment. They were frequently given as informal additions to important ceremonies such as the Busk.

Medicine men derived some of their power from the supernatural and some from such natural remedies as herbs. While some of these were efficacious according to the standards of modern science, most were probably not. Their curing method consisted mostly of psychotherapy and was effective against the many fears and anxieties of native life; but against smallpox, measles, and other diseases of European origin, for which the Indian had no racial immunity, it was unsuccessful, and mortality was high. A neat distinction between natural and supernatural was not made by these Indians, because, even when plant remedies were used, the medicine men had to collect and administer them along with verbal formulas in a manner satisfactory to the supernatural. The distinction between the shaman, who derives his power directly from the supernatural, and the priest, who learns rituals, songs, and verbal formulas from another priest, is not sharply drawn for this area. The same individuals often did both. For this reason the simpler term, medicine man, has been chosen.

There were several classes of medicine men among the Creeks: a class of diviners, called "knowers," who prophesied future events and diagnosed disease (twins were likely to belong to this class); the graduates of the medicine men's school; controllers of the weather (mostly rain) or of floods in streams, and dew makers; witches or wizards, who were not always known because of the evil nature of their activities. The latter were supposed to be filled with lizards, which forced them to commit murder, but they might be cured of this impulse by being made to vomit up the lizards.

The medicine men's school was taught by an experienced "priest" of the highest degree, who tutored each student individually, sending him to an isolated spot to sweat, fast, and take medicines in order to attain direct contact with the supernatural. A student who succeeded in his first four-day attempt and obtained his "degree" was eligible to try again for the second "degree" a year or so later, with his second isolation period extended to eight days. Along with this vision seeking went a considerable amount of instruction in songs, dances, verbal formulas, and concocting of medicines—all for a price, because the graduate medicine man always charged the laymen for his services. The third and final "degree" was obtained after a twelve-day vigil. The war leader and the head medicine man for town ceremonies were chosen from this group of third "degree" graduates, although proper sib affiliation also was a factor. This was the class of medicine men which was officially recognized and whose leaders might hold permanent town offices. Individuals wore insignia indicative of their achievements—a buzzard feather for one who could heal gunshot wounds; a foxskin for one who could cure snake bite; an owl feather if he could trail the enemy in the dark.

Native classification of causes of disease is nonexistent or unreported. Instead, we are given long lists of reptiles, birds, mammals, meteorological phenomena, mythological phenomena, and mythological characters as causers of specific ailments. For example, when mumps was caught from Whites in the eighteenth century, the Indians thought it was caused by cattle, because they were beginning to eat beef at that time. Their choice of cattle from among the dozens or hundreds of things they had derived from the Whites by that date reflects the persistence of the native notion that animals cause most disease. There is a suggestion in one account that the wrath of an animal spirit was inflamed by the breaking of some taboo in connection with the manner of hunting or disposing of its body parts. The cures were plant medicines which had to be concocted and administered in the correct way with the proper songs, dances, verbal formulas, and motions. Most of these medicines were taken internally. The gourd rattle was the instrument used to accompany the singing and dancing of the doctor, which were done more often to diagnose the disease than to cure it.

That foreign physical materials were thought to enter the body and cause disease is demonstrated by the bloodletting and sucking techniques to remove them. This is equivalent to lancing and poulticing an area of infection or poison, and was certainly efficacious for such things as snake bite. The shaman sometimes sucked directly with his mouth, at other times through a bison horn, the large end of which was cupped over the wound. When nothing unusual was removed from the infected area, the shaman would plant some small object in the discharge to convince the patient that he had extracted the cause of the ailment.

The sweat bath was prescribed by both laymen and doctors to cure disease. A dome-shaped hut, covered with hides or mats, was built especially for this purpose, and into this were rolled hot stones on which water was sprinkled to create water vapor. When the patient had

had all of this he could endure, he plunged into the waters of the nearest stream. From the many accounts of this custom from many tribes of Indians, it seems quite possible that the heat was sufficient to induce an artificial fever, which would aid recovery from some ailments. The shock experienced by plunging into cold water after the sweat bath is parallel to hydrotherapy treatments so commonly used today for patients suffering from nervous tension. Therefore it was probably effective for ailments of a psychosomatic nature.

Bandages and splints were employed, and the sick were transported on litters. A doctor who lost a patient was suspected of witchcraft, and might himself be killed by the deceased patient's relatives.

THE VISION QUEST OF THE SANPOIL

The Sanpoil, who lived in eastern Washington state, in the Plateau culture area, had the minimum of social, political, and religious organization. Their emphasis was on the vision quest, the spirit helpers obtained on the quest, and the multiple souls possessed by humans. Because every man went on a vision quest, and practically all claimed on return to have contacted the supernatural, there was no sharp distinction between shaman and layman. Shamans merely possessed a greater number of spirit helpers or more powerful ones than the layman, and any layman might be upgraded to the position of shaman if he acquired more power or more spirits on another vision quest. Such quests were repeated throughout life, and any unusual good fortune that befell a man was thought to have come from the supernatural. The concept of magic probably existed among the Sanpoil, but it was overshadowed by the plethora of spiritual personalities. Priests were totally absent because there were no religious organizations or standardized rituals. Natural diseases were more clearly distinguished from those of supernatural causation than is generally the case with Indians.

The Sanpoil distinguished six kinds of spiritual personalities. The first was the god Sweat Lodge, who was the creator of animals and spirits and perhaps of human beings as well. He was a benevolent deity, and answered the prayers of all who appealed to him by sweating in a sweat lodge and praying in song. The second kind was the soul, which animated the living human body and resided in the viscera near the heart. Death would result if it left the body. When a person died, the soul left his body, going either at once to the land of the dead or roaming about on earth after being transformed into a ghost. Ghosts belonged to the third kind of spiritual beings. The fourth kind consisted of spirits who had never resided in the bodies of human beings. They took on the forms of animals, plants, inanimate objects, and physical phenomena of nature. It was a spirit of this type which every youth sought on his quest for a spirit helper, who became so identified with his human host that departure brought on sickness or death. When a person died, his spirit helper did not cease to exist but underwent a transformation comparable to that from soul to ghost mentioned above. This transformed spirit, which belongs to a fifth kind, may be called a "spirit-ghost." Such spirit-ghosts could form an association with a relative of the deceased or with a shaman as an additional source of supernatural power, secondary to the primary spirit which everyone of any consequence acquired early in life. The sixth category included all dangerous supernatural personalities, embracing ogres, monsters, demons, and evil dwarfs. The Sanpoil made no attempt to quantify the numbers of spiritual beings in each of the six categories; but it is apparent that they totaled at least double the number of human beings on earth, because most living persons possessed two.

A soul was possessed by human beings of all ages, including the unborn child. Because it never left the body without undergoing transformation, it was not assigned any visible form. Unconsciousness, as well as death, was attributed to soul loss, and no distinction in the Sanpoil language is made between unconsciousness and death. Here we have a fundamental difference between native ideology and that of modern medical science.

At death, the soul had two alternatives: it could go at once to the land of the dead at the end of the Milky Way in the sky; or it could be transformed into a ghost and remain on earth. If it went to the land of the dead, it never returned to earth or communicated with men on earth. It gave up all individual activity and assumed a nirvana-like status, which—strangely—was a desirable one. Everyone hoped his soul would attain the limbo of the land of the dead and not remain on earth as a ghost in a condition of perpetual torment. Ghosts varied from complete visibility to invisibility, but generally were shadowy or vague in outline. Some were without heads or other body parts, but they were usually garbed in opaque clothing. They appeared both in the daytime and at night, but never to more than one person at a time. Ghosts remained on earth for different reasons: if a person before death had hidden an object of value in a place unknown to any human being, his ghost would stay on to watch the object; if hair or nail parings of the deceased were left undestroyed, the ghost would hover around to watch them also. If a spirit helper was buried with the corpse, or if the deceased had failed to confess some wrongdoing before death, the ghost was likewise compelled to remain on earth.

Spirits were most commonly animals, and every known animal functioned as a spirit helper for somebody in the society. However, rocks, lakes, mountains, and even some inanimate objects possessed spirits, as did also whirlwinds and clouds. Such spirits were not arranged in a neat hierarchy of authority, although some were generally regarded as being more powerful than others. Although spirits were never equated with the souls and ghosts associated with human beings, they always assumed human form when appearing before men, only to change back again to their original forms when an interview was ended. Such spirits usually appeared to man only during vision quests, in dreams, at the winter dances, and in times of trouble. The loss of one's spirit helper resulted in sickness and, if not found and returned to its host, in death. Shamans both recovered lost spirit helpers and stole them on other occasions.

Every boy was compelled to seek a spirit helper at an early age, and girls went on such quests if their parents encouraged them to do so. A young man past puberty who had failed to acquire a spirit helper could look forward to only the most meager kind of life with the minimum of rewards. Not more than 10 per cent of youths failed to acquire spirit power in this manner. Perhaps 70 or 80 per cent of the girls did not obtain spirit helpers but, as this was not mandatory for success in feminine pursuits, they led satisfactory lives without this experience. Most men boasted of more than one spirit helper, and it was taken for granted that the most successful men possessed more than one such power. The greatest Sanpoil shaman possessed six spirit helpers and one spirit-ghost.

A boy went on his first spirit quest, a vigil of only one night, at about eight years of age. As he became older, the period was gradually extended to several nights. An old man, most often a grandfather, instructed the boy in the technique of acquiring a vision. The youngster would be told to go to the top of a certain mountain or to the shore of a particular lake where he was likely to find a spirit. The boy stayed out alone all night, sitting beside a fire on the mountain or diving repeatedly into the cold waters of the lake. To make sure that the boy went to the designated spot, the old man would give him a peculiarly shaped stick or piece of hide to leave at the spot, so that the old man could find the object the next day and confirm the fact that the boy had indeed been there. The youth was supposed to stay awake all night, but it is said that that rule was often broken.

The vision involved seeing a spirit in the guise of a human being in a dream or hallucination. The spirit revealed its true identity to the child, told him the activities in which he would be especially successful as an adult, and listed the kinds of harm from which it would protect him. For instance, the lad might be told that he would be lucky in gambling, would be a great hunter, would be able to bring rain in time of drought, or that he would be protected from injury in battle. Then the spirit taught the boy a song, which was supposed to be an original one different, at least in detail, from every other song; when this was sung at a later date, it called forth the boy's supernatural power and assured his success in the undertakings listed by his spirit helper. In addition to the loneliness and fear experienced by the boy, fasting from food and water on the longer quests increased his discomfort and helped induce the hallucinations or illusions regarded as visitations of spirits.

Shamanistic power was obtained in exactly the same manner as any other kind of power, and a young man could tell from the spirit's instructions and song whether he would become a successful shaman. Shamans normally possessed both more numerous spirit helpers and more powerful ones than other men. Spirit helpers were not sought in all-night vigils after the age of adolescence, but they were thought to contact men on their own volition up to almost any age.

The results of the first successful vision quest in childhood or adolescence were not disclosed to anyone for many years. Then, when the visionary was twenty-five or thirty years of age, and had achieved full adult status, his spirit helper would return. This caused him to get spirit sickness, a feeling of lonesomeness and despondency, which usually came on in the early winter. Only a shaman could cure such sickness. The shaman first located the spirit in the patient's body, then removed it, held it in his hands long enough to learn the song it had given the patient, and, finally, blew it back into the patient's body. Next, the shaman sang the song, with the patient joining in before it was finished or repeating it a second time. After thus receiving back his spirit and his song, the patient recovered and was able to leave his bed, but he was not entirely well until he had sung the new song almost continuously for several days.

During the coldest part of the winter, when it was almost impossible to fish or hunt, the Sanpoil lived on stored foods for about two months. It was at this time that spirits most often recontacted their human hosts, and public dances were held to validate this renewal of spirit power. Such "winter dances" were sponsored most often by a shaman, but never by a group of shamans because they were not organized in any way. Sometimes, however, such a dance was sponsored by the individual who had received the power, or by one directed to do so by his spirit helper. A winter dance lasted two or three nights, and was attended by every adult who cared to witness the ceremony. Each person who had recently received supernatural power impersonated his spirit helper in a dance. Many such dances occurred during the winter period, and a single person might attend all within accessible distance of his home. These dances served as initiation ceremonies, in which the shaman helped the young man to entice his spirit helper to come to the dance house and ensconce itself in his body. This was the proof that the youth had acquired a personal spirit.

In Chapter 20, we pointed out again and again that the principal purpose of sodality initiations was to facilitate contact between the initiates and supernatural personalities. The Sanpoil winter dances had the same function, but the absence of any organization of shamans or other participants rules out the sodality there. Like the sodality ceremonies, the Sanpoil winter dances also gave the experienced shaman a chance to demonstrate his control over his supernatural powers, sometimes with the aid of illusory tricks.

Disease among the Sanpoil was divided into two major classes: natural and supernatural. Natural ailments included headaches, the common cold, injuries from such inanimate objects as sharp stones, and tuberculosis. Supernatural illnesses were divided into five subclasses: injuries inflicted by animate beings other than men; diffuse internal illnesses; afflictions of the mind; spirit illness; magical "poisoning."

In the first supernatural subclass are included serious wounds resulting from attacks by bears, wolves, and snakes, which were interpreted as being caused by the spirits of the animals. The reason that these animal spirits wished to harm a man might be his failure to follow the dictates of his spirit helper, or jealousy between his spirit helper and the animal spirit.

The second subclass includes fevers and contagious diseases caused by intrusion into the body of foreign matter, and this, in turn, might be

caused by the breaking of taboos or by sorcery initiated by an un-
friendly shaman.

Afflictions of the mind were thought to be caused by a shaman
projecting one of his spirit helpers into the body of the victim. Such
spirit intrusion brought on raving, delirium, and insanity, and could be
cured by a more powerful shaman removing the foreign spirit.

Spirit illness was caused either by the sudden return of one's spirit
helper or by its equally sudden departure. Loss of one's spirit came
about by burying it with a corpse or by its being stolen by a shaman.
The former case was hopeless, but the latter could be cured by the
recovery of the stolen spirit by a more powerful shaman.

Magical poisoning was a form of contagious magic, and was
engaged in only by lay women—not men—and not women shamans. A
lock of hair, some nail parings, or a piece of the victim's clothing was
ground up in a witches' mixture of a certain root, red paint, the body of
a bat, and a bit of bone from a corpse. As the mixture was being ground,
the name of the victim and his desired fate were muttered, after which
the stuff was placed in the victim's food or tossed on the dirtiest refuse
heap in the vicinity. Soon the victim would wither away or break out in
sores over his body. A cure was difficult, even for a shaman.

The first task of the shaman was to diagnose the ailment. After
smoking a pipe of tobacco for a few moments, the shaman placed a
hand on various parts of the patient's body, singing his doctoring songs
at the same time. The audience then joined in the songs, beating time
with sticks on the floor planks or on a log. When the intrusive object or
spirit was located in the body of the patient, the shaman attempted to
remove it by making a drawing-out motion with his hands or by
"sucking" with deep inhalation an inch or two from the afflicted area
of the body. The extracted spirit or object was immersed in a basket of
water, where it was harmless. Shamans were paid only if they effected a
definite cure. Some, however, used their power to cause illness in order
to obtain the fee for curing it.

The Sanpoil used plant remedies to cure the ailments regarded as of
natural causation. Verne Ray (1932: 217–22) lists forty-three species
used for this purpose, but cautions that many such remedies have been
forgotten and that the total would probably include half the total
number of species available in the area. Knowledge of medicinal plants
was not secret, and was shared by both men and women. Plants were
most often crushed, boiled in water, and applied both externally and
internally, according to the nature of the ailment. The sweathouse was

used for the curing of natural illnesses, except for the common cold. Growths over the eye and warts anywhere on the body were removed by surgery, and boils were lanced.

THE POSSESSIONAL SHAMANISM OF THE ESKIMO

Possessional shamanism was the rule everywhere in the Arctic; although it was not lacking in other areas, this is the only area where it was universal. A soul or spirit from without was thought to enter the body of the shaman and take possession, causing the body to talk, sing, dance, and otherwise behave as if possessed. In most cases interpreted as spirit possession, the shaman seemed to have been unconscious, because he did not remember how he behaved when possessed. In other instances, however, the shaman consciously put on an act to impress his audience; and the same man might achieve possession at one seance and not at another. Perhaps the other most definitive aspect of Eskimo religion was "soul flight." The shaman sent his soul to the spirit world to recover a stolen soul or to get a direct answer from the spirits concerning some question that had arisen on earth. Disease was most often attributed to breach of taboo and the theft of the patient's soul by offended spirits.

The Eskimo believed in many spirits or souls residing in persons, animals, inanimate objects, and places. Three kinds of human souls were generally distinguished: the immortal spirit, which left the body at death and went to live in a spiritual world; the breath and warmth of the body, which ceased to exist at death; and the name soul, which lived for a time in a spirit world and was later reincarnated into the body of a baby descendant.

Disease was believed to be caused by soul loss, apparently of the first and third souls, because shamans were supposed to be able to recover them. Old or ill persons sometimes changed their names in the hope of acquiring a fresh name soul to improve their health. Disease was less frequently thought to be caused by the intrusion into the body of an evil spirit. Soul loss or spirit intrusion usually resulted from the breaking of taboos, and isolation with dietary and other restrictions usually set the matter right. It was most often the shaman who diagnosed the difficulty and prescribed the cure.

Souls or spirits residing in animals, objects, and places were invariably called by terms translated as "man" or "person." This is substantial evidence for the concept of the unity of the soul. Rephrasing this idea, we might say that the soul was the personality of the animal, object, or place. The kinship between man and the animals has been amply illustrated in Chapter 6 in the section on religious aspects of hunting. Inanimate objects which possessed souls included parts of the bodies of animals (bones, teeth, claws), quartz crystals, iron, and carved images of humans or animals, including masks. Places believed to possess souls were burial cairns, peculiar geographical features, and other less definable isolated places where shamans went to obtain spirit helpers.

In addition to this indeterminate number of spirits or souls which flitted about continuously almost everywhere, there were several more powerful figures which were believed in by everyone and constituted a sort of pantheon. The most important of these was Sedna, a goddess who lived beneath the sea and controlled sea mammals. According to a myth, Sedna had run away from her husband to live with another man. Her father, being of a moral nature, went after her in a boat to bring her back to her first husband. On the return trip, a storm arose, and her father, fearing the wrath of spirits toward his sinful daughter, decided to get rid of her. He threw her overboard, but she clung to the gunwale with her hands. He picked up a hatchet, and chopped off the first joints of her fingers, and, when she still clung to the boat, finally, the other joints. At last she lost her grip and was drowned. Her finger joints were transformed into sea mammals, and that is why the Eskimo always propitiate her when they are about to hunt sea mammals.

The moon was regarded as a male deity who lived in an incestuous relationship with his sister, the sun. He controlled human reproduction—menstruation, fertility, pregnancy, childbirth—and punished taboo violators. He was supplicated to increase the ratio of boy babies to girls. To a lesser degree, he controlled the reproduction of game animals, so that the breaking of human sexual taboos angered him and caused him to curtail the reproduction of the animals. His least important function was to control the tides.

The sun was much less important than the moon. She was not worshiped or propitiated in any way. A minority of localities celebrated the return of the sun in the spring by putting out all lamps and relighting them from new fire made with a drill; or they made string figures (cat's cradles) only when the sun was absent in winter.

There was also a spirit of the air called Sila, who was vaguely regarded as half-personal and half-impersonal. This was a purely spiritual essence, apparently sexless and without any former earthly connections. It controlled the weather and, through the weather, the abundance or scarcity of game. When angered by a breach of taboo, it sent storms. This completes the pantheon.

Between the four deities and the multitude of souls of animals and ghosts of the dead was a class of spirits called Tornait. These were a legendary race of people who formerly lived in Arctic regions, and some anthropologists believe they should be equated with the actual people of the Thule culture, which has been established by archeologists as having formerly existed almost everywhere in central and eastern Eskimo territory. These spirits served as shamans' helpers and escorted shamans' souls en route to Sedna beneath the sea or to the moon or Sila through the air. Some were like ghosts, that is, human in form; others were of grotesque and freakish appearance unlike any animal or human. On the whole they were malevolent, but they sometimes cooperated with persons whom they served as spirit helpers.

Shamans were predominantly men, but included in their ranks some women past the menopause. They were religious intermediaries between man and the spiritual world, and had the power to send their souls to any of the spiritual personalities enumerated above and to plead for aid to man.

Supernatural power in the form of a spirit sometimes first appeared, unsought by the shaman-to-be, in a dream or hallucination. At other times, a person who wanted to become a shaman would go to a lonely spot where spirits were thought to dwell and seek contact with them there. This contact, when it came, was in the same form: dream or hallucination. These subjective experiences were interpreted as real by both the shaman and the public. The neophyte shaman saw or heard, and occasionally felt, a spirit which was most often in the form of either a human being or an animal, sometimes rather grotesque. This might be a common ghost, a Tornait, or an animal spirit.

Shamans attempted to predict or control weather and the supply of game animals whose habits and hunting depended on weather. They also cured disease, brought fertility to barren women, and applied the head-lifting test to suspected taboo breakers. In order to impress the public with their powers, they used ventriloquism and sleight of hand and allowed themselves to be bound hand and foot by a rope from which they miraculously escaped. Like our modern stage magicians, the shamans performed these tricks in semidarkness.

Possessional shamanism was universal. Every shaman went into a trance, at which time the spirit of some divinity was thought to enter his body and speak magical words, usually in a special brand of archaic language not understood by the people and doubtfully understood by shamans themselves.

A shaman might go into a trance and, instead of his body becoming possessed by an entering spirit, he might send his soul on a journey to contact his spirit helper or some divinity, such as Sedna. The psychological explanation is a simple one: he dreamed that he went on these journeys. On regaining consciousness he would tell the people present what he had experienced on his soul flight and would often predict the future or prescribe behavior which would be aimed at improving the plight of the people.

The routine for making a barren woman fertile usually included her sleeping with the shaman. In cases where a husband was sterile, this might have real efficacy. Shamans usually received fees, or demanded that some compensation be given to the spirit who had brought good health to a sick person. This payment to a spirit might amount to a female relative of the sick person sleeping with the shaman, or the patient herself doing the same after recovering. The material payment might be an article of clothing, a weapon, or an art object. When the shaman performed publicly during a time of famine, he received no specific pay other than personal advertising.

Spoken formulas, passed on from one shaman to another in the archaic language, were thought to bring definite results. Their effect was compulsive; the spirits or supernatural forces were forced to comply. They were therefore magical in character. Such magical formulas were sometimes bought and sold, or willed to another at the point of death. Other less secret verbiage could be heard and later uttered by anyone.

If there is any recurrent theme threading through all Eskimo religion, it is the consistent association of everything religious with the food quest. In a hostile environment where hundreds starved to death every winter, it is no wonder that the naïve person alleviated his anxieties over hunger by imagining that help could be obtained from the supernatural. Religion thus became an outlet for anxieties over problems beyond natural solution; the antics and verbalizations indulged in to influence the supernatural served to reduce highly charged emotions and ease tensions.

CONCLUSIONS

The number of spiritual personalities thought to exist probably exceeded that of living human beings everywhere in native North America, for the simple reason that every people believed in ghosts and there were as many ghosts as there were people who had died. There was a strong tendency to arrange gods in a ranked hierarchy in areas where people were ranked in similar manner, and to ignore such ranking where egalitarianism dominated human societies. Thus the peoples of Meso-America carefully ranked their gods, while those in the Arctic, Sub-Arctic, Plateau, and Great Basin believed in large numbers of spirits of about equal rank. Other areas tended to be intermediate in this respect. Among the Pueblos, where many spiritual personalities were widely enough recognized to be designated as gods, there was little tendency toward ranking, just as there was near equality among human beings.

The number of public religious ceremonies, the number of participants, and the number of spectators is correlated not only with the density of population but with general culture complexity and with a surplus of food and other necessities which made mass participation in the luxury of ceremonies possible. Here again, Meso-America surpasses all other areas, while the Arctic, Sub-Arctic, and Great Basin fall at the other end of the scale. The Pueblo and Navaho of the Southwest may have devoted as much time per capita to religious activities as did the Meso-Americans, but their populations were much smaller and the total effect less spectacular.

Specialization in the priesthood paralleled that in economic activities. Again Meso-America leads all other areas with its full-time priests, as well as in numbers of part-time participants in ritual. The Pueblos, on the other hand, had no full-time priests; all priests worked part time at some primarily economic activity to earn their livings. If there were any full-time priests in the East, they were only to be found on the coastal plain of the Southeast, where the political ruler was linked with the sun, inherited his position, and had the power of life and death over all his subjects. In the Arctic, Sub-Arctic, Plateau, Great Basin, and probably Northeast Mexico, there were no priests at all because there were no religious organizations, except in a few localities bordering on areas where organized religion prevailed. In these four or five culture areas, shamans dominated religion, magic, and medicine. On the Northwest Coast, in California, in much of the Southwest, on the Plains and Prairies, and in most of the East, religious leaders shared the attributes of both priests and shamans. They belonged to cults, performed carefully memorized rituals, and sometimes appealed to generally recognized gods or powerful spirits; but, at the same time, they had visions and other direct contact with the supernatural, from which they obtained what were regarded as original songs, cures, and the like. Shamans occurred even in Meso-America, and some of the priests there possessed attributes more characteristic of shamans elsewhere. The dichotomy of the priest as opposed to the shaman therefore fits about half of the culture areas of North America if only the major attributes of these religious functionaries are considered. It cannot be applied with much meaning to the other areas. The term "medicine man" has been applied where it is difficult to choose between "priest" and "shaman."

Concerning medicine, we found that most ailments were thought to have been caused by the supernatural and could therefore be cured only with the aid of the supernatural. Where plant remedies were used, the Meso-Americans tended to mix a number of plants together into a single prescription for a single ailment. Peoples in the East and the Southwest concocted fewer plant mixtures, and those in remaining areas tended to prescribe a single plant for each ailment. Theories of disease show much variation, but intrusion of a foreign object may be the most frequent and a near universal. Intrusion of a disease-causing spirit is less often reported although perhaps almost as common. Soul loss, or loss of spirit helper, was formerly thought to be common only in the north, but more recent evidence has turned up some cases in every culture area, although the known continental frequency would be less than that of the other two major causes of illness.

Sorcery, by definition, is never condoned by Indian societies in which it is practiced, but the social scientist may regard it as a substitute for murder and other forms of physical aggression. A number of Indian societies, including the Canadian Ojibwa (Hallowell, 1955: 277–90), have never heard of a case of murder. No one has ever been known to kill by physical means a member of his own group; but invariably such societies practice witchcraft. If a person feels he has been wronged by another, he attempts to injure or kill the offender by witchcraft. Although some persons become ill or may even die as a result of knowing they are being bewitched, many anthropologists believe that the mortality from witchcraft in these societies is less than that from murder in societies where murder takes place. Mortality from witchcraft has certainly been less among the Ojibwa than death by murder among the Eskimo. The total amount of anxiety which sorcery creates in a society and the amount of disability such anxiety causes cannot be objectively measured; but neither can anxiety be measured in societies where murder is common. With mortality as the measure of disharmony, many anthropologists believe a society in which witchcraft occurs without physical murder is better off than one in which actual murder is committed.

Social scientists possess no criteria for scaling Indian religions according to their total value for their believers. As examples of science, they all fail to measure up; but as forms of psychotherapy, they all have been demonstrated to be efficacious. There is no unanimity of opinion in the anthropological profession on what to do about native religions in connection with modern programs of economic, medical, and educational aid to the Indians. Many persons would agree, however, that there is no point in trying to eliminate native religions until something else has been supplied to replace them. After the standard of living has been raised, modern medicine introduced, mortality reduced, and perhaps a program of insurance initiated, Indians will become less dependent psychologically on their own religions and will be willing to rely increasingly on these more tangible forms of security.

REFERENCES

CANNON, 1942; CASO, 1958; ELMORE, 1944; FENTON, 1942; HALLOWELL, 1955; KLUCKHOHN, 1944; PARSONS, 1939; RAY, 1932; REICHARD, 1950; RICHTER, 1957; SAHAGÚN (ANDERSON AND DIBBLE), 1950–58; SKINNER, 1911; SWANTON, 1928; VAILLANT, 1941; WEYER, 1932.

24

Personality and Culture

THE WORD "personality" is used in psychology to refer to the total responses of a single individual, as opposed to other individuals, in a society. It includes emotional or physiological responses as well as overt behavior and language. Common synonyms for "personality" are "character," "disposition," and "temperament." Social psychologists, as well as laboratory and clinical psychologists, treat the individual person as the unit of investigation. Generalizations about groups of persons are derived by statistical methods from the responses of individuals.

Anthropologists, on the other hand, have extended the concept of personality, character, or temperament to social groups, often without making observations on a truly representative sample of all individuals in the group. Just as "culture" refers to the way of life shared by an entire society, "personality" may also refer to the composite personality of an entire society. Although all anthropologists recognize individual variation in personality within the small groups they study, their chief interest has been the typical or modal personality of the group as a whole.

The term "modal personality" is derived from the mode of the statistician, which is the interval on any scale of measurement where the largest number of persons (cases) are located. For instance, if we measure the stature of a group of college men to the nearest inch, we might find that more men are 5 feet 9 inches tall than 5 feet 8 inches, 5 feet 10 inches, and so on. If that is true, then 5 feet 9 inches is the modal stature of the group. The mode is usually close to the average, and the two may be, but are not always, identical

Just as hundreds of measurements and other observations may be taken on the human body, so hundreds of measurements and observations of a psychological nature may be made on human responses. There may be as many modes for the personality of a single society as there are scales of measurement for traits of personality. Psychological

431

statisticians have developed objective techniques for integrating the results of any number of separate measurements on the members of a society into a smaller number of clusters or factors, which describe the society as a whole. Guilford (1968) reports that in the United States alone as many as eighty distinct (uncorrelated) mental abilities have been discovered. He predicts that this number will soon reach 120. If there are 120 uncorrelated scales of mental ability in a single nation using a single language, there may be thousands in the entire world. What anthropologists have accomplished so far, largely with impressionistic writing, has scarcely scratched the surface of this complex problem. However, the concept of modal personality, as used by anthropologists, implies that it is a composite mode derived from a representative sample of all the kinds of responses made by all the members of the society.

At the present time, many anthropologists believe that the thousands of societies in the world that we can now distinguish on the basis of race, language, and culture could also be distinguished from one another in composite modal personality if our knowledge were more complete. Experience with the data of bioanthropology, language, and culture shows that if enough observations were obtained, the peoples of the world could be differentiated into very many units, each one distinguishable in some respect from every other one. On the basis of language alone, the American Indians of both continents have been divided into from one to two thousand entities, each with its own language. Add to this what we know of bioanthropology and culture differentiae, and the number would swell to many thousands. If we possessed enough observations on personality, it too should yield a large number of composite modal personality types, each one differing significantly from every other.

Modal personality patterns are similar to the national character constructs of historians. Historians have not only distinguished the national character of such nations as England, France, and Germany, but have also recognized differences within a single nation at different periods in its history. Thus the national character of the British would show differences at the times of Elizabeth I, Cromwell, Victoria, and Elizabeth II. Historians have also recognized differences in personality in Europe according to social class. Nobles behave differently from commoners or slaves, and the rich show significant differences in behavior from the poor.

The above qualifications apply with equal force to Indian societies.

Indian personality of a single tribe would be expected to change over the centuries since the first White contact as well as to differ from tribe to tribe. For example, early Spaniards in Mexico universally reported the Indians' gaiety, wit, and keen sense of humor. By the nineteenth century, the Indian was represented as sad, dismal, and withdrawn, much as Oscar Lewis found the people of Tepoztlán in the 1940's (Cumberland, 1968: 54–55). In societies with social classes, the modal personality of each class should be distinguishable from that of every other class. But so far no one has studied Indian personality with this multiple-modal approach.

United States historians, up to a few decades ago, had tended to describe the personality of the Indian as that of a bloodthirsty savage struggling for survival in a howling wilderness. The Indian was viewed chiefly as an impediment to the spread of European civilization and Christianity, and was eliminated by some pioneers almost as ruthlessly as dangerous beasts, such as wolves, bears, and mountain lions. Little attention was given to personal relations within Indian society, except by a few romantic writers, such as James Fenimore Cooper. The anthropologist today is concerned primarily with in-group personal relations, and only secondarily with out-group relations. The result is that the anthropologist gives a much more sympathetic picture of Indian personality than does the historian. The whole truth includes both views.

Two of the many determinants of personality, largely neglected by anthropologists today, are malnutrition and organic disease. A society in which malnutrition is widespread is not going to give forth bursts of energy or respond energetically to the anthropologist, colonial administrator, or businessman. The scarcity of food in the Great Basin area of North America must have contributed to the dull, unresponsive personalities that field workers have so often found there. Chronic diseases, such as malaria, yaws, and tuberculosis, obviously limit the full participation of the sick in any kind of activity. An anthropologist recently studied personality in an Eskimo community without knowing that most of the population had tuberculosis. They had largely ceased to hunt not because of some purely psychological defeatism but principally because they did not have the physical strength to do so.

The proof that psychosomatic disease is the cause of a person's symptoms demands the elimination of organic disease by a series of careful and thorough laboratory tests. Only modern hospitals are equipped to diagnose accurately a wide range of organic diseases. For instance, when I was in Mexico on a field trip, a woman from the United States became seriously ill with jaundice, which a laboratory test identified as infectious hepatitis. Her Mexican servants and other unsophisticated local people, however, attributed her sickness to an argument she had had with her children's tutor. Her anger had made her ill, they thought. They said that such cases were common among the Mexicans. The moral of this tale is that we cannot take an informant's word for the causation of disease. Informants in many primitive cultures believe that all disease is caused by the supernatural; but the anthropologist should not interpret this to mean that practically all disease in the culture is of psychogenic origin. By extension, when a case of a person being killed by sorcery is reported by informants, the cause of death should not be labeled "psychogenic" by the anthropologist unless an autopsy revealing no organic disease has been performed by a well-equipped pathology laboratory.

There has also been considerable confusion between the actual behavior of persons and the ideal behavior that informants often prefer to talk about when speaking to an outsider. Much of the older ethnography seems to consist largely of an idealized picture derived from a small number of old informants who loved to glorify the past. Recent field reports tend to be much more candid, and usually attempt to distinguish between ideal and manifest behavior.

Before narrowing down to descriptions of modal personality types in restricted areas, we can profit by quoting a recent general statement about Anglo-American Indian personality by George and Louise Spindler (1957).

Without attempting to document the many sources from which inferences and data were drawn, we can tentatively describe the psychological features most widely exhibited among the North American Indians as a whole in the following way: nondemonstrative emotionality and reserve accompanied by a high degree of control over interpersonal aggression within the in-group; a pattern of generosity that varies greatly in the extent to which it is a formalized social device without emotional depth; autonomy of the individual, a trait linked with socio-political structures low in dominance-submission hierarchies; ability to endure pain, hardship, hunger, and frustration without external evidence of discomfort; a positive valuation of bravery and courage that varies sharply with respect to emphasis on highly aggressive daring in military exploit; a generalized fear of the world as dangerous, and particularly a fear of witchcraft; a "practical joker" strain that is nearly everywhere highly channelized institutionally, as in the common brother-in-law joking prerogative, and that appears to be a safety valve for in-group aggressions held sharply in check; attention to the concrete realities of the present—what Rorschachists would call the "large D" approach to problem solving—practicality in contrast to abstract integration in terms of long-range goals; a dependence upon supernatural power outside one's self—power that determines one's fate, which is expressed to and can be acquired by the individual through dreams, and for which the individual is not held personally accountable, at least not in the sense that one's "will" is accountable for one's acts in Western cultures. (Spindler and Spindler, 1957: 148–49.)

THE CONTROVERSIAL PUEBLOS

The modal personality of the Pueblo Indians of the Southwest was first described in detail by Ruth Benedict in her famous book *Patterns of Culture* (1934). She concentrated on the Zuñi, among whom she had done field work. The present sketch will embrace both Hopi and Zuñi, between whom there are few differences with respect to personality and culture.

According to Benedict, the Pueblos are more wrapped up in religious ceremony than in any other aspect of their way of life, and they value sobriety and inoffensiveness above all other virtues. Most prayers are magic formulas which must be recited verbatim to bring the desired result. They are not spontaneous outpourings of the troubled heart, but carefully memorized, emotionally mild requests asking for an orderly life, pleasant days, and protection from violence. Their religious dances, likewise, must be done exactly as prescribed by the gods themselves in order to carry enough appeal to the supernatural to be sure of bringing results to man. Practically all religious authority is vested in the four major and eight minor priesthoods, and all public religious ceremonies are conducted by one or the other of these groups. Almost all ceremonial activity is for the benefit of the entire Pueblo, and even ceremonies to cure a sick person often include rainmaking or fertility features. Benedict sums up the modal personality of the Pueblo people with the term "Apollonian," which Nietzsche opposed to "Dionysian." The Apollonian personality is modest, gentle, and cooperative, and does not indulge in disruptive psychological states. He is temperate, enjoys his sobriety to a moderate degree, and avoids the heights of ecstasy as well as the depths of despair.

Dorothy Eggan (1943) found the Hopi a much more disturbed group of adults than Benedict found at Zuñi.

In any prolonged contact with the Hopi Indians, an investigator who is interested in the psychic as well as in the more tangible phenomena of culture is struck with the mass maladjustment of these people, maladjustment being here defined as a state in which friction predominates in personal relations, and in which the worst is anxiously and habitually anticipated. The comment has been made by numerous persons who have worked with them that one Hopi is a delightful friend; two are often a problem; and more than that number are frequently a headache. Discord is apparent in inter-tribal relations as well, as most Hopi will testify; the younger ones particularly express annoyance over the needless arguments which accompany any group attempt to reach a decision in tribal matters. Gossip is rampant throughout the villages; witchcraft is an ever present threat, one's relatives as well as others being suspect; and in some cases individuals fear that they may be witches without being aware of it. Even sisterly love in this strongly matrilineal society seldom runs smoothly, although sisters present a united front to the rest of their world. (Dorothy Eggan, 1943: 357.)

Dorothy Eggan reviews the generally accepted gentleness and permissiveness in the child-parent relationship, the threat of punishment from the spirits if the child does not behave properly, and the emotional shock that initiation brings to girls as well as boys. She concludes:

In summary, this preliminary study of Hopi psychology suggests that the first five or six years of childhood among them may have a different significance than Freudian theory allows. . . . It seems evident that the Hopi were not subject to the same set of early pressures which encompass western children, and even when the pressures were similar, they were much less intensely instigated. . . . Of greater weight in Hopi personality development were the frustrating acculturation influences, the fears of various kinds which were ever present and inadequately sublimated, and the suppression of physical aggression. Probably the rather sudden shift from indulgence to control [at initiation] was also an important precipitating factor in personality formation. (Dorothy Eggan, 1943: 373).

Laura Thompson and Alice Joseph (1944) used eight psychological tests on a sample of 190 Hopi children aged from six to eighteen years, and wrote a modest volume on Hopi personality. This was the most scientifically oriented study of personality in the Southwest up to its time. Thompson later (1945) summed up her views of the ideal Hopi man:

Thus the *hopi* individual is: (1) strong (in the Hopi sense, i.e., he is psychically strong— self-controlled, intelligent, and wise—and he is physically strong); (2) poised (in the Hopi sense, i.e., he is balanced, free of anxiety, tranquil, "quiet of heart" and concentrated on "good" thoughts); (3) law-abiding (i.e., responsible, actively cooperative, kind and unselfish); (4) peaceful (i.e., non-aggressive, non-quarrelsome, modest); (5) protective (i.e., fertility-promoting and life-preserving, rather than injurious or destructive to life in any of its manifestations, including human beings, animals, and plants); (6) free of illness. (Thompson, 1945: 733.)

Another challenge of Benedict's Apollonianism comes from Esther Goldfrank (1945*a*). Her interpretation holds that Pueblo personalities have their share of tension, suspicion, anxiety, hostility, fear, and ambition, but that outward manifestations of such emotions are suppressed by those in authority and repressed by the fear on the part of the individual of being accused of witchcraft or of being bewitched.

Large-scale cooperation deriving primarily from the needs of irrigation is therefore vitally important to the life and well-being of the Pueblo community. It is no spontaneous expression of good-will or sociability. What may seem voluntary to some is the end of a long process of conditioning, often persuasive, but frequently harsh, that commences in infancy and continues throughout adulthood. (Goldfrank, 1945a: 519.)

To the need of irrigation we would like to add the need of defense against enemy raids, which was very real before and after the Spanish gained control.

Goldfrank attacks the Freudian view that the treatment received in infancy and early childhood determines, to a great degree, the adult personality. All writers on Pueblo peoples agree that their treatment of infants is unusually loving, gentle, and permissive. They are nursed when hungry, picked up whenever they fuss or cry, given a very gentle toilet training, and never slapped or spanked. However, when the child goes through his first initiation ceremony, he experiences harsh treatment, which is a threat of worse things to come if he does not conform to the adult personality pattern.

But it is eminently clear that a study of the period of infancy alone would give few clues to the personality structure exhibited by the Pueblo adult. . . . But in the Pueblos where both severe discipline and substantial rewards derive from external agents who function most importantly in the "later" years, a study of the society as a whole and over time is absolutely necessary for any satisfactory understanding of the building of adult personality. (Goldfrank, 1945a: 537.)

The four descriptions of Pueblo personality, all published within a span of twelve years, clearly fall into two groups, as John W. Bennett (1946) has pointed out: the Benedict-Thompson Apollonian view; the Eggan-Goldfrank maladjusted view. How are these differences to be explained? First, it seems likely that sampling variability among the Pueblo persons contacted by the four writers produced some of the differences. Only Thompson and Joseph studied a large sample of persons, and they were mostly children. Second, the personal biases of the researchers are probably reflected in their descriptions of the Pueblos. Benedict and Thompson may have brought more sweetness and light with them, and Eggan and Goldfrank more controversy and dissent. Third, there are probably true differences from east to west in the Pueblo area and possibly significant differences between every combination of two Pueblos. The differences found in these studies emphasize the need for more explicit sampling techniques and research designs.

THE EGOCENTRIC NORTHWEST COAST MEN

Benedict's (1934) account of the culture and personality of the Northwest Coast peoples will be considered first. Although the Northwest Coast peoples did not farm, they lived in permanent villages and accumulated more in the way of material possessions than did the Pueblos. Fish were so plentiful and easy to catch that the time spent in obtaining food was no greater than that of most farming peoples, and the inexhaustible supply of wood and other materials, plus the skill of the people in working these materials, provided a relatively rich and varied way of life. No other area of equal size without agriculture anywhere in the world enjoyed as much material prosperity as did the Northwest Coast.

Kwakiutl religion was loaded with intense emotional states, and those who did not have definite visionary experiences often had the chance to play the role of a person possessed by a powerful spirit in public performances. Initiates into the highest-ranking organization, the Cannibal Society, pretended that they had been seized by a cannibal spirit and could not restrain themselves from eating human flesh (see page 348). The potlatch (described on pages 209–11) was the occasion for giving away huge amounts of corporeal property to guests, who later made return gifts to the donor. The man who gave away the most property was the winner of these contests. These give-aways were always associated with a transfer of status and title from one individual to another. Thus if a rich man died, his heir could not claim title to any of his inherited possessions until he had given a potlatch to validate or confirm his right to the inheritance. Destruction of property was the most extreme form of wealth display. A man who was so rich that he could afford to destroy valuable possessions, instead of giving them away with the expectation that he would later receive return gifts of greater value, was indeed a great figure in the society.

Although marriage was the principal means of acquiring enhanced rank in the culture, a man sometimes achieved it by murdering another man and appropriating his titles, crest, and privileges. A man could even raise his rank by claiming to have killed a supernatural being, thus proving that he was more powerful than the spirit. By becoming a medicine man, one could receive all the trapping of noble rank directly from the spirits, and medicine men competed in contests to demonstrate their supernatural powers. They collected large fees for curing the sick, and were the highest-ranking group in the culture.

Behavior on the Northwest Coast was dominated by the desire of every individual to show himself superior to his rivals. The speeches of chiefs at potlatches, which Benedict (1934: 190–93) quotes at length, were outbursts of self-glorification which she labels "megalomania." The kings of Africa and Europe were modest in self-praise compared with Kwakiutl chiefs. Along with this bragging about one's self went ridicule of one's rivals; the greatest insult was to call a man a slave.

The Kwakiutl response to failure and frustration was sulking and acts of violence. Even when, through no fault of his own, a man's child died, he felt it necessary to redeem his loss in some concrete manner. After sulking on his bed for several days without speaking or eating, he arose and distributed property, went headhunting, or committed suicide. There are no accurate figures on the frequency of suicide, but many cases are reported, often for reasons we would consider trivial. For instance, when a man's son stumbled in his initiation dance and failed to qualify as a secret society member, the man committed suicide because he was ruined financially. He had invested everything he owned in this ceremony to raise his son's status, and knew that he could not raise enough material goods for a second try the next year.

Benedict sums up her description of the ideal Northwest Coast man by combining the term "paranoid" with the previously used "megalomania," and points out that our culture regards such behavior as abnormal. But what we regard as abnormal is the ideal personality of the Kwakiutl and their neighbors on the Northwest Coast, as she sees it.

Helen Codere (1956) has challenged Benedict's position with respect to Kwakiutl culture in a paper aptly entitled, "The Amiable Side of Kwakiutl Life: The Potlatch and the Play Potlatch."

Field work among the Kwakiutl in 1951 produced evidence of a kind of potlatching, play potlatching or potlatching for fun, that has never been described but is of the greatest importance for an understanding of Kwakiutl life. The existence of playfulness in relation to potlatching requires reinterpretation of the character of both this institution and of the people participating in it. The 1951 field data include much new material on home life, child rearing, and humor that supports Boas' claim that the private life of the Kwakiutl possessed many amiable features, but it is the aim of this presentation to show that even in the public life of the ceremonials and potlatches there was mirth and friendliness....

Even in those parts of Kwakiutl life in which a competitive, paranoid, atrocious character seems most unrelieved, there is evidence that such an extreme and unqualified characterization cannot be made. . . . The Kwakiutl are more real, more complex, more human than they have been represented to be. Even in their potlatches, their most extreme and flagrant institution, there are elements of humor and great complexity of thought and feeling: they are not single-minded; they are not lacking in insight; they do not put themselves and their most exigent interests beyond reflective thought and criticism. (Codere, 1956: 334–50.)

It seems apparent from Codere's remarks that Benedict has again exaggerated almost to the point of caricature her portrait of Northwest Coast, and especially Kwakiutl, personality. Again Benedict has concentrated on an ideal personality, while Codere is more interested in manifest behavior over its entire range as well as at its central tendency. If we realize that Benedict selected her evidence to produce as sharp a contrast as possible with the Pueblo personality pattern, and that other evidence exists to modify her conclusions, we can still give her credit for first calling attention to the many differences in the ideal personalities of the Pueblos and Northwest Coasters.

What about the personality of the slaves, who are estimated to have made up from 10 to 20 per cent of the population on the Northwest Coast? It is obvious that the concept of modal personality patterns is not adequate to describe personality patterns of class-structured societies, which are presumably multiple. Because about half the peoples of the world possess definite systems of rank or social classes, this is a serious limitation. This problem can be solved by introducing the concept of multiple modes, which, in the present stage of personality studies in anthropology, would demand multiple essays, one on each of the distinguishable social classes in each society. Where class distinctions are clear, as between freemen and slaves on the Northwest Coast, this would not be difficult to do; but where the presence or absence of class structure is debatable, the personality investigator would be compelled to help solve that problem, perhaps in part with his personality data.

THE MANLY-HEARTED PLAINS PEOPLE

Benedict (1932) gave a brief description of Plains modal personality, which did not elicit as much controversy as had her characterizations of the Pueblos and Northwest Coast Indians. Later writers, such as Lewis (1941, 1942), Goldfrank (1943, 1945b), and Devereux (1951), enlarged her views and added more in the way of psychoanalysis.

Plains Indian mothers often nursed their children for years and treated them with considerable tenderness. Children were much more closely attached to the mother than to the father. Fathers were often away hunting or on the warpath, and mortality of fathers must have been about twice that of mothers. The mother, then, was not only the child's principal source of affection and security but was his chief disciplinarian as well. The concept of the "manly-hearted woman" reflects the role many women played on the Plains. The result was that the child developed more hostility toward the mother than toward the father, thus transferring the Oedipus complex from the father to the mother. From the mother this hostility tended to be projected to the wife and even to other women. Chastity in females was valued everywhere on the Plains although not expected of all of them, and ritual continence was also common. Along with this went a legitimized stealing of other men's wives for a few days by members of certain men's sodalities. Conflicts arose from the notion that a woman should be chaste while a man should engage in sex adventures at every opportunity. Thus a man would feel impelled to defend the honor of his wife and sisters at one moment and to seek to dishonor another man's wife or sister at the next. A man who was able both to protect his wife and sisters from the sexual advances of other men and at the same time to achieve many conquests of other women enjoyed the most prestige.

Rivalry and hostility between men were more institutionalized and given a healthier set of outlets by the culture. A man could raise his status by a successful vision quest, by public self-torture in the Sun Dance, by giving away horses and other property, by being a good hunter, and—above all—by defeating the enemy in war. The individual success of a man in male pursuits was generally of benefit to his entire band or tribe. Some men, however, had such a strong aversion to this ultramasculine role that they would have been complete failures in the society if there had not been an escape for them. They donned the clothing of women, did women's work, and sometimes lived homosexually with another man. As *berdaches*, they were accepted by their societies and were even allowed, like women, to carry scalps in the victory dance on the return of a successful war party.

All the Plains tribes observed the custom of recounting coup. On certain public occasions, it was proper for a man to tell, in a boastful manner, about his triumphs in war. Some tribes even permitted a man to recount coup on women, to boast of his sexual exploits in public. Such examples of exhibitionism gave the partially rejected Plains male a chance to reinflate his ego.

The volatility of Plains emotions is well illustrated by the 1890 Ghost Dance religion, which swept the entire Plains area in a few years and continued for about a decade (Mooney, 1896). By 1890, the Plains Indians had all been defeated in wars with the Whites; most of them had been rounded up and confined to reservations; the buffalo were nearly exterminated; and many persons were starving. An Indian prophet from Nevada told them that he had experienced visions which indicated that all the Indians, dead as well as living, would be reunited upon a regenerated earth to live a life of happiness again, free from the Whites, misery, disease, and death. This package of prosperity was so attractive to the depressed, oppressed, repressed, and suppressed personality of the defeated Plains Indians, that they became converted to the new religion in droves. They actually thought a transformation of the world was about to take place, and discussed the dates when it was supposed to happen.

Benedict characterizes the personality of the Plains people, as well as that of the Northwest Coasters, as Dionysian, given to extreme indulgence in violence, grief, trance, and other emotional states. While this is acceptable as far as it goes, Plains culture lacked the extreme egocentrism of the Northwest Coast, which pointed in the direction of megalomania and paranoia. On the Plains, there was nothing as extreme as the potlatch. Generosity was regarded as a virtue, but property given away did not always bring a reciprocating gift, as on the Northwest Coast. There was less hereditary wealth on the Plains, and high honors were achieved principally by brave deeds in war. Plains culture was therefore much more democratic; a man of humble origin could rise to the top by his own achievements. Physical aggression against the enemy provided a socially approved outlet for rivalries and hostilities arising within the family, band, and tribe.

THE PSEUDO-APOLLONIANS OF THE SUB-ARCTIC

A significant series of studies in this area is that of A. Irving Hallowell (1955). He describes the Ojibwa of the Berens River, a small stream flowing into Lake Winnipeg from the east. This locality falls within the Eastern Sub-Arctic culture area.

The care of infants and children seems to have been as gentle and permissive as elsewhere in North America. The mother-child relationship is the warmest of any in the society. The infant is bound to the cradle board most of the time until he is able to walk, and is weaned gradually without marked emotional disturbance. Parents seldom inflict corporal punishment on their children, and Hallowell never witnessed boys and girls exchanging blows. The sexual activities of parents or other adults in the one-room dwellings are not concealed from children as they grow up. There is a little sex play among prepubescent children, but most of it is confined to those who are potential marriage mates: cross-cousins of the opposite sex. In former days, all boys were sent out by their parents to obtain visions at the age of puberty or a little younger. If a boy had experienced sex before his vision quest, the supernatural would not bestow on him the blessings absolutely necessary to every man's successful life. To avoid this catastrophe, parents probably watched their boys more carefully than their girls. After the vision quest of boys and the first menstruation of girls, which was kept as secret as possible, premarital sex activity took place.

Genital sex activity was the only approved outlet, as in our society. All other kinds were not only frowned upon but regarded as causes of illness. Marriage was polygynous until recent times, and was the only wholly approved form of sexual gratification. Neither impotence nor frigidity was understood by Ojibwa informants; they had never heard of a case of either. Younger men were expected to have intercourse nightly, and if a man failed to perform regularly, his wife might suspect him of carrying on an adulterous affair with another woman.

Perhaps the most noticeable characteristic of adult Ojibwa personality is the restraint exercised over almost all emotions in public; love, joy, hate, and fear are all repressed to an extreme degree. The one exception is laughter. There is a great deal of joking and laughing, even during time of hunger, fatigue, and anxiety, and even their sacred myths contain Rabelaisian humor. The greatest amount of joking is between cross-cousins of the opposite sex. Furthermore, face-to-face verbal quarreling or criticism of another is almost unheard of, although derogatory gossip behind a person's back is general. Along with this go: a hesitancy to command others; ready assent to a request from another; and much lending, sharing, and hospitality. Competition is discouraged, and discretion is considered the better part of valor. Physical aggression and violence are totally unknown—no cases of murder have been reported; wars with other

Indians or Whites are unknown in the memory of twentieth-century informants; suicide is unknown; theft and brawls are extremely rare. To the casual observer, laughter, harmony, cooperation, modesty, patience, and self-control are the high points of Ojibwa modal personality. Here we seem to have as clear an example of the Apollonian ideal as can be found among the Pueblos or perhaps anywhere in the world.

But when we inquire into the reasons for this Apollonian behavior, we find it is fear of illness and death. Serious illness can be caused by only two things: wrongdoing and sorcery. Wrongdoing includes all forms of deviant sexual behavior, cruelty to animals as well as to human beings, inconsiderate treatment of the dead, insult and ridicule of others, failure to share one's worldly goods, and a host of other acts running contrary to the cultural norm. Bad conduct is not punished by spirits or by any legal machinery, to which one may appeal his case, but directly according to a law of moral compensation. Punishment always takes the form of illness or death.

The other cause of illness and death is sorcery, inflicted on a person by a hostile human being, who may magically inject a poison object into his victim or may steal his soul. In almost every case, the sorcerer is thought to be someone whom the victim has wronged in some way. Because physical aggression is wholly suppressed by the society, the wronged individual can get even only by making his enemy sick or by killing him with sorcery. Everyone believes himself to be in danger of being bewitched, even by his own relatives; and everyone is, at the same time, a potential sorcerer. Physical murder is unknown, but murder by witchcraft is thought to be common. Such a belief has social value as an inhibitor of aggressions against one's neighbor in a society which has no true government and little else in the way of social control.

Fear of sickness and death is therefore the principal sanction which produces the pseudo-Apollonian behavior of the Berens River Ojibwa. Instead of achieving a truly Apollonian adjustment to life, they have emotions that remain ambivalent, shifting from the satisfactions derived from friendliness and sharing to the fear of retaliation if they do not please their associates. The threat of starvation in the past and the temptation to solve it by cannibalism are related to a psychosis in which the afflicted person imagines himself to be transformed into a cannibalistic monster. This is the most severe emotional disturbance occurring among these people, but its frequency is apparently low. The repeated confession of bad conduct serves as a better barometer of their maladjustment; yet their ability to enjoy a full sex life, even up to old age, and their perpetual laughter suggest that their maladjustment on the whole is not extreme.

A comparison of the Berens River Ojibwa with the Kaska, who live over a thousand miles to the northwest in the Mackenzie drainage, suggests that modal personality in the Sub-Arctic is fairly uniform. Honigman (1949, 1954: 4–10) describes the Kaska's extreme distaste for overt hostility and acts of aggression, his suppression of all strong emotion, his relative independence and emotional isolation from his associates, and his employment of sorcery to harm an enemy. Sorcery, however, seems less developed than among the Ojibwa.

THE AGGRESSIVE BUT INSECURE IROQUOIANS

William Fenton (1948) compares Iroquois personality with that of the Berens River Ojibwa described by Hallowell. The Iroquois also stressed speaking kindly to others and avoiding argument and anger. Along with this went a strong individualism, which permitted no one to give orders to another and contributed to the lack of real authority on the part of chiefs and a parallel absence of real cohesion in the League of the Iroquois. Membership in war parties was on a volunteer basis; warriors were never drafted. Parents were permissive with their children, never struck or whipped them, and lived in fear of child suicide, which actually happened occasionally. Child suicide suggests that there may have been too abrupt a change from indulgence to discipline. The Iroquois also resorted to sorcery to right wrongs inflicted on them by others, but it does not seem to have been as common as among the Ojibwa. Polite and impersonal forms of speech were used in public lest one's remarks be construed as personal criticism likely to arouse anger. Gossip and slander were ideally avoided, and seem to have been less frequent than among the Ojibwa, although by no means absent. Laughter, funny stories, and jesting songs provided escape from the severe emotional restraint in public. Hospitality, lending, and sharing were the rule in both private and public affairs. At the game of lacrosse, the player who did not get angry was the ideal, although, in practice, these hotly contested matches often ended in brawls between the two sides. To nurse a grudge until an opportunity arose to even the score by ambush or sorcery was regarded as deplorable, although it sometimes occurred.

Like the Pueblos, and other Indians as well, the Iroquois withheld leadership from the man who was overanxious for prestige. Failing to keep an appointment was a breach of social form, and a group of local officials or the tribal council would always ignore a person's request if he did not show up to plead his case. After the petitioner had made his appeal, he was asked to withdraw from the meeting while the officials discussed the issue; they seldom came to a decision on the same day. Thus they avoided criticizing an individual to his face and arousing him to anger, and put off their decision until he had had time to become calm. The successful negotiator learned to divide up his request in the hope that if part was rejected the remainder might be accepted. A great deal of latitude was allowed in personal behavior so long as it did not affect the fate of the sib, tribe, or league; when it did, the councils denied the requests of the individual. Ideally, chiefs were even-tempered, mild-mannered men who neither engaged in nor paid attention to gossip. Their internal rule was by persuasion and reason, but their external rule of subject peoples was direct and backed by the threat of war.

Anthony Wallace (1958) contributes much to our knowledge of Iroquoian personality by his study of the dreams recorded by missionaries, mostly in the seventeenth century. We learn that dreams were regarded as wishes of the soul which must be satisfied lest the dreamer experience sickness or death. A person who was awakened after dreaming he was bathing got up and took a bath no matter how cold the weather. A man who dreamed he was a captive being tortured by the enemy insisted that his friends tie him up and burn his flesh the next day, in the belief that this would satisfy his soul's desire and prevent him from actually being captured by the enemy and tortured to death.

Sexual dreams created a problem. The Iroquois permitted premarital sex relations between unrelated young people in different sibs, who were therefore eligible as marriage mates, and divorce and remarriage were easy for adults. As with the Pueblos, it was the wife who most often divorced her husband, simply by tossing his personal possessions outside the longhouse door. But they were often rather shy in heterosexual contacts, and chastity in the young and marital fidelity in the mature were regarded as virtues. Nevertheless, when a certain man had a dream in which the culture hero ordered him to go to a certain village and cohabit with two married women for five days, his dream fulfillment was permitted by the village authorities for fear that the spirit would bring disaster upon them if disobeyed. Such sexual dreams were common.

Dreams of torture at the hands of the enemy were common among warriors. When one man who had had such a dream told it to others, a council was held. The chiefs agreed that steps should be taken to avoid the ill fortune that the dream foretold. They seized the dreamer and tortured him with fire, telling him that they pitied him and that he should take courage in his hour of agony. Finally, the dreamer ran out of the ring of fires, seized a dog, and offered it as a sacrifice to a war spirit. The dog was killed, roasted in the flames, and eaten in a public feast, just as they would eat a human captive. This routine was supposed to prevent the defeat, capture, and torture of warriors from the village where the dreamer lived. In one case, it took the dreamer six months to recover from the burns his own tribesmen inflicted on him.

If a man dreamed he had killed a person, he felt impelled to commit murder. In one instance, a Cayuga man dreamed he had killed a girl and eaten her flesh. He called the chiefs of the tribe to his cabin and asked them to guess his dream, as was the custom. When one chief finally guessed that he desired to eat human flesh, all of them became frightened to the point that they went out and selected a victim. When the dreamer was about to deal the death blow to the innocent girl, remorse seized him; he decided that his dream had been satisfied, and the girl's life was spared.

Boys at puberty went on vision quests to acquire a personal spirit helper. They sought isolation in the woods, fasted, and denied themselves comforts so that spirits would take pity on them and come to their aid. After such experience, dreams about the spirit helper recurred throughout life, and it was important to do whatever the spirit told a man to do. The sick also commonly had dreams which they had to fulfill in order to recover from their illnesses. Many religious ceremonies were initiated by dreaming, each type of dream being associated with a particular ceremony. It is easy to see that illnesses and states of anxiety caused by emotional disturbances could be cured by a dream and its reenactment. The most successful members of Iroquoian society were those who had had many visions and dreams.

William Fenton's study (1941a) of suicide shows how the frustrated and rejected individual turned his aggressions on himself. Women committed suicide most often because of husbands deserting them in middle age; children because of too much restraint by elders; and men as an escape from torture by the enemy or from death by blood revenge at the hands of the relatives of a murdered man. Taking a plant poison was the most common method of doing away with one's self, especially for women; men more often strangled, stabbed, or shot themselves with firearms. Public opinion tended to condemn suicides of men to escape physical suffering, but it condoned the suicides of women mistreated by lovers.

We see from this brief sketch of Iroquoian personality that although men were strong, brave, aggressive, and ultramasculine on the surface, they had their share of insecurity, anxiety, and fear on the inside. Few could maintain the hypermasculine role without some form of inner emotional repercussion. The Iroquoians seem closest in modal personality to the peoples of the Sub-Arctic and the Plains; yet the differences with both appear to be significant.

THE AMBIVALENT ESKIMO

One of the best descriptions of Eskimo personality is that of Robert F. Spencer (1959) in his excellent monograph *The North Alaskan Eskimo*.

Children were wanted and were treated as indulgently as in other areas of native North America. Infants were nursed at their mother's breast whenever they cried from hunger. Weaning was a gradual process; a mother might even nurse two children of different ages at the same time. Although toilet training was started as early as two or three months by setting the infant over one of the wooden vessels used as a urinal by the family, there was no punishment for bed wetting or other "accidents." On the whole, toilet training was gentle.

Infants slept with their mothers or with both parents. Parents resumed intercourse soon after a birth, apparently in one or two months, and the child was not barred from the bed on those occasions. Therefore, neither the father nor the infant was rejected in favor of the other by the mother. Infants were never left alone or completely rejected by members of the household. If the mother was busy at some household task, there was always another person to hold the child and otherwise take care of it. Infants were not forced to walk or to talk. Boy babies were subjected to a single unpleasant experience: they were sometimes placed outdoors naked for a time when the north wind blew. This was thought to increase their ability to withstand the cold.

Boys and girls were separated much of the time in childhood. Girls stayed at home with their mothers, from whom they gradually learned household tasks. Boys accompanied their fathers on hunting expeditions as soon as they were old enough and began to learn the activities of men. Although children were encouraged to become as proficient at necessary activities as they were able, boasting was frowned upon, and modesty was held up as the ideal. A good runner took care not to win races too often for fear of being regarded as too self-assertive. Industriousness, cooperation, generosity, and truthfulness were among the cardinal virtues.

The change from childhood to adulthood was not marked by formal initiations. For boys, the piercing of the lower lip near the corners of the mouth for labrets ended the period of adolesence and marked the beginning of manhood. At first menstruation, girls were secluded from the rest of the family inside the house, were subject to restrictions on food and drink, and could not prepare food for others, but the taboo period lasted for only five days. Their chins were tattooed soon afterward, and they were regarded as women ready for marriage.

Premarital sexual relations were the rule for both young men and young women, although the latter were warned not to become involved with several men lest they confuse the obligations between families which began with sexual ties and were aimed at marriage. Ideally, parents preferred to arrange marriages for their children. This was often associated with bride service, where the young man lived in his future bride's household and assisted her father in hunting for a year or more before the marriage.

Although most marriages seem to have been satisfactory to both parties, neither expressed feelings for the other. In fact, no one in Eskimo culture verbalized his feelings about anything. Feelings were repressed most of the time, but were occasionally expressed in outbursts of violence. If a man's wife was dissatisfied with her marriage but her relatives approved of her husband, the husband could punish her severely. He might tear her clothes to pieces. If she were a scold, he could rip her cheeks open from the corners of her mouth; and if she ran away too often, he might cut the Achilles tendons in her legs, so that she could not walk far. Two wives in a polygynous union seem to have got along well with each other, and even two husbands in a polyandrous union with one wife generally had no difficulty. However, there was a definite taboo on the marriage of a man to two sisters or of a woman to two brothers. Both the sororate and the levirate were likewise forbidden; a widower could not marry his dead wife's sister, nor could a widow marry her dead husband's brother.

Old men, except possibly shamans, tended to lose prestige as their physical prowess waned. Old women, in contrast to men, sometimes became shamans after the menopause, or the wife of a shaman might take an active part in her husband's profession at this time. Those who were not shamans were often thought to possess evil supernatural powers with which they could harm another.

The grandmother and, to a lesser extent, the grandfather often became the baby-sitters and guardians for their grandchildren. When rejected by a parent, a child frequently sought refuge in the arms of a grandparent. If we add to this the fact that children were usually given the names of deceased grandparents and were thought to have derived their souls from the same source, we see that the grandparent-grandchild relationship was second only to that of parent and child.

In a succinct but excellent paper entitled "Alaskan Eskimo Cultural Values," Margaret Lantis (1959), sheds much light on Eskimo personality. The Eskimo placed a premium on the self-reliance, self-confidence, quick thinking, and skill of the successful hunter; this included skill in manufacturing weapons as well as skill and ingenuity in using them. Lack of skill meant starvation and death. Hunting achievements contributed most to a man's prestige and to his high ego ideal. After these traits had given a man a generous supply of the world's goods, he was expected to share them freely with others. There was even rivalry in public generosity; those with the most competed to see who could give away the most. Men even shared their wives with friends and guests.

Physical aggression toward other Eskimos was inhibited to the point of becoming completely repressed most of the time. Patience and a philosophy of fatalism were highly valued. So strong was the socialization of the individual that community survival was valued above individual survival. Infanticide, suicide, and the killing of invalids are to be explained in these terms. Eskimo religion placed greater value on human and animal souls than it did on the bodies. Thus it was proper to kill and eat a sea mammal if this was done in a manner which would not offend the animal's soul. Such was the ideal pattern of Eskimo personal values and behavior.

When an Eskimo group was confined in cramped quarters by bad weather for a number of days, or when hunters came home empty-handed and starvation became a threat, tensions rose and were relieved by aggression. The killing of animals was probably the most frequent outlet for hostility, but beating one's dogs in anger was common. Aggression often took the form of sorcery against another person and, less often, of physical violence. Other outlets were the destruction of property and wife stealing, as well as the aggressions by a husband against his own wife, mentioned above. The most common social mechanism for dealing with such antisocial behavior was avoidance; the offender or the offended took to flight. But ultimately the culprit might be apprehended and forced to pay with his life for his deviations.

Frustrated individuals sometimes obtained relief by means of dreams or visions which were interpreted as soul flights and contact with spirits, and mythology constituted a kind of group fantasy or therapy. The personality of the shaman is largely to be explained in this manner.

If the ideal Eskimo personality described above was general throughout all of Eskimo territory, the amount of deviation from this ideal must have varied from one locality to another. For example, among the Musk-Ox Eskimo of the central region, every adult man had killed at least one other man in a duel. This suggests a wide deviation from the ideal of cooperation, generosity, and friendliness. If more were known about personality and culture, a number of cultures might be scaled according to the amount of adjustment or maladjustment of each to the ideals it professed. That some discrepancy between the ideal and the actual is general is suggested by the other sections in this chapter.

THE NEGATIVE MESO-AMERICAN COMMONERS

The concept of a single modal personality can scarcely be applied to Meso-America because of the class structure present there. Some excellent studies have been made of the personality of contemporary Indian minorities in Meso-America, but they portray only the character of the common man after four centuries of domination by an alien culture. One of the best descriptions of this kind is that by Oscar Lewis (1951) of the people of Tepoztlán, an Aztec village two hours' drive south of Mexico City. The Tepoztecans exercise a great deal of emotional restraint and reserve, and rarely show any spontaneity in public. They prefer not to attract attention by word or deed; even in large public gatherings regarded as social occasions, there is the minimum of noise. In the street, most faces are somber masks,

smiles minimal, and laughter rare. Women and girls walk with downcast eyes lest they be accused of being too flirtatious, and adolescent
girls maintain an emotionless facial expression because a smile or
even a glance of interest may act as an invitation to some emotionally
starved young male. Considerable restraint is practiced even at home
and with relatives. Deviations from this straight and narrow path are
tolerated only in the aged and in drunken men.

The lack of emotional expression is reflected in the limited development of arts and crafts. There are practically no traditional crafts such
as basket making, pottery making, or weaving. Cultural missions sent
by the Mexican federal government have introduced crocheting,
embroidery, and other feminine crafts, but the designs used are all
copied from patterns in stores or in style magazines; they are not
created by the worker. There are no traditional dances for men and
women together, and the men perform only a single simple Spanish
dance. All music is imported; there are no local composers and little
individuality in performing.

The shyness and restraint generally characteristic of the Tepoztlán
personality apply also to the relations between the sexes. People do not
express their affections warmly, and generally avoid bodily contact.
The principal exception to this rule is the mother-child relationship
during the nursing period, when the mother shows genuine affection
for her child. The double standard for adolescents is the rule. Boys are
expected to have their sexual adventures, but girls are severely
punished if caught.

The negative emotions of anger, hate, fear, and envy are more easily
expressed than the positive emotions of love, kindness, sympathy, and
joy. But because all emotions tend to be suppressed, the negative ones
often take the form of suspicion and distrust or the harboring of a
grudge. They may be expressed more definitely, however, in gossip,
ridicule, stealing, destruction of another's property, and sorcery.
Successful persons tend to be targets of envy, criticism, and malicious
gossip. Tourists, federal government agents, and other outsiders,
whether Mexicans or from foreign nations, are ridiculed in private; no
common citizen would dare to say such things in public, much less in
face-to-face contact. Even the Catholic priest is not above criticism.

The repression of the negative emotions of envy, hate, anger, and
the like sometimes gives rise to an illness called *muina*. The symptoms
are loss of appetite, vomiting, loss of weight, and very often death.
This sickness is primarily found among adults of both sexes, but

sometimes occurs among children. It may be precipitated by misfortune, humiliation, or insult, according to native belief.

Aggression sometimes takes the form of beating one's wife,
children, younger brothers or sisters, or domestic animals. But such
cases seem to be the exception rather than the rule, and wife beating is
usually limited to times when the husband is drunk. People throw
stones at the objects of their anger; husbands displeased with food
may throw it on the ground; and wives sometimes toss around household objects when angered. Small children have temper tantrums, and
boys sometimes fight in the absence of adults. There is absolutely no
sense of chivalry in fights between men. Face-to-face fights occur only
when one or both men are drunk. At other times the aggressor attacks
his enemy from behind, usually at night, and, after a few shots or
slashes with a machete, runs away to hide without any effort to
determine how much damage he has done.

To offset fear, anxiety, and insecurity, the Tepoztecans rely on the
moral virtues of hard work and thrift. A man who can provide his
family with plenty of food, clothing, and shelter is a successful man.
Those who accomplish less console themselves with the thought that
they are hard-working and thrifty men, and measure their worth as
much by the amount of their labor as by their economic gain. Men are
reluctant to lend, borrow, or share with other men, and prefer to
remain independent; yet they share almost everything within the
nuclear families they support, and may expect a little sharing with more
distant relatives in time of need. Most men work alone in their fields
or with the help of a son. This daily isolation probably contributes to
the withdrawn character of the men. But family life does have its
rewards. Even a poor provider remains the head of his household and
maintains the respect of his children, who make few demands upon
their parents. Few parents feel that they are poor providers for their
children even though they fall below the average in objective terms.

With the negative emotions dominating the positive ones, it might
be inferred that there was a great deal of competition within the society,
but such is not the case. On the contrary, the people lack a competitive
drive, and do not try very hard to improve their lot or outdo their
neighbors. They do not feel that they have much chance of bettering
themselves, and are resigned, if not content, to plod along from year to
year. Most young men aspire to nothing more than the life of a farmer,
like their fathers, and girls look forward to marrying and performing
the household tasks.

Lewis' description of Tepoztlán was published in 1951 but was the result of field work done in the 1940's. Lewis has returned to Tepoztlán since that time and has found many changes. Many young men have gone as laborers (*braceros*) to the United States and returned with a little capital, the first they have ever acquired in their lives. Many now operate small businesses of their own and never expect to farm. So great is the shift away from the farm that land, which had been getting progressively scarcer up to about 1945, now often goes unworked. After four centuries of little change in the rural areas, Mexico is finally on the move, and Lewis' 1951 picture of Tepoztlán will soon be history. We can be certain that changes in personality are accompanying those in economics.

CONCLUSIONS

In this section, a few of the theories of personality formation will be tested against the examples just described. The Freudian notion that the treatment of infants in the first few years of life is more important than any other period of comparable length in the life span does not seem to hold. The above survey shows that infants were treated lovingly, affectionately, and permissively in all the Indian cultures described in this chapter. If infant care is uniformly gentle, it cannot explain the differences in adult personality revealed by the examples described above.

Pettitt (1946: 12) suggests that the binding of infants to cradling devices, which restrict arm as well as leg movements, may account in part for the general absence of overt expression of emotions. The "deadpan" face or "wooden Indian" restraint so common among North American Indians may be related to this physical restriction in infancy. An opposing view holds that swaddling or binding the limbs gives the infant a feeling of security comparable to that of the womb or the mother's arms rather than frustrating him. Superficial comparison of personality in the Arctic and tropical areas of North America, where infants are not swaddled or bound to cradling devices, suggests no marked differences in adult personality between these areas and the rest of the continent. Therefore, for areas where binding is the rule, this aspect of infant treatment seems to have little to do with adult personality.

North American Indians reveal no strong cases of the Oedipus complex anywhere. There are several reasons for this. First, the gentle and affectionate treatment of infants would tend to keep hostilities at the minimum. Second, the transfer of discipline to the supernatural, as described in Chapter 22, would tend to prevent the accumulation of much hostility by children toward either parent. Third, the extended family pattern, dominant in about half of our Indian societies, would tend to diffuse a child's emotional responses to a number of relatives rather than to concentrate them on one or two. Fourth, matrilocal residence and matrilineal descent, in areas where they occurred, would tend to weaken the role of the father and to substitute the mother's brother for him. For these reasons the Oedipus complex was weak in aboriginal North America.

It is clear that while impressionistic studies of modal personality made in the past are acceptable as pioneer efforts, they have not achieved enough precision to satisfy contemporary researchers in the field of culture and personality. The trend is toward experimentation and psychological testing in all its myriad ramifications, which must include intricate statistical methods if it is to satisfy the critical standards of the behavioral sciences today. Anthropologists intending to do research in this controversial field must get the more technical part of their training from psychologists and psychiatrists rather than in anthropology departments. Although studies in personality and culture are less frequent and less fashionable in anthropology now than they were ten years ago, anthropologists are needed as collaborators with other behavioral scientists in this important field of study.

REFERENCES

BENEDICT, 1932, 1934; BENNETT, 1946; CODERE, 1956; DEVEREUX, 1951; DOROTHY EGGAN, 1943; FENTON, 1941*a*, 1948; GOLDFRANK, 1943, 1945*a*, 1945*b*; GUILFORD, 1968; HALLOWELL, 1955; HONIGMAN, 1949, 1954; LANTIS, 1959; LEWIS, 1941, 1942, 1951; MOONEY, 1896; SPINDLER AND SPINDLER, 1957; THOMPSON, 1945; THOMPSON AND JOSEPH, 1944; WALLACE, 1952, 1958.

25

History and Culture Change in Mexico

THE AVOWED purpose of the first voyage of Christopher Columbus was to discover a new route to the Far East which would be shorter and easier to negotiate than that around the Cape of Good Hope in Africa. Such a route would have given the Spanish an advantage in the trade with the East and would have increased the wealth of their royalty and upper classes. The Spaniard in the lower ranks hoped to gain favor in the eyes of his upper-class sponsor and to earn a fortune large enough to permit a speedy return to Spain and a life of leisure there.

After the Spanish realized that they had discovered new continents teeming with millions of unsaved souls, their colonization included a religious crusade to Christianize the masses in the New World. The "Christian Kings," Ferdinand and Isabella, fresh from their victory over the Moors, wished to spread Christianity to their new colonies across the seas. They and their devout successors Charles I and Philip II sent many Dominicans, Franciscans, and—later—Jesuits to the Americas for this purpose; and even their military representatives conquered the Indians in the name of their God as well as their king. The Indians were judged by a papal bull in 1537 to be fully human and in possession of immortal souls.

Luckily for the Spanish, they encountered the wealthiest Indians in the New World in Mexico and Peru. They promptly defeated them in war, robbed them of their gold and other valuables, deposed their political and religious leaders, appointed Spaniards in their places, and proceeded to operate these colonies according to the economic system of Spain. Largely because the Indians of Mexico and Peru had paid taxes and taken orders from overlords of some kind literally from time immemorial, they knew no model for general rebellion and yielded to the iron hand of the Spaniards. The population in these areas was so large and so dense that it was impossible for most of the Indians to flee to some place of refuge. Another thing which helped the Spanish to regiment the Indian in Mexico and Peru was the latter's habit of daily labor, at farming, mining, crafts, and on public works, which had been going on for centuries before the Spanish arrived. Indian men did most of the farm work and all other labor away from home, while the women performed household tasks and sometimes wove cloth or made pottery vessels. Men accustomed to daily work will submit to forced labor or excessive taxation much more readily than those who habitually only hunt and fight.

After conquering the Aztecs in 1521, the Spanish rapidly regimented all available Indian labor to mine, farm, and produce export goods in factories. Spain thus produced more gold and silver than all the rest of Europe combined in the colonial period, but most of the crown's share went to pay the debts that the kings had incurred to launch their conquests of the New World, to fight religious wars against the new Protestants or general wars against its rivals in commerce, to build new cathedrals and palaces, and to stock them with the finest works of European art. Second to metals in export value was the red cochineal dye, made from the blood of insects raised on cultivated cactus plants. Of imports, textiles accounted for over half the total value, with paper, distilled alcoholic beverages, mercury, and iron making up most of the remainder (Cumberland, 1968: 84–112).

The commercial explosion of the sixteenth century took a terrible toll of the Indian laborers. European and African diseases, for which the Indians had no hereditary immunity, killed the greatest numbers; the mercury used in the silver refining process in Mexico in the sixteenth century poisoned many others; and malnutrition and the absence of safety devices in mines and construction work were equally lethal. Dobyns (1966: 415) estimates that the population of Mexico was reduced from between 30 and 37·5 million to a mere 1·5 million between 1520 and 1650. Although I think that his estimate of aboriginal population is too high, reducing it to 20 million would still allow a drop to 7·5 per cent of the pre-Columbian figure by 1650.

Partly as a result of this squandering of most of the human resources in the sixteenth century, labor became so scarce that the entire commercial system ground almost to a halt. The seventeenth century in Mexico was one of business depression and a retreat to the rural areas where the hacienda system had begun about 1540. The hacienda owner (*hacendado*) obtained his land from the king or viceroy; although he had no authority to commandeer Indian labor, he could lend individual Indians enough money to establish little homesteads on or near his land and to work for him on a sharecrop or part-time basis, and could even pay their tribute to royal authorities. The hacienda owner also operated a "company" store, where he supplied merchandise on credit. Most Indians failed to pay off such debts and became debt peons bound to their employer and his land.

The evils of the hacienda system were offset to some extent by the crown's grants of lands to many Indian communities. Each community was given six and a half square miles of land on which to establish a self-sustaining economic and social unit. Such land could be sold only on approval of the viceroy, the king's chief executive in New Spain, and the hacienda owners had no control over it or the Indians on it. The officers of the crown retained the right to judge such major crimes as murder and litigation between two communities, but the internal affairs of each community were controlled by its own Indian officers and council as long as they did not conflict with the demands of Church and State. These officers directed the labor and levied the taxes, part of which was paid to the crown and the remainder deposited in a community fund. The social and religious life of the community was also directed by its own officers, who were in charge of the elaborate fiestas that were blends of Spanish and Indian religion, pageantry, and art.

During the War of Independence which freed Mexico from Spain, 1810–21, José Morelos and other Mexican leaders issued a number of decrees concerning Indians. These abolished slavery of persons of all races in 1810—half a century ahead of the United States—and eliminated the plethora of such labels as *mulatto* and *casta* for the many people of mixed ancestry. The decrees of 1810–21 also abolished all enforced service of Indians short of slavery (*mita*) to corporations, civil officials, or parish priests, and demanded that Indians be given control of the lands they worked and the produce from these lands. Because these humanitarian decrees were never enforced, the Indians gained nothing from them during the ensuing century. In 1810, the best fields and pastures were owned and operated by only 4,944 ranchers (*hacendados*), and it is estimated that in 1910 as few as 830 families owned 97 per cent of all farm and ranch land in Mexico.

After the War of Independence, the Church acquired more and more land, until by 1840 it held at least half the farm and ranch land in Mexico. During the period called the *Reforma*, 1854–76, attempts were made to wrest some of this land from the Church and give it to small freeholders, including Indians. Thus the law of the reformer

Miguel Lerdo of 1856 demanded that the Church sell all its land not devoted to religious purposes and pay a heavy sales tax to the national treasury. Because the lower classes had no money to buy these lands, it was the *hacendados* who bought them and benefited by the law. In addition, the government divided the collective farms of the Indians into small plots assigned to individual heads of families, many of whom lost their small holdings to the *hacendados* in a few years. Finally the sale of so-called vacant lands to raise money to repel the French invaders deprived Indians of more land because their titles to it had often not been registered in any government office, making their lands technically vacant. This scheme was executed by the full-blooded Zapotec Indian Benito Juárez, president of Mexico twice during this period, in his effort to save the political independence of the nation.

In the early years of the Revolution of 1910–20, a series of decrees reiterated the right of farm laborers, including Indians, to own the land on which they worked, and some of these were incorporated into the Constitution of 1917. Its Article 27 states that the nation shall have at all times the right to impose upon private property such restrictions as the public interest may require in order to conserve and equitably distribute the public wealth, and declares void all previous laws which had deprived *rancherías*, *pueblos*, *congregaciones* (reservations), tribes, and other corporations of their lands, forests, and water.

Gradually, for the first time in Mexican history, the property laws were enforced. Between 1910 and 1968 the Mexican government obtained from the *hacendados* and distributed to independent small holders and to small farmers' communities (*ejidos*) 148 million acres, a total area almost as large as the state of Texas. This is 58 per cent of all of Mexico's farm and grazing land, which totals about 254 million acres. The most powerful leader in this land reform movement was Lázaro Cárdenas, a full-blooded Tarascan Indian and president of Mexico from 1934 to 1940. In 1968, over half the total population of Mexico, including many Indians, was participating in the *ejido* system, though the *ejidos* in that year were less productive, on either a per-acre or a per-capita basis, than privately owned lands (Cumberland, 1968: 303, 369).

From 1917 to 1968, a number of federal agencies were established to funnel aid and education to Indians, best defined in this period as those still speaking Indian languages and living in communities largely made up of such speakers. These programs, the first of their kind in Latin America, have served as models for other nations. In 1948, the National Indian Institute (Instituto Nacional Indigenista) was created by law to coordinate such programs. Some of the figures from an annual report of this agency for 1964–65 give an idea of its varied activities. Its education program taught 45,000 pupils in 531 primary schools, and 25,910 new textbooks were issued. Its health program included: 68,165 consultations with outpatients; 595 surgical operations; 37,832 hypodermic injections to cure extant ailments; and 90,000 immunizations against smallpox, polio, diphtheria, whooping cough, and tetanus. In a campaign against typhus, 600,000 pieces of clothing were sterilized (Aguirre Beltrán, 1965).

Economic and agricultural aid to Indians for the same year from the National Indian Institute included loans for the improvement of forest resources and agricultural operations. Fifty thousand new fruit trees were planted in 1,500 orchards, and 150,000 coffee trees in 1,000 new coffee plantations. Breeding stock, for better varieties of cattle, hogs, and chickens, was distributed to Indians, and about 20,000 animals and chickens were given inoculations against disease. These examples demonstrate the realistic nature of the federal aid to Indians in Mexico.

The remainder of this chapter will give the main trends of Mexican culture change by topic in approximately the same order as that of the previous chapters of this book.

Food.—Food production changed less after A.D. 1492 than most other facets of culture in Meso-America. The Indians continued to raise almost all of the plant foods they had grown before the Spanish arrived, but with reduced acreage because the Spanish appropriated grazing land for animals and required the Indians to raise crops that were exported or consumed by the colonists. The two main products raised for the local consumption of the Spanish colonists were wheat and wine grapes. The Spanish introduced a form of the ancient Mediterranean scratch plow pulled by oxen with yokes attached to their horns, but it was used more on the fields of the Spanish overlord than on the plots cultivated by the Indians for themselves. Recent tests in modern Tepoztlán have shown that plow cultivation produces only half as much corn per hectare as hoe cultivation (Wolf, 1959: 198). Its only virtue is that it saves human labor.

The Spanish brought over most of the livestock found in Latin America today: horses for riding and prestige; cattle for plowing and cart pulling, meat, hides, and tallow; mules and donkeys for packing and riding; sheep for meat and wool; goats for milk and meat; pigs for meat and lard; chickens for eggs and meat; and bees for honey. Although Indians had contact with these animals on the Spanish ranches, few of them in the beginning could afford to acquire any for themselves and to give them the care required for their survival. Later, the Indians acquired the smaller animals in considerable numbers: donkeys, sheep, goats, pigs, and chickens. The donkey could live off the country, be ridden, pack loads heavier than a man normally carried, go longer without water than a horse, was docile and easy to control, and not expensive to breed or purchase. The Spanish never allowed Indians to own and ride horses.

The diet of the Indians changed only a little, partly because they preferred native American fare and partly because they could not afford as much meat as the Spaniards. As late as 1965, the production of maize in Mexico was over four times that of wheat, the second most important cereal crop, and over half of all crop land was planted in maize (*Statistical Yearbook of the United Nations for* 1966). Sheep, goats, pigs, and chickens improved the diet as they gradually became more common in the new blend of Spanish and Indian culture.

Maize is still prepared for food by the old Indian process in Mexico. It is first soaked in lime water, which furnishes an abundance of calcium for growing children, whose teeth are generally healthier than those of children in Europe and the United States. Then it is ground wet on a three-legged stone *metate*, which is still in enough demand to be mass-produced and sold in rural markets. Next, the wet dough is patted between the hands to form a thin pancake of Indian origin but called by the Spanish word *tortilla*. It is finally baked on a grill of pottery and is ready for eating. In many localities in Mexico, the wet corn is at present ground between two cylindrical stones, European style, and this mill is powered by gasoline or electricity. The rest of the process remains unchanged in rural areas. Corn used to make tortillas must have a higher protein content than the hybrid corn fed to live-stock in the United States; otherwise, it would not hold together. Native corn is therefore of superior nutritional value for human consumption, although its yield in bushels per acre is much less than that of hybrid corn. However, a new strain of corn recently developed in laboratories in the United States, called opaque-2 maize, is higher in protein content; experimental animals fed this new corn have shown much more rapid growth rates than those fed on ordinary hybrid corn (Mertz *et al.*, 1965).

Corn production in the colonial period in Mexico averaged about one million metric tons per annum; in the period from 1877 to 1946, it averaged about two million. After 1946, production increased rapidly to nearly nine million in 1965. This recent increase was brought about by scientific agriculture with its better seeds, fertilizers, insecticides, tractors, and mechanical planters. Other crops showed similar increases (Cumberland, 1968: 369–72).

The cattle of the Spanish increased rapidly in the highland areas of Meso-America, where there was a lush growth of grass. There was such a surplus of beef in the sixteenth century that one military officer complained that his men in the ranks were tired of beef and demanding more food of other kinds. By the middle of the seventeenth century, however, overgrazing had reduced much of this rich grassland to semidesert produced by the invasion of desert shrubs into areas formerly dominated by grass. Much of it remains semidesert to this day.

Some of the Spanish religious ideas associated with farming also diffused to the Americas. San Isidro is the patron saint of agriculture everywhere in Latin America, and in Mexico seed is usually blessed at Mass on May 15. Beliefs about weather prediction and the phases of the moon also follow the Spanish model. Domesticated animals are blessed on the day of St. Anthony; the notion that the evil eye may harm animals as well as people seems to have been derived from Spain.

The dominant process of acculturation for domesticated plants and animals was one of simple diffusion of Spanish elements which were added to those of Indian origin without much replacement of the latter. On Spanish ranches, the Spanish-style farming predominated; but the Indian peasant farmers largely retained their Indian heritage on the smaller plots that they controlled, and added only a modest number of Spanish features. The entire inventory of farming practices in Spain is much larger than that taken to the New World, which comes mainly from two provinces in southwestern Spain near the ports from which the ships sailed. This process of reduction of Spanish inventory in Spain, followed by very wide diffusion of the selected items in the New World, is characteristic of other aspects of culture as well (Foster, 1960: 50–69).

Indian fishing methods continued to be used in Mexico by individuals seeking a few fish for home consumption. Commercial fishing, in contrast, is almost wholly of Spanish origin. The pocket seine, the gill net, the circular hand-thrown net, and the trot line with multiple hooks all have Spanish names and are obviously of Spanish origin.

Tobacco and Alcohol.—Tobacco, before European contact, was smoked, chewed, snuffed, or drunk in concoctions principally by priests, shamans, and others seeking rapport with the supernatural. Daily smoking was unknown to the masses. It was only after tobacco was carried to Europe and smoking habits established there that it was diffused to the masses, mostly in the form of cigarettes, throughout Latin America. Alcoholic beverages were consumed in quantity by religious practitioners, but were also regularly drunk by the masses. The consumption of fermented *Agave* juice (pulque) in Mexico still exceeds that of all other alcoholic drinks combined, as it did before A.D. 1492. The grape wines and distilled brandies introduced by the Spanish are consumed mainly by the upper classes in Mexico, although tequila and mescal, distilled from native products, are imbibed by persons of lower rank also. The distillation technique itself was invented in Europe and introduced by the Spanish into Mexico. The other drugs mentioned in Chapter 7 have never been widely used in either pre-Columbian or post-Columbian times with the exception of peyote, which has had its greatest acceptance in the United States.

Housing.—Those Latin American nations with the largest Indian populations—Mexico, Guatemala, Ecuador, Peru, and Bolivia—still house many of these Indians in dwellings much like those of the pre-Columbian period. They are mostly rectangular in ground plan with the earth for a floor, and lack stoves and chimneys, windows, running water, electricity, sanitary facilities, and sometimes tables and chairs. In Peru, Mexico, and the Pueblo Southwest, walls were often made of stone or adobe in the pre-Columbian period, and nearly flat roofs were the rule in parts of highland Mexico and among the Pueblos of the Southwest. Solid-walled houses with flat roofs have been built in the Middle East and around the Mediterranean for thousands of years and are certainly independent historically of generically similar types in North America. Even the multistoried Pueblo apartment houses are paralleled many places in the Middle East.

The Spanish *cuarto*, a single room nearly square, with four vertical masonry walls and a nearly flat roof with a single slight pitch, diffused to many parts of Mexico and the Southwest. The wealthier Spaniards or mestizos often built a series of such rooms around a patio, with the doors opening on the patio and the back walls left solid for defense. A single gate opened onto the street. So nearly parallel are some of the features of this Spanish *cuarto* style to those of some Indian houses that one must know the archeology and history of an area in order to be sure of the Spanish or Indian origin of the dwellings. Perhaps the most conspicuous feature derived from Spain is the tile roof, which is widespread in Spanish America. Iron railings around balconies are also Spanish, but are limited to homes of the more well-to-do. Other Spanish elements include wooden doors of milled lumber with iron hinges and locks, glass in windows, and sometimes bathrooms. The flush toilet and sewage disposal are twentieth-century innovations in Spanish America, as they are in many areas of the world, and came from northern Europe or the United States. They are still missing in all but a small minority of houses in rural Latin America.

Town plans in the Old World and the New also have some interesting parallels. In the New World, ceremonial centers date back to the Olmecs, 1500 B.C. to A.D. 300, and continued to be built up to the time of European contact. Although subject to much variation, they ran generally to rectangular patterns for the main pyramids, temples, palaces, and connecting streets. In the Old World, rectangular grids of streets broken by a central plaza can be found in the Middle East well before the Christian era, and some Greek and Roman cities follow such a plan. Foster (1960: 34–49) shows that conscious town planning, resulting in a rectangular grid plan of streets and a rectangular central plaza, dates back to the twelfth century in Spain. The Spanish were able to achieve their ideal town plan more frequently in the New World because they built many new towns in new locations where no municipality had existed before; or they destroyed the Indian town completely and used the stone for their own buildings. In Spain, during the same period, there were too many old buildings and streets running counter to the ideal grid plan to achieve as great a uniformity there. The concentration of Indians in the new towns in greater numbers than in their former villages unfortunately facilitated the spread of epidemic diseases.

Sociologically, the Hispanic American plaza achieves greater importance than the Spanish plaza. It is consistently faced by a church, a city hall, the homes of the wealthy, the finest shops, and sometimes the open market. Promenades around the plaza every evening are the rule for unmarried young people, with the boys and girls walking in opposite directions. The girls are often chaperoned by their parents, who sit on a park bench most of the time. Fiestas, with their processions, take place in the plaza or terminate a longer journey through the town at the plaza. Although the physical details of the grid plan and plaza can be traced back to Spain, socially it has reached its greatest florescence in the New World.

Clothing.—Although the conquerors did not allow the Indians to wear Spanish dress, and forced them to retain their Indian costumes, the latter soon became mixtures of Indian and Spanish materials and styles. In some areas at least, the men put on trousers, shirts or boleros, and straw hats, specifically different but stemming from Spanish models. Because women were already dressed in skirts and blouses not so different from Spanish women's dress, their costumes underwent less change than the men's. The sleeveless blouse (*huipil*) and the poncho-styled upper garment (*quesquemetl*) are still to be seen in Mexico today. In the cooler areas, women welcomed skirts of wool from sheep introduced by the Spanish. The men likewise took to woolen ponchos with head holes, a blend of Spanish material and Andean design. Woolen blankets without head holes, however, were derived from Spain (Foster, 1960: 102). Wool and cotton soon replaced maguey fiber, which had been the most common clothing material before the Conquest. Cowhide sandals became the standard footwear for Indian soldiers and porters in the service of the Spanish, and were derived from both pre-Columbian Indian models and Spanish types. They have been continuously worn down to the present time, although the majority of people probably went barefoot until the twentieth century, as they had done before European contact. In 1960, 60 per cent of Mexicans were wearing shoes, 23 per cent sandals or huaraches, and 17 per cent (including children) went barefoot. The shawl or stole of the women, the ubiquitous rebozo, is ultimately of Spanish origin though much modified. The so-called Indian styles of clothing worn today are all colonial hybrids of Indian and Spanish costume.

Crafts.—The Indian hand loom, one end of which is attached to the waist of the weaver, and the spindle whorl are still used in the more conservative villages of Mexico and Guatemala, but are fast losing ground to more efficient spinning wheels and looms. The Indian loom was first replaced by the Spanish flat-bed loom with foot treadles to move the heddles. This was a much more efficient loom than the Indian model, but it, in turn, is being replaced rapidly in this century by high-speed powered looms designed by weaving engineers. A majority of Mexican women still cut and sew their own clothing, but from mass-produced yard goods purchased in stores. The sewing machine is increasingly facilitating this work. During the past hundred years—and here and there even today—men have worn white pajama-like costumes of muslin made by their wives from factory-made yard goods purchased at the store or market. But most men's clothing in Mexico today is made entirely in clothing factories, as it is in Europe and the United States.

Pottery making in rural villages underwent little change after Spanish contact. The kiln, which raised the temperature of the firing process enough to permit glazing, was the principal addition. The Spanish potter's wheel was seldom adopted by Indian or mestizo rural potters, although it was used in cities where Spaniards had set up shops. Indian-type molds continued to be used for mass production in pottery-making centers and were just as efficient as the wheel. Indian pottery is more generally used in the household today; because it exhibited a greater variety of both shape and decoration than that from Spain, the Mexicans had little incentive to copy Spanish models. Black ware, produced by slowing down the firing process to impregnate the surface with the carbon in the smoke, was independently invented in Spain and Meso-America (Foster, 1960: 102), and again in the Southwest at San Ildefonso by the famous María Martínez.

Spanish basket weaving had even less influence on Meso-American basketry, where the same essential techniques had long before been independently invented by Indians. Spanish steel needles and dyes are about the only additions to this largely Indian tradition.

The Spanish introduced the tanning of leather with tannic acid, which eventually became widespread in Hispanic America. The leather thus produced was the only kind used, at least for the horse trappings of the army and the ranches.

Iron smelting and working were wholly Spanish—the Indians had never known the use of iron. Iron tools and weapons, along with other trade goods, were sometimes given to Indians as a friendly gesture to get them to settle down on ranches or to join the army as porters or wranglers. Indian metallurgy, mostly limited to body ornaments and lacking the bellows, rapidly went out of fashion when the Indian elite, who wore the metal ornaments, were deposed by the Spanish. Silver working in Spanish style has replaced the earlier Indian metal-working techniques, and tourists have encouraged its manufacture.

Art.—The modest folk art, which manifested itself principally in the decoration of utilitarian objects, such as baskets, pots, and textiles, was much less disturbed by the Conquest, and has survived with modification in rural areas where Indian culture is least changed.

The greatest works of American Indian art and architecture were deliberately destroyed by the Spanish conquerors as soon as they gained control of the New World. This was because the art had been inextricably integrated with politics and religion, nobles and priests. By destroying the Indian "idols" and the buildings on which they were depicted or placed as well as the sacred pictographs in the codices, and by robbing the rich of their jewelry and most elaborate costumes, the Spanish eradicated all but a few of the best examples of Indian art. At the same time, Indians who acquiesced and became devout Catholics were trained in European styles of painting, sculpture, and even architecture, and produced much of the work seen in Mexican colonial churches today.

After the revolution of 1910–20, a new art style sprang up in Mexico. It included both Spanish and Indian motifs, most often took the form of huge mural paintings or tile mosaics, and was politically slanted in favor of the Indian and others in the economically depressed class.

Architecture had the same fate as other Indian arts. Every Indian edifice of any consequence in the cities occupied by the Spanish was torn down and the stone used to build government buildings for the viceroy and lesser representatives of the crown as well as churches and cathedrals in which to worship the Christian God. No city of comparable size in Europe up to the sixteenth century was built as rapidly as was the new Mexico City. The only examples of Indian art and architecture to survive in Mexico City were those that somehow got buried in the grading of the sites for new buildings or that were buried by the Aztecs at an earlier date when they built Tenochtitlán. These have reappeared in the twentieth century when excavations for the foundations of taller and taller buildings have been dug deeper and deeper. Because most of the Maya cities were located in a tropical jungle, a number were so completely overgrown with vegetation that they were never found by the Spanish and were not discovered until archeologists of the late nineteenth and the twentieth centuries searched for them. Fortunately, some of these have preserved the most superb examples of Mayan art, which rivals that of the Olmecs for first position in the American Indian field. At this writing, archeologists are uncovering monumental ruins in other New World areas and thus continuing to rediscover many dramatic examples of Indian art and architecture.

Music.—Indian music has disappeared more completely than other Meso-American arts, partially because there was no true musical notation. The recovery of a few musical instruments by archeologists tells us little of the structure of the music itself. Furthermore, it was closely associated with Indian religion and ceremony. Just as the Roman Catholic Church rapidly substituted its own art and architecture for the Indian varieties, so it also taught its music to the Indians at the expense of the earlier native styles. At the popular level, Spanish guitars, other instruments, and folk songs almost wholly replaced the modest amount of Indian folk music that may have persisted for a time. The small remnant of Indian music that survived into the early twentieth century was eroded first by Spanish music and instruments and later by the radio, jukebox, and television, which have enormously sped up musical acculturation. Fortunately, a little of the flavor of Indian music survives in the compositions of a few twentieth-century composers, such as Carlos Chávez.

Trade, Transportation.—The Spanish permitted the Indians to continue to operate their native local markets, but put them on weekly or biweekly schedules. Mules and donkeys packed the loads of the Spanish merchants, but many Indians continued to back-pack their loads to and from the market with the aid of the strap across the forehead. Although Foster (1960: 104) found the forehead strap in use in Galicia and a few other Spanish provinces, its more frequent use over the entire New World at White contact suggests independent origin in the two hemispheres, unless one speculates that the early Indian immigrants to the Americas brought it from Asia. The carrying pole may also have a dual origin. I am inclined to believe that most of the New World examples are of Spanish origin, since they are found only in areas where the Spanish arrived before the end of the sixteenth century. However, a design on a spindle whorl from the coast of Ecuador, dated at 200 B.C., clearly shows a carrying yoke which may have been introduced from Asia (Jennings, 1968: 175). In Mexico today, the carrying pole is used principally to carry water buckets, as it is also in the Pyrenees (Foster, 1960: 105).

The solid-wheeled oxcart, the horn yokes, the mules and donkeys, the packing technique, the management of the pack train, and the vocabulary associated with these are all of Spanish origin. The trails used, however, were often those of local Indian traders or of the itinerant merchants of the Aztecs, who were largely liquidated by the Spanish.

The first Mexican railroad began operation in 1850, but it was only eight miles long. By 1910, Mexico had 12,000 miles of railroads, and has continued to build more mileage all through the twentieth century. Cars, trucks, and modern highways were few before 1940, but increased rapidly after that date to 58,000 miles of highways (33,000 paved), 771,000 cars, and 389,000 trucks in 1965. All cars and trucks were imported until the 1940's, when the first assembly plants in Mexico were built. By 1964, thirteen assembly plants produced about 100,000 motor vehicles of all kinds, and planned expansion will soon supply all of Mexico's automotive needs (Cumberland, 1968: 320, 374).

The modest amount of Indian sea trade, largely in the hands of the wealthy, was curtailed by the Spanish, who replaced it with a much larger operation to and from Spain and the Philippines. The chief exports from Spain were arms, paper, textiles, books, wine, olive oil, and soap. The production of competitive goods of these kinds in the colonies was prohibited or restricted.

Slaves and Serfs.—In order to insure an adequate labor force to produce the New World export items, the crown condoned slavery in the first half of the sixteenth century and the *encomienda* (royal land grant) system for a longer period. The crown gave the *encomendero* (trustee) the right to receive tax payments and labor service from Indians living in certain villages on certain lands; needless to say, the Indians became serfs or virtual slaves in the factories. The true slaves were mostly Negroes imported from Africa. From the seventeenth to the nineteenth century, many Indians became debt peons on the *haciendas*, which were owned outright by the *hacendados*.

Property.—Property rights, such as those of the Aztecs in land (Caso, 1963) were drastically altered by the Spanish. The king was regarded at first as the owner of all land; his viceroy and lesser officials managed it or loaned it to Spaniards under the *encomienda* system. Indian commoners and serfs, however, remained on their lands, but the former paid taxes to the crown while the latter did not. As a result, many commoners posed as serfs, whose tax-free status was preferred. When Indian committees were established, they were given collective titles to land and allowed to manage their own affairs as long as they paid taxes to the crown and did not break the laws of Church and State. Sons continued to farm the plots of their fathers in these community-owned lands as they had done before the Conquest. The drastic land reforms of the twentieth century have already been mentioned above.

Kinship.—Kinship relationships were less disturbed by the Spanish than political affairs were. Except for the lineages of the nobility, Indian kinship authority had been limited to the household or the village, where the Spanish allowed it to continue. For instance, the patrilineal sibs of most of the Mayan-speaking peoples survive to this day, though with altered functions. The demes (*calpulli*) of the Aztecs of Tenochtitlán were wiped out because of their political importance in the capital city of the leading Indian military power. Elsewhere, some paternal kinship groups were lost in the shuffle of the Conquest, and the Indians were regrouped in the communities approved by the crown. In the areas where Indian languages are still spoken, mostly south of Mexico City, it is still possible to collect kinship terminologies in the native languages. The behavior of various combinations of kin to one another is less patterned, however, than it was before the Conquest. There has been a deculturation of kin relationship, with few new forms to replace the old. The monogamous family, consisting of a man, his wife, and their children, is the most common kinship unit. An unmarried man or woman is not included in the adult members of the society, and a childless couple cannot fully participate in the system. The economic and biological qualifications of marriage partners take precedence over romantic love. The more Hispanicized groups have large extended families with more emphasis on kinship, as in Europe.

The wedding ceremony itself is largely Spanish because it is prescribed by the Church. Informal aspects of courtship that stem from Spain are: forms of divination to determine who a girl's husband will be; prayers to San Antonio; serenades; and the use of guide books to successful courtship (Foster, 1960: 140). Elopement is reported both from Spain and from early Mexican sources. The so-called wife stealing in Mexico, which in most cases was elopement, seems to have been a blend of Indian and Spanish custom, although its reporting in early sources on Indians inclines some scholars to favor Indian priority in some areas. In addition, there were many informal marriages, without the sanction of the Church, in order to avoid the heavy expense of a wedding.

Government.—Immediately following the Conquest, the Spanish took over the functions of the Indian ruling class at the regional and national level. A few of the deposed Indian rulers moved to town, learned to speak Spanish, and dressed and behaved like Spaniards. As they were given many of the privileges of Spanish nobility, some became *encomenderos*, employing Indian serfs and Negro slaves, thus maintaining their positions of wealth and leadership. Most of them remained in the Indian communities and were reduced in status, although there were some local offices which only a noble could fill. The complete elimination of Indian nobility was not accomplished until Mexico won her independence from Spain in the early nineteenth century (Carrasco, 1961).

All offices in Indian communities rotated annually, so that over a period of time many mature men participated in the system. Each group of officers was responsible for the purchase and distribution of the food, liquor, candles, incense, fireworks, and everything else consumed in the elaborate religious fiestas. In the early colonial period, most of the wealth consumed in these great public fiestas came from the taxes in the local civil treasury, the produce from the collective farm, and the coffers of local religious sodalities. But as more and more land and labor was grabbed by the *hacendados* and the Spanish Church, public resources at the Indian village level were reduced to the point where an individual contributed most of the wealth consumed in fiestas. It often took a man years to accumulate enough wealth to sponsor such an affair, or it took him years to pay back the debts he incurred in so doing. But he attained the maximum of religious and social prestige in this manner. This is how the term *mayordomo*, originally applied to the steward or manager of a collective landholding, has become the general term for the man who finances a religious festival with his own personal wealth (Carrasco, 1961: 492–93. Pozas, 1962). After a man served his turn as *mayordomo*, he was qualified and often required to accept one of the rotating political offices. The officers also managed the civil affairs of the village; they allocated land to individual farmers, settled boundary disputes, judged and punished thieves, disarmed potential troublemakers, and dealt with officers of outside communities.

Warfare.—The war system of the Aztecs, with its hundreds of tons of tribute and its thousands of captives for human sacrifice, collapsed when the Spanish conquered them in 1521. About the only item from the Aztec materials of war that was taken over by the Spanish was the quilted cotton armor, which they put on their horses as well as themselves. The reed arrows and darts of the Aztecs often split when they struck the Spanish chain mail and kept right on going. Cotton armor stopped these missiles better than chain mail. After the defeat of the Aztecs, the domination of the Spanish was assured, and they were able to recruit large numbers of Indians of many tribes to serve as foot soldiers in the ranks, as porters of loads carried on their backs, and "skinners" of mules and donkeys in the pack trains. These Indian allies took part in all of the subsequent military campaigns of the Spanish. Those who were soldiers were instructed in the use of Spanish arms.

Life Cycle.—Life cycle ceremonies and behavior show considerable Spanish influence. Foster (1960: 112–24) lists a number of pregnancy and birth similarities attributable to informal diffusion from Spain, such as satisfying a woman's cravings for food during pregnancy, so that the child will not have birthmarks; the taboo on the pregnant woman winding yarn or string around her neck, lest the umbilicus strangle her infant at birth; the use of the Spanish term *partera* or *comadrona* for the midwife; the confinement (*cuarentena*) of the mother for forty days after birth; calling an unbaptized infant a *moro* (Moor); the baptism itself; and the institution of *compadrazgo*.

Foster (1960: 122–23) believes that the godparent-godchild relationships *(compadrazgo)* in Spain and Hispanic America are historically connected, but points out the principal difference—namely, that in Spain the primary relationship is that between godchild and godparents, while in America it is between godparents and the parents of the child.

Social and religious patterns of behavior at a death all over Latin America are dominated by Catholic dogma and ritual derived from Spain. The sacrament of extreme unction is given to a dying person when possible; a wake is held the night of the death; and the body is usually buried the next day in a wooden coffin. Disposal of the body in caves or by cremation ceased as soon as the Spanish gained control. A novena (series of prayer services) is held on the nine following evenings at the home of the deceased. Dead children are called little angels (*angelitos*) because they are believed to die without sin and to go directly to heaven. A few Spanish behaviors seem to have diffused informally without the sanction of the Church: throwing out all the water in the house because it is thought that the departing soul had bathed itself in the water; and closing the eyes of the corpse so that it will not call other members of the family to death.

Inheritance.—Before the Conquest, offices, real estate, and male chattels tended to be inherited from father to son, but there was never any rule of primogeniture or ultimogeniture. In the case of offices and real estate, the son had to be approved by some government agency, such as the deme council or, for high office, the national council.

Because this tendency toward patrilineal inheritance was more marked among nobility than among commoners, the downgrading of most of the nobility by the Spanish did away with much patrilineal inheritance. The general rule of bilateral inheritance today, with the survivors receiving equal shares, is therefore of both Spanish (Foster, 1960: 156) and Indian commoner origin, and is consistent with the deemphasis on kinship relations after the Conquest.

Education.—The educational system of the Aztecs was compulsory for all males for a period of at least five years, and therefore surpassed, at least in its universality and hours in school, the educational system in Spain at the time of the Conquest. It was completely eliminated by the Spanish because its military and religious emphasis was a threat to Spanish domination. The Catholic Church established schools for education in Spanish language and culture within a few years after the Conquest. It also permitted a few priests, such as the famous Bernadino de Sahagún, to do research on Aztec culture and to record in the Aztec language, with the help of Aztec scholars, everything available about the Aztecs. The 1960 Mexican census shows that 96 per cent of the people speak Spanish; some 1966 estimates of literacy in Spanish were as high as 78 per cent, although many people did not read and write very well.

Medicine.—The Spanish recognized the efficacy of Aztec medicine and considered it superior to their own for the treatment of native American diseases. They studied the prescriptions and methods of Aztec physicians and recorded them for European use. A course in Aztec medicine, taught by the best available Aztec physicians, was included, along with philosophy, logic, the Aztec and Latin languages, arithmetic, and music, in the regular curriculum of the College of Santa Cruz, established by the Franciscans in 1536. At this college, native Aztecs produced the first American medical book, now known as the Badianus Manuscript. This Aztec herbal, written in Aztec by Martinius de la Cruz and translated into Latin in 1552 by his colleague Badianus, is a worthy companion to the great medieval herbals still in use in sixteenth-century Europe. Except for the use of the Latin language and a few minor technicalities, it is a purely Mexican product, without European influence, written, illustrated, and translated by native Indians. Yet its formulas, with their odd mixture of efficacious medicines, magical animal substances, and precious stones, are fascinatingly reminiscent of medieval and Renaissance prescriptions (Emmart, 1940).

Modern scientific medicine has improved health standards enormously. General mortality has dropped from thirty-three per thousand inhabitants in 1910 to ten in 1965; that for the United States in 1965 was nine. Infant mortality has dropped from about three hundred per thousand live births in 1910 to sixty-one in 1965. Population doubled between 1940 and 1965, and the standard of living per capita has also risen. In 1964, Mexican universities graduated as many medical doctors per capita as did their United States counterparts (Cumberland, 1968 : 322, 323, 366).

Religion.—In contrast to the Spanish army officers, landowners, and mine operators, who had little respect for the lives of Indians, the Spanish priests made a tremendous effort to protect the Indians from exploitation as well as to save their souls. In the long run, they saved more souls than bodies, but their devotion to those at the bottom was sincere, and some gave their own lives to protect their flocks. The rapidity of the mass conversion of a large majority of Indians to the Roman Catholic faith has probably set a world record for missionary zeal and efficiency. The Christian doctrine of equality of all men in the eyes of God had tremendous appeal to those whose worldly possessions and status had been reduced to the very minimum. In addition, there were many demonstrations of the impotence of the Indian gods. When men in the Spanish army dashed the Indian idols to pieces, as was the practice everywhere, the idols failed to respond by harming the Spanish in any way. The myth that the pyramid of Cholula contained water which, if released, would drown anyone in its path was shown to be false when the Indian priests removed the keystones and nothing happened to the advancing Spanish army. In hundreds of such demonstrations, the old gods proved to be powerless.

The number of parallels between the leading Meso-American religions and Roman Catholicism are truly amazing. Both asserted a highly structured and stratified supernatural world, with the most powerful but least approachable gods at the top, and the less powerful but much more available spirits at the bottom. The Catholic saints were equated with the Indian gods who had made crops fertile, brought rain, and kept away illness; the wooden figures of the Spanish saints were an easy substitute for native images of clay and stone. Quetzalcoatl was equated with Saint Thomas the Apostle; Hummingbird-on-the-Left with Saint James; Tlaloc with the Christian Señor de Sacromonte; a God of the Cave with the Lord of Chalma; and Our Lady Spirit with the Virgin of Guadalupe. Both religions also unofficially embraced folk medicines, depended on omens, and believed in witches who could readily change from human to animal form. Both religions also shared a rite of baptism, the concept of confession, and a ritual of communion; both burned incense in churches, fasted, did penance, went on pilgrimages to holy places, had houses of celibate virgins, celibate priests, believed in a virgin birth, and used the cross as a symbol (Wolf, 1959: 168–72). Although no two members of these pairs were identical, they were close enough so that the Indians readily made the transfer.

Because the Catholic faith holds that the baptism of an infant or older person who understands no word of Latin or any other European language somehow changes the soul for the better, some priests were willing to baptize thousands of Indians as speedily as possible. Thus the Franciscan Pedro de Gante, kinsman of King Charles I of Spain, baptized Indians in Mexico City at a daily rate of 14,000 (Wolf, 1959: 173). Other priests, however, insisted on some knowledge of dogma and catechism, and faithfully instructed all converts. All Protestants, in contrast, demanded some knowledge of their creed from their adult converts, and never engaged in mass baptism. This difference in standards of conversion is one of the reasons why Catholics in Mexico made more apparent converts than did Protestants in Anglo-America.

The feast days considered most essential by the Church are observed in all Latin American nations: Epiphany, Candlemas, Lent, Holy Week and Easter, San Isidro, Corpus Christi, San Juan, All Saints' Day, All Souls' Day, and Christmas. Secular activities associated with these fiestas and derived from Spain include climbing a greased pole, masked dancers, fireworks, bullfights, and horse races. The wars between the Moors and Christians in pre-Conquest Spain and between the French and Mexicans in the nineteenth century are both reenacted at fiesta time in Mexico today. Associated or parallel features of Indian origin are: the Virgin of Guadalupe, who first revealed herself at the site of the temple of Tonantzin (the Aztec goddess of motherhood); the blowing of conch-shell trumpets; the beating of Indian drums in a few of the out-of-the-way churches; the spectacular *volador* act, in which men swing from ropes tied to the top of a high pole in imitation of birds; and the continued worship of Indian idols in the hills by burying food offerings and burning copal incense on the fiesta days (Foster, 1960: 167–226).

Personality.—Although we know much less about personality changes after the Conquest than about overt behaviors, it seems clear that the extreme domination of the Spanish over the Indians, the inhuman treatment that reduced population so drastically, the breakup of Indian social units and the regrouping of the Indians in villages and later as peons on haciendas—all had the effect of producing frustration, despair, and a more sullen, hostile, and withdrawn personality than existed before the Conquest. The personality syndrome in the Tepoztlán of Oscar Lewis (1951) has probably been approached, if not actually duplicated, in many other towns in Mexico. (See Chapter 24 for a summary of Tepoztlán personality.)

Rank and Class.—Since about 90 per cent of Spanish colonists were unmarried men, they cohabited with and married Indian women in large numbers, thus producing a large mestizo class. By the middle of the seventeenth century, Mexico had about 1,270,000 Indians, 120,000 persons socially defined as White, and 130,000 persons originally called *castas* but later mestizos. By the end of the eighteenth century, the mestizo group had risen to 2,270,000, as compared to 5,200,000 Indians, and today they make up a majority of Mexican population (Wolf, 1959: 235). Not being identified with land as either a landlord, a peon, or a member of an Indian collective farm, the mestizo became an opportunist and relied on his own initiative and individuality. His hostility took the form of self-assertiveness or aggression instead of withdrawal. He took pride in being very male *(muy macho)*, in possessing as many women as he could, and dominating his wife more than did the Indian husband. He indulged more in alcohol, gambling, and talk in bars and other public places. It was from this emerging mestizo group that most of the leaders of the 1910–20 Revolution came. They joined forces with those at the bottom *(los de bajos)*, and made room for the growing middle class that we know today in Mexico.

In Mexico today, there is much less discrimination against dark skin or any other physical characteristic than in the United States. A person is judged more by his dress, speech, education, and manners—in other words, by his language and culture, not his race. But because one's language and culture are determined in part by economic level and opportunity to acquire the valued proficiencies, there are marked differences in social rank in Mexico, and most scholars recognize social classes. That Indian ancestry is not a social and political handicap is amply demonstrated by the careers of Benito Juárez, 1806–72, and Lázaro Cárdenas, 1895. Juárez was a Zapotec, and Cárdenas a Tarascan, and both achieved the highest office in the nation, the presidency of Mexico—Juárez achieved it long before the Revolution of 1910–21 (Herring, 1963: 329, 376–383).

Language.—Language acculturation proceeded in both directions. Indian languages borrowed many Spanish words associated with the new culture thrust upon them, with the result that every Indian language is salted with many Spanish terms which have no Indian equivalents. Although almost everyone in Mexico today speaks Spanish, this vocabulary contains thousands of Indian words. The huge three-volume *Diccionario General de Americanismos*, by Francisco J. Santa María, gives tens of thousands of such words of Indian origin for all of Spanish America. The principal explanation of this wholesale borrowing of Indian words is that there were no Spanish words at all for many of the new plants, animals, material objects, and places found in the New World. Another explanation is the small number of Spaniards in the New World. In the entire colonial period, the numbers of Spaniards never exceeded 5 per cent of the total population in the American colonies as a whole, although Wolf's figures of 1650, quoted above, indicate that Whites were about 10 per cent of the population at that time in Mexico. Regardless of minor differences in numbers from place to place and time to time, the Spaniard was so outnumbered by Indians that he was forced to learn some of their language to communicate with them at all. The pillow talk of the mixed Spanish man and Indian woman concubinages and marriages probably also hastened this process. In Anglo-America, where Whites outnumbered Indians from about 1700 on, there was no wholesale incorporation of Indian words into English.

If the amounts of change for biological traits, language, and culture are compared for Mexico today, it is clear that biology shows the least change. Although almost everyone in Mexico today is of mixed ancestry, the Indian genes that went into the mixture are about 80 per cent of the total, with Spanish genes about 10 per cent, and those of all other ethnic groups, including Negroes, the remaining 10 per cent. Language has shown the greatest amount of change; in 1960, the percentage of exclusive Spanish speakers was 89 per cent, that of bilinguals in Spanish and an Indian language another 7 per cent, leaving only 4 per cent speaking only Indian languages. Culture change is more difficult to quantify, but would fall in an intermediate position between biology and language. Different aspects of culture have changed at different rates; for instance, the dominance of maize and pulque in the diet is as great as that of Indian genes in the population, while clothing is now almost wholly acculturated to Spanish and United States styles and materials. On the whole, the cultures of the Spanish and Indians in Mexico have blended better than those of the Anglos and Indians in the United States. In some cases, the blend is so complete that historians and anthropologists have difficulty in separating the Spanish and the Indian contributions.

REFERENCES

Aguirre Beltrán, 1965; Carrasco, 1961; Cumberland, 1968; Dobyns, 1966; Emmart, 1940; Foster, 1960; Gamio *et al.*, 1958; Herring, 1963; Jennings, 1968; Lewis, 1951; Mertz *et al.*, 1965; Pozas, 1962; Santa María, 1942; *Statistical Yearbook of the United Nations for* 1966; Tax, 1952; Wolf, 1959.

26

Indian-White Relations in the United States

NOT UNTIL 1607 were the English able to found a permanent colony in the New World—that at Jamestown in what is now Virginia. From Maryland and Virginia southward, the English colonies were founded by businessmen who organized trading companies chartered by the crown and privy council. These companies included many investors of many ranks. Although the colony was often headed by a lord, the colonists included persons of all ranks and statuses, many of whom intended to remain in the colony for the rest of their lives. Some loafed on the job, feeling themselves too important for physical labor, and thereby contributed to the collapse or near failure of the first colonies.

In New England and the Middle Atlantic States, the first colonists were religious idealists from the middle and lower classes, such as the Puritans in New England and the Quakers in Pennsylvania. The Protestant ethic of these groups demanded hard work on the part of everyone, including a handful of officials, and physical labor was not considered degrading, as it was in the Spanish colonies and, to a lesser extent, in the more southern English colonies. These new England and Middle Atlantic settlers were looking for unoccupied land on which to live out their lives in a freer and economically fuller environment unfettered by the Church and State of England. They had no desire to enslave or enserf Indians, and little desire for Indian women because the men had brought wives, daughters, and a few unattached single women with them.

The English had no legal mechanism comparable to the Spanish *encomienda* system which gave them the right to the labor of the Indians in a certain territory. Furthermore, most of the Indians in what is now the United States had never been regimented in an aboriginal class structure such as that of Meso-America, and would not have submitted to rigid control by anyone. In addition, it was mostly the Indian women who cultivated the crops and worked constantly at some form of labor, not the men. The principal occupations of the men were hunting and fighting, both arduous, risky, and essential, but not the plodding routine required of a plantation worker. The presence of English women in the colonies and the strict Protestant moral codes prevented the creation of a mestizo class from large numbers of mixed concubinages and marriages.

Another contrast with Spanish colonization was the slower and less effective missionary effort of the English. Their earliest attempt, the sending of fifty Anglican missionaries to Virginia in 1619, was followed, as soon as 1622, by an Indian uprising in which at least 347 Englishmen, including many of the missionaries, were killed. One of the reasons for this explosion was the separating of Indian children by force from the unholy atmosphere of their families in the name of* God and on orders from the Virginia Company (Hagan, 1961 : 9). The Puritans were too narrow-minded on the whole to have devoted much effort to Christianizing the Indians, whom they regarded as the agents of Satan. When large numbers of Indians died of disease or were killed in war, the Puritans thanked God for helping them get rid of the unbelievers. No English missionary ever boasted of the large number of Indians he had baptized in a single day, as did some of the Spanish priests, and baptism without previous instruction in Protestant belief and moral behavior was not considered beneficial to either the Indian or the Church.

Still another contrast was the difference in Indian patterns of warfare in Meso-America and the Eastern United States. War efforts of the major powers in Meso-America were tightly controlled by the political, military, and religious hierarchy, and a group of individuals who unofficially went on a war raid would have been regarded as outlaws and killed on their return home. Not so in the Eastern United States. Most war actions were initiated by individuals who thought they had experienced direct contact with the supernatural through dreams or visions. Although the better-organized tribes, such as the Iroquois, insisted on council approval of a war expedition, this was almost always granted. As tribal organization broke down under the stress of Indian and White conflict, many attacks were initiated by incensed individual Indians and their followers without any approval of a governing body. It was impossible to make a lasting peace with a tribal chief when he could not control all of his brash, hot-blooded young men anxious to become war heroes.

Another difference in the Spanish and English systems had its roots in the Indian utilization of land in the two regions. In Meso-America, most of the best land was already occupied and farmed by the Indian peasants in the system, who derived almost all of their living from plant cultivation. It was easy to determine what lands the Indians occupied and used. The Indians of the Prairies and East had a mixed economy in which hunting and fishing commonly provided as much as half of the diet, and in some cases even more. Population was sparse, and the areas farmed were a very small fraction of the total landscape. The English colonists tended to regard all land not occupied by Indian farms or houses as open territory to be appropriated by them at will. The result was a series of clashes over land that is still going on to this day, although now much hedged by legal red tape.

Hagan very succinctly sums up the relations of the English and the Indians for the entire colonial period.

Scores of Indian tribes, such as King Philip's Wampanoags, had been corrupted and eliminated by the Whites. The outline of events in such tragedies was clear. The traders first employed the Indians to gather furs and tribal standard of living rose as they acquired firearms and metal tools. Then as the game diminished and the frontier line pressed upon the Indian holdings the second act opened. It closed with the tribesmen having been forced or seduced into selling their land. Occasionally this act would include an Indian war with a standard script calling for an outburst of violence by the tormented natives, scalpings, burning, and the horrors of torture embellished by that early American form of literature, the captivity narrative. The third act would find the Indian resistance crushed and the inevitable treaty written ceding even more land to the whites. The principal problem remaining would be the ultimate disposition of the tribe. The Indians might settle the problem temporarily by migrating westward to compete with already established tribes for their hunting grounds and set the stage for a repetition of the last two acts. Or, if the defeat in the war had been overwhelming, the few tribesmen remaining might be absorbed by neighboring bands or located on a reservation. The usual result was that the reservation Indians frustrated their well-wishers and co-operated with their oppressors by dying off rapidly. (Hagan, 1961: 29–30).

The following chronology will be of help in keeping track of the many events crowded into this chapter.

1492   Columbus discovered America.
1539–42 De Soto explored the Southeast for Spain.
1540–41 Coronado explored the Southwest for Spain.
1598   Oñate established the first Spanish colony on the Rio Grande, in what is now New Mexico, and gained control of the Pueblo Indians there.
1604–35 Champlain explored and colonized the Northeast for France.
1607   First permanent English colony founded at Jamestown, Virginia.
1611   First Jesuit missionaries sent to New France.

1619   First English missionaries, fifty Anglicans, sent to Virginia. First African slaves landed in U.S., Virginia.

1620   *Mayflower* arrived at Plymouth to found the first colony in New England.

1622   First Indian uprising in an English colony (Virginia) in the New World.

1672–76 Defeat of Indians in King Philip's War ended organized resistance of southern New England tribes.

1680   The Pueblo Indians rebelled against the Spanish and drove them south to about the present United States–Mexican border.

1692   The Spanish returned, and reconquered the Pueblo Indians on the Rio Grande in the next few years.

1756–63 French and Indian War. The English defeated the French and took possession of the entire Northeast by 1763.

1763   The British crown removed jurisdiction over Indians from the colonies, and regarded each tribe as an independent nation to be dealt with by the crown.

1767   Secularization of the missions in New Mexico, ending the Spanish mission program there.

1768   The British reneged on the Proclamation of 1763, and gave the control of trade and Indian affairs back to the colonies.

1769   Spanish occupied California and established first mission.

1775–83 United States won independence from England in the Revolutionary War.

1778   Continental Congress made first treaty with an Indian tribe, the Delaware.

1787   Northwest Ordinance approved by Confederation Congress.

1789   United States Constitution ratified by the states, and George Washington elected first president. Indian rights of 1787 reaffirmed.

1790   Congress enacted first law regulating trade and land sales with Indians.

1795–1822 United States operated trading posts.

1803   Louisiana Purchase.

1810–21 The Mexicans won their independence from Spain.

1812–14 War of 1812 between England and the United States—the last war in which Indians allied themselves with a foreign colonial power against the United States.

1819   First appropriation by Congress of a fund ($10,000) to civilize the Indians.

1824   The Bureau of Indian Affairs was established in the War Department of the United States government.

1830   Indian Removal Act passed by Congress, legalizing removal of all Indians east of the Mississippi to lands west of that river.

1832   Chief Justice John Marshall issued the opinion that state law does not apply to Indians on tribal lands. Position of Commissioner of Indian Affairs created in War Department.

1834   Administrative structure of Bureau of Indian Affairs amplified. Indian Trade and Intercourse Act, including prohibition of sale of intoxicants to Indians.

1846–48 War between the United States and Mexico.

1849   The Bureau of Indian Affairs shifted to the Department of the Interior. Gold rush to California.

1861–65 Civil War in United States.

1870   Congress appropriated first sum earmarked for federal administration of Indian education.

1871	Congress passed a law putting an end to further treaties with Indian tribes.
1878	Congress appropriated first funds for Indian police.
1879	Carlisle Indian School founded.
1885	The Major Crimes Act (with later amendments) listed ten offenses which were federal crimes to be judged in federal courts.
1886	Geronimo and his rebel band of Apaches captured, ending Indian fighting in the Southwest.
1887	Dawes Severalty Act (General Allotment Act) passed by Congress.
1890	Massacre of nearly three hundred Indians by Whites at Wounded Knee, South Dakota. Last major bloodshed involving Indians in United States.
1892-97	More laws passed providing for schools and giving truant officers the right to force Indian children to attend. Federal support of church schools withdrawn.
1902	All employees of Bureau of Indian Affairs put under civil service.
1910	Medical Division established in Bureau of Indian Affairs.
1922	First meeting of All-Pueblo Council.
1924	All Indians made citizens by act of Congress, thereby being given the right to vote.
1928	"Meriam Survey" stressed that Indian assimilation could not be forced, and paved the way for a change of policy.
1933	John Collier appointed Commissioner of Indian Affairs by Franklin D. Roosevelt.
1934	Congress passed Wheeler-Howard (Indian Reorganization) Act.
1941-45	World War II.
1944	Founding of National Congress of American Indians.
1946	Congress established Indian Claims Commission to judge all tribal claims.
1948	Court rulings in Arizona and New Mexico enforced the right of Indians to vote, which had been denied them in those states since 1924.
1951	A general relocation program organized to find employment for Indians in cities.
1953	Congress adopted House Concurrent Resolution 108, which asked for the termination of the special treatment of Indians as rapidly as possible.
1955	Medical services on reservations transferred from Bureau of Indian Affairs to Public Health Service.
1961	American Indian Chicago Conference. Anthropologist Philleo Nash appointed Commissioner of Indian Affairs. Founding of National Indian Youth Council.
1964	"Fish-in" in Washington state.
1968	Six titles dealing with Indians in Civil Rights Bill (H.R. 2516) passed by Congress.

Hagan's drama had run its course for most of the Indians east of the Appalachians by the time of the Revolutionary War and the founding of the new government of the United States of America, but the tribes a little farther inland, such as the Iroquois, survived in attenuated numbers. Because the Iroquois had suffered in their first encounter with Whites at the hands of a French force commanded by

Champlain, they continued to regard the French as enemies most of the time and sided with the English in the French and Indian War. They came out on the winning side, but when most of them sided with the English in the Revolutionary War, they lost and moved to Canada to remain under the protection of the English there. Those who remained in the United States were put on reservations, beginning in 1784.

Treaties.—The first treaty made with an Indian tribe (the Delaware) by the budding new nation was that of 1778 ratified by the Continental Congress. This had been foreshadowed by the British crown's treaties with New England tribes from 1664 and its later removal of jurisdiction over Indians from all the colonies from 1763 to 1768 in order to prevent further unjust land grabbing by the colonists. The standard set by the Continental Congress in 1778 was continued by the Confederation Congress and later by the Congress of the United States. Between 1778 and 1871, when Congress put an end to treaty making with Indian tribes, a total of 389 treaties had been made and remade with Indians. Treaties were remade again and again with the same tribe as conditions changed, the record number being forty-two separate treaties each for the Potawatomi and Chippewa (Oswalt, 1966: 502). In these treaties, the government set aside a homeland territory (reservation) for the tribe, paid them for land transferred to the United States, and sometimes agreed on periodic distributions of cash, food, or other material goods. The Indians, in turn, pledged themselves to peace with the United States and alliance with it in wars with foreign nations. Because the payment for land averaged less than ten cents per acre and the government sometimes resold it for as much as $1.25 per acre, few of these treaties are regarded as just today (Lurie, 1968: 33).

Northwest Ordinance.—In 1787, the Confederation Congress passed the Northwest Ordinance, which promised that land and other property would not be taken from Indians without their consent, except in just and lawful wars authorized by Congress. Because Congress never declared war officially on an Indian tribe, no exceptions of this kind ever occurred. The Indian rights of 1787 were reaffirmed in the Constitution of the United States, which was ratified by the last state in 1789. A year later, Congress enacted another law regulating trade and land sales with Indians in greater detail.

Trading Posts.—From 1795 to 1882, the United States operated Indian trading posts, to provide trade goods at cost to the Indians and thus buy friendship. The first two posts were established in the Southeast among the Creek and Cherokee, whose attachment to the British and Spanish was close enough to cause alarm. In 1806, Thomas Jefferson proposed that United States trading posts operate at a loss, if necessary, in the Northeast in order to win over Indians from the British, whose firms were active in that area. After the War of 1812, the threat of the British was diminished, and the Spanish had by then abandoned their trading bases in Florida. With competition less keen and John Jacob Astor lobbying in Washington for private enterprise in the fur business, Congress terminated the government trading posts in 1822 (Hagan, 1961: 45, 58, 66–67).

Bureau of Indian Affairs.—Indian problems were still increasing at a more rapid rate than solutions for them. In order to centralize government effort, the Bureau of Indian Affairs was established in 1824 in the War Department, which up to that time had been involved with Indians more than any other federal department. As early as 1786, the administration of Indian affairs had been placed under the Secretary of War. In 1849, the Bureau of Indian Affairs was shifted to the newly created Department of the Interior, where it has remained ever since. Until 1892, when physicians and teachers were put under civil service, all employees of the Bureau were political appointees given jobs simply for helping to win elections. Such incompetents became less numerous after 1902, when all employees except the commissioner and assistant commissioner were placed under civil service (Lurie, 1968: 40). Over half of the Bureau's 16,000 employees in 1968 had Indian ancestry.

Removal.—After the Louisiana Purchase in 1803, the United States came into possession of a vast territory which President Jefferson and others thought had plenty of room for all the Indians east of the Mississippi. The Civilized Tribes of the Southeast had made such progress in their acculturation that Congress considered forming an Indian state there and admitting it to the Union. In 1821, a Cherokee named Sequoyah invented a syllabic system for writing his language, and within a few years thousands of Cherokee had learned to read and write. But the Southern states, especially Georgia, were already threatening secession from the Union if they could not get more land from Indians to expand their plantations. At first, individual chiefs were persuaded, with the aid of medals, officer's uniforms, alcoholic beverages, and gold, to cede or sell their lands to the United States.

Finally, in 1830, Congress passed the Indian Removal Act, calling for the removal of all Indians east of the Mississippi to lands farther west. Congress appropriated only $500,000 to compensate Indians for loss of lands and the expenses of moving and getting established in the new region. Although some Indians moved out rapidly, many did not possess the transportation facilities to make the move and others resisted removal in every way they could. Whole tribes—men, women, and children—trudged along on foot, hurried on their way by soldiers of the United States army, who sometimes would not permit them to stop even to care for the sick or bury the dead. Thousands died, and the journey is still known as the Trail of Tears (Foreman, 1934). The final result was the resettlement of about 100,000 Indians, most of them in Indian Territory, in what is now Oklahoma. The campaign against the Seminole alone, who hid out in the Everglades of Florida, cost the United States the lives of 1,500 soldiers and an expenditure of about $50,000,000 (Hagan, 1961: 66–91). The price in lives, including those of Indians, of the entire removal program was enormous. The Seminole were finally allowed to remain in Florida, and the Cherokee who had remained in North Carolina bought themselves a reservation there. Smaller remnants of other tribes managed to remain in or near their home territory east of the Mississippi.

Although the United States had promised to protect the removed tribes in their new homes west of the Mississippi, they rarely had provided enough troops to do the job, and sometimes failed to supply enough guns and ammunition for the new arrivals to protect themselves. There was no territorial vacuum in the West, and the tribes already there resented the invasion of their hunting territories by those recently removed from the East. Armed conflict was the rule, not the exception.

Mexican War.—The removal business was far from settled when the war between the United States and Mexico (1846–48) broke out. Mexican histories rightfully call this war the "invasion by the North Americans". In the end, the United States appropriated almost half of the territory of the Mexican nation: what is now California, Nevada, Utah, Arizona, New Mexico, Texas, and part of Colorado. There were about 150,000 Indians in this territory at that time. In order to understand the impact of the United States on these Indians it is necessary to sketch briefly their earlier contact with the Spanish and Mexicans.

Spanish and Mexicans in the Southwest.—Although Coronado in 1540 and 1541 and other Spaniards had explored much of the Southwest before 1598, it was not until that year that an attempt was made to found a permanent colony. The leader of this expedition was Oñate, who led a group of settlers, soldiers, and priests northward from Chihuahua into the Rio Grande Valley of New Mexico. Emissaries with military escort were sent at once to some sixty pueblos, where the leaders of the Indians were told that they were henceforth to be followers of the Spanish king and the Christian religion. Not realizing what they were doing, but anxious to avoid clashes with the more heavily armed Spaniards, all of the pueblos acquiesced.

Oñate's group included thirty-five soldier-citizens who had been given *encomiendas* in New Mexico by the viceroy of New Spain as an incentive to join the expedition (Dozier, 1961: 128). This gave them the authority to put the Indians to work on the appropriated land at meager wages or for a small share of the crops or domesticated animals produced on the land. The priests likewise regimented Indians, first, to build churches and chapels and, later, to farm the church's lands and herd its animals. By 1630, ninety chapels had been built, but there were so few priests (thirty-three in 1680) that services were held only once a month in most of them (Dozier, 1961: 147). The military and civil officials, in turn, needed Indians to act as servants and to work on their ranches. The Indians were also put to work at weaving on Spanish looms, at blacksmithing, making carts and wagons, woodworking, and gathering large quantities of pine nuts for export to Mexico City.

The Spanish might have accomplished the regimentation of large amounts of Indian labor if they had not been so militant about religious matters. They attempted not only to convert the Indians to the Catholic faith but also to stamp out entirely the native religions. In 1661, the Spanish raided the Indian kivas, where the most sacred ceremonies were performed, and seized a total of 1,600 kachina masks, the most sacred object among all the Indians' religious paraphernalia. The masks were later burned (Dozier, 1961: 95). Indians who strayed from the straight and narrow path of Catholicism were flogged at the whipping post, hung by their arms, forced to stand in a small circle for hours, and eventually hanged by the neck until dead if they continued to defy their Spanish masters.

The accumulation of such inhuman treatment over the years

brought about the Pueblo rebellion in 1680. For the first and last time in their history, most of the pueblos united their fighting men against the Spanish and drove them south out of Pueblo territory at considerable loss of life. After twelve years in which to get reinforcements and additional financial backing, a larger Spanish force returned in 1692 and reconquered the pueblos one by one in the next few years. By this time the Pueblos were quarreling with one another, and failed to unite against the common enemy.

The eighteenth century was a period of more relaxed relations between the Pueblos and their Spanish masters. Although the number of Spanish colonists in New Mexico continued to increase, the *encomienda* system was not revived after the rebellion. The smaller number of friars—only twenty in 1776—put less religious pressure on the Indians and permitted them to give more attention to their own religions, which were in a period of resurgence at this time. Nomad raids by Navahos, Apaches, and Comanches increased in the eighteenth century. The horses, sheep, and many other things introduced by the Spanish had produced a richer inventory to steal from, and the horse increased the mobility of the raiders. Both the pueblos and the Spanish settlements were raided, and, although the Spanish made an honest effort to protect their Pueblo Indian charges, who were legally citizens of Spain, they were frequently unable to do so. The raids diminished the amount of control by the Spanish over the Pueblo Indians because the former were too occupied with the nomad problem to give as much attention to the latter as they had in the previous century.

The biological and ecological result of the Spanish domination in New Mexico was a reduction of the Pueblo Indian population from about 40,000 in 1600 to about 10,000 in 1800. By 1810, on the eve of Mexico's rebellion against Spain, only nineteen of the sixty-six pre-Spanish Rio Grande pueblos were left, and only four were still in their original locations (Spicer, 1962: 169).

There was little change in the Rio Grande Valley in the Mexican period from 1821 to 1846. The number of resident priests in the pueblos had dwindled to only five, and the Indians were allowed to carry on their religions with less fear of persecution. Ceremonies which had been held underground in the kivas were now performed in the public plazas for all to see. The civil authorities were fully occupied with the threat of invasions from Texans and other Anglos and the still recurring raids by nomadic Indians. Relations between the

Pueblos and the poorer "Hispanos" became closer, and the two groups even joined in two abortive rebellions against the tax-levying officials.

United States in the Southwest.—In 1846, General Stephen Kearny of the United States took Santa Fe, the capital of Spanish and Mexican New Mexico, without firing a shot; the Mexican authorities had already headed south. A month after Kearny's arrival, some Navahos stole several head of cattle from the general's own beef herd at Algodones and went on to raid settlements around Albuquerque, killing seven or eight settlers and absconding with thousands of cattle, sheep, and horses. This was too much for the general, who initiated a series of campaigns against the Navaho that ended in the impounding of 8,500 of these Indians in Fort Sumner from 1864 to 1868. Only after United States troops had killed or captured most of their sheep and destroyed their crops, did the Navaho surrender. The numbers of sheep stolen by the Navaho and other nomads are almost unbelievable. It has been estimated that between 1846 and 1850 the Navahos and Apaches stole over 450,000 sheep from Hispanos (Vogt, 1961: 296). In 1863, after the United States army had gone into the sheep-stealing business, the Navaho stole 24,389 sheep from Pueblos and Hispanos, and the United States troops took 24,266 from them in reprisal. Before that date, the Navaho had come out ahead in the exchange; but in 1864, the Navaho stole only 4,250 sheep, while the army took 12,284 from them (Vogt, 1961: 313). This put an end to Navaho raiding. Their incarceration in Fort Sumner was a warning to the other bands of nomads, and was the turning point after two and a half centuries of nomad raids on livestock. It was apparent to all that the United States was going to rule with a much firmer hand than had the Spaniards and Mexicans. In 1868, the Navaho were given a reservation in their homeland with some sheep to raise on it, and there they have lived peacefully ever since.

Last Indian Wars.—The Civil War (1861–65) drew the attention of the Anglos away from the Indian problem for a time, but many of the Indians were forced to choose a side. Those in Oklahoma chose the Confederate side for the most part and, after the Union victory, were discriminated against by the victors. The Mexican War and the gold rush to California in 1849–50 had increased the number of wagon trains from east to west across the continent and through the lands of many tribes en route. The end of the Civil War freed considerable numbers of trigger-happy Union officers and troops who stayed with the army to get in on the Indian fighting in the West. There followed many so-called Indian wars, with the Indians winning only a few battles, such as that of the Little Big Horn, where Custer and all his men lost their lives and scalps in 1876, exactly one hundred years after the Declaration of Independence. With the capture of Geronimo and his Apache band in 1886, Indian fighting stopped in the Southwest. On the Plains, the last mass bloodshed was in 1890, when United States troops massacred nearly three hundred men, women, and children of the Sioux tribe who had assembled at Wounded Knee, South Dakota, to put on a Ghost Dance ceremony. Allegedly, the Indians had refused to lay down their arms when first ordered to do so, but many had done so when the shooting began.

California.—In California, the first Spanish mission was founded at San Diego in 1769, and the last at Sonoma in 1823. Soon after the later date, the missions were secularized by the Mexican government, and the program ended. As elsewhere, the priests saved the souls but lost the bodies of a large majority of Indians in the "mission strip", a territory along the coast about fifty miles wide and stretching from San Diego to Sonoma. The gold rush of 1849–50 brought into California a large number of Anglos who were single men and less responsible than colonists in other areas. The impact was so sudden that few Californian Indians had the weapons or knowledge to save themselves from extinction. In Northeastern California, however, a small group of Modocs barricaded themselves in the lava beds and fought Whites in the Modoc War of 1872–73. This ended organized Indian resistance in California (Knight, 1960), but a small group hid out until this century, when, in 1911, the last wild Indian in the United States, Ishi, gave himself up (Theodora Kroeber, 1961).

Indian Police.—In 1878, Congress appropriated the first funds for Indian police. The appointing of the more acculturated Indians to these positions was a step toward mediation between Indians and Whites, whose relationship was still marked by hostility. These police served as truant officers, arrested offenders, and occasionally became executioners when they were resisted. By 1884, Indian police forces had been established on forty-eight of the sixty existing agencies. Many police also acted as judges—a double role of dubious merit. This system had a short life, and began to deteriorate within a decade as conditions changed. As more United States marshals became available, the need for Indian police became less; the passing of the Major Crimes Act by Congress in 1885 removed ten offenses, including murder, from Indian courts and made them federal crimes to be tried in federal courts. The Indian courts of the Five Civilized Tribes in Indian Territory (now Oklahoma) were eliminated by the Curtis Act of Congress in 1898, which expanded the jurisdiction of federal courts there (Hagan, 1966).

Dawes Severalty Act.—The Dawes Severalty Act (General Allotment Act), passed by Congress in 1887, and amended in 1891, 1906, and 1910, not only made Indian police and judges less necessary but challenged the whole reservation system. It authorized the president to parcel tribal land to individual members in tracts of forty, eighty, or 160 acres, called "allotments". The purpose of this act was to phase out reservations and encourage each Indian family head to manage his own affairs like White citizens of the United States. Proponents of the act thought that individual ownership would provide the incentive for an Indian to become a farmer or a rancher and support himself and his family. Opponents of the act portrayed it as a deliberate mechanism to make it possible for Whites to grab more Indian lands. Whatever the intentions of Congress, the second alternative was the one actually realized. Many Indians first rented their land to Whites, eventually sold it to Whites, spent the money, and were still dependent on the federal government (Lurie, 1966: 50–52). In 1887, tribal landholdings were about 138 million acres; in 1934, when the allotment system was stopped by law, the tribes held only 48 million acres on which to support more Indians than existed in 1887 (Brophy and Aberle, 1966: 18–20). In 1968, there were 50 million acres held in trust for Indians by the federal government—39 million for tribes, and 11 million for individuals (Bennett, 1968).

Indian Education.—The first step toward educating the Indian began in 1819, when Congress appropriated a Civilization Fund of $10,000 per annum. At first, this money was given to churches and benevolent societies because the government had no machinery to screen, employ, and evaluate teachers and programs. By the 1840's, the federal fund was still the same, but private organizations and individuals were contributing $150,000 per annum to Indian education. In addition, many treaties included federal funds for establishing model farms, sawmills, blacksmith shops, and other applied programs. These manual-labor schools also taught the three R's, and girls were instructed in household tasks. Only a few Indian schools in this period taught such ivory-tower subjects as Greek, Latin, and astronomy (Hagan, 1961: 87–91).

In 1870, Congress appropriated the first funds earmarked for federally administered education in schools. By 1889, over $2,500,000 was being expended annually on 148 boarding schools and 225 day schools, with a total of about 20,000 Indian children attending. This number changed little up to 1950, when 27,000 children attended federal schools; but by 1967, it had risen to 47,000. In addition, 84,000 Indian children were enrolled in public schools, and 9,000 in mission and other private schools in 1967, bringing the total to 140,000 (Zellers, 1968). The dropout rate, however, was higher than that of Whites; half of the Indian children in high school dropped out before graduation. In 1966, the Bureau of Indian Affairs spent $121,000,000 on its education programs (*Indian Voices,* July, 1966: 19). The progress of the program in the early years was blunted by the use of force to bring children to schools, much too severe punishment for infractions of petty rules of behavior—such as the prohibition of the use of Indian languages—and a vindictive attitude on the part of most teachers toward Indian religions and value systems. Many graduates of these schools returned to their Indian ways after going home. The literacy rate rose from 44 per cent in 1900, to 75 per cent in 1930, to 88 per cent in 1959. In the decade from 1950 to 1960, the number of Indians attending college rose from 6,500 to 17,000 (Steiner, 1968: 31), and was probably double the latter figure in 1968. The college dropout rate is also higher than that for Whites, and the principal causes are emotional difficulties rather than inadequate intelligence. A smaller number of Indians have gone on into graduate work, and a few have earned doctoral degrees.

In 1968, hearings before the Senate Subcommittee on Indian Education, chaired by Robert F. Kennedy, revealed that the Indians want more control of the federally subsidized schools (including some public schools as well as those of the Bureau), which 57 per cent of all Indian children attend. The emotional disturbance created by an all-White curriculum that downgrades Indian cultures and languages contributes to a dropout rate twice the national rate and a suicide rate several times the national one. Boarding schools received especially heavy criticism because of the isolation of the child from his family and relatives (*Indian Affairs,* 70: 1, April–May, 1968).

All-Pueblo Council.—In 1922, the first meeting of the All-Pueblo Council was held. This was the first time that these Indians had engaged in concerted action since the Pueblo rebellion of 1680. The issue that brought them together was a threat to their lands. Because the Pueblo Indians were full citizens under the Spanish and Mexican governments, and the United States had agreed, in the treaty that ended the Mexican War in 1848, to make all Mexican nationals United States citizens, the United States law that prohibited unlawful entry on Indian lands did not apply to the Pueblo people, who were technically not Indians. By 1922, 3,000 non-Pueblo families, totaling about 12,000 persons, were living on former Pueblo land. In that year, the Bursum Bill was introduced in Congress, requiring that the Indians prove their right of ownership. This precipitated the first meeting and the formation of the All-Pueblo Council, which is still functioning. The publicity created by the meeting defeated the bill in Congress and led to the creation by Congress of the Pueblo Land Board and a more equitable procedure for determining ownership of disputed lands (McNickle, 1964: 53–55). The All-Pueblo Council was strengthened in 1966 by the adoption of a constitution signed by the members.

Indian Citizenship.—All Indians were made full citizens by an act of Congress in 1924, and were thereby given the right to vote in local, state, and national elections. As early as 1817, a few Indians were granted citizenship by treaties, and the number increased over the years, so that a majority had already become citizens by 1924. The act of that year made it universal, and followed the awarding of citizenship in 1919 to the many Indian men who had served in the armed forces in World War I. (They were enlistees because Indians were not subject to the draft at that time.) However, some states failed to react to the change, and in 1938 seven states still refused to allow Indians to vote. It was not until 1948, when Indians won voting rights in Arizona and New Mexico by court decisions, that the franchise was generally extended to Indians (Oswalt, 1966: 498–99). The largest tribes, especially the Navaho, with its 35,750 registered voters in 1966 (*Indian Voices*, November, 1966: 7), have become a political force that is now being given attention by candidates of all major political factions and parties.

Lewis Meriam Report.—In the mid-1920's, a privately endowed foundation, the (Brookings) Institute for Government Research, was requested by the Secretary of the Interior to make a field survey of living conditions and achievements of Indians on reservations. This resulted in the Lewis Meriam report published in 1928, which emphasized the need for educational and medical improvements and the raising of personnel standards in the Indian Service, and also cast a critical eye at the allotment system, which alone was not enough to make Indians into self-supporting citizens. This report further voiced the impossibility of integrating the Indian into United States culture in a few decades, and recommended a program of longer range.

Indian Reorganization Act. — The recommendations in the Meriam Report and the views of John Collier, Commissioner of Indian Affairs under Franklin Roosevelt from 1933 to 1946, were built into the Indian Reorganization (Wheeler-Howard) Act of 1934. This act stopped the alienation of tribal lands in the individual allotment system, authorized appropriations to purchase new holdings for tribes, established a system of federal loans, recognized the principle of self-determination for Indian communities, and provided a plan for organizing Indian groups into corporations with officers and councils. An important safeguard in the beginning was that the new plan could be accepted only by those tribes in which a majority voted in its favor. At the outset, 189 tribes (129,750 Indians) accepted the new program, and seventy-seven tribes (86,365 Indians) rejected it. Other tribes that did not get around to voting in time were later included, and in 1936 the program was extended to include peoples in Alaska and Oklahoma but without their vote of approval. Each tribe that accepted the plan was given a free hand at writing its own constitution, and most of them did so (Brophy and Aberle, 1966:20–21. Oswalt, 1966:507–8. Hagan, 1961:155–58. Witt, 1968: 59–60).

Although not every provision of the Indian Reorganization Act of 1934 was a success, the act as a whole accelerated the growth of Indian prosperity and well-being. Indians were also encouraged to revive their native crafts, not in order to turn the path of progress backward but to sell the products to tourists and other Whites. In 1966, the National Congress of American Indians, in Denver, Colorado, published complete listings of Indian-made products. In some localities, sales of goods, services, and entertainment to tourists is now the most profitable source of cash income to the tribe and has increased per-capita income many fold. That almost all Indians accepted the responsibility of managing their own tribal affairs is proved by their high rate of repayment on loans. From 1934 to 1960, 96.6 per cent of primary loans from the United States to tribal corporations, credit associations, and cooperative groups had been repaid on their date due; 0.5 per cent had been extended;

0.5 per cent had been canceled; and only 2.2 per cent had been declared delinquent ("Declaration of Indian Purpose", 1961; 25).

World War II.—World War II was, on the whole, a boon to Indians, although some lost their lives fighting for the nation that had conquered them less than a hundred years before. About 25,000 Indians served in the armed forces, and nearly twice that number were drawn into industry as the flow of federal funds for Indian reservations decreased and that for war industries increased (Hagan, 1961: 158). The Indians were subject to the draft, as were other citizens, but, among those tribes with a former strong war tradition, the voluntary enlistment rate was high. In one of the few tribes that opposed participation in the war effort, draft dodging was aided by assigning youths to long vacant offices in religious organizations so that they could claim exemption on religious grounds. For the first time in their lives, many young men who went to war were immersed in White culture. It was an exposure much more complete than that of the boarding school of the previous half-century. On returning to the reservation after the war, the Indian G.I. became more self-assertive on the whole and helped remove Arizona's and New Mexico's ban on voting for Indians in 1948 and the federal taboo on the off-reservation purchasing of liquor in 1953. The amount of acculturation during the war years was greater than that accomplished by all government programs up to that time.

Claims Commission.—In 1946, Congress made it legal for a period of ten years (later extended) for Indian tribes to present suit for claims of all kinds against the United States, and provided positions for three claims commissioners to hear and judge all the cases. This was the beginning of a change in policy; a desire to settle all grievances with Indians by a large cash payment, and then to cut off most of the annual kinds of aid in the federal budget. It was thought that many Indians were staying on the reservation to be sure of their cut in any federal payment that might materialize, and that if sizable sums were paid each tribe, many individuals would leave the reservation and get jobs on the outside. Most of the claims were for land taken from Indians by Whites. By 1951, the deadline year for filing, a total of 852 claims had been filed by Indian tribes (Hagan, 1961: 167) for about twice as much acreage as exists within the boundaries of the United States (minus Alaska and Hawaii). This was because many of the claims overlapped or because one tribe was represented by two rival law firms, each of which filed a claim. For instance, two law firms each claimed to represent all the Indians of California. Only after the commissioners told both groups that neither case would be heard and judged until they had combined their two cases into one, did the two factions join together. The fees of the lawyers representing each Indian tribe were limited to 10 per cent of the judgment, plus expenses, that the tribe obtained from the United States; so it is no wonder that some lawyers, like ambulance chasers, made claims that were unrealistic, if not downright dishonest, to increase their fees. Others went bankrupt when their years of work on a case failed to obtain a judgment.

More than fifty anthropologists participated as expert witnesses in these hearings, most of them on the side of the Indians and against the United States. Anthropologists employed by the Department of Justice to aid in the defense were regarded as anti-Indian by most members of the profession. Few anthropologists realized that an inadequate defense would have made it possible for the tribes whose cases came up early in the sequence to have grabbed more than their fair share of the land. Tribes with cases heard at later dates would have come out on the short end, because part of their land would have been assigned already to another tribe.

The amount of the claim depended not only on the amount of land but also on its value per acre. The values used in these lawsuits were the values of the land at the time it was unjustly taken from the tribe. This was sometimes a hundred years ago, and the planned compensation of $1.25 per acre was nowhere near enough for much of the land in the mid-twentieth century. Inflation of the dollar has been ignored in all Indian land claims cases; but the spending of the awards today is geared to a highly inflated currency. As of June 30, 1968, 122 cases had been awarded claims totaling $251,504,544.05, and 133 had been dismissed without recovery (personal communication from Ralph Barney, chief, Indian Claims Section of Department of Justice).

The use Indians made of the claim moneys was sometimes disappointing in the beginning. For instance, the claim of about $31,000,000 won by the Ute Indians of Colorado and Utah in a federal Court of Claims amounted to only a few thousand dollars per family after some was spent for public improvements on the reservation and to pay back earlier federal loans. Some families spent their share in a year or two on passenger cars and other nonproductive items instead of on trucks, bulls, fences, and corrals that were needed to make a success of a stock-raising operation. However, the trend for the past decade has been to invest more and more of the awards in business and industry on the reservation, community recreation and social services, scholarship funds, and leadership training programs. The fact that the United States has paid out such sums in land-claims lawsuits is the best proof obtainable that many of the land deals with Indians in the past were unjust. Needless to say, the payment of claims has not resulted in a mass exodus from the reservations.

The legal experience gained in these lawsuits against the federal government has greatly benefited the Indians. At present, almost all tribes retain legal counsel on a permanent basis. In addition to representing the Indians in disputes with the federal government, the Indian-employed attorney also deals with state and local governments and even individuals. The denial by states of Indian rights awarded by the federal government is progressively becoming less common as states have lost one lawsuit after another to Indians. Attorneys for the Indians, acting as lobbyists, have persuaded both state and federal government officials to make concessions to Indians without the expense of a court trial. They have also negotiated contracts with White business interests for lumbering, mining, and farming on Indian lands, in one case obtaining as much as forty-five times the revenue of the previous contract. Anthropologists and other specialists have also been employed by Indian tribes (Dobyns, 1968).

Relocation and Employment Assistance.—A program for relocating Indians and helping them find jobs in cities was begun in 1951. It was first called the Branch of Relocation (of the Bureau of Indian Affairs), later became the Voluntary Relocation Program in 1953, but is now known as Employment Assistance. In the beginning, it advanced enough money for transportation to the city, located housing, and took care of living expenses until a job was found. A majority of Indians succeeded from the beginning in the new environment, although most of them were unskilled and poorly prepared, but 20 to 30 per cent failed and had to be helped by private persons and agencies to return to the reservation. Most of those who were able to hold their jobs regarded the city as a good place to earn money but not to live in permanently. Eventually, most of this group will also return to the reservation. By the end of fiscal year 1967, about 61,500 Indians had been helped to find employment (*Answers to Your Questions about American Indians*, 1968: 18).

Since 1961, the emphasis of Employment Assistance has moved

toward more and better education to prepare the Indian to compete with Whites in job proficiency. These education programs include better prevocational education in the three R's and better and more varied vocational training, including on-the-job training. The amount appropriated by Congress for this fairly successful program rose from $3,500,000 in 1951 to $15,000,000 in 1967, and 10,000 Indians were given job training in the latter year. Companies with government contracts for training Indians have been located in Arizona, New Mexico, Oklahoma, Montana, North Dakota, Minnesota, Wisconsin, and North Carolina. In the decade from 1957 to 1966, about 50,000 Indians were relocated successfully in off-reservation communities (*Indian Voices*, April–May, 1966: 10).

In spite of the programs just described, over half of the Indian labor force was unemployed in 1968, as against 3.5 per cent for the rest of the population. The proportion of Indian families with annual incomes below the $3,000 poverty line was 75 per cent. The total earned income of all Indians under the jurisdiction of the Bureau of Indian Affairs was only about 150 million in 1967, as compared with about 450 million of federal aid from all departments in the same year (*Answers to Your Questions about American Indians*, 1968: 17. Bennett, 1968: 11, 15).

A program to establish industry on the reservations was launched in 1957. At the end of fiscal 1967, more than a hundred industrial and commercial enterprises had been established in Indian areas, providing over 9,000 jobs. New developments in 1967 included an electronics plant on the Seminole reservation in Florida, the General Dynamics missile parts plant and the EPI-Vostron assembly plant on the Navaho reservation, and an expansion of the Sequoyah Carpet Mills in Osage County, Oklahoma (Bennett, 1968).

Termination.—The presidency of Franklin D. Roosevelt, 1933–45, was sympathetic to Indians and initiated legislation favorable to them, but the regime of Harry S. Truman, 1945–52, retrogressed in this respect. When Eisenhower, a Republican, took office in 1953, economy measures were advocated, and an effort to phase out appropriations for Indians was made again. It took the form of House Concurrent Resolution 108, passed by Congress in 1953. This was technically not a statute, but, since it represented the opinion of the majority of federal politicians, it was followed by administrative action in the same direction. In part, the resolution reads:

It is the policy of the Congress, as rapidly as possible, to make the Indians within territorial limits of the United States subject to the same laws and entitled to the same privileges and responsibilities as are applicable to other citizens of the United States, to end their status as wards of the United States, and to grant them all the rights and prerogatives pertaining to American citizenship. .... ("Declaration of Indian Purpose," 1961: 32).

From 1954 through 1960, sixty-one tribes, groups, communities, *rancherías*, or allotments were terminated by withdrawing federal services and protection (Brophy and Aberle, 1966: 187). Most of these units were small, so that the number of individuals involved was not as great as the sixty-one total terminations suggests. However, the Klamath and Menomini lost great stands of timber when their reservations were terminated, and Indians in five states (including California, with about 80,000 Indians in 1968) became subject to state laws, which were less sympathetic than federal controls. The members of the Klamath tribe voted by more than two to one in favor of termination and the relatively large cash settlement for the land and timber that it brought; but after they have spent the money, they will be more dependent than before on welfare checks from the outside.

Termination of federal aid and protection of Indians was far from new. Federal aid and protection for Choctaws, who refused to move to Indian Territory and remained in Mississippi, were terminated in 1830, the same year the Removal Act was passed; that for the Kickapoos terminated in 1862; for the Cherokees who remained in North Carolina, in 1868; for part of the Winnebagos in 1875; and for the Five Civilized Tribes in Oklahoma in 1906 (Brophy and Aberle, 1966: 180–81). The stampede toward termination, begun in 1953, raised so much protest from Indians, anthropologists, and other minorities that the Secretary of the Interior, in a public speech in 1958, promised that no tribe would have its federal aid terminated without its consent. But even though a tribe consents, as did the Klamath, it may be inadvisable to terminate it.

Medical Services.—In 1955, medical services on reservations were transferred from the Bureau of Indian Affairs to the Public Health Service. This was in no sense a termination, since the appropriations for Indian medical services have increased since that date.

Commissioner of Indian Affairs.—When John F. Kennedy, a Democrat, assumed the office of president in 1961, he appointed Philleo Nash to the position of Commissioner of Indian Affairs. Nash was the first anthropologist to hold this position. He not only held a doctorate in anthropology from the University of Chicago but he had been Lieutenant Governor of Wisconsin. This unique combination of anthropology and politics gave him ideal qualifications for the job. But when Nash advocated, in a speech in 1965, that Indians should be allowed to continue their tribal way of life if they chose, this proposal ran counter to Secretary of the Interior Udall's view that they should be pushed toward assimilation into White society as rapidly as possible. Nash resigned the next year, and President Johnson appointed Robert L. Bennett to succeed him (McNickle, 1966). Bennett is an Oneida Indian, the second Indian to hold the office. The first held the office ninety-seven years ago.

American Indian Chicago Conference.—This conference was held in June, 1961, with Sol Tax, a prominent anthropologist at the University of Chicago, as coordinator. The object was to give Indians of all tribes an opportunity to give their opinions about their rights and needs and their ideas on what kind of government policy they preferred. The conference was attended by over 500 Indians representing ninety tribes and bands. The result was a document entitled "The Declaration of Indian Purpose," in which a large majority of the delegates expressed their desire to maintain their identity as Indians and their right to choose some aspects of the White man's culture and to reject others. They further expressed opposition to mandatory termination of federal services to Indians.

> What we ask of America is not charity, not paternalism, even when benevolent. We ask only that the nature of our situation be recognized and made the basis of policy and action. In short, the Indians ask for assistance, technical and financial, for the time needed, however long that may be, to regain in the America of the space age some measure of the adjustment they enjoyed as the original possessors of their native land ("Declaration of Indian Purpose," 1961:20. Lurie, 1961).

A direct result of this conference was the establishment, at the University of Chicago, of a news sheet called *Indian Voices*, which, unfortunately, was terminated in 1968 for lack of funds.

Organizations.—The extended family is still functioning in most Indian societies today. Although individuals and nuclear families may go to the city to earn money, most keep in touch with their relatives in their home locality and return there to visit and often eventually to stay. Since the Indian Reorganization Act (1934), most Indians have had an affiliation with a "tribal" or community organization, which today is legally a corporation with a constitution and paid officers. Many individuals and "tribes" also belong to a national organization.

The first national organization was the National Indian Association, founded in 1879. Although now extinct, it has been followed by other associations of national scope. One of the most active of these is the National Congress of American Indians, founded in Denver, Colorado, in 1944, so that the "Indians themselves could freely express their views and wishes on national legislation and policy." This was the first all-Indian national organization; it includes both individuals and "tribes" in its membership, and also permits non-Indians to join on a nonvoting basis. More than a hundred tribes and bands were represented in 1968, with greatest strength in the Plains area. Soon after its founding it opened an office in Washington, D.C., and registered as a political lobby. In the beginning, it helped various tribes to make more effective use of the Indian Reorganization Act (1934), and in the 1950's was active in opposing termination of federal aid and protection for Indians. In 1964, it backed the National Indian Youth Council (described below) in its "fish-in" in the state of Washington. It also publishes a little magazine, called *The Sentinel*, and holds meetings of its executive committee and annual conventions in various states to keep in touch with local personnel and organizations. Its first executive director, first vice-president, and first secretary were women; and in 1968, three of its regional vice-presidents were women. Since 1961, it has chosen an increasing number of its officers from the National Indian Youth Council.

The National Indian Youth Council was founded in 1961 at the American Indian Chicago Conference, where five college men and five college women got together and, after considerable discussion, unabashedly elected each other to the ten offices of the organization. In the beginning, the membership was "all chiefs and no Indians." Discussion by some of this group had begun in 1954 in the Kiva Club of the University of New Mexico. The National Indian Youth Council membership is made up of individual Indians of high-school and college age, not tribes; it permits non-Indians to affiliate as nonvoting members. It publishes a news sheet called *Americans before Columbus*, and another called *The Aborigine*. In looking around for a cause to sponsor, it became aware of the Indian-White fishing hassle in the state of Washington, and was the principal organization behind the "fish-in" in 1964, where it was joined by the National Congress of American Indians, the Civil Liberties Union, and the movie actor Marlon Brando, who was the most widely known person in the group. It has also been active in opposing termination of federal aid and protection in the 1960's, and has promoted the formation of state Indian commissions, which, by 1968, existed in Arizona, California, Michigan, Minnesota, Montana, New Mexico, and North Dakota.

Although the least-acculturated old Indians will have nothing to do with these national organizations, the younger and best-educated ones are rapidly becoming aware of the benefits that are already being realized from the greater visibility being given Indians in the national scene. (For further details on Indian organizations, see indexes in Levine and Lurie, 1968, and Steiner, 1968.)

Civil Disobedience.—The "fish-in" in Washington state in 1964 was the first large-scale intertribal civil disobedience involving direct defiance of White laws. The controversy started in 1854 with the Treaty of Medicine Creek, in which the Indians of what later became Washington state agreed to give up most of their lands if the federal government would guarantee their fishing rights. This treaty was signed by representatives of the Indians and the federal government, and was followed by many similar treaties involving salt as well as fresh water. After Washington became a state, it passed a series of laws restricting the fishing of Indians in the waters specified in the federal treaties. A major blow came in the 1950's, when a large dam built at The Dalles on the Columbia River eliminated the Indians' fishing places guaranteed by federal treaty.

In 1964, the local Washington tribes, with the help of the National Indian Youth Council, sent urgent messages to fifty tribes to come to a council meeting to discuss what to do. Representatives of more than forty came. The result was a gathering of over a hundred Indians from fifty-six tribes and a larger number of Whites at the state capitol. When this accomplished nothing, hundreds of Indians deliberately fished in the waters forbidden by the state. Dozens were arrested by the overworked game wardens, at whom Indian women and children threw sticks and stones. No one was seriously injured by this token violence.

The Indians in the Puget Sound region hired lawyers and fought their case in the state courts. In 1966, the United States Department of Justice took the side of the Indians in an appearance before the Supreme Court of Washington state (Steiner, 1968: 48–64). In late 1967, the United States Supreme Court granted the Puyallup tribe's petition for review of the Supreme Court of Washington state's decision which had denied that tribe the fishing rights given them in a federal treaty. But in late 1968 the United States Supreme Court decided against the Puyallup and thus dampened the hopes of other tribes with similar claims.

Political Offices.—In 1968, an Indian from South Dakota, Ben Reifel, was elected to his fifth term in the United States House of Representatives. In 1967 and 1968, eighteen Indians were seated in the legislatures of six Western states and Alaska, and more held offices at the county and local level. Although only a few Indians voted as recently as a decade ago, many are voting today; ninety per cent of the eligible Indian voters of one tribe turned out and won in a recent state election. In the states with the largest Indian populations, the Indian vote can be decisive in a closely contested election, and politicians are beginning to recognize this fact (Steiner, 1968: 231–49. *Answers to Your Questions about American Indians*, 1968: 7).

Civil Rights Bill.—In the Civil Rights Bill (H.R. 2516), passed by Congress in 1968, there are six titles dealing with the rights of American Indians. The most important provision requires tribal consent before a state may assume civil and criminal jurisdiction over Indian reservations within its borders (*Indian Affairs*, 70: 1, April–May, 1968). The American Indian Civil Rights Council was founded in Washington, D. C., in 1967 by Sioux Indians. Indians joined the Poor People's March on Washington in June and July, 1968, and intend to continue to participate in demonstrations and picketing (*Indian Voices*, February and March 1967: 10; Winter of 1968: 12).

"Omnibus" Bill.—The "Omnibus" Bill, called the "Ominous" Bill by some Indians, is pending in Congress as of 1968.

"For the purpose of securing loans guaranteed or pursuant of this act, Indian tribes are authorized, subject to the approval of the Secretary [of the Interior], to execute mortgages, or deeds of trust, land title to which is held by the United States . . . [Section 416]. Property mortgaged or hypothecated pursuant of this section shall be subject to foreclosure and sale in accordance with the laws of the state in which the land is located . . . without the approval of the Secretary . . . [Section 102]."

The proponents of this bill argue that it is a boon to Indians because private lending institutions will lend them more money if Indian property can be used as collateral. Opponents of the measure point out that most Indians are not yet ready to compete with Whites in economic matters, and are likely to lose sizable portions of their land. Again, it is impossible to be sure of the motives of the Congressmen promoting the bill and of what would happen if it were approved by Congress (Steiner, 1968:252. *Americans before Columbus*, May, 1967).

Civil Rights Goals.—A comparison of the civil rights activities of Negroes and Indians reveals a tendency toward convergence in the 1960's with both minorities clamoring for more equal opportunities but self-imposed segregation. Most Indians have always wanted to maintain their tribal and community organizations and to accept only those aspects of White culture that they find useful. This has run contrary to the plan of the Bureau of Indian Affairs and other federal agencies, which have tried for a hundred years to assimilate the Indian into the society at large and to phase out all activities and organizations which keep the Indian segregated. The Negroes in the 1950's, in contrast, demanded not only equal opportunity but integration with Whites into a single great society. In the 1960's, the "Black Muslims" and other Black-power groups switched to a self-imposed segregation with more or less militant organizations for Blacks only. The problem in the United States in 1968 is how to persuade Congressmen, who must be elected by voters who are almost 90 per cent White, to raise taxes, if necessary, and appropriate enough money to raise the standard of living of the Browns, Blacks, and Reds, as the Indians are beginning to call themselves. Although private business has already initiated sizable programs to recruit, educate, and later employ colored minorities, most of the initiative and funding must come from governments, with the federal government taking the lead.

REFERENCES

Americans before Columbus, 1967; *Answers to Your Questions about American Indians*, 1968; BARNEY, personal communication; BENNETT, 1968; BROPHY AND ABERLE, 1966; "Declaration of Indian Purpose," 1961; DOBYNS, 1968; FOREMAN, 1934; HAGAN, 1961, 1966; *Indian Affairs*, 1968; *Indian Voices*, 1963–1968; KNIGHT, 1960; THEODORA KROEBER, 1961; LEVINE AND LURIE, 1968; LURIE, 1961, 1966, 1968; MCNICKLE, 1964; OSWALT, 1966; SPICER, 1962; STEINER, 1968; VOGT, 1961; WITT, 1968; ZELLERS, 1968.

27

Indian Culture Change in the United States

Food.—The principal change in food consumption of Indians was a lowering of protein in the diet as game animals became depleted. This began on the East Coast in the seventeenth century, and most of the game there was gone by the end of the eighteenth century. West of the Appalachians, in the Midwest, the cycle came a little later and, on the Plains, resulted in the near extermination of the buffalo in the 1880's. By that date, little meat could be obtained from hunting, even in the Far West. It was only in the Southwest among the Pueblos, where cultivated plants were the staples at first Spanish contact, that diet was not radically altered, but the virtual elimination of meat protein from a diet already short of it must have had a deleterious effect on health.

The diminution of game was offset to some extent here and there by the acquisition of domesticated animals from Europe, but most Indians did not possess such animals in sufficient numbers to anywhere near compensate for loss of game. Even the Plains Indians, with their large herds of horses derived from the Spanish, chose to starve in the 1880's and 1890's, after the buffalo were gone, rather than to eat their horses. The sheep that the Spanish brought to the Southwest more nearly balanced the loss of protein from diminishing wild game, especially among the Navaho. That the sheep were important in their diet is proved by their quick surrender to the United States troops after the latter had captured most of the Indians' sheep. It is only in the past few decades that beef cattle have been raised by Indians in sufficient numbers effectively to improve diet as well as cash income. Dairying was unknown to Indians before White contact, and has since been much less important than beef production to them.

In the Southeast and Southwest areas especially, the Indians cultivated a number of plants introduced by Europeans. The principal ones were wheat, sweet potatoes, "Irish" potatoes, peaches, apricots, apples, pears, watermelons, muskmelons, and tomatoes. Both kinds of potatoes are native to South America, and were first domesticated by Indians there long before Columbus discovered America, but they were introduced into what is now the United States by Europeans. Tomatoes were brought to the Southwest by the Spanish, although they too are native to America.

The turkey is the only animal of any significance that the Indians of the United States gave to the Whites, but it was wild turkeys that were served at the first Thanksgiving in New England. Domestic breeds were developed later.

Tobacco.—Although most Indians used tobacco before White contact, those in North America smoked mostly the *Nicotiana rustica* species. The European explorers and colonists in the New World preferred to smoke the milder *Nicotiana tabacum* from the West Indies; and it was this species, introduced into North America by them, that became the tobacco of worldwide commerce. It was raised commercially on plantations in Virginia and other Southern states and sold to Indians as a trade item. It replaced other species of tobacco to some extent, but Indians on the whole smoked it less than Whites, and the native species survived in some localities in religious ritual. A few Indians in the United States took up tobacco chewing in emulation of Whites after the tobacco industry prepared and marketed chewing tobacco.

Alcoholic Beverages.—Alcoholic beverages were known only to a few Indians in the United States (Map 12) before White contact, and were used sparingly. After Europeans arrived, alcohol became a standard item in the list of trade goods, to the detriment of Indians and Whites alike. The immediate reaction of the more warlike tribes to alcohol was violence, although not all individuals lost their self-control under its influence. After the sale of alcohol to Indians was banned by the United States government, many Indians still obtained it from bootleggers or from Indians of mixed ancestry who could pass as White. Today, alcoholism is a major Indian problem. The drink-associated crime rate of Indians is twelve times higher than the national rate (Stewart, 1964:61).

Housing.—Indian housing in what is now the United States was generally used by European explorers and travellers only when European housing was not available. It was only among the Pueblos in the Southwest, whose native houses resembled those of the Spanish, that Indian housing was regarded as comparable to that of Whites. Therefore the dominant type of change was the modification of

Indian housing to conform to that of Whites. There was a great deal of variation in the kinds of change and in the time that it occurred from tribe to tribe and area to area. For instance, the Iroquois stopped building palisades around their towns in 1690, abandoned clan towns by 1710, replaced the bark-covered longhouse with a log-walled house by about 1800, and gradually acquired frame houses of milled lumber in the nineteenth century (Fenton 1957: 33).

In 1862, most of the Hidatsa, Mandan, and Arikara, in the extreme northwestern part of the Prairies culture area, lived in earth lodges; but by 1883, the log house had almost replaced the earth lodge, and by 1886, when they moved onto a reservation, the earth lodge was eliminated entirely in favor of log cabins. These began to be replaced with houses of milled lumber soon after that date, and the latter are dominant today (Bruner 1961: 244). The more nomadic tribes, such as the Sioux, continued to live in hide-covered tipis until the buffalo were near extinction in the 1880's, and very reluctantly shifted to log cabins supplemented by canvas tents when they too were confined to a reservation. In the Great Basin and Rocky Mountain regions, canvas-covered tipis, wickiups, and tents carried over into the twentieth century and are still used in some localities.

The Pueblos in the Southwest have continued to live in houses essentially like their pre-Spanish ones down to the present time, but with modifications. The corner fireplace, the outdoor domed oven, and doors at street level began to appear in the eighteenth century, but in the late nineteenth century some houses were still entered only by way of ladders and hatchways in roofs. In the twentieth century, the communal pueblo is no longer built, but some are still occupied. All new houses are separate for each family, spaced some distance apart. A few pueblos enjoy electricity, running water in outside faucets or occasionally inside the house, and many now have Anglo-type furniture; and those with electricity even have television sets, which are replacing live storytellers (Dozier, 1961: 149, 162, 173).

On the Northwest Coast (Oregon and Washington), the native plank houses began to be replaced gradually by houses made of milled lumber in the last half of the nineteenth century. Today, all the Indians have shifted to White-type houses, and the more well-to-do have furnished them so completely in the White manner that the whole ensemble is no longer distinguishable from that of Whites.

Structures used primarily for religious purposes tended to lag behind dwellings in the sequence of change. For instance, the Iroquois in Canada in the 1950's were still using a log-cabin type longhouse for religious ceremonies (*Longhouse People*, Encyclopaedia Britannica Films). The Pueblo peoples still use their underground or semi-underground kivas, which have changed little since the Spanish first came to the scene. The Indians of central California still build their religious structures in the round shape of the semisubterranean earth lodge, but they are wholly above ground and are made of milled lumber.

The earliest-known dwelling of the Navaho was the conical hogan with a forked pole in the center. Archeological data show a few stone-walled houses in Navaho territory in the period from 1745 to 1812, but these are probably the pueblitos of Pueblo refugees. Between 1812 and the end of the Mexican period in 1846, the Navaho built some five-, six-, and eight-sided dwellings of horizontal logs (Vogt, 1961: 294, 303). The six-sided log variety is the most common today, although it, in turn, is being replaced by White-type structures of milled lumber. The doors of the latter type still face the east in traditional style. A hospital built with federal funds had the entrance facing west instead of east, and many Navaho refused to enter the building for this reason.

A 1962 survey of 563 Navaho homes by the Environmental Sanitation Branch of the United States Public Health Service reveals shockingly low standards of sanitation:

291 of the homes had no water sources on the premises; of 325 water sources inspected, 90 per cent were unsatisfactory, and of the 294 storage and distribution systems surveyed, *all* were unsatisfactory; more than 55 per cent of the homes had no facilities whatever for disposing of excreta, and 84 per cent of the privies and 92 per cent of sewage-disposal facilities were unsatisfactory; provisions for refuse disposal were 98·5 per cent unac-cepatable; and 87 per cent of the food-sanitation practices inspected were not satisfactory (Brophy and Aberle, 1966: 168).

If the results of this survey are offensive to Indian readers of this volume, they should remember that their need for better housing must be made known before they can obtain outside funds to build it. In other localities, however, Navaho housing is much better, and electricity has reached a few Navaho settlements.

On the other side of the ledger, eighty tribes by the end of fiscal 1967 had established housing authorities and applied for funds to initiate new housing units with standards comparable to those of Whites, and 1,200 new units had been built and 1,000 more were under construc-tion. In addition, these tribes have asked for materials with which Indians too poor to make the down payment on White-standard houses can build do-it-yourself units that will be better than most of those occupied previously. About 700 houses were completed under this plan by 1967, and 2,900 more were in the planning stage. The Bureau of Indian Affairs placed the housing need of all Indians under its jurisdiction at 65,000 units in the same year. (*Answers to Your Questions about American Indians*, 1968: 21. *Indian Affairs*, 66: Apr.-July, 1967, 5, and 69: Jan.-Mar., 1968, 5). In fiscal 1967, the federal government appropriated $13,500,000 for construction of sanitation facilities, more than three times the fiscal 1962 figure (*The Year's Highlights*, 1967-68).

Clothing.—Changes in clothing materials and styles began almost everywhere with the establishment of trading posts by Europeans, because items of dress were included in all inventories of trade goods. Blankets of wool and—less frequently—cotton were popular with Indians and were wrapped around the body for warmth in place of the earlier robes of fur. The European man's coat, with full-length sleeves and the opening in front, was soon copied in buckskin or fur material by Indians. The breechcloth and leggings of Indians in the Plains, Prairies, and East were sewn together to imitate European trousers. White pioneers, such as Daniel Boone, wore both coats and trousers of buckskin. As the trade goods poured in, the wealthier Indians bought coats and trousers of cloth and even a few top hats, and yachting caps had a great vogue on the Plateau.

Wherever the Indian women went topless, the missionaries hastened to cover them up with blouses or dresses. The "squaw dress" of the Southwest was copied by Indian women from the dresses of the wives of United States army officers in the early years of the Anglo period, and Indian girls at boarding schools were taught to make such dresses. Where Indian women's clothing covered the body sufficiently to satisfy White prudes, as on the Plains and in the Pueblos, it tended to persist, at least as a ceremonial costume, with little alteration. Thus the Plains women's long dress of buckskin is wholly acceptable to Indians and Whites alike and is still worn on special occasions. The woven pre-Spanish cotton dress, dyed black, is the standard ceremonial dress of all Pueblo women today on such occasions as the Corn Dance, performed in the plaza and open to the public. Today it is said these dresses are made only by the Hopi, who trade them to the other Pueblo peoples.

Footgear changed more slowly. Moccasins have persisted almost everywhere, and are always worn with traditional costumes. The

Pueblo women's boot, with the wrap-around upper almost to the knee, is still worn as ceremonial dress. White-type shoes on Indians date almost entirely within the twentieth century.

In the Southwest and in other areas where cattle are raised, the Indian men wear the standard cowboy costume today: shirt, blue jeans, riding boots, and broad-rimmed hat. Earlier Spanish influence is apparent in velvet shirts, wide-bottomed trousers, and bright colored sashes, more common among the older Indian men today. Women's dress in the same area also shows the bright colors and shawls of the Spanish and Mexican periods.

Plains Indian clothing styles have diffused in all directions and have almost produced a pan-Indian costume in the twentieth century. From the Iroquois in New York to the West Coast, such costumes are worn by Indians of many tribes at rodeos, Fourth of July celebrations, and Indian ceremonial occasions. It is principally in the Southwest that this diffusion has been resisted, probably because the Indians there already possessed rich and colorful costumes.

Trade.—Indian-White trade greatly influenced Indian arts and crafts because European trade goods included a host of new materials and tools. The earliest trading activities on the East Coast of what is now the United States began in the sixteenth century, but the first trading post that survived long enough to do a substantial business was that of the Dutch on Manhattan Island, established in 1612. This was soon followed by English trading posts from New England to Georgia. The Hudson's Bay Company was founded in 1670 and, although its original character limited it to the basin of Hudson Bay, it soon expanded west and south into what are now the northern states of the United States. By the end of the seventeenth century, Indian-White trade had crossed the Appalachians everywhere and reached the Mississippi in some places. Spain engaged in trade in New Mexico in the same century, but there were few furs in that area and the pattern was different. On the West Coast, European ships with trade goods began to stop regularly from about 1775 on.

Furs were everywhere the principal commodity obtained from the Indians, who received, in return, a great variety of European trade goods. Of the latter, the most ubiquitous were glass beads, most of which were manufactured in Venice, Italy, up to the end of the eighteenth century. After 1800, many other nations went into the bead business. Beads cost little to make, were highly valued by Indians, and were therefore the most profitable item handled. Their appeal to Indians probably stemmed from the native shell beads which were widely used as standards of value and media of exchange. The value of the shell beads was high because the shells were available only on the coasts and the Indian manufacturing process was very time-consuming. When pump drills and grindstones arrived from Europe, the technique of manufacture was sped up so much that the oversupply deflated the value. Similarly, where one kind of glass bead was traded in exceedingly large numbers, it too became less valuable; the European traders soon learned to switch colors and sizes frequently in order to create a steady demand.

The trade objects of most economic value to the Indian were those of metal: steel awls and axes; brass rings and wire; iron wire; guns, bullets, and shot; fishhooks; copper or brass kettles; steel knives, including pocketknives with folding blades and special scalping knives; iron pickaxes; needles, scissors, and shears; steels and flints to strike together to make fire; steel swords; steel and iron hatchets and tomahawks; table ware of pewter; steel razors; sleigh-type bells; and even jews harps (Woodward, 1965: 2-4).

Articles of clothing were often less serviceable than the predominantly hide and fur clothing of the Indians, but were valued as prestige symbols. These included: cloth of many kinds and colors, blankets of wool, coats, waistcoats, caps, hats, shirts, trousers, shoes, ribbons, and even dyed feathers (Woodward, 1965: 2-4).

Of food and drink items, the most common were sugar, salt, molasses, rice, wheat flour, coffee, tea, whiskey, and rum. Other miscellaneous trade items were: combs, glass bottles, chinaware, glass mirrors, pipes, tobacco, paints of many colors, dyestuffs, gunpowder, powder horns, lace, thread, twine, stockings, saddles, bridles, candles, eyeglasses, burning glasses, playing cards, and soap (Woodward, 1965: 2-4).

In addition to acquiring the new objects fully manufactured in advance, the Indians often used the new White materials to improve their own tools and weapons. This is illustrated by the burning of wrecked ships in the early days to obtain the iron and sometimes other metals from the ashes. The iron was then used for such things as arrowheads, spear points, harpoon heads, knives, awls, and adz blades.

Although the objects received from Europeans were generally regarded by the Indian as superior to his corresponding native forms, this was not always true for all purposes. A muzzle-loading gun was very awkward to reload on horseback and took much more time than to release the next arrow from the bow. It was only after breech-loading guns and cartridge ammunition became available that the gun could compete with the bow and arrow in buffalo hunting on horseback; only after the repeating rifle appeared, was the bow finally made completely obsolete for those who could afford the rifle.

The effect of the European trade on the lives of the Indians and the far-reaching changes it brought about have already been described in Chapter 13. We need only repeat here that it produced a cycle that began with an initial period of greater prosperity when the Indian had most of his pre-Columbian culture plus the many trade items; this was followed by a middle period of competition with other tribes for the best fur-producing areas, giving rise to much bloodshed; finally, there came a period of complete disaster, when the fur-bearing animals were destroyed, and food as well as income from exchange dropped drastically. Shimkin (1947: 280–81) was one of the first to argue that while the horse and European trade increased the total amount of Wind River Shoshoni activity, there was no real gain and the system could not support any more people on the land than could the pre-horse culture. Levy (1961: 23) comes to the same conclusion for the southern Plains, but hastens to add that the Sioux, at least, in the northern Plains did show an increase in population on the upswing of the cycle.

Crafts.—Crafts responded to the new tools made available by the European trade. The preparing of plant materials was facilitated by the use of steel knives to peel, scrape, and split the stems and roots for basket making; and the steel awl improved some kinds of coiling technique. The technique of making splint basketry in the Southeast spread northward beyond the Canadian border in the nineteenth century, because splint baskets made with a steel knife could be made faster than any other kind. Such baskets are still made in the north by Indians and sold to Whites as a source of cash income. The making of watertight twined and coiled baskets in the West for stone boiling disappeared rapidly as metal containers became available in trade.

The Spanish flat-bed loom in the Southwest crowded out native weaving among the Rio Grande Pueblos by the early nineteenth century (Dozier 1961: 174). Navaho weaving is unquestionably derived from that of the Pueblos, most likely between 1700 and 1750, when large numbers of Pueblo refugees from Spanish oppression were living among the Navaho. By 1799, Navaho woolen blankets were being woven for the Spanish market (Vogt 1961: 296, 301). Tourists in the twentieth century have purchased large numbers of Navaho blankets, used as rugs or as wall hangings, and have vastly expanded the weaving business of the Navaho. Unfortunately, the Navaho woman who does the labor often gets a smaller portion of the retail price than the middleman or the retailer, and the work is so time-consuming that a few years ago it was estimated that the weaver earned only ten or twelve cents per hour.

Pottery vessels gave way to metal containers in all areas where pottery had been made by Indians. This change came quickest to Plains tribes after they acquired the horse, because pottery was too fragile to withstand the frequent moving. The sedentary Pueblos, in contrast, were the last to give up most of their pottery making, and enough of it has survived into the twentieth century to make it possible to revive the craft for the tourist trade. Some Pueblos today earn more cash from sales of pottery to tourists than from any other source. Neither the potter's wheel nor molds were ever introduced in trade in the United States, so that pottery-making methods in the Southwest are substantially the Indian ones.

Skinning animals killed in the hunt and skin dressing were speeded up by the steel knives and iron blades for fleshers and scrapers obtained in trade, but tanning with tannic acid was never done by Indians in the United States, except for a little in the Southwest under Spanish supervision.

Indians north of Meso-America had no true metallurgy before White contact, but those in the Southwest were quick to learn silver working with the aid of hammers, anvils, pliers, molds, and the pump drill brought in by the Spanish. The making of silver and turquoise jewelry for sale to tourists is now a major activity in the Southwest (Adair, 1944).

Art.—The wood carving and painting of the Indians in western Washington benefited from the steel ax heads, adz blades, knives, chisels, and paint obtained in trade from Europeans from about 1775 on. Houses, canoes, boxes, and carvings of the human figure all became larger and more impressive. It was a change in quantity more than in quality. The dog-wool blankets made by finger weaving could not compete with the power-loomed blankets of the trading companies, and soon disappeared. Wood carving is also almost a lost art on the Northwest Coast today.

In the Plains and Prairies areas especially, work with skins was greatly aided by trade needles. Before needles arrived, all sewing was done by punching a hole with a bone awl and then threading it with the fingers. Every stitch was as laborious as threading a needle. Even a metal awl was a big improvement over the bone awl. The needle also helped in the sewing of buffalo hides together for tipi covers, as tipis grew larger after the horse was introduced. The needle was likewise indispensable to the elaborate beadwork of the nineteenth century; the beads of course were glass trade ones from Europe. The new paints and dyes also lent more color to the earlier porcupine quill embroidery and to designs painted on hides. While the Indian men were fighting their last wars with Whites and conditions were generally disturbed in the last half of the nineteenth century, the women patiently embroidered small glass trade beads on buckskin shirts, dresses, moccasins, mittens, gloves, belts, and bands. Bead work reached its florescence in this period (Hunt, 1951).

The paints, brushes, canvases and papers introduced by Anglos in the Southwest in the twentieth century, as well as teaching of art in the Indian schools starting in the 1920's, have helped launch a new art program there. Sales of paintings, mostly in Santa Fe and Taos, have brought much needed income to the growing number of Indian artists, and have given them the opportunity to create a new art style which is a blend of Indian, Spanish, and Anglo (Dunn, 1968. Tanner, 1957). The presence of Anglo art colonies in Taos and Santa Fe has aided Indian artists by attracting patrons in larger numbers than the Indian art alone could have done. In the Eastern United States, Indian art is almost a thing of the past, although it survives in modified form in areas where Indians are still numerous, for instance, among the Cherokee of North Carolina, the Seminole of Florida, and various tribes around the Great Lakes. In the latter area, the Menomini, Meskwakie, Winnebago, and Potawatomi are experiencing a resurgence of ribbon appliqué panels on women's skirts of blanket cloth, worn with silk overblouses ornamented with ribbon and silver, and with German silver brooches copied from heirlooms and museum originals of the late eighteenth and early nineteenth centuries. These costumes are now edging out Plains-style buckskin dresses which have long been popular at powwows. The nearby Ojibwa are reviving the black velvet shift dress with tie-on sleeves of the early trade period.

The Association of American Indian Affairs opened a nonprofit Indian Art Center in New York City in 1964; in 1967–68, it grossed over $100,000 (*The Year's Highlights*, 1967–68). The total sales of art and craft objects made by Indians in the Southwest in recent years are estimated at $7,000,000 annually, but the White retailers and middlemen get most of this.

Music.—Indian music experienced a brief period of florescence as songs spread from tribe to tribe in the religious revitalization movements, such as the Drum Dances, Ghost Dances, and the Peyote religion. In the Plains and Great Lakes areas, new Peyote songs have been composed to honor men who went to war in World War I, World War II, Korea, and Vietnam. Because Indian music is so extremely different from European music in so many ways—in voice projection, intervals, progressions, and instruments—there has been little tendency for the two to blend. In areas where Indians have survived in large numbers and still perform many of their ceremonies, especially in the Plains and Southwest, some of their native music has survived almost intact. The inventory is probably nowhere still complete, and will diminish as the old ceremonial leaders pass away, but the less esoteric songs sung by choruses in public may continue for another hundred years. At present, tape recorders are widely used by Indians to preserve songs, to teach them to younger singers, and to diffuse them from tribe to tribe.

Kinship.—Kinship groupings, behavior, and terminology of Indians have been profoundly modified by White contact. The most general trend has been away from unilocal and unilateral organization to bilocal and bilateral systems. This was not a simple diffusion from Anglo to Indian culture, but rather a historical or evolutionary cycle which began with a change in subsistence, in ownership and inheritance of land and chattels, in family composition, in descent groupings, and generally ended with a change in kinship terminology.

In the Southeast, the breakup of the Indian matrilineal systems began in the eighteenth century with the appearance of missionaries, traders, and colonial officials. The removal of most of these Indians to Oklahoma in the 1830's hastened the process, as did the later pressures from Whites in Indian Territory. The assignment of land to men as heads of nuclear families instead of to women, the paying of doles and the rationing of food to men instead of women, and the election of new political officials by men only on a territorial rather than a kinship basis—all tended to push kinship away from the native matrilineal system toward the bilateral and patrilineal structure of Whites. The regulation of marriage by law, with widows entitled to dower rights, and a man's children rather than his sister's children inheriting his estate, plus the replacement of the old clan and town rituals by church activities, also exerted pressure in the same direction. The Choctaw changed the most, while the Chickasaw, who had less White contact, changed the least. The Cherokee who remained behind in North Carolina showed little change up to the 1930's, but those who went to Oklahoma showed greater change as early as the time of the Civil War. The Yuchi may have run the whole gamut of change from matrilineal (Crow) to patrilineal (Omaha) kinship terminology, but only after close contacts with the Shawnee, Sauk, and Fox, all of whom were patrilineal (Omaha). Among the Yuchi, diffusion from, and acculturation by, other Indians triggered the change (Eggan, 1966: 15–36).

Most of the Plains tribes speak Algonquian and Siouan languages, and most of these had unilateral descent at an earlier period when they lived in the Prairies area to the east. On the Prairies, they farmed, lived in villages, inherited farm plots from relatives, had matrilocal or patrilocal residence, a corresponding matrilineal or patrilineal descent, and a corresponding Crow or Omaha type of kinship terminology. After acquiring the horse, moving out on the high Plains, abandoning farming, and regrouping along band and tribal lines, their social organizations shifted from unilocal toward bilocal residence, from unilateral toward bilateral descent, and from Crow or Omaha kinship terminologies toward the Hawaiian (bilateral-generation) type. Some tribes proceeded further than others in the cycle of change, but almost all moved in the same general direction.

The Crow Indians, for instance, originally had a farming economy in which women owned the fields and did the farm work, matrilocal residence in earth lodges owned by women, matrilineal descent, and a Crow-type kinship terminology. After they abandoned their farms in the Dakotas and moved west into Montana to follow the buffalo, their residence shifted to bilocal or patrilocal, the matrilineal sibs survived but without the localization of members on the land, and the Crow kinship terminology survived in reference but gave way to Hawaiian (generation) terms for siblings in address. Thus they had passed about halfway through the cycle of change when studied by Robert H. Lowie in the first decade of the twentieth century (Eggan, 1966: 45–77).

The Southwest also lends itself to a similar interpretation. There is good reason to believe that the earliest farmers there were women, who owned their farm plots and inherited them from mother to daughter, and that residence was matrilocal, descent matrilineal, and kinship terminology of Crow type. Today, this system survives most clearly among the Hopi. As one proceeds eastward, to Zuñi, Acoma, Laguna, and other Keresan pueblos, the system becomes more bilocal and bilateral, until the Tanoans on the Rio Grande are reached. Eggan (1966: 112–41) believes that the Tanoans may have lost their matrilineal organization when they abandoned such places as Mesa Verde and Chaco Canyon in the late thirteenth century and moved southeastward to the Rio Grande Valley. The appearance of the Spanish as early as 1598 may have obliterated the last traces of matrilineal organization among the Tanoans, because none of them except the Jemez were found to be matrilineal by nineteenth- and twentieth-century scholars. The Jemez probably acquired their system from contact with Keresans rather than retained it from the thirteenth century.

It was mentioned above that the Navaho acquired domesticated plants and weaving from the Pueblo refugees who lived with them from about 1700 to 1750. That their kinship organization also was influenced by that of the Pueblos at this time is evident because some of their matrilineal sibs are named after Pueblos: Jemez sib, Zia sib, and the "Black Sheep People" sib, the last-named derived from San Felipe. The Western Apache, in turn, derived their matrilineal sib system principally from the Navaho, because their traditions hold that most of their sibs are descended from one of three archaic sibs of the Navaho (Vogt, 1961: 301–2).

White contact with most California Indians was so catastrophic that changes in kinship organization are hard to trace. It seems likely, however, that the Wappo and one Pomo tribelet, since they had a Crow type of kinship system, must have had at least a maternal lineage system at first White contact. If so, it must have been lost in the Indian-White scuffle, because no field anthropologist has been able to obtain satisfactory evidence of it. Elsewhere in California, the predominantly patrilocal extended families and more restricted paternal lineages and moieties lost most of their functions rapidly without being replaced by any new Indian kind of social organization. Other areas in the West were bilateral to begin with, and, although their native kinship organization soon began to change or lose its functions, there is no clear general trend toward, or away from, unilaterality as demonstrated for other areas.

From these examples it is clear that kinship organization changes in response both to an altered ecology and economy and to contacts with other peoples having different kinds of systems. It is not necessary to decide which of these two causes of change is generally paramount: each may be dominant in different times and places, or both may be of about equal potency in other examples of change.

The decision-making power of women in kinship affairs among the Iroquois has been shown to have increased during the historic period. As the prestige of men was lessened by severe losses in numbers and defeats in warfare, by lack of opportunity to do much hunting on the reservations after the Revolutionary War, and by the subservient status they were forced to assume as wards of White governments, the prestige of women in family affairs rose to new highs. A seventeenth-century source states that choice of spouse at marriage was made by the principals: the bride and groom. In the eighteenth century, the principals and their parents jointly made the choice; but in the nineteenth century, it was the mothers of the principals who made the decision. With respect to the marriage of relatives, seventeenth-century sources say that neither cousins nor other relatives were permitted to marry; but by the nineteenth century, marriage was permitted between paternal relatives if they were not closer than first cousins, and matrilineal exogamy applied to all members of one's matrisib whether related or not. Thus there was a shift from bilateral to matrilineal extension of incest taboos. Disposal of children at divorce shows a similar direction of change: in the seventeenth century, there were no clear rules, the matter being negotiated in each instance; in the nineteenth century, the mother kept the children at divorce or disposed of them as she saw fit. Thus the authority of women in kinship affairs, formerly thought to have been the pre-White norm, has been shown by Richards (1957) to have been increased by post-contact conditions.

Political Organization.—From archeological evidence it is generally assumed that tribal organization with a hierarchy of officials capable of controlling the common man by force, if necessary, existed in the East and Prairies at least as early as the Hopewell culture, 200 B.C. to A.D. 400. By the time of the Mississippian climax, A.D. 1200–1500, the largest of these native governments must have embraced tens of thousands of persons, and some tribal organizations may have been joined together to form confederacies or alliances. De Soto saw these Mississippian groups in his famous journey of 1539–42, but a century later most of them seemed to have been finished off by the first shock of White contact. In the seventeenth century, the Iroquois confederacy was the dominant one, the traditional date of its founding being 1570. It split up during the Revolutionary War and never re-formed because those who had sided with the British had fled to Canada. As the Whites became a threat to the Indians in other areas, the latter formed many confederacies or alliances as a means of better resisting a common enemy, but most of them lacked sufficient economic resources as well as singularity of purpose to last more than a few years. Various Plains tribes united at different times in the nineteenth century, most successfully when a mixed army of Sioux, Cheyennes, and Arapahos under Sitting Bull and Crazy Horse annihilated George A. Custer and his troops in 1876.

In the Southwest, a Spanish decree of 1620 created a group of officers for each pueblo except those of the Hopi. The highest officer was the governor, who dealt directly with the Spanish. The lieutenant governor helped the governor and succeeded him when the occasion arose. There were also: a sheriff (*alguacil*), to maintain law and order; a sacristan to assist the priest in the church; a number of *fiscales* to maintain discipline within the pueblo; and the *mayordomos* to super- intend the construction and maintenance of irrigation ditches (Dozier, 1961 : 138–39). The Indians retained their native government, which largely went underground, where it has remained to this day. The Spanish system was a superficial overlay that was never integrated with the native organization. The Anglos in the United States failed to impose as uniform a system on their Indian subjects until 1934.

After a progressive diminution of the number of tribal governments in the United States and of the authority they possessed down to 1934, the Indian Reorganization Act of that year provided a model of democratic tribal government that most groups of Indians accepted. A considerable number in the West that had never had any pre-White tribal organization went along with the new plan and organized themselves for the first time.

Warfare.—During the colonial period, the Whites and Indians on the East Coast exchanged weapons and war tactics freely with each other. The Indians eagerly accepted the guns in exchange for furs, and the White pioneers learned the Indian guerrilla ways of taking cover behind rocks and trees and making surprise attacks. The fate of the close ranks of the British in Braddock's defeat was a bitter lesson to the British and their colonists, and George Washington, who witnessed the defeat, never later placed his own revolutionary army in such an untenable position. In the protracted contest between the British and the French, both sides paid bounties for scalps of Indians, presumably those on the opposing side. As early as 1703, the colonial government of Massachusetts was paying twelve pounds for every Indian scalp (Stewart, *in* Spencer and Jennings, 1965: 496). As late as the Revolutionary War, the Americans claimed that the British were still paying bounties for scalps, including White American ones, but the British denied it.

The general view in the United States is still that the Indians committed more inhuman atrocities than did the Whites. At this date, it is impossible to obtain satisfactory documentation for such a broad generalization on this subject, but a single instance of White atrocities against Indians will suffice to make the point that White hands are not clean in this respect.

In the summer of 1864, bands of Cheyennes and Arapahos in Colorado raided isolated ranches and stagecoach terminals, killing and scalping one family within twenty miles of Denver. One band reported to Fort Lyon on the upper Arkansas river, made peace with the military detachment there, and settled for the winter at a place called Sand Creek. In late November of that year, a column of Colorado militia led by Colonel J. M. Chivington, a Methodist minister, made a surprise attack on the camp. They killed about one-third of the five hundred in the Indian group, mostly women, children, and the aged, who could not defend themselves. Eyewitnesses told of Indian children being clubbed to death and pregnant women being disemboweled. General Nelson A. Miles, who was later to gain fame fighting Apaches in the Southwest, termed the massacre the "foulest and most unjustifiable crime in the annals of America" (Hagan, 1961: 107–8).

The skill and courage exhibited by Indians in wars with Whites in the United States have never been exceeded by any human group on earth. Man for man, gun for gun, and horse for horse, the Indians were superior. It was only because the Whites had larger numbers of men and a greater quantity of armament and other supplies that they were able to subdue the Indians. It was estimated in 1870 that it had cost the United States government about a million dollars for every Indian killed (Loram and McIlwraith, 1943: 142). Considering the much greater value of the dollar at that time, such a figure indicates how heavily the odds were stacked against the Indians.

Rank and Social Classes.—Rank and social classes responded to the changing conditions in the historic period. Those Indians who were more successful at trade with Whites became richer and more independent of tribal authority. Before White contact, intertribal trade in the Plains, Prairies, and East had sometimes been controlled by chiefs who managed to get the lion's share of the profit, but after trading posts were established the White traders were generally willing to do business with anyone. This lowered the prestige of the chief and raised that of the individual trader.

In dealings with Indians, White formality and legal red tape often required the signature (an ✗ mark) of the chief or some other person with tribal authority. Indians who knew English, French, or Spanish and could communicate the most easily with Whites were often raised to a position of authority by virtue of their participation in the negotiations. Some individuals who started as mere interpreters ended up as signers of legal documents and virtual chiefs, thus scrambling the traditional power structure. In the long run, however, the statuses of all Indian officials became drastically lowered as White governments gained more and more control over Indians.

In the Plains area, the acquisition of large numbers of horses, more than any other single factor, accentuated differences in wealth and rank where they had scarcely existed before. Ewers (1955), Mishkin (1940), and Wilson (1963) go so far as to say that social classes were created in this manner. Lowie admits that distinctions of rank occurred but denies the existence of hereditary social classes.

All that can be said in this respect is that, as everywhere, the children of distinguished men enjoyed certain advantages. As the son of a Rockefeller or Morgan has a better chance to become a great businessman than has a guttersnipe, so a Cree chief's son was more readily acclaimed a brave than an orphan would be (Lowie, 1954: 112).

However, the southern Plains tribes had stronger tendencies toward class structure than those in the north, probably from indirect contacts with Southeastern peoples who undeniably had social classes. The large herds of horses in the south provided a mechanism for the southern Plains tribes to emulate their neighbors in the Southeast.

The acquisition of large numbers of sheep by the Navaho did not create social classes, nor did the considerable numbers of horses among Apaches as well as Navahos have such an effect. This is easily explained by the history of these peoples: their origin in the north as hunters and gatherers and their later contact with the very equalitarian Pueblos. Most of the Plains tribes, in contrast, had been farmers on the Prairies, and probably brought some distinctions of rank with them from the Prairies area, where such distinctions were more developed. The eastern Caddo were sedentary Southeastern farmers with a class system, and this surely had some influence on the leaning toward class structure of the Plains Caddoans, who formerly lived in or adjacent to the Southeast.

Sodalities.—White contact spelled the doom of most Indian sodalities but, at the same time, gave rise to new sodalities or encouraged the diffusion of old ones to new peoples who had not had them before. Hickerson (1963) shows how the principal development and spread of the Midewiwin took place after White contact. This was not a revitalization movement at a time when the Chippewa were suffering deprivation, but was a florescent development at the height of a period of prosperity from the trade with Whites. Although it is more difficult to find documentation for the Plains area in the eighteenth century, there is good reason to believe that the increased contacts brought about by the horse aided the diffusion of men's societies at this time.

In other areas, certain sodalities are remarkable examples of persistence in the face of heavy odds against survival. The Iroquois of Canada still have a False Face sodality within the Longhouse religion, and the Pueblos in the Southwest still maintain some of their sodalities. Partly because Pueblo sodalities were secret to begin with and habits of secrecy were firmly inculcated in the membership, they continued to hold their secret meetings all through the Spanish and Mexican periods. Most of the attrition of these organizations has taken place in the twentieth century; late-nineteenth-century observers, such as Frank Cushing, found these sodalities fully alive and active in the society.

Life Cycle.—Indian beliefs and practices associated with the life cycle survive to a considerable extent in the areas where Indian population is most numerous. Because life cycle ceremonies were often small family affairs attracting little attention, they survived in areas where large public religious ceremonies were discouraged or prohibited. Many infants today are brought into the world by nonliterate Indian midwives, in much the same way as they were in pre-Columbian times. Boys' initiations at puberty have almost entirely disappeared, but girls at first menstruation are secluded and indoctrinated with the same old native taboos in many localities. Among the Apaches of the Southwest, the girl's puberty ceremony was formerly held for each girl just after she came of age. Her relatives invited everyone to attend, provided food and drink for the guests, and sometimes paid the professional performers. After the Apaches were rounded up on reservations, the United States government forbade them to assemble at any time except between the first and the fourth of July, for fear that they would start a war dance and go on the warpath. Because the girl's puberty ritual was the most important one in the whole culture, the Apaches changed what had been an individual rite into a group affair and put on the ceremony for every girl who had come of age during the past year. After the ban on public assemblies was lifted, they continued to hold their girl's puberty rites between the first and the fourth of July.

Funeral and memorial ceremonies for the dead have disappeared or become attenuated for the most part, but continue to be held in areas where large numbers of Indians live together and otherwise maintain much of their native culture. The Mohave, for example, still cremate their dead much as they did in the past. Burial above ground in caves, trees, and on scaffolds is forbidden by law in the United States, and disappeared in the nineteenth century. Burial in the ground, which satisfies Christian doctrine as well as civil laws, has increased in frequency during the historic period.

Religion.—Indian religion has survived to some extent in areas where there are large numbers of Indians living together and maintaining some of their traditional culture. In spite of noble efforts on the part of missionaries, Indians in the United States have responded slowly to Christianity. The uncompromising attitude of most Protestant missionaries to the beliefs and practices of the Indians, the many attempts of United States officials and citizens to stamp out Indian religions, and the insistence that the Indian become acculturated to White ways in general before being accepted as a full member of a Protestant sect, have retarded conversion to Christianity. The dominant trend in the historic period has been the formation of new religious organizations by Indians. Although these religions do contain some Christian elements, their original inception and subsequent acquisition of followers have been independent of organized Christianity. Wallace (1956) has called these religions "revitalization movements."

The principal revitalization movements of Indians in the United States began with that led by Pope, a Tewa medicine man, whose following fomented the rebellion of the New Mexican Pueblo Indians against the Spanish in 1680. In the eighteenth century, a Delaware prophet preached the rejection of Christianity and a return to a modified form of earlier Delaware religion; and in the early nineteenth century, a Shawnee prophet preached a parallel doctrine. About 1800, the Seneca prophet Handsome Lake began preaching a return to Indian religion and a rejection of the Quaker brand of Christianity to which he had been exposed. About 1870, the first Ghost Dance movement, prophesying the removal of the White man, got under way in Nevada, California, and Oregon; and in 1890, a derived religion, again called the Ghost Dance, also starting in Nevada, spread east to the Plains tribes, where it disappeared in a few years. Other revitalization religions include: the Drum or Dream Dance, which originated in the 1870's among the Santee Sioux and spread to neighboring peoples in the northern Prairies area; the 1801 Chumash affair, which spread to other California tribes; the 1881 beginning of the Indian Shaker cult in the state of Washington; the 1884 religion of Smohalla along the Columbia river; and the Peyote religion, to be described in more detail below (partly from Stewart, *in* Spencer and Jennings, 1965: 498-99).

The Peyote religion, known technically today as the Native American Church, is the largest of the new Indian religions, with an estimated 250,000 members in 1968. For this reason, it will be described in more detail. Its history has already been sketched in Chapter 7 and summarized on Map 13. The doctrine includes the belief in supernatural power, in spirits, and in the incarnation of power in human beings. Spirits consist of: the Christian Trinity (the Father, Son, and Holy Ghost); other Christian spirits, such as the devil and the angels; and still other spirits derived exclusively from Indian religions. The Christian spirits tend to be equated with comparable Indian spirits: God is the Great Spirit; Jesus is the culture hero, guardian spirit, or intercessor between God and man; the devil is an evil spirit bent on harming man; the angels are often the spirits of the four winds or cardinal directions, and are sometimes represented as being dressed like Indians. The pantheon is thus seen to include about an equal mixture of Indian and Christian spiritual beings.

The ethics of the Native American Church also closely parallel those of Christianity. Members should exhibit brotherly love by being helpful, friendly, honest, and truthful to one another, as in the Golden Rule (Matthew 7: 12; Luke 6: 31). Married couples should cherish and care for each other and their children, and should not commit adultery. Members should work steadily and reliably at their jobs to earn a good living, and, above all, should avoid alcohol.

Peyote ritual, however, is heavily weighted in favor of Indian elements, such as the eagle-bone whistle, cedar incense, the fan of bird tail feathers, the bundle of sage sprigs, the gourd rattle, and the water drum. Ritual behavior too is principally Indian in character. Eating peyote induces rapport with the supernatural and brings visions of spirits or departed loved ones, sometimes with aid in solving personal problems or with warning to abandon evil thoughts and deeds. Visions occur also in Christianity, in both the Old and the New Testament. To sum up, the Native American Church is a happy blend of about equal portions of Christian and Indian elements and patterns, and provides a stabilizing force for the personalities of its followers (Slotkin, 1956). At the same time, it has divided many tribes into three groups: traditionalists, Peyotists, and Christians.

Health.—Before White contact, Indian religions took care of every phase of human activity; there were rituals to increase success in every imaginable human action as well as to cure disease and to bring about good health. After the gun and the fur trade had finally destroyed the game animals and there was no more hunting to do, hunting rituals were dropped or reinterpreted for other purposes. After the disastrous military defeats and incarcerations on reservations, rituals to ensure success were likewise turned to other purposes. One after another, religious behaviors and beliefs were either dropped from the inventory or altered to adjust to the new circumstances. But there was one kind of ritual that never became obsolete because the need never disappeared. That was ritual to cure injuries and diseases and to protect persons from these harms in the future. Health ceremonies loomed larger and larger in the Indian religions; the pre-White ones were never lost, and rituals for vanished purposes were converted to health-helping routines. The increase in alleged witchcraft in the historic period has also encouraged the development of ceremonies to counteract it. Although all of such routines were and are efficacious as psychotherapy, none of them can cure injuries such as fractures, internal disturbances like ruptured appendixes or gallstones, or diseases caused by microbes or viruses. However, they can aid in postoperative recovery, and many White physicians with Indian patients have learned in recent years to allow the medicine man to sing his harmless songs or perform other ritual to bolster the patient's confidence (Adair, 1960).

On the whole, Indians have been slow to accept the White man's medical aid because of general distrust of the group that exhibited so much overt hostility toward them. The rate of acceptance has been increasing in the past few decades, however, and better medical programs are reaching more and more Indians.

The first Congressional appropriation for Indian health was made in 1832. By 1880, the Bureau of Indian Affairs had provided four hospitals and seventy-seven physicians; in 1892, physicians were put under civil service. In 1910, a medical division was established in the Bureau of Indian Affairs, but progress was slow until after 1934, when there was an upswing in health services. In 1955, the Division of Indian Health of the United States Public Health Service took over all the health activities of the Bureau of Indian Affairs and, by 1962, had taken full jurisdiction over Indian health services in other federal agencies. It now administers the construction and alterations of hospitals and clinics, field health services, contract patient care, sanitation facilities, and quarters for medical personnel. The budget for Indian health for fiscal 1967 was about $100,000,000.

From the 1960 census, the median age of Indians was found to be under twenty, as compared with thirty in the general United States population. This reflects the shorter life span of Indians, which was forty-four years in 1967 while that for the general population was sixty-five years. The greatest number of Indian deaths is among infants and children: infant mortality in 1944 was 135 per thousand live births, but in 1968 it had been reduced to thirty-five, showing a great deal was accomplished in health programs from 1944 to 1968; but thirty-five is still twelve points above the national rate of twenty-three. However, an Indian baby born in 1968 can expect to live to age sixty-four, as compared to seventy for the total United States population (*Answers to Your Questions about American Indians*, 1968:72).

Causes of Indian deaths in 1959 show sharp differences from those of the general United States population. The following causes of death were from three to eight times more frequent among Indians: intestinal infections, tuberculosis, accidents, homicide, influenza, and pneumonia. On the other hand, certain other causes of death among Indians are only about half as frequent as among the general population: malignant neoplasms (cancer), heart diseases, and vascular lesions affecting the central nervous system (strokes). This difference is to be explained by the shorter life span of the Indians as well as by any possible genetic difference in susceptibility to diseases of old age. For the most common contagious diseases not necessarily causing death, the Indian rates are from two to twelve times higher than those for the general population. In general, Indian statistics for illness and death are comparable to those for Whites in the early part of the twentieth century.

The Indian birth rate in 1959 was 41.4 live births per thousand of the population, almost twice the rate of 24·1 for the general population. However, it was higher for some tribes; that of the Ute Mountain Ute in 1960 was 55·8. Again, these figures are comparable to those for Whites two generations or more ago. It is obvious that if voluntary family planning (birth control) could reduce the Indian birth rate to that of Whites, the problem of first taking care of the Indians and then raising their standard of living to that of Whites would be much easier. The statistics above compared Indian rates with those for the general population, which includes other underprivileged groups. If all of these minorities were separated from the remaining "Whites," and Indian rates were compared with those of the latter, the contrast would be sharper.

A sentimental view held by some is that we should not breathe a word about family planning to Indians until they have increased about tenfold to their pre-Columbian level. A realistic appraisal of the amount of support that is likely to be obtained from the federal government and other sources for Indians makes this view impractical, regardless of its ideal of compensating for the terrible toll of Indian lives since first White contact. A saner view would be to extend to the Indians the same freedom of choice in family planning as is available to many Whites in the United States and to many people of other nations.

One of the impediments to better health service for Indians is their fear and distrust of White physicians and hospital staffs, brought about as much by the Indian patient's poor facility with English as by his superstitions about the cause of illness. To remedy this difficulty, the Public Health Service launched a program in 1967–68 to train 260 Indians as community health aides (*The Year's Highlights*, 1967–68).

Population.—Indian population in the United States minus Hawaii and Alaska reached a low of about 250,000 in 1890. It has risen sharply in the twentieth century, as the following figures show: 1900, 271,000; 1920, 336,000; 1940, 355,000; 1960, 509,000; 1968, over 600,000. These figures were compiled by the Bureau of Indian Affairs and the United States Census. If those with only a small fraction of Indian blood who live as Whites are counted, an educated guess is that the 1968 figure might be 1,000,000 or more. In 1960, 308,000 were members of tribes, bands, and other communities under the jurisdiction of the Bureau of Indian Affairs; the remaining 201,000 lived outside reservations and were economically more independent. The five states with the most Indians in 1960 were: Arizona, 83,000; Oklahoma, 65,000; New Mexico, 56,000; California, 39,000; North Carolina, 38,000. The stampede of Indians to California cities, especially Los Angeles, in the 1960's has increased Indian population in California enough to raise its rank to first or second in 1968.

Powwows.—The latest "American Indian Calendar" of the Bureau of Indian Affairs lists 385 powwows, religious ceremonies, fairs, festivals, dances, rodeos, athletic contests, and other gatherings in which Indians and Eskimos participate in the continental United States including Alaska. The numbers of such celebrations in the leading states are: Alaska, 75; New Mexico, 65; Montana, 43; Oklahoma, 39; Arizona, 28; South Dakota, 28. All of these are open to tourists and the general public, and art and craft objects made by Indians are sold at many such celebrations. Indians are no longer ashamed to be identified as Indians, and many who live as Whites off the reservation return to play roles in these traditional celebrations.

Language.—Nearly all Indians today speak English, and about 90 per cent read and write it to some extent. At the same time, most of them still speak one of about a hundred Indian languages still extant in the United States. On the reservations, where a majority of Indians still live, almost all still speak their native language; but off the reservations, especially in cities, the Indian languages are rapidly being dropped. Formal education in schools for reservation Indians has been tremendously handicapped by the virtual absence of bilingual teachers. A child in the first grade who knows only his Indian language learns very little from a program wholly in English. However, this is now being remedied with better "English as a second language" programs for pupils and Indian language programs for teachers (Bennett, 1968: 5).

There is no question that the personality of the Indian generally became hostile, sullen, and withdrawn as a result of White pressures of all kinds over the centuries. This tendency probably reached its peak at about the same time that the total number of people reached its nadir, about 1890. Since that time, Indians have become more responsive at an increasing rate, and much more so in the past decade. If we can imagine our own reaction to being conquered and regimented by beings from outer space, we can perhaps understand the Indians a little better.

The two contrasting images of the Indian—the noble savage versus the bloodthirsty savage—have been discussed in historical perspective at some length by Stewart (*in* Spencer and Jennings, 1965: 495-96). He points out that the image of the noble savage goes back to Montaigne in the sixteenth century and did not originate with Rousseau in the eighteenth, although the latter's writings on this subject are more widely known. The downgrading of Indian personality began with the Puritans in New England, who believed the Indians were controlled by the devil, and got progressively worse until the last half of the nineteenth century. Since that time, White attitudes toward Indians have softened a great deal. The enlightened view at the present time is that Indian personality is not determined by heredity but by the environmental conditions under which Indians grow up and live out their lives. By giving the Indians more opportunity and treating them as equals in the consumption of the amenities of our civilization, even though they are not yet equal in the production of these amenities, we can increase their response to our way of life to the mutual benefit of both parties.

REFERENCES

ADAIR, 1944, 1960; "American Indian Calendar," n.d.; *Answers to Your Questions about American Indians*, 1968; BROPHY AND ABERLE, 1966; BRUNER, 1961; DOZIER, 1961; DUNN, 1968; EGGAN, 1966; EWERS, 1955; FENTON, 1957; HAGAN, 1961; HICKERSON, 1963; HUNT, 1951; LEVY, 1961; LORAM AND MCILWRAITH, 1943; LOWIE, 1954; MISHKIN, 1940; RICHARDS, 1957; SHIMKIN, 1947; SLOTKIN, 1956; SPENCER AND JENNINGS, 1965; STEINER, 1968; STEWART, 1964; TANNER, 1957; VOGT, 1961; WALLACE, 1956; WILSON, 1963; WOODWARD, 1965; *The Year's Highlights*, 1967-68.

28

History and Culture Change in Canada, Alaska, Greenland

THE EUROPEANS who first explored and later settled Canada, Alaska, and Greenland, mostly north of the 49th parallel of latitude, were interested primarily in trade. Since fur was the most valuable product to be obtained from this huge territory, and since the Indians and Eskimos did most of the hunting and trapping, the Europeans needed these natives to make their economic operation a success. There was no attempt to drive the natives off their land to make way for settlers, except in small areas in what is now southern Canada. Neither was there any desire to regiment the Indians in agriculture or factories, because farming was practiced only in the southeastern part of Canada in the colonial period and manufacturing was minimal at that time. The Eskimos and almost all of the Indians had lived by hunting and fishing before White contact, knew nothing of farming or animal husbandry, and would not have performed indoor labor.

Although the English and French brought more of their own women to the colonies in what is now Canada than did the Spanish in Hispanic America, the nature of the fur trade was such that many Englishmen and Frenchmen led single lives on the ship, at the trading post, or traveling in search of bargains in furs. Frenchmen more often than Englishmen traveled alone or in groups of two or three and lived with Indians because there was nobody else to provide food and lodging. Some of the Frenchmen spent their entire lives as hunters and trappers in the company of Indians. There were enough French-Indian marriages and concubinages to produce a sizable number of hybrids, which are recognizable in the population today. A French-speaking group of mixed French and Indian ancestry, called the *métis*, lived undisturbed for about a century in southern Manitoba and united to form a political faction at about the time dominion status was achieved.

The missionary effort of the French Jesuits was greater than any parallel program of the English, but nowhere near as successful as that of the Spanish in Meso-America. The Canadian Indians were not as credulous and docile as Meso-Americans after the defeat of the Aztecs, and they often drove out or killed the French Jesuits. Missionary work was most successful in Greenland, where the Eskimo, unlike the Indians in Canada, were not caught between French and English political and military rivalries.

Almost all of the natives north of the 49th parallel lacked tribal organization and well-developed patterns of warfare. Only the Iroquoians and their immediate neighbors south of that line, and a few Plains tribes north of it, offered serious resistance to White intrusion. This is in sharp contrast to the Aztecs of Mexico and practically all the tribes east of the Rocky Mountains in what is now the United States.

Another difference was the very sparse population over most of Canada, Greenland, and Alaska. At least in the early stages of the fur trade, there was room for everybody. Except in a few localities in the south and on the coasts, the natives were not literally overrun by a horde of settlers, as they were in the United States.

The following chronology highlights some of the principal events in the area of this chapter.

A.D. 10th to 15th century	Norse settlers in Greenland.
1497	John Cabot's first voyage for England.
1534	Cartier's first voyage for France.
1604	First permanent French colony in North America founded at Port Royal, Nova Scotia.
1610	Hudson discovered Hudson Bay for England.
1611	First Jesuits in New France.
1670	British king instructed governors of the colonies to protect Indians desiring it. Hudson's Bay Company formed.
1713	Treaty of Utrecht between France and England.
1721	First lasting settlement of Danes in Greenland.
1741	Vitus Bering reached Alaska from the west.
1755	British appointed first Indian superintendent for colonies and territories.
1756–63	French and Indian War (Seven Years' War); New France conquered by English.
1764	Moravian missions founded in Labrador.
1775–83	American Revolutionary War.
1784	Northwest Company was formed.
1788	First United States vessels reached the Northwest Coast.
1789	Mackenzie reached the mouth of the Mackenzie River on the Arctic Ocean.
1793	Mackenzie reached the Pacific Ocean via the Fraser River.
1818	Polar Eskimo discovered by John Ross at Thule in northwest Greenland.
1821	Merger of Northwest and Hudson's Bay companies.

1833	First exploration of interior Alaska by Russians.
1848	Start of intensive commercial whaling in north Bering Sea, mostly by United States ships.
1861	First Eskimo-language newspaper in Greenland.
1867	Dominion of Canada formed. United States purchased Alaska from Russia.
1870	First Riel rebellion.
1876	Parliament of Canada consolidated Indian legislation in First Indian Act.
1884	East Greenland Eskimo discovered by Holm.
1890's	Siberian reindeer introduced and missions established in Alaska.
1896	Gold discovered in Alaska.
1900–05	First Hudson's Bay Company trading posts in Canadian Arctic.
1903	Canadian government began to establish permanent stations in Arctic.
1912	Territorial legislature created in Alaska.
1921	Danish sovereignty extended to all of Greenland.
1929	Canadian government purchased first reindeer in Alaska and drove them to lower Mackenzie area for Indians there.
1941	Greenland made temporary protectorate of United States.
1951	Denmark and United States agreed to jointly defend Greenland. United States air and radar base established at Thule. Canadian Parliament passed the Second Indian Act.
1953	Greenland became a county of Denmark, with two representatives in Danish Parliament.
1955–57	Construction of Distant Early Warning (DEW) radar line from Alaska to Baffin Island.
1957	Canada began a relocation and employment service for Indians: the Individual Placement Program.
1959	Alaska became a state.

CANADA

John Cabot's voyages in 1497 and 1498 established a British claim on eastern Canada and were followed by fish-drying stations on Newfoundland. In 1534–42, Cartier sailed up the St. Lawrence as far as Montreal but failed to establish a permanent French colony, which was not achieved until 1604 at Port Royal, Nova Scotia. In the meantime, the English continued to fish from ships and fishing stations on the coast, and the French traveled up the St. Lawrence in search of furs. Henry Hudson discovered Hudson Bay in 1610 and claimed it for the English, who later established fur trading posts on its southern shores. By 1635, New France was a complete colony, with traders, farmers, priests, and soldiers at its capital Quebec.

The British gradually turned from fishing to fur trading and carried on a running battle with the French throughout the seventeenth century. The Hudson's Bay Company was founded by the British in 1670; by the next year, this company had ships anchored off the south shore of the bay to trade with Indians, and soon built trading posts on land. A temporary peace was established in 1713 by the Treaty of Utrecht, which gave England Newfoundland, Acadia, and the Hudson Bay drainage; France was given the central region, including the St. Lawrence drainage, the Great Lakes, and the entire Mississippi drainage west to the Rocky Mountains. Hostilities soon broke out again, and culminated in the French and Indian War, 1756–63, in which France lost to England all of New France east of the Mississippi and, for a short time, the area west of the Mississippi—called Louisiana—to Spain. The latter area was purchased from France by the United States in 1803 (Brown, 1944. Creighton, 1960).

Indians on the east coast began receiving trade goods from the English and French in the sixteenth century. By the end of that century, these Indians were dependent on the Europeans for metal kettles, knives, guns, hatchets, and other utilitarian trade items. The most prized fur was that of the beaver, from which were made the large hats so popular in Europe at the time. In the period from 1600 to 1663 the fur trade moved up the St. Lawrence and Ottawa rivers. By 1635, the Hurons had exhausted the supply of beaver in their own territory, and by 1641, the Iroquois were in the same predicament. This precipitated the trade rivalry between the Iroquois and Hurons that ended in the annihilation of the latter (see Chapter 13).

From about 1663 to 1713, the fur trade moved west to the Great Lakes and Hudson Bay, bringing quantities of European goods to the Indians in these areas. From 1713 to 1763, it moved on to the Saskatchewan drainage that flowed into Hudson Bay from the west. By 1770, so many independent traders had established posts inland closer to the source of furs that the business at the Hudson's Bay Company posts on the bay had declined alarmingly. In 1770–71, the Hudson's Bay Company employed Samuel Hearne to lead an expedition to the Coppermine River, which flows into the Arctic Ocean. This he succeeded in doing, and later, in 1774, established the first inland trading post of the Hudson's Bay Company, on the Saskatchewan River (Innis, 1962).

The independent traders joined together to form the Northwest Company in 1784; their most daring member, Alexander Mackenzie, reached the Arctic Ocean in 1789 and the Pacific in 1793. The entire continent from Atlantic to Pacific was soon linked by a series of trading posts which brought European goods to practically all Indians.

In 1821, the two rival fur companies—the Hudson's Bay Company and the Northwest Company—merged. But by 1869, the fur trade had declined to the point where it was more profitable to sell the company's rights in the Hudson Bay drainage to the new Dominion of Canada, created in 1867, than it was to try to continue as a trade monopoly. This the company did in that year. This alarmed the *métis*, the French-speaking French-Indian mixed bloods, who feared that more English-speaking settlers from what is now Ontario would squat on their land and otherwise disturb them. The *métis*, numbering about nine thousand and led by Louis Riel, demanded separation from Ontario and autonomy, which was finally partly achieved by establishing the province of Manitoba in 1870. The French were permitted to continue teaching the French language in the schools. In 1885, when the buffalo were gone and the *métis* were being pressed by more Anglos from Ontario, Riel led a second rebellion of Indians as well as *métis*; but it failed, and he was hanged for treason. This second rebellion hastened the establishment of the province of Saskatchewan, however. After this, the authority of the Dominion government was unchallenged in the west (Brown, 1942. Innis, 1962).

The Indian Act of 1876, passed by the Canadian Parliament, was the most important piece of legislation for Canadian Indians in the nineteenth century. It provided for the control of Indian lands and the moneys invested by Indian groups in the Indian Trust Fund, which was established to protect the money Indians received from the sale of natural resources on their lands. This act also recognized the responsibility of the Dominion government for the health, welfare, and education of the Indians and for aid in their agricultural and industrial enterprises. It also specified how an Indian could become a full citizen with voting rights (Oswalt, 1966: 504), and it prohibited the use of alcohol by Indians. This law was revised in 1951, the liquor prohibition removed and liquor control placed in the hands of the provinces and territories, about half of which now permit Indians to consume alcoholic beverages.

Voting rights of Canadian Indians varied over the years. The Indian Act of 1876 provided that any Indian with a university education or its equivalent must become a citizen with voting rights and relinquish his special tax-free rights as an Indian. In 1880, the mandatory aspect was made voluntary, but in 1933, mandatory enfranchisement became the law again. The present rule, based on the Indian Act of 1951, is that an adult may become a full Canadian citizen, with voting rights and taxation, by presenting character references and proof that he can earn a living outside the reservation. Response to this opportunity has been slow; until 1960, there were only 122 Indians who had acquired voting rights in this manner. However, the total number of Indian voters in Canada, including war veterans and Indians outside reservations, was 20,000 out of an estimated total of 60,000 adults (Hawthorn, 1966: 258–59).

In 1680, Louis XIV of France granted land to a group of Iroquois in Quebec. This grant was later honored by the British, and the Iroquois still occupy the land. The Proclamation of 1763 prohibited the taking of land from Indians without their consent and the approval of the British crown. In 1784, the Iroquois who had sided with the British in the American Revolutionary War were granted nearly 700,000 acres of land as a reward for their loyalty. By 1821, they had sold or lost nearly half of this land and were forbidden by law to alienate any more of it. Treaties made with Indians always contained agreements about land, the first being that with the Ojibwa in 1850. This was followed by one more treaty before confederation in 1867, and by thirteen more between 1871 and 1923, when the last was negotiated (Oswalt, 1966: 503, 509–10). About half the Indian population of Canada today is under a formal treaty agreement.

The administration of Indian Affairs in Canada has been allocated to nine different governmental departments or divisions since 1816, and is now the Indian Affairs Branch of the Department of Citizenship and Immigration (Oswalt 1966: 504). In spite of these changes in administration, the treatment of Indians by the Canadian government has been better than that by the United States. The more modest budget for Indian aid has fluctuated less from one political administration to another. The Church in Canada played a more dominant role, with its mission programs, often taking care of health, education, and economic assistance locally in the field; the Hudson's Bay Company posts performed similar functions as a matter of course. The demand for Indian land was much less than in the United States, and there was never any mass removal of Indians from large areas. Canada has rarely repudiated treaties with Indians or turned its back on violations by irresponsible Whites, as has occurred many times in the United States.

So far, nothing about the Eskimo in Canada has been included in this section. They were few in numbers before White contact, which occurred in the late nineteenth century for many, with little culture change until the twentieth. There were not even trading posts or stations of the Royal Canadian Mounted Police—who were un-mounted in Eskimo territory—until the first decade of this century. For most of the Eskimo groups, there has been more culture change since World War II than before that time. Eskimos were under the jurisdiction of Northern Affairs—rather than Indian Affairs—until 1967 (when the two were combined); the former agency has shown more imagination and better judgment in handling the Eskimos than the latter in its treatment of Indians.

Food.—Food habits changed as the animals on which the Indians depended diminished in numbers or became practically extinct. At first, the gun and other metal tools improved the efficiency of hunting and increased the food supply. In the far north, these increased the amount of meat for Eskimo dogs, and for fox bait as well, and the size of dog teams increased. But as early as the first half of the seventeenth century, the beavers of the Iroquois and Hurons were so depleted that these tribes fought over the role of middleman in the trade from the interior. Other game became progressively scarcer, and by the time of the American Revolutionary War, hunting was a minor activity in the St. Lawrence Valley. In most other areas, the only difference was the time of depletion, which became progressively later to the west and north.

In 1907, Ernest Thompson Seton estimated that there were 30,000,000 caribou in all of Canada, a figure regarded by other game experts as too high. In 1938, the estimate was down to 2,500,000; by 1948–1949, it was only 670,000 from Hudson Bay to the Mackenzie River, which probably included nine-tenths of these animals in all of Canada; by 1955, the figure in this same area had dropped to 277,000. The principal cause of this decline was excessive slaughter by humans, although the many forest fires and lumbering had reduced the spruce-lichen forests, which provided the winter forage of the animals. The lichens and sedges, the chief plants on which the caribou feed, were heavily impregnated with strontium 90 and cesium 137 from the atomic bomb tests of the 1950's, and the caribou meat was heavily loaded with the same radioactive materials. If this did not further deplete the caribou, it at least made the meat less safe for human consumption for a time (Hughes 1965: 18). Now that most such tests have gone underground, this danger has passed, at least temporarily.

The moose population has survived better than the caribou, and has actually increased in some areas in this century. Knight (1965) has shown that moose have benefited by forest fires, because they feed on the shrub foliage and grassy weeds that spring up in a burned-over area. The fires destroy the lichens and sedges eaten by caribou, and these plants come back very slowly. The solitary nature of the moose also protects it from the mass slaughter inflicted on the herd-minded caribou. The musk-ox in the eastern Arctic was practically annihilated because its habit of making a stand in a group with horns outward to impale attacking wolves did not work against guns. The shortage of game was partly alleviated in the lower Mackenzie region by the importing of reindeer from Alaska in 1929. By 1967, the numbers of reindeer in this locality reached 8,000, enough to make a substantial contribution to the Indian diet (Hill, 1967: 148).

There is still enough game left in many parts of Canada to respond to conservation programs. The following table from Hawthorn *et al.* (1958: 105) shows that the number of beaver in three provinces more than doubled in a short span of seven years.

	Number of Beaver Pelts	
	1945	*1952*
Manitoba	3,379	27,875
Saskatchewan	1,646	17,618
Ontario	47,276	106,000

This sharp increase was made possible by a joint program of the Dominion and provincial governments. In 1954, in British Columbia, where no such programs had been applied, only 401 Indians out of a total population of 31,077 were earning most of their living by trapping. In 1964, about 40 per cent of the furs produced in Canada came from fur farms (*Encyclopaedia Britannica*, 1964: Canada).

The European foods obtained at the trading posts, such as wheat, flour, rice, sugar, tea, and coffee, were generally lacking in proteins, vitamins, and minerals, and were inferior to the usual staples in the native diet. Malnutrition and complete starvation have been common in Canada as a result of the depletion of game. Where fish are available, they have been sought more intensively to bolster the diet, leading some scholars to believe that fish provided more food than did meat before White contact. This I doubt, but fish are today furnishing the greater share in many areas of the Sub-Arctic, and commercial fishing is now a major source of income for Indians ("Indians of Ontario," 1966: 34–35). On the whole, northern Indians and Eskimos are today dependent to some extent on White foods, and most prefer them.

Population.—Population figures for human beings reflect in part the loss of game, but European diseases, often reinforced by malnutrition, were the principal causes of population decline. In the smallpox epidemic of 1781–82 among northern Athapaskans, Hearne estimated that nine-tenths of these Indians died (Innis, 1962:152). If we compare another set of population figures for a single group—the southern Kwakiutl—a sharp decline is evident: 7,500–8,000 in 1835, 2,264 in 1882, 1,208 in 1911, and 1,039 in 1924 (Codere 1961:456–57). The Kwakiutl were a coastal people with the maximum amount of contact with Europeans of many nationalities not only in their home territory but also in Victoria, British Columbia, the principal port on Vancouver Island. The figures given by Hawthorn *et al.* (1958:23, Table 1) for all of the Indians of British Columbia cover only the years from 1885 to 1954. For interior groups in British Columbia, the nadir is 9,708 in 1890, and the zenith 13,287 in 1954; for coast groups, the nadir is 12,133 in 1917 and the zenith 17,690 in 1954. The nadir for interior groups corresponds closely in time to that for the United States, but the nadir for the coast groups is much later. Unfortunately, these figures are too late to give any idea of the size of the pre-White population, which was surely larger than that in 1954. In 1958, the birth rate for all the Indians of British Columbia was over twice that of Whites and the infant mortality rate four times that of Whites (Hawthorn *et al.*, 1958:285–86). The nadir date for the Arctic and Sub-Arctic may have been as late in some localities as 1920, when the influenza epidemic struck.

On the whole, there seems to have been less aboriginal population decline after White contact in Canada than in the United States or Mexico. Kroeber's low pre-White estimate (1939:134–41), totals only about 264,000 Indians and Eskimos for all of Canada. If this is compared with the figure given by Lagassé (1966) for 1965 of 200,000 Indians and 12,000 Eskimos, it suggests a moderate decline, even though the low point around 1900 was a great deal less than the 1965 figure. In addition, Lagassé estimated 250,000 persons of mixed Indian and European ancestry who live as Whites. The truth for Canada as a whole probably lies somewhere between the extremes of rapid decline, as given by Hearne and Codere, and little decline, according to Kroeber's figures. An educated guess would be that the percentage of population loss in Canada was about half what it was in the United States and Mexico. Owing to better nutrition and medical services, the

Indians and Eskimos of Canada are increasing at about twice the rate of the White population (Hawthorn, 1966:97).

Although sharp declines for Eskimos can be demonstrated in some localities—such as Labrador, where a permanent European settlement dates back to 1764—close contact did not reach some of the Eskimo until the twentieth century. By this time, traders and government officials were more concerned with the welfare of natives than in earlier times, and medical science had much more to offer them. For example, the commissioner of the Royal Canadian Mounted Police reported in 1959: that, from 1949 to 1959, seven nursing stations had been opened in the Arctic and six more were planned; that only 197 active cases of tuberculosis had been discovered from 6,459 X rays taken; and that the death rate from 1954 to 1957 was less than half what it had been a decade earlier (Hughes 1965:14).

Housing.—Indian and Eskimo housing changed only slightly in response to trade goods in the early period of contact. Later, in southern Canada and on the coasts, where White settlers were most numerous, native housing borrowed milled lumber and frame construction from Whites. In other areas, where Indians and Eskimos continued to live largely by hunting and trapping, native housing continued to be used throughout the nineteenth century and on into the twentieth in some localities. The more nomadic Indian groups still build temporary housing of essentially aboriginal type in the camps they occupy in the summer, and some of the Eskimo still live in snow houses in the winter. Thus native housing in Canada has persisted longer than in the United States.

The size of the frame houses of milled lumber of the Indians of British Columbia in the 1950's averaged about 5,000 cubic feet, the equivalent of 25 feet in length, 20 feet in width, and 10 feet in height. More than three-fourths of them were occupied by a single nuclear family. A comparison of the frequency of electric lights, central heating, running water, inside flush toilets, and other appointments showed lower percentages in the interior than on the coast and lower percentages among Indians of both groups than among the general population of British Columbia (Hawthorn *et al.*, 1958:232–33).

Where Whites have congregated in large numbers at military posts, trading posts, mines, and lumbering operations, natives also have tended to assemble in large numbers for economic opportunities (including employment) and for the handouts that they have received in recent decades. In such localities, they often build inferior shacks of any cast-off material available and live at a lower housing level than they did before White contact.

To alleviate this difficulty, the Canadian government has built a number of housing projects, the largest of which is that east of Aklavik in the Mackenzie delta. In the early 1950's, the government began the construction in that locality of a planned community for Whites as well as natives that eventually cost $50,000,000. It met every White standard of engineering and health, and even had a central heating system. By 1959, however, only about one-third of the people in the old town of Aklavik had moved into the new buildings, and a study was undertaken to find out the reason why. The human relations factors of the native population had been neglected, and the people simply did not like the new apartments, the many rules and restrictions associated with them, and the overbearing attitude of the White personnel who screened applicants and inspected their living quarters from time to time. By 1963, however, the new community housed two-thirds of the people in the Aklavik area and thus may be regarded as a success (Hughes 1965: 23).

Clothing.—Clothing went through a cycle parallel to that of housing. At first, the gun and other trade goods brought in more game, furs, and needles to sew better hide and fur garments. The full-length sleeves and trouser legs of European men's clothing were imitated in hide and fur in non-Arctic Canada, and provided warmer clothing than was known before White contact. Then as game became scarce and White clothing more available, the natives shifted to White clothing, which offered less protection in the extremes of winter than had fur. Since World War II, such military-type garments as parkas designed for cold weather have been acquired by many Eskimos and Indians in the north, and these are an improvement over conventional White clothing.

Arts and Crafts.—Arts and crafts were heavily influenced by White contacts. Metal kettles quickly replaced hide, bark, basketry, pottery, and wooden cooking containers as soon as they were available, and the making of the aboriginal types ceased. Steel adz blades and axes increased the size and quantity—if not the quality—of Northwest Coast woodwork. The knife made the making of splint baskets in southeastern Canada profitable, and needles and trade beads of glass enhanced northern Plains beadwork at the expense of the earlier porcupine quill embroidery. The ceremonial garments in areas where native religions have survived or revitalizations generated are now

often made of machine-made cloth, but the cut and design are all or part Indian. Since about 1950, missionaries, traders, and government officials have encouraged both Indians and Eskimos to make their own style of art objects for sale to Whites. The Eskimos especially have produced large quantities of carvings in stone and ivory, stone prints on paper, embroidery on skins, and little dolls for export; these have become the principal sources of money income for some. For most persons, however, the making of native objects for sale is only a part-time occupation; with proper promotion, the demand can be increased.

A nonprofit marketing organization, the Canadian Arctic Producers, Ltd., was created in 1965 to sell the art work of Canadian Eskimos to dealers in wholesale lots. Prints are made in limited editions of not more than fifty each. Ayre (1967) reproduces eighty-four such prints.

Employment.—In 1957, the Indian Affairs Branch inaugurated a program to train Indians and find them jobs in White-managed industries ("Indians of Ontario," 1966: 35). In the census of Indians in 1959, it was found that earned income per capita was only $300, as compared to $1400 for Canada as a whole. This difference is exaggerated by the larger number of Indian children under 16 years of age, which is double that of the White population. About half of the employed Indians worked at such traditional tasks as trapping, fishing, guiding White hunters and fishermen, handicrafts, and forestry. The other half worked mostly at skilled labor (lumbering, mining, and in factories), at unskilled labor (including most farm labor), on their own farms, or in their own businesses. Skilled laborers constituted only 14 per cent of the employed group, but their earnings came to 46 per cent of the Indian total because of higher wages and more regular employment (Hawthorn, 1966: 45–47). On the whole, Eskimos have responded better than interior Indians to the job opportunities that have arisen during and since World War II in connection with the building and maintenance of military bases. By far the largest opportunity of this kind came with the construction of the Distant Early Warning (DEW) radar line across the Arctic from Alaska to Baffinland in 1955–57 at a cost of $600,000,000. This line consists of a total of about fifty stations, and 9,000 Whites from Canada and the United States were employed on the job, a number equal to almost all the Eskimos in Canada at that time. The project gave jobs to Eskimos in actual construction, in maintenance, and in moving supplies into the bases in the summer, and it exposed them suddenly to the wonders of modern science. The other side of the coin was the mushroom growth of shantytowns near the stations and the health problems these created (Hughes, 1965).

Land Tenure.—The effect of White contact on the landownership and social organization of the Eastern Sub-Arctic area has already been discussed in Chapter 16. In the Mackenzie Sub-Arctic, the changes are less clear, and the suggestions derived from the recent works of Helm (1965, 1968) are that bilocal and bilateral land-using groups have been the rule in the area from the earliest contact period and have not changed down to the present time. There has been no "atomization" of society into small family groups as in the Eastern Sub-Arctic; perhaps the social groups around twentieth-century trading posts and fishing lakes are larger than those before White contact.

Kinship.—Kinship relations among Indians and Eskimos have become less and less important on the whole, as they have elsewhere where new economic opportunities and wage work have made individuals more independent of each other. In the Eastern Sub-Arctic, band organization has given way to nuclear or small extended families, each spending the winter on its own trapping territory. Among the Chippewa, there was a two-directional change: from patrilocal and patrilineal localized kin groups to multiple-clan villages, and then to the breakdown of clans and isolation in the small family trapping territories (Hickerson, 1966, 1967). It is probable that all peoples in the Eastern Sub-Arctic once practiced cross-cousin marriage and had a kinship terminology with no separate terms for in-laws (who were also blood relatives). In the next later stage, cross-cousin marriage was dropped, but the kinship terminology and behavior toward relatives short of marriage was retained; and in a third stage, the behavior patterns began to change, but the terminology still remained the same. And, from the third stage, Eggan (1966: 91) predicts that cross-cousins will soon be differentiated from siblings-in-law in a new terminology.

Among the Eskimo, the same general trend away from extended families toward greater independence of nuclear families is the rule. The rifle made individual hunting of the caribou and seals possible; fishnets obtained in trade increased the efficiency of individual fishing; the demand for furs rewarded the individual trapping enterprise; and wages from work for Whites likewise went to the individual, thus making him independent economically of his kin. An example of a countertrend observed in some localities is the motorboat complex. A number of men, not necessarily relatives, pool funds and jointly purchase a motorboat, thus forming a new kind of group economic venture. In other localities, a band or a patrilocal extended family might purchase and operate a motorboat, thus reinforcing an aboriginal social unit (Hughes, 1965: 24–25). Thus there were at least three kinds of economic and social responses of Eskimos to White contact.

Government.—The tribal and confederal organization of the Iroquoians lost authority as Whites gained more and more control, and the same can be said of tribal organization on the northern Plains. Band organization, at least in the Eastern Sub-Arctic, gave way to more emphasis on nuclear and small extended families, each with its own trapping territory. One instance of a countertrend to this progressive atomization of society was that of the Chippewa, cited above, who first grouped their localized clan-bands into multiple-clan villages before abandoning these for family trapping territories. In other areas, which had only village or band organization before White contact, the general trend was toward a disintegration of such units. This has been offset to some extent in the past few decades by the formation of economic cooperatives.

Rank and Class.—Rank and social classes on the Pacific coast, where they were most marked, suffered both ups and downs in the historic period. War raids and slavery were stopped by the British as soon as they gained control—by about 1850 in most localities—and whatever prestige the winner and slave owner enjoyed was brought to an abrupt end. Potlatches and Winter Ceremonies, on the other hand, became larger, and the men who sponsored them rose higher in rank from first White contact until about 1920. In terms of the quantities of gifts given to guests, the largest Kwakiutl potlatch was given in 1921. The total wealth of the Kwakiutl, as measured by material possessions, actually increased in the historic period until about 1920. The swan song of the potlatch came in the 1930's, when the last was given, and since that date the Kwakiutl have adapted their economic efforts rapidly in the direction of those of Canadians generally. The material ambitions of the Kwakiutl were not very different from those of the European Protestants from whom most Canadians of today stem, and their psychological adjustment to the modern world around them was less traumatic than that of most Indians (Codere, 1961).

Sodalities.—Sodalities have survived, with modifications, in areas where they were strong before White contact. Iroquois religious sodalities have been retained by the Longhouse religion, and the Midewiwin society still meets in some Chippewa communities. Men's societies still functioned in 1939, when Goldfrank (1945b: 40–43) did field work among Blackfoot on the northern Plains, but the members were mostly old men. The elaborate secret societies of the Northwest Coast are not mentioned by Hawthorn *et al.* (1958) or by Codere (1961), and apparently are extinct. The Peyote religion (Native American Church) did not reach northern Plains tribes until the twentieth century, and is strong there today. The British Columbia Native Brotherhood, founded in the twentieth century, favors Christianity and White economic, educational, and health programs, and also serves as a bargaining agency with the government and the fish-canning industry (Drucker, 1965: 230–31).

Life Cycle.—Life cycle behavior has changed greatly since first White contact, and large public ceremonies in the few areas where they occurred have mostly been discontinued. Rituals confined to the home have survived longer. Christianity and scientific medicine have reached the majority of Indians and Eskimos by now, and have replaced most of the aboriginal behavior patterns associated with birth, adolescence, and death. Confinement of girls in the home at puberty was still practiced on the Northwest Coast in the early twentieth century; a difference of opinion about this in one family is described in Chapter 21. Behavior at death is largely guided by White standards, although old persons may still retain the old beliefs.

Religion.—Aboriginal religious ceremonies in most localities have undergone secularization, as they have in the United States. Performers still put on the costumes and go through the dances, but with less and less knowledge of the meaning. Religious leaders of today often read the printed data which the anthropologist has obtained concerning an earlier period, so that they can keep up on their tribal lore. On the Northwest Coast, the Winter Ceremonials of Boas' time—1895—emphasized the prestige and rank of the sponsors more than the purely religious aspects, and the optical and auditory illusions produced by performers (see Chapter 20) were almost a prostitution of the older religious beliefs. On the other hand, my wife witnessed what were called "spirit possessions" among Indians in the late 1940's in Washington state near the Canadian border. In this ceremony, attended by perhaps a hundred Indians from British Columbia and a larger number from Washington state, dozens of individuals appeared to achieve a psychological state of trance or hypnosis that was wholly Indian. Rates of acculturation have varied from place to place and from one type of religious experience to another. On the whole, Christianity has been more widely accepted by Indians in Canada than in the United States.

Education.—Traditional education has largely given way to White education. In 1945, there were 3,650 Indian children attending school in British Columbia; but by 1955, the figure was 7,665—more than double in ten years. In 1955, about three-fourths of the students were attending schools administered by the Indian Affairs Branch of the government, while the remainder attended the regular provincial schools or private schools along with Whites. The private schools were mostly those of Christian religions, which played a role comparable to that of the denominational schools in the United States in the late nineteenth century. As in the United States, Indian children were more retarded than White children; they showed higher median ages than Whites in the same grade (Hawthorn *et al.*, 1958, 291–92). As mentioned in Chapter 27, this is not due to biological inheritance but to the great differences in the preschool environments in the home. A large majority of Canadian Indian children now attend some kind of White-administered school. In 1957, a new educational program was begun, with better financing, school committees made up of Indian adults, and a larger scholarship fund ("Indians of Ontario," 1966: 39).

In the Arctic, there were only missionary schools until after World War II, when the Canadian government established schools there. In 1959, some 860 Eskimo children out of a total of 1,900 in the Canadian Arctic, minus the Mackenzie delta, were attending school, and the percentage has surely risen since that time. Since only about 5 per cent of Eskimo adults at that time were acquainted with the three R's, this represents a tremendous step forward in education.

Personality.—Indian personality has changed more slowly than Indian material culture. Hallowell (1955) has shown, from much field work and the results of psychological tests, that the personality of the Ojibwa near Lake Winnipeg remained largely Indian well into the twentieth century, even though these Indians had had about two centuries of contact with White trading posts. Where aboriginal Indian personality and value systems differed markedly from those of Whites, as they did in the Sub-Arctic, acculturation of the inner person has been slow and painful. But where many of the goals of life matched those of Whites, as on the Northwest Coast, the change has been more rapid and freer from conflict. The Eskimo in the Arctic have responded more rapidly to Whites than have the Indians in the Sub-Arctic, possibly owing in part to a difference in personality.

Language.—Indian languages and the one Eskimo language are still spoken by a majority of Canadian aborigines today, but almost all also speak English. Probably more Indian and Eskimo words are used in the spoken English of Canada than in that of the United States, although a significant difference in the written word is not to be expected. A glance at a detailed map of Canada suggests an enormous number of Indian-derived place names, easily as many as in the United States.

ALASKA

The first European explorer to reach Alaska was Vitus Bering, a Russian, who came by way of Siberia in 1741. About the same time, Russian fur traders reached the Aleutian Islands from the west and exploited the Aleuts in every possible way. They sometimes took furs at the point of a gun, enslaved the men, killed those who resisted, raped or stole their wives, and spread diseases among them. The result was the extinction of Aleut traditional culture before an adequate description of it could be obtained.

The Eskimo on the mainland were a little more fortunate. The interior of Alaska was not explored until 1833, and whaling in the Bering Sea was not intensive until after 1848. From that date on, the Eskimo on the Bering Sea were exploited seasonally by the whaling crews and traders. The depletion of their sea mammals, on which they depended for food as well as for furs to trade, and the contracting of European diseases took a huge toll of their lives, but they survived in relatively larger numbers than the unfortunate Aleuts. The purchase of Alaska from Russia by the United States in 1867 sped up the acculturation of Eskimos and Indians. Under the Russians only the sea mammals had been seriously depleted, but within a few years after the United States took over, fishing companies owned by Whites appropriated every major salmon stream and drove the Indians off when they attempted to fish in their traditional places. River grabbing was substituted for land grabbing. The Indians had no alternative other than to work for wages for the Whites who had taken their principal source of food from them. Indians were not allowed to file squatter's claims for their own land until 1924, because their citizenship status was in doubt until that date, when all Indians and Eskimos were legally made citizens of the United States (Drucker, 1965: 213–16).

Food.—To bolster the food supply, a missionary, who later became general agent for education, introduced Siberian reindeer in the 1890's, at first with Chukchi and later with Norwegian Lapp herders to instruct the Eskimo in the care of the animals. The number of reindeer increased for several decades and made a substantial contribution of furs for clothing as well as meat for the table, but by 1930 it began to decline. Some of the reindeer joined the herds of wild caribou in their seasonal migrations, and wolves constantly preyed on the herds, but the principal cause of decline was the overgrazing of forage. For instance, on St. Lawrence Island there were several thousand reindeer for about thirty years, but this number dropped to 2,500 in 1946 and to only about one hundred in 1955. On Nunivak Island, the animals were better managed, with the help of Whites, and today this island exports meat to mainland Eskimo, few of whom have any reindeer left. Musk-oxen have also been introduced on Nunivak Island, but it is too soon to evaluate this program.

The wild caribou herds in the northern interior of Alaska have increased in the past twenty-five years or so because the Eskimo have left the region for the coast. Before White contact, the inland Eskimo exchanged caribou hides with the coastal Eskimo for seal oil, used for heating, cooking, and lighting, and the coastal Eskimo used the caribou hides to make clothing. With the acquisition of White textile clothing, from World War II on, by the coastal people, the demand for caribou hides on the coast fell off and the supply of seal oil for inland bands dropped to the point where they could no longer live in the interior but were forced to move to the coast. Thus the acquisition of large quantities of mass-produced White clothing on the north coast of Alaska has increased the numbers of wild caribou in the interior. For once a game animal benefited from increased White contact (Hughes 1965: 33).

The supply of salmon, which was the staple food of Eskimos and Indians on the Yukon, Kuskokwin, and other rivers south of Bering Strait, has been reduced since White occupation. The introduction of the fish wheel in the late nineteenth century at first provided more fish for everyone but later diminished the numbers. Natives have also benefited temporarily from employment in fish canneries, but attempts by White officials to establish Indian-owned canneries have failed because of poor planning.

Population.—As of 1960, the Bureau of Indian Affairs estimated 23,000 Eskimos, 5,700 Aleuts, and 14,500 Indians, but the United States Public Health Service estimated only 18,000 Eskimos and 4,000 Aleuts for the same year. Kroeber (1939: 135) estimated 40,000 Eskimo and 16,000 Aleuts before White contact. Comparing these figures with those for Canada, we can see that there has been a greater reduction of native population in Alaska than in Canada, regardless of whether one subscribes to Dobyns' (1966) largest estimate or Kroeber's (1939) smallest estimate of aboriginal population (Hughes, 1965: 30).

Health.—Before World War II, Alaska Eskimo were scattered in two hundred or more settlements, with only twenty having more than 200 inhabitants. During the war, they flocked to military bases for employment, formed villages of a thousand or more, and in most cases have remained in the larger communities. The overcrowding in inadequate housing during the war years increased the incidence of a wide spectrum of contagious diseases, but since 1950 health has improved. A campaign against tuberculosis reduced the frequency from 6·5 deaths per 1,000 in 1950 to only one in 1957, but there are still many active cases to care for. In 1950, the death rate of Eskimos, Indians, and Aleuts combined from all causes was seventeen per 1,000 but by 1960 it had been reduced to nine. During the same period, the infant mortality for the same population dropped from ninety-five per 1,000 live births to forty-three. The birth rate for the same population in 1960 was forty-eight per 1,000, as compared to thirty per 1,000 for Whites (Hughes, 1965: 30–31. Tiffany, 1966: 20).

Employment.—The fur of the sea otter, which dominated the fur market from about 1750 until 1850, was no longer obtainable after the animal became extinct in far northern waters in the last half of the nineteenth century. The white fur of the Arctic fox was the most valuable one in the early twentieth century, and in the 1920's some individual Alaskan Eskimos and Indians earned as much as $8,000 per year from fox trapping alone. The market for this fur fell in the 1930's and is today an unreliable source of income.

Although Alaskan Eskimo have handled some money for half a century, the big change to cash income came with World War II. Since that time many have been employed in construction and maintenance of military bases, in unloading supply vessels, in the commercial fishing industry, and recently as hunting guides for sportsmen. During this period they have also become aware of their eligibility for compensation for disability, unemployment, old age, and dependent children. Furthermore, some earn a little from membership in National Guard units in coastal villages. Still others sell a few furs, collect the bounties on wolves and eagles, and sell art and craftwork. During the construction of the DEW line, three-fourths of the men in one villages earned wages of $600 per month. Most of such income was spent on new material goods brought in by Whites.

Kinship.—As elsewhere, the most noticeable change in the realm of kinship has been the decreasing number and cohesiveness of extended families and the increasing number and independence of nuclear families. Residence, formerly bilocal or patrilocal in the extended families, is now more often neolocal. Boat crews are less often composed of relatives than in the past. Trade partnerships between male nonrelatives, which often included wife exchange, are also vanishing, and the institution known as the men's house is on the way out. The church, school, restaurant, and movie theater are now the rallying points for men as well as women (Hughes, 1965: 38–40).

Leadership.—Leadership patterns have shown changes among Alaskan Eskimos. The Eskimo whaling captain and the shaman of pre-White times competed with the White trader, missionary, and teacher before World War II. Since that time, ability to handle English and to communicate well with the Anglos in authority has become a prerequisite to leadership. The presidents and even members of newly established village councils are looked up to as leaders, as are lay preachers, National Guard sergeants, bosses of work crews, and store managers. In a few localities where whaling is still done, the whaling captain has retained his position of authority, but the shaman has everywhere lost out to the churches, medical personnel, and the gun, which made the hunting rituals obsolete.

Education.—After the United States purchased Alaska in 1867, missionaries soon established schools in which the teaching was in English. By 1914, the Bureau of Education of the United States Department of the Interior had established public schools in most Alaskan Eskimo villages. Since World War II, there has been a sharp increase in education, and today a majority of Eskimo and Indian children attend school. A school census for the year 1963–64 showed 14,182 Eskimo, Aleut, and Indian children in elementary schools, 2,623 in high schools, and 763 in post-high schools and colleges (Logan and Johnson, 1965: 7). Education in Alaska has been hampered by lack of special textbooks with vocabulary and illustrations adapted to the life of Alaska, but these are now in the making and should speed up the learning of English.

The Alaska Native Brotherhood, founded in 1912, is a Christian organization aimed at acculturating the natives to White ways as rapidly as possible. It was the model for the British Columbia counterpart mentioned above. It has made progress toward its goal of equal rights and opportunities for Indians, although these have not yet been fully achieved (Drucker, 1965: 222–24).

GREENLAND

Greenland was occupied by a maximum of 3,000 Norse between the tenth and the fifteenth centuries. The colony died out when the climate became colder and its farming and animal husbandry failed. In 1721, Hans Egede, a Danish missionary, arrived to minister to the Norse settlements there and discovered that they no longer existed. Instead of returning to Denmark, he stayed in Greenland to Christianize and civilize the Eskimo according to the Danish Lutheran tradition.

The blubber whales were reduced in numbers by European whalers from the seventeenth century on, and by the twentieth century the open whaling boat, which had been the pride of the men, was reduced to a transportation barge rowed by women. As early as 1774, the Danes established a trade monopoly to earn enough to pay for part of the cost of maintaining the colony and to prevent the Eskimo from being exploited by anyone who landed on Greenland. This trade monopoly was in effect until 1951, and succeeded admirably in the purposes for which it was designed. The Polar (Thule) Eskimo were not discovered until 1818, when John Ross found them, and those of East Greenland not until 1884 by Holm. (The principal references used throughout this short section are: Birket-Smith, 1959, and Hughes, 1965. They will not be repeated at the end of every paragraph.)

The missionaries set up missions, schools, and trading posts all along the west coast of Greenland. With much more foresight than was usual at that time, they taught the Eskimos to read and write in their own language, and in 1861 published the first Eskimo-language newspaper. Today, there is a considerable and rapidly growing literature available in Eskimoan, far more than was produced in

Labrador, the only other place where the written Eskimo language was taught to natives. Education in Greenland has long been compulsory, with the result that every adult is literate in Eskimoan and between 10 and 15 per cent in Danish. Seven years of bilingual education for children between seven and fourteen years of age are now required, and enrollment in 1967 was 14,000 (Christensen, 1966:78).

In the 1860's, the Danes also established democratic government in the form of councils on a local, regional, and provincial basis. The local council consisted of the missionary as chairman, the trading post manager, a medical officer (if one was in residence), a post assistant, and a number of elected Greenlanders, as the Danes refer to the Eskimos there. These councils maintained law and order, made loans for housing, administered relief, and obtained their operating funds from a tax collected on native products sold through the store. This system continued with minor modifications until Greenland became a county of Denmark in 1953 with two representatives in the Danish Parliament. This change required the creation of one governing body for all of Greenland and thirteen regional councils.

In the second decade of this century, a warming trend in the ocean water off the southwest coast of Greenland drove the few remaining seals farther north and brought cod and other fish from the south to take their place. This necessitated the organizing of a commercial fishing industry to provide food, jobs, and income for Greenlanders. The first fishing station was established in 1910, and by 1964 there were seventy-three stations where cod were butchered, salted, packed, and shipped and seven canneries. In 1948, the world's second largest prawn-shrimp beds were discovered near Christianshaab and Jakobshavn, and two canning and quick-freezing factories were built to handle the catch. All fishing is done with motor boats today. Where sea mammals are still available, north of 70° latitude, Eskimos are encouraged to hunt them at sea.

Domesticated animals have also been introduced in the southwest. The most successful are sheep, which numbered about 27,000 in 1964; but the more recently introduced reindeer, about 3,000 in 1964, are increasing rapidly. A few cattle are raised in the extreme south, but they do not do as well as the other two animals.

The diet of Greenlanders has of course adapted to changing conditions. All are dependent to some extent on imported foods purchased at the trading posts and markets.

The aboriginal skin tents have given way to canvas in the more nomadic areas or seasons, and the turf house is being rapidly replaced by wooden frame structures. Likewise, the oil lamp has been abandoned in favor of Primus stoves or kitchen ranges. In general, the trend has been away from nomadism to a more settled life and from small villages to larger towns. In 1956, there were thirteen "colonies" visited regularly by passenger and supply ships, and these had populations ranging from 100 to 2,000 persons. In addition there were fifty-three trading centers with forty to three hundred inhabitants each and a church, school, and store. Finally, there were 106 settlements of from three to 300 persons with only a school but access to a neighboring trading post. In 1963, the trading centers were growing most rapidly.

Hide and fur clothing has largely been abandoned in the more southerly and populous region, as much from lack of furs as from a change in preference. Imported factory-made textile clothing is the rule for the men, with women making some of their dresses from yard goods purchased at the store.

Population figures for Greenland are as follows: aboriginal, 10,000 (Kroeber, 1939: 134); 1805, 6,046; 1905, 12,000; 1950, 23,642; 1961, 31,304; 1966, 39,000. All but the first of these figures include Europeans, who numbered 3,000 in 1966. On the assumption that European diseases alone would have reduced population in the beginning, the nadir point may have been earlier than 1805. At any rate, since that time population has steadily increased, and the rate has accelerated in the twentieth century after scientific medicine came of age. Health facilities in 1961 included thirty-five physicians, eighteen dentists, ninety-two trained nurses, a great number of midwives, and seventeen hospitals in addition to sanatoria. The largest hospital had two hundred beds. There is one physician for about nine hundred persons, which is near the Danish ratio. Most Greenlanders today have some Danish ancestors in their family trees, but, as in Mexico, aboriginal genes predominate by a wide margin.

Over the years, Denmark has invested more in Greenland than she has derived from the trade, as has been the recent history of colonialism almost everywhere. Her program has been far more enlightened than that of England, Canada, the United States, Spain, or Mexico. The insularity and comparatively small size of inhabited Greenland made the problem simpler, but does not detract from the more humanitarian and intellectual tradition and the superior administration of the Danes.

REFERENCES

Ayre, 1967; Birket-Smith, 1959; Brown, 1944; Christensen, 1966; Codere, 1961; Dobyns, 1966; Drucker, 1965; Eggan, 1966; *Encyclopaedia Britannica*, 1964; Goldfrank, 1945*b*; Hallowell, 1955; Hawthorn, 1966; Hawthorn *et al.*, 1958; Helm, 1965, 1969; Hickerson, 1966, 1967; Hill, 1967; Hughes, 1965; "Indians of Ontario," 1966; Innis, 1962; Kroeber, 1939; Lagassé, 1966; Logan and Johnson, 1965; Oswalt, 1966; Tiffany, 1966.

29

Achievements and Contributions

THE DISCOVERY of America by Christopher Columbus initiated the most dramatic and far-reaching cross-fertilization of cultures in the history of the world. Although European peoples also expanded into Asia, Africa, and Oceania after A.D. 1492, close contact and colonization of these areas came later in most instances than it did in the Americas. The impact of these Old World peoples on European cultures was less sudden and precipitous than that of the Indians.

Food.—A glance at the common names for Indian domesticated plants (Table 3) reveals many species available in markets in the United States today. Some of these plant foods may be found in every nation of the Americas and probably in every nation of the Old World as well. Table 5 gives figures on world production of leading crops, taken from the *Statistical Yearbook of the United Nations* for 1967 (referring to the year 1966).

TABLE 5

WORLD PRODUCTION IN METRIC TONS OF STAPLE CROPS IN 1966

Wheat	308,695,000
Potatoes	293,539,000
Rice	253,490,000
Maize	238,102,000
Barley	115,065,000
Sugar (cane and beet)	61,655,000
Oats	47,997,000
Soybeans	39,031,000
Rye	31,044,000
Cottonseed	19,987,000
Peanuts	15,690,000

It is clear from this list that the quantity of the first four crops exceeds that of all others by a wide margin. Of these leading crops, the two from the New World—potatoes and maize—total 531,641,000 metric tons as compared to a total of 562,185,000 metric tons for the two from the Old World—wheat and rice. The next five plants are all from the Old World, but cottonseed is derived from both Old World and New World species, and peanuts are New World plants. From these figures, it is clear that New World plants first domesticated by American Indians produce almost half of the world's plant food supply.

The leading continent for potato production in 1966 was Europe, and the leading nation the U.S.S.R. The history of the potato (Salaman, 1949) is a fascinating chapter in culture history. The potato was widely raised by Indians in the Andean highlands of South America in pre-Columbian times, and was first taken to Europe by the Spaniards in about 1570. Although it has been grown in Spain and other southern European countries continuously down to the present time, it has never been as important in the diet of southern Europe as it has in northwestern Europe. Its first recorded appearance in England was in 1596, over a century after Columbus discovered America, and, by coincidence, it was first mentioned by French writers in the same year. But it was in Ireland that it achieved its greatest importance in the diet. The earliest certain date for the presence of the potato in Ireland is 1606. Within the next fifty years, it became the most important single source of food in that country. The climate and soils were ideal for the potato, and it was raised in increasing quantities until attacked by blight in 1845. The resulting potato famine initiated the emigration of large numbers of Irish to the United States. The term "Irish potato" was first used by an English herbalist in 1693, and the potato was first transferred from Ireland to the United States by a group of Irish Presbyterians in 1719 (Salaman, 1949: 188). Thus it reached the United States by way of Europe over two centuries after Columbus' discovery of America, and has since become one of the staples of our diet. The potato also diffused northward from South America to Mexico, where it is called by the Peruvian term *papas*, but its rate of consumption in Mexico has never equaled that in the Andean region of South America, where it has maintained its prominent role in the diet in spite of the introduction of European foods after the Spanish Conquest.

More maize (corn) is raised on the North American continent than on any other, and the United States leads all other nations in its production, but most of its maize is fed to cattle and hogs. The Mexicans, in contrast, produce much less maize than the United States but use more of it to feed people. The only part of the United States where maize forms a considerable part of human diet is the South, where cornbread and hominy are standard items on the menu. Corn was raised in the Indian manner in hills, spaced a yard or so apart, by the earliest colonists. After oxen and horses became more common, it was planted in rows spaced far enough apart for animals to walk between. With the recent mass production of fertilizers, weed killers, insecticides, and mechanized planting and harvesting equipment, the rows of the past decade or two have become narrower and the bushels per acre much greater.

Peanuts, of South American origin, are raised today in greatest quantity in southern Asia, with India leading all other nations, and are also an important export crop in west Africa. Another plant of New World origin which is raised in greater quantities today in the Old World is the Cacao tree, the source of cocoa and chocolate. Cocoa and chocolate production is highest in Africa, where these are important export items for a few of the new nations in tropical latitudes; world production was only 1,530,000 metric tons in 1964. Cocoa and chocolate are consumed principally in Europe and the United States in sweetened drinks, candies, cakes, and pastries. Of the other plants of American origin grown in the Old World, but not mentioned in the United Nations source, cassava or manioc (from which tapioca is derived) and the sweet potato are probably the most important in the diet of peoples in tropical latitudes, while tomatoes are widely eaten in many forms on all continents of the globe.

If the American Indians had not domesticated any food plants, the world today would have less to eat and population would consequently be smaller. Because each plant grows best in a limited range of soils and climates, Old World domesticated plants would not flourish as well in the regions most suited to New World domesticates. It took centuries to domesticate a plant to the point of high yield of nourishing food; if the Indians had not achieved this for maize, potatoes, cassava, sweet potatoes, and some other food plants, it is doubtful if Europeans would ever have accomplished it for these plants. Europeans would almost certainly have devoted their attention to improving rice, wheat, and other plants familiar to them and would not have recognized the nutritional potential of the scrubby wild relatives of the American domesticates.

The turkey is the only American animal to be raised commercially on a large scale for food today, and it has had its greatest acceptance in the United States in connection with Thanksgiving. At the first Thanksgiving, in what is now Massachusetts, the turkeys eaten were wild ones. The nearest domesticated turkeys were those of the Pueblos in the Southwest, who kept them for feathers and rarely ate them, although the Meso-Americans raised them mainly for food before A.D. 1492 as well as later.

Of the narcotics and stimulants mentioned in Chapter 7, tobacco is the most widely used in the world today. Now that cigarette smoking has been proved by medical research to be causally related to circulatory failures, lung cancer, and other diseases, it would be out of place to praise it here as a contribution to human welfare. The history of tobacco, however, is well known and illustrates the speed of diffusion and the wide acceptance of a product from a people and culture regarded as inferior by most Europeans. It was brought to two European nations independently: to Spain in 1558, where it was regarded as a medical panacea; to England in 1586 by Sir Walter Raleigh, who introduced it to the upper class, from which it spread quickly to the commoners. From these two nations it diffused rapidly over most of the Old World despite the opposition of priests and kings. Tobacco users were fined and imprisoned in Switzerland, tortured in Russia, and executed in Turkey. Tobacco finally reached Alaskan Eskimos by way of the Russians from Siberia by 1700 (Stewart, *in* Spencer and Jennings, 1965: 491). Thus it encircled the globe in less than two centuries, with the word for it still recognizable at the end of the journey. New varieties became established in many parts of the Old World, and some, such as Turkish, are imported back into the New World today.

More than two hundred drugs used by Indian tribes have been listed in the official *United States Pharmacopeia* since its first edition in 1820, or in the *National Formulary*, first published in 1888. About two dozen of these drugs were first produced in Latin America and later imported into the United States. The best known of these Indian substances are: coca (*Erythroxylon coca*), used in cocaine and novocain to relieve pain, especially by dentists; quinine from cinchona (*Cinchona pubescens*) bark, until about 1940 the only remedy for malaria; Jimson weed (*Datura* sp.) in pain relievers; ipecac for stomach ailments; jalap as a laxative; curare (*Strychnos toxifera*) in recent surgery to stop breathing for an instant while a rubber tube is inserted into the windpipe to prevent a person under anesthesia from choking to death; and copaiba, tolu, and Peru balsams.

Some of the better-known substances of medicinal value which Indians in what is now the United States may have been the first to discover are: cascara (*Rhamnus purshiana*) and mayapple (*Podophyllum peltatum*), used as laxatives; pinkroot (*Spigelia*), to destroy intestinal worms; dogwood (*Cornus*), a remedy for fever; lobelia (*Lobelia*) and bloodroot (*Sanguinaria canadensis*), as emetics; Virginia snakeroot (*Aristolochia serpenteria*), to increase perspiration; alumroot (*Heuchera americana*), an astringent; boneset (*Eupatorium perfoliatum*), as a stimulant; blue cohosh or squawroot (*Caulophyllum thalictroides*), as an antispasmodic and promoter of menstrual discharge.

Since 1880 there has been a decline in the number of such drugs because they have been replaced by modern antibiotics and synthetics of all kinds. The *United States Pharmacopeia* of 1960 lists only about a dozen of the Indian-type drugs derived from indigenous plants. However, the fact remains that most of the natural drugs made by Whites from plants in the Americas were known in some form by Indians (Vogel, 1967).

The Virginia Houses of Burgesses in 1738 rewarded Dr. John Tennent with a hundred pounds for using Seneca rattlesnake root in treating pleurisy. Senecas still sell sassafras on the streets of Buffalo, New York, and Pamunkeys until recently have sold it in Washington, D. C. Many Indian medicine shows traveled widely in the United States in the nineteenth and early twentieth centuries, the most famous ones being those of the Kickapoo Indians (Hallowell, 1957, 1959). That drug businesses still anticipate discovering new drugs from Indian medical practitioners is proved by an offer within the past ten years of partial support by a drug firm for anthropological field work if the study included ethnobotany and use of plants in medicine.

The Indians were the first to make useful objects out of rubber, such as balls, enema tubes and syringes, and waterproof clothing. Columbus took samples of rubber to Europe, but the English were apparently the first to put it to practical use erasing pencil marks, hence the word "rubber." The manufacture of pneumatic tires for motor vehicles in the twentieth century has been economically the most important use of rubber. Rubber was first produced in quantity for export in the vicinity of Manaus, on the Amazon River in Brazil, which is the native habitat of the tree. By 1910 Brazil furnished nine-tenths of the world's rubber, but by 1921 it provided less than one-tenth. A British scientist had taken seeds of the rubber tree to England, and by 1895 the first British rubber plantations were operating in what is now Malaya and Indonesia. They eventually ran Brazil out of business by producing larger quantities of rubber more cheaply (Herring, 1963: 754–56). In 1964, the total world production of natural rubber was 2,280,000 metric tons; it was heavily concentrated in Southeast Asia and nearby islands, with Malaya first and Indonesia second in amount produced (*Statistical Yearbook of the United Nations for 1965*).

Indian housing was used by explorers, traders, and missionaries when no other kind was available, and was indispensable to their survival in the Arctic and Sub-Arctic areas as late as this century. The Sibley tents of the army are modifications of Plains Indian tipis. In the Southwest, both Spanish and Pueblo influence on housing and architecture is apparent. In New Mexico, public buildings in the capital at Santa Fe and those at the University of New Mexico in Albuquerque emulate either Spanish or Pueblo architecture or a blend of both. The laboratories of the National Center for Atmospheric Research at Boulder, Colorado, designed by I. M. Pei and completed in 1967, were inspired by the thirteenth-century pueblos at Mesa Verde National Park, Colorado (*Time*, September 22, 1967: 78-79). Architecture in Mexico since the 1910–21 Revolution has made use of Indian themes. In an exclusive residential district of Mexico City, the Pedregal, tile roofs and iron balconies of Spanish origin are forbidden in order to encourage a return to Indian motifs. Public buildings in Mexico City, especially those of the National University, definitely show Indian influence.

The one item of Indian furniture which has had wide acceptance all over the world is the hammock, for centuries the dominant sleeping place on both merchant and naval ships.

The Indians of Meso-America never came up to the standards of Greece and Rome in the engineering aspects of their architecture. They lacked the true arch, except in a single instance (cited under "Architecture" in Chapter 8), and their corbeled arch produced thick and heavy walls more bulky than the room space within. Yet the originality of the design of their temples and palaces and their artistic embellishment has produced one of the world's great and distinctive architectural styles. Knowledge of this style is still being augmented by new discoveries by archeologists.

Textile fibers used today are of both Indian and Old World origin, because the cottons grown commercially were independently domesticated in both hemispheres before 1492. World production of cotton fiber in 1966 totaled 10,727,000 metric tons and far outdistanced wool, with about 2,500,000 metric tons. The second most common fiber, however, is no longer wool; 3,370,000 metric tons of rayon and acetate fibers were produced in the same year. The amount of cotton, nevertheless, is still greater than wool and synthetics combined. The United States is the world's greatest producer of cotton, a position maintained only by federal subsidy for that industry. Maguey fiber (sisal), formerly used for clothing in Mexico, is raised there, as well as in Africa and other Old World areas, commercially for export as rope fiber.

Indian clothing styles have had only modest diffusion to Whites in the Americas and to peoples of the Old World, except for the parka. The parka, modeled on that of the Eskimo, but made of cotton, wool, or synthetic fibers instead of fur, has been a standard article of issue by the military for troops in cold climates in the twentieth century. It is also commonly used in winter sports costumes and as everyday winter wear for children in the United States. The South American poncho, modified in both cut and material, was the general issue raincoat of World War I for the United States troops and is widely used as such in Latin America today. Moccasins are worn as house slippers by Anglos in the United States, and the moccasin toe in shoes of tanned leather is common, especially in heavy shoes and boots for outdoor winter wear. The *quesquémetl*, a poncho-like women's upper garment of Mexico and still worn there, is diffusing at least to college campuses in the United States at the present time.

Weaving reached a peak in pre-Columbian Peru, where some of the world's finest textiles were produced by hand methods. The fineness of the cotton or vicuña thread, the almost unbelievable variety of weaves, and the intricate designs of these weavers have never been surpassed and are only rarely equaled in modern textiles. Today we excel Peruvian weavers only in speed of production. Because the finest weaving was done by virgin nuns, called the "chosen women," and because the Inca religion was rapidly destroyed by the Spanish, the weaving done today in Peru does not come up to its pre-Columbian standards. For the same reason, Peruvian weaving has not had much influence on weaving in the modern world. It remains an isolated peak of perfection to be admired by those privileged to study it, but unlikely to be equaled, much less excelled, by weavers in the future.

The beautiful Indian jewelry cast by the lost-wax method from Mexico to Peru has found its place in displays in leading art galleries and museums in both the Americas and Europe and represents a great achievement in arts and crafts. Since the Indians knew nothing of iron, their metal tools, utensils, and weapons were less effective than those of Europeans and ceased to be made soon after White contact.

Pottery making has been revived in the Southwest for the tourist trade, and the best pots are careful replicas of aboriginal types. Some of the modern Pueblo potters visit the museums and scratch around in the garbage dumps of their pueblos to find pieces of broken pottery from the past to give them authentic designs to reproduce on the new vessels. In one pueblo at least, hundreds of pots are hastily slapped together, painted, and sold to tourists without firing. If filled with water, they will melt away. However, most pots sold in the Southwest are fired; if the buyer is in doubt, he may ask the vendor.

Navaho blankets, each an individual work of art, have found their way into many White homes as rugs or wall hangings. Although some are made with modern aniline dyes, the superior native vegetal dyes are being revived and, when combined with dark as well as light wool, produce more authentic and artistic colors. Navaho and Pueblo jewelry of silver and turquoise, appropriate with either Indian or White clothing, has become so popular that cheap imitations are to be found in novelty shops throughout the United States. The Indians have had to institute a campaign to educate prospective buyers to discriminate between genuine Indian handcrafted products and inferior factory-made imitations.

Eskimo carving in ivory and stone has been revived by missionaries and government officials and is becoming increasingly common in art and craft shops in the United States and Canada. Some of it, along with prints by Eskimos, has attracted the attention of art collectors and is widely exhibited in leading art galleries. A distinctive style of Indian painting, showing influence of both aboriginal and European traditions, has arisen in the past few decades in New Mexico. In other states, a number of Indian painters are using Indian themes to produce new and original works of art. Unfortunately, much of their contemporary painting has not yet received suitable exhibition and critical review.

As mentioned in Chapter 11, American Indian art has only recently been granted a place among the great art styles of the world. The art of Africa and Oceania, however, has had more influence on contemporary European art than has that of the American Indian. This is due in part to the fact that much of African and Oceanian art depicts the human figure, which is less common in American Indian art. From the time of the ancient Greeks, the human figure has dominated European art, and the striking heads and complete figures carved in the hard tropical woods of Africa and Oceania have had enormous appeal to European artists from about a century ago to the present time. In comparison, American Indian art is more geometric and abstract or, when the human figure is attempted, a bit stiff and awkward. Exceptions to this characterization are the superb pottery heads of pre-Incan Peru and the most naturalistic painting and sculpture of the Olmecs and Mayas of Mexico and adjacent Central America.

Mexico, more than any other contemporary American nation, has developed a national art style, which is an integration of Spanish and Indian elements. This is largely a twentieth-century development. For centuries the two art styles remained separated for the most part. European statues and paintings were conspicuous in churches, government buildings, and the homes of the Spanish families in the colonial period. Indian art was left to the Indians, who formed the lower class. After Mexico won her independence from Spain in the war of 1810–21, there was no significant change; but it was the revolution of the lower classes against the upper classes and the Church, starting in 1910, that produced the kind of nationalism which could give rise to a new and integrated art style.

At the hands of such masters as Diego Rivera, José Clemente Orozco, David Alfaro Siqueiros, Rufino Tamayo, Miguel Covarrubias and Juan O'Gorman, this art came to life; it may be seen today in Mexico City in such public places as the Bellas Artes, the National Palace, and the National University of Mexico. In the work of all these men, the Indian face and figure are portrayed beside those of the European. Many huge indoor mural paintings of this group depict important historical events in the history of Mexico, including the class struggle of the twentieth-century revolution. The buildings of the National University are adorned with mosaics full of eagles, serpents, jaguars, sun symbols, and other motifs derived from Indian art. These are combined with human figures in European as well as Indian dress, with horses, churches, buildings of classic architecture, and references to great Old World scholars, such as Ptolemy and Copernicus. As if this variegated mixture were not enough, cries of the revolution, such as *Viva la Revolución* and *Tierra y Libertad*, are also displayed in these unusual tile mosaics. Mexico also has its school of more modern, abstract, and imaginative art; here also the human faces and figures are as often Indian as European.

The earliest known attempt in the United States to utilize Indian themes in music composed for White consumption was that of James Hewitt in 1794. He used Cherokee themes in the musical play *Tammany*. A century later, Edward MacDowell, in his effort to develop national qualities in United States music, turned to the first published collection of Indian melodies, which appeared in 1882. The result was MacDowell's *Indian Suite*, written in 1891–92 and first performed in 1896. The next modern composition to use Indian musical motifs was Skilton's *Indian Dances*, published in 1915. These works of MacDowell and Skilton were among the twenty-seven compositions of twelve composers which had the greatest number of performances in the United States from 1919 to 1926 (Hallowell 1957, 1959). The contemporary composer George Frederick McKay has made considerable use of authentic Indian themes in his orchestral compositions. On the whole, Indian music has had much less effect than has African Negro music on the total amount of all music heard today on radio, television, records, tapes, and in live performances in churches and places of entertainment. Musical educational programs in universities and conservatories stem almost wholly from Europe; the Africanisms are mainly at the popular level. In Latin America, on the other hand, the compositions of Carlos Chávez in Mexico and of Heitor Villa-Lobos in Brazil, based in part on Indian themes, are generally regarded as significant contributions to twentieth-century musical style.

English has far fewer loan words from Indian languages than does Spanish, but the number is still considerable. Huge numbers of geographical place names for lakes, rivers, mountains, towns, counties, and states throughout the United States and Canada are derived from Indian languages. Long ago Kroeber (1916) found 196 place names of certain Indian origin in California, and more recently Huden (1962) has listed and translated about 5,000 Indian place names for all of New England. These and other similar studies suggest that there are tens of thousands of such geographical terms in the entire United States and as many more in Canada and Greenland. Twenty-four of our states have Indian names: Alabama, Arizona, Arkansas, Connecticut, North Dakota, South Dakota, Idaho, Illinois, Iowa, Kansas, Kentucky, Massachusetts, Michigan, Minnesota, Mississippi, Missouri, Nebraska, Ohio, Oklahoma, Tennessee, Texas, Utah, Wisconsin, and Wyoming. Indian words incorporated into English include "tobacco," "hominy," "succotash," "toboggan," "moccasin," "wampum," "wigwam," "tipi," "squaw," "papoose," and thousands of others. A number of phrases—such as "go on the warpath," "bury the hatchet," "smoke the pipe of peace," and "run the gauntlet"—are meaningful only in the light of Indian culture.

Literature produced in the Americas since A.D. 1492 also reflects the influence of the Indian. No doubt every reader knows of Henry Wadsworth Longfellow's *Hiawatha* and James Fenimore Cooper's "Leatherstocking tales." In the novels of Cooper, written from 1823 to 1841, his hero Natty Bumppo became the epitome of pioneer character, with a combination of the best personality traits of both Indians and Whites. He was reverent about religion, fearless of danger, and fair and just in his dealings with his fellow man. Chingachgook, the old Delaware warrior, is a more tragic figure, lonely, frustrated, drunken, yet proud. Every novel set in the pioneer period, which was as late as 1900 in some parts of the West, gives some space to Indians and their culture.

The Indian also figures prominently today in motion pictures and television melodramas of the West. Western pictures have never been more popular than at the present time, and the character of the White heroes of these tales is certainly influenced by that of the Indian. The strong, silent, fearless male talks softly with little outward emotion, but flies into action against evil "when the chips are down." Some of this personality type may be that of the generalized Anglo-American pioneer, and as true of Australia and South Africa as of America; but the American Indian was instrumental in producing the particular kind of Western personality so admired at a popular level in the United States today.

On a more serious level, the psychoanalyst Carl Jung (1928) thought he could observe an Indian component in the character of some of his American patients. Although his American patients exhibited significant differences from Europeans, it is questionable how much of this was derived from generalized frontier personality and how much was specifically Indian. Some certainly belongs to the latter category.

The largest governmental unit in the New World before A.D. 1532 was the Inca empire in the Andes of South America, with a population of perhaps fifteen million (Dobyns, 1966, estimates thirty million) and a territory 2,500 miles long. This compared in size with the pre-Christian empires of the Old World. It had a divine emperor at the top, a number of royal lineages related to that of the emperor, a lower class of nobility, and commoners at the bottom. Although recent research by Sally Moore (1958) suggests that the Inca government was less neatly centralized and organized than the classic sources claim, it remains one of the world's outstanding political accomplishments.

The Inca government, like that of the Aztecs, was liquidated by the Spanish and had no effect on the development of political thought in Europe. In contrast, the "noble savage" concept, as propounded by Rousseau and other eighteenth-century writers, included much about the equality of man and the democratic tribal organizations of Indians north of Mexico. This contributed to the rise of democratic ideals in France, England, and the thirteen English colonies in America. The League of the Iroquois was held up as a model of federal organization by Benjamin Franklin, and the more general ideal of Indian democracy permeated the thinking of other framers of the United States Constitution.

In the realm of science and mathematics, the Indians made a few outstanding innovations. Perhaps the highest achievement of this kind was the mathematics, astronomy, and calendar system of the Maya. By some two thousand years ago, the Maya had perfected a calendar accurate to the day for a period of 374,400 years (Morley, 1955: 183). This was almost equaled in accuracy by the 1582 calendar associated with Pope Gregory XIII, about 1500 years later in Europe. The Maya calendar was superior to those of such famous Old World civilizations as Egypt, Babylonia, Pakistan (Indus River), China, Greece, and Rome. The Maya priests in charge of the calendar were able to predict eclipses and the heliacal rising and setting of Venus.

The accurate recording of dates was made possible by a place numeral system with a symbol for zero. The Chinese of the first century B.C. also achieved a place numeral system, but without a symbol for zero. The zero was indicated by leaving an empty space (Goodrich, 1959: 48). A still earlier zero was invented by the Babylonians about 500 B.C. (Kroeber, 1948: 469–72). And finally a fourth invention of the zero occurred in India about A.D. 500. The Arabs adopted the Hindu place numeral system, and passed it on to Europe as the Arabic system. Because the symbols for zero differ in all four localities, and the values of the places in the place numeral systems were different for all except the Chinese and Hindu (which were decimal), it seems highly probable that there were three or four independent inventions or discoveries of the concept. The Maya therefore take their place beside Babylonia, India, and China as one of the cradles of intellectual achievement.

REFERENCES

DOBYNS, 1966; FENTON, 1942; GOODRICH, 1959; HALLOWELL, 1957, 1959; HERRING, 1963; HO, 1955; HUDEN, 1962; JUNG, 1928; KROEBER, 1916, 1948; MOORE, 1958; MORLEY, 1955; SALAMAN, 1949; SPENCER AND JENNINGS, 1965; *Statistical Yearbook of the United Nations for 1965 and 1967*; VOGEL, 1967.

MAPS

MAP 1

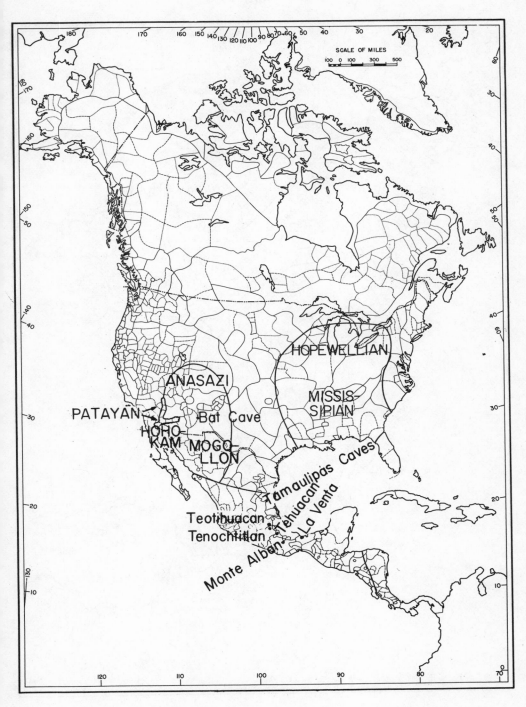

SCALE OF MILES
100 0 100   300   500

HOPEWELLIAN

ANASAZI

MISSIS-
SIPIAN

PATAYAN   Bat Cave

HOHO-
KAM   MOGO-
LLON

Tamaulipas Caves

Teotihuacan   Tehuacan Caves
Tenochtitlan   La Venta

Monte Alban

Some Archeological Cultures and Sites

MAP 2

CULTURE AREAS. After Driver and Massey

MAP 3

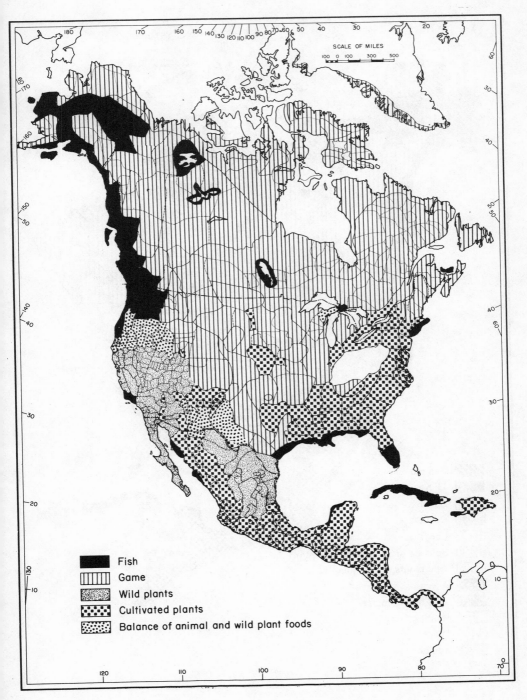

SCALE OF MILES
100 0 100   300   500

Fish

Game

Wild plants

Cultivated plants

Balance of animal and wild plant foods

DOMINANT TYPES OF SUBSISTENCE. Driver and Massey

MAP 4

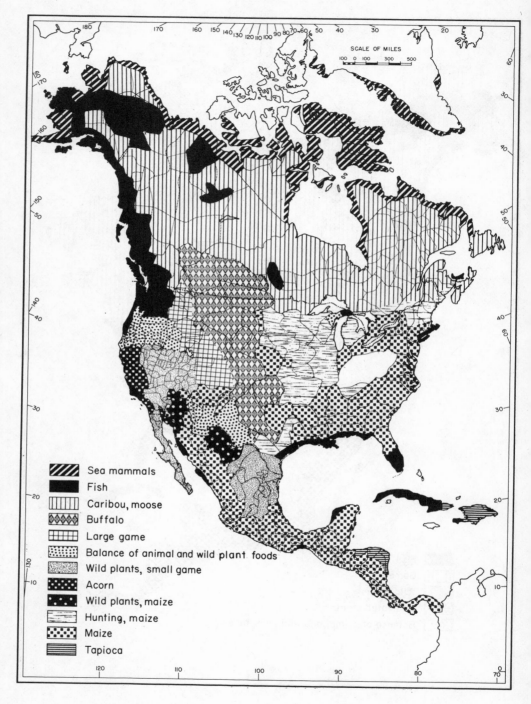

Legend:

- Sea mammals
- Fish
- Caribou, moose
- Buffalo
- Large game
- Balance of animal and wild plant foods
- Wild plants, small game
- Acorn
- Wild plants, maize
- Hunting, maize
- Maize
- Tapioca

SCALE OF MILES
100 0 100 300 500

SUBSISTENCE AREAS. Driver and Massey

MAP 5

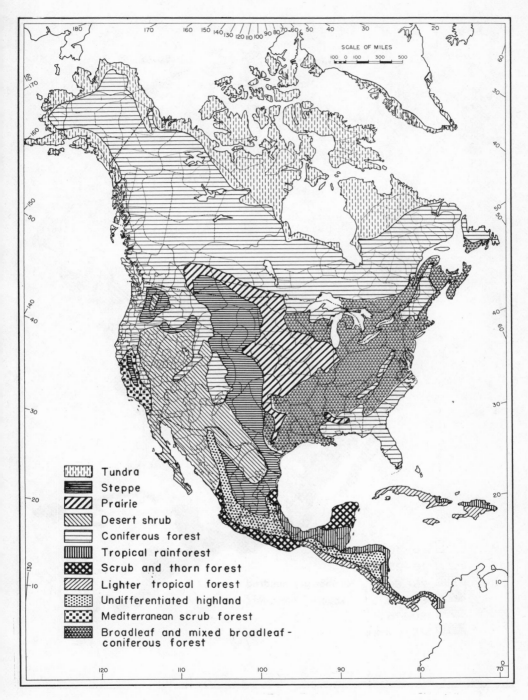

Legend:
- Tundra
- Steppe
- Prairie
- Desert shrub
- Coniferous forest
- Tropical rainforest
- Scrub and thorn forest
- Lighter tropical forest
- Undifferentiated highland
- Mediterranean scrub forest
- Broadleaf and mixed broadleaf-coniferous forest

SCALE OF MILES
100 0 100 300 500

NATURAL VEGETATION AREAS. Driver and Massey

MAP 6

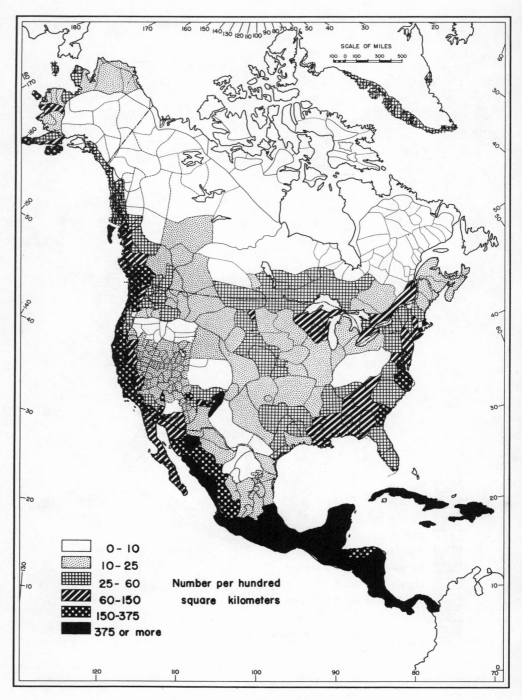

0 – 10	
10 – 25	
25 – 60	Number per hundred
60 – 150	square kilometers
150 – 375	
375 or more	

SCALE OF MILES
100 0 100 300 500

NATIVE POPULATION DENSITY. After Driver and Massey

MAP 7

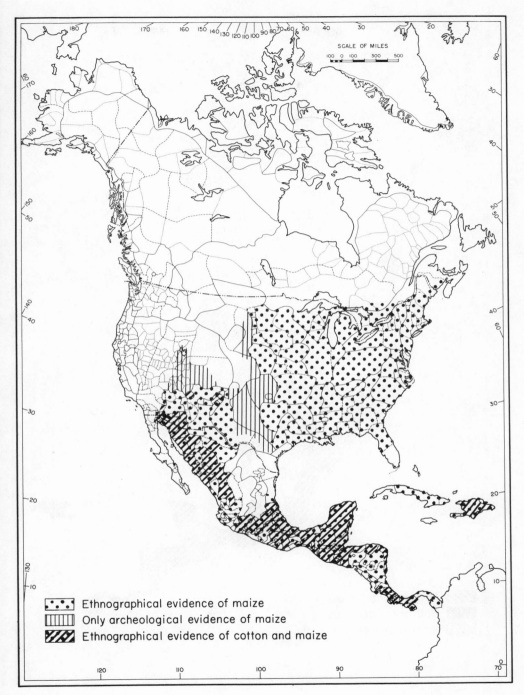

Ethnographical evidence of maize
Only archeological evidence of maize
Ethnographical evidence of cotton and maize

MAIZE AND COTTON. Driver and Massey

MAP 8

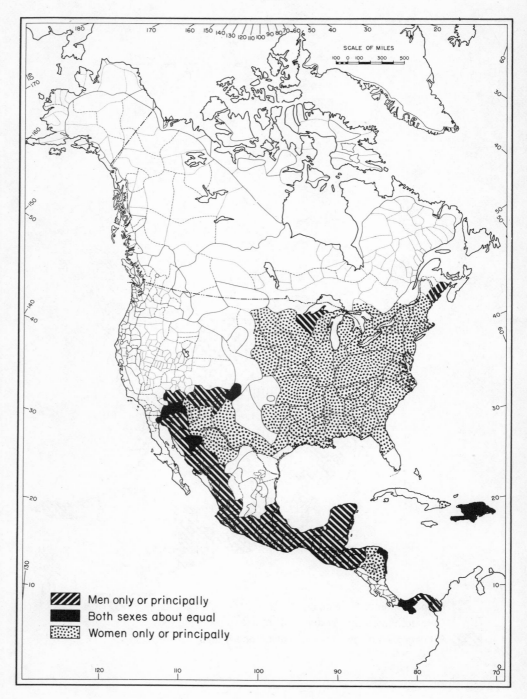

SCALE OF MILES

Men only or principally

Both sexes about equal

Women only or principally

HORTICULTURAL SEXUAL DIVISION OF LABOR. Driver and Massey

MAP 9

SCALE OF MILES

Salt (Sodium Chloride)

SALT. Driver and Massey

MAP 10

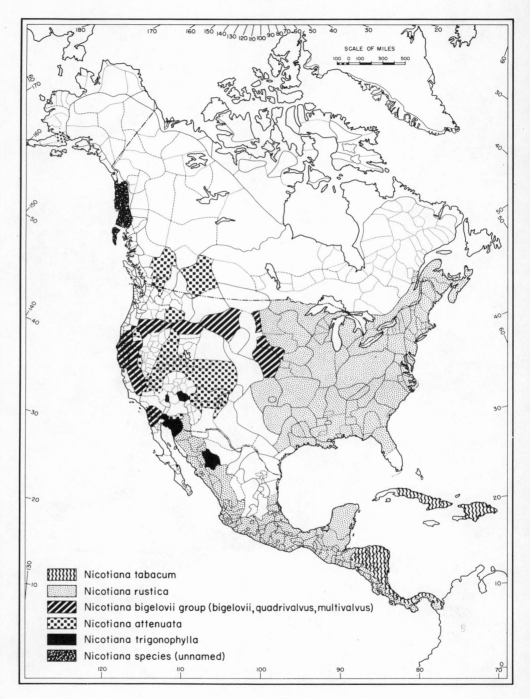

Legend:

- Nicotiana tabacum
- Nicotiana rustica
- Nicotiana bigelovii group (bigelovii, quadrivalvus, multivalvus)
- Nicotiana attenuata
- Nicotiana trigonophylla
- Nicotiana species (unnamed)

DOMINANT SPECIES OF TOBACCO. Driver and Massey

MAP 11

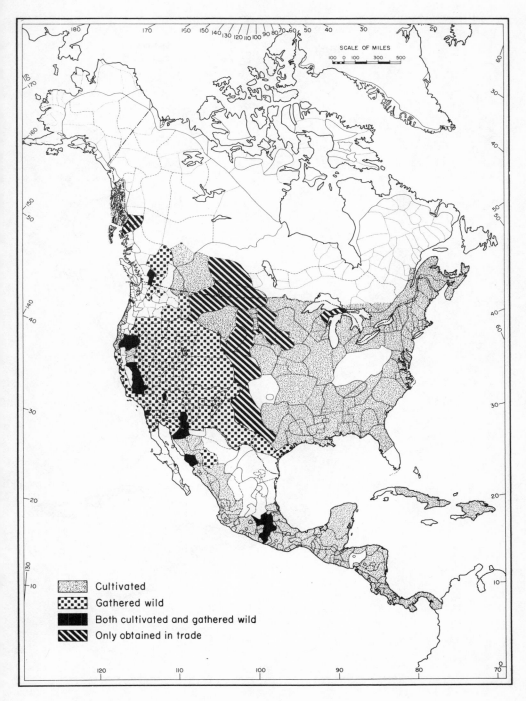

SCALE OF MILES
100 0 100   300   500

Cultivated

Gathered wild

Both cultivated and gathered wild

Only obtained in trade

PROBABLE ABORIGINAL SOURCES OF TOBACCO. Driver and Massey

MAP 12

ALCOHOLIC BEVERAGES

MAP 13

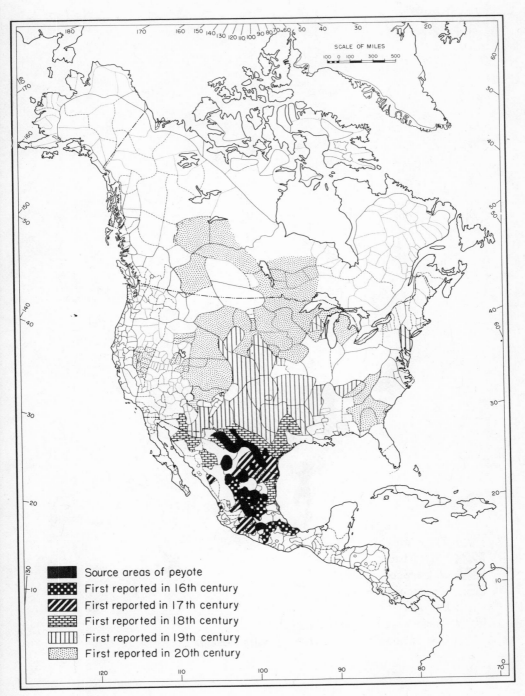

SCALE OF MILES
100 0 100 300 500

■ Source areas of peyote
▨ First reported in 16th century
▧ First reported in 17th century
▦ First reported in 18th century
▥ First reported in 19th century
▒ First reported in 20th century

PEYOTE. After Driver and Massey

MAP 14

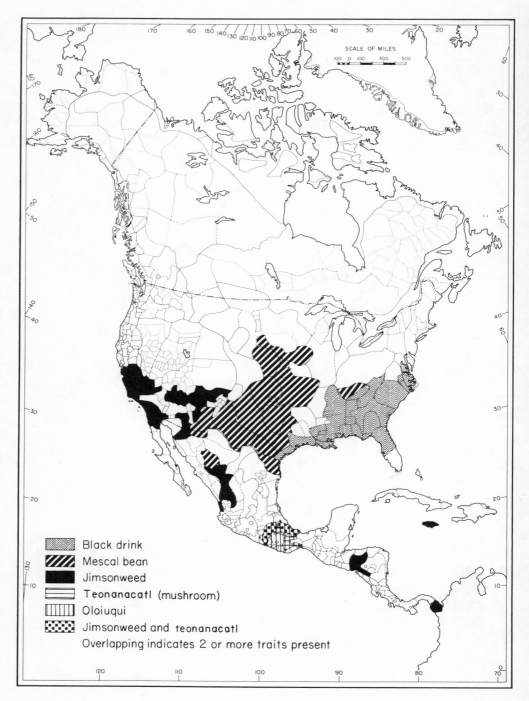

Black drink
Mescal bean
Jimsonweed
Teonanacatl (mushroom)
Oloiuqui
Jimsonweed and teonanacatl
Overlapping indicates 2 or more traits present

OTHER NARCOTICS. After Driver and Massey

MAP 15

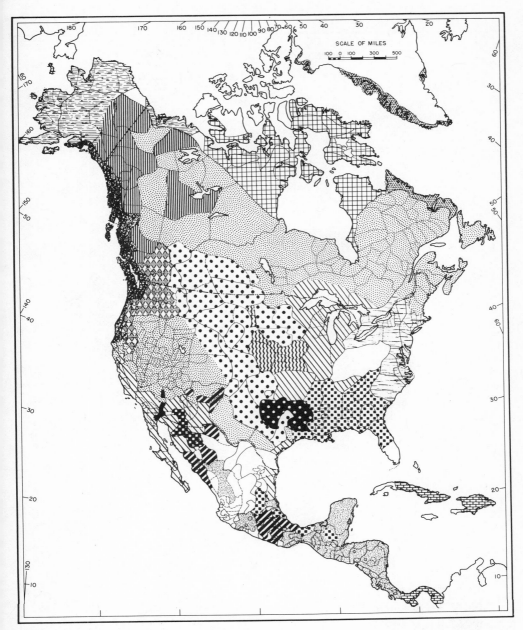

Double lean-to

Rectangular plank house

Semi-subterranean Plateau house

Prairie-Southeast earth lodge

Mohave type, 4-pitch-roof house

Crude conical tipi

Plains tipi

Rectangular, flat roof house

Rectangular, domed roof house

Pyramidal or hip-roof rectangloid house

Conical roof on cylinder, thatched

Gothic dome, thatched house

Rectangular, gabled house, thatched

Domed bark, mat, thatch, hide house

Rectangular, barrel-roofed house

Rectangloid earth-covered Alaskan house

Domed snow house

Domoid stone-earth-whalebone house

DOMINANT HOUSE TYPES. Driver and Massey

MAP 16

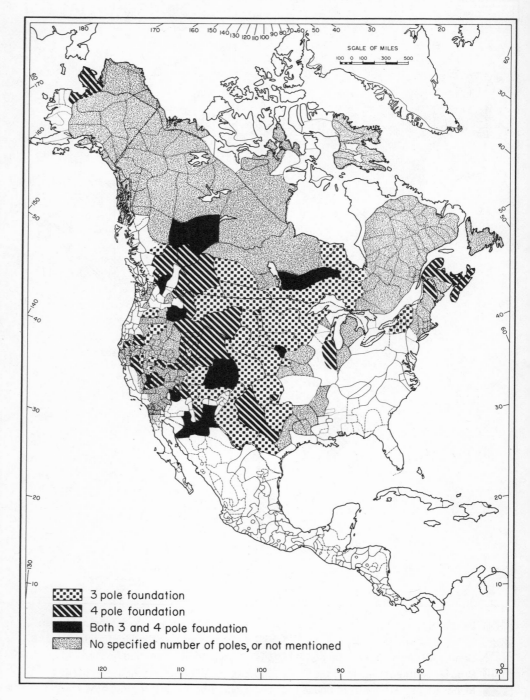

SCALE OF MILES
100   0   100   300   500

3 pole foundation
4 pole foundation
Both 3 and 4 pole foundation
No specified number of poles, or not mentioned

CONICAL AND SUB-CONICAL HOUSES. Driver and Massey

MAP 17

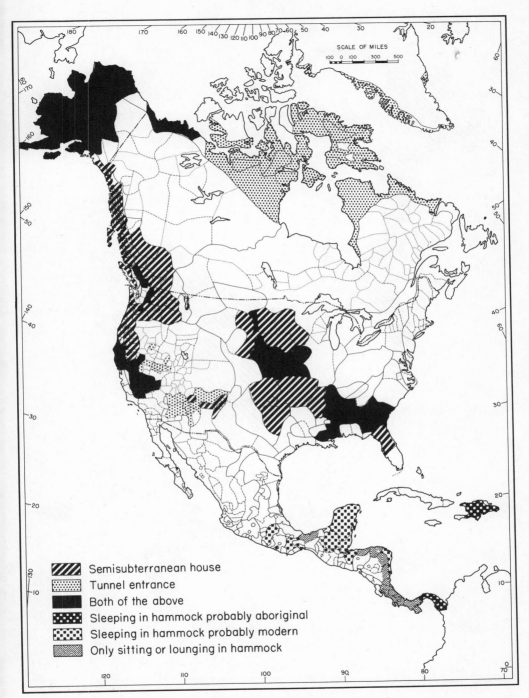

SCALE OF MILES
100 0 100   300   500

	Semisubterranean house
	Tunnel entrance
	Both of the above
	Sleeping in hammock probably aboriginal
	Sleeping in hammock probably modern
	Only sitting or lounging in hammock

SEMISUBTERRANEAN HOUSES, TUNNEL ENTRANCES, AND HAMMOCKS
Driver and Massey

MAP 18

SCALE OF MILES
100 0 100 300 500

Two or more nuclear families in same dwelling

MULTIFAMILY HOUSES. Driver and Massey

MAP 19

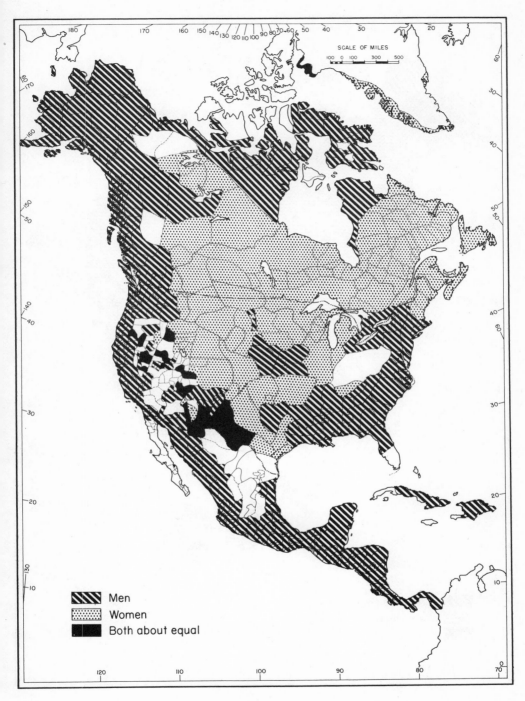

SCALE OF MILES

| Men |
| Women |
| Both about equal |

DOMINANT HOUSE-BUILDING DIVISION OF LABOR. Driver and Massey

MAP 20

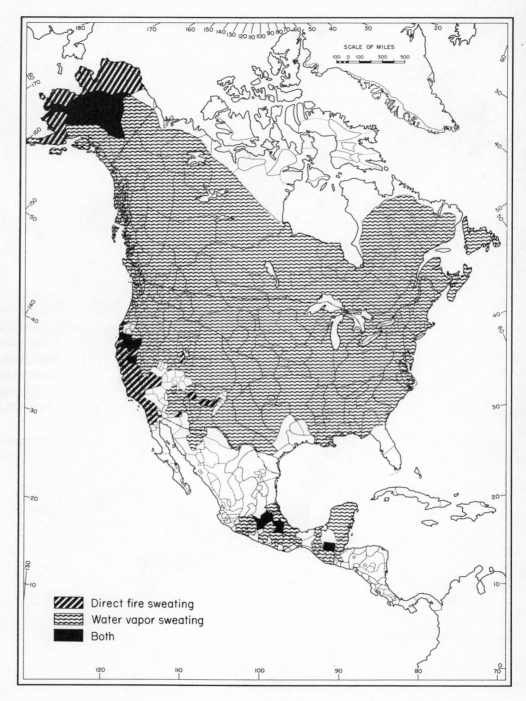

SCALE OF MILES

Direct fire sweating

Water vapor sweating

Both

SWEATING. Driver and Massey

MAP 21

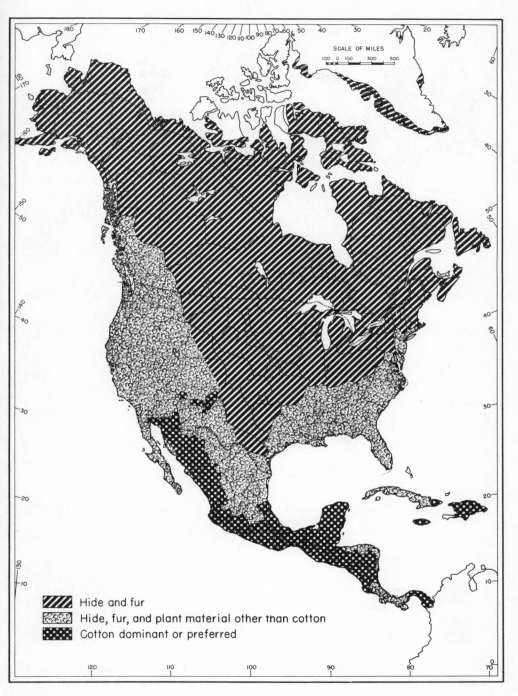

SCALE OF MILES

100 0 100   300   500

Hide and fur

Hide, fur, and plant material other than cotton

Cotton dominant or preferred

DOMINANT CLOTHING MATERIALS. Driver and Massey

MAP 22

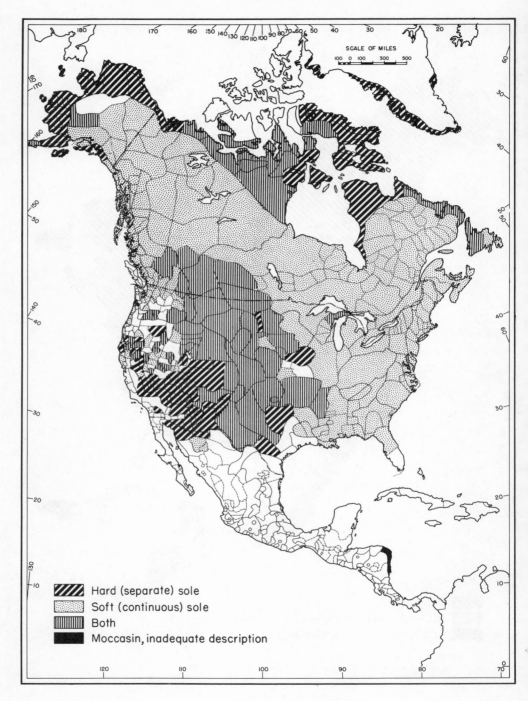

SCALE OF MILES
100 0 100 300 500

Hard (separate) sole
Soft (continuous) sole
Both
Moccasin, inadequate description

Moccasins. Driver and Massey

MAP 23

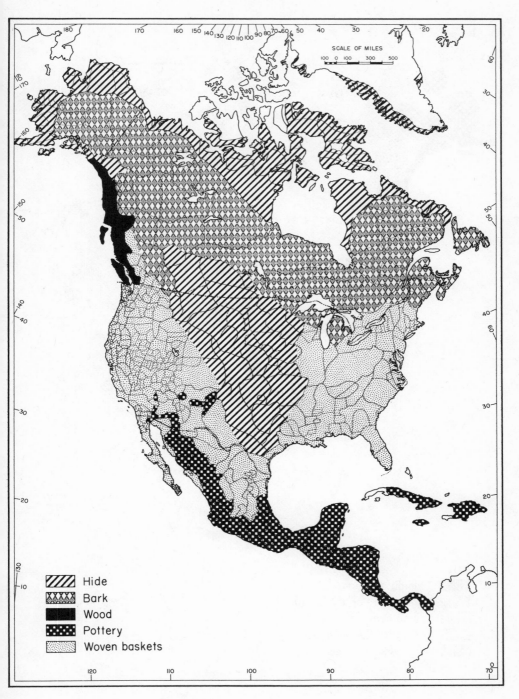

SCALE OF MILES
100 0 100 300 500

Hide
Bark
Wood
Pottery
Woven baskets

DOMINANT NON-COOKING CONTAINERS. Driver and Massey

MAP 24

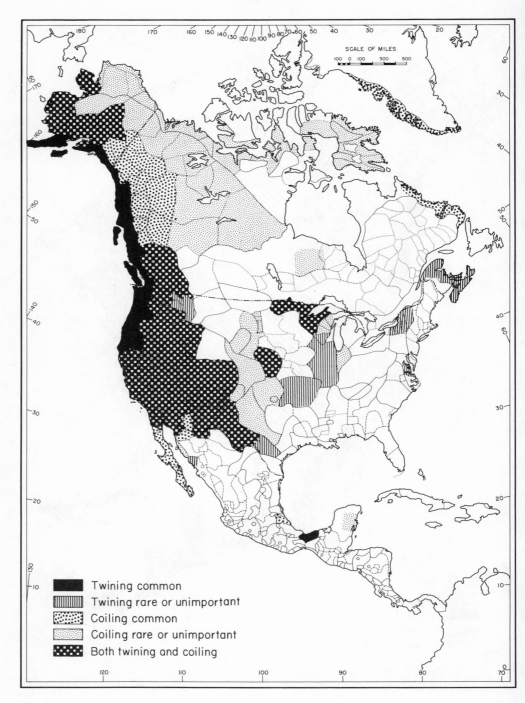

SCALE OF MILES
100 0 100 300 500

Twining common
Twining rare or unimportant
Coiling common
Coiling rare or unimportant
Both twining and coiling

TWINING OR COILING OF BASKETS, BAGS, OR MATS. Driver and Massey

MAP 25

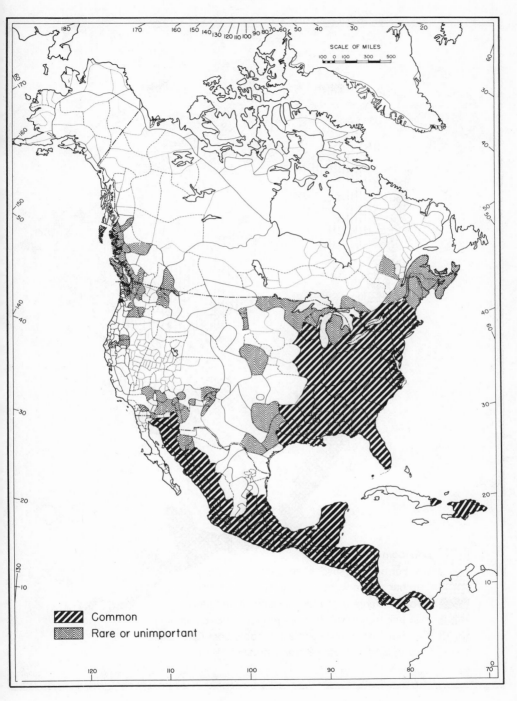

SCALE OF MILES
100 0 100 300 500

Common
Rare or unimportant

PLAITING OF BASKETS, BAGS, OR MATS. Driver and Massey

MAP 26

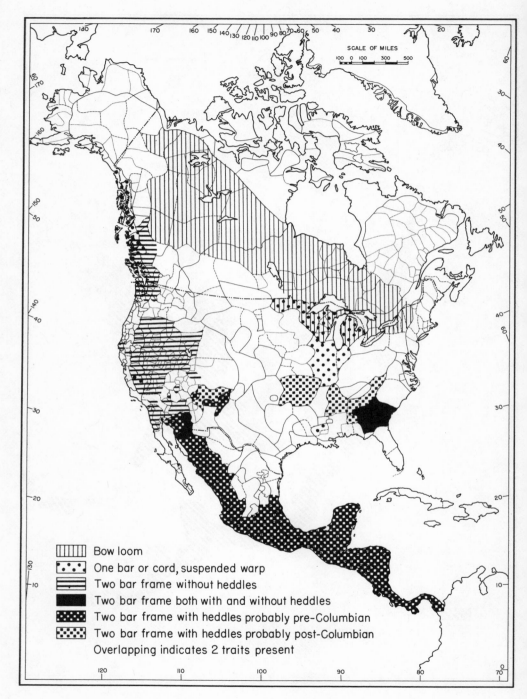

SCALE OF MILES
100 0 100   300   500

Bow loom
One bar or cord, suspended warp
Two bar frame without heddles
Two bar frame both with and without heddles
Two bar frame with heddles probably pre-Columbian
Two bar frame with heddles probably post-Columbian
Overlapping indicates 2 traits present

Weaving Devices. Driver and Massey

MAP 27

SCALE OF MILES
100 0 100   300   500

▨ Ethnological data
▨ Only archeological data

POTTERY VESSELS. Driver and Massey

MAP 28

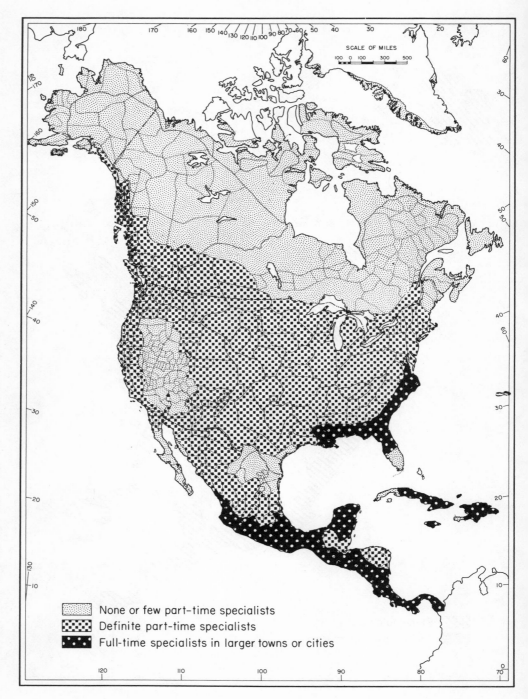

SCALE OF MILES

None or few part–time specialists
Definite part–time specialists
Full-time specialists in larger towns or cities

CRAFT SPECIALIZATION. After Driver and Massey

MAP 29

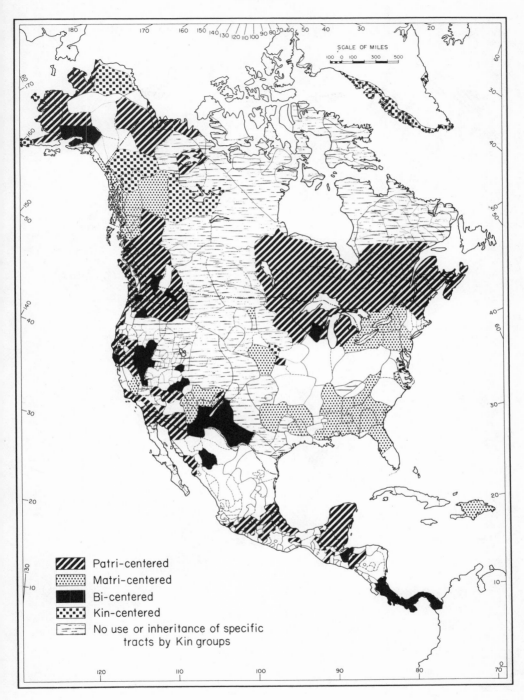

▨	Patri-centered
▦	Matri-centered
■	Bi-centered
▩	Kin-centered
≡	No use or inheritance of specific tracts by Kin groups

SCALE OF MILES
100 0 100   300   500

LAND TENURE. After Driver and Massey

MAP 30

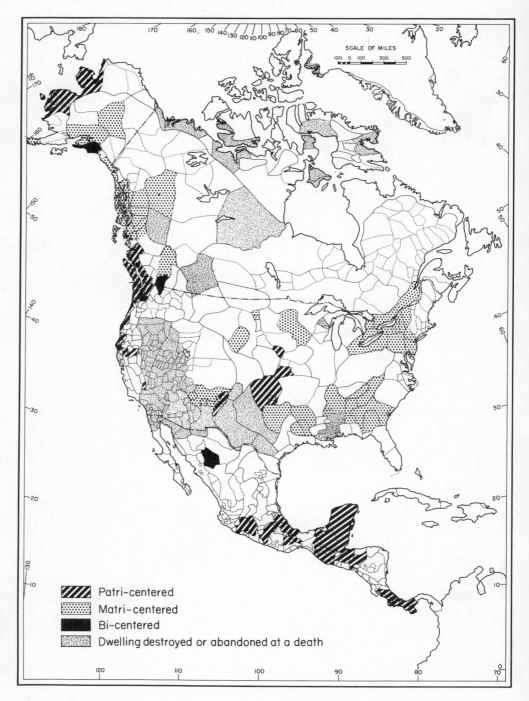

SCALE OF MILES
100 0 100   300   500

Patri-centered
Matri-centered
Bi-centered
Dwelling destroyed or abandoned at a death

OWNERSHIP AND INHERITANCE OF DWELLINGS. Driver and Massey

MAP 31

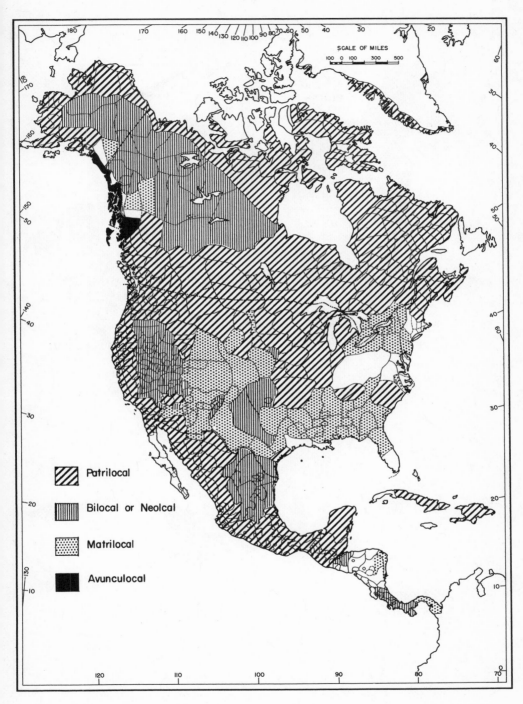

Patrilocal

Bilocal or Neolcal

Matrilocal

Avunculocal

POST-NUPTIAL RESIDENCE. After Driver and Massey

MAP 32

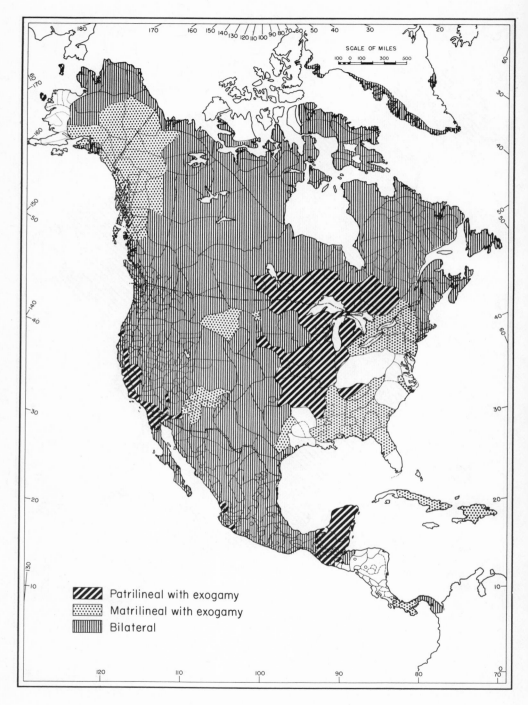

SCALE OF MILES
100 0 100   300   500

Patrilineal with exogamy
Matrilineal with exogamy
Bilateral

DESCENT. Driver and Massey

MAP 33

NUMBER OF MULTIPLE SIBS. Driver and Massey

MAP 34

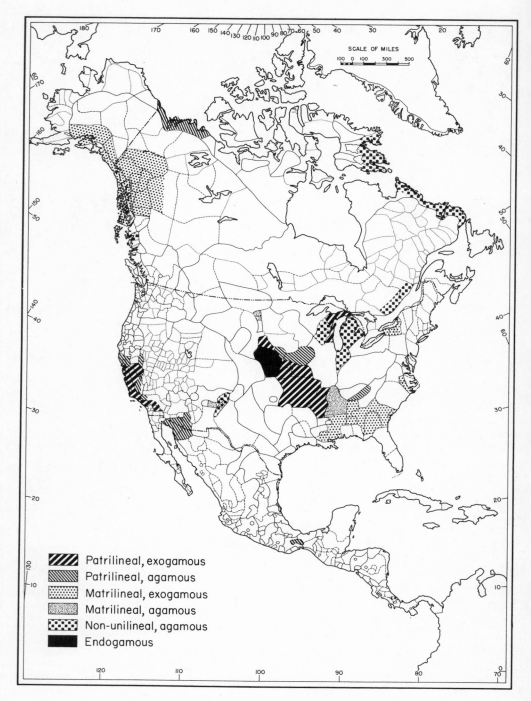

SCALE OF MILES
100 0 100   300   500

Patrilineal, exogamous
Patrilineal, agamous
Matrilineal, exogamous
Matrilineal, agamous
Non-unilineal, agamous
Endogamous

MOIETIES. Driver and Massey

MAP 35

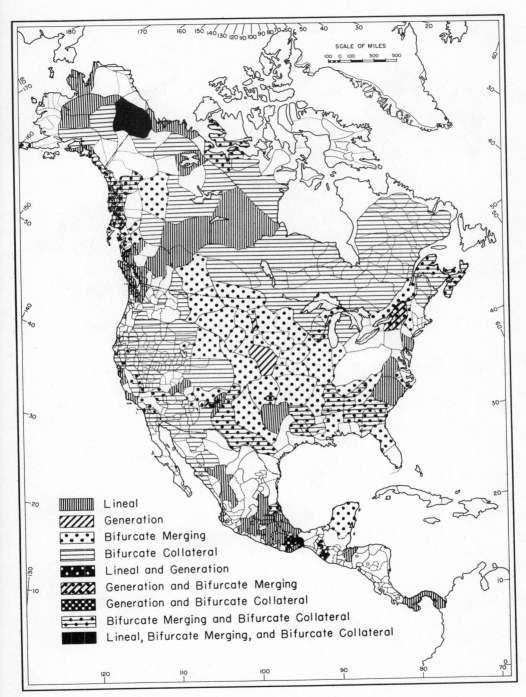

SCALE OF MILES
100 0 100   300   500

Lineal
Generation
Bifurcate Merging
Bifurcate Collateral
Lineal and Generation
Generation and Bifurcate Merging
Generation and Bifurcate Collateral
Bifurcate Merging and Bifurcate Collateral
Lineal, Bifurcate Merging, and Bifurcate Collateral

MOTHER-AUNT TERMS OF REFERENCE. After Driver and Massey

MAP 36

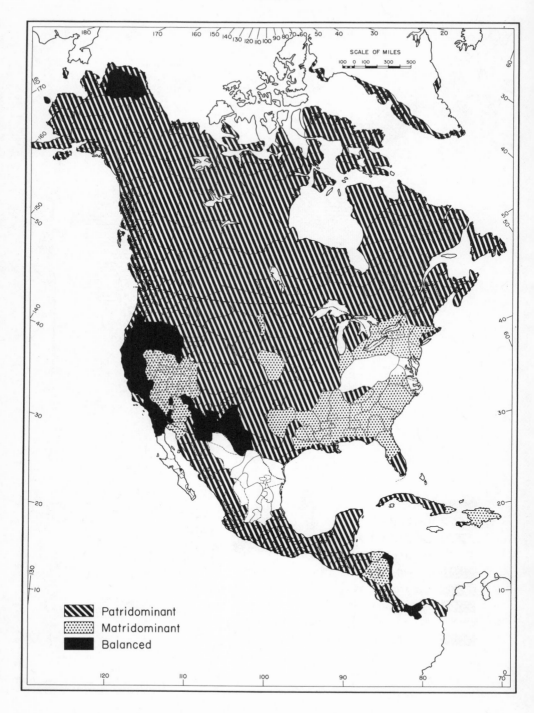

SEXUAL DOMINANCE IN SUBSISTENCE PURSUITS. Driver and Massey

Legend:
- Patridominant
- Matridominant
- Balanced

MAP 37

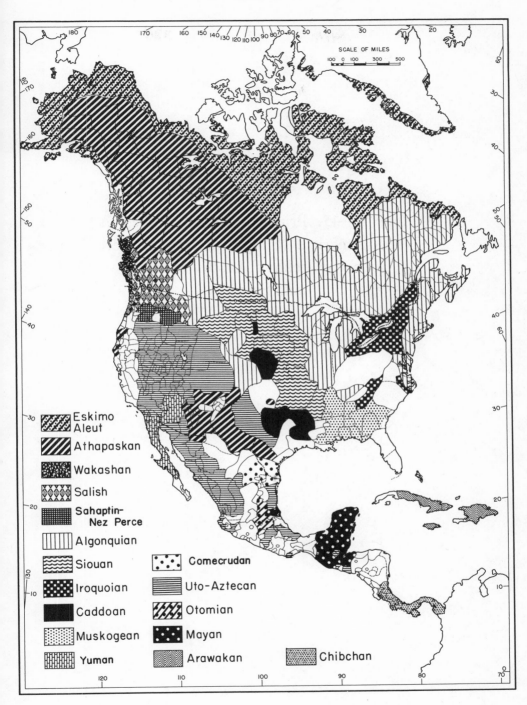

SCALE OF MILES
100 0 100   300   500

Eskimo Aleut
Athapaskan
Wakashan
Salish
Sahaptin-Nez Perce
Algonquian
Siouan
Iroquoian
Caddoan
Muskogean
Yuman
Comecrudan
Uto-Aztecan
Otomian
Mayan
Arawakan
Chibchan

LANGUAGE FAMILIES

Maps 38–45. Principal Indian Tribes of North America. (Simplified from Driver, Cooper, Kirchhoff, Libby, Massey, and Spier.)

MAP 38

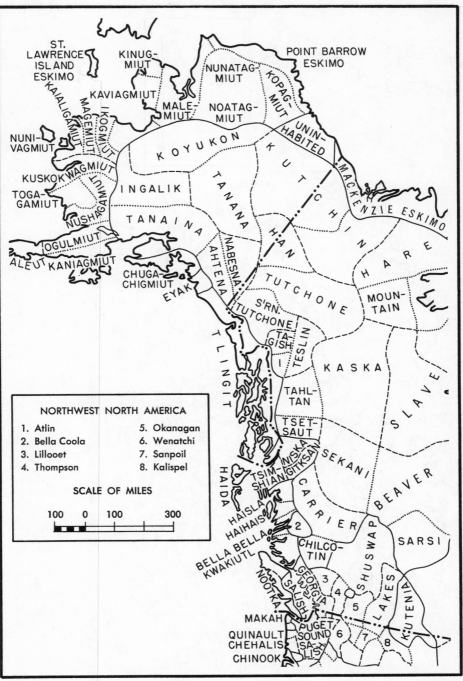

ST. LAWRENCE ISLAND ESKIMO

KINUG- MIUT

KAVIAGMIUT

KAIALIGAMIUT

MAGEMIUT

IKOGMIUT

MALE- MIUT

NUNATAG- MIUT

NOATAG- MIUT

KOPAG- MIUT

POINT BARROW ESKIMO

UNIN- HABITED

NUNI- VAGMIUT

KUSKOKWAGMIUT

TOGA- GAMIUT

NUSHAGAMIUT

OGULMIUT

ALEUT

KANIAGMIUT

KOYUKON

KUTCHIN

MACKENZIE ESKIMO

INGALIK

TANANA

HAN

HARE

TANAINA

NABESNA

AHTENA

CHUGA- CHIGMIUT

EYAK

S'RN TUTCHONE

TUTCHONE

MOUN- TAIN

TA- GISH

TESLIN

KASKA

SLAVE

TLINGIT

TAHL- TAN

TSET- SAUT

SEKANI

BEAVER

HAIDA

TSIM- SHIAN

NISKA GITKSAN

CARRIER

SHUSWAP

SARSI

HAISLA

HAIHAIS

CHILCO- TIN

2

LAKES

KUTENIA

BELLA BELLA KWAKIUTL

NOOTKA

GEORGIA SALISH

3

4

5

MAKAH

QUINAULT

CHEHALIS

CHINOOK

PUGET SOUND

ISA- LISH

6

7

8

NORTHWEST NORTH AMERICA

1. Atlin
2. Bella Coola
3. Lillooet
4. Thompson

5. Okanagan
6. Wenatchi
7. Sanpoil
8. Kalispel

SCALE OF MILES

100   0   100   300

MAP 39

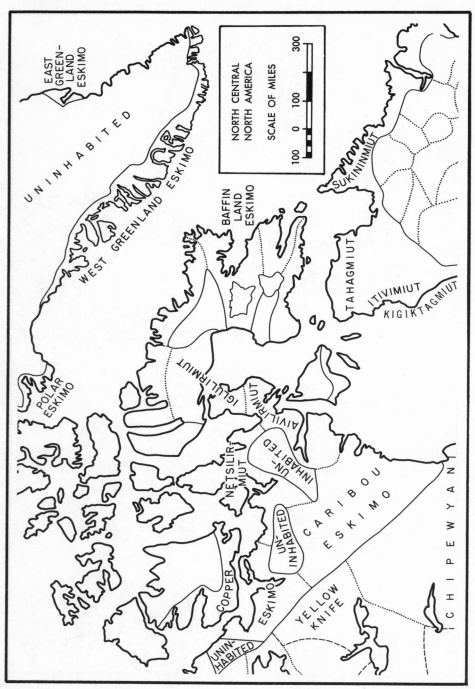

EAST GREEN- LAND ESKIMO

UNINHABITED

WEST GREENLAND ESKIMO

BAFFIN LAND ESKIMO

POLAR ESKIMO

NORTH CENTRAL NORTH AMERICA

SCALE OF MILES

300

100

0

100

SUKININMIUT

TAHAGMIUT

ITIVIMIUT

KIGIKTAGMIUT

IGLULIRMIUT

AIVILIRMIUT

NETSILIRMIUT

UN- INHABITED

UN- INHABITED

CARIBOU ESKIMO

COPPER ESKIMO

YELLOW KNIFE

UNIN- HABITED

CHIPEWYAN

MAP 40

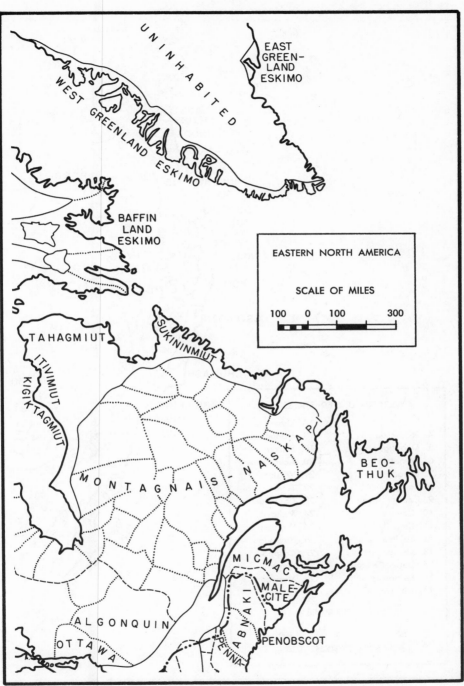

UNINHABITED

EAST
GREEN-
LAND
ESKIMO

WEST GREENLAND ESKIMO

BAFFIN
LAND
ESKIMO

EASTERN NORTH AMERICA

SCALE OF MILES

100   0   100   300

TAHAGMIUT

SUKININMIUT

ITIVIMIUT

KIGIK-TAGMIUT

MONTAGNAIS - NASKAPI

BEO-
THUK

MICMAC

MALE-
CITE

ABNAKI

PENOBSCOT

ALGONQUIN

OTTAWA

PENNA-

MAP 41

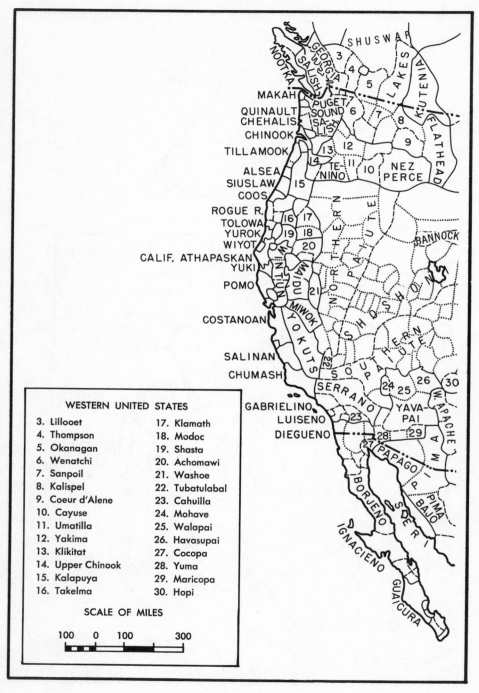

SHUSWAP

GEORGIA

NOOTKA

SALISH

LILLOOET 3

4

5

LAKES

KUTENAI

FLATHEAD

MAKAH

QUINAULT

CHEHALIS

CHINOOK

PUGET
SOUND
SALISH

6

7

8

WENATCHI

SANPOIL

KALISPEL

COEUR D'ALENE 9

TILLAMOOK

13

12

14

TE-
NINO

11

10

NEZ
PERCE

ALSEA

SIUSLAW

COOS

15

ROGUE R.

TOLOWA

YUROK

WIYOT

16

17

19

18

20

NORTHERN

PAIUTE

BANNOCK

CALIF. ATHAPASKAN

YUKI

POMO

WINTUN

MAIDU

21

SHOSHONI

COSTANOAN

MIWOK

YOKUTS

22

SOUTHERN PAIUTE

SALINAN

CHUMASH

SERRANO

24

25

26

30

W A P A C H E

GABRIELINO

LUISENO

DIEGUENO

23

YAVA-
PAI

28

29

MAM

27

PAPAGO

PIMA
BAJO

BORJENO

S. DE RI

IGNACIENO

GUAICURA

WESTERN UNITED STATES

3. Lillooet
4. Thompson
5. Okanagan
6. Wenatchi
7. Sanpoil
8. Kalispel
9. Coeur d'Alene
10. Cayuse
11. Umatilla
12. Yakima
13. Klikitat
14. Upper Chinook
15. Kalapuya
16. Takelma

17. Klamath
18. Modoc
19. Shasta
20. Achomawi
21. Washoe
22. Tubatulabal
23. Cahuilla
24. Mohave
25. Walapai
26. Havasupai
27. Cocopa
28. Yuma
29. Maricopa
30. Hopi

SCALE OF MILES

100   0   100   300

MAP 42

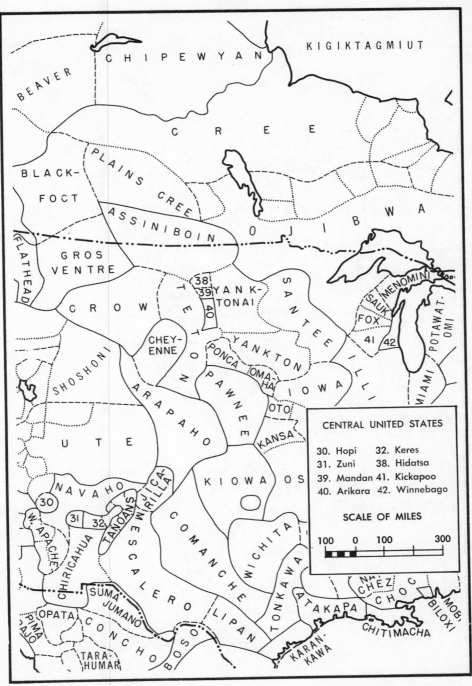

KIGIKTAGMIUT

CHIPEWYAN

BEAVER

CREE

BLACK-
FOCT

PLAINS CREE

ASSINIBOIN

OJIBWA

FLATHEAD

GROS
VENTRE

CROW

TETON

38
39
40

YANK-
TONAI

SANTEE

MENOMINI

SAUK
FOX

41 42

ILLI

POTAWAT-
OMI

MIAMI

CHEY-
ENNE

YANKTON

SHOSHONI

ARAPAHO

PONCA
OMA-
HA

IOWA

PAWNEE

OTO

UTE

KANSA

NAVAHO

JICA-
RILLA

TANOANS

CHEY

30

W. APACHE

31

32

CHIRICAHUA

MESCALERO

KIOWA

OS

COMANCHE

WICHITA

KANSA

SUMA
JUMANO

LIPAN

TONKAWA

ATAKAPA

NA-
CHEZ

CHOC

MOB'

BILOXI

OPATA

CONCHO

BOSO

KARAN-
KAWA

CHITIMACHA

PIMA
JAJO

TARA-
HUMAR

CENTRAL UNITED STATES

30. Hopi   32. Keres
31. Zuni   38. Hidatsa
39. Mandan 41. Kickapoo
40. Arikara 42. Winnebago

SCALE OF MILES

100   0   100   300

MAP 43

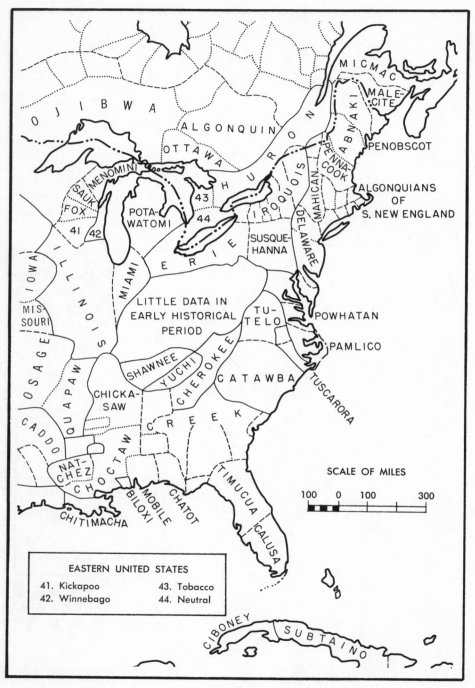

OJIBWA

ALGONQUIN

OTTAWA

MICMAC

MALE-
CITE

PENOBSCOT

ABNAKI

PEN-
NA-
COOK

MAHICAN

ALGONQUIANS
OF
S. NEW ENGLAND

MENOMINI

SAUK

FOX

POTA-
WATOMI

41

42

IOWA

ILLINOIS

HURON

43

44

ERIE

IROQUOIS

SUSQUE-
HANNA

DELAWARE

MIAMI

MIS-
SOURI

LITTLE DATA IN
EARLY HISTORICAL
PERIOD

TU-
TELO

POWHATAN

PAMLICO

OSAGE

QUAPAW

SHAWNEE

YUCHI

CHEROKEE

CATAWBA

TUSCARORA

CHICKA-
SAW

CADDO

CREEK

NAT-
CHEZ

CHOCTAW

MOBILE

BILOXI

CHATOT

TIMUCUA

CALUSA

CHITIMACHA

SCALE OF MILES

100   0   100   300

EASTERN UNITED STATES

41. Kickapoo   43. Tobacco
42. Winnebago   44. Neutral

CIBONEY

SUBTAINO

MAP 44

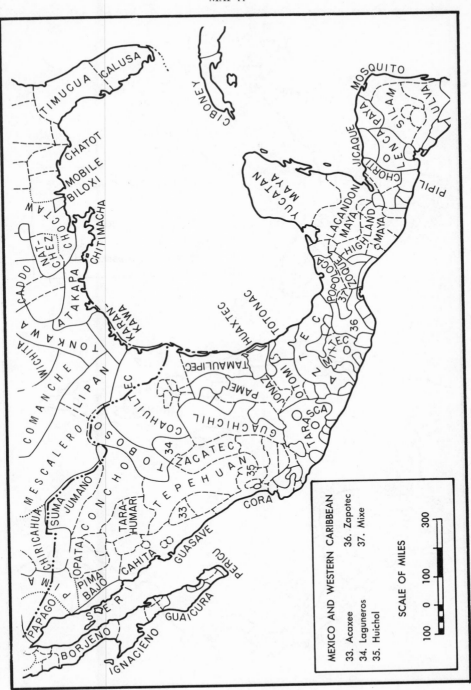

MEXICO AND WESTERN CARIBBEAN

33. Acaxee
34. Laguneros
35. Huichol
36. Zapotec
37. Mixe

SCALE OF MILES

100   0   100   300

MAP 45

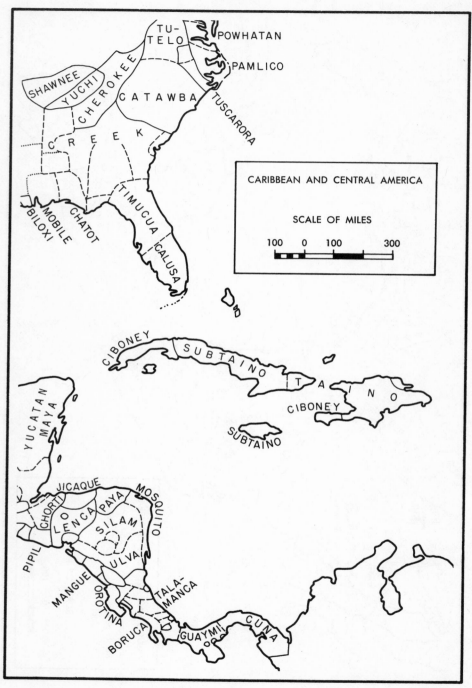

SHAWNEE

YUCHI

CHEROKEE

TU-TELO

POWHATAN

PAMLICO

CATAWBA

TUSCARORA

CREEK

BILOXI

MOBILE

CHATOT

TIMUCUA

CALUSA

CARIBBEAN AND CENTRAL AMERICA

SCALE OF MILES

100   0   100   300

CIBONEY

SUBTAINO

TAINO

CIBONEY

SUBTAINO

YUCATAN MAYA

JICAQUE

MOSQUITO

CHORTI

PAYA

LENCA

SILAM

ULVA

PIPIL

MANGUE

OROTINA

TALA-MANCA

BORUCA

GUAYMI

CUNA

Bibliography

ABERLE, DAVID F. 1966. *The Peyote Religion among the Navaho*. Chicago.

ABERLE, DAVID F., and STEWART, OMER C. 1957. *Navaho and Ute Peyotism*. University of Colorado Series in Anthropology, No. 6.

ACOSTA SAIGNES, MIGUEL. 1945. "Los Pocheta," *Acta Antropológica*, I, No. 1, 1–55. Mexico, D.F.

ADAIR, JOHN. 1944. *Navaho and Pueblo Silversmiths*. Norman, Okla.

———. 1960. "The Indian Health Worker in the Cornell-Navajo Project," *Human Organization*, XIX, 59–63.

AGUILAR, C. H. 1946. "La Orfebrería en el México Precortesiano," *Acta Antropológica*, II, No. 2, 1–140. Mexico, D.F.

AGUIRRE BELTRÁN, GONZALO. 1965. "Informe de Labores Llevadas a Cabo por el Instituto Nacional Indigenista de México, de Septiembre de 1964 a Junio de 1965," *Anuario Indigenista*, XXV, 111–15.

ALEXANDER, H. B. 1939. "The Horse in American Indian Culture," *in* DONALD BRAND and F. E. HARVEY (eds.), *So Live the Works of Men*, 65–74. Albuquerque.

ALFORD, THOMAS W. 1936. *Civilization: As Told to Florence Drake*. Norman, Okla.

American Indian Calendar. n.d. Bureau of Indian Affairs, Washington, D.C.

Americans before Columbus. Magazine of the National Indian Youth Council, Box 118, Schurz, Nevada 89427.

AMSDEN, CHARLES. 1932. "The Loom and Its Prototypes," *American Anthropologist*, XXXIV, 216–35.

Answers to Your Questions about American Indians. 1968. Bureau of Indian Affairs. Washington, D.C.

ARISS, ROBERT. 1939. "Distribution of Smoking Pipes in the Pueblo Area," *New Mexico Anthropologist*, III, 53–57.

ARREOLA, J. M. 1920. "El Temezcal o Baño Mexicano de Vapor," *Ethnos*, I, No. 2, 28–33.

AYRE, ROBERT. 1967. *Eskimo Graphic Art*. Canadian Arctic Producers, Ltd., 141 Catherine St., Ottawa.

BANDELIER, ADOLPH F. 1877. "On the Art of War and Mode of Warfare of the Ancient Mexicans," *Peabody Museum Annual Report*, II, 95–161.

BARBEAU, MARIUS. n.d. "Tsimshian Songs," *in* GARFIELD, VIOLA E., PAUL S. WINGERT, and MARIUS BARBEAU, *The Tsimshian: their Arts and Music*. American Ethnological Society Publ. XVIII, 97–157.

BARNETT, HOMER G. 1938. "The Nature of the Potlatch," *American Anthropologist*, XL, 349–58.
———. 1968. *The Nature and Function of the Potlatch.* Department of Anthropology, University of Oregon, Eugene.
BARNEY, RALPH. 1968. Personal Communication.
BARTLETT, KATHERINE. 1933. *Pueblo Milling Stones of the Flagstaff Region and Their Relation to Others in the Southwest.* Museum of Northern Arizona, Bulletin 3.
———. 1936. *The Utilization of Maize among the Ancient Pueblos.* University of New Mexico Bulletin 296, pp. 29–34, Anthropological Series, Vol. I, No. 5. Albuquerque.
BASEHART, HARRY W. 1960. *Mescalero Apache Subsistence Patterns and Socio-Political Organization.* The University of New Mexico Mescalero-Chiricahua Land Claims Project Contract Research No. 290–154, Section II.
BEAGLEHOLE, ERNEST. 1937. *Notes on Hopi Economic Life.* Yale University Publications in Anthropology, No. 15.
BEALS, RALPH L. 1932a. *The Comparative Ethnology of Northern Mexico.* University of California *Ibero-Americana*, No. 2.
———. 1932b. "Unilateral Organization in Mexico," *American Anthropologist*, XXXIV, 467–75.
———. 1943. *The Aboriginal Culture of the Cáhita Indians.* University of California Ibero-Americana, No. 19.
BEALS, RALPH L.; CARRASCO, PEDRO; and MCCORKLE, THOMAS. 1944. *Houses and House Use of the Sierra Tarascans.* Smithsonian Institution, Institute of Social Anthropology, No. 1.
BEALS, RALPH L. and HARRY HOIJER. 1965. *An Introduction to Anthropology.* 3d ed. New York.
BEARDSLEY, RICHARD K.; HOLDER, PRESTON; KRIEGER, ALEX D.; MEGGERS, BETTY J.; and RINALDO, JOHN B. 1956. *Functional and Evolutionary Implications of Community Patterning. Seminars in Archaeology*: 1955, Society for American Archaeology Memoir XI, 131–57.
BELL, WILLIS H., and CASTETTER, EDWARD F. 1937. *The Utilization of Mesquite and Screwbean by the Aborigines in the American Southwest.* University of New Mexico Bulletin, Biological Series, Vol. V, No. 2.
BENEDICT, RUTH. 1932. "Configurations of Culture in North America," *American Anthropologist*, XXXIV, 1–27.
———. 1934. *Patterns of Culture.* New York.
BENNETT, JOHN W. 1946. "The Interpretation of Pueblo Culture: A Question of Values," *Southwestern Journal of Anthropology*, II, 361–74.
BENNETT, ROBERT L. 1968. *Indian Affairs 1967.* Bureau of Indian Affairs. Washington, D.C.
BENNETT, WENDELL C., and ZINGG, ROBERT M. 1935. *The Tarahumara: An Inland Tribe of Northern Mexico.* Chicago.
BERGSLAND, KNUT, and VOGT, HANS. 1962. "On the Validity of Glottochronology," *Current Anthropology*, III, 115–53.
BIRKET-SMITH, KAJ. 1929. *The Caribou Eskimos: II, Analytical Part. Report*

of the Fifth Thule Expedition 1921-24, Vol. V, Part II. Copenhagen.
————. 1936. *The Eskimos*. New York.
————. 1945. *Ethnological Collection from the Northwest Passage: Report of the Fifth Thule Expedition, 1921-24*, VI 218-88. Copenhagen.
————. 1953. *The Chugach Eskimo*. Nationalmusetts Skrifter Etnografish Raekke, VI. Copenhagen.
————. 1959. *The Eskimos*. Rev. ed. London.
BIRKET-SMITH, KAJ, and LAGUNA, FREDERICA DE. 1938. *The Eyak Indians of the Copper River Delta*. Copenhagen.
BOAS, FRANZ. 1897. *The Social Organizations and Secret Societies of the Kwakiutl Indians, Based on Personal Observations and Notes Made by George Hunt*. Report of the United States National Museum for 1895.
BOLTON, HERBERT EUGENE, and MARSHALL, THOMAS MAITLAND. 1936. *The Colonization of North America*. New York.
BONNERJEA, B. 1934. "Hunting Superstitions of the American Aborigines," *International Congress of Americanists*, XXXII, 167-84.
BRANT, CHARLES S. 1950. "Peyotism among the Kiowa-Apache and Neighboring Tribes," *Southwestern Journal of Anthropology*, VI, 212-22.
BRIEGER, F. G.; GURGEL, J. T. A.; PATERNIANI, E.; BLUMENSCHEIN, A.; and ALLEONI, M. R. 1958. *Races of Maize in Brasil and Other Eastern South American Countries*." National Academy of Sciences–National Research Council, Publication No. 593, Washington, D.C.
BROPHY, WILLIAM A., and ABERLE, SOPHIE D. 1966. *The Indian: America's Unfinished Business*. Norman, Okla.
BROWN, GEORGE W. 1944. *Building the Canadian Nation*, Toronto and Vancouver.
BROWN, W. L., and ANDERSON, EDGAR. 1947. "The Northern Flint Corns," *Annals of the Missouri Botanical Garden*, XXXIV, 1-28.
————. 1948. "The Southern Dent Corns," *Annals of the Missouri Botanical Garden*, XXXV, 255-68.
BRUMAN, H. J. 1946. "Aboriginal Drink Areas in New Spain." Ph.D. dissertation, University of California, Berkeley.
BRUNER, EDWARD. 1961. "Mandan," *in* EDWARD H. SPICER (ed.), *Perspectives in American Indian Culture Change*, 187-277, Chicago.
BUSHNELL, David I. 1908. "Ethnographic Material from North America in Swiss Collections," *American Anthropologist*, X, 1-15.
————. 1919. *Native Villages and Village Sites East of the Mississippi*. Bureau of American Ethnology, Bulletin 69.
————. 1922. *Villages of the Algonquian, Siouan, and Caddoan Tribes West of the Mississippi*. Bureau of American Ethnology, Bulletin 77.
CALDWELL, JOSEPH R. 1958. *Trend and Tradition in the Prehistory of the Eastern United States*. American Anthropological Association Memoirs, No. 88.
CANNON, WALTER B. 1942. "Voodoo Death," *American Anthropologist*, XLIV, 169-81.
CARR, L. 1897. "Dress and Ornaments of Certain American Indians," *Proceedings of the American Antiquarian Society*, N.S., XI, 381-454.

CARR, LLOYD G. 1947. "Native Drinks in the Southeast and Their Values, with Special Emphasis on Persimmon Beer," *Proceedings of the Delaware County Institute of Science*, X, 29–43.

CARRASCO, PEDRO. 1961. "The Civil-Religious Hierarchy in Meso-American Communities: Pre-Spanish Background and Colonial Development," *American Anthropologist*, LXIII, 483–97.

CARTER, GEORGE F. 1945. *Plant Geography and Culture History of the American Southwest*. Viking Fund Publications in Anthropology, No. 5.

———. 1963. "Maize to Africa," *Anthropological Journal of Canada*, I, No. 2.

CARTER, GEORGE F., and ANDERSON, EDGAR. 1945. "A Preliminary Survey of Maize in the Southwestern United States," *Annals of the Missouri Botanical Garden*, XXXII, 297–322.

CASO, ALFONSO. 1958. *The Aztecs: People of the Sun*. Norman, Okla.

———. 1963. "Land Tenure among the Ancient Mexicans," *American Anthropologist*, LXV, 863–78.

CASTETTER, EDWARD F. 1935. *Uncultivated Native Plants Used as Sources of Food*. University of New Mexico Bulletin, Biological Series, Vol. IV, No. 1.

———. 1943. "Early Tobacco Utilization and Cultivation in the American Southwest," *American Anthropologist*, XLV, 320–25.

CASTETTER, EDWARD F., and BELL, WILLIS. 1937a. *The Utilization of Mesquite and Screwbean by the Aborigines in the American Southwest*. University of New Mexico Bulletin, Biological Series, Vol. V, No. 2.

———. 1937b. *The Aboriginal Utilization of the Tall Cacti in the American Southwest*. University of New Mexico Bulletin, Biological Series, Vol. V, No. 1.

———. 1938. *The Early Utilization and Distribution of Agave in the American Southwest*. University of New Mexico Bulletin, Biological Series, Vol. V, No. 4.

———. 1942. *Pima and Papago Indian Agriculture*. University of New Mexico, Inter-American Studies, No. 1.

———. 1951. *Yuman Indian Agriculture*. Albuquerque.

CATLIN, GEORGE. 1841. *Letters and Notes on the Manners, Customs, and Conditions of the North American Indians*. New York.

CHAMPLAIN, SAMUEL DE. 1619. *Voyages*, ed. by BIGGARS, III, 1–230.

CHARD, CHESTER S. 1950. *Pre-Columbian Trade between North and South America*, Kroeber Anthropological Society Papers, No. 1, 1–27.

CHRETIEN, C. DOUGLAS. 1962. "The Mathematical Models of Glotto-chronology," *Language*, XXXVIII, 11–37.

CHRISTENSEN, N. O. 1966. "Greenland," MAJA VAN STEENSEL (ed.), *in People of the Light and Dark*, 77–80, Department of Indian Affairs and Northern Development, Ottawa.

CLAVIGERO, FRANCISCO J. 1945. *Historia Antigua de México*, Vol. II, Mexico, D.F.

CODERE, HELEN. 1951. *Fighting with Property*. Monographs of the American Ethnological Society, No. 18.

———. 1956. "The Amiable Side of Kwakiutl Life: The Potlatch and the Play Potlatch," *American Anthropologist*, LVIII, 334–51.

————. 1957. "Kwakiutl Society: Rank without Class," *American Anthropologist*, LIX, 473–86.

————. 1961. "Kwakiutl," *in* EDWARD H. SPICER (ed.), *Perspectives in American Culture Change*, pp. 431–516. Chicago.

COLINVAUX, PAUL A. 1967. "Bering Land Bridge: Evidence of Spruce in Late-Wisconsin Times," *Science*, CLVI, 380–83.

COLTON, H. S. 1941. "Prehistoric Trade in the Southwest," *Scientific Monthly*, LII, 308–19.

CONN, RICHARD. 1952. "A Classification of Aboriginal North American Clothing." M.A. thesis, University of Washington.

COOK, SHERBURNE F. 1946. "Human Sacrifice and Warfare as Factors in the Demography of Pre-Colonial Mexico," *Human Biology*, XVIII, 81–102.

COOPER, JOHN M. 1938. *Snares, Deadfalls, and Other Traps of the Northern Algonquians and Northern Athapaskans*. Catholic University of America Anthropological Series, No. 5.

————. 1939. "Is the Algonquian Family Hunting Ground System Pre-Columbian?" *American Anthropologist*, XLI, 66–90.

COVARRUBIAS, MIGUEL. 1954. *The Eagle, the Jaguar, and the Serpent: Indian Art of the Americas*. New York.

CREIGHTON, LUELLA B. 1960. *Canada: The Struggle for Empire*. Toronto and Vancouver.

CRESSON, F. M., JR. 1938. "Maya and Mexican Sweat Houses," *American Anthropologist*, XL, 88–104.

CUMBERLAND, CHARLES. 1968. *Mexico: the Struggle for Modernity*. New York, London, Oxford.

CUSHING, FRANK H. 1894. "Primitive Copper Working," *American Anthropologist*, VII, 93–117.

DAHLGREN DE JORDAN, BARBRO. 1954. *La Mixteca: Su Cultura e Historia Pre-hispánicas*. Mexico, D.F.

DAIFUKU, HIROSHI. 1952. "The Pit House in the Old World and in Native North America," *American Antiquity*, XVIII, 1–6.

DAMAS, DAVID. 1963. *Igluligmiut Kinship and Local Groupings*. National Museum of Canada, Bulletin 196, Ottawa.

DAVIDSON, D. S. 1935. "Knotless Netting in America and Oceania," *American Anthropologist*, XXXVII, 117–34.

DAWSON, WARREN. 1929. *The Custom of Couvade*. Publications of the University of Manchester, No. 194, Ethnological Series, No. 4.

"Declaration of Indian Purpose," American Indian Chicago Conference, University of Chicago, 1961.

DEMBO, A., and IMBELLONI, J. 1938. *Deformaciones Intencionales*. Buenos Aires.

DENHARDT, ROBERT M. 1948. *The Horse of the Americas*. Norman, Okla.

DENSMORE, FRANCES. 1926. *The American Indians and Their Music*. New York.

————. 1929. *Chippewa Customs*. Bureau of American Ethnology, *Bulletin 86*.

DEVEREUX, GEORGE. 1951. *Reality and Dreams: Psychotherapy of a Plains Indian*. New York.

————. 1955. *A Study of Abortion in Primitive Societies*. New York.

DIENES, ANDRE DE. 1947. "Costumes of the Southwest Indians," *Natural History*, LVI, 360–67.

DINGWALL, E. J. 1931. *Artificial Cranial Deformation*. London.

DOBYNS, HENRY F. 1966. "Estimating Aboriginal American Population," *Current Anthropology*, VII, 395–449.

————. 1968. "Therapeutic Experience of Responsible Democracy," *in* STUART LEVINE and NANCY O. LURIE (eds.), *The American Indian Today*, 171–85, Deland, Fla.

DOCKSTADER, FREDERICK J. 1964. *Indian Art in Middle America*. Greenwich, Conn.

————. 1966. *Indian Art in America: The Arts and Crafts of the North American Indian*, 3d ed. Greenwich, Conn.

DORSEY, J. OWEN. 1897. "Siouan Sociology," *Annual Report of the Bureau of American Ethnology*, No. 15, 213–44.

DOUGLAS, FREDERICK H. 1932. *New England Houses, Forts and Villages: Colonial Period*. Denver Art Museum Indian Leaflet Series, No. 39.

DOUGLAS, FREDERICK H., and D'HARNONCOURT, RENÉ. 1941. *Indian Art of the United States*. New York.

DOZIER, EDWARD P. 1961. "Rio Grande Pueblos," *in* EDWARD H. SPICER (ed.), *Perspectives in American Indian Culture Change*, 94–186, Chicago.

DRIVER, HAROLD E. 1936. *Wappo Ethnography*. University of California Publications in American Archaeology and Ethnology, XXXVI, 179–220.

————. 1937. *Culture Element Distributions: VI Southern Sierra Nevada*. University of California Anthropological Records, I, 53–154.

————. 1941. *Girls' Puberty Rites in Western North America*. University of California Anthropological Records, VI, 21–90.

————. 1953a. "The Acorn in North American Indian Diet," *Proceedings of the Indiana Academy of Science*, LXII, 56–62.

————. 1953b. "The Spatial and Temporal Distribution of the Musical Rasp in the New World," *Anthropos*, XLVIII, 578–92.

————. 1964 (ed.). *The Americas on the Eve of Discovery*. Englewood Cliffs, N.J.

————. 1968. "On the Population Nadir of Indians in the United States," *Current Anthropology*, IX, 330.

DRIVER, HAROLD E., and DRIVER, WILHELMINE. 1963. *Ethnography and Acculturation of the Chichimeca-Jonaz of Northeast Mexico*. Indiana University Research Center in Anthropology, Folklore, and Linguistics, Publication 26.

————. 1967. *Indian Farmers of North America*. Chicago.

DRIVER, HAROLD E., and MASSEY, WILLIAM C. 1957. *Comparative Studies of North American Indians*. Transactions of the American Philosophical Society, XLVII, 165–456.

DRIVER, HAROLD E., and RIESENBERG, SAUL H. 1950 *Hoof Rattles and Girls' Puberty Rites in North and South America*. Indiana University Publications in Anthropology and Linguistics, Memoir 4.

DRIVER, HAROLD E., and SANDAY, PEGGY. 1966. "Factors and Clusters of Kin Avoidances and Related Variables," *Current Anthropology*, VII, 169–76.

DRUCKER, PHILIP. 1939. "Rank, Wealth, and Kinship in Northwest Coast Society," *American Anthropologist*, XLI, 55–65.

———. 1940. *Kwakiutl Dancing Societies*. University of California Anthropological Records, II, 201–30.

———. 1955. *Indians of the Northwest Coast*. New York.

———. 1965. *Cultures of the North Pacific Coast*. San Francisco.

DRUCKER, PHILIP, and HEIZER, ROBERT F. 1967. *To Make My Name Good: A Reexamination of the Southern Kwakiutl Potlatch*. Berkeley and Los Angeles.

DUNN, DOROTHY. 1968. *American Indian Painting of the Southwest and Plains Areas*. Albuquerque.

EDMONSON, MUNRO S. 1958. *Status Terminology and the Social Structure of the North American Indians*. American Ethnological Society, Seattle.

EGGAN, DOROTHY, 1943. "The General Problem of Hopi Adjustment," *American Anthropologist*, XLV, 357–73.

EGGAN, FRED. 1950. *Social Organization of the Western Pueblos*. Chicago.

———. 1955. "Social Anthropology: Methods and Results," *in* FRED EGGAN (ed.), *Social Anthropology of the North American Tribes*, 485–551. Chicago.

———. 1966. *The American Indian*. Chicago.

EKHOLM, GORDON F. 1964. "The True Arch in Pre-Columbian America," *Current Anthropology*, V, 328–29.

ELLIS, FLORENCE HAWLEY. 1951. "Patterns of Aggression and the War Cult in Southwestern Pueblos," *Southwestern Journal of Anthropology*, VII, 177–201.

ELMORE, FRANCIS H. 1944. *Ethnobotany of the Navaho*. Monographs of the School of American Research, No. 8, Santa Fe, N.M.

EMMART, EMILY W. 1940. *The Badianus Manuscript*. Baltimore.

Encyclopedia Britannica. 1964. Chicago.

EWERS, JOHN C. 1939. *Plains Indian Painting*. New York.

———. 1955a. "The Bear Cult among the Assiniboin and Their Neighbors of the Northern Plains," *Southwestern Journal of Anthropology*, XI, 1–14.

———. 1955b. *The Horse in Blackfoot Indian Culture*. Bureau of American Ethnology, Bulletin 159.

FAIRBANKS, C. H. 1946. "The Macon Earth Lodge," *American Antiquity*, XII, 94–108.

FARABEE, W. C. 1921. "Dress among the Plains Indian Women," *University of Pennsylvania Museum Journal*, XII, 239–51.

FARMER, MALCOLM F. 1957. "A Suggested Typology for Defensive Systems of the Southwest," *Southwestern Journal of Anthropology*, XIII, 249–67.

FENTON, WILLIAM N. 1936. *An Outline of Seneca Ceremonies at Coldspring Longhouse.* Yale University Publications in Anthropology, No. 9, 1–23.

———. 1941a. *Iroquois Suicide: A Study in the Stability of a Culture Pattern*. Bureau of American Ethnology, Bulletin 128, 79–137.

———. 1941*b*. "Masked Medicine Societies of the Iroquois," *Annual Report of the Smithsonian Institution for 1940*, 397–430.

———. 1942. "Contacts between Iroquois Herbalism and Colonial Medicine," *Annual Report of the Smithsonian Institution for 1941*, 503–26.

———. 1948. "The Present Status of Anthropology in Northeastern America," *American Anthropologist*, L, 494–513.

———. 1953. *The Iroquois Eqgle Dance, an Offshoot of the Calumet Dance.* Bureau of American Ethnology, *Bulletin 156*.

———. 1957. "Long-Term Trends of Change among the Iroquois," *Proceedings of the 1957 Annual Spring Meeting of the American Ethnological Society*, 30–35.

FEWKES, VLADIMIR J. 1944. "Catawba Pottery Making," *Proceedings of the American Philosophical Society*, LXXXVIII, 69–124.

FISCHER, J. L. 1964. "Solutions of the Natchez Paradox," *Ethnology*, III, 53–65.

FISHER, R. G. 1939. "An Outline of Pueblo Government," *in* D. D. BRAND and F. E. HARVEY (eds.), *So Live the Works of Men*, 147–57, Albuquerque.

FLANNERY, KENT V. 1965. "The Ecology of Early Food Production in Mesopotamia," *Science*, CXLVII, 1247–56.

FLANNERY, KENT V.; KIRKBY, ANNE V. T.; KIRKBY, MICHAEL J.; and WILLIAMS, AUBREY W., JR. 1967. "Farming Systems and Political Growth in Ancient Oaxaca," *Science*, CLVIII, 445–54.

FLANNERY, REGINA. 1939. *An Analysis of Coastal Algonquian Culture.* Catholic University of America Anthropological Series, No. 7.

———. 1946. "The Culture of the Northeastern Indian Hunters: A Descriptive Survey," *in* FREDERICK JOHNSON (ed.), *Man in Northeastern North America.* Papers of the Robert S. Peabody Foundation for Archaeology, III, 263–71.

FOREMAN, GRANT. 1934. *The Five Civilized Tribes.* Norman, Okla.

FOSTER, GEORGE M. 1948. "Some Implications of Modern Mexican Mold-Made Pottery," *Southwestern Journal of Anthropology*, IV, 356–70.

———. 1949. "Sierra Popoluca Kinship Terminology and Its Wider Relationships," *Southwestern Journal of Anthropology*, V, 330–44.

———. 1955. *Contemporary Pottery Techniques in Southern and Central Mexico.* Tulane University Middle American Research Institute, No. 22.

———. 1959. "The Coyotepec *Molde* and Some Associated Problems," *Southwestern Journal of Anthropology*, XV, 53–63.

———. 1960. *Culture and Conquest: America's Spanish Heritage.* Viking Fund Publications in Anthropology, No. 27.

GAMIO, MANUEL, *et al.* 1958. *Legislación Indigenista de México.* Instituto Indigenista Interamericano, Ediciones Especiales, Numero 38, Mexico, D.F.

GAYTON, ANN H. 1945. "Yokuts and Western Mono Social Organization," *American Anthropologist*, XLVII, 409–26.

———. 1928. "The Narcotic Plant *Datura* in Aboriginal American Culture." Ph.D. dissertation, University of California, Berkeley.

GIDDINGS, J. L. 1960. "The Archeology of Bering Strait," *Current Anthropology*, I, 121–38.

GIFFEN, NAOMI M. 1930. *The Roles of Men and Women in Eskimo Culture.* University of Chicago Publications in Anthropology, Ethnological Series.

GIFFORD, EDWARD W. 1916. *Miwok Moieties.* University of California Publications in American Archaeology and Ethnology, XII, 139–94.

———. 1926. "Miwok Lineages and the Political Unit in Aboriginal California," *American Anthropologist,* XXVIII, 389–401.

———. 1928. *Pottery-Making in the Southwest.* University of California Publications in American Archaeology and Ethnology, XXIII, 353–73.

———. 1932. *The Southeastern Yavapai.* University of California Publications in American Archaeology and Ethnology, XXIX, 177–252.

———. 1936. *Northeastern and Western Yavapai.* University of California Publications in American Archaeology and Ethnology, XXXIV, 247–354.

———. 1944. "Miwok Lineages," *American Anthropologist,* XLVI, 376–81.

GODDARD, PLINY E. 1945. *Indians of the Northwest Coast.* New York.

GOGGIN, JOHN M. 1949. "Plaited Basketry in the New World," *Southwestern Journal of Anthropology,* V, 165–68.

GOLDFRANK, ESTHER S. 1943. "Historic Change and Social Character, a Study of the Teton Dakota," *American Anthropologist,* XLV, 67–83.

———. 1945*a.* "Socialization, Personality, and the Structure of Pueblo Society," *American Anthropologist,* XLVII, 516–39.

———. 1945*b. Changing Configurations in the Social Organization of a Blackfoot Tribe during the Reserve Period.* American Ethnological Society Monographs, No. 8.

GOLDMAN, IRVING. 1941. "Alkatcho Carrier: Historical Background of Crest Prerogatives," *American Anthropologist,* XLIII, 396–418.

GOLDSCHMIDT, WALTER R. 1948. "Social Organization in Native California and the Origin of Clans," *American Anthropologist,* L, 444–56.

GOLDSCHMIDT, WALTER R., and HAAS, THEODORE H. 1946. *Possessory Rights of the Natives of Southeastern Alaska. Report of the Commissioner of Indian Affairs,* Washington, D.C.

GOODRICH, L. CARRINGTON. 1959. *A Short History of the Chinese People.* 3d ed. New York.

GOODSPEED, THOMAS HARPER. 1954. "The Genus *Nicotiana,*" *Chronica Botanica,* XVI, 1–536.

GOODWIN, GRENVILLE. 1942. *The Social Organization of the Western Apache.* Chicago.

GRABURN, NELSON H. H. 1964. *Taqagmiut Eskimo Kinship Terminology.* Northern Co-ordination and Research Center, Department of Northern Affairs and National Resources, Ottawa.

GREENBERG, JOSEPH H. 1953. "Historical Linguistics and Unwritten Languages," *in* A. L. KROEBER (ed.), *Anthropology Today,* 265–86, Chicago.

GRIFFIN, JAMES B. 1935. "Aboriginal Methods of Pottery Manufacture in the Eastern United States," *Pennsylvania Archaeologist,* V, 19–24.

———. (ed.) 1952. *Archaeology of Eastern United States.* Chicago.

———. 1967. "Eastern North American Archaeology: A Summary,"

Science, CLVI, 175-91.
GRIFFIN, JAMES B., and KRIEGER, ALEX D. 1947. "Notes on Some Ceramic Techniques and Intrusions in Central Mexico," *American Antiquity*, XII, 156-68.
GROBMAN, ALEXANDER; SALHUANA, W.; and SEVILLA, R. 1961. *Races of Maize in Peru and Their Origins, Evolution and Classification*. National Academy of Science–National Research Council, Washington, D.C., Publication 915.
GUERRA, F., and OLIVERA, H. 1954. *Las Plantas Fantásticas de México*. Mexico, D.F.
GUILFORD, J. P. 1968. "Intelligence Has three Facets," *Science*, CLX, 615-20.
GUNTHER, ERNA. 1928. *A Further Analysis of the First Salmon Ceremony*. University of Washington Publications in Anthropology, II, 129-73.
———. 1945. *Ethnobotany of Western Washington*. University of Washington Publications in Anthropology, X, 1-61.
HADLOCK, WENDEL S. 1947. "Warfare among the Northeastern Woodland Indians," *American Anthropologist*, XLV, 204-21.
HAGAN, WILLIAM T. 1961. *American Indians*. Chicago.
———. 1966. *Indian Police and Judges*. New Haven and London.
HAINES, FRANCIS. 1938a. "Where Did the Plains Indians Get Their Horses?" *American Anthropologist*, XL, 112-17.
———. 1938b. "The Northward Spread of Horses among the Plains Indians," *American Anthropologist*, XL, 429-37.
HALLOWELL, A. IRVING. 1937. *Cross-Cousin Marriage in the Lake Winnipeg Area*. Publications of the Philadelphia Anthropological Society, I, 95-110.
———. 1949. "The Size of Algonkin Hunting Territories," *American Anthropologist*, LI, 35-45.
———. 1955. *Culture and Experience*. Philadelphia.
———. 1957. "The Impact of the American Indian on American Culture," *American Anthropologist*, LIX, 201-17.
———. 1959. "The Backwash of the Frontier: The Impact of the Indian on American [U.S.A.] Culture," *Annual Report of the Smithsonian Institution for 1958*, 447-72.
HART, C. W. M. 1943. "A Reconsideration of the Natchez Social Structure," *American Anthropologist*, XLV, 374-86.
HATT, GUDMUND. 1916. *Moccasins and Their Relation to Arctic Footwear*. American Anthropological Association Memoirs, No. 3, 149-250.
HAURY, EMIL W. 1947. "A Large Pre-Columbian Copper Bell from the Southwest," *American Antiquity*, XIII, 80-82.
HAWTHORN, H. B., ed. 1966. *A Survey of the Contemporary Indians of Canada, Part I*, Indian Affairs Branch, Ottawa.
HAWTHORN, H. B.; BELSHAW, C. S.; and JAMIESON, S. M. 1958. *The Indians of British Columbia*. Berkeley, Los Angeles, Toronto.
HEISER, CHARLES B., JR. 1951. "The Sunflower among the North American Indians," *Proceedings of the American Philosophical Society*, XC, 432-48.
———. 1965. "Cultivated Plants and Cultural Diffusion in Nuclear America," *American Anthropologist*, LXVII, 930-49.

HEIZER, ROBERT F. 1940. "The Botanical Identification of Northwest Coast Tobacco," *American Anthropologist*, XLII, 704–6.
———. 1953. *Aboriginal Fish Poisons*. Bureau of American Ethnology, *Bulletin 151*, pp. 225–84.
HELM, JUNE. 1965. "Bilaterality in the Socio-territorial Organization of the Arctic Drainage Dene," *Ethnology*, IV, 361–85.
———. 1969. "A Method of Statistical Analysis of Primary Bonds in Community Composition," *in* DAVID DAMAS (ed.), *Proceeding of the Conference on Band Organization*, National Museum of Canada Bulletin, Ottawa.
HELM, JUNE, and DAMAS, DAVID. 1963. "The Contact-Traditional All-Native Community of the Canadian North," *Anthropologica*, V, 9–21.
HERRING, HUBERT. 1963. *A History of Latin America*. 2d ed. rev., New York.
HERSKOVITS, MELVILLE J. 1948. *Man and His Works*. New York.
———. 1952. *Economic Anthropology*. New York.
HERZOG, GEORGE. 1928*a*. "Musical Styles in North America," *Proceedings of the Twenty-third International Congress of Americanists*, 455–58.
———. 1928*b*. "The Yuman Musical Style," *Journal of American Folklore*, XLI, 183–231.
———. 1934. "Speech-Melody and Primitive Music," *Musical Quarterly*, XX, 452–66.
———. 1935*a*. "Plains Ghost Dance and Great Basin Music," *American Anthropologist*, XXXVII, 403–19.
———. 1935*b*. "Special Song Types in North American Indian Music," *Zeitschrift für Vergleichende Musik-wissenschaft*, III, 23–33.
———. 1936. *Materials and Resources in Folk and Primitive Music in the U.S.A.* American Council of Learned Societies, Bulletin 25.
———. 1938. "A Comparison of Pueblo and Pima Musical Styles," *Journal of American Folklore*, XLIX, 283–417.
———. 1949. "Salish Music," *in* SMITH, MARIAN E. (ed.), *Indians of the Urban Northwest*, pp. 93–110. New York.
HICKERSON, HAROLD. 1963. "The Sociohistorical Significance of Two Chippewa Ceremonials," *American Anthropologist*, LXV, 67–85.
———. 1966. "The Genesis of Bilaterality among Two Divisions of Chippewa," *American Anthropologist*, LXVIII, 1–26.
———. 1967. "Some Implications of the Theory of the Particularity, or 'Atomism,' of Northern Algonkians," *Current Anthropology*, VIII, 313–43.
HICKERSON, NANCY P. 1950. "The Institution of Slavery in Societies of Northwestern North America." M.A. thesis, Indiana University.
HILL, RICHARD M. 1967. *Mackenzie Reindeer Operations*. Department of Indian Affairs and Northern Development, Ottawa.
HILL, W. W. 1938. *The Agriculture and Hunting Methods of the Navaho Indians*. Yale University Publications in Anthropology, XVIII, 1–194.
HIND, H. Y. 1863. *Explorations in the Labrador Peninsula*. 2 vols. London.
HO, PING-TI. 1955. "The Introduction of American Food Plants into China," *American Anthropologist*, LVII, 191–201.
HOEBEL, E. ADAMSON. 1939. "Comanche and Hekandika Shoshoni Relationship Systems," *American Anthropologist*, XLI, 440–57.

———. 1940. *The Political Organization and Law-ways of the Comanche Indians.* American Anthropological Association Memoirs. No. 54.

———. 1941. "Law-Ways of the Primitive Eskimos," *Journal of Criminal Law and Criminology*, XXXI, 663–83.

———. 1960. "The Authority Systems of the Pueblos of the Southwestern United States," in *Akten des 34 Internationalen Amerikanistenkongresses*, 555–63. Vienna.

———. 1966. *Man in the Primitive World*, 3d ed. New York.

HOFFMAN, WALTER J. 1891. "The Midewiwin or Grand Medicine Society of the Ojibwa," *Bureau of American Ethnology Annual Report for 1885–1886*, VII, 143–300.

———. 1897. "The Graphic Art of the Eskimos," *Report of the United States National Museum for 1895*, 739–968.

HOIJER, HARRY (ed.). 1954. *Language in Culture.* American Anthropological Association Memoirs, No. 79.

———. 1956a. "The Chronology of the Athapaskan Languages," *International Journal of American Linguistics*, XXII, 219–32.

———. 1956b. "Athapaskan Kinship Systems," *American Anthropologist*, LVIII, 309–33.

HONIGMAN, JOHN J. 1946. *Ethnography and Acculturation of Fort Nelson Slave.* Yale University Publications in Anthropology, No. 33.

———. 1949. *Culture and Ethos of Kaska Society.* Yale University Publications in Anthropology, No. 40.

———. 1954. *Culture and Personality.* New York.

HOWARD, JAMES H. 1957. "The Mescal Bean Cult of the Central and Southern Plains," *American Anthropologist*, LIX, 75–87.

HUDEN, JOHN C. 1962. *Indian Place Names in New England.* Contributions of the Museum of the American Indian, XVIII.

HUGHES, CHARLES C. 1965. "Under Four Flags: Recent Culture Change among the Eskimos," *Current Anthropology*, VI, 3–69.

HUNT, GEORGE T. 1940. *The Wars of the Iroquois.* Madison, Wis.

HUNT, WALTER BERNARD. 1951. *American Indian Beadwork.* Milwaukee, Wis.

HUNTER, H. V. 1940. *The Ethnography of Salt in Aboriginal North America.* Philadelphia.

HUTCHINSON, SIR JOSEPH. 1962. "The History and Relationship of the World's Cottons," *Endeavor*, XXI, 5–15.

HYMES, DELL H. 1957. "A Note on Athapaskan Glotto-chronology," *International Journal of American Linguistics*, XXIII, 291–97.

———. 1959. "Genetic Classification: Retrospect and Prospect," *Anthropological Linguistics*, I, 50–66.

———. 1960. "Lexicostatistics So Far," *Current Anthropology*, I, 3–44.

——— (ed.). 1964. *Language in Culture and Society.* New York.

IMBELLONI, JOSÉ. 1958. "Nouveaux Apports à la Classification de l'Homme Américain," *Miscellanea Paul Rivet, Octogenaria Dictata*, I, 107–36. Mexico, D.F.

Indian Affairs (magazine). Association on American Indian Affairs, Inc., 432 Park Ave. South, New York, N.Y. 10016.

Indian Historian, The, (magazine). American Indian Historical Society, 206 Miguel Street, San Francisco, Calif. 94131.

"Indians of Ontario." 1966. Indian Affairs Branch. Ottawa.

Indian Voices (magazine). University of Chicago, 1126 East 59th Street, Chicago, Ill. 60637.

INNIS, HAROLD ADAMS. 1962. *The Fur Trade in Canada*. Rev. ed. Toronto.

INVERARITY, ROBERT BRUCE. 1950. *Art of the Northwest Coast Indians*. Berkeley and Los Angeles.

IZIKOWITZ, KARL G. 1935. *Musical and Other Sound Instruments of the South American Indians*. Göteborg.

JABLOW, JOSEPH. 1951. *The Cheyenne in Plains Indian Trade Relations, 1795–1840*. Monographs of the American Ethnological Society, No. 19.

JACOBSON, OSCAR B. 1952. *North American Indian Costumes*. Nice, France.

JENNESS, DIAMOND. 1932. *Indians of Canada*. Bulletin of the Canada Department of Mines, No. 65, National Museum of Canada, Ottawa.

JENNINGS, JESSE D. 1957. *Danger Cave*. Memoirs of the Society for American Archaeology, No. 4.

———. 1968. *Prehistory of North America*. New York.

JENNINGS, JESSE D., and NORBECK, EDWARD. 1964. *Prehistoric Man in the New World*. Chicago.

JOHNSON, IRMGARD WEITLANER. 1953. "El Quechquemitl y el Huipil," *in* IGNACIO BERNAL and EUSEBIO DÁVALOS HURTADO (eds.), *Huastecos, Totonacos y sus Vecinos*, Revista Mexicana de Estudios Antropológicos, XIII-2-3, 241–47.

JONES, VOLNEY H. 1944. "Was Tobacco Smoked in the Pueblo Region in Pre-Spanish Times?" *American Antiquity*, IX, 451–56.

JONES, VOLNEY H., and MORRIS, ELIZABETH ANN. 1960. "A Seventh-Century Record of Tobacco Utilization in Arizona," *El Palacio*, LXVII, 115–17.

JUDD, NEIL M. 1948. "Pyramids of the New World," *National Geographic Magazine*, XCIII, 105–28.

JUNG, CARL G. 1928. *Contributions to Analytical Psychology*. London.

KELEMEN, PÁL. 1956. *Medieval American Art*. New York.

KELLY, ISABEL. 1943. "West Mexico and the Hohokam," *in El Norte de México y el Sur de los Estados Unidos*, 206–22. Mexico, D.F.

KELLY, ISABEL and PALERM, ANGEL. 1952. *The Tajin Totonac*. Smithsonian Institution, Institute of Social Anthropology, Publication No. 13.

KELLY, WILLIAM H. 1942. "Cocopa Gentes," *American Anthropologist*, XLIV, 675–91.

KENT, KATE P. 1957. *The Cultivation and Weaving of Cotton in the Prehistoric Southwestern United States*. Transactions of the American Philosophical Society, XLVII, 457–732.

KING, ARDEN R. 1947. "Aboriginal Skin Dressing in Western North America." Ph.D. dissertation, University of California, Berkeley.

KINIETZ, VERNON. 1940. *Notes on the Roached Headdress of Animal Hair among the North American Indians*. Papers of the Michigan Academy of

Science, Arts, and Letters, XXVI, 463–67.

KLUCKHOHN, CLYDE. 1944. *Navaho Witchcraft*. Harvard University Papers of the Peabody Museum of American Archaeology and Ethnology, XXII, 1–149.

KNIGHT, OLIVER. 1960. *Following the Indian Wars*. Norman, Okla.

KNIGHT, ROLF. 1965. "A Re-examination of Hunting, Trapping, and Territoriality among the Northeastern Algonkian Indians," *in* LEEDS, ANTHONY and ANDREW P. VAYDA (eds.), *Man, Culture, and Animals: The Role of Animals in Human Ecological Adjustments*, pp. 27–42. American Association for the Advancement of Science, Washington, D.C.

KNOWLES, NATHANIEL. 1940. "The Torture of Captives by the Indians of North America," *Proceedings of the American Philosophical Society*, LXXXII, 151–225.

KRICKEBERG, W. 1939. "The Indian Sweatbath," *Ciba Symposia*, I, 19–35.

KRIEGER, ALEX D. 1964. "Early Man in the New World," *in* JESSE D. JENNINGS and EDWARD NORBECK (eds.), *Prehistoric Man in the New World*, 23–81. Chicago.

KRIEGER, H. W. 1929. "American Indian Costumes in the United States National Museum," *Annual Report of the Smithsonian Institution for 1928*, 623–61.

KROEBER, ALFRED L. 1916. *California Place Names of Indian Origin*. University of California Publications in American Archaeology and Ethnology, XII, 31–69.

———. 1925. *Handbook of the Indians of California*. Bureau of American Ethnology, Bulletin 78.

———. 1928. *Native Culture of the Southwest*. University of California Publications in American Archaeology and Ethnology, XXIII, 375–98.

———. 1932. *The Patwin and Their Neighbors*. University of California Publications in American Archaeology and Ethnology, XXIX, 253–364.

———. 1934. "Native American Population," *American Anthropologist*, XXXVI, 1–25.

——— (ed.). 1935. *Walapai Ethnography*. Memoirs of the American Anthropological Association, No. 42.

———. 1937. "Athabascan Kin Term Systems," *American Anthropologist*, XXXIX, 602–9.

———. 1939. *Cultural and Natural Areas of Native North America*. University of California Publications in American Archaeology and Ethnology, XXXVIII.

———. 1940. "Stimulus Diffusion," *American Anthropologist*, XLII, 1–20.

———. 1941. *Salt, Dogs, and Tobacco*, University of California Anthropological Records, VI, 1–20.

———. 1948. *Anthropology*. New York.

———. 1955. "Nature of the Land-Holding Group," *Ethnohistory*, II, 303–14.

KROEBER, THEODORA. 1961. *Ishi in Two Worlds: A Biography of the Last Wild Indian in North America*. Berkeley and Los Angeles.

KURATH, GERTRUDE P. 1953. "Native Choreographic Areas of North

America," *American Anthropologist*, LV, 60–73.

———. 1966. *Michigan Indian Festivals*. Ann Arbor.

———. 1968. *Dance and Song Rituals of Six Nations Reserve, Ontario*. National Museum of Canada, Bulletin 220.

KURATH, GERTRUDE P., and MARTÍ, SAMUEL. 1964. *Dances of Anáhuac*. Chicago.

LABARRE, WESTON. 1938*a*. "Native American Beers," *American Anthropologist*, XL, 224–34.

———. 1938*b*. *The Peyote Cult*. Yale University Publications in Anthropology, XIX, 1–188.

———. 1960. "Twenty Years of Peyote Studies," *Current Anthropology*, I, 45–60.

LAGASSÉ, JEAN-H. 1966. "Indians of Canada," *América Indigena*, XXVI, 387–94.

LAGUNA, FREDERICA DE. 1932–33. "A Comparison of Eskimo and Paleolithic Art," *American Journal of Archaeology*, XXXVI, 477–508; XXXVII, 77–107.

———. 1940. "Eskimo Lamps and Pots," *Journal of the Royal Anthropological Institute of Great Britain and Ireland*, LXX, 53–76.

LANTIS, MARGARET. 1938. "The Alaskan Whale Cult and Its Affinities," *American Anthropologist*, XL, 438–64.

———. 1947. *Alaskan Eskimo Ceremonialism*. Monographs of the American Ethnological Society, No. 11.

———. 1959. "Alaskan Eskimo Cultural Values," *Polar Notes*, No. 1, pp. 35–48. Dartmouth College, Hanover, N.H.

LAS CASAS, GONZALO DE. 1944[1574]. *La Guerra de los Chichimecas*. Mexico, D.F.

LAWSON, JOHN. 1860. *History of Carolina*. Raleigh, N.C.

LEACOCK, ELEANOR. n.d. *The Montagnais Hunting Territory and the Fur Trade*. American Anthropological Association Memoirs, No. 78.

———. 1955. "Matrilocality in a Simple Hunting Economy," *Southwestern Journal of Anthropology*, XI, 31–47.

LEES, ROBERT B. 1953. "The Basis of Glottochronology," *Language*, XXIX, 113–27.

LEONARD, IRVING A. 1942. "Peyote and the Mexican Inquisition," *American Anthropologist*, XLIV, 324–26.

LEVINE, STUART, and LURIE, NANCY O. (eds.). 1968. *The American Indian Today*. Deland, Fla.

LEVY, JERROLD E. 1961. "Ecology of the South Plains," *Proceedings of the 1961 Annual Spring Meeting of the American Ethnological Society*, 18–25.

LEWIS, OSCAR. 1941. "Manly-Hearted Women among the North Piegan," *American Anthropologist*, XLIII, 173–87.

———. 1942. *The Effect of White Contact upon Blackfoot Culture*. Monographs of the American Ethnological Society, No. 6.

———. 1951. *Life in a Mexican Village: Tepoztlán Restudied*. Urbana, Ill.

LIBBY, DOROTHY RAINIER. 1950. *Girls' Puberty Observances among Northern Athapaskans*. Ph.D. dissertation, University of California, Berkeley.

LID, N. 1948. "On the Dual Division of North American Tribes," *Proceedings of the International Congress of Americanists*, Paris, 1947, 277–82.

LINTON, RALPH. 1924a. *Use of Tobacco among North American Indians*. Field Museum of Natural History Anthropological Leaflets, No. 15.

———. 1924b. "The Origin of the Plains Earth Lodge," *American Anthropologist*, XXVI, 247–57.

———. 1936. *The Study of Man*. New York and London.

———. 1942. "Land Tenure in Aboriginal America," *in* OLIVER LA FARGE (ed.), *The Changing Indian*, pp. 42–54, Norman, Okla.

———. 1944. "North American Cooking Pots," *American Antiquity*, IX, 369–80.

LIPS, JULIUS E. 1947. *Naskapi Law (Lake St. John and Lake Mistassini Bands): Law and Order in a Hunting Society*. Transactions of the American Philosophical Society, XXXVII, 379–492.

LLEWELLYN, K. N., and HOEBEL, E. ADAMSON. 1941. *The Cheyenne Way*. Norman, Okla.

LOEB, E. M. 1932. *The Western Kuksu Cult*. University of California Publications in American Archaeology and Ethnology, XXXIII, 1–138.

———. 1933. *The Eastern Kuksu Cult*. University of California Publications in American Archaeology and Ethnology, XXXIII, 139–232.

LOGAN, EUNICE, and JOHNSON, DOROTHY NADEAU. 1965. *We Teach in Alaska*. Bureau of Indian Affairs. Juneau, Alaska.

LONG, JOSEPH K. 1966. "A Test of Multiple-Discriminant Analysis as a Means of Determining Evolutionary Changes and Intergroup Relationships in Physical Anthropology," *American Anthropologist*, LXVIII, 444–64.

LOPATIN, IVAN A. 1960. "Origin of the Native American Steam Bath," *American Anthropologist*, LXII, 977–93.

LORAM, C. T., and McILLWRAITH, T. F. (eds.). 1943. *The North American Indian Today*. Toronto.

LORM, A. J. DE. 1945. *Kunstzin der Eskimós*. The Hague.

LOTHROP, SAMUEL K. 1952. *Metals from the Cenote of Sacrifice, Chichén Itzá, Yucatán*. Harvard University Memoirs of the Peabody Museum of American Archaeology and Ethnology, X, No. 2.

LOWIE, ROBERT H. 1916. *Plains Indian Age-Societies*. Anthropological Papers of the American Museum of Natural History, XI, 877–992.

———. 1935. *The Crow Indians*. New York.

———. 1940. *An Introduction to Cultural Anthropology*. Rev. ed. New York.

———. 1948. *Social Organization*. New York.

———. 1951. "Some Aspects of Political Organization among the American Aborigines," *Journal of the Royal Anthropological Institute of Great Britain and Ireland*, Vol. LXXVIII, Parts 1–2, 11–24.

———. 1954. *Indians of the Plains*. New York.

LURIE, NANCY O. 1961. "The Voice of the American Indian: Report on the American Indian Chicago Conference," *Current Anthropology*, II, 478–500.

———. 1966. "Women in Early American Anthropology," *in* JUNE HELM (ed.), *Pioneers of American Anthropology*, pp. 29–81, Seattle.

———. 1968. "Historical Background," *in* STUART LEVINE and NANCY O. LURIE (eds.), *The American Indian Today*, pp. 25–45. Deland, Fla.

McALLESTER, DAVID P. 1954. *Enemy Way Music*. Papers of the Peabody Museum of American Archaeology and Ethnology, Vol. XLI, No. 3.

McGUIRE, J. D. 1897. "Pipes and Smoking Customs of the American Aborigines," *Report of the United States National Museum for 1897*, pp. 351–645.

MACLEOD, W. C. 1925. "Certain Mortuary Aspects of Northwest Coast Culture," *American Anthropologist*, XXVII, 122–48.

———. 1926. "Priests, Temples and the Practice of Mummification in S.E. North America," *Proceedings of the International Congress of Americanists*, XXII, 207–30.

———. 1933. "Mortuary and Sacrificial Anthropophagy on the Northwest Coast," *Journal de la Société des Américanistes*, XXV, 335–66.

MacNEISH, RICHARD S. 1955. "Ancient Maize and Mexico," *Archaeology*, VIII, 108–15.

McNICKLE, D'ARCY. 1964. *The Indian Tribes of the United States*. London.

MANDELBAUM, DAVID. 1949. *Selected Writings of Edward Sapir*. Berkeley and Los Angeles.

MANGELSDORF, PAUL C.; MacNEISH, RICHARD S.; and GALINAT, WALTON C. 1964. "Domestication of Corn," *Science*, CXLIII, 538–45.

MANGELSDORF, PAUL C.; MacNEISH, RICHARD S.; and WILLEY, GORDON R. 1964. "Origins of Agriculture in Middle America," *in* ROBERT WAUCHOPE (ed.), *Handbook of Middle American Indians*, I, 427–45. Austin, Tex.

MARQUINA, IGNACIO. 1951. *Architectura Prehispánica*. Mexico, D.F.

MARTIN, PAUL S.; QUIMBY, GEORGE I.; and COLLIER, DONALD. 1947. *Indians before Columbus*. Chicago.

MARTÍNEZ, MAXIMINO. 1936. *Plantas Utiles de México*. Mexico, D.F.

MARTÍNEZ DEL RÍO, P. 1954. "La Comarca Lagunera a Fines del Siglo 16 y Principios del 17 Según las Fuentes Escritas," *Publicaciones del Instituto de Historia*, XXX, 63–98.

MASON, J. ALDEN. 1924. *Use of Tobacco in Mexico and South America*. Field Museum of Natural History, Anthropological Leaflets, No. 16.

———. 1948. "The Tepehuan and other Aborigines of the Mexican Sierra Madre Occidental," *América Indígena*, VIII, No. 4, 289–300.

MASON, OTIS T. 1891. "Aboriginal Skin-Dressing," *Report of the United States National Museum for 1889*, pp. 553–89.

———. 1904. "Aboriginal American Basketry," *Report of the United States National Museum for 1901–2*, pp. 171–548.

MEIGHAN, C. W.; PENDERGAST, D. M.; SWARTZ, B. K.; and WISSLER, M. D. 1958. "Ecological Interpretation in Archaeology," *American Antiquity*, XXIV, 1–23; 131–50.

MENDIZÁBAL, MIGUEL DE. 1930. "Influencia de la Sal en la Distribución Geográfica de los Grupos Indígenas de México," *Proceedings of the Twenty-third International Congress of Americanists*, 1928, 93–100. New York.

———. 1942. "La Evolución de las Culturas Indígenas de México y la División de Trabajo," *Cuadernos Americanos*, I, No. 1, 121–31.

MERA, HARRY P. 1937. *The "Rain Bird": A Study in Pueblo Design*. Laboratory of Anthropology Memoirs, No. 2. Santa Fe.

———. 1939. *Style Trends of Pueblo Pottery*. Laboratory of Anthropology Memoirs, No. 3. Santa Fe.

MERRIAM, ALAN P. 1964. *The Anthropology of Music*. Evanston, Ill.

———. 1967. *Ethnomusicology of the Flathead Indians*. Chicago.

MERTZ, EDWIN T.; VERNON, OLIVIA A.; BATES, LYNN S.; and NELSON, OLIVER E. 1965. "Growth of Rats Fed on Opaque-2 Maize," *Science*, CXLVIII, 1741–42.

MICKEY, BARBARA HARRIS. 1955. *The Family among the Western Eskimo*. Anthropological Papers of the University of Alaska, IV, No. 1, 13–22.

MILLER, CARL F. 1950. "Early Cultural Horizons in the Southeastern United States," *American Antiquity*, XV, 273–88.

MILLER, WALTER B. 1955. "Two Concepts of Authority," *American Anthropologist*, LVII, 271–89.

MISHKIN, BERNARD. 1940. *Rank and Warfare among the Plains Indians*. American Ethnological Society Monograph, No. 3.

MOONEY, JAMES. 1896. *The Ghost-Dance Religion. Bureau of American Ethnology, Annual Report for 1892–1893*, XIV, No. 2.

MOORE, SALLY F. 1958. *Power and Property in Inca Peru*. New York.

MORGAN, LEWIS H. 1871. *Systems of Consanguinity and Affinity*. Smithsonian Institution Contributions to Knowledge, XVII.

———. 1877. *Ancient Society*. Chicago.

———. 1881. *Houses and House-Life of the American Aborigines*. Contributions to North American Ethnology, IV, 1–281.

MORLEY, SYLVANUS G. 1955. "The Maya of Yucatan," *in* MATTHEW W. STIRLING, *National Geographic on Indians of the Americas*, 183–216. Washington, D.C.

MORRIS, EARL H., and BURGH, ROBERT F. 1941. *Anasazi Basketry*. Carnegie Institution of Washington, Publication 533.

MÜLLER, WERNER. 1954. *Die Blaue Hütte: Zum Sinnbild der Perle bei Nordamerikanischen Indianern*. Studien zur Kulturkunde, No. 12. Wiesbaden, Germany.

MÜLLER-BECK, HANSJÜRGEN. 1966. "Paleohunters in America: Origins and Diffusion," *Science*, CLIV, 1191–1210.

MURDOCK, GEORGE P. 1949. *Social Structure*. New York.

———. 1957. "World Ethnographic Sample," *American Anthropologist*, LIX, 664–87.

———. 1967. "Ethnographic Atlas: A Summary," *Ethnology*, VI, 109–236.

NADEAU, GABRIEL. 1944. "Indian Scalping Techniques in Different Tribes," *Ciba Symposia*, V, No. 10, 1677–84.

NELSON, E. W. 1899. *The Eskimo about Bering Strait. Bureau of American Ethnology, Annual Report*, for 1896–1897, XVIII, 3–518.

NETTL, BRUNO. 1954. "North American Indian Musical Styles," *Journal of American Folklore*, LXVII, 45–56, 297–307, 351–68.

NEUMANN, GEORG K. 1940. "Evidence for the Antiquity of Scalping from Central Illinois," *American Antiquity*, V, 287–89.
———. 1952. "Archaeology and Race in the American Indian," *in* JAMES B. GRIFFIN (ed.), *Archaeology of the Eastern United States*, 13–34. Chicago.
NEWCOMB, W. W. JR. 1950. "A Re-examination of the Causes of Plains Warfare," *American Anthropologist*, LII, 317–30.
NEWMAN, MARSHALL T. 1962. "Evolutionary Changes in Body Size and Head Form in American Indians," *American Anthropologist*, LXIV, 237–57.
NISHIYAMA, I. 1963. "The Origin of the Sweet Potato Plant," *in* J. BARRAU (ed.), *Plants and the Migrations of Pacific Peoples*, 119–28, Honolulu.
NUTTALL, ZELIA. 1902. "Sorcery, Medicine and Surgery in Ancient Mexico," *Johns Hopkins Hospital Bulletin*, XIII, 1–133.
OLSON, RONALD L. 1927. *Adze, Canoe, and House Types of the Northwest Coast*. University of Washington Publications in Anthropology, II, 1–38.
———. 1933. *Clan and Moiety in Native America*. University of California Publications in American Archaeology and Ethnology, XXXIII, 351–422.
O'NEALE, LILA M. 1945. *Textiles of Highland Guatemala*. Carnegie Institution of Washington, Publication 567.
OPLER, MORRIS E. 1941. *An Apache Life Way*. Chicago.
ORCHARD, W. C. 1929. *Beads and Beadwork of the American Indians. Contributions of the Museum of the American Indian*, XI, 3–140.
OSGOOD, CORNELIUS. 1936. *Contributions to the Ethnography of the Kutchin*. Yale University Publications in Anthropology, XIV, 1–189.
———. 1937. *The Ethnography of the Tanaina*. Yale University Publications in Anthropology, XVI, 1–229.
OSWALT, WENDELL. 1953. "Northeast Asian and Alaskan Pottery Relationships," *Southwestern Journal of Anthropology*, IX, 395–407.
———. 1966. *This Land Was Theirs*. New York, London, Sydney.
PARKER, SEYMOUR. 1962. "Eskimo Psychopathology in the Context of Eskimo Personality and Culture," *American Anthropologist*, LXIV, 76–96.
PARSONS, ELSIE C. 1939. *Pueblo Indian Religion*. 2 vols. Chicago.
PASSIN, HERBERT. 1944. "Some Relationships in Northwest Mexican Kinship Systems," *El México Antiguo*, VI, 205–18.
PATTERSON, BRYAN, and HOWELLS, W. W. 1967. "Hominid Humeral Fragment from Early Pleistocene of Northwestern Kenya," *Science*, CLVI, 64–66.
PAUL, BENJAMIN D. and LOIS. 1952. "Life Cycle," *in* SOL TAX, (ed.), *Heritage of Conquest*, 174–92, Chicago.
PETTITT, GEORGE A. 1946. *Primitive Education in North America*. University of California Publications in American Archaeology and Ethnology, XLIII, 1–182.
PIDDOCKE, STUART. 1965. "The Potlatch System of the Southern Kwakiutl: A New Perspective," *Southwestern Journal of Anthropology*, XXI, 244–64.
PIERCE, JOE E. 1957. "A Statistical Study of Consonants in New World Languages," *International Journal of American Linguistics*, XIII, 36–45, 94–108.

POLLOCK, H. E. D. 1936. *Round Structures of Aboriginal Middle America.* Carnegie Institution of Washington, Publication 471.

PORTER, MURIEL N. 1948. "Pipas Precortesianas," *Acta Antropológica,* III, No. 2.

POWELL, J. W. 1891. *Indian Linguistic Families North of Mexico.* Bureau of American Ethnology, *Annual Report for 1885–1886,* VII, 1–142.

POZAS, RICARDO. 1962. *Juan the Chamula.* Berkeley and Los Angeles.

PROCTOR, VERNON W. 1968. "Long Distance Dispersal of Seeds by Retention in Digestive Tract of Birds," *Science,* CLX, 321–22.

QUIMBY, GEORGE I. 1946. "Natchez Social Structures as an Instrument of Assimilation," *American Anthropologist,* XLVIII, 134–37.

———. 1948. "Culture Contact on the Northwest Coast, 1784–1795," *American Anthropologist,* L, 247–55.

RAY, VERNE F. 1932. *The Sanpoil and Nespelem.* University of Washington Publications in Anthropology, V, 1–237.

———. 1939. *Cultural Relations in the Plateau of Northwestern America.* Publications of the Frederick Webb Hodge Anniversary Publication Fund, No. 3. Los Angeles, Southwest Museum.

———. (ed.). 1960. "Windigo Psychosis," *Proceedings of the 1960 Annual Spring Meeting of the American Ethnological Society,* Seattle.

REICHARD, GLADYS A. 1950. *Navaho Religion.* 2 vols. New York.

RICHARDS, CARA B. 1957. "Matriarchy or Mistake: the Role of Iroquois Women through Time," *Proceedings of the 1957 Annual Spring Meeting of the American Ethnological Society,* 36–45, Seattle.

RICHTER, CURT P. 1957. "On the Phenomenon of Sudden Death in Animals and Man," *Psychosomatic Medicine,* XIX, 191–98.

RICKARD, T. A. 1934. "The Use of Native Copper by the Indigenes of North America," *Journal of the Royal Anthropological Institute of Great Britain and Ireland,* LXIV, 265–87.

RIVET, PAUL, and ARSANDAUX, H. 1946. *La Metallurgie en Amérique Precolombienne.* Travaux et mémoires de l'Institut d'Ethnologie, XXXIX. Musée de l'Homme, Paris.

ROBERTS, HELEN H. 1936. *Musical Areas in Aboriginal North America.* Yale University Publications in Anthropology, XII, 1–41.

ROE, FRANK G. 1939. *From Dogs to Horses among the Western Indian Tribes.* Proceedings and Transactions of the Royal Society of Canada, 3d Ser., Vol. XXXIII, Sect. 2, pp. 209–75.

———. 1952. *The North American Buffalo.* Toronto.

———. 1955. *The Indian and the Horse.* Norman, Okla.

ROEDIGER, VIRGINIA M. 1941. *Ceremonial Costumes of the Pueblo Indians.* Berkeley and Los Angeles.

ROJAS, G. F. 1942. "Estudio Histórico-etnográfico del Alcoholismo entre los Indios de México," *Revista Mexicana de Sociología,* IV, No. 2, 111–25.

ROSS, JOHN. 1819. *A Voyage of Discovery.* London.

ROSTLUND, ERHARD. 1952. *Freshwater Fish and Fishing in Native North America.* University of California Publications in Geography, No. 9.

ROYS, RALPH L. 1943. *The Indian Background of Colonial Yucatan.* Carnegie

Institution of Washington, Publication 584.

————. 1957. *The Political Geography of the Yucatán Maya*. Carnegie Institution of Washington, Publication 613.

RUPPERT, KARL; THOMPSON, J. ERIC S.; and PROSKOURIAKOFF, TATIANA. 1955. *Bonampak, Chiapas, Mexico*. Carnegie Institution of Washington, Publication 602.

SAFFORD, W. E. 1917. "Narcotic Plants and Stimulants of the Ancient Americans," *Annual Report of the Smithsonian Institution for 1916*, 387–424.

SAHAGÚN, FRAY BERNARDINO DE. 1950–58. *Florentine Codex: General History of the Things of New Spain*. Translated from Aztec to English by ARTHUR J. O. ANDERSON and CHARLES E. DIBBLE. Sante Fe and Salt Lake City.

SALAMAN, REDCLIFFE N. 1949. *The History and Social Influence of the Potato*. Cambridge, England.

SALAS, ALBERTO M. 1947. "Armas de la Conquista: Venenos y Gases," *Cuadernos Americanos*, Año 6, Vol. XXXII, 135–52.

SANFORD, TRENT ELWOOD. 1947. *The Story of Architecture in Mexico*. New York.

SANTA MARÍA, FRANCISCO J. 1942. *Diccionario General de Americanismos*. 3 vols. Mexico, D.F.

SAPIR, EDWARD. 1921. *Language*. New York.

SATTERTHWAITE, LINTON, JR. 1952. *Piedras Negras Archaeology: Architecture*: Part V, *Sweathouses*. University Museum, University of Pennsylvania.

SAUER, CARL O. 1935. *Aboriginal Population of Northwestern Mexico*. University of California. "Ibero-Americana," No. 10.

————. 1939. *Man in Nature*. New York.

————. 1950. "Cultivated Plants of South and Central America," in *Handbook of South American Indians*. Bureau of American Ethnology, *Bulletin 143*, Vol. VI, 487–543.

————. 1952. *Agricultural Origins and Dispersals*. New York.

————. 1959. "Age and Area of American Cultivated Plants," *Congrès International des Americanistes* 33, I, 215–29.

————. 1960. "Maize into Europe," *Akten des 34 Internationalen Amerikanistan Kongresses*, 777–88. Vienna.

SAVILLE, MARSHALL H. 1920. *The Goldsmith's Art in Ancient Mexico*. Museum of the American Indian, Indian Notes and Monographs.

SCHULTES, R. E. 1940. "Teonanacatl, the Narcotic Mushroom of the Aztecs," *American Anthropologist*, XLII, 429–43.

SECOY, FRANK R. 1953. *Changing Military Patterns on the Great Plains*. American Ethnological Society Monograph, No. 21.

Sentinel (magazine). National Congress of American Indians, 1765 P Street, N. W., Washington 6 D.C.

SETCHELL, W. A. 1921. "Aboriginal Tobaccos," *American Anthropologist*, XXIII, 397–414.

SHAFER, ROBERT. 1952. "Athapaskan and Sino-Tibetan," *International Journal of American Linguistics*, XVIII, 12–19.

SHIMKIN, DEMITRI B. 1941. "The Uto-Aztecan Systems of Kinship Terminology," *American Anthropologist*, XLIII, 223–45.

———. 1947. *Wind River Shoshone Ethnogeography*. University of California Anthropological Records, V, 245–88.

SINCLAIR, A. T. 1909. "Tattooing of the North American Indians," *American Anthropologist*, XI, 362–400.

SKINNER, ALANSON. 1911. *Notes on the Eastern Cree and Northern Saulteaux*. American Museum of Natural History Anthropological Papers, IX, 117–77.

SLOTKIN, J. S. 1952. *Menomini Peyotism. Transactions of the American Philosophical Society*, Vol. XLII, Part 4.

———. 1955. "Peyotism, 1521–1891," *American Anthropologist*, LVII, 202–30.

———. 1956. *The Peyote Religion: A Study in Indian-White Relations*. Glencoe, Ill.

SLOTKIN, J. S., and SCHMIDT, KARL. 1949. "Studies of Wampum," *American Anthropologist*, LI, 223–36.

SMITH, A. L. 1940. "The Corbeled Arch in the New World," *in The Mayas and Their Neighbors*, 202–21. New York.

SMITH, C. EARLE, JR., and MACNEISH, RICHARD S. 1964. "Antiquity of American Polyploid Cotton," *Science*, CXLIII, 675–76.

SMITH, MARIAN W. 1938. "The War Complex of the Plains Indians," *American Philosophical Society Proceedings*, LXXVIII, 425–64.

———. 1951. *American Indian Warfare. New York Academy of Sciences Transactions*, Ser. 2, Vol. XIII, pp. 348–65.

SNYDERMAN, GEORGE S. 1948. *Behind the Tree of Peace: A Sociological Analysis of Iroquois Warfare. Pennsylvania Archaeologist*, Vol. XVIII, Nos. 3–4.

SOLIER, W. DU. 1950. *Indumentaria Antigua Mexicana*. Mexico, D.F.

SOUSTELLE, JACQUES. 1956. *La Vida Cotidiana de los Aztecas en Vísperas de la Conquista*. Mexico, D.F.

SPECK, FRANK G. 1911. "Huron Moose Hair Embroidery," *American Anthropologist*, XIII, 1–14.

———. 1915. *Family Hunting Territories and Social Life of Various Algonkian Bands of the Ottawa Valley*. Canadian Department of Mines, Geological Survey, Memoir 70, Anthropology Series, No. 8.

———. 1917. *The Social Structure of the Northern Algonkian*. American Sociological Society *Proceedings*, N.S. XII, 82–100.

———. 1918. "Kinship Terms and the Family Band among the Northeastern Algonkian," *American Anthropologist*, XX, 143–61.

———. 1919. *The Functions of Wampum among the Eastern Algonkian*. American Anthropological Association *Memoirs*, VI, 3–71.

———. 1920a. *Decorative Art and Basketry of the Cherokee*. Public Museum of the City of Milwaukee, *Bulletin 2*, 53–86.

———. 1920b. "Correction to Kinship Terms among the Northeastern Algonkian," *American Anthropologist*, XXII, 85.

———. 1928. *Chapters on the Ethnology of the Powhatan Tribes of Virginia*.

Museum of the American Indian, *Indian Notes and Monographs*, I, 225–455.

——. 1931. "Birch-Bark in the Ancestry of Pottery Forms," *Anthropos*, XXVI, 407–11.

——. 1935. *Naskapi*. Norman, Okla.

——. 1937. "Analysis of Eskimo and Indian Skin-dressing Methods in Labrador," *Ethnos*, II, 345–53.

——. 1938. "The Question of Matrilineal Descent in the Southeastern Siouan Area," *American Anthropologist*, XL, 1–12.

——. 1945. *The Iroquois, a Study in Cultural Evolution*. Cranbrook Institute of Science, *Bulletin 23*.

SPECK, FRANK G., and EISELEY, LOREN C. 1939. "The Significance of Hunting Territory Systems of the Algonkian in Social Theory," *American Anthropologist*, XLI, 269–80.

——. 1942. "Montagnais-Naskapi Bands and Family Hunting of the Central and Southeastern Labrador Peninsula," American Philosophical Society *Proceedings*, LXXXV, 215–42.

SPENCER, ROBERT F. 1959. *The North Alaskan Eskimo*. Bureau of American Ethnology, *Bulletin 171*.

SPENCER, ROBERT F.; JENNINGS, JESSE D.; *et al*. 1965. *The Native Americans*. New York, Evanston, London.

SPICER, EDWARD H. 1962. *Cycles of Conquest*. Tucson.

SPIER, LESLIE. 1925. "The Distribution of Kinship Systems in North America," University of Washington *Publications in Anthropology*, I, 69–88.

——. 1928. *Havasupai Ethnography*. American Museum of Natural History *Anthropological Papers*, XXIX, 83–392.

SPINDLER, GEORGE D. and LOUISE S. 1957. "American Indian Personality Types and Their Sociocultural Roots," *Annals of the American Academy of Political and Social Science*, CCCXI, 147–57.

SPOEHR, ALEXANDER. 1947. *Changing Kinship Systems*. Field Museum of Natural History, Anthropological Series, XXXIII, 153–235.

Statistical Yearbook of the United Nations. 1965, 1966, and 1967. New York.

STEINER, STAN. 1968. *The New Indians*. New York.

STEVENSON, MATILDE COXE. 1904. *The Zuñi Indians: Their Mythology, Esoteric Societies, and Ceremonies*. Bureau of American Ethnology Annual Report for 1901–1902, XXIII.

STEVENSON, ROBERT. 1952. *Music in Mexico*. New York.

STEWARD, JULIAN H. 1938. *Basin-Plateau Aboriginal Socio-political Groups*. Bureau of American Ethnology, *Bulletin 120*.

STEWART, KENNETH M. 1947. "Mohave Warfare," *Southwestern Journal of Anthropology*, III, 257–78.

STEWART, OMER C. 1944. *Washo–Northern Paiute Peyotism*, University of California Publications in American Archaeology and Ethnology, XL, 63–142.

——. 1964. "Questions Regarding Indian Criminality," *Human Organization*, XXIII, 61–66.

STRACHEY, WILLIAM. 1849. *The Historie of Travaile into Virginia Britannia.* London.

STRONG, WILLIAM D. 1929. "Cross-cousin Marriage and the Culture of the Northeastern Algonkian," *American Anthropologist,* XXXI, 277–88.

STURTEVANT, WILLIAM C. 1960. *The Significance of Ethnological Similarities between Southeastern North America and the Antilles.* Yale University Publications in Anthropology, No. 64.

———. 1961. "Taino Agriculture," in JOHANNES WILBERT, (ed.), *The Evolution of Horticultural Systems in Native South America: Causes and Consequences,* pp. 69–82, Caracas. Editorial Sucre, Antropológica Supplement No. 2.

SUTTLES, WAYNE. 1958. "Private Knowledge, Morality, and Social Classes among the Coast Salish," *American Anthropologist,* LX, 497–507.

SWADESH, MORRIS. 1952. "Athapaskan and Sino-Tibetan," *International Journal of American Linguistics,* XVIII, 178–81.

———. 1959a. "The Mesh Principle in Comparative Linguistics," *Anthropological Linguistics,* I, 7–14.

———. 1959b. *Mapas de Clasificación Lingüística de México y las Américas.* Cuadernos del Instituto de Historia, Serie Antropológica, No. 8. Universidad Nacional Autónoma de México.

———. 1960. *La Lingüística como Instrumento de la Prehistoria.* Instituto Nacional de Antropología e Historia.

———. 1962. "Linguistic Relations across Bering Strait," *American Anthropologist,* LXIV, 1262–91.

SWANTON, JOHN R. 1909. *Contributions to the Ethnology of the Haida.* American Museum of Natural History *Memoirs,* VIII, 1–300.

———. 1911. *Indian Tribes of the Lower Mississippi Valley and Adjacent Coast of the Gulf of Mexico.* Bureau of American Ethnology, *Bulletin 43.*

———. 1928. "Religious Beliefs and Medical Practices of the Creek Indians," Bureau of American Ethnology *Annual Report for 1924–1925,* XLII, 473–672.

———. 1946. *The Indians of the Southeastern United States.* Bureau of American Ethnology, *Bulletin 137.*

TANNER, CLARA LEE. 1957. *Southwest Indian Painting.* Tucson.

TAX, SOL, (ed.). 1952. *Heritage of Conquest.* Chicago.

———. 1953. *Penny Capitalism: A Guatemalan Indian Economy.* Smithsonian Institution, Institute of Social Anthropology, No. 16.

THOMPSON, J. ERIC S. 1940. *Mexico before Cortez.* New York.

———. 1954. *The Rise and Fall of Maya Civilization.* Norman, Okla.

THOMPSON, LAURA. 1945. "Logico-Aesthetic Integration in Hopi Culture," *American Anthropologist,* XLVII, 540–53.

THOMPSON, LAURA, and JOSEPH, ALICE. 1944. *The Hopi Way.* Chicago.

TIFFANY, WARREN I. 1966. *Old Ways for New: Selected Material on Alaska Native Culture and Education.* Bureau of Indian Affairs. Juneau, Alaska.

Time Magazine. September 22, 1967, 78–79.

TOOKER, ELISABETH. 1963. "Natchez Social Organization: Fact or Anthropological Folklore?" *Ethnohistory* X, 358–72.

TROIKE, RUDOLPH C. 1962. "The Origins of Plains Mescalism," *American Anthropologist*, LXIV, 946–63.

UNDERHILL, RUTH. 1939. *Social Organization of the Papago Indians*. Columbia University Contributions to Anthropology, No. 30.

———. 1948. *Ceremonial Patterns in the Greater Southwest*. Monographs of the American Ethnological Society, No. 13.

———. n.d. *Workaday Life of the Pueblos*. Washington, D.C.

United Nations Statistical Yearbook. 1965, 1966, 1967. New York.

VAILLANT, GEORGE C. 1941. *Aztecs of Mexico*. New York.

VAN DER MERWE, NICHOLAAS J. 1966. "New Mathematics for Glotto-chronology," *Current Anthropology*, VII, 485–500.

VOEGELIN, C. F., and F. M. 1966. *Map of North American Indian Languages*. American Ethnological Society.

VOEGELIN, ERMINIE WHEELER. 1944. *Mortuary Customs of the Shawnee and Other Eastern Tribes*. Indiana Historical Society, Prehistory Research Series, II, 227–444.

VOGEL, VIRGIL J. 1967. "American Indian Influence on Medicine and Pharmacology," *The Indian Historian*, I, 12–15.

VOGT, EVON Z. 1961. "Navaho," *in* EDWARD H. SPICER (ed.), *Perspectives in American Indian Culture Change*, 278–336, Chicago.

WALLACE, ANTHONY F. 1952. *The Modal Personality of the Tuscarora Indians: As Revealed by the Rorschach Test*. Bureau of American Ethnology, *Bulletin 150*.

———. 1956. "Revitalization Movements," *American Anthropologist*, LVIII, 264–81.

———. 1958. "Dreams and the Wishes of the Soul: A Type of Psychoanalytic Theory among the Seventeenth Century Iroquois," *American Anthropologist*, LX, 234–48.

WATERMAN, T. T. 1924. "North American Indian Dwellings," *Geographical Review*, XIV, 1–25.

WAUCHOPE, ROBERT. 1962. *Lost Tribes and Sunken Continents*. Chicago.

———. 1964–67. *Handbook of Middle American Indians*. 6 vols. Austin.

WELLHAUSEN, E. J.; ROBERTS, L. M.; HERNÁNDEZ, E.; and MANGELSDORF, P. C. 1952. *Races of Maize in Mexico*. Cambridge: Bussey Institution of Harvard University.

WELLHAUSEN, E. J.; FUENTES, O. A.; and CORZO, A. HERNÁNDEZ. 1957. *Races of Maize in Central America*. National Academy of Science-National Research Council, Washington, D.C., Publication 511.

WELTFISH, GENE. 1930. "Prehistoric North American Basketry Techniques and Modern Distributions," *American Anthropologist*, XXXII, 454–95.

WEST, G. A. 1934. *Tobacco, Pipes, and Smoking Customs of the American Indians*. 2 vols. Public Museum of the City of Milwaukee, *Bulletin 17*.

WEYER, EDWARD M. 1932. *The Eskimos*. New Haven, Conn.

WHITAKER, THOMAS W., and CARTER, GEORGE F. 1954. "Oceanic Drift of Gourds. Experimental Observations." *American Journal of Botany*, XLI, 697–700.

WHITAKER, THOMAS W.; CUTLER, HUGH C.; and MACNEISH, RICHARD S.

1957. "Cucurbit Materials from Three Caves near Ocampo, Tamaulipas," *American Antiquity*, XXII, 352–58.

WHITAKER, THOMAS W., and DAVIS, G. N. 1962. *Cucurbits: Botany, Cultivation and Uses*. London.

WHITING, JOHN W. M.; KLUCKHOHN, RICHARD; and ANTHONY, ALBERT. 1958. "The Function of Male Initiation Ceremonies at Puberty," *in* E. E. MACCOBY; T. H. NEWCOMB; and E. L. HARTLEY (eds.), *Readings in Social Psychology*, 359–70. New York.

WILLEY, GORDON R. 1966. *An Introduction to American Archaeology*, Volume One: *North and Middle America*. Englewood Cliffs, N.J.

WILSON, GILBERT L. 1917. *Agriculture of the Hidatsa Indians: An Indian Interpretation*. University of Minnesota Studies in Social Sciences, No. 9.

———. 1924. *The Horse and the Dog in Hidatsa Culture*. Anthropological Papers of the American Museum of Natural History, XV, 125–311.

———. 1934. *The Hidatsa Earth Lodge*. Anthropological Papers of the American Museum of Natural History, XXXIII, 341–420.

WILSON, H. CLYDE. 1963. "An Inquiry into the Nature of Plains Indian Cultural Development," *American Anthropologist* LXV, 355–69.

WINTENBERG, W. J. 1942. "The Geographical Distribution of Aboriginal Pottery in Canada," *American Antiquity*, VIII, 129–41.

WISSE, JAKOB. 1933. *Selbstmord und Todesfurcht bei den Naturvölkern*. Zutphen, Holland.

WISSLER, CLARK. 1908. "Types of Dwellings and Their Distribution in Central North America," *Proceedings of the Sixteenth International Congress of Americanists*, 477–87.

———. 1914. "The Influence of the Horse in the Development of Plains Culture," *American Anthropologist*, XVI, 1–25.

———. 1916. *Costumes of the Plains Indians*. Anthropological Papers of the American Museum of Natural History, XVII, 39–91.

———. 1926. *Indian Costumes in the United States*. American Museum of Natural History Guide Leaflet Series, No. 63, pp. 1–32.

———. 1938. *The American Indian*. New York.

———. 1941. *North American Indians of the Plains*. New York.

WITT, SHIRLEY HILL. 1968. "Nationalistic Trends among American Indians," *in* STUART LEVINE and NANCY LURIE (eds.), *The American Indian Today*, 53–75. Deland, Fla.

WITTHOFT, JOHN. 1949. *Green Corn Ceremonialism in the Eastern Woodlands*. Museum of Anthropology, University of Michigan, *Occasional Papers*, No. 13.

WOLF, ERIC. 1959. *Sons of the Shaking Earth*. Chicago.

WOODWARD, ARTHUR. 1965. *Indian Trade Goods*. Metropolitan Press for Oregon Archaeological Society, Portland.

WORMINGTON, H. M. 1957. *Ancient Man in North America*, 4th ed., rev. Denver Museum of Natural History "Popular Series," No. 4.

WRIGHT, H. E., JR. 1968. "Natural Environment of Early Food Production North of Mesopotamia," *Science*, CLXI, 334–39.

YANOVSKY, E. 1936. *Food Plants of North American Indians*. United States

Department of Agriculture *Miscellaneous Publications*, No. 237.

YANOVSKY, E., and KINGSBURY, R. M. 1938. "Analysis of Some Indian Food Plants." *Journal of the Association of Official Agricultural Chemists*, XXI, 648–65.

YARROW, H. C. 1880. *Introduction to the Study of Mortuary Customs among the North American Indians*. Washington, D.C.

———. 1881. *A Further Contribution to the Study of Mortuary Customs among the North American Indians*. Bureau of American Ethnology *Annual Report*, I, 89–203.

lighlights. 1967–68. Association on American Indian Affairs, rk Avenue South, New York, N.Y. 10016.

LES N. 1968. *Statistics Concerning Indian Education*. Bureau airs. Washington, D.C.

Index

ships, 388; as prestige symbol, 326, 511; of semitailored hide or fur, 136, 148, 149; of tailored hide of fur, 3, 4, 5, 136, 137, 138, 140, 147, 149, 212, 387, 540, 552; of untailored hide or fur, 139, 141; of woven animal hair, 141, 143; of woven fur strips, 147; of woven plant fibers, 138, 139, 141, 147, 151. *See also* Coats; Headgear; Moccasins; Parka; Regalia; Sandals

Clubs (organizations). *See* Sodalities

Clubs (weapons), 3, 85, 319, 324

Coahuila, 115

Coahuiltecan language isolate, Table 2 (p. 44), Map 37

Coats, 150

Cocaine, 105, 557

Cochimi, 51, 350

Cochineal insect and dyes, 189, 457

Cochise culture, 92

Coconut, 77, Table 2 (p. 74)

Cocopa, 60

Cod, 56

Codere, Helen, 439, 440

Codices, books, manuscripts, 50, 51, 145, 188, 190, 191, 358, 394, 467

Coffee, 511

Coffins, 375

Cognate words, 42, 43, 48, 76

Coiling: of basketry, bags, mats, 156, 157, Fig. 26, Map 24; of pottery, 162, 163, 164

Colima, 252

Collective farms, 459, 469, 471, 476

Collier, John, 483, 494

Colombia (S.A.), 67, 168, 178

Color symbolism in art, 185

Color terms in language, 34, 35

Colorado Plateau, 60

Colorado River, 11, 61, 78, 80, 82, 126, 248, 281, 282, 297, 318

Colorado (state), 10, 18, 20, 21, 130, 214, 237, 486, 496, 501, 520, 559

Columbia River, 20, 93, 150, 178, 213, 315, 334, 347, 369, 502, 524

Columbus, Christopher, 81, 105, 106, 219, 456, 481, 554, 555, 558

Comanche, 20, 49, 130, 238, 260, 299, 488

Combination suit (of clothes), 138

Commissioner of Indian Affairs, 482, 483, 499–500

Commoners, 337, 339, 340, 341, 432

Communal ownership, 269, 273, 277

Communities, 98, 101, 111, 208, 222, 225, 227, 232, 247, 248, 251, 253, 269, 270, 272, 273; Arctic, 99, 450, 540, 548; California, 252, 279; East, 102, 252, 265; Meso-America, 174, 252, 458, 469, 470, 471; Northwest Coast, 252; Prairies, 252, 354; Southwest, 113, 281; Sub-Arctic, 354. *See also* Bands; Local groups; Villages

Comparative analysis of housing, 129–32

Compensation, blood money, indemnity, weregild, 314, 315, 316, 317, 323, 324

Composition in art, 181, 191

Compulsory military service, 324

Confederacies, confederations, leagues, 302, 303, 304, 306, 309, 310, 318, 321, 323, 341, 445, 446, 518, 519, 543, 565

Confederation Congress, 482, 484

Congress of U.S., 484, 485, 486, 490, 491, 492, 493, 498, 503, 526

Conical and sub-conical houses, 20, 116, 120, 125, 127, 129, 130, 132, Map 16. *See also* Tipis

Coniferous forest, 18, 19, Map 5

Connecticut, 563

Constitution of U.S., 482, 484, 565

Containers, kettles, vessels, 154, 178, 189, 212, 213, 215, 369, 511, 513, 540, 561, Map 23. *See also* Bark; Basketry, Hide; Pottery; Wood

Continental Congress, 482, 484

Conventionalization in art, 179, 180, 185, 187, 188, 189, 190

Convergences in language, 35, 37, 39, 40, 47

Cooking. *See* Boiling; Broiling and roasting; Food preparation and preservation

Cooper, James Fenimore, 433, 564

Copal, 51

Copan, Honduras, Fig. 19

Copper, 13, 78, 146, 166, 167, 168, 171, 178, 188, 203, 212, 213, 216, 217, 407, 511. *See also* Tools and utensils

Copper Eskimos, 212

Copper plate as symbol of prestige and wealth, 210

Coppermine River, 166, 212, 533

Coptic language, 40

Corn. *See* Maize

Coronado, Francisco de, 481

Coronation Gulf, 55